Pittsburgh Series in Composition, Literacy, and Culture

David Bartholomae and Jean Ferguson Carr, Editors

For Michael B. Katz
with my thanks:
on a winter's evening in 1971
he started it all

The Labyrinths of Literacy
Reflections on Literacy Past and Present

Harvey J. Graff

Revised and Expanded Edition

University of Pittsburgh Press

Pittsburgh and London

First published by The Falmer Press, 1987. Revised edition published by the University of Pittsburgh Press, Pittsburgh, Pa. 15260

Library of Congress Cataloging-in-Publication Data
Graff, Harvey J.
    The labyrinths of literacy : reflections on literacy past and present/Harvey J. Graff.—Rev. and expanded ed.
        p. cm.—(Pittsburgh series in composition, literacy, and culture)
    Includes bibliographical references and index.
    ISBN 0-8229-5562-8 (alk. paper)
    1. Literacy—North America—History.   2. Literacy—Europe—History.   3. Literacy—Social aspects—North America.   4. Literacy—Social aspects—Europe.   I. Title.   II. Series.
LC149.G629   1995
302.2'244—dc20   95-2687
                                                                          CIP

A CIP catalogue record for this book is available from the British Library.

Eurospan, London

Contents

Contents

Foreword

Moving through the pages of this revised and expanded version of *The Labyrinths of Literacy* is like a walk through a refreshing garden in full bloom, with a vibrant mixture of new hybrid plants and botanical varieties dating back centuries. Guiding us on this walk is an expert whose interests combine botany and horticulture, who lets us in on the secrets of science while offering hints on how to tend our own gardens and whispering occasional tales of ancient gardeners.

As Graff indicates in his own overview of the paths ahead in this volume, he has been in this garden longer than most contemporary scholars of literacy. Moreover, his perspectives have been considerably stretched in the years since 1987 across not only new parts of the world, but also into new arenas of debate for literacy—politics, education reform, and institutional continuities and discontinuities. What Graff offers here are not only what have become some of the classics of revisionist work in the history of literacy in North America, but also an intellectual history of literacy scholarship and politics in the years following the original publication of this volume.

It is rare that scholars and social movements coincide in their interest in specific societal issues. Literacy over the past decade or so represents an exception to this pattern, for scholars, grass-roots groups, education and welfare institutions, and the public press have joined in what will, no doubt, be looked on in the next twenty years as a social movement. Literacy (and illiteracy) have captured the attention (and sometimes the imagination) of volunteers, local theater groups, storytelling programs, and teen mother services; and even corporate boardrooms and shop floors have taken up "workplace literacy." Literacy programs have offered reading and writing opportunities along with children's literature sessions, basic computer skills, and health programs for women and children.

The problem-solving, knowledge-creating, and communication side-benefits that come along with literacy have been increasingly recognized and have helped move reading and writing away from old descriptors such as "basic economic survival." New arenas of decision making, technological expertise, and mental health now surround literacy programs that encourage learners to write and read in connection with their own needs and interests and to gain a growing sense of self-efficacy as they do so. Unlike earlier simplistic linkages between literacy and "getting a job," more and more literacy studies and practical programs have come to focus on literate behaviors that benefit social community, self-pride, group resourcefulness, and strong family ties.

The essays here reflect Graff's engagement with current issues such as the influence of "cultural literacy" on policies and curricula, jobs programs, and re-formed development approaches around the world. Along with struggles over these contemporary debates about just what a literacy program should include and accomplish, however, come historical frames that help explain the continued ties in the minds of far too many citizens between crime and illiteracy and the acquisition of literacy and employment. Graff moves back and forth across the decades, weakening such simple cause-and-effect notions, while also addressing some newly developed contemporary myths. He chides readers for believing that literacy, once injected, remains in its original potency, and points out that literacy skills, like other language skills, tend to diminish if not practiced. He attempts to demolish notions that associate alphabetic rote learning with literacy and stresses that meaningful interpretation of holistic portions of text can precede recognition of specific letters of the alphabet and their sounds. He lets us know that even though many of us would claim we cannot sing the musical note A below middle C, we *can* sing "Twinkle, twinkle, little star." Learning the song does not depend on either knowing the name of its first note or being able to produce that sound in isolation.

In my foreword to the 1987 edition, I naively wrote: "Finally, he [Graff] has put to rest simple correlations linking literacy with higher earnings, increased civility, great citizen participation, and higher forms of thought" (p. vii). Certainly, in the past decade, these notions and their more simplistic companions noted earlier have not been "put to rest." Many programs still struggle to let their students know that in the economy of the final decade of the twentieth century, literacy skills alone will not offer even a job, and certainly increased literacy skills will not necessarily bring higher wages. In an era when fewer and fewer voters exercise the privilege of the ballot in the United States, citizen participation in voting does not correlate with literacy rates. When the best educated societies in the world have the highest crime rates, it is hard to claim that literacy brings civility or positive attitudes toward one's family members and neighbors.

In that foreword, I also noted Plato's warning that only the knowledge gained through spirited debate "is written in the soul of the learner." Plato further argued that those who have gained and given most from the reading and writing in their society have been those who were also capable of oral argumentation and per-suasion. I pointed out that Graff's essays gave little comforting evidence that either those who study literacy or those who plan and direct literacy programs recognized the close links between oral and written language facility and between retention of literacy skills and having a community of listeners and talkers whose interests are linked to reading and writing. The essays in this new volume similarly offer little encouragement on these points. Graff cannot tell us that we have come very far in facilitating these associations for the retention and development of literacy (as distinct from its mere acquisition). Lacking still are studies of the conditions for oral transmission and transformation of knowledge gained from written sources. We still know little about how family and community norms of recreation and family interaction promote or discourage talk about information gained from reading. The role of community associations of service, religious life, and the arts remains disassociated from the bulk of attention given to literacy programs for "beginnners."

Since Plato's day, we have heard again and again that beginners grow in and with their literacy skills in connection with their opportunities for oral debate and performance within a community of learners and learning. A glimmer of recognition of some of these points has come in a few of the evaluations of workplace literacy programs that show ties between uses of literacy on the job with increased reading opportunities for reading and talking about books in family times with young children. But much more needs to be done to tell us how the opportunities for debate and reference to written stories or recommendations for action instill problem-solving skills, powers of argumentation and persuasion, and a buildup of the literate behaviors so critical within academic settings and across an increasingly broad range of job settings.

Also still missing from the essays in which Graff summarizes trends in literacy programs is evidence that the special challenge of small-scale societies in developing nations has been met. More often than not, communities in these nations do not speak the language of national affairs, and village primary schools offer the only access to reading and writing most youngsters will have. Of the more than four thousand languages in the world, about three hundred are in regular use in written form. Though missionaries have provided writing systems and some primers in more than a thousand languages, habitual use of the written form across a variety of functions—mercantile, literary, and religious—rarely follows. In many nations of the world, when those who establish educational systems choose the language of instruction, it is often not the mother tongue for major segments of the population. We still know little of the interplay of early language socialization, parental values of child-rearing, and motives for developing literate behaviors within these communities. These local factors have become even more complex since the first edition of Graff's book, because of uncertainties about how changes in the global economy will affect low-skill job opportunities in developing nations. The breach between local factories, small farm efforts, and local nongovernmental organizations, on the one hand, and global corporate enterprises, agribusinesses, and state bureaucracies, on the other, leaves little hope that low-level literacy skills available in primary schools and adult literacy programs will translate into either jobs or citizen participation in a communication network dependent on print and other technologies.

The intellectual history embedded throughout this collection should stir readers to look ahead and to consider what a version of this volume might contain in another decade or so. Is the will in place to address remaining questions, and are the advances in programs, theory, and research strategies that Graff describes strong enough to persist in spite of the power of old simplistic views and new myths? What new connections between research and practice will be necessary to answer the questions we now acknowledge as well as those that will surely emerge as the global economy continues to change? As with his earlier volume, this collection offers challenges and makes it clear that neither tilling the same ground in the same old ways nor tossing new hybrid ideas without preparation of the environment will benefit us in the decades to come.

Shirley Brice Heath
Stanford University

Acknowledgments

These essays originally appeared in the following publications and are reprinted here, sometimes in slightly revised form, by permission, for which I am extremely grateful:

"Reflections on the History of Literacy: Overview, Critique, and Proposals." *Humanities in Society* 4 (1981): 303–333.

"Literacy Past and Present: Critical Approaches in the Literacy-Society Relationship." *Interchange: A Journal of Educational Studies* 9 (1978): 1–21. Reprinted by permission of Kluwer Academic Publishers.

"Literacy and Social Development in North America: On Ideology and History." In *Aspects of Literacy in the Eighteenth and Nineteenth Centuries*, ed. W. B. Stephens. Leeds: Museum of the History of Education, University of Leeds, 1983.

" 'Exaggerated Estimates of Reading and Writing as Means of Education (1867),' " by W. B. Hodgson, ed. Harvey J. Graff. *History of Education Quarterly* 26 (1986): 377–393.

"Critical Literacy Versus Cultural Literacy: Reading Signs of the Times." *Interchange* 20 (1989): 46–52. Reprinted by permission of Kluwer Academic Publishers.

"Literacy, Education, and Fertility, Past and Present: A Critical Review." *Population and Development Review* 5 (1979): 105–140. Reprinted with the permission of the Population Council.

"On Literacy in the Renaissance: Review and Reflections." *History of Education* 12 (1983): 69–885. Reprinted by permission of Taylor & Francis Ltd.

"Literacy in History: Review Essay." *History of Education Quarterly* 15 (1975): 467–474.

"Respected and Profitable Labour: Literacy, Jobs, and the Working Class." In *Essays in Canadian Working Class History*, ed. Gregory S. Kealy and Peter Warrian. Toronto: McClelland and Stewart, 1976. Reprinted by permission of the publisher.

" 'Pauperism, Misery, and Vice': Illiteracy and Criminality in the Nineteenth Century." *Journal of Social History* 11 (1977–78): 245–268.

"Literacy in Literature and in Life: An Early Twentieth-Century Example." *History of Education Quarterly* 23 (1983): 279–296.

"Literacy, Libraries, Lives: New Social and Cultural Histories." *Libraries and Culture* 26 (1991): 24–43.

"*On Literacy:* Review Essay." *Language and Society* 12 (1983): 559–563. Reprinted by permission of Cambridge University Press.

"National Literacy Campaigns in Historical and Comparative Perspective," with Robert F. Arnove. In *National Literacy Campaigns in Historical and Comparative Perspective,* ed. Arnove and Graff. New York: Plenum, 1987. Reprinted by permission of the publisher.

"Whither the History of Literacy? The Future of the Past." *Communication* 11 (1988): 5–22. Reprinted by permission of Gordon and Breach Science Publishers.

"Literacy, Myths and Legacies: Lessons from the History of Literacy." Forthcoming in a volume of essays on literacy presented as public lectures at Indiana University under the sponsorship of the Indiana University Literacy Forum, with excerpts from essays forthcoming in volumes of papers from the 1992 United Nations Conference on Adult Literacy: An International Urban Perspective, and the 1993 Griffith University, Australia, Conference on Critical Literacy: Difference, Silence and Textual Practice.

Some of the many persons whose assistance and counsel was vital to the writing and/or appearance of these essays are thanked in the notes to the essays. Many others, too numerous to acknowledge here, including institutions and granting agencies, are recognized in the acknowledgements to my earlier books. At Falmer Press, the interest and support of Malcolm Clarkson has been essential to this project. As recognized in the dedication, Michael Katz's role has been seminal and radical, in the historical sense of both words. Last, but far from least, Vicki L. W. Graff deserves my thanks: she has lived with the entire enterprise!

Harvey J. Graff
Dallas, Texas
Winter–Spring, 1986

In preparing this revised edition, the interest, enthusiasm, and support of David Bartholomae, co-editor of the Pittsburgh Series in Composition, Literacy, and Culture and of Catherine Marshall, editor-in-chief at the University of Pittsburgh Press, have been invaluable. Working with them has been a pleasure.

Harvey J. Graff
Dallas, Texas
Fall, 1993

Introduction to the 1995 Edition

In 1986, as I completed editorial work on three book-length projects relating to the history of literacy, I told myself and significant others that I could, and would, now stop writing on the subject that had been my central scholarly (pre)occupation for almost a decade and one half. *The Legacies of Literacy: Continuities and Contradictions in Western Culture and Society,* the first edition of *The Labyrinths of Literacy: Reflections on Literacy Past and Present,* (co-edited with Robert Arnove) saw print in 1987. Beginning with a second-semester graduate school seminar paper (discussed in the 1987 introduction to this book), which led to my first academic publication, my various studies of literacy had yielded three earlier books: *The Literacy Myth: Literacy and Social Structure in the Nineteenth-Century City* (1979, new edition, 1991); *Literacy in History: An Interdisciplinary Research Bibliography* (1981); and the edited volume, *Literacy and Development in the West* (1981). Combined with articles, reviews, conference papers, informal talks, and occasional university courses, this output struck me as much more than enough for one person on one subject, albeit a very large topic that I had sought, with demonstrable success, to make even larger. Others no doubt agreed with the former assessment.

With some surprise, I discovered in the spring of 1993 how poorly I had fared in meeting that sensible goal. To all intents and purposes, I had failed! In preparing an overview of "The History of Literacy in the 1990s" to open the Conference on Writing and Reading in Western Europe in Valencia, Spain, in June 1993, and in reviewing my lecture, article, and review files in planning a conference and lecture tour in Australia, June–July 1993, I found that my production of texts about literacy had continued fairly steadily and that the stack of pages mounted, even somewhat alarmingly. This occurred, moreover, as I shifted my active research program to focus first on the history of growing up—children, adolescents, youth—not wholly unrelated to literacy, among several long-standing interests.

On reflection, of course, I am not surprised. As friends and mentors assured me, sometimes impolitely, when I announced this apparent clash between avowed intentions and subsequent results, this was neither surprising nor unexpected. As one longtime mentor and friend put it, "one is always associated with (or remembered by) the subject of the first book." Since my first book on literacy turned into an armload, the various demands and solicitations to which I responded during the six odd years following 1987 were numerous.

In scanning my accumulated writings on literacy during that period, I am struck by some of the reasons why. Many of them are historical and/or professional. This has been an exceptionally important era in the annals of late modernity's many contradictory discourses and "crises" of literacy—and other things, sometimes related directly to literacy, often less directly but no less revealingly for that. Many of the occasions for my continuing to speak and write fall directly in that path. It is no accident that the latest proclamation on the condition of popular literacy—*Adult Literacy in America: A First Look at the Results of the National Adult Literacy Survey,* September 1993—sits on the desk a few feet from the keyboard I am tapping. Connecting perceived crises in literacy to their contexts is itself a major historical task to which a number of the chapters in the book contribute.

Six new chapters combine with the original material of the 1987 edition to extend but also to transform the substance and thrust of the book.[1] Most simply but still significantly, the new chapters extend the old in several directions: in designating trends and problems in research and interpretation, connecting the past to the present and possible futures, updating and reviewing newer works in the major fields related to literacy studies. Updating but also conducting almost a conversation over a period of more than one-and-one-half decades, chapters 15 and 16, in particular, speak, supplement, refine, and advance chapters 1 and 2.

On one hand, the social and cultural criticism that linked the parts of the original edition is also advanced in those chapters along with the new chapter 5 and also 4, which take different routes toward their critique. On the other hand, all these pieces continue to speak to my concerns about the critical evaluation of theory and expectations by confronting them with the evidence of practice, historical and more recent. Here the new chapters 12 and 14 are especially relevant in their empirical examples and comparative perspectives. The newer thread and theme of explicit "lessons from history" takes the effort beyond the limits of stocktaking review and evaluation toward new questions and conceptualizations.

Overall, this edition goes well beyond the original in advocating, exploring, and explicating the historicity, complexity, problematic nature and conditions of literacy whether our gaze turns toward past or present or seeks to connect them. The power of the past, the presence and interaction of many literacies, and the interdisciplinary imperative for literacy studies confirm the vitality of this research vein and its contemporary importance. Between 1987 and today, that import has only heightened. There is no sign of its abating.

Most of the recent works included in this new edition owe their existence to conferences, special issues, collective books, and other projects that were conceived more or less directly as responses to current events or perceived currents. As such, they may be "read" (a particular use of literacy, to be sure) as marks on the contemporary intellectual, cultural, and political landscapes. Chapter 5 below, for example, critically discusses the substance and the phenomenon of E. D. Hirsch's *Cultural Literacy*. It was presented orally at a not unrelated event: the 1988 conference in Vancouver on the Legacy of J. S. Woodsworth and the Welfare State in Canada. My decision to reprint (as chapter 4) W. B. Hodgson's remarkably prescient 1867 commentary, "Exaggerated Estimates of Reading and Writing as Means of Education," was unabashedly a response to and itself a sign of the times in the early to mid-1980s. The editors of the *History of Education Quarterly,* Paul Mattingly and Ed McClellan, grasped my purpose.[2]

Adding the cross-national, cross-cultural, and struggles for national liberation to the stimuli to which we responded, Robert Arnove and I developed an explicitly comparative as well as historical approach to the exploration of national literacy campaigns over an almost five-hundred-year range in our collection, *National Literacy Campaigns in Historical and Comparative Perspective* (Plenum Publications, 1987), the introduction to which appears below (chapter 14).

Most clear and most explicit in evoking and attempting to make these kinds of connections is my series of "myths, legacies, and lessons" from the history of literacy lectures, talks, and essays (chapter 16, below).[3] The first of these serial installments was prepared at the invitation of the 1991 Bard College Conference on Education for Complexity in the Twenty-first Century. In addition to outlining a series of key "lessons," often in the forms of myths and legacies (to use my lexicon) from the history of literacy, to be learned and then applied to contemporary conditions, that particular version concluded by contemplating school and university curricula revised or reformed to place historical context, interpretation, and understanding at their core.[4] Bracketing the chronological span of these essays' origination and underscoring the power of cultural politics, one version of chapter 1 below was presented at the 1981 Bard College Conference on Crisis in Literacy: Cultural Hard Times, where I had the privilege of sharing the podium with Eric Havelock. In the intervening ten years, it is safe to say, my own and Bard College Conferences' sensitivity to the central issues grew.

Another version of my "lessons" focused on the question of "functional" literacy. This target arose in response to an invitation to present a historical key-note address to the International Conference on Attaining Functional Literacy: A Cross Cultural Perspective, sponsored by Tilburg University and the Netherlands Commission for UNESCO in 1991. The agenda for this forum followed from the return of "functional" literacy to the top of the international policy, planning, and assessment agendas raised during International Literacy Year 1990, especially at its centerpiece conference in Jomtien, Thailand. This emphasis, I must admit, took scholars like myself by surprise. Some of us at Tilburg and many elsewhere, in our relative isolation and hubris, were certain that our critical efforts had largely buried the once frequent and loose use of terms like "functional" or "nonfunctional" literacy. We were wrong! Renewed critical efforts recommenced in the early to mid-1990s. It is too early to assess their results.[5]

Additional opportunities to hone that perspective and reiterate historical critical analysis came hand-in-hand with the hand-wringing at home and abroad over fears of declining and inadequate literacy skills. For a major public conference, on whose planning I advised, the New Hampshire Humanities Council directed attention to Literacy, Myths, and Lessons, new and old, in the fall of 1991. Entitled in recognition of my work on literacy, the conference also honored me with presentation of the opening keynote address. I spoke on "Myths, Legacies, and Lessons" in general, the text resembling the first version presented in chapter 16. This was a rare, public and scholarly confirmation of the value of history in confronting a difficult contemporary public issue.[6]

An invitation to keynote the summer, 1992 Conference on Adult Literacy: An International Urban Perspective, sponsored by UNESCO, City University of New York, and the City of New York, and held at the United Nations in New York City, prompted my developing an explicitly urban focus and interpretation. The second version included in chapter 16 comprises the text of that presentation, where I returned to more solidly historiographic grounds than I held when addressing contemporary curricular reforms or "function-alities." The demands of an international audience of scholars, teachers, literacy practitioners, planners and evaluators, politicians, as well as scholars made for a tricky balancing of elements, emphases, and expressions. The opportunity, and its honor, were very special. But, again, the fact that a historian was called upon to deliver the keynote address stands as another sign of shifting sands of time.[7]

An invitation to serve as opening keynote speaker to the June 1993 Griffith University, Australia, Conference on Literacy and Power: Difference, Silence, and Textual Practice, turned my attention to a target largely new to my sights: "critical literacy." As with "functional" literacy, here, too, the return of a seemingly old label at first surprised me, for most explicit talk of "critical" literacy or literacies had surrounded Paulo Freire's seminal efforts in the late 1960s and 1970s.[8] Whereas that served as one pillar of the new discussion, linguistics, and especially in Australia, systemic linguistics and its conflicts with genre-based approaches, served as another. Workplace literacy problems and programs and feminist theory, singly and sometimes together, formed other bases for a complicated conversation that ranged in- and outside the academy's boundaries and across all school and age grades, but didn't quite converge.

Between and among these approaches, I endeavored to survey and then follow a course of criticism and clarification by way of lessons from the history of literacy. The substance of this perspective appears as the third version in chapter 16. Chapter 16 is one historian's still developing response to John Fowles's *The French Lieutenant's Woman*. I leave it for readers to decide which is/are fiction and nonfiction, and where those shifty lines fall.

Less immediate but still contemporary and timely in their stimuli were the origins of the other new chapters. In the format included here, replacing an earlier, less complete version, chapter 15 assesses the current status, future needs, and likely agenda of historical and also other studies of literacy. It was drafted by invitation for inclusion in the 1988 special issue on the history of literacy for the journal *Communications*. Among academic disciplines, this was a notable event, no longer rare but not yet common: a major journal in the area of communication studies embracing, at least for the subject of literacy and a special issue, a historical approach. As the issue's editor, John Nerone, writes in his introduction, "Literacy commands urgent attention these days. . . . Behind all this discussion are common beliefs that literacy is central to modern societies. . . . these beliefs imply a history. . . . This anonymous history is what gives controversies over literacy today their sense of apocalypse. It also makes explicitly historical research more compelling. . . . [Essays in this special issue] offer important lessons both to the discussion of contemporary literacy and to broader research in the history of communication."[9] Nerone's and *Communication*'s recognitions have continued to gain assent across the academy during the past decade or two. That is one measure of the import and success of the historical approaches that this collection represents. The distance remaining to be traversed is vast.

The other addition to the collection, chapter 12 on "Literacy, Libraries, Lives," has its origins in an invitation to present a Distinguished Plenary Address to Library History Seminar VIII, the once-every-five-years gathering of library historians. An early installment in my uneven and incomplete career as an "after (and sometimes before) dinner (or lunch) speaker," on this occasion in spring 1990, I also followed a group of "Sweet Adeline" harmonic singers, a singular experience. The audience I confronted was by facial expressions and other signs perhaps the least inviting I have faced! Not only did the occasion rise above those temporarily limiting circumstances, but the situation provided me with a happy opportunity to bring together my long-standing interest and expertise in the history of literacy (which brought me the invitation) and my newer research into a large number of first-person sources (autobiography, diary, memoir, letters, etc.) to study the history of growing up. For this presentation, I selected examples from the larger group of testimonial sources that addressed reading, writing, libraries, and changing lives in the context of American social history.[10] A personal, sometimes a lighter side among the larger pool of evidence and approaches does not diminish the significance of the larger tasks to which they contribute. This kind of evidence offers new opportunities for empirical precision and refinement.

As my incipient after-dinner speaking career illustrates, the motives and rewards that lie behind my continuing activities in the literacy history and literary studies fields are neither all historical nor academic or professional, as those categories are narrowly and normatively construed. On the one hand, there are ever-present daily pushes from outside as well as inside the academy toward new ways of confronting especially challenging and irascible contemporary issues like literacy. The compelling needs for and the very real satisfactions of history applied and public are major motivators whose benefits are salient if not always tangible. On the other hand are benefits more personal: wide travels, fascinating new acquaintances, lasting friendships, diverse and sometimes distinctive audiences that cross disciplines, nations, cultures, among other divides, to challenge and sway. These are special opportunities. I appreciate my good fortune in having many opportunities to seize them.[11]

Together these various developments illustrate not only the growing recognition of the value of a historical approach to literacy. They also confirm that history has won a place in literacy studies, unlike its usual neglect in many (most?) other contemporary and policy areas. This is indeed exceptional. Due in part to my own work and certainly that of other students of the history of literacy, it has become exceedingly difficult, even tendentious, to ignore the role of the past, of literacy's history, in shaping the present.[12] This is sometimes the case for approaches that range from language and composition, to social development, educational implementation, and evaluation. A striking cross-, multi- and interdisciplinarity and an openness to explicit comparisons also mark the most important studies.

This achievement, to be sure a rare one, is far from complete. It may give both pause and hope, if not sanguineness. Far from all persons interested or actively involved in literacy work today are aware of or influenced by the new histories of literacy. Much remains to be done. This revised collection of essays is dedicated to that effort.

My most recent thinking—including serious stock-taking in chapters 15 and 16, among others—concentrates on assessing in general terms what we have learned from the past two decades' research into literacy, historically and contemporarily, conceptually and empirically, and determining what remaining tasks are most critical.[13] Part of the new literacy history's contribution to the present moment comes in the form of "lessons" from the past. My earlier work pointed discursively and diffusely in their direction; my later writing probes and develops these conclusions more precisely.

From recent studies, a set of common conclusions and major persisting problems emerge, despite differences of opinion and interpretation on many questions. Among the former, especially prominent and powerful, and supported with historical evidence and interpretation, are:

1. The *historicity* of literacy. Reading and writing and whatever other abilities or attributes are assigned to literacy take on their meaning and acquire their value in concrete historical circumstances that mediate in specific terms whatever supposedly general or "universal" attributes or concomitants are claimed for literacy. Research in many disciplines, from anthropology to philosophy and literary criticism, and inter-disciplines, joins in this first lesson. Present-day conceptions, arrangements, and practices of literacy, as well as schooling, are *historically founded and grounded.*
2. Despite common notions to the contrary, literacy is *fundamentally complex* practically and theoretically, complicated and problematic conceptually and operationally. This recognition makes mockery of

the simple dichotomies and "great divides" that plague considerations of the subject, from literate versus illiterate, literate versus oral, print versus script, and so forth, to the long roster of supposedly more "modern" and "advanced" individual and societal attributes from sophisticated to self-mobilized. To the contrary, many common notions about literacy are rather fragile when probed or tested; expected consequences from its acquisition are anything but "universal" or "unmediated." In particular, "strong" theories of literacy fail.

3. No more often confirmed by research and criticism is the myth of literacy as value neutral. *No mode or means of learning and communicating is neutral;* they all reflect and incorporate the assumptions and expectations, the biases and emphases of their production, acquisition, use, maintenance, and preservation, even as they vary from culture to culture and time to time. This ranges from so-called school literacy to other forms of textual and media access and transmission. Modes and media—like the stereotypically opposed "literate" and "oral"—tend to interact dynamically and complexly in specific practices and specific contexts.

4. Alphabetic literary—reading and writing as we believe we know them—is *one exceptionally valuable set of competencies among others* with which it interacts. Not only do common constructions of "traditional" alphabetic literacy exaggerate the power of literacy *by itself,* they neglect the place of any one mode or form of literacy operating in interaction with many others. Considerations of "new," "other," and "many" literacies, while increasingly frequent, tend to oppose and dichotomize rather than compare and interrelate. Potentially revolutionary remaking of elementary and even higher and adult learning and of concepts of literacy themselves may follow from serious recognition of the many, if not infinite forms of literacies, from, for example, the alphabetic to the numeric or mathematic (numeracy); scientific, geographic, or spatial (graphicacy); to that of the human body, among the countless "new literacies," many of them silly or worse, sometimes proclaimed. Care in designation and description is an obvious mandate here. History as well as anthropology provide laboratories in which to explore interactions.

5. The long domination of practical and theoretical presumptions that elevate the literate, the written, to the status of the dominant element in the "Grand Dichotomy," as Jack Goody termed it, *have caused massive damage* to individuals and societies who paid high prices for their presumed lack of literacy or failures to learn.

6. Equally slighted and part of the same "modernization" by literacy parcel is a thoroughgoing awareness of *the difficulties regularly, perhaps normally experienced* by those attempting to gain, practice, and master the elements of alphabetic literacy. Learning literacy(ies) is

hard work that needs to be appreciated in and of itself as well as a means to other ends. Recognition of the *"many literacies"* may contribute to this reconfiguration and revaluation.

7. Historical and other perspectives underscore the presence and significance of *multiple paths of learning literacy:* a wide variety of environments and contexts for learning at varying points along the human life and developmental courses. These stand in striking contrast to modern expectations—embedded and formalized in theories, policies, and laws—of the "normally" inseparable intertwining of early age, formal institutional settings explicitly designed for the purpose, and acquisition of literacy. To the extent that this configuration was achieved as goal and image as well as reasonable if never complete description, it was the culmination of a lengthy historical struggle and centuries of reforms and reformers. Of course, at no time past or present has it encompassed the experience of all persons. As a normative expectation against which "deviants" are judged as failing, it does great harm, resulting in what Leon Botstein calls "damaged literacy" and Elspeth Stuckey deems the "violence of literacy." Ironically, under pressing late-twentieth-century demands for elevating mass literacy levels for social order, productivity, "human capital investments," citizenship, and the like, programs in adolescent, adult, workplace, family, and other literacy targets seek to establish flexible images of learning throughout life. The irony is that a history of learning at many ages in fields, workshops, factories, dame schools, class and ethnic and gender associations, among many other informal and formal, integrated and segregated locations, was obscured in the triumph of one correct path. The costs are inestimable, the losses irreplaceable.

8. During centuries of reforms, particularly during the last two hundred years, expectations and common practices *equated literacy learning with elementary education,* a kind of foundationalism that has served to restrict and socially stratify both literacy and education. Coupled with the suspect conclusion that once one had those "basics," then building upon that foundation—using literacy and advancing—was easy, led to the equally easy presumption that failure to learn and advance was primarily the fault of the individual learner, not the schools or society. That is a lesson learned over and over and over, seemingly never sufficiently.

9. Just as individuals took different paths to literacy, *societies and nations have also taken different paths* toward attaining rising levels of popular literacy. Despite expectations and theories of *one* sure road to progress, inscribed in "strong" theories and "standard versions," historical (and more recent developmental) research demonstrates that there is *no one* route to near-universal literacy and associated "modern" con-

comitants. Similarly, there is *no one* route with respect to literacy to economic development, industrialization, democraticization, and the like. At some times and places, literacy served causally, indirectly or directly. At others, it came as a consequence, an effect rather than a cause. And at yet others, dis-connections with and/or negative impacts to literacy predominated. Similar considerations and dis-/connections, we are still learning, relate to quantitative and qualitative levels of literacy and uses of abilities, workplace demands on literacy, among other key relationships, despite simpler and more sanguine expectations.

Together, these lessons—and this set is selective and unavoidably biased in terms of my research and interests—attest to the power of historical learning, the hegemony of common myths and legacies, and the imperative need to shatter that domination in an effort to reconstruct literacy and literacies for today and tomorrow. Our debts to history are mixed. We best repay them by beginning to heed their lessons across the disciplines, ages, environments, and other structured separations.

As I explain particularly in chapter 15, the past two decades' studies also point to a roster of central complications, problems in the research and interpretation of literacy that also span and link disciplines and other concerns. These include such issues as reconceptualizing research away from too close a focus on literacy in and of itself; greater efforts in comparative and ethnographic studies; more flexible conceptualization of *contexts* for acquiring, practicing, and using literacy(ies), alphabetic and other. As the latter issue implies, there is a sharp demand that arches over many other questions and issues for a thoroughgoing critical reconceptualization of literacy itself, as skill, attribute or characteristic or orientation; as factor or "variable" dependent or independent—or both—or. . . . Issues of quantity and quality here stumble over questions of the limits or expansiveness of literacies learned and practiced in specific social or cultural contexts, and questions about "consequences," "implications," or "concomitants" of literacy or literacies. Literacy(ies)' roles in the making and communicating of meaning follow in this roster of topics theoretical, conceptual, and very practical. From there, the reconstruction of policy and popular expectations surrounding transmission, practice, and uses of literacy new and old, and with them the refashioning of learning places, teachers, learners, and learning itself writ large awaits their takers as we turn toward the twenty-first century with a newly heightened understanding and appreciation of the powers of the past.

Notes

1   After due reflection and discussion with the series editor, I chose to retain the original chapters, for historiographic and interpretive, and, may I say, "historical" purposes,

    while adding six new essays. Only in the case of the original chapter 11 have I deviated, replacing that version with a later, fuller version.

2   It is not coincidental that "Reading, Writing and Power," a 12 September 1993 *New York Times* OpEd piece by WALTER ANDERSON, makes the same points that HODGSON did 120 year earlier.

3   As explained there, the version presented in this book uses the concluding sections of three different editions of the presentation to illustrate the applications and targets of "lessons" from the history of literacy: in general, for cities, and with respect to critical literacy. Other editions focus on functional literacy.

4   Parts of that presentation appear in "Literacy, Myths and Legacies: Lessons from the Past/Reflections for the Future," *Interchange* 24 (1993), not included in this collection.

5   See, for example, in addition to chapter 16 below, GRAFF, "Assessing the History of Literacy in the 1990s." presented to the Conference on Writing and Reading in Western Europe, Valencia, Spain, 1993, forthcoming in the conference proceedings; my own and others' contributions to the book of Tilburg conference papers, *Functional Literacy: Theoretical Issues and Educational Implications,* ed. LUDO VERHOEVEN (Amsterdam: JOHN BENJAMINS, 1994); BRIAN STREET, ed., *Cross-Cultural Approaches to Literacy* (Cambridge: Cambridge University Press, 1993); SHERYL GOWEN, *The Politics of Workplace Literacy: A Case Study* (New York; Teachers College Press, 1992).

6   In fact, the other keynote address, by the historian CARL KAESTLE, was also historical in substance and understanding. Several other historians spoke, and one session promoted a brief exchange about "new" literacies and the challenge of hypertext between JAY BOLTER and myself. On "new" literacy(ies), see below and, for example, MYRON C. TUMAN, *Word Perfect: Literacy in the Computer Age* (Pittsburgh: University of Pittsburgh Press, 1992).

7   The second keynote, beset by erroneous allusions to classical mythology and contemporary issues, but none to history, was presented by a U.S. congressman whose participation was limited to his own session.

8   See PETER MCLAREN and PETER LEONARD, eds., *Paulo Freire: A Critical Encounter* (London; Routledge, 1993); a second volume, edited by MCLAREN and COLIN LANKSHEAR is forthcoming; LANKSHEAR and MCLAREN, ed., *Critical Literacy* (Albany: SUNY Press, 1993); IRA SHOR, *Empowering Education* (Chicago: University of Chicago Press, 1992).

9   Credit goes to JOHN NERONE, but also to the journal's editor and a longtime practitioner and supporter of historical approaches, JAMES CAREY. NERONE's quotation appears in "Introduction," *Communication* 11 (1988): 1.

10 The larger study, entitled *Conflicting Paths: Growing Up in America,* is forthcoming from Harvard University Press in 1995.

11 It should be noted here that, regardless of any appearances to the contrary, I am not reprinting all new or relevant pieces.

12 Major historical works are cited in many of the chapters in this book. The final chapter ends with a relatively up-to-date reference list of historical and selected contemporary studies.

13 See especially chapters 15 and 16 below, and my "Assessing the History of Literacy in the 1990s," for amplification.

Introduction

Only the fortunate scholar and writer gains the opportunity to gather together his or her major essays on a single topic and to place them in the form of a unified book. Grateful for this relatively rare moment early in my career, I want to seize the chance to reflect critically on the problematics that literacy studies—be they historical, contemporary, or futuristic—represent to concerned persons in the latter years of the twentieth century. That set of problematics, in the manner considered here, pivots around historical and current traditions of thinking about and studying literacy, principally the assumptions, expectations, and ideologies that dominate those traditions; my own efforts to confront and recast them critically and usefully; my shifting reflections about those efforts; and the place of literacy in contemporary culture and society, and in contemporary thought, theory, and planning.

History

Central to those themes, especially as they intricately interplay and intertwine with one another in many formulations, are certain distinctive elements. Perhaps most prominent in the pages that follow, and most strongly felt in my convictions and intellectual foundations, is the centrality and significance of *history*: the complex relationships that irrevocably tie *past and present*, and, for that matter, *future* too. The questions, critiques, and struggles to posit new conceptualizations that mark all the chapters of this volume flow from that point of origin: my own belief that understanding itself is historically rooted, and that failure to grasp and to proceed seriously from that first premise is an inescapably limiting factor. In part, this constitutes one lesson that recent history suggests may have been forgotten—to the detriment of us all and the suffering of many persons.

At this juncture, I should clarify the kind of historical conception, or historical epistemology and metaphysic, from which I begin. I refer neither to a naive historicism, a historical determinism of any kind, nor any form of chronologically or narratively oriented historical practice. Rather, I advance from a conception of historical inquiry and understanding that is at once critical, theoretical, comparative, interdisciplinary, and reflexive. History, in this sense, constitutes a series of opening moves rather than a delimiting or enclosing mode.

My form of historical practice is at once self- and other-critical. It begins with the general conviction that history provides an especially significant form of understanding. It continues with its presumption that past and present can never be dichtomously divided, and that neither can be grasped without due attention to the other, reciprocally and dialectically. Thus, the constant constellations of contradictions are never ignored but instead placed at the center of the explicandum and explanation. A third element emphasizes that history reveals simultaneously the restrictions on human agency and choice, and the liberating potentials before humanity. A fourth focuses upon history as a 'laboratory' in which the processes of human choices may be studied with reference to the alternatives considered and the outcomes. In sum, my historical orientation activates this mode of human understanding's greatest contribution: its role as *the* discipline of human context in the venues that the other presumptions provide.

In the terms of the pages that follow, the 'case' of literacy, in particular, is one arena in which these perspectives are at once most visible and practicable—and desperately required—in comprehending what is so often termed our contemporary 'crisis' of literacy, regardless of its domains: 'civilization', culture, security, social order, human capital, technology, or 'minimal competency'. The continuities, as well as the transformations and contradictions, that so starkly mark the subject literally cry out for an explicitly historical perspective to any level of its comprehension. The approach is no less valuable in viewing that historical outcome critically, and in considering alternative approaches and responses, and alternative futures.

Literacy*

Less than two decades ago, the place and meaning of the concept and the fact of *literacy* in scholarly and popular understanding were simple and secure. In the social sciences, for example, tied closely to the 'liberal', post-Enlightenment synthesis of modernization theory, literacy was seen as a central variable among that complex of factors that distinguished modern, developed or developing, and advanced societies *and* individuals from the lesser developed areas and persons of the world. Literacy, moreover, was typically conceptualized more as an independent variable than as a dependent factor.

Support for this set of propositions was drawn, on the one hand, from a set of once commonsensical assumptions and expectations, rooted in a special view

---

*This section draws upon my article 'Literacy' in Kuper, Adam, and Kuper, Jessica (Eds), *The Social Science Encyclopedia*, London: Routledge and Kegan Paul, (1985)

of the nature of (historical) development that emphasized the linearity and certainty of progress and, on the other hand, from a number of 'aggregate macrolevel ecological correlations' that saw literacy levels relatively highly associated with many of the other indicators of social development ranging from fertility rates to measures of economic development.

Although literacy itself was at best vaguely defined and variously measured, a diffuse positivism and functionalism undergirded the prominence it was accorded in many formulations. Strong assumptions were paralleled by surprisingly few empirical or critical studies, in fact. Important questions were few; expectations of literacy's key contribution to social and economic development, political democraticization and participant citizenship, widening awareness and identification, seizure of opportunities, and action orientations dominated. As such, promotion of literacy often featured as a central element in plans for the development of underdeveloped areas, especially by North American and Western European social scientists, governments, and foundations.

Such an understanding no longer maintains its hegemony. In fact, in the late-1980s, no central theory governs expectations about the roles and meanings of literacy. Its very nature has itself become problematic and a problematic that arouses contention and an increasing degree of critical attention. From its formerly secure status as critical independent variable, literacy is now conceptualized more as a dependent factor; the linearity of its contributions is also debated. Ironically, as the status—so to speak—of literacy as an independently determinative, necessary if not always sufficient variable has declined, its place on the agenda of social science research and discussion has risen. There are lessons in that transformation, explored in this book.

Many sources account for this change. Among them are the discovery of the limits of modernization theory and the theoretical synthesis on which it was based; increasing awareness of the differences (and different effects) among literacy, schooling, and education—terms too often used interchangeably and confused conceptually; recognition of the problematic nature of literacy; and the conceptual and empirical difficulties that the subject represents.

For example, by the 1960s, the severe problems of measuring literacy, comparing measures and resulting rates for different places and periods, and assessing associations and contributions were frequently noted; a variety of measures and definitions, with a trend toward their inflation, proliferated. Whether literacy's impacts were attitudinal and ideational, cognitive, skill-linked, concrete or more abstract, all-pervasive or more selective—questions arising from empirical studies and from critical conceptual analyses—sparked further discussion and weakened common bases of understanding. In addition, the often conservative functions and consequences of literacy and, indeed, certain 'noneffects' received renewed attention. Empirical studies became more sensitive to weak and contradictory findings; discussions of literacy 'gaps' and time 'lags' in association with other expected aspects and concomitants of development punctuated the literature. International attention increased: from the twin sources of UNESCO's calls for action and analysis and pathbreaking national literacy campaigns in the Third World.

The discovery of persisting *il*literacy in the advanced societies led to the identification of *il*literacy, and sometimes literacy too, as a 'social problem', and national welfare, and the promise of democratic life. Rapid changes in communications technology, especially of nonprint and nonalphabetic forms (in contrast to the traditional bases of literacy) not only led to sometimes frenzied questions about the 'future' and 'decline' of literacy and print, but also stimulated more questions about definitions, measures, and levels of individual and national skills requisite for survival and advancement in late modern societies. Whereas literacy was seldom deemed *un*important or nonconsequential, or *il*literacy *not* an obstacle or liability, its precise contributions and impacts could no longer be simply assumed.

The challenge of a number of revisionist 'critical theories' was also important. So too was the development of a historical analysis of literacy and illiteracy, much of which aimed specifically at testing the literacy-modernization linkages. Examples of both appear below. In a number of careful, often statistical studies, historians throughout Europe and North America sharply qualified traditional expectations of a series of direct connections tying rising levels of literacy to developments in societies, economics, polities, and cultures.

This is one area in which historians, and other 'human scientists', and social scientists have had much of importance to contribute to one another. In part, historians discovered relatively high levels of literacy in advance of 'modernization'; they simultaneously located important 'takeoffs' prior to 'mass' or even moderately high literacy rates. Literacy's linkages to the spread of modern attitudes and its relationship to individual advancement have been questioned. Notions of stages or 'threshold levels' have also been criticized. Many macrolevel correlations seem to break down in disaggregated testing.

There are, importantly, a number of critical points at which recent historical and social scientific analyses reflect one another conceptually and empirically. These include the nature of literacy as a *dependent* variable; its dependence on *context*; the *limits* of universal impacts and generalized consequences (which have major implications for literacy's place in social science theories); the epistemological complications of *defining and measuring* literacy levels at the societal plane or literacy abilities at the individual; the weakness of the traditional literacy-illiteracy *dichotomy*; and the fact that changes in literacy levels may ofen *follow from* rather than precede basic social, economic, political, or cultural transformations. Literacy, increasingly, is connected to the larger network of communicative competencies (the oral and electronic, for example), not contrasted dichotomously and developmentally from them; it is also conceptualized more as a *continuous, widely varying, and nonlinear* attribute. Its importance as shaper of attitudes and as a symbol and symbolic influence stands beside, in partial independence from, its role in cognitive and skill determination. To speak of literacy in the abstract is now considered hazardous, if not quite meaningless.

Among the most critical of contemporary research approaches to literacy is the emerging social psychology of literacy. Scribner and Cole (1981) document the limits of literacy by itself and the theoretical assumptions that link it universally to higher forms of thought and practice; they point toward a formulation of literacy as *practice and context* ethnographies of literacy in use and nonuse, whose promise is great (Whiteman, 1981; Tannen, 1982; Heath, 1983).

Historical studies continue their pathbreaking relevance (Graff, 1979, 1981, 1986; Lockridge, 1974; Furet and Ozouf, 1977). By contrast, the sociology and economics of literacy find their theoretical presuppositions and empirical methods challenged and seek new paradigms (*Harvard Educational Review*, 1981; Stanley, 1979; Bataille, 1976). The future of literacy studies can be an exciting, and vastly important one. Of that, this book is but one sign.

My 'history with literacy' is the connection that joins the preceding sections. As a part of that transformation, I have been at once deeply influenced by the various trends forcing and promoting criticism and reconceptualization and also a contributor, for over a decade now, to that process. My personal involvement stems from, and begins with my 'coming of age' in the throes of the 1960s and the variety of activities in which I found myself engaged and/or influenced. Questions, often very basic and radical ones, about education and schooling on the one hand—their methods, assumptions, 'uses', ends, human consequences—and about their relations to culture, society, economy, and polity, on the other hand, were ever present.

Following my decision, at the end of that decade, to pursue graduate study in history and having the good fortune to discover a pioneering social history in process of development with Michael B. Katz and his 'Hamilton Project' at the University of Toronto and Ontario Institute for Studies in Education, I began to find ways in which to blend interests, influences and practice. Of course, only in retrospect is this a clear and consistent, let alone a conscious set of experiences.

As chance would have it, a specific focus on literacy, historically studied and understood, emerged in a first-year graduate seminar on 'the historical study of social structure'. In this setting, one which combined a variety of approaches to the subject with quantitative methodology and an explicit focus on social theories, each student was required to prepare a research paper based on the exploitation of quantitative social data. Sparked most immediately by reading Stone's (1969) and Cipolla's (1969) now classic but then novel essays on the history of literacy and influenced by concurrent work in a seminar on the history of education, I undertook to examine the usefulness of nineteenth-century manuscript census data, for the city of Hamilton, Ontario, Canada, for the history of literacy in the social structure. I now recognize how concerns, issues, and questions with which I had literally grown up, deeply influenced this path. With that very preliminary essay—which itself grew into a Masters Thesis and my first two scholarly publications (Graff, 1971, 1972, 1973)—began a major occupation and preoccupation for the next decade and a half! My own growing belief in the necessity for a explicitly historical dimension—typically ignored—to literacy studies and criticism was only reinforced.

Not only did literacy provide the subject for initial graduate study; in the end it also grew into the doctoral dissertation and writings that resulted in important, influential encounters with a wide range of audiences and a lengthy series of publications. Here too the consequences have been reciprocal.

From a rather narrow testing and elementary manipulation of numerical data on one nineteenth-century city, the bounds of my inquiries and explorations grew. They early touched on rural society, although my interests fell most often on the urban, but also probed for a more global perspective within the shifting contexts of time and space. From my first book on literacy, *The Literacy Myth: Literacy and Social Structure in the Nineteen-Century City* (1979) through my culminating interpretive synthesis, *The Legacies of Literacy: Continuities and Contradictions in Western Society and Culture* (1986) which spans the several millenia of the Western experience with literacy, and the co-edited explicitly contrapuntal volume, *National Literacy Campaigns in Historical and Contemporary Perspective* (1987), the chronological, geographical, and interpretive scope have been transformed, a requisite for deeper understanding. To borrow a phrase from family sociologist Glen Elder, employed in assessing developments in his own field, this was at heart 'the discovery of complexity' and regular contradiction.

Paralleling that process was another: an appreciation of the uncounted ways in which literacy—in thought and life experiences—touched, reflected, refracted so many of the key issues and developments of the diverse courses of historical change. Thus, literacy emerged as a topic not only consequential in and of itself but as a thread which ran through many seams whose stitching, unravelling, and repair were at once worthy of direct focus and tracing along the paths of otherwise apparently loose ends. Readers will see this shifting in comparing, for example, Chapter 2 with Chapter 1 and 11 in this volume. As with the subject writ large, to paraphrase the title of my general history, 'continuities *and* contradictions' pervade, and integrate, the remnants into its larger fabric. Questions about focus, and at which points to begin—with literacy itself or toward literacy in its contexts—develop as important theoretical and methodological concerns in their own right.

These are not the only foci or transformations. Inseparable from them have been concurrent methodological discrimination and dissatisfaction, an emergent theoretical and conceptual critique, and a search for more satisfactory and appropriate foundations and formulations. Beginning with a critical perspective but a fairly normative social scientific historical approach and methodology, much of my first work now seems inherently narrow and restricted by a latent functionalism and technical linearity. This limited not only a more sophisticated recasting, but also the ability to connect and to move across and among the social (or sociological), economic, and political domains—with which I began, and the cultural, anthropological, psychological, linguistic, communicative, and ideological dimensions, on whose larger linkages I came to focus. The same dilemma also surfaces in the problem of simultaneously considering the roles of and the impacts for the individual and the aggregate. In part, this is another reflection of the boundaries of academic traditions, training, and research-interpretive practice; it also underscores the especially refractory—indeed rather slippery—nature of the subject.

Yet another key dimension of this search pivots on limiting dichotomies and potentially liberating dialectics. This emerges clearly in the chapters, especially if they are compared with reference to their dates of initial publication (and drafting) and their relative datedness. Literacy, as discussed in detail below, is, perhaps more than other topics, especially marked by the range and number of dichotomies that wrack its understanding; of these the literate/illiterate is but one example of many.

In learning to transcend these oppositions, but also to grasp the significance of their regular presence and the uses to which they are put, I have struggled to follow and to play out the 'dance of the dialectic'. Over time and gradually, this emerged as absolutely central to my developing conceptualizations, as the chapters illustrate. Among the core moves, this has involved, for example, learning to embrace—without invidiously dichotomizing—literacy's simultaneous capabilities for hegemony and control, and for individual and collective realization of potential and actions, sometimes of a transcending nature. In this, of course, literacy's limits, its contextualized meanings, and its contributing/facilitating—rather than independently determining—impacts can never be forgotten. Again, as the essays suggest on a number of different levels, the subject and its traditions, and the assumptions and expectations that mark them both, demand a dialectical as well as a historical approach. In no other manner can the regular patterns of central contradictions be apprehended.

The ideological nature of literacy studies and literacy's place in thought and theory accompanies these points. Despite traditions of positing literacy as 'neutral', as a 'variable', this can no longer be tolerated. The word—I use this term in several senses at once—'literacy', as concept, principle, condition, goal, etc., is itself the product of its own history. Indeed, part of scholars' squabbles, educators' errors, and popular panegyrics is the failure to appreciate that simple but inescapable 'fact'. Among the many consequences is the easy manipulability of the word 'literacy'—typically for derogation—and the problems of communication that pervade and surround it. As the first chapter essays, literacy must be 'deconstructed', to borrow a term from literary criticism, before it can be meaningfully reconstructed. That mental act must also be a historical one. That has been one focus of my efforts.

Equally relevant here is not only that different commentators 'mean' different things by reference to 'literacy' and that the same persons sometimes implicitly contradict themselves in their employment of 'literacy'; we also must recognize that there is no one 'literacy'. As recent thinking in a variety of disciplines and fields now underscores, distinctions need to be made and kept consistent between different forms of literacy—alphabetic, mathematic, graphic, visual, musical, physical, oral/aural, among the many—as between differing quantitative and qualitative levels of literacy. Failure to discriminate here is only complicated by gross ignorance about how the different 'literacies' may actually relate, or not relate, to one another. Therein lies the next agenda, I aver, for psychological and educational researchers.

The Essays*

Rereading the chapters that constitute this volume, recognizing their points of commonality and divergence, reflecting on the developments they document (visible at least to their author!), and remembering the occasions that prompted their first writing and the circumstances of the draftings themselves is a moving personal experience. I am struck perhaps more by certain levels of consistency, of echoes and reciprocal reflections than by core differences, although I am mindful of changes in perspective, shifts in understanding, and, I hope, an increasing sophistication.

A concern with empirical research within a practice informed by conceptual and theoretical criticism, conceptual questioning and explicit testing of different formulations, and a concern with comparing and relating theory and practice—often in historical circumstances—mark the chapters. So does the historical-rootedness of the subject itself. This holds true despite their many differences. The latter include the occasions and purposes of their writing, the forms and formats of their construction and appearance, the levels of criticism targeted, the explicitness of theoretical (in some cases) and policy (in other cases) orientations. Some, it should be clear, were written first for oral or public airing; some developed relatively independently from research in progress; others were invited or solicited interim statements, research reports, or forms of overview. The introductory notes and the notes to the chapters themselves indicate some of these considerations.

Equally noteworthy are issues of audience. Chapters 5–9 were published in journals read overwhelmingly by historians; Chapter 10 was first an essay review in a linguistics and language journal, Chapter 1 in an interdisciplinary humanities forum, Chapters 2 and 11 in an educational journal, Chapter 3 in a collection aimed at historians, historians of education, and educationists, and Chapter 4 in a journal of population and policy. Revealing of the lines that the subject crosses, this diversity also implicitly raises further questions about cross- and interdisci-

---

*After careful consideration and with some hesitancy, I have chosen to reprint the following chapters largely as they originally appeared, but in a topical rather than a chronological ordering. I think that their aggregate purpose is best served, and their fullest flavor conveyed, in this manner. Brief section introductions begin Parts II and III; Parts I and IV, with one chapter each, require no such discussion.

plinary research and thinking, and about faciliting (and the limitations on) communication within and without the academy.

All the chapters, to my rereading, share central concerns, regardless of their sometimes rather basic—and telling—differences. These, I think, should be highlighted. The eleven chapters, from one format and angle of refraction or another, speak to overarching issues of ideologies, assumptions, concepts and conceptualizations, and theories and practices. All are galvanized around the many ways in which the past speaks to the present: shaping, conditioning, influencing it, and the future(s), as well. A dialogue, cast in a dialectical set of relationship, is called for and exemplified on occasion. A number of the chapters, especially those focusing on planning and policy, fertility, economic development and individual advancement, and criminality and punishment, should be read as exemplars in this quest, as well as monographic or review essays in their own right.

A concern about political and social policies aimed at promoting literacy and about the 'uses' of literacy in other policy debates and formulations also permeates the chapters. The striking, sometimes distressing and depressing parallels and continuities between past and present require little additional emphasis here, alas. But the use of history as a policy 'arena' or 'laboratory', suggested in some chapters, remains novel and underexplored. Finally, examples of case study approaches, critical commentaries, and synthetic approaches may be compared and contrasted in reading and evaluating the substance of this collection. In sum, the entire collection may usefully be read as an intended, but still incomplete exemplar in terms of the revision and re-visioning of literacy anew. Should it prove useful as part of a continuing dialogue in at least some of the terms proposed here, I will be more than satisfied, however limited or further revised it may prove.

The Present Moment

The currency and topicality of this material need not, I am certain, be belabored. At present, as so very many indications daily remind us, we are at a critical juncture in the history of literacy—and in the history of the Western, indeed the entire world. That conjuncture is not coincidental; that is one point of the present work, of course. But as the recent writings by Street (1984) Kozol (1985), and Levine (1982), for example, serve to underscore, there have been few if any points in history at which the needs and potential costs have been so great. The core process of criticism, reflection, and rethinking toward which this book is directed carries an unmistakable urgency.

In sum, the limits of these efforts should also be recognized. Those of the individual chapters are readily apparent to all critical readers. What I would rather stress is that they are but one part of a much larger, multifaceted intellectual and practical struggle on the part of many persons at this moment. Among those who might be recognized here, I mention only a handful of scholars whose work has prodded, stimulated, complemented mine, and whose writings should be read for those comparisons and contradictions: Carlo Ginzburg (1980), Sylvia Scribner and Michael Cole (1981), Shirley Brice Heath (1983), David Olson (in progress), and Brian Street (1984). Their efforts and place in the larger dialogue add to the agenda found in the first and the final chapters of this book. They too realize that the questions and the resulting answers and actions, appearances sometimes to the contrary, are more than academic.

References

BATAILLE, LEON (Ed.) (1976) *A Turning Point for Literacy.* Oxford: Pergamon Press.
CIPOLLA, CARLO (1969) *Literacy and Development in the West.* Harmondsworth: Penguin.
CLAMMER, J.R. (1976) *Literacy and Social Change: A Case Study of Fiji.* Leiden: E.J. BRILL.
FURET, FRANÇOIS and OZOUF, JACQUES (1977) *Lire et Écrire: L'Alphabetisation des français de Calvin à Jules Ferry,* 2 vols. Paris: Editions de Minuit (English translation, *Reading and Writing.* Cambridge University Press, 1983).
GINZBURG, CARLO (1980) *The Cheese and the Worms.* Baltimore: Johns Hopkins University Press.
GOODY, JACK (Ed.) (1968) *Literacy in Traditional Societies.* Cambridge: Cambridge University Press.
GOODY, JACK (1977) *The Domestication of the Savage Mind.* Cambridge: Cambridge University Press.
GRAFF, HARVEY J. (1971) 'Notes on methods for studying literacy from the manuscript census,' *Historical Methods,* 11–16.
GRAFF, HARVEY J. (1972) 'Towards a meaning of literacy: Literacy and social structure in Hamilton, Ontario,' *History of Education Quarterly,* 12, 411–431.
GRAFF, HARVEY J. (1972) 'Approaches in the historical study of literacy,' *Urban History Review,* 1, 6–11.
GRAFF, HARVEY J. (1973) 'Literacy and social structure in Elgin County, Canada West,' *Histoire sociale/Social History,* 6, 25–48.
GRAFF, HARVEY J. (1979) *The Literacy Myth: Literacy and Social Structure in the Nineteenth-Century City.* New York and London: Academic Press.
GRAFF, HARVEY J. (Ed.) (1981) *Literacy in History: An Interdisciplinary Research Bibliography.* New York: Garland Press.
GRAFF, HARVEY J. (Ed.) (1981) *Literacy and Social Development in the West: A Reader.* Cambridge: Cambridge University press.
GRAFF, HARVEY J. (1981) 'Reflections on the history of literacy: Overview, critique, and proposals', *Humanities in Society,* 4, 303–333.
GRAFF, HARVEY J. (1986) *The Legacies of Literacy: Continuities and Contradictions in Western Society and Culture.* Bloomington: Indiana University Press.
GRAFF, HARVEY J. and ROBERT ARNOVE (Eds.) (1987) *National Literacy Campaigns in Historical and Comparative Perspective.* New York: Plenum.
HARMON, DAVID (1970) 'Illiteracy: An overview', *Harvard Educational Review,* 40, 226–243.
HARVARD EDUCATIONAL REVIEW (1981) 51, No. 1, 'Education as Transformation: Identity, Change, and Development' (entire issue).
HEATH, SHIRLEY BRICE (1983) *Ways with Words.* Cambridge: Cambridge University Press.

KOZOL, JONATHAN (1985) *Illiterate America.* Garden City, New York: Doubleday.

LEVINE, KENNETH (1982) 'Functional literacy: Fond illusions and false economies,' *Harvard Educational Review*, 52, 249–266.

LOCKRIDGE, KENNETH (1974) *Literacy in Colonial New England.* New York: Norton.

OXENHAM, JOHN (1980) *Literacy: Writing, Reading and Social Organisation.* London: Routledge and Kegan Paul.

SCRIBNER, SYLVIA and COLE, MICHAEL (1981) *The Psychology of Literacy.* Cambridge, Mass.: Harvard University Press.

STANLEY, MANFRED (1978) *The Technological Conscience.* New York: Free Press.

STONE, LAWRENCE (1969) 'Literacy and education in England, 1640–1900,' *Past and Present*, 42, 61–139.

STREET, BRIAN (1984) *Literacy in Theory and Practice.* Cambridge: Cambridge University Press.

TANNEN, DEBORAH (Ed.) *Spoken and Written Language: Exploring Orality and Literacy*, Vol. 9, Advances in Discourse Processes. Norwood, NJ: Ablex.

WHITEMAN, MARCIA FARR (Ed.) *Writing: The Nature, Development, and Teaching of Written Communication*, Vol. 1, Variations in Writing, Hillsdale, NJ: Lawrence Erlbaum Associates.

Part I
The Legacies and Contradictions of Literacy

1 Reflections on the History of Literacy: Overview, Critique, and Proposals

Let us set the stage. These statements, from a variety of disciplinary and ideological perspectives, help us prepare for a reconsideration and reconceptualization of literacy:

> In the popular imagination, literacy is the most significant distinguishing feature of a civilized man and a civilized society. Expressions of these attitudes are readily culled from the popular press. . . . The assumption that nonliteracy is a problem with dreadful social and personal consequences is not only held by laymen, it is implicit in the writings of academics as well.[1]
>
> Since popular literacy as earlier noted depends not alone on the alphabet but on instruction in the alphabet given at the elementary level of child development, and since this is a political factor which varies from country to country, the alphabetized cultures are not all socially literate.
>
> . . . For whereas historians who have touched upon literacy as a historical phenomenon have commonly measured its progress in terms of the history of writing, the actual conditions of literacy depend upon the history not of writing but reading. In dealing with the past, it is obviously much harder to be certain about the practice of reading, its conduct and extent, than about writing. For the latter can simply exist in an artifact. . . . [Literacy] is a social condition which can be defined only in terms of readership.[2]
>
> Not long ago anthropologists equated civilization with literacy. Many archaeologists working in the Near East still believe that writing is highly likely to develop as a data-storage technique when a given level of complexity is reached. This seems to be supported, for example, by the apparently extensive use of writing for bureaucratic purposes in ancient Egypt. . . . Yet, the evidence from Africa and the New World reveals that complex societies can exist without fully-developed (initially logosyllabic) writing systems and that those early civilizations that lacked writing were

3

of comparable complexity to those that had it . . . there is no obvious reason why some of these should have developed writing systems and not the rest.[3]

Literacy is for the most part an enabling rather than a causal factor, making possible the development of complex political structures, syllogistic reasoning, scientific enquiry, linear conceptions of reality, scholarly specialization, artistic elaboration, and perhaps certain kinds of individualism and of alienation.

Whether, and to what extent, these will in fact develop depends apparently on concomitant factors of ecology, intersocietal relations, and internal ideological and social structural responses to these.[4]

For certain uses of language, literacy is not only irrelevant but is a positive hindrance.[5]

These statements may seem too sweeping and too vast to some. They are, to the contrary, important examples of the correctives and revisions only now beginning with respect to understanding the presumed impacts and consequences of literacy.[6] For until quite recently, scholarly and popular conceptions of the value of the skills of reading or writing have almost universally followed normative assumptions and expectations of vague but powerful concomitants and effects presumed to accompany changes in the diffusion of literacy. For the last two centuries they have been inextricably and inseparably linked with post-Enlightenment, 'liberal' social theories and contemporary expectations regarding the role of literacy and schooling in socioeconomic development, social order, and individual progress. This set of conjunctures—in theory, thought, perception, and expectation—is enormously important. The implications are far too numerous to recount in this brief chapter. Yet, they constitute what I have come to call a 'literacy myth,' which I have discussed for the nineteenth century in my recent book of that title and have sketched for the past five thousand years of Western civilization in my new work, *The Legacies of Literacy: Continuities and Contradictions in Western Society and Culture.*

Along with other tenets of a world view dominant in the West for the greatest part of the past two centuries, the 'literacy myth' no longer serves as a satisfactory explanation for the place of literacy in society, polity, culture, or economy.[7] Given the massive *contradictions* that complicate and confuse our understanding of the world we inhabit, it is hardly surprising that a perceived 'crisis' and 'decline of literacy' rank among the other fears of our day. Because our comprehension of this crisis and decline is no more firm than that of the historical relevance of literacy itself, now is the time to ask new, if challenging and difficult, questions that may lead to new views about literacy and its roles. If the present teaches us nothing else, we must heed the lesson that the presumed places of literacy and schooling are neither sacrosanct nor well understood. That awareness—especially in tandem with the advantages only a historical perspective can yield—can be tremendously liberating; that, I think, is what is urgently required. For, 'if we have learned anything from modern European sociology, it is that historical and social interest, not systems of logic, determine what shall count as knowledge.'[8] From this perspective, we turn to a historical understanding of literacy, for what it may teach us anew about that important past itself, and also for the illumination that it sheds upon pressing questions of the present.

Literacy, I have come to believe, is *profoundly misunderstood.* That is one 'natural' consequence of the long-standing tyranny of the 'literacy myth,' which, along with other social and cultural myths, has of course had sufficient grounding in social reality to insure its wide dissemination and acceptance. Misunderstanding of literacy is as true for the past as for the present; these two elements are in fact but one, we must recognize. And this misconstrual of the meanings and contributions of literacy, and the interesting contradictions that result, is not only an evidential and empirical problem but also a failure in conceptualization and, even more, epistemology. That, indeed, constitutes my largest and most important point.

Discussions about literacy are surprisingly facile (at least *I* used to be surprised), whether they come from the pen of a Marshall McLuhan or a contemporary social and educational critic like Paul Copperman, author of *The Literacy Hoax.* Without supporting the point with extended examples or quotations, I find that virtually all such discussions, regardless of purpose or intent, flounder because they slight any effort to formulate consistent and realistic *definitions of literacy,* have little appreciation of the *conceptual complications* that the subject of literacy presents, and ignore—often grossly—the vital role of *sociohistorical context.* As a historian, I find the last to be the greatest sin of the three, but it would be unfounded to maintain that the first two are less severe as obstacles to informed understanding.

The results of such failures surround us. They preclude our knowing even the dimensions of qualitative changes in popular abilities to employ usefully or functionally the skills of reading and writing today.[9] *Expectations* and *assumptions* of the primacy and priority of literacy and print, for society and individual; the necessity of 'functional' skills for survival (whatever they might be); or the mass condition of literacy as an index of the condition of civilization—all stand unsatisfactorily and inadequately as substitutes for a deeper, grounded understanding of the issues and problems. Clearly, this cannot be regarded as surprising to us; it is the result of an important historical development: the ideological origins of our own world and society, and the place of literacy within them.

This has often been recognized more cogently by nonhistorians than by those of us who ought to know better. David Olson, an educational psychologist, for example, has observed:

> But such an overwhelming concern with literacy can only increase one's
> suspicions that the significance of a universal high degree of literacy is
> grossly misrepresented. It is overvalued partly because literate people,
> such as educators, knowing the value of their own work, fail to recognize
> the value of anyone else's. More importantly, literacy is overvalued be-

cause of the very structure of formal schooling—schooling that, in Bruner's words, involves learning 'out of the context of action, by means that are primarily symbolic.' The currency of schools is words—words, as we saw earlier, that are shaped up for the requirements of literacy.

We may have a distorted view of both the child and of social realities if we expect that the values and pleasures of literacy are so great that everyone, whether it is easy or difficult for him, or whether it leads to wealth or power . . . or not, is willing to invest the energy and time required to reach a high level of literacy.[10]

The reading methodologists Nan Elsasser and Vera John-Steiner also comment:

In spite of the belief, widely held in America, that education in and of itself can transform both people's sense of power and the existing social and economic hierarchies, educational intervention without actual social change is, in fact, ineffective.[11]

We are familiar with these notions; the extent to which we permit them consciously and systematically to reorient our thinking about the roles and relevances of literacy and schooling, past and present, remains too separate and distinct an issue. Consequently, we overvalue literacy, by itself, and in so doing, we remove it from its sociocultural context.

The *first* point to consider is definitional. This is at once an insolubly complex problem and a deceptively simple issue. It is depressing but instructive to note how rarely debates and discussions about literacy levels pause to consider what is meant by reference to literacy. Part of the inattention to context, this failure, on one hand, invalidates most discussions at their outset and, on the other hand, permits commentators to use the evidence of changes in such measures as Scholastic Aptitude Tests, undergraduate composition abilities, Armed Forces Qualifying Tests, and random written or textual evidence to be taken as appropriate representations of literacy. Although I am *not* claiming that the evidence of such measures should be ignored (although I urge a greater caution in their interpretation), I emphasize that whatever these indicators reveal, it is typically little or nothing directly about the skills of literacy: *the basic abilities to read and write.*

To study and interpret literacy, on the contrary, requires three tasks. The *first* is a consistent definition that serves comparatively over time and across space. *Basic or primary levels of reading and writing* constitute the *only* flexible and reasonable indications or signs that meet this essential criterion; a number of historical and contemporary sources, while not wholly satisfactory in themselves, may be employed (see table 1.1). Included here are measures ranging from the evidence of written documents, sources that reveal proportions of signatures and marks, the evidence of self-reporting (surprisingly reliable, in fact), responses to surveys and questionnaires, test results, and the like.[12] Only such basic but systematic and direct indications meet the canons of accuracy, utility, *and* comparability that we must apply consistently. Otherwise, quantitative and qualitative dimensions and changes cannot be known, and only confusion and distortion

Table 1.1 Sources for the Historical Study of Literacy in North America and Europe

Source	Measure of literacy	Population	Country of availability	Years of availability	Additional variables
Census	Questions: read and write, read/write Signature/mark (Canada 1851, 1861 only)	Entire 'adult' population (in theory): ages variable, e.g., over 20 years, 15 years, 10 years	Canada, United States	Manuscripts: Nineteenth century	Age, sex, occupation, birthplace, religion, marital status, family size and structure, residence, economic data
Wills	Signature/mark	20–50% of adult males dying; 2–5% of adult females dying	Canada, United States, England, France, etc.	Canada, eighteenth century on. US 1660 on, others from sixteenth-seventeenth century on	Occupation, charity, family size, residence, estate, sex
Deeds	Signature/mark	5–85% of living landowning adult males; 1% or less of females	Canada, United States	Eighteenth century on	Occupation, residence, value of land, type of sale
Inventories	Book ownership	25–60% of adult males dying; 3–10% of adult females dying	Canada, United States, England, France, etc.	Seventeenth-eighteenth century on (quantity varies by country and date)	Same as wills
Depositions	Signature/mark	Uncertain: potentially more select than wills, potentially wider Women sometimes included	Canada, United States, England, Europe	Seventeenth-eighteenth century on (use and survival varies)	Potentially, age, occupation, sex, birthplace, residence

Source	Measure of literacy	Population	Country of availability	Years of availability	Additional variables
Marriage records	Signature/mark	Nearly all (80% +) young men and women marrying (in England)	England, France, North America	From 1754 in England; 1650 in France	Occupation, age, sex, parents' name and occupation, residence (religion—North America)
Catechetical examination records	Reading, memorization, comprehension, writing examinations	Unclear, but seems very wide	Sweden, Finland	After 1620	Occupation, age, tax status, residence, parents' name and status, family size, migration, periodic improvement
Petitions	Signature/mark	Uncertain, potentially very select; males only in most cases	Canada, United States, England, Europe	Eighteenth century on	Occupation or status, sex, residence, political or social views
Military recruit records	Signature/mark or question on reading and writing	Conscripts or recruits (males only)	Europe, esp. France	Nineteenth century	Occupation, health, age, residence, education
Criminal records	Questions: read, read well, etc.	All arrested	Canada, United States, England	Nineteenth century	Occupation, age, sex, religion, birthplace, residence, marital status, moral habits, criminal data

Source	Measure of literacy	Population	Country of availability	Years of availability	Additional variables
Business records	Signature/mark	1. All employees 2. Customers	Canada, United States, England, Europe	Nineteenth-twentieth century	1. Occupation, wages 2. Consumption level, residence, credit
Library/mechanics institute records	Books borrowed	Members or borrowers	Canada, United States, England	Late eighteenth, early nineteenth century	Names of volumes borrowed, society membership
Applications (land, job, pensions, etc.)	Signature/mark	All applicants	Canada, United States, England, Europe	Nineteenth-twentieth century	Occupation, residence, family career history, etc.
Aggregate[1] data sources	Questions or direct tests	Varies greatly	Canada, United States, England, Europe	Nineteenth-twentieth century	Any or all of the above

Note: 1 Censuses, educational surveys, statistical society reports, social surveys, government commissions, prison and jail records, etc.

Sources: Graff, *The Literacy Myth*, Appendix A, pp. 325–27. This is a modified and greatly expanded version of Table A in Lockridge, *Literacy*.

result. Some may question the quality of such data; others argue that tests of basic skills are too low a standard to employ.

To counter such common objections requires moving to a *second* task in defining literacy. This is to stress, to underscore the fact, that literacy is above all *a technology or set of techniques for communications and for decoding and reproducing written or printed materials:* it cannot be taken as anything more or less. Similarly, despite the protestations of recent scholarship to the contrary, printing is also a technique or tool, a mechanical innovation. Neither writing nor printing alone is an 'agent of change'; their impacts are determined by the manner in which human agency exploits them in a specific setting. Literacy must be seen as a basis, a foundation, not as an end or conclusion. What follows from that foundation is perhaps a greater concern than literacy *per se.* Literacy, moreover, is a learned or acquired skill, in a way in which oral ability or nonverbal, nonliterate communicative modes are not. As I shall explain later, we need to be wary of drawing overly firm lines between the oral and the literate.[13]

Writings about the imputed 'consequences,' 'implications,' or 'concomitants' of literacy have assigned to literacy's acquisition a truly daunting number of cognitive, affective, behavioral, and attitudinal effects. These characteristics include, in typical formulations or listings, attitudes ranging *from* empathy, innovativeness, achievement orientation, 'cosmopoliteness,' information and media awareness, national identification, technological acceptance, rationality, and commitment to democracy, *to* opportunism, linearity of thought and behavior, or urban residence! Literacy is sometimes conceived as a skill but more often as symbolic or representative of attitudes and mentalities. That is suggestive. On other levels, literacy 'thresholds' are seen as requirements for economic development, 'take-offs,' 'modernization,' political development and stability, standards of living, fertility control, and on and on. The number of asserted consequences and ecological correlations is literally massive; large volumes easily could be filled with them. The evidence, however, is much less than the expectations and presumptions, as a review of the literature quickly reveals.

One major contradiction in the literacy-as-a-path-to-development enterprise (or should we say 'industry'?) is the disparity between theoretical assumptions and empirical findings. The latter are, first, much less frequent than the former. When they are attempted, second, the results of macro-level, aggregative, or ecological studies are usually much less impressive either statistically or substantively than the normative theories and assumptions. Schuman, Inkeles, and Smith's ingenuous effort to account for this is revealing: 'Rather than finding literacy to be a factor which completely pervades and shapes a man's entire view of the world, we find it limited to those spheres where vicarious and abstract experience is essentially meaningful. The more practical part of a man's outlook, however, is determined by his daily experience in significant roles.'[14] The conclusion is that literacy in the abstract is at most viewed as a technique or set of techniques, a foundation in skills that can be developed, lost, or stagnated. At worst, literacy in the abstract is meaningless.

Hence, understanding literacy requires a *further, large* step: into precise, historically specific material and cultural contexts. As psychologist M.M. Lewis recognized, 'The only literacy that matters is the literacy that is in use. Potential literacy is empty, a void.'[15] The first two points are preparations for the major effort; they help us to clear the air of so much noise and unfounded generalizations. The major problem, which lags far behind in efforts to study literacy whether in the past or present, is that of reconstructing the contexts of reading and writing: how, when, where, why, and to whom literacy was transmitted; the meanings that were assigned to it; the uses to which it was put; the demands placed on literate abilities; the degrees to which those demands were met; the changing extent of social restrictedness in the distribution and diffusion of literacy; and the real and symbolic differences that emanated from the social condition of literacy among the population. To be sure, answers to these kinds of questions are never easy to construct; nevertheless, the point remains that an awareness of their overriding methodological and interpretive importance is only beginning to appear in research and discussion. The meaning and contribution of literacy, therefore, cannot be presumed; they must themselves be a distinct focus of research and criticism. Here contemporary debate is most often incomplete.

Without the space for detailed examples, I must risk the danger of vagueness and abstraction. Let me point to several examples of research orientations that fall within the more general categories. The context in which literacy is taught or acquired is one significant area. The pioneering work of the crosscultural cognitive psychologists Michael Cole and Sylvia Scribner with the Vai people in Liberia and elsewhere points to the enormously suggestive conclusion that the *environment* in which students acquire their literacy carries a major impact on the cognitive consequences of their possession of the skill and the uses to which it can be put. Children who were formally educated in schools designed for that purpose acquired as part of their training a set of skills rather different from those of children who learned more informally. Cole and Scribner point toward an interpretation that contradicts the usual view 'that literacy leads inevitably to higher forms of thought.' 'Rather,' they argue, 'we advocate an approach to literacy that moves beyond generalities to a consideration of the organization and use of literacy in different social contexts.' Whereas previous empirical studies did not test literacy itself but rather confounded it with schooling, as do most historians, Scribner and Cole attempt to distinguish the roles and contributions of the two. In contrast with other researchers, they find,

> we concluded from these data that the tendency of schooled populations to generalize across a wide range of problems occurred because schooling provides people with a great deal of practice in treating individual learning problems as instances of general classes of problems. Moreover, we did not assume that the skills promoted by schooling would necessarily be applied in contexts unrelated to school experience.
>
> As in previous research, improved performance was associated with years of formal schooling, but literacy in the Vai script did not substitute

for schooling. Vai literates were not significantly different from nonliterates on any of these cognitive measures, including the sorting and reasoning tasks that had been suggested as especially sensitive to experience with a written language.

Some psychological consequences were in fact associated with personal engagement in reading and writing, but they were both limited and highly specific to activities with the Vai script.[16]

This set of findings, of restricted impacts of literacy, has wide implications. It can usefully enrich historical as well as contemporary analyses of literacy, especially regarding the time and place in which literacy is acquired and transmitted in circumstances outside the environment of the schoolroom and in formal institutional settings.[17] Such research may also control the assumptions and expectations that students carry to studies of literacy—such as presupposing literacy to be 'liberating' or 'revolutionary' in its consequences. There are, I suggest, better reasons to expect the opposite to be more often the case. We therefore ask: What kind and quality of literacy have schools sought to provide? What lessons, cognitive or noncognitive, have accompanied it? Conclusions must reflect these issues; only then may ability levels be understood.

A second example involves the 'tyranny of *conceptual dichotomies*' in the study and interpretation of literacy. Few research areas suffer more from the obstruction to understanding that rigid dichotomizing represents than literacy studies. Consider the common phrases: literate *and* illiterate, written *and* oral, print *and* script, and so on. None of these polar opposites usefully describes actual circumstances; all of them, in fact, preclude contextual understanding. The oral-literate dichotomy is the best example. Despite decades of scholars who have proclaimed a decline in the pervasiveness and power of the 'traditional' oral culture from the advent of moveable typographic printing onward, it remains equally possible and significant to locate the persisting power of oral modes of communication. The work of Eric Havelock on classical Greek literacy and that of Michael Clanchy on medieval English literacy, to cite only two of the possible cases, illustrate the workings of cultural and communicative processes especially richly. Clanchy reveals nicely the struggle that writing and written documents waged for their acceptance from the eleventh through the thirteenth centuries—a time of rising lay literacy. Early written documents, impelled by the state and the interests of private property, faithfully reproduced the 'words' of oral ceremonies and the rituals that traditionally had accompanied formal agreements; they were also adorned with the traditional badges of sealed bargains.[18]

Oversimplifying a complicated and sophisticated sociocultural process of interchange and interaction, we may say that Western literacy, from its 'invention' in the Greek alphabet and first popular diffusion in the city-states of classical times, was *formed, shaped,* and *conditioned* by the oral world which it penetrated. In earliest times, literacy was highly restricted and a relatively unprestigious craft; it carried relatively little of the association with wealth, power, status, and knowledge that it later acquired. It was a tool, useful, as it would remain, first for the needs of state and bureaucracy, church, and trade. This 'triumvirate' of literacy and writing, although reshaped with the passage of time, has remained incredibly resilient in its cultural and political hegemony over the social and individual functions of literacy and schooling. Yet, it was established and continued in a world in which communications were comprised overwhelmingly of the oral and the aural. As reading and writing began to spread, irregularly and inconsistently, among the population (especially the free males), their links with the larger cultural world of speech and hearing, and seeing too, were articulated ever more elaborately. Writing was used to set down the results of speech; it was also used, perhaps seminally by Plato if Havelock's arguments are correct, to facilitate patterns of thought and logic that were exceedingly difficult without the services that its technology could supply. Even with the encroachment of literacy, the ancient world remained an oral world, whether on street corners, marketplaces, assemblies, theaters, villas, or intellectual gatherings. The word as spoken was most common and most powerful. This tradition continued from the classical era through the thousand years of the Middle Ages and beyond; it is not dead today and may well have been reinforced by the impact of the newer electronic media. Contemporary confusion, I think, reflects the impact of changing modes of communications in a context of inflexible, historically rooted assumptions.

What needs to be grasped is that the oral and the literate, like the written and the printed, need not be opposed as simple choices. Human history and human developments did not transpire in that way. Rather, they allowed a deep and rich process of reciprocal interaction and conditioning to occur as literacy gradually spread and gained in acceptance and influence. The poetic and dramatic word of the ancients was supplanted, if not replaced, by a new Word: a religion of Christ rooted in the *Book* but propagated primarily by oral preaching and teaching. Analogously, classical and other forms of education long remained oral activities; any contradictions within the transmission of literacy by oral instruction are modern misconstruals of traditional ways that apparently succeeded as well as any we know now. They are no more inexplicable as contradictions than many others that punctuate the historical or contemporary understanding of literacy. The written and then printed words were spread to many semiliterates and illiterates via the oral processes; information, news, literature, and religion were spread far more widely than purely literate means could have allowed. For many centuries, reading itself was an oral, often collective activity and not the private, silent one we consider it to be.

Literacy, in the form of the Western alphabet, was first shaped by a powerful oral culture. Similarly and analogously, writing and written literature were also so conditioned, just as printing was by traditions of both the oral and the manuscript cultures. On the other side, it cannot be ignored that reading, writing, and printing have had their impacts upon traditional and oral cultural modes, media, and processes. To search out the interactions and evaluate the nature and impact of the resulting patterns is the task of the student of culture and society.

One point of special significance may be raised at this juncture. This is a question of chronology: the comparatively *late* invention of alphabetic literacy and the striking recency of the invention of moveable typographic printing, despite the sanctity with which we hold them. First, we 'listen' to Eric Havelock:

> The biological-historical fact is that *homo sapiens* is a species which uses oral speech, manufactured by the mouth, to communicate. This is his definition. He is not, by definition, a writer or reader. His use of speech, I repeat, has been acquired by processes of natural selection operating over a million years. The habit of using written symbols to represent such speech is just a useful trick which has existed over too short a time to have been built into our genes, whether or not this may happen half a million years hence. It follows that any language can be transliterated into any system of written symbols that the user of the language may choose without affecting the basic structure of the language. In short, reading man, as opposed to speaking man, is not biologically determined. He wears the appearance of a recent historical accident. . . .[19]

The chronology is devastatingly simple: *homo sapiens* as a species is about one million years old; writing dates from approximately 3000 B.C., so is about five thousand years old (.5 percent of humanity's existence); Western literacy from about 600 B.C., making it roughly twenty-six hundred years old (.26 percent of the species' life); and printing from the 1450s, now aged a mere 430 years. The numerical exercise may appear frivolous to many fearful persons today; still, I contend that a reflection upon this time sequence and its implications can be both liberating—from the chains of the present moment or the recent past—and stimulating to new points of view. It assists us in placing literacy and the primacy with which we hold it in a larger, proper context.

Let us return to the issues central to the necessary reconceptualization of literacy and its history. We must recognize that the history of literacy is typically conceived, and virtually always written, in terms of *change*—usually major kinds of changes in individuals, societies, or states. That is, the epistemological underpinnings governing most thought about literacy are evolutionary ones; the assumption is that literacy, development, growth, and progress are inseparably linked, especially in the modern period. Literacy becomes one of the key elements in the larger parcel of characteristics and processes that remade a traditional, premodern world into the modern West. It has not sufficed to model the history of the West itself in this way; social scientists during the past three decades have argued that the development of the underdeveloped areas must (or, normatively, *should*) recapitulate that of the West and sometimes have attempted to put that vision into practice. This is the moving spirit of the major works by such scholars as McLuhan, Elizabeth Eisenstein, Lawrence Stone, Jack Goody and Ian Watt, and Carlo Cipolla, although to make the point we need not erase their differences in emphasis or interpretation nor their real contributions.[20] Thus, it is not surprising that the history of literacy is also commonly a truncated one: most studies ignore, as irrelevant or inaccessible, the first two thousand years of Western literacy—the ages before the so-called advent of printing—despite the major insights that that historical experience provides for us.

My argument, my *re*vision, is that this perspective is an unduly limiting and distorting one. Its simplicity and linearity obstruct and complicate our understanding. The reconceptualization that I urge, and that underlies my research and writing, is a perspective that emphasizes *continuities* and *contradictions* in the history of Western society and culture especially with respect to the place of literacy and considers the extent of change, and discontinuity, in that framework. On one hand, this is a corrective to the long-standing interpretation that slights the roles of continuities and traditions, the legacies of literacy as I call them. On the other hand, it constitutes a mode of analysis and set of theoretical assumptions that seem to explain literacy's complex history more fully and effectively than the former approach has done. The examples presented above give an indication of what I mean by this.[21]

Continuity, as a historical concept, has an impressively broad meaning and applicability, despite historians' traditional abhorrence of this aspect of change and development. Among the insidious dichotomies that confuse more than they instruct, continuity versus change surely ranks highly. To focus on continuities, however does not require any neglect of changes or *dis*continuities. As the economic historian Alexander Gerschenkron has made clear in a valuable essay, continuity is an important and quite useful approach and one that has many meanings. He notes, for example, that

> it does not require long semantic expeditions through the current uses of the term 'continuity' to discover that it denotes a good deal more than stability. Confused and inconsistent as that usage is, unmistakably it refers time and again to the nature of change rather than its absence. Hence the phrase 'continuous change' is by no means a contradiction in terms; by the same token, the phrase 'discontinuous change' need not be pleonastic at all. It is precisely because continuity and discontinuity can relate to a certain kind of change that the two concepts may be expected to prove useful in historical research.

Concepts of continuity involve comparisons over time as well as awareness of the need to determine the relationship between elements of change and continuity simultaneously operating in any historical moment or situation. Nevertheless, it is useful to employ the language of continuity and its implications when describing circumstances in which development and change tend to be more gradual than rapid. This is the case with respect to the history of literacy, especially when that history encompasses a chronology more inclusive than one beginning in the fifteenth or sixteenth centuries.

Particularly impressive within the *longue durée* of literacy's full history—from the classical Greek civilizations onward—is the role of traditions and legacies. The use of elementary schooling and learning one's letters, for example, for political and civic functions such as moral conduct, respect for social order, and participant citizenship, begins in the Greek city-states during the fifth century before Christ and constitutes a classical legacy regularly rediscovered and reinterpreted by persons in the West: during the late Middle Ages, the Renaissance, the Reformation, the Enlightenment, and again during the great institutional reform movements of the nineteenth century. (For a summary of key points in the history of literacy, see table 1.2.)

Recognizing this series of continuities, or legacies of literacy, is not reductive; rather, it allows us to consider the similarities and differences in rates of literacy, schooling configurations, practical and symbolic uses of literacy, and the like that accompany renewed recognition of the positive value of expanded popular literacy within the differing social or economic contexts. Gerschenkron expresses it: 'At all times and in all cases, continuity must be regarded as a tool forged by the historian rather than as something inherently and invariantly contained in the historical matter. To say continuity means to formulate a question or a set of questions and to address it to the material.'[22] In other words, this conceptualization provides an appropriate model with which to approach and reinterpret the history of literacy in culture and society.

Table 1.2   *Key Points in the History of Literacy in the West*

Ca. 3100 B.C.	Invention of writing
Ca. 3100–1500 B.C.	Development of writing systems
Ca. 650–550 B.C.	'Invention' of Greek alphabet
Ca. 500–400 B.C.	First school developments, Greek city-states, tradition of literacy for civic purposes
Ca. 200 B.C.–A.D. 200	Roman public schools
0 +	Origins and development of Christianity
800–900	Carolingian language, writing, and bureaucratic developments
1200 +	Commercial, urban 'revolutions,' expanded administration and other uses of literacy and especially writing, development of lay education, rise of vernaculars, 'practical' literacy, Protestant heresies
1300 +	Rediscovery of classical legacies
1450s	Advent of printing, consolidation of states, Christian humanism
1500s	Reformation, spread of printing, growth of vernacular literatures, expanded schooling (mass literacy in radical Protestant areas)
1600s	Swedish literacy campaign
1700s	Enlightenment and its consolidation of traditions, 'liberal' legacies
1800s	School developments, institutionalization, mass literacy, 'mass' print media, education for social and economic development: public and compulsory
1900s	Non-print, electronic media
late 1900s	Crisis of literacy . . . and other things . . .

To take another case, we may point briefly to the issue of the oral and the literate in Western culture, mentioned earlier. We now observe that the exaggerated emphasis on change and discontinuity, in addition to the excesses of radical dichotomization, are principally responsible for the neglect of the important contribution of oral communications and traditions in receiving, conditioning, shaping, and even accepting the penetration of reading and writing—from the time of the Greeks through the Middle Ages, the early modern period, and on to the present. Third is the equally impressive power of the 'trinity' of literacy's primary uses: for reasons of state and administration, theology and faith, and trade and commerce, from the preliterate early centuries in which writing technologies evolved and in which writing was a highly restricted but relatively low-status craft, through the early modern transition to mass literacy in selected (primarily but not exclusively) religiously reforming areas within the West. The priority of these demands for and uses of literacy has remained, regardless of the degree of social restrictiveness that regulated the supply curve of popular diffusion. They also have played vital roles in determining the degree of restriction, the opening and closing of opportunities for the transmission and the acquisition of the skills of reading and writing. Commerce and its social and geographical organization, for example, stimulated rising levels of literacy from the twelfth century onward in advanced regions of the West.[23]

The significant link between literacy and religion forms one of the most vital, if (often but not always) conservative, legacies within the larger number. This critical connection is perhaps the best example of the intricate role of continuities and contradictions in the nearly three millennia of Western literacy. The sixteenth-century reformations, both Protestant and Catholic, are the most striking examples of this phenomenon. But the religious impulse for reading for the propagation of piety and faith long predates that time. Its history is closely tied to the history of Western Christianity, and the contradictions within one are often those of the other. Within the religious tradition, as well, the dialectic between the oral and the written has played a major part, with different balances being struck in different periods, places, and sects, to be sure. Literacy served to record for time immemorial the Word, but its influence and diffusion came, for centuries, overwhelmingly through oral means of teaching and preaching. Still, many who never came themselves to take the cloth or the collar learned their letters through the agencies of the universal medieval Christian church, using them for the service of state, commerce, letters, or selves. This need not have been a conservative end. The Reformation, however, constituted the first great literacy campaign in the history of the West, with its social legacies of individual literacy as a powerful social and moral force and its pedagogical traditions of compulsory instruction in public institutions specially created for the purposes of the indoctrination of the young for explicitly social ends. One of the great innovations of the German or Lutheran Reformation was the recognition that literacy, a potentially dangerous or subversive skill, could be employed—if controlled—as a medium for popular schooling and training on a truly unprecedented scale. The great reform was hardly an unambiguous success in its time, but it may well have contributed more to the cause of popular literacy than to that of piety and religious practice.[24] We might add, a bit blithely perhaps, that Luther had a dream which depended on universal literacy and schooling for its success, that the eighteenth-century Enlightenment prophets of progress and institutional solutions found the means, and that the nineteenth-century builders of mass institutions and promoters of school and schooling put them into practice! The twentieth century, we might conclude, lives with the legacies, and the continuities and contradictions.

We see the workings of *contradictions* in social, economic, and cultural development at the core of the processes that shaped the historical movement of literacy in the West. They are suggested in the examples presented here. Conceptually, this orientation requires a sensitivity and awareness of the fact that 'the social order produced in a process of social construction contains contradictions, ruptures, inconsistencies, and incompatibilities in the fabric of the social life.' Some contradictions are order-threatening or destructive; others are embedded within the ongoing processes of development. They are present regardless of the extent of continuity or discontinuity, although outcomes certainly differ. Sociologist Kenneth Benson usefully summarizes this perspective: a dialectical conceptualization

> differs from conventional strategies in treating these orderly patterns as created, produced arrangements with latent possibilities which can be transformed. The dialectical vision of the future [or past, for that matter] is not one of continuous, predictable development through an extension or consolidation of the present order; rather, the future [or past] has many possibilities and the final determination depends upon human action or praxis.
>
> Contradictions grow out of social production in two ways. First, there is in any social setting a contradiction between ongoing production and the previously established social formation. . . . Second, the production process is carried out in different social contexts producing multiple and incompatible social forms.[25]

It is indisputable that the history of Western literacy is a story of contradictions and that an explicit recognition of this is a prerequisite to a fuller understanding of that history. The relatively recent historical conjuncture between the deep faith we place in the efficacy and utility of mass literacy and schooling and the more fragile evidence of the power of literacy's own contribution is only explicable in this perspective. So too are the apparent limits to literacy, and the dimensions of a crisis rooted in perceptions of its presumed decline.

Other examples are revealing. They exist on a number of social and cultural levels, including disjunctures between the promoted uses of literacy and the social purposes that propel its widest diffusion; between the functional and *non*functional uses; between the self-activating potentials of literacy and the realities of its more common contributions and typical uses; between the social theories and experimental realities; between the liberating potentials and the integrating, homogenizing, controlling uses; and, finally, between quantity and qualities. To understand literacy, therefore, means that contradictions—oppositions, negations, countervailing factors, or dialectical processes—should be expected to result from the ongoing processes and developments within culture, polity, economy, and society. These are neither ironic nor paradoxical, as some call them, but fundamentally *historical*.[26]

Literacy's relationship with the processes of economic development, from the Middle Ages through the nineteenth century, provides one of the most striking examples of patterns of contradictions. Contrary to popular and scholarly wisdom, major steps forward in trade, commerce, and even industry took place in some periods and places with remarkably low levels of literacy; conversely, higher levels of literacy have not proved to be stimulants or springboards for 'modern' economic developments. More important than high rates or 'threshold levels' of literacy, such as those postulated by Anderson and Bowman or E.G. West, have been the educational levels and power relations of key persons, rather than the many; the roles of capital accumulation, 'cultural capital,' technological innovations and the ability to put them into practice; or the consumer demands and distribution-marketing-transportation-communication linkages.

Major 'take-offs,' from the commercial revolution of the Middle Ages to eighteenth-century proto-industrialization in rural areas and even factory industry in towns and cities, owed relatively and perhaps surprisingly little to popular literacy abilities or schooling. Early industrialization, the evidence from a number of studies agrees, owed little to literacy or the school; its demands upon the labor force were rarely intellectual or cognitive in nature. In fact, industrialization often reduced opportunities for schooling and, consequently, rates of literacy fell as it took its toll on the 'human capital' on which it fed. In much of Europe, and certainly in England—the paradigmatic case—industrial development (the 'First Industrial Revolution') neither was built on the shoulders of a literate work force nor served to increase popular levels of literacy, at least in the short run.

In other places, typically later in time, however, the fact of higher levels of popular education *prior* to the advent of factory capitalism may well have made the process different, varying in different needs and results. The presence of a literate *and* formally schooled population may have contributed to a rapid but smoother, less violent and conflict-ridden transition to the market and factory. The sequence of earlier school development served to prepare the future work force for the conduct, habits, behavior, rhythms, and discipline required by the factory. Or so it currently seems. Literacy, by the nineteenth century, became vital to the process of 'training in being trained.' Finally, it may also be the case that the 'literacy' required for the technological inventiveness and innovations that made the process possible was not a literacy of the alphabetic sort at all, but rather a more visual, experimental one.[27] Today, we confront claims and imagery of a labor force growing at once in 'functional illiteracy' or under-education *and* in overeducation for available jobs.

There are many kinds of 'literacies,' a crucial point insufficiently recognized. We need to distinguish not only between basic or elementary kinds of literacy and higher levels of education and schooling but also among the alphabetic, visual and artistic, spatial and graphic (what geographers are beginning to call 'graphicacy'), mathematical ('numeracy'), symbolic, technological, and mechanical, among other varieties of literacy.[28] The point, of course, is not to proliferate names or terminologies—that will only increase confusion. Rather, an understanding of any one type of literacy requires special care in qualifying terms and specifying what precisely is meant by reference to 'literacy.' These many 'literacies,' we note, are all conceptually distinct but nonetheless interrelated. The nature of those relationships requires sustained conceptual and empirical attention. In these pages, however, the focus is on alphabetic literacy.

In conclusion, let us turn to several additional aspects of the history of literacy in the Western world. Our goal here is twofold. On one hand, we may learn more about the emerging results of recent literacy studies; on the other hand, and equally important, we may note some of the 'lessons of the past.' For the proper study of the historical experience of literacy has more than antiquarian interest; it has much to tell that is relevant to policy analysis and policy making in the world in which we live today.[29]

Consider first the idea of multiple paths to the making of literate societies and states. The history of literacy shows clearly that there is no *one* route to universal literacy, and that there is no *one* path destined to succeed in the achievement of mass literacy. In the history of the Western world, one may distinguish the roles of private and public schooling in the attainment of high rates of popular literacy, as well as the operation of informal and formal, voluntary and compulsory education. Mass literacy was achieved in Sweden, for example, without formal schooling or instruction in writing. High rates of literacy have followed from all of these approaches in different cases and contexts. The developmental consequences are equally varied. The importance of these facts lies precisely in that

> perhaps the most striking feature of UNESCO discussions on literacy since 1965, when a campaign to wipe out world illiteracy got going, is that it is remarkably little based on either experiment or historical precedents. Rather, in spite of Adam Curle's careful warnings in 1965, action seems as much based on self-evident axioms and hope as on anything else. UNESCO assumes that literacy is a good thing—more latterly, functional literacy. Furthermore, in no clearly defined or understood way poverty, disease, and general backwardness are believed connected with illiteracy; progress, health, and economic well-being are equally self-evidently connected with literacy. UNESCO is committed to what amounts to a modernization theory to the effect that economic progress follows upon a change in man from illiterate to literate, preferably in one generation, and, even better, in the very same man. It is presupposed that such a change will lead, if not immediately then inevitably, to such

changes and values in a society that economic progress—and in its train good health, longevity, and, perhaps, peace—is possible.

The past, not surprisingly, provides a different set of experiences than those that lie behind the UNESCO expectations. Although neither all the research nor the balance sheet of historical interpretation is in, we may argue that historical experiences furnish a more appropriate and accurate guide to such crucial questions as how and to what degree basic literacy contributes to the economic and individual well-being of persons in different socioeconomic contexts, and under what circumstances universal literacy can be achieved. The costs and benefits of the alternative paths can be discerned too. Thus, the connections and disconnections between literacy and commercial development, a favorable relationship, and literacy and industrial development, often an unfavorable linkage at least in the short run of decades and half-centuries, offer important case studies and analogs for analysis. If nothing else, the data of the past strongly suggest that a simple, linear, modernization model of literacy as a prerequisite for development and development as a stimulant to increased levels of schooling will not do. Too many periods of lags, backward linkages, setbacks, and contradictions existed to permit such cavalier theorizing to continue without serious challenge and criticism.

The example of Sweden is perhaps most important in this respect. Not only does this case provide the most richly documented illustration of a transition to mass literacy in the Western world, but it also has much to teach us. As shown by the pioneering researches of Egil Johansson, near-universal levels of literacy were achieved rapidly and permanently in Sweden in the wake of the Reformation. Under the joint efforts of the Lutheran Church and the state, from the seventeenth century reading literacy was required under law for all persons. Within a century, remarkably high levels of literacy among the population existed—without any concomitant development of formal schooling or economic or cultural development that demanded functional or practical employment of literacy; moreover, literacy grew in a manner that led to its being defined by reading and not by writing. Urbanization, commercialization, and industrialization had nothing to do with the process of making the Swedish people perhaps the most literate in the West before the eighteenth century. Contrary to the paths of literacy taken elsewhere, this campaign, begun by King Charles XI, was sponsored by the state church. By legal requirement and vigilant supervision that included regular personal examination by parish clergy, the church stood above a system rooted in home education. The rationale of the literacy campaign, one of the most successful in Western history before the last two decades, was conservative; piety, civility, orderliness, and military preparedness were the major goals. The first was as important as the other reasons, and in the end it was the decisive one. Ian Winchester succinctly summarizes the conclusions of the Swedish scholarship:

> A Protestant in order to receive the sacraments or to marry must be able to read God's word directly. With the enactment of laws restricting marriage to the literate, a direct incentive upon which the parish priests could

act was in the hands of the Swedish church. The net effect was that the custodians of reading became the parish priests and their instruments the families in the Swedish farming villages. From the time of Charles XI onward the priest, with increasing rigour, made annual tours of every household, testing the reading and understanding level of every Swede with respect to Luther's Little Catechism (the Swedish translation of the Bible was a little delayed). The annual testing program was standardized early and the results survive in manuscript form for the bulk of the population.

Significantly, the home and church education model fashioned by the Swedes not only succeeded in training up a literate population, but it also placed a special priority on the literacy of women and mothers. This led to Sweden's anomalous achievement of female literacy rates as high as male rates or higher, a rare pattern in the Western transitions to mass literacy. Sweden also marched to its impressive levels of reading diffusion without writing; it was not until the mid-nineteenth century and the erection of a state-supported public school system that writing, in addition to reading, became a part of popular literacy and a concern of teachers in this Scandinavian land. Finally, we note that the only other areas that so fully and quickly achieved near-universal levels of literacy before the end of the eighteenth century were places of intensely pious religion, usually but not always Protestant: Scotland, New England, Huguenot French centers, and places within Germany and Switzerland. There are lessons to be learned from this past.[30]

A second important example is literacy's relationships with the paths to economic development. This was surveyed above. A third is the connection of literacy with social development, also hinted at above. In this case, we again discover a history full of continuities and contradictions, and of variable paths to societal change and maturity. From the classical period forward, leaders of polities and churches, reformers as well as conservers, have recognized the uses of literacy and schooling. Often they have perceived unbridled, untempered literacy as potentially dangerous, a threat to social order, political integration, economic productivity, and pattern of authority. But, increasingly, they concluded that literacy, if provided in carefully controlled, formal institutions created expressly for the purposes of education and supervised closely, could be a powerful and useful force in achieving a variety of important ends. Precedents long predated the first systematic mass efforts to put this conception of literacy into practice, in Rome, for example, and in the visionary proposals of the fifteenth and sixteenth-century Christian humanists. But for our purposes the Reformations of the sixteenth century represented the first great educational campaigns. As the Swedish case reminds us, they were hardly homogeneous efforts, in either design or degree of success. Nonetheless, they were precedent setting and epochal in their significance for the future of Western social and educational development. In their own times, many of wealth and power still doubted the efficacy of schooling the masses.

With the Enlightenment and its heritage came the final ideological under-pinnings for the 'modern' and 'liberal' reforms of popular schooling and institu-tional building that established the network of educational-social-political-and-economic relationships central to the dominant ideologies and their social theoretical expressions for the past century and a half. Prussia, revealingly, took the lead, and provided a laboratory that United States, Canadian, English, French, and Scandinavian school promoters and reformers regularly came to study. North Americans and Swedes followed in Prussia's wake, and, in time and in their own ways, so did the English, French, and Italians.

We must not slight other important uses of literacy, such as for personal advancement, entertainment, or collective action in cultural, political, or eco-nomic terms. These crucial topics are not my main focus in this essay, although the significance and potential of literacy to individuals and groups throughout history are undoubted. There is a large, if uneven, volume of studies with this emphasis, highlighting the value of literacy to individual success, the acquisition of opportunities and knowledge, collective consciousness, and action. The writings of Robert K. Webb, Richard Altick, Thomas Laqueur, Michael Clanchy, among others, make this case with force and evidence. The role of class and group-specific demands for literacy's skills, the impact of motivation, and the growing perceptions of its values and benefits are among the major factors that explain the historical contours of changing rates of popular literacy. Any complete un-derstanding and appreciation of literacy's history must incorporate the large, if sometimes exaggerated and decontextualized, role of demand (in dialectial rela-tionship to supply) and the very real benefits that literacy may bring. Literacy's limits must also be appreciated.

The subtleties and complexities of the process of 'enlightenment,' 'liberation,' or 'demystification' with the assistance of literacy emerge nicely in Henry Dobyns' account of social change in a Peruvian Indian village. He observes that economic growth and education were in fact positively correlated but that the relationship was 'a correction between two independent processes that happened to be oc-curring concurrently without being causally related.' The increase in farm pro-duction and in participant democracy in the village of Vicos did benefit from classroom training; they also make the latter possible. The nature of the process and the relationships may be seen:

> The burst of economic productivity achieved in Vicos resulted from prac-tical enlightenment of adults who made immediate decisions about farm-ing practices. . . . The initial increase in economic production in Vicos was accomplished, moreover, before the formal classroom educational process had significantly increased the level of literacy and other formal knowledge in the population. Impressive improvement in economic pro-ductivity was achieved by illiterate Indian serfs on the basis of enlight-enment in their own language and with practical demonstration to impact simple skills.

At the same time, the villagers began to govern their own community and manage their own affairs. Nevertheless, 'after the Vicos Indians assumed the management of their own affairs, literacy and writing skills assumed more importance in connection with the community farm enterprise. Still, nearly all the councilmen continued to be illiterate farmers . . . Ten years of agricultural development occurred under the leadership of a small handful of literates—less than 1 per cent of the total population.' Literacy increased, however, and with it came new roles and new kinds of power relationships in families, in the community, and with the larger society.[31]

It remains nevertheless important to stress the integrating and hegemony-creating functions of literacy provision through formal schooling. Especially with the transition from preindustrial social orders based in rank and deference to the class societies of commercial and then factory capitalism, schooling became more and more a vital aspect of the maintenance of social stability, particularly during periods of massive but often confusing social and economic changes, and a regular feature of the life course. Many persons, most prominently social and economic leaders and social reformers, grasped the uses of schooling and the vehicle of literacy for the promotion of the values, attitudes, and habits considered essential to the maintenance of social order and the persistence of integration and cohesion.[32] The people's acceptance of literacy's import forms the other dimension of this history.

A final aspect focuses on the question of the *quality*, as opposed to quantity, of literacy. Because of the nature of the evidence, virtually all historical studies have concentrated on the measurement of the extent and distribution of reading and writing; issues involving the level of the skills themselves and the abilities to use those skills have not attracted much attention. What research has been conducted, however, comes to a common conclusion that qualitative abilities cannot be deduced simply or directly from quantitative levels of literacy's diffusion. Studies of early modern England, eighteenth- and nineteenth-century Sweden, and urban areas in the nineteenth century all suggest that there is a significant disparity between the levels of the possession of literacy and the usefulness of those skills. In Sweden, for example, where systematic evidence exists, a great many persons who had attained high levels of *oral* reading skill did not have comparable abilities in *comprehension* of what they read. Other data lend support for similar interpretations for other places.

The implications of such findings are *enormous*. First, the measurement of the distribution of literacy in a population may in fact reveal relatively little about the uses to which such skills could be put and the degree to which different demands on personal literacy could be satisfied with the skills commonly held. Second, it is also possible that with increasing rates of popular literacy did not come ever-rising capabilities or qualitative abilities (or declining abilities, either). Third, and potentially most important today, such evidence places the often-asserted contemporary decline of literacy in a new and distinctive context, leading to a fresher and historical perspective. That is: the possibility that mass levels of ability to use literacy may have, over the long term, lagged behind the near-universality of literacy rates. For some, like black Americans, great progress has occurred. The recent decline, so often proclaimed but so ineffectively measured and little understood, may be *much less a major decline than we are told.* We should perhaps pay more attention to longer term trends than those of a decade or two and to changes in popular communicative abilities and compositional effects among students than to 'competency examinations' and SAT test scores. Or so I suggest.[33] This, however, does not mean that real, even grave, problems do not exist.

Having begun with quotations to set our stage, I should like to conclude in like manner. First, we need to understand that:

> the old gray mare was never what she used to be. Very few people read many books in this or any other country, and I think that a source of delusion is that many of us who think a lot about these things grew up in book-oriented homes and had book-oriented childhoods, and, hence, tend to project our childhood experiences back in the recollection of that era. I think this is certainly true of a lot of what we perceive as a dramatic new problem of marginal literacy, or illiteracy, in the core city populations of our country. We forget that this marginal literacy or illiteracy was there all along.[34]

And, then:

> What would happen if the whole world became literate? Answer: not so very much, for the world is by and large structured in such a way that it is capable of absorbing the impact. But if the world consisted of literate, autonomous, critical, constructive people, capable of translating ideas into action, individually or collectively—the world would change.[35]

Literacy is not the only problem, nor is it the only solution.

Notes

This essay represents a summary statement of the emphases and interpretations presented in my book, *The Legacies of Literacy: Continuities and Contradictions in Western Society and Culture* (Bloomington: Indiana University Press, 1986). This is a lengthy, interpretive survey history of literacy in Western society and culture spanning the five millennia from the invention of writing to the 'future.' For assistance to date, I wish to acknowledge the important contributions of the American Council of Learned Societies, the Spencer Foundation, the Newberry Library, and the National Endowment for the Humanities. The essay and most of the first draft of the book on which it is based were written while I was an NEH Fellow at the Newberry Library and a Visiting Professor at Simon Fraser University: the support of these scholarly agencies has made my progress more rapid, satisfying, and enjoyable than it might otherwise have been. Those individuals who have aided me in one way or another are too many to list here; I hope they know my gratitude.

1 DAVID OLSON, 'Toward a Literate Society,' *Proceedings of the National Academy of Education, 1975–1976,* pp. 111, 112.

2   ERIC HAVELOCK, *Origins of Western Literacy*. Toronto: Ontario Institute for Studies in Education, 1976, pp. 83, 18, 19.
3   BRUCE G. TRIGGER, 'Inequality and Communication in Early Civilizations,' *Anthropologica* 18 (1976): 39.
4   KATHLEEN GOUTG, 'Literacy in Kerala,' in GOODY, JACK (Ed.) *Literacy in Traditional Societies,* Cambridge: Cambridge University Press 1968, p. 153.
5   WALTER J. ONG, *The Presence of the Word*. New York: Simon and Schuster, 1970, p. 21.
6   Among a literature growing rapidly, see my *Legacies of Literacy: Continuities and Contradictions in Western Culture and Society,* esp. introduction, chap. 1, epilogue. *The Literacy Myth: Literacy and Social Structure in the Nineteenth-Century City.* New York and London: Academic Press, 1979. *Literacy in History: An Interdisciplinary Research Bibliography.* Chicago: The Newberry Library, 1976, addendum, 1979, rev. ed. New York: Garland Publishing, 1981; GOODY, (Ed.), *Literacy;* JACK GOODY, *The Domestication of the Savage Mind.* Cambridge: Cambridge University Press, 1977; JACK GOODY and IAN WATT, 'The Consequences of Literacy,' in *Literacy,* (Ed.) GOODY, pp. 27–68; G.H. BANTOCK, *The Implications of Literacy.* Leicester: Leicester University Press, 1966; DAVID R. OLSON. 'From Utterance to Test: The Bias of Language in Speech and Writing,' *Harvard Educational Review* 47 (1977): 257–81; OLSON, 'Toward A Literate Society,' pp. 109–78; Michael Cole *et al., The Cultural Context of Learning and Thinking.* New York: Basic Books, 1971; JACK GOODY, MICHAEL COLE, and SYLVIA SCRIBNER, 'Writing and Formal Operations: A Case Study Among the Vai,' *Africa* 47 (1977): 289–304; SYLVIA SCRIBNER and MICHAEL COLE, 'Studying Cognitive Consequences of Literacy' (unpublished paper, 1976), 'Cognitive Consequences of Formal and Informal Education,' *Science* 182 (1973): 553–59, 'Literacy Without Schooling: Testing for Intellectual Effects,' *Harvard Educational Review* 48 (1978): 448–61; MICHAEL COLE, 'How Education Affects the Mind,' *Human Nature,* April 1978, pp. 51–58; SCRIBNER and COLE, *The Psychology of Literacy.* Cambridge, Mass.: Harvard University Press, 1981; MICHAEL T. CLANCHY, *From Memory to Written Record, England, 1066–1307.* Cambridge, Mass.: Harvard University Press, 1979; WALTER J. ONG, *Presence, Interfaces of the Word.* Ithaca: Cornell University Press, 1977, and *Rhetoric, Romance, and Technology.* Ithaca: Cornell University Press, 1971; DANIEL P. RESNICK and LAUREN B. RESNICK, 'The Nature of Literacy: An Historical Exploration.' *Harvard Educational Review* 47 (1977): 370–85; DAVID CRESSY, *Literacy and the Social Order.* Cambridge: Cambridge University Press, 1980; FRANÇOIS FURET and JACQUES OZOUF, *Lire et Ecrire.* Paris: Les Editions de Minuit, 1977; KENNETH A. LOCKRIDGE, *Literacy in Colonial New England.* New York: Norton, 1974, 'L.' Alphabètisation en Amèrique,' *Annales: e, s, c* 30 (1977): 503–18: EGIL JOHANSSON, *The History of Literacy in Sweden, in Comparison with Some Other Countries, Educational Reports,* Umeà, 12. Umeà, Sweden: University of Umeà and School of Education, 1977. Some of the most important historical writings have been collected into an anthology entitled *Literacy and Social Development in the West,* which I edited, Studies in Oral and Literate Culture. Cambridge: Cambridge University Press, 1981.
7   Among a truly daunting, if not always helpful, literature, see, for example, the interesting papers in LEON BATAILLE, (Ed.), *A Turning Point for Literacy.* New York and Oxford: Pergamon Press, 1976; GRAFF, *Literacy Myth,* and 'Literacy Past and Present: Critical Approaches to the Literacy-Society Relationship,' *Interchange* 9 (1978): 1–21; GOODY, *Domenstication;* G.H. DOUGLAS, 'Is Literacy Really Declining?' *Educational Records* 57 (1977): 140–48; JOHANSSON, 'The Postliteracy Problem—Illusion or Reality in Modern Sweden?' in *Time, Space, and Man,* (Ed.) JAN SUNDIN and ERIK SODERLUND. Stockholm: Almqvist and Wiksell, 1979, pp. 199–212; ROGER FARR, LEO FAY, and HAROLD H. NEGLEY, *Then and Now: Reading Achievement in Indiana*

(1944–45 and 1976). Bloomington: University of Indiana School of Education, 1978, ROGER FARR et al., *Then and Now: Reading Achievement in the U.S.* Bloomington: University of Indiana School of Education, 1974; J.R. BORMUTH, 'Value and Volume of Literacy,' *Visible Language* 12 (1978): 118–66.

8 LAURO MARTINES, *Power and Imagination: City-States in Renaissance Italy.* New York: Knopf, 1979, p. 201; GRAFF, 'Literacy Past and Present,' and the reply and rejoinder; ROBERT NISBET, *Social Change and History.* New York: Oxford University Press, 1969; PHILLIP ABRAMS. 'The Sense of the Past,' *Past and Present* 52 (1972): 18–32; GEOFFREY HAWTHORN, *Enlightenment and Despair.* Cambridge: Cambridge University Press, 1977.

9 COPPERMAN, *The Literacy Hoax.* New York: Morrow, 1978, among a large literature. See also note 7, above, and my *Literacy in History* for a guide to this writing. For informed criticism, see MANFRED STANLEY, 'Literacy—The Crisis of a Concept,' *School Review* (1972): 373–408; and HENRY F. DOBYNS, 'Enlightenment and Skill Foundations of Power,' in *Peasants, Power, and Applied Social Change: Vicos as a Model,* (Ed.) HENRY F. DOBYNS, P.L. DOUGHTY, and H.D. LASSWELL, Beverly Hills: Sage, 1971, pp. 137–66.

10 OLSON, 'Toward a Literate Society,' pp. 149, 170.

11 ELSASSER and JOHN-STEINER, 'An Interactionist Approach to Advancing Literacy,' *Harvard Educational Review* 47 (1977): 361–62. See also Jonathan Kozol, 'A New Look at the Literacy Campaign in Cuba,' *ibid.* 48 (1978): 341–77; PAULO FREIRE, *Pedagogy of the Oppressed.* New York: Herder and Herder, 1971, and *Education for Critical Consciousness.* New York: Seabury, 1973.

12 For the most important examples, see table 1; my *Literacy Myth,* introduction, appendixes; ROGER S. SCHOFIELD, 'The Measurement of Literacy in Pre-industrial England,' in *Literacy,* (Ed.) Goody, pp. 311–25; Lockridge, *Literacy in Colonial New England;* CLANCHY, *From Memory;* FURET and OZOUF, *Lire;* CRESSY, *Literacy and Social Order;* JOHANSSON, *Literacy in Sweden.*

13 See the studies cited in note 6 above, and MARSHALL MCLUHAN, *The Gutenberg Galaxy.* Toronto: University of Toronto Press, 1962, *Understanding Media.* New York: McGraw-Hill, 1964; ELIZABETH L. EISENSTEIN, *The Printing Press as an Agent of Change.* Cambridge: Cambridge University Press, 1979; LAWRENCE CREMIN, *American Education: The Colonial Experience.* New York: HARPER and ROW, 1970; ALEX INKELES and DAVID H. SMITH, *Becoming Modern.* Cambridge, Mass.: Harvard University Press, 1974. See also the useful introductions in JOHN OXENHAM, *Literacy: Reading, Writing and Social Organization.* London: Routledge and Kegan Paul, 1980 Havelock, *Origins.*

14 HOWARD SCHUMAN, ALEX INKELES, and DAVID H. SMITH, 'Some Social Psychological Effects and Non-effects of Literacy in a New Nation,' *Economic Development and Cultural Change* 16 (1967): 7; INKELES and SMITH, *Becoming Modern;* and a large body of literature including the well-known writings of DAVID MCCLELLAND, DANIEL LERNER, MARY JEAN BOWMAN and ARNOLD ANDERSON, and LUCIEN PYE. For a summary, citations, and critique, see, for example, *Literacy Myth,* introduction and chap 5.

15 LEWIS, *The Importance of Illiteracy.* London: Harrap, 1953, p. 16.

16 SCRIBNER and COLE, 'Literacy without Schooling,' pp. 449, 450, 452, 453; GOODY, (Ed.), *Literacy,* and GOODY, *Savage Mind;* GOODY, SCRIBNER, and COLE, 'Writing,' and other studies by SCRIBNER and COLE; DOBYNS, 'Enlightenment'; STANLEY, 'Crisis of a Concept.'

17 MARGARET SPUFFORD, 'First Steps in Literacy: The Reading and Writing Experiences of the Humblest Seventeenth-Century Spiritual Autobiographers,' *Social History* 4 (1979): 407–35, *Contrasting Communities.* Cambridge: Cambridge University Press, 1974; THOMAS LAQUEUR, *Religion and Respectability.* New Haven: Yale Uni-

versity Press, 1976, 'The Cultural Origins of Popular Literacy in England, 1500–1800,' *Oxford Review of Education* 2 (1976): 255–75, 'Working-Class Demand and the Growth of English Elementary Education, 1750–1850,' in *Schooling and Society,* (Ed.) LAWRENCE STONE, Baltimore: Johns Hopkins University Press, 1976, pp. 192–205; R.K. WEBB, *The British Working Class Reader.* London: Allen and Unwin, 1955; Johansson, *Literacy in Sweden;* MICHAEL W. APPLE, 'The Other Side of the Hidden Curriculum: Correspondence Theories and the Labor Process,' *Interchange* 11 (1980–81): 5–22; *Ideology and Curriculum* (Boston: Routledge and Kegan Paul, 1979).

18 Among a large and diffuse literature, see RUTH FINNEGAN, *Oral Literature in Africa.* Oxford: Oxford University Press, 1970, *Oral Poetry.* Cambridge: Cambridge University Press, 1979; HAVELOCK, *Origins, Preface to Plato.* Cambridge, Mass.: Harvard University Press, 1963, 'The Preliteracy of the Greeks,' *New Literary History* 8 (1977): 369–92; BIRGER GERHARDSSON, *Memory and Manuscript: Oral Tradition and Written Transmission in Rabbinic Judaism and Early Christianity.* UPPSALA, LUND, and COPENHAGEN: Acta Seminarii Neotestamentici Upsaliensis, XII, 1961: Clanchy, *From Memory;* F.L. GANSHOF, *The Carolingians and the Frankish Monarchy.* Ithaca: Cornell University Press, 1971; E. LEROY LADURIE, *Montaillou: Promised Land of Error.* New York: George Braziller, 1978; NATALIE Z. DAVIS, 'Printing and the People,' in her *Society and Culture in Early Modern France.* Stanford: Stanford University Press, 1975, pp. 189–226; H-J MARTIN, 'Culture écrite et culture orale, culture savante et culture populaire dans la France d'Ancien Régime,' *Jounarle des Savants* (1975): 225–82; PETER BURKE, *Popular Culture in Early Modern Europe.* New York; Harper and Row, 1978; MARGARET ASTON, 'Lollardy and Literacy,' *History* 62 (1977): 347–71; CARLO GINZBURG, *The Cheese and the Worms,* trans. JOHN and ANNE TEDESCHI. Baltimore: Johns Hopkins University Press, 1980; GOODY *Domestication;* E.P. THOMPSON: 'Eighteenth-Century Society.'

19 HAVELOCK, *Origins,* p. 12.

20 For citations, see notes above and Lawrence Stone, 'Literacy and Education in England, 1640–1900,' *Past and Present* 42 (1969): 69–139; CARLO CIPOLLA, *Literacy and Development in the West.* Harmondsworth: Penguin, 1969; ROBERT DISCH, (Ed.), *The Future of Literacy.* ENGLEWOOD CLIFFS, NJ: Prentice-Hall, 1973. Readers may also wish to consult Eisenstein's series of articles that preceded the publication of her *Printing: History and Theory* 6 (1966); *Past and Present* 45 (1969); *Journal of Modern History* 40 (1968); *American Historical Review* 75 (1970); *Annales, e, s, c* 26 (1971). Professor Eisenstein proclaims her independence from my depiction; I leave the evaluation to readers. Goody has reevaluated and revised his interpretation in recent writings.

21 See, for example, my *Literacy Myth;* LOCKRIDGE, *Literacy in Colonial New England;* SCHOFIELD, 'The Dimensions of Illiteracy in England, 1750–1850,' *Explorations in Economic History* 10 (1973): 437–54; CRESSY, *Literacy and Social Order,* 'Educational Opportunity in Tudor and Stuart England,' *History of Education Quarterly* 16 (1976): 301–20, 'Levels of Literacy in England, 1530–1730', *Historical Journal* 20 (1977): 1–23.

22 GERSCHENKRON, 'On the Concept of Continuity in History,' in his *Continuity in History and Other Essays.* Cambridge, Mass.: Harvard University Press, 1968, pp. 13, 38.

23 Among the relevant literature are GOODY, (Ed.), *Literacy;* TRIGGER, 'Inequality'; WILLIAM A. BRUNEAU, 'Literacy, Urbanization, and Education in Three Ancient Cultures,' *Journal of Education* (British Columbia) 19 (1973): 9–22; CLANCHY, *From Memory;* CIPOLLA, *Literacy and Development.*

24 LOCKRIDGE, *Literacy in Colonial New England;* LADURIE, *Montaillou, The Peasants of Languedoc.* Urbana: University of Illinois Press, 1975; ASTON, 'Lollardy'; GERHARDSSON, *Memory;* DAVIS, 'Printing'; GINZBURG, *Cheese;* GERALD STRAUSS, *Luth-*

er's House of Learning. Baltimore; Johns Hopkins University Press, 1979; MARY JO MAYNES, 'Schooling the Masses' (Ph.D. diss., University of Michigan, 1977), 'The Virtues of Anachronism The Political Economy of Schooling in Europe, 1750–1850.' *Comparative Studies in Society and History* 21 (1979): 611–25; CIPOLLA, *Literacy and Development;* JOHANSSON, *Literacy in Sweden;* GRAFF, *Literacy Myth.*

25 J. KENNETH BENSON, 'Organizations: A Dialectial View,' *Administrative Science Quarterly* 22 (1977): 4, 5, *passim,* and the literature cited there. See also ROBERT L., HEILBRONER, *Marxism: For and Against.* New York: Norton, 1980, pp. 33–44.

26 For other examples, see my *Literacy Myth.* A good recent example is MARY RYAN, *Cradle of the Middle Class.* New York: Cambridge University Press, 1981.

27 Among a large literature on these issues, see, for example, E. VERNE, 'Literacy and Industrialization—The Dispossession of Speech,' in *Turning Point,* (Ed.) BATAILLE, 211–28: my *Literacy Myth,* esp. chap. 5; MARIS VINOVSKIS, 'Horace Mann on the Economic Productivity of Education,' *New England Quarterly* 43 (1970): 550–71; ALEXANDER J. FIELD, 'Educational Reform and Manufacturing Development in Mid-Nineteenth Century Massachusetts' (PhD. diss., University of California, Berkeley, 1974), 'Educational Expansion in Mid-Nineteenth Century Massachusetts,' *Harvard Educational Review* 46 (1976): 521–52, 'Economic and Demographic Determinants of Educational Commitment: Massachusetts, 1855,' *Journal of Economic History* 39 (1979): 439–59, 'Occupational Structure, Dissent, and Educational Commitment: Lancashire, 1841, '*Research in Economic History* 4 (1979): 235–87; SAMUEL BOWLES and HERBERT GINTIS, *Schooling in Capitalist America.* New York: Basic Books, 1976; MICHAEL B. KATZ, 'The Origins of Public Education: A Reassessment,' *History of Education Quarterly* 14 (1976): 381–407, 'Origins of the Institutional State,' *Marxist Perspectives* 1 (1978): 6–22; CARL KAESTLE and MARIS VINOVSKIS, *Education and Social Change in Nineteenth-Century Massachusetts.* Cambridge: Cambridge University Press, 1980; RICHARD JOHNSON, 'Notes on the Schooling of the English Working Class, 1780–1850,' in *Schooling and Capitalism,* (Ed.) R. DALE, G. ESLAND, and M. MACDONALD. London: Routledge and Kegan Paul, 1976, pp. 44–54: Scholfield, 'Dimensions'; FRANÇOIS FURET and JACQUES OZOUF, 'Literacy and Industrialization.' *Journal of European Economic History* 5 (1976): 5–44; MARK BLAUG, 'Literacy and Economic Development,' *School Review* 74 (1966): 393–417; W.G. BOWEN, 'Assessing the Economic Contribution of Education,' in *The Economics of Education,* Vol. 1, (Ed.) MARK BLAUG, Harmondsworth: Penguin, 1968, pp. 67–100; DAVID C. MCCLELLAND, 'Does Education Accelerate Economic Growth?' *Economic Development and Cultural Change* 14 (1966): 257–78; MICHAEL SANDERSON, 'Literacy and Social Mobility in the Industrial Revolution,' *Past and Present* 56 (1972): 75–105, and the critique by Laqueur with reply by Sanderson, *ibid.* 64 (1974): 96–112; MICHAEL SANDERSON, 'Education and the Factory in Industrial Lancashire,' *Economic History Review* 20 (1967): 266–79, 'Social Change and Elementary Education in Industrial Lancashire,' *Northern History* 3 (1968): 131–54; DAVID LEVINE, *Family Formation in An Age in Nascent Capitalism.* New York and London: Academic Press, 1977, 'Education and Family Life in Early Industrial England' *Journal of Family History* 4 (1979): 368–80; W.B. STEPHENS, 'Illiteracy and Schooling in the Provincial Towns, 1640–1870,' in *Urban Education in the 19th Century.* (Ed.) DAVID REEDER. London: Taylor and Francis, 1977, pp. 27–48, among his studies; PETER FLORA, 'Historical Processes of Social Mobilization,' in *Building States and Nations,* (Ed.) S.N. EISENSTADT and S. ROKKAN, Beverly Hills: Sage, 1973, 4: 213–58; SIDNEY POLLARD, *The Genesis of Modern Management.* Harmondsworth: Penguin, 1968, esp. chap. 5; E.P. THOMPSON, 'Time, Work-Discipline, and Industrial Capitalism,' *Past and Present* 38 (1967): 56–97; HERBERT GUTMAN, 'Work, Culture, and Society in Industrializing America, 1815–1919,' *American Historical Review* 78 (1973): 531–88;

RONALD DORE, *Education in Tokugawa Japan.* London: Routledge and Kegan Paul, 1967.

> For contrary views, see E.G. WEST, *Education and the Industrial Revolution.* London: Batsford, 1975, 'The Role of Education in 19th Century Doctrines of Political Economy,' *British Journal of Educational Studies* 12 (1964): 161–74, 'Literacy and the Industrial Revolution,' *Economic History Review* 31 (1977): 369–83; C.A. AN-DERSON, 'Literacy and Schooling on the Development Threshold,' in *Education and Economic Development,* (Ed.) C.A. ANDERSON and M.J. BOWMAN, Chicago: Aldine, 1965, pp. 247–63; M.J. BOWMAN and C.A. ANDERSON. 'Concerning the Role of Education in Development,' in *Old Societies and New States,* (Ed.) CLIFFORD C. GEERTZ, New York: Free Press, 1963, pp. 247–79, 'Education and Economic Modernization in Historical Perspective,' in *Schooling and Society,* (Ed.) STONE, pp. 3–19; INKELES and SMITH, *Becoming Modern.*

> On inventiveness, see EUGENE FERGUSON, 'The Mind's Eye: Nonverbal Thought in Technology,' *Science* 197 (1977): 827–36; A.F.C. WALLACE, *Rockdale.* New York: Knopf, 1978, 237 ff; WILLIAM M. IVINS, JR., *Prints and Visual Communications.* Cambridge, Mass.: MIT Press, 1953.

28   'Literacy: Power or Mystification?' *Literacy Discussion* 4 (1973): 409, 389–414. Among a large literature see also STANLEY, 'Crisis of a Concept'; DOBYNS, 'Enlightenment'; GOODY, *Domestication;* FREIRE, *Pedagogy.*

29   Among the relevant studies cited above, see those by GRAFF, JOHANSSON, RESNICK, SCHOFIELD, and my 'Literacy, Education, and Fertility, Past and Present: A Critical Review,' *Population and Development Review* 6 (1979): 105–40; IAN WINCHESTER, 'How Many Ways to Universal Literacy?' (paper Presented to the Ninth World Congress of Sociology Uppsala, 1978, and the University of Leicester Seminar on the History of Literacy in Post-Reformation Europe, 1980).

30   WINCHESTER, 'How Many Ways,' pp. 1, 4; JOHANSSON, 'Literacy in Sweden,' 'Literacy Studies in Sweden: Some Examples,' in *Literacy and Society in a Historical Perspective: A Conference Report.* (Ed.) EGIL JOHANSSON, *Educational Report.* Umeå, 2, Umeå: University of Umeå and School of Education, 1973, pp. 41–66; LOCKRIDGE, *Literacy in Colonial New England;* STRAUSS, *Luther's House of Learning.* See also BATAILLE, (Ed.), *Turning Point.*

31   DOBYNS, 'Enlightenment,' pp. 150–51, *passim.*

32   See for example, FURET and OZOUF, *Lire;* GRAFF, *Literacy Myth, Legacies;* Kaestle, " 'Between the Scylla of Brutal Ignorance and the Charybdis of a Literacy Education": Elite Attitudes Toward Mass Schooling in Early Industrial England and America,' in *Schooling and Society,* (Ed.) STONE, pp. 177–91; CREMIN, *American Education;* LOCKRIDGE, *Literacy in Colonial New England;* HENRY MAY, *The Enlightenment in America.* New York: Oxford University Press, 1976; DONALD H. MEYER, *The Democratic Enlightenment.* New York: Putnam's Sons, 1976; H.S. COMMAGER, *The Empire of Reason.* Garden City: Doubleday/Anchor, 1977; HYMAN KURITZ, 'Benjamin Rush: His Theory of Republican Education,' *History of Education Quarterly* 7 (1967): 432–51; LINDA K. KERBER, 'Daughters of Columbia: Educating Women for the Republic, 'in *The Hofstadter Aegis,* (Ed.) STANLEY M. ELKINS and ERIC L. McKITRICK. New York: Knopf, 1974, pp. 36–60; STANLEY E. BALLINGER, 'The Idea of Progress through Education in the French Enlightenment,' *History of Education Journal* 10 (1959): 88–99; PETER GAY, *The Enlightenment: The Science of Freedom.* New York: Knopf, 1969, esp. chap. 10; ROLAND MORTIER, 'The "Philosophes" and Public Education,' *Yale French Studies* 40 (1968): 62–76; KARL A. SCHLEUNNES, 'French Revolution and the Schooling of European Society,' *Proceedings of the Consortium on Revolutionary Europe* (1977): pp. 140–50; THOMAS NIPPERDEY, "Mass Education and Modernization—The Case of Germany,". *Transactions of the Royal Historical Society* 27 (1977): 155–72; H.B. APPLEWAITE and D.G. LEVY, 'The Concept of Mod-

ernization and the French Enlightenment,' *Studies on Voltaire and the Eighteenth Century* 84 (1971): 53–98; JAMES A. LEITH, 'Modernization, Mass Education, and Social Mobility in French Thought, 1750–1789,' in *Studies in the Eighteenth Century*, vol. 2, (Ed.) R.F. BRISSENDEN, Canberra: Australian National University Press, 1973, pp. 223–38; ROBERT R. PALMER, 'The Old Regime Origins of the Napoleonic Educational Structure,' in *De L'Ancien Régime a la Révolution Française*, (Ed.) ALBERT CREMER. Gottingen: Vandenhoeck and Rupprecht, n.d., pp. 381–33; MICHEL VOVELLE, 'Y a-t-il une révolution culturelle au XVIII siècle?' *Revue d'histoire moderne et contemporaine* 22 (1975): 89–141. 'Maggiolo en Provence, 'Collogue sur le XVIIIéme siècle et l'éducation, *Revue de Marseille* 88 (1972): 55–62; MAYNES, 'Schooling the Masses'; JOYCE APPLEBY, 'Modernization Theory and the Formation of Modern Social Theories in England and America.' *Comparative Studies in Society and History* 20 (1978): 259–85; JOHANSSON, 'Literacy in Sweden'; 'Facets of Education in the Eighteenth Century,' (Ed.) JAMES A. LEITH, *Studies on Voltaire and the Eighteenth Century* 167 (1977).

33 For some evidence and analysis, see GRAFF, *Literacy Myth*, chap. 7; CRESSY, *Literacy and Social Order;* JOHANSSON, 'Literacy Studies,' See also note 7, above.

34 DAN LACY, 'The View from the World of Publishing,' in *Television, the Book, and the Classroom*. Washington, D.C.: Library of Congress, Center for the Book, 1978, pp. 82–83.

35 JOHAN GALTUNG, 'Literacy, Education, and Schooling—for What?' in *Turning Point*, (Ed.) BATAILLE, p. 93.

Part II
The Ideologies of Literacy, Past and Present

Introductory Note to Part II

In contrast to most of the other chapters, those in Part II take the phenomenon and complications of the ideological aspects of literacy and literacy's inseparability from ideology in any formulation or consideration as central themes. That commonality ties essays otherwise disparate in subject matter and emphasis.

Chapter 2 was written in 1976 in response, in part, to the publication of the *Final Report* of the 1975 International Symposium for Literacy, in Persepolis, Iran, a joint effort of the UNESCO International Co-ordination Secretariat for Literacy, in Paris, and the Government of Iran. Thus, this chapter explicitly uses that *Final Report* as a take-off point for a much wider-ranging critical review of recent thinking about literacy. Cast in and showing its rootedness in a novel historical perspective, the essay also demonstrates the possibilities and values of historical criticism. Criticism, on one hand, and the bases for revision and reconceptualization, on the other hand, are the twin features.

Happily, that effort, whose terms and conceptions were then alien to the respondent that the journal *Interchange* asked to react formally as part of an 'interchange', is much less novel today. Interested readers might well compare J.C. Cairns' response and my rejoinder in the original issue (*Interchange*, 9 [1978–79], pp. 21–29) with the manner in which more contemporary writings make regular reference, at least, to historical literature and interpretations. Street's *Literacy in Theory and Practice* (Cambridge University Press, 1984) and Heath's *Ways with Words* (Cambridge University Press, 1983) are just two examples among an increasing number. My contribution to the 1985 *Social Science Encyclopedia* A. Kuper and J. Kuper, (Eds.) London: Routledge and Kegan Paul) is another, a sign of new openness within the 'establishment'. Of course, the penetration of this new perspective is still in its early stages. The lines of its further development are central to today's agenda.

Cairns' response revealed the large gap between and among 'critical' views toward literacy, its relationships, and developmental notions. He asserted a transformation of conception and conceptualization that simply could not then be located in the body of literature at issue, including the Persepolis *Final Report* or the papers themselves. The greatest area of miscommunication linked the critical view of literacy and its concomitants to the utility of historical formulations. That issue, it must be emphasized, is far from a final settlement, and in part Chapter 2, in some respects the most dated of all the chapters, is included early in the book to provoke that discussion toward a continuing dialogue.

Chapter 3, in contrast, seems at first more a historian's brief in its focus on the ideological aspects of important recent empirically based histories of literacy. The paper was solicited to serve as a North American counterpart in a collection of essays on the history of literacy in Great Britain, though I chose to raise theoretical and interpretive questions by way of my evaluation of the North American studies. Its larger point, however, transcends issues of historiography and links it to the preceding chapter. That is the manner, sometimes simply and other times quite subtly, in which ideology influences—one way or another—*all* efforts to deal with the subject of literacy, regardless of approach or level of discourse. That is one of the special distinguishing and erascible elements of the topic itself.

To make this point is hardly novel today. Yet the depth of its centrality to the subject of literacy, critically and practically both, remains, I think, insufficiently appreciated. Here then, we may grasp the ways in which it permeates both historical and contemporary thinking and penetrates to their cores. Only with the fullest embrace of that conjuncture may hopes for original, potentially liberating reconceptualizations and re-visions find common ground and progress together.

Added to the two chapters that originally constituted Part II is an 1867 text that I reprinted in the *History of Education Quarterly* in 1986, with an introduction that is also included here. W. B. Hodgson's idiosyncratic but powerfully fresh "Exaggerated Estimates of Reading and Writing as Means of Education," presented to the Social Science Association in Belfast in 1867 and printed in the next year, reminds us that important precedents exist for today's critical attitudes that emphasize limits of literacy. Hodgson's prescient views, relatively rare in his lifetime, are more common today, but still not as widely accepted as they deserve to be. I, for one, have no shame in admitting that Hodgson argued some of the ideas that I developed in the 1970s and published in *The Literacy Myth* and other places, including the other chapters in this section and Chapter 1 above. Both in themselves, as a significant historical statement, but also in reflection of debates 125 years later, Hodgson's words merit auditors today. Past and present continue to reshape each other dialectically.

(1993)

2   Literacy Past and Present: Critical Approaches in the Literacy / Society Relationship

On the desk beside my typewriter is the *Final Report* of the International Symposium for Literacy, a summary of the proceedings of the 1975 conference at Persepolis, Iran, on literacy in the modern world. This is hardly a startling or insightful document; nor is it innovative or critical. Nevertheless, it has a special importance for the student of literacy. It is a fitting representative as well as a culmination of two centuries of Western-biased and -based thinking about literacy and the literacy / society relationship. To a remarkable degree, it mirrors virtually all the clichés, assumptions, and uncritical writing and theorizing which dominate conceptualizations of the role of literacy in our models of development, modernization, and demographic progress.

The International Symposium stemmed from the joint efforts of the Iranian Government and the International Co-ordination Secretariat for Literacy, a UNESCO agency in Paris, and commemorated the tenth anniversary of the Teheran 'World Congress of Ministers of Education on the Eradication of Illiteracy.' Its purpose was the evaluation of 'a decade of international reflection and action on the subject of literacy teaching, with a view to extending and intensifying adult literacy teaching throughout the world' (1975, p. 3). Thus, while its perspective was not a critical one, the Symposium explicitly set out to evaluate past programs and progress.

The summary of the debates reveals several curious features. Most striking is the tension which marks the discussion of each of the major themes: a political split—capitalist versus socialist or communist; and a theoretical split—the role of literacy-training as politically oriented. Not surprisingly, the more critical perspective on the second issue seems to follow from the position on the former. A second feature is the dominance of traditional, progressive interpretations of literacy and education. This signifies the pervasiveness of the 'literacy myth' even among those critical of past literacy campaigns, traditional provision and distribution of literacy, and the uses of literacy, and among those who propose 'revolutionary' uses (socially or individually) of literacy. As in past-discussions of literacy and education, the speakers at the Symposium, regardless of their political persuasions, reflect a central tendency to overemphasize the power of literacy.

The purpose of this chapter is to present a first step toward a needed reconsideration of the literacy / society relationship. As the 1975 Persepolis Symposium reveals, among the world's experts in literacy-training and literacy studies, and even among those critical of past uses of literacy, a progressive, optimistic, liberationist, and fundamentally democratic set of assumptions governs thinking about literacy. The dominance of the evolutionary perspective holds whether the subject is social change, individual development, mobility, or economic modernization. Significantly, the controlling assumptions, the pervasive metaphors, derive from the period encompassing the last third of the eighteenth century through the first third of the nineteenth. The experts are, in many ways, Children of the Enlightenment and reflect an explicit faith in both the progress of civilization and humankind's ability to rationally improve itself—hence, the need for literacy and education.

A Historical Perspective

Historically, many grasped quickly the importance of print and the presumptions of individual and societal advancement which would follow from the achievement of mass literacy, yet disagreement raged and sputtered until about the end of the first third of the nineteenth century (Graff, 1975a, 1975b; Stone, 1969). Many conservatives feared the acquisition of education by the masses, thinking (probably quite erroneously) that they would be unfitted for grueling manual labor, unsettled in their stations, and lacking respect for their betters. Without traditional deference, reinforced by ignorance of print and communication, the masses would become undisciplined, unwilling to labor at sub-subsistence levels and to accept their lack of power. Moreover, the dangers of protest, civil strife, and even revolution, which so many feared in that Age of Revolution, would only be heightened. Of course, in many places, literacy continued to be restricted and even systematically withheld from certain segments of the population. Slaves in the United States South offer one such illustration.

This reactionary tendency, which feared schooling for the poor and working class, succumbed to the triumph of liberal progressive school promotion in the first half of the nineteenth century. Conservatives were out-argued and beaten down by sheer numbers, as well as by the fact and forces of rapid social change, the accompanying problems, and the urgent need for solutions. Education on both sides of the Atlantic was a typical Victorian obsession and remedy to changes often beyond the comprehension of middle class men and women. As we can now see, the systematic and institutional provision of literacy and education for the masses formed a central element in strategies for establishing control in society. As control by traditional rank deference and the 'moral economy' were replaced by emergent class divisions, education was seen as the new social cement (Graff, 1975a).

In this progressive formulation, the socializing powers of print were not lost on the leaders of social reform, those individuals most powerful and influential in attempts to reorder society. As opposition to mass schooling diminished in the West, a new consensus was rather rapidly achieved, stressing schooling for social stability and dominating the goals of educational promoters throughout the Anglo-American world and beyond. In later years this consensus became an integral commodity exported to underdeveloped nations as part of the Western parcel of modernization theory and strategy. This view emphasized aggregate social goals: the reduction of crime and disorder, the instillation of proper moral (and Protestant) values and, to a more limited extent, increased economic productivity rather than individualistic goals of intellectual development and personal advancement. These aims, rooted in perceptions demanding social and industrial discipline, work habits suited for factory and commercial capitalism, and respect for property, pervaded the rhetoric which surrounded the creation of systems for mass schooling and represented the primary motives for the properly controlled training of children (and adults) in literacy.

Implicitly people asked what were the uses of literacy, just as the participants at the Persepolis meeting did. Their answer lay in the moral arena, derivative of nondenominational Protestantism. Of the panoply of reasons offered by school promoters in this period, the inculcation of morals was supreme. This was an issue upon which virtually all agreed, regardless of differences over tactics and sectarian influences. Consequently, and crucial for us to recognize, literacy was only rarely seen as an end in itself. More often, its possession or absence was assumed to represent either a symbol or a symptom of the progress in moral and social training which had transpired or which remained to be accomplished through the creation of educational systems embracing all the children of the community. Schooling in literacy, thus, was useful to the efficient training of the population to the social order; its attainment ideally represented the sign that the operation was under way. Literacy was hardly a goal, for isolated from its moral basis, literacy was feared as potentially very dangerous. Rather, it was the literacy of properly schooled, morally restrained men and women that symbolized and guaranteed the goal of school promoters and social developers.

The roots of this controlling perspective on the place of literacy in social training predated the rise of institutionalized, systematic schooling and the rush to construct networks of educational facilities to mold the masses. The initial impetus was sectarianism, as religious groups competed for the souls of the poor and struggled to morally uplift them. Religion, and particularly Protestantism, was the driving force in those few societies which achieved universal adult literacy before the nineteenth century. As Lockridge (1974, pp. 99–101). concluded:

> In all this world the only areas to show a rapid rise in literacy levels
> approaching universality were small societies whose intense Protestant-
> ism led them widely to offer to compel in some way the education of

their people. . . . The motive force behind this action was the common
Protestant impulse to bring to all men the Word of God . . . the conservation of Piety.

The conservation of piety symbolized well the conservative influences at work. In
succeeding centuries both explicitly religious groups and nonsectarian (but reli-
giously-inspired) parties have been instrumental in furthering educational campaigns. The role of churches and missionaries (including Catholics) in education,
home and abroad, must not overlooked. As in the earlier period, the Bible served
as the vehicle for indoctrination, the moral message deriving from the pages of
the printed Scriptures. This was neither an intellectual nor a liberating act; it was
primarily ritualistic, with the level of literacy required often quite minimal. Literacy—and sometimes not much at that—symbolized in theory the observance
of an ordained and approved social order.

As the quest for social stability became nore important in the nineteenth
century and acquired an urgency not yet lost, education increasingly became the
dominant tool, regardless of the evidence revealing its limitations as an agent for
individual development. The Persepolis Symposium attests to this. Moral precepts
formed the basis of tutelage in literacy, and instruction was properly to teach and
inculcate the correct rules for social and economic behavior in a changing and
modernizing society. Literacy became a crucial vehicle for that process, as reformers seized upon the socializing powers of print and as morality and literacy
became intertwined. They were to be taught together: literacy speeding and eas-
ing moral instruction and morality guiding and restraining the potentially dangerous uses of unbridled literacy. Formal education, the only way in which to
dispense mass literacy securely, was intended to elevate the population and insure
peace, prosperity, and social cohesion. An efficient replacement for deference
and paternalism (a key concept), education would produce discipline and aid in
the inculcation of the values and habits required for an urban and industrial
society (Graff, 1975a; Thompson, 1976; Pollard, 1963).

In the past as in the present, the institutional structure of the school furthered
the inculcation of correct behavioral patterns. In ways beyond its stated objectives
and curricular intent, the school has been, and apparently continues to be, an
effective environment for training in approved patterns of conduct—i.e. the inculcation of normative behavior. The rational organization of the school acts as a
'hidden persuader' which contributes to learned rules for personal action. Consciously and unconsciously, formally and informally, the organization of work and
social relations is implicitly encapsulated in the microcosm of the school to be
understood and assimilated. Indeed, this is a frequently-ignored mechanism of
early socialization, which students of literacy in their somewhat misplaced concentration on adult education commonly overlook. Thus, the moral and social
bases of literacy gained reinforcement directly from the environment constructed
to transmit them (Dreeben, 1968, Inkeles and Smith, 1974; Graff, 1975a).

The purpose of literacy, in the past as in the present, was to integrate society
and to foster progress by binding men and women in its web and instilling in

them the guidelines for correct behavior. The importance of print and the concomitant ability to read and write were grasped by those most interested in social order. They saw, on the one hand, that more and more men and women were becoming literate, able to use their literacy without restraint. They saw, on the other hand, individuals without literacy—especially the young but sometimes adults too. Both elements represented a threat and an obstacle, a barrier to the spread of middle class values considered essential to social order and economic progress. The result, of course, was dispensation of print and literacy in environments carefully structured for that specific purpose, and instruction in the normative code and the socially approved uses of literacy.

During the second half of the nineteenth century, major influences in social thought—idealism, scientism, evolutionism, positivism, and progressivism—reinforced already-pervasive assumptions, securing the maintenance of traditional theories and insuring their permanence. In this century, moreover, the development and key concepts of social science, social theory, educational reform, and democratic liberalism continue to guarantee the dominance of the legacy of literacy's primacy—in the face of all problems and difficulties. This brief historical background is offered to illustrate my theme: the pervasive and often unproven progressive and optimistic assumptions which have guided and continue to condition our thinking and social theories about literacy and its relation to development and individual advancement. It is offered in support of my overriding belief that a firm comprehension of the historical forces which have shaped modern society is required to understand present developments and trends. Literacy represents just one aspect of this larger epistemological issue (Nisbet, 1969; Tipps, 1973).

The primary focus of this chapter, nonetheless, is the development (an initial one) of a systematic critique of the place of literacy (and, by extension, schooling) in modernist assumptions, developmental theories, and modernization schemes. The approach is historically-based, as good social science must be. The failings of literacy campaigns and education / development theories derive specifically from largely uncritical acceptance of assumptions formulated over the past two centuries.

In the remainder of the chapter, I shall return to the examination of the *Final Report* of the Symposium, continuing the critical exposition of its approaches to literacy. Then, turning to a series of discrete but interrelated aspects of the literacy / society relationship, I will attempt to show how the maintenance of these progressive assumptions influences a wide range of issues and obstructs a full understanding of the interrelatedness of critical factors in individual life and social development. Included among these topics are problems in defining and measuring literacy; the 'myth' of literacy's recent decline, literacy's relationships to communications, economic development, industrialization, and work; individual progress, social order and revolution; and, finally, democracy. Underlying all these concerns is my conclusion that a new paradigm is required in literacy studies and campaigns and that controlling orthodoxies from the past must be revised. The various strands of my discussion may constitute the beginnings of a new viewpoint; this is implicit in my presentation. However, the articulation of a unified theory is not my purpose here.

The Symposium: Four Themes

We now return to the Symposium of September, 1975. The participants focused on four themes central to contemporary literacy promotion and understanding.[1] The first theme, an appraisal of the past decade's adult literacy work, revealed the error of an exclusive concentration on adult training while allowing the literacy instruction of children to continue in unexamined modes, changing only in strategy and technique but not in assumptions or intent. The role of political and statist influences, a concern which continued throughout the other sessions, was also stressed. It was maintained, rather vaguely, that the 'political will' of the state was a 'necessary, though not sufficient, condition of success' for literacy programs (1975, pp. 8–9). One must note the vagueness, ambivalence, and ambiguity which permeate all pages of the proceedings of the Symposium. This removes any chance for the creation of a critical edge; of more importance, it is typical of discussions of literacy, awash in the sea of assumptions as they are. Political considerations, consequently, are not fully addressed after this initial appearance in the proceedings. For example, the intrinsic political act of sponsoring or obstructing literacy provision is barely recognized and hardly debated. As the historical introduction indicates, instruction in literacy has always been colored by the social (and concomitant political) goals of the sponsoring agencies. Today, it is no different.

Several other issues were central to the discussion of the first theme. Overall, there was an instructive amount of disagreement about whether progress had been made in the 'eradication' of illiteracy. Some participants assured the gathering that if controls for population growth were used, advance had been made; others stressed the overall failures. Similarly, controversy arose over the issue of *quantitative versus qualitative* assessments of literacy and their relative validities (1975, p. 9). Assuredly, there is a distinction to be made, one which too many students and policy-makers fail to realize. But the need to use both forms of measurement separately and conjointly as required, rather than arguing over the choice and exclusion, was not recognized, complicating further discussion of defining and measuring literacy.

The relationship of literacy's increasing distribution in connection with social structural and technological development formed a third issue. Here the political allegiances of the national representatives were strikingly visible, as seen in the emphases on literacy as one factor in strategies for social and revolutionary transformations. The legacy of social theories about education was most pervasive: literacy was related to liberty, initiation of social and economic change, national destiny, social justice, the transformation of mentalities, and the 'awakening of autonomous, critical, constructive minds, capable of changing man's relationship with man and with nature' (1975, p. 10). Indeed, one speaker summarized aptly one of the central and fallacious assumptions of the past: literacy instruction 'is concerned with propagating . . . an ideology of hope.' The historical and contemporary limits of educational reforms, so familiar to readers of periodicals such as this one, the errors of neoclassical economics and the human-capital school, and the lack of social mobility for many throughout the world . . . all attest to the failure of those who refuse to revise assumptions about the role of education in society. It is time such formulations were re-examined.

The Symposium's second theme stressed the 'functionalities' of literacy in terms of economic activities, health, culture, and social reform. The optimistic emphasis on the power of literacy is most striking in the discussion of this topic, as literacy is related directly to the 'need to satisfy the essential needs of man' (1975, p. 11). Participants seemed well aware that, historically, the 'functionality' approach to literacy had its origins in the improvement of labor productivity. Yet their feeling was that only recently had this been broadened to include other social and economic issues. They appeared unaware that *only one* of the roots for mass provision of literacy was industrial and economic; the social upheavals accompanying the commercial and industrial revolutions propelled educational promotion at least as directly as industrialization itself. Moreover, it is crucial to distinguish conceptually industrialization from the more general phenomena of modernization, as Wrigley has argued in an important paper (1972; Tipps, 1973).

Once more the basic, perhaps irreconcilable, divisions among participants came to the fore. This is seen clearly in the split regarding the need for literacy as a stimulant to economic functions and to cultural developments—'from primary consciousness to critical consciousness' (1975, pp. 11–14). Apparently no one argued about the crucial linkages tying ideology, culture, and consciousness to the structural bases of social and economic life. Thus, the Symposium went on with its business of creating distinctions where there need have been none, and missing connections which, if grasped, would have aided the proceedings. This failing is all the more unfortunate in view of some representatives' important recognition of literacy training's dependence upon 'the political and ideological functions it is expected to fulfill, both in the productive, set up and in society as a whole,' and their realization of the reactionary *as well* as the progressive uses of literacy and education.

Significantly, in one of the most 'enlightened' passages of the summaries, one speaker explicitly condemned the 'present state of chaos engendered' by the acceptance of Western educational systems and functionalist developmental models. This speaker identified excessive specialization, dispossession and dequalification of work, sterilization of inventive and innovative faculties, and the increasing dependence of the underdeveloped nations (1975, pp. 13–14). Literacy, quite explicitly, has been a tool of Western imperialism; the social control of education and knowledge is a useful agent indeed, as Altbach (1975) has recently hinted. Nevertheless, the complexities of literary colonialism are but barely comprehended, both in the Report and in other literature. Local or internal controls are not sufficient in themselves to prevent normative or reactionary uses of literacy; *nor* is rejection of all external or Western literature a path to progress.

A further complication results from the fact that literacy is never defined. This stems from the lack of conceptualization in virtually all discussions, from the aura of vagueness surrounding them, and from the unrealistic expectations held about the power of literacy. Thus commentators and speakers make tremendous leaps from campaigns to provide instruction in the technical skills of reading and writing to literacy as the source of independent, critical, and constructive thought processes. Literacy *may* be a key cause for this further activity (necessary but not sufficient). But we must certainly agree with E.P. Thompson (1967a) that the ability to read is only an elementary technique and that the ability to handle abstract and consecutive argument is by no means inborn. Reports by psychologists and learning specialists only reinforce this conclusion; critical powers are developed through hard effort and constant practice and their relationship to reading and writing is more ecological than casual. Just as the literacy leaders of Persepolis expect too much from a literacy which they fail to conceptualize or define, conversely so do they anticipate too little from a theoretically-conceived state of universal illiteracy: 'nothing less than the end of civilization, without a doubt' (1975, p. 13).

To recast their perspective on literacy to include these much broader considerations would require more than just a new term, as some participants suggested. It would necessitate the abandonment of literacy and literacy campaigns, as those in the Symposium know them, for an emphasis on more advanced (and presumably ideological) education, requiring important changes in the social structure and work routine of most societies. While this may indeed be needed, the Symposium, even if it were prepared to advocate it, could hardly serve to produce such changes.

The third theme (1975, pp. 14–16) of the meeting confronted directly 'the determination to introduce deep changes in the living conditions of man and in social structures as a *sine qua non* of literacy undertakings.' Although the phrasing leaves something to be desired, this topic certainly reveals the persistence of the assumptions discussed above. As noted earlier, the relationship of literacy to politics was reiterated. It was also emphasized by some that there was no such thing as a politically neutral education (1975, p. 14). Significantly, there seemed to be less than full agreement on this primary precept, and more than a few speakers rose to qualify the assertion. They stated that the technical and methodological aspects of literacy training could be considered neutral. Ah, the myth of objective techniques!

Similarly, the conference experienced considerable discomfort about the relationship of educational systems to material, social structural, and historical circumstances. Opinion, not surprisingly, was divided over the use of schooling to reproduce the dominant ideology, the social relations of production, and the structures of inequality. Those unwilling to accept this formulation attempted to argue that, on the contrary, any type of education, regardless of the context, tends to strengthen 'the learners' autonomy of decision and therefore to enhance their capacity for change . . .' (1975, p. 15). Evidence, alas, is lacking, particularly with regard to the role of the structural bases of educational provision. Literacy may certainly open up paths to knowledge; equally surely, its possession does not automatically provide knowledge, especially where literature is censored and book distribution is carefully regulated.

The final theme (1975, pp. 76–77) need not detain us; this was the evaluation of the role of new literacy experiments in reforming teaching and training systems. Of course, this is a critical issue, regardless of one's position on the uses of literacy. Moreover, its importance is heightened by the simple fact that teachers of reading fail to agree about the success of any given method and that reading methodology remains one of the most confused areas in education today. The Symposium, as far as the *Final Report* reveals, contributed little to clarification. More generally, the discussion reinforced the common ambiguities and misassumptions. On this note, the thematic discussions concluded. The observer and the student of literacy, past or present, would certainly be justified in asking in what ways had the Symposium for Literacy advanced our understanding of contemporary issues facing literacy campaigns, the changing uses of literacy, and the relationship of literacy to a whole series of important social and individual developments. The answer, I must conclude, would not be a positive one.

As its final and undoubtedly major action, the Symposium produced a document which will receive wide attention. This is the 'Declaration of Persepolis,' the tone of which is consistent with that of the proceedings themselves. The uncritical acceptance of past assumptions is especially striking, the myths about literacy equally pervasive. There is little awareness of the contradictory uses of literacy and certainly none of the historical factors. The Declaration is a fitting testament to two hundred years of Western social thought and social-developmental theories about the relationship of literacy to modernization, both individual and structural.

Definition and Measurement

This evaluation of the Persepolis Symposium for Literacy has revealed the major variables in the literacy / society relationship. Let us consider several of these issues directly.

Difficulties in definition and measurement of literacy severely restrict most attempts to discuss the subject. Even generally, discussions of literacy are fraught with confusion. Two sources principally account for this: first is the vagueness which surrounds the conception of what it means to be literate and how this might be determined; the second derives from our lack of knowledge about the benefits of literacy—thus, the dependence on assumptions and their survival.

Definitions of literacy are highly problematic, for the present as well as the past (Graff, 1975a; Schofield, 1968). As Harman (1970) recounts, until the early 1950s most governments considered the ability to read, to write and to do simple arithmetic the constituents of individual literacy. As UNESCO expressed it: 'a person is literate who can, with understanding, both read and write a short simple statement on his everyday life.' How was this determined? Most often, a census-style question, asking respondents, or their families or neighbors, if an individual were able to read and write, constituted the test. The decade of the 1950s witnessed an increasing tendency to distinguish between a literate and a functionally literate person, defined by the 'essential knowledge and skills which enable him to engage in all those activities in which literacy is required for effective functioning in his group and community, and whose attainments make it possible for him to use these skills towards his own and the community's development' (Harman, 1970, p. 227). Crucially, nowhere are the critical concepts of 'effective functioning,' 'knowledge and skills,' or 'development' defined or even discussed. Nowhere is the key notion of functional literacy ever addressed; nor are the implications explored.

Most governments employ the first definition, with all its ambiguity, in conjunction with an elementary school grade completion equivalency, most often the fourth or fifth grade. For example, the US Bureau of the Census considers literacy the ability to read and write a simple message and uses a fifth grade level, as does the Bureau of the Census of Statistics Canada. Yet, the US Bureau simultaneously admits that 'the completion of no one particular grade of school corresponds to the attainment of literacy.' Still they use the equivalencies as do bureaus throughout the world. Aside from this self-criticism, we might also object to the lack of comparability over units large or small. The implications of reading and writing a message are apparently never considered; in other words, there is *no specified context* for literacy to serve either the individual or society. Attempts to define and measure a 'functional' literacy do not succeed in this direction; nor are there even attempts at controls for changing demands and socio-economic requirements.

In the 1970s, there have been several more interesting definitional efforts, although they continue to be plagued by many of the same failings of specification and context (Graff, 1975a, Introduction). For example, several sociologists operating on a smaller scale than a national or regional census have taken different approaches. Subjects have been asked if they can read their native language, and then tested for comprehension, sometimes orally and other times by written test. Such tests do represent an improvement on census-type measures of literacy; the definitions which accompany them, however, do not give a close fit with the test. Writing, to take one case, is never measured. More importantly, functions are never specified or related to test questions; consequently, no serious attempt has yet been made to relate literacy to a hierarchy of skills, job or social, or to specific contextual needs. Researchers are not always aware that literacy is a process, different for different roles and that its requirements change with individual and social changes. The meaning and uses of literacy are much more complex than the simple questions or examinations would suggest to many readers (and to many researchers).

Vagueness and ambiguity of definition and measurement also influence modes of analysis and the questions which contemporary students employ (Graff, 1975a, Introduction). Functional necessity very often is translated into attitudes and values rather than behaviours or skills. Of this there are many examples, and they are indicative more of literacy's important role in attitude and values-inculcation than in skill-provision. This subtle connection is rarely seen, however. Thus, rather than isolating the role literacy plays in work of life-chances researchers inquire into such abstractions as empathy, achievement orientation, and 'cosmopoliteness.' Other questions concern the media, political knowledge, and opinion, while very few address functional abilities.

The most recent attempts to supplement such definitions make an effort to overcome some of these limitations. David Harman (1970), for instance, proposes a three-stage conceptualization of literacy: as a tool, an achievement of skills, and, finally, the application of the skills in ways meaningful to the individual. 'Each stage is contingent upon the former; each is a necessary component of literacy.' This approach makes good sense; nevertheless, it continues to make key assumptions without either support or rationale, and it does not go far enough in dispelling the aura of vagueness which has traditionally pervaded discussions of literacy. Literacy is assumed to be a tool. But what kind of a tool and for what ends? In fine, the discussion has remained for well over a century at the level which Harman (1970, p. 228) accepts: 'few would dispute the significance of literacy for either individual or national development.'

The Myth of Decline

An important contemporary concomitant of this faith in literacy is the 'myth' of literacy's decline. As the newspapers and the other media inform us daily *ad nauseam,* standards of literacy achievement have rapidly declined in recent years. Blame is cast upon the school, the curriculum, the family, television and other media, and of course on youth and society. I for one am not yet persuaded by the evidence for this decline. For one, it is the gut reflex of a social order whose basic premises have become outmoded and whose ideological supports are crumbling. The death of Western industrially-based liberalism and the demise of the Enlightenment legacy of rationality are now surfacing into official and academic consciousness; literacy of course is a central aspect. More directly, the so-called decline has yet to be established even statistically over a meaningful longitudinal span. Comparable test results do not exist for much more than the last decade, and when comparisons are made, controls are not always applied for such basic considerations as recent changes in the socioeconomic and demographic profiles of the student populations, in both senior high schools and in higher education.

This latter factor does, in fact, account for a very large degree of the variation. Much of the evidence adduced to proclaim contemporary crises of decline, however, is anecdotal; students twenty, thirty, or forty years ago *of course* knew more; they read and wrote better, and graduated with more useful skills. Thus, we must retrench to the basics and reinforce instruction in the 3 Rs. Is it even necessary to mention that such evidence is wholly unsystematic?

There are other considerations too, which the domination of our myths and assumptions prevent us from realizing. Basic channels of communication are changing. Print media no longer hold their traditional importance; radio, TV, sight and sound, as well as symbolic representation, are increasing in importance. This is not to say, however, that sight, sound, and symbol were not important before the advent of electronic media—they were indeed, as the historian should be well aware. Their importance, however, is increasing now. Focusing on excessive media exposure as a primary cause for the decline of literacy obstructs from understanding the fact that as a society and culture change, channels of communications do as well. One simply cannot talk about decline without a firm comprehension of change and the place of literacy in the process. I would suggest that literacy may be changing in its forms of utility now—becoming more technologically-oriented rather than declining. Surely, the schools could do a better job in the provision of basic skills, especially if all the latent and covert moral and social controlling factors were admitted or revised. It should be clear that many assumptions need to be reconsidered for changes to begin; paranoia about an unproven decline will not advance these important changes.

A final factor is the discovery that high or universal levels of literacy in the nineteenth century or earlier do not usually correlate with high ability to understand the written page or to employ usefully or practically the literacy taken from the schoolhouse (Graff, 1975a, Ch. 7; Johansson, 1973). Estimation of popular qualitative levels of literacy is difficult and more so for the past than for the present. Nevertheless, initial research hints at the fallacy so commonly made of assuming that statistical levels of literacy inform our knowledge about qualitative levels.

Some Common Illusions

Communication modes return us to the topics of the Persepolis meetings. Several times, participants spoke of the necessity for literacy to insure effective social functioning for cooperation and communication. First, channels of communication are indeed changing; traditional conceptions of reading and writing, which are prominent in all literacy campaigns, are insufficient to meet new needs. Furthermore, there is a growing body of evidence that possession of literacy, even of a high quality, is no guarantee of its employment. For example, publishing and book distribution are densely concentrated among the wealthier (and generally Western) nations (Altbach, 1975); nevertheless, in these industrialized societies, many who can read simply do not. In Italy and Hungary, to take one case, 40 per cent of the population do not read to any extent, and in France, 53 per cent do not. In 1970, an average French man or woman read no more than one book (Graff, 1975a, Introduction). To those operating with traditional assumptions, this is disturbing news, but it is necessary to ask: what effect did this have on their lives; were they less functional or less productive members of their communities, etc.?

Recent studies of literacy in underdeveloped areas reinforce this need for revision (reviewed in Graff, 1975a). In East Pakistan (Bangladesh), literacy was found to bear no relationship to growing material self-interest; nor did it relate to the recognition of differing opinions among fellow men. In fact, literacy correlated *negatively* with contentment with material possessions, despite two hundred years of literacy promotion! Significantly, literacy has been only slightly correlated with media exposure, suggesting that literates do not read to any important extent and / or illiterates have direct access to newspapers or other sources of information. Illiterates in fact do buy newspapers (48 per cent of them in one study) and have the journals read to them. In another report 19 per cent had newspapers read, and 6 per cent had magazines read. It was found that even among Colombian peasants, most households contain at least one literate person. Sources of information and channels of communication may indeed be open to those without literacy; conversely, many with literacy make little attempt to use such mechanisms. Finally, in spite of the promises of liberating literacy campaigners, individuals—and not the media or print sources—are considered the best sources of information, and many opinion leaders in underdeveloped nations are far from literate.

I should not want this interpreted as an 'anti-literacy' argument. I am certainly not opposed to literacy provision or to the many uses of literacy (I do make my living through manipulation of oral and written words after all). Rather, what I seek is the revision of pervasive, uncritical, and outmoded assumptions about the place of literacy in social and individual development. Literacy, as the work of Paulo Freire (1971) has movingly illustrated, may be a tool for liberation and social change. In most cases, however, the dominant employment of literacy has been conservative, regardless of promises to the contrary. The origins of the promotion of mass literacy were tied to the reordering of society at a time of transformation; this strong element of social order has never been lost. Moreover, it pervades modern social theories and certainly colors Western modernization thinking.

In the latter years of the eighteenth and the first third of the nineteenth century, many persons of power and property feared that the education of the poor and working classes would lead to revolution. Contact with secular works, the writings of the Paines, Godwins, and Wollstonecrafts, and the increasingly anti-religious emphasis frightened these individuals (Graff, 1975a, 1975b). They held that reading and print (and rationality) were powerful and dangerous tendencies. Not only would the working class draw upon books and often outlawed papers and pamphlets but also they would be able to communicate much more effectively with one another and to use the printing press to their advantage. The result, many were certain, would turn the world upside down (Webb, 1955). Nonetheless, overwhelmingly it was middle class radicals and the upper ranks of the working class who seized upon the revolutionary (or, perhaps more properly, the reformist) uses of print. This movement barely touched the lives of the majority of the poor and working class or common laborers, whose energies and bodies were required for larger social action. In England, the failure of Chartism and the course of electoral reforms provide two examples among many. Ironically, too, among violent rebels, such as the rural Captain Swing movement, illiterate men and women tended to dominate.

Even the common assumption of the intimate connection between literacy and revolution must be qualified. The successful movements of the last two centuries were propelled by middle class intellectuals (I use the term loosely) and the newly literate masses. A case could be defensibly advanced that the widespread distribution of literacy has served more of a safeguard role than the opposite (Graff, 1975a). The power of the morally-laced and morally-based curriculum which provided the substance of literacy training, the experience of that training itself, the institutional structures (hidden and overt), all combined with the economic insecurities and poverty of the working class and poor—and with the much more open and obvious mechanisms of control—to prevent revolutionary outbursts. We must take caution, of course, against overemphasizing the effectiveness of literacy in its conservative aspects. Literacy, I believe, has a lesser influence than the experience of 'training in being trained' and the social message which underlies and permeates skill-learning. In other words, the noncognitive aspects of the educational experiences are more influential than the cognitive ones, as Bowles and Gintis (1976) and Dreeben (1968) have also recently argued.

Progress, social order, and stability were closely connected in nineteenth century thought. Literacy, if properly dispensed, would prevent disruption and criminality, as it might prevent pauperism and vice (Graff, 1975a, 1976a, 1977–78, 1978). Conversely, it was expected that those who were poor, illiterate, irreligious, and often immigrant were the greatest offenders against civil law and property. And of course, these were precisely the persons who were arrested most often: vagrants, homeless women, the laboring class, Irish Catholics. Patterns, of arrest and conviction, I have found, were quite systematic—systematic and regular to the extent that one finds the operation of a self-fulfilling prophecy: those expected to perpetrate criminal acts were arrested whether guilty or not and most often found to be guilty. Systematic patterns of discrimination followed from the assumptions which governed social thought. How much does the present deviate from the course of the past?

In terms of working class organization, culture, and communications, it may well be that informal processes were more important than literacy-oriented ones. One reader could inform a much larger number, and reading circles were prominent features of nineteenth century taverns, pubs, and ports of call (Thompson,

1967a; Graff, 1975a). In addition, it was not uncommon for artisans and other shop and factory workers to employ a young man to read to them as they worked. Work was obtained informally and bureaucratic application procedures were at a minimum. Finally, cooperatives and businesses on occasion replaced ledgers and money with color-coded tickets. A primacy on literacy did not exist. Present-day life, especially in less developed areas, might usefully be re-examined in this light.

Literacy and Economic Growth

One of the most central of the many assumptions in our inherited set of literacy / society relationships is that of joining literacy to economic development and work. An entire school of economic thought, the so-called 'human capital' school initiated by Becker and Schultz, has its roots in this precept, and it has been equally prominent in modernization theory and tactics. I shall not comment specifically on the philosophical weaknesses of the human capitalists; they are obvious from even the sketchiest familiarity. Perhaps most instructive of the overall conceptual failings here is the work of the 'social indicators' researchers with respect to literacy.

The general lack of recognition of literacy for the purposes it truly serves, together with its controlling assumptions, conditions the place accorded to literacy in schemes of development (Cipolla, 1969). It has been given a vague and superficially powerful role. Economists, sociologists, planners, and governments have found that literacy rates correlate with literally scores of factors, including individual attitudes, economic growth and productivity, industrialization, urbanization, migration, per capita wealth and GNP, income, political stability, participatory democracy, fertility and mortality rates, population density, communications and related media productions, health and food consumption, rates of mobility, and technological advances, to cite just some of the correlations reported in such volumes as *The World Handbook of Social and Political Indicators*. Of course, there is a certain logic in many of these relationships, but it is important to question whether there is a significance beyond the statistical one. There remain no accompanying explanations, beyond the most superficial; nor have there been any specific analyses of literacy's role as an independent variable or even as a dependent one. The assumptions, ambiguities, and contradictions implicit in many of these modernization approaches have begun to be justly criticized, especially by Nisbet (1969) and Tipps (1973), and I need not repeat that debate here. What must be stressed; however, are the limitations of the literacy-modernization-development approach, which derive from the acceptance and perpetuation of past assumptions, the vagueness which surrounds the meaning of literacy, the failure to specify contexts for its role and, most importantly perhaps, the fundamental ignorance about the functional benefits of literacy. This also relates to the surveys of individual literacy which stress attitudes and not behavior, action, or accomplishments—making many, if not most, of the large-scale cor-relations, regression, and factor analyses less than meaningful in current status.

In this context, it is useful to re-examine briefly the literacy / economic de-velopment relationship. In various studies, Anderson and Bowman (1965, 1963) have attempted to demonstrate the ways in which literacy should be considered essential to economic development. From the premise that education is one of the few sure roads to economic growth and increasing factor productivity, they find a tendency to 'justify' education (especially primary schooling) in economic terms, à la human capitalists. They have claimed (1965), for example, that 'about 40 per cent' adult' literacy or primary enrollment is a 'threshold' for economic development. True, they are aware that the level of education alone is an insuf-ficient condition for 'take-off' in a society lacking other prerequisites. Throughout their writings, however, Bowman and Anderson stress the necessity, if not the sufficiency, of a literacy threshold for sustained growth, a stage which would be maintained until a level of 70–80 per cent literacy were reached. Significantly, they have failed to show with any precision that these thresholds have meaning in any historical context.

McClelland (1966), on the other hand, finds that investment in education at the primary or literacy level is inadequate and does not correlate positively with growth rates. He concludes that elementary school attendance has a 'doubtful relationship' to economic improvement. He also advances (1966, p. 262) the im-portant, historically-validated point that 'the marginal product of a primary school education would seem likely to be low, because skilled artisans may function as well without being literate.' We now know (Thompson, 1967a; Pollard, 1963) that the training of such illiterate producers was a severe complication to the devel-opment of factory industrialization, with its emphasis on disciplined work habits and time. Furthermore, McClelland discovers that primary schooling is not suf-ficient to lift a person to jobs characteristic of the middle class, hinting at the perilousness of the mobility promise of the school promoters. A strong relation-ship, however, derives from post-primary education, especially if the lagtime be-tween training and the impact on the economy is considered. As he summarizes: 'education is a long-term investment from the economic point of view.' This view and his supporting evidence strike squarely in the face of many modernizers and literacy campaigners.

On a broader and more historically-based level, recent work in economic history and development has begun to contradict the received wisdom that edu-cation is central to the process of industrialization and that it must logically pre-cede a 'take-off into sustained growth.' Education and economic growth, as McClelland suggests, need not be collateral or sequential processes; productivity and wealth do not necessarily follow from mass literacy, as the histories of Sweden and Scotland demonstrate. Both achieved near universal literacy before the nine-teenth century, but both remained desperately poor.

The larger issue is embraced by Schofield (1968, p. 312), who observes that today literacy is considered to be a necessary precondition for economic devel-opment.

The necessity of literacy as a precondition for economic growth is a persistent theme running through many UNESCO publications. Correlations between measures of industrialization both in the past and in the present are established in UNESCO *World Illiteracy at Mid-Century* (Paris, 1957), pp. 177–89. These measures are very general and throw no light on the question of why literacy should be considered essential to economic growth.

Just as with the social indicators! What about the past? What lessons has it to offer? Talbott (1971, p. 141) concludes 'in the first decades of industrialization, the factory system put no premium on even low-level intellectual skills. Whatever relationships existed between widespread literacy and early industrial development must have been quite roundabout.'

Ironically for those who seek a productive value for education, past or present, the relationship at least in England was less than 'roundabout.' Early industrialization disrupted education, and adult literacy levels probably fell as a result (Sanderson, 1967, 1972). The demand for child labor, in North America too, greatly reduced the chances for a lower-class child to attend school. Factory schools were, on the whole, rare, ineffectual, and very irregularly attended. Secondary education was unheard of for the children of the working class.

The result was reflected in the literacy rates for late eighteenth- and early nineteenth-century England. Scholars now are producing evidence that the Industrial Revolution cannot be seen as one 'nourished' by rising educational standards at the primary level. Crucially, the decline in literacy did not impede the upsurge in economic growth because the very nature of industrialization made very low literacy demands. Schofield (1973, pp. 452–3) puts it well:

> Thus, insofar as economic growth in this period entailed the acquisition of a large number of practical skills by a growing proportion of the population, developments in literacy and education were probably largely irrelevant to it. And, insofar as economic growth resulted from the increased productivity of labor brought about by the shift from domestic to factory production, literacy and education were also probably largely irrelevant for many of the new industrial occupations recruited a mainly illiterate work force.

'Knack', as one student put it, was of far greater importance than book-learning in the process of industrialization. I suggest that this historical analogy has much to offer contemporary developmental theorists.

England, it appears, reached Bowman and Anderson's 'forty per cent threshold' level of literacy by 1750 (for males at least[2]), and it remains for searchers to isolate an exceptional case to that rule of thumb. The threshold level may well be so general as to be meaningless. Secondary levels may have been more influential, but more research is required to firmly establish the relationship. Overall, the causal relationship between literacy and economic development might be reversed. The reduction in illiteracy in nineteenth-century England then would appear more as a cultural change wrought by economic growth than as a cause of growth.

If not education for productive labor in early industrialization, then what? The principal problem for economic development, I would argue, is the organization and indoctrination of the work force. The laboring population, in underdeveloped areas today as in early nineteenth-century England, had to be trained for factory work and taught industrial habits, rules and rhythms. Traditional social habits and customs did not fit new patterns of industrial life; they had to be discredited (or more actively removed) and replaced with new, 'modern' forms of behavior. Literacy was often far from central in the creation of an industrial workforce, although its potential for assimilation was soon realized (Graff, 1975a). Primarily, capitalists and managers saw that it was not the better worker but the stable one who was of greater value (Pollard, 1963). The problem was one of discipline, and factory owners with difficulty forced workers to change their habits and identify themselves with unvarying regularity and machine-driven work paces. Discipline was required to produce goods on time and rules became the norm.

To 'educate' the workers was the problem. It was not an education in reading and writing, but rather it was the need to train them to a new work discipline, permeated with the middle class obsession with character and morality. This was as true of North America and also pervades discussions of the requirements for Third World development. Precise and mechanically-maintained clocktime symbolized the emerging order. Here schools had a direct role to play; they aided in the inculcation of 'time thrift,' teaching industry, frugality, order, regularity, and punctuality (Thompson, 1967b). As a factory owner expressed it, by the time a child reached six or seven, he or she should be 'habituated, not to say naturalized, to Labour and Fatigue.' The parallels between the rules of the school and those of the factory were many—and certainly continue to be (Bowles and Gintis, 1976). With both, the new universe of disciplined time and conduct were supreme; both were agents for instruction in the behavior and values required for industrialization, productivity, and socially-approved habits (Inkeles and Smith, 1974).

In England, America, and much of the rest of the world, the value of formal education was increasingly grasped, and its importance in the inculcation of industrial habits among the working class and the poor was certainly not viewed in terms of literacy alone. Literacy, though, could ease the transition if provided in carefully structured institutions designed for that purpose. The destruction of traditional habits and attitudes was not easy; nor was it accomplished in one generation. As a result, the process of assimilation was closely related to the spread of literacy. Literacy, then, constitutes a training in being trained. A person who in childhood has submitted to some processes of disciplined and conscious learning is more likely to respond to further training, whether in an army, a factory, or in participatory activities. This training is the critical job preparation and the problem for industrial development; simultaneously it has been the first task of the school and *one* critical use of literacy.

Literacy and Individual Achievement

The issue most closely allied with the work and industrial associations of literacy is of course the impact of literacy on the individual. As seen throughout this chapter, the key questions have consistently been more complex than current formulations and traditional assumptions would allow. Here we must ask just how important have literacy and education been to occupational and economic success at the individual level? Traditional wisdom, modern sociology and educational theory, the rhetoric of modernization as well as of nineteenth century school promoters . . . all sing out the glorious relation of education to success. Not surprisingly, not all the evidence, past or present, lends credence to this view. As we shall see, the relationship of education / literacy to work, occupation, and mobility is an imprecise one, complex and often contradictory (Graff, 1975a, 1976a).

In the first place, there is a curious set of findings from recent studies of literacy. As noted above, they remain largely in the realm of attitudes and values, and not in that of skills or behaviors as the promoters of success through schooling have promised. There are fundamental contradictions within this set of relationships, and only a very few relate to 'functionalities': innovativeness, opportunity awareness, and achievement seeking. These are basically attitudinal and are not skills in a direct sense.

In terms of jobs, literacy research has found little to support the promise of educationists who claim that education and literacy will be well compensated in the open marketplace. Contemporary sociological debate also continues to focus on the relationship between educational and occupational achievement. Recent data join with historical evidence, contradicting assumptions of the direct link connecting school achievement and job attainment. Blau and Duncan's methodological classic, *The American Occupational Structure* (1967), marked a watershed in the current controversy. They maintained that the changes of upward occupational mobility are directly related to education, mobility is a function of education and social origins, and occupational status in 1962 (the year of their special CPS questionnaire) is apparently influenced more strongly by education than by first job. Blau and Duncan qualified these sweeping generalizations, claiming that educational status was historically increasing in importance, that social origins were indeed important in determining both education and occupation, and that the impact of education and origin decreases with age and experience. Nevertheless, in their conclusions, they remain firmly convinced of the primacy of education.

Other researchers have been quick to supplement the Blau-Duncan findings, and have attempted to revise them in evaluating the contribution of education. Berg (1971), for one, has demonstrated that the commonly-perceived relationships are an endemic part of modern democratic mythology. He concludes that it is impossible to construct an occupational scale according to the intellectual abilities required by diverse occupational demands. He also presents 1950 and 1960 census data which contradict Blau and Duncan's conclusions. Rather than illustrating an increasing primacy for education, his data reveal a drift of 'better' educated people into 'middle' level jobs and a reduction in the number of less educated people moving up into middle level positions. Education has expanded more rapidly than net changes in skill requirements. The attitudes fostered by the schooling process suffer from the frustrating consequences of underemployment.

Significantly, Berg's examination of job requirements found self-fulfilling prophecies about the value (rampant among managers) of educated workers. Not only was there overeducation for job requirements but also there was little, if any, relationship between changes in educational levels and changes in output per worker! In fact, less productive workers were slightly better educated. Education did not predict promotion, but at the professional level, educational achievement rather than skill or performance was rewarded.

> To argue that well-educated people will automatically boost efficiency, improve organizations, and so on may be to misunderstand in a fundamental way the nature of American education, which functions to an important, indeed depressing extent as a licensing agency. (1971, p. 104).

These arguments, a direct legacy from the past, we have good reason to doubt, then and now. Further, studies of social mobility since Blau and Duncan have pointed increasingly to a lack of movement in society over long periods of time, to an increasing emphasis on social origins and other ascribed social characteristics, to the exclusion of achieved characteristics, and to a large-scale shift from 'achievement to ascription,' just the opposite of what modernization theory would lead us to expect.

Throughout the past two centuries, working men and women, organized and unorganized, have displayed an instructive ambivalence in their attitudes toward formal schooling (Graff, 1975a, 1976a). To a certain extent, the working class has accepted the wisdom of middle class school promoters in seeking the benefits of education, especially for their children. Why should they be immune to the powerful controlling assumptions? Nevertheless, labor's views have been marked by a tension between a hunger for education and doubts about both the usefulness and the form of that schooling. To them, education often meant something more than a socially mobile, well-trained worker. Workers have historically desired that education be accessible to them, that it be practical and job-oriented, tied to rising wages and promotion. At the same time, as one nineteenth-century Canadian labor paper expressed it: 'educated workmen, skilled workmen, and moral workmen [make] labor respected as well as profitable' (Graff, 1976a). They wanted less bourgeois moral philosophy, more concentration on developing critical abilities, and graduates with a range of knowledge and flexible skills—what the primary curriculum certainly was not designed to provide. They also admired the successes of the self-educated and the uneducated. Finally, the workers asked that their children not simply *be* educated—that 'they must educate themselves to think; they must also learn to think for themselves.'

It would be inaccurate to argue that the working class and their spokesmen did not embrace the all-pervasive assumptions about the value of schooling in job preparation and social mobility, and that they did not send their children to school when they could afford to do so. Of course they responded to the promises of the school promoters. It would be equally inaccurate, however, to suggest that they never questioned the primarily moral and attitudinal training, the social control of the school. At times, their analyses cut to the core. But there was little they could do, in all reality, other than try to play the game and to win when they could: win more often for the next generation, they believed.

One aspect of the labor perspective on literacy is especially interesting. Reading was often discussed in terms of amusement, comfort, consolation, and leisure (Graff, 1975a). Relief from hard labor could come from reading and literature. Furthermore, the impulse to establish mechanics' institutes, working men's reading rooms, and ancillary public institutions came from reasons beyond the literary ones. Workmen, it was thought, needed places to meet one another, to share interests, and to organize gatherings. Here a political analysis or political action could be advanced to which literacy's contribution might be secondary at best. Thus, labor had uses for literacy, but not always were they the same as those the middle class promoted.

Were the workers' specific economic benefits related to literacy? No clear answer can yet be given, but the results of research in several nineteenth-century places offer a beginning (Graff, 1975a; Sanderson, 1972). Systematic comparison of the stratification of literate and illiterate adults reveals an important finding: the structures of inequality—both in occupational and wealth stratification—paralleled almost perfectly the stratification of literacy. The distribution of literacy by class, occupation, economic rank, ethnicity, race, age, and sex presented the same rank order as the patterns of social stratification; provision of literacy was firmly tied to the ordering of groups in society and was hardly free, universal, or open to all. Literacy and its provision were hardly neutral, but tied to the social structure quite directly.

This is not all. As the social structure of literacy paralleled the larger structures of inequality, the groups most literate were of course those most highly ranked, just as their children were provided with more literacy and schooling. In theoretical terms, the social order was a highly *ascriptive* one, as distribution of both literacy and reward were tied to the facts of birth: ethnicity, social and economic origins, race, sex and age. A literate person from a group ranking low on the class ladder (and also low in literacy) had far greater chances of working and earning at a low level.

The achievement of literacy was rarely sufficient to enable individual men or women to overcome the facts of their ascribed characteristics. Acquisition of literacy was often not rewarded occupationally or economically. This of course belied the democratic and progressive promises of the middle class school promoters, whose own status was much more secure.

57

Only rarely did education counteract some of the effects of the unequal social system; probably these cases were enough to give the mobility promise some visible validity. Overwhelmingly, however, literacy's role *reinforced* the steep social rigidity, re-emphasizing patterns of social and ethnic inequality—hardly a liberating role (Graff, 1975a).

Literacy and Democracy

The final topic in this all-too-schematic chapter is perhaps that most ridden by assumptions and cherished legacies. This is the relationship between literacy, education, and modern participatory democracy. A full exposition of this problem requires greater attention to the social and philosophical bases of liberal democratic theory than I can now give. Thus I shall be very brief.

Among the most central and undoubtedly most proudly-held of our Enlightenment notions is that a free, self-governing people must be educated; one must be able to read and write and be trained in critical skills in order to make the critical choices which democracy requires and in order to perform the duties of responsible citizenship. I do not wish to quibble with this basic formulation, but I do want to emphasize that the hope implicit in this tenet of modern social thought does stem from an overestimation of the powers of literacy and education as explored here. More importantly, I want to suggest an essential qualification: literacy and education are better viewed as necessary and *not* sufficient prerequisites for popular rule and democratic rights. The powers of literacy and schooling for control, the negative aspects of education, must be fully recognized. Literacy *can* and *has* been employed for social control and for political repression as well. We must be fully cognizant that education by itself is not a cause for freedom, and that schooling for responsibility and social change requires much more emphasis on critical and independent thinking than public schooling has ever allowed. Certainly this is true of literacy at elementary levels. Literacy must be seen for what it has been historically and what it is contemporarily, as well as for what it may be in the future.

My hope in writing this piece has been to direct critical attention to past formulations about literacy and its connections with society and individuals within it. I have attempted to link the past with the present, showing both the roots of modern social thought and the pervasiveness of traditional assumptions. I also have tried to suggest, in many examples and through many aspects of the relationship, that a new paradigmatic formulation is needed. My analysis, while hardly a systematic and synthetic construction of that paradigm, may well offer to a larger audience the lines which such a new articulation might take.

Notes

This article was written while the author's work was supported by a grant from the National Endowment for the Humanities.

1   It is unfortunate that the Report does not identify commentators specifically and that the entire papers were unavailable at the time of writing. A selection was published in 1977: LEON BATAILLE (Ed.), *A Turning Point for Literacy*. New York: Pergamon Press; the collection merits examination.

2   Historically, as contemporarily, there has been a wide disparity in the education achievements of the sexes. Discrimination against equal education for women, which International Women's Year conferences strongly opposed, dates for centuries. It seems that sexual stratification is central to social inequality. Interestingly, only in Sweden did women's literacy equal men's; there it derived from an emphasis on home education.

References

ALTBACH, P.G. (1975) 'Literary colonialism: Books in the third world.' *Harvard Educational Review,* 45, 226–236.

ANDERSON, C.A. (1965) 'Literacy and schooling on the development threshold', in ANDERSON, C.A. and BOWMAN, M.J. (Eds.), *Education and Economic Development,* Chicago: Aldine, pp. 347–362.

ANDERSON, C.A. and BOWMAN, M.J. (1963) 'Concerning the role of education in development', in GEERTZ, C.C. (Ed.), *Old Societies and New States.* New York: Free Press, pp. 247–279.

BERG, I. (1971) *Education and Jobs: The Great Training Robbery.* Boston: Beacon.

BLAU, P. and DUNCAN, O.D. (1967) *The American Occupational Structure.* New York: John Wiley.

BOWEN, W.G. (1968) 'Assessing the economic contribution of education', in BLAUG, M. (Ed.), *Economics of Education.* Harmondsworth: Penguin, I, pp. 67–100.

BOWLES, S. and GINTIS, H. (1976) *Schooling in Capitalist America.* New York: Basic Books.

CIPOLLA, C. (1969) *Literacy and Development in the West.* Harmondsworth: Penguin.

DISCH, R. (Ed.) (1973) *The Future of Literacy.* Englewood Cliffs: Prentice-Hall.

DREEBEN, R. (1968) *On What Is Learned in School.* Reading, Mass.: Addison-Wesley.

FREIRE, P. (1971) *Pedagogy of the Oppressed.* New York: Herder and Herder.

GOODY, J. (Ed.) (1968) *Literacy in Traditional Societies.* Cambridge: Cambridge University Press.

GRAFF, H.J. (1975a) 'Literacy and social structure in the nineteenth-century city', unpublished PhD dissertation, University of Toronto (published as *The Literacy Myth: Literacy and Social Structure in the Nineteenth-Century City.* New York and London: Academic Press, 1979).

GRAFF, H.J. (1975b) 'Literacy and history'. *History of Education Quarterly,* 15, 467–474.

GRAFF, H.J. (1976a) 'Respected and profitable labour': Literacy, jobs, and the working class,' in KEALEY, G.S. and WARRIAN, P. (Eds.), *Essays in Canadian Working Class History.* Toronto: McClelland and Stewart, pp. 58–82, 202–207.

GRAFF, H.J. (1976b) *Literacy in History: An Interdisciplinary Research Bibliography.* Chicago: Newberry Library.

GRAFF, H.J. (1977–78) " 'Poverty, misery and vice": Illiteracy and criminality in the nineteenth century'. *Journal of Social History,* 11, 245–268.

GRAFF, H.J. (1978) 'The reality behind the rhetoric: The social and economic meanings of literacy in the mid-nineteenth century'. MCDONALD, N.G. (Ed.), *Egerton Ryerson and His Times*. Toronto: Macmillan of Canada.

HARMAN, D. (1970) 'Illiteracy: an overview'. *Harvard Educational Review*, 40, 226–243.

HOGGART, R. (1961) *The Uses of Literacy*. Boston: Beacon.

INKELES, A. and SMITH, D.H. (1974) *Becoming Modern*. Cambridge, Mass.: Harvard University Press.

INTERNATIONAL SYMPOSIUM FOR LITERACY (1975) *Final Report*. Persepolis, Iran, 3–8 September 1975.

JOHANSSON, E. 'Literacy studies in Sweden: Some examples', in JOHANSSON, EGIL (Ed.), *Literacy and Society in a Historical Perspective—A Conference Report*. Umea: Umea University Press, pp. 41–66.

LOCKRIDGE, K.A. (1974) *Literacy in Colonial New England*. New York: Norton.

MCCLELLAND, D.C. (1966) 'Does education accelerate economic growth?' *Economic Development and Cultural Change*, 14, 257–278.

NISBET, R. (1969) *Social Change and History*. New York: Oxford University Press.

POLLARD, S. (1963) 'Factory discipline in the industrial revolution'. *Economic History Review*, 16, 254–271.

SANDERSON, M. (1967) 'Education and the factory in industrial Lancashire'. *Economic History Review*, 20, 266–279.

SANDERSON, M. (1972) 'Literacy and social mobility in the industrial revolution in England'. *Past and Present*, 56, 75–104.

SCHOFIELD, R. (1968) 'The measurement of literacy in pre-industrial England', in GOODY (Ed.), *op. cit.*, pp. 311–325.

SCHOFIELD, R. (1973) 'Dimensions of illiteracy, 1750–1850'. *Explorations in Economic History*, 10, 437–454.

STONE, L. (1969) 'Literacy and education in England, 1640–1900'. *Past and Present*, 42, 61–139.

TALBOTT, J. (1971) 'The history of education'. *Daedalus*, 100, 133–150.

THOMPSON, E.P. (1967a) *The Making of the English Working Class*. New York: Vintage.

THOMPSON, E.P. (1967b) 'Time, work-discipline and industrial capitalism'. *Past and Present*, 56–97.

TIPPS, D.C. (1973) 'Modernization theory and the comparative study of civilizations'. *Comparative Studies in Society and History*, 15, 199–226.

WEBB, R.K. (1955) *The British Working Class Reader, 1790–1848*, London: Allen and Unwin.

WRIGLEY, E.A. (1972) 'The process of modernization and the industrial revolution in England'. *Journal of Interdisciplinary History*, 3, 225–259.

3   *Literacy and Social Development in North America: On Ideology and History*

During the past decade, literacy became a subject of worldwide concern. Questions, concerns, fears, and phobias all were felt in nations new and old, underdeveloped and developed alike. Historians were not immune from these issues; and, as one result, a major new interest arose among social, cultural, educational, and economic historians. A body of important, often pioneering scholarship is now appearing where but fifteen years ago, there was virtually none.[1]

I

Students of the North American past, in their own ways, share in these scholarly interests. Indeed, much about their researches resembles those of their European colleagues; international cooperation and exchange is one important theme.[2] Yet, in important ways, North American studies distinguish themselves from those elsewhere. To understand the development of a historical approach to literacy on the western shores of the Atlantic requires grasping both the common and the differentiating forces that impelled and conditioned North American approaches and interpretations. This chapter attempts to unravel some of those threads, and in so doing, to present an evaluation of the evolving historiography of literacy in the United States and Canada.

Two themes immediately strike one who surveys the literature. They are the relative tardiness of North American historians in their beginnings of active, primary research into the subject, and the manner in which ideology—that is, the ideology implicit in historical interpretations, an essentially epistemological issue—has influenced approaches to literacy. These themes, not surprisingly, are deeply inter-related; they have reciprocally reinforced one another in the making and shaping of the field of study. In fact, the role of the second has been to reinforce the first theme: ideology long substituted for historical study. More recently, since the first half of the 1970s, progress has been made. A moderate take off *and* an expression of real interest in the significance of the subject and its relevance to a previously unappreciated wide range of issues have been felt.

Nevertheless, the dominance of ideological issues of an especially American nature has served to restrain the interpretive possibilities of this research. On one hand, many studies—empirical as well as the more speculative and sweeping—have found it difficult to break with the 'received wisdom' of what I have termed elsewhere 'the literacy myth' and which has proved strongest and most resilient in its American versions.[3] On the other hand, the perceived, but nonetheless real, need to counter the hegemony of this interpretive stance has meant that it continues to shape the field, even among those who argue for its frailty[4] and for its replacement. It has continued to obstruct efforts to interpret freshly the growing bodies of primary evidence and to limit the necessary tasks of framing new questions and reconceptualizing the issues.[5]

What is meant by this ideology, which I claim has so influenced North American considerations of the history of literacy? There are a number of intertwined elements of which it is comprised, none of them unique to North America, but which have all proved particularly powerful, especially in the United States. In part is the long-standing assumption of 'American uniqueness': the lack of a 'feudal' past with an established aristocracy and a bound peasantry; colonial origins in the wake of 'modernizing' revolutions in England and on the continent; national origins in the midst of a period of Enlightenment; major liberal, democratizing, nineteenth-century developments.[6] To make a complex subject overly simple, a historiographic legacy long proclaimed that the United States (and sometimes North America itself) was born 'different' and 'modern': its past and its future diverged from the 'Old World's.' From that set of assumptions, it was not difficult to make yet another: North America as born 'literate'. Social theories, dating from the eighteenth-century *philosophes,* but codified into the canons of twentieth-century social science in the form of modernization theory, have come to undergird these historical understandings. Bound into an apparently natural and logical bundle of epistemological underpinnings, they long made the conduct of research into the history of literacy all but redundant.[7]

II

The 'received wisdom' about the historical contours and the origins of North American literacy is well expressed in the major writings of Samuel Eliot Morison, Bernard Bailyn, and Lawrence A. Cremin.[8] From their landmark works on early American cultural life and educational configurations, several generations of historians gained the ABCs of literacy's history. In his paeon to *The Intellectual Life of Colonial New England,* Morison surveyed the then quite limited and unrepresentative data collected in counts of signatures and marks. Though aware of some of the limitations and biases of the data and aware that the number of readers might well exceed that of signers or writers (also drawing attention to the order of learning in schools), Morison concluded that literacy prevailed from early times at impressively high levels: in excess of 90 per cent. Noting that 'Literacy was lowest among women, since little provision was made for their education outside the home' and that the 'poorest people, indentured servants and the like, had slight opportunity to sign deeds or petitions', nevertheless, he argued, 'it is certain that very many, perhaps a major part of the colonists, not only in New England but in the Middle Colonies and Virginia, [even including those] who were unable to write their names could read the King James Bible and other simple English texts.'[9]

For more than three decades, such conclusions were repeated; their apparent soundness pre-empted any need to study literacy directly. Three early twentieth-century exercises at counting New English signatures sufficed, for the results accorded with interpretations and assumptions that emphasized the levels of Puritan pioneers' literacy and the exceptional origins of American culture and character.[10]

Twenty-five years after Morison, Bailyn retold the tale. Although he called for new studies of literacy itself and urged Americanists to begin their stories in Europe where the roots of North America lay, he endorsed a strong version of exceptionality. Rather than a direct transfer of culture, Bailyn sketched a drama of 'the rapid breakdown of European society in its wilderness setting. In the course of adjustment to a new environment, the pattern of education was changed'. To him, the informal functioning of family, community, and church—for the provision of literacy, among other things—by necessity gave way to formal, legal provisions: in a frenzy of parental fear that their children might succumb to a savage environment. In his *Education in the Forming of American Society,* Bailyn had surprisingly little to say about literacy *per se;* yet, it hangs in the interstices between the lines as a constant goal of the settlers and their descendants, for which basic arrangements had been transformed; in large part as a result of that goal itself. The exceptional primacy of literacy was never lost, and, in fact, during the eighteenth century, the Revolution's effects were to free the trends of the colonial period from legal and institutional encumbrances and to confirm them, to formalize them, to give them the sanction of law in a framework of enlightened political thought'. Colonial education thus stimulated 'typical American individualism, optimism, and enterprise' as it promoted the diversity and mobility that are claimed increasingly to characterize early American society. With literacy's acquisition as part of this socialization process, the modernizing impact of literacy was asserted, much as recent social scientists would have it.[11]

Conventional wisdom received its finest casting in the hands of Lawrence Cremin. First, in his magisterial *American Education: The Colonial Experience,* then a decade later in *The National Experience,* Cremin artfully spun out the story from late medieval England to post-Enlightenment America. In contrast to his predecessors, Cremin added to the empirical evidence about the distribution of colonial literacy. His students counted signatures in several communities in different regions of the colonies: Dedham, Massachusetts; Elizabeth City County,

Virginia; New York City; and Philadelphia. In all cases, data from wills and deeds (and some other signatory sources), pointed to high and growing (nearly universal) levels of literacy among men and rising rates among women. Cremin concluded, from these surveys of upwardly-biased sources, 'these rates are extraordinary, and stand as eloquent testimony to the power the tradition of learning had acquired in the minds of provincial Americans'.[12]

Cremin's theme was the eighteenth-century expansion of formal schooling and, consequently, of literacy rates. This he normatively explained by reference to economic growth and social mobility, sectarian competition, growing participation (politicization) in public affairs: in other words, functional and ecological explanations. Thus, 'As almanacs, newspapers, pamphlets, and books dealt with matters of topical interest, especially after the Stamp Act crisis of the 1760s, a premium was placed on literacy in segments of the population where illiteracy had long been no stigma.' This in turn increased the pressure for more schools and schooling, and yielded a 'rapid spread of literacy among the population'.

That was not all. Cremin further asserted the spread of 'a more liberating literacy, in which a growing technical competence is combined with expanding motivation, expanding need, and expanding opportunity', in distinction to a more 'inert literacy'. Therefore, 'it is with this meaning in mind that one can assert with some confidence, for example, that eighteenth-century literacy rates were generally higher in the American colonies than in Ireland, and roughly equivalent as between English and American white males, with the Americans possibly having a slight edge'. The odds were growing, Cremin felt, that colonials could and did develop 'liberating literacy—that is, that one would reach out to intellectual worlds beyond one's own—via the schools'. This was the culmination of the colonial experience and the eve of nationhood:

> Now, it is the historical interaction of a relatively expansive literacy with a relatively inclusive politics that explains much of the character of American society during the latter decades of the eighteenth century. As popular interest in public affairs mounted, a greater number of readers fed the press, which in turn only heightened the motivation to read among ever larger segments of the population.

Fruition came in the struggle for Independence and the creation of a Republic. In this formulation, literacy was tied intimately to an interpretation of the birth of a nation and the presumed course of social development: a uniquely American popular achievement.[13]

Seldom has the history of literacy been presented more dramatically; rarely has so much been so strongly associated with its quantities and qualities. But, increasingly, the drama has been challenged: more of a melodramatic tone may now be heard among literacy's North American students. Kenneth Lockridge, in *Literacy in Colonial New England: An Enquiry into the Social Context of Literacy in the Early Modern West,* took the major step in this rescripting. Instructively, both Lockridge, and Allan Tully, whose study of literacy in rural Chester and

Lancaster, Pennsylvania, preceded Lockridge's, framed their analysis in the familiar terms. The 'received wisdom' continued to shape interpretive efforts.[14]

Lockridge's work remains the most important study of the pre-1800 era. Boldly, sometimes brashly, he not only erected a time-series of signatory data for the course of New English literacy, but he also compared that history with Pennsylvania, Virginia, England, Scotland, and Sweden. Lockridge further inquired into literacy's impact on attitudinal change, essaying a test of Bailyn and Cremin and of recent social science emphases. It is important to note the limited interest and impact that this original study has had. Despite an initial flurry of incisive, if critical reviews, the book has thus far stimulated few efforts to extend, test, or revise its findings or interpretations.[15] This is as revealing of my argument as it is disappointing. It marks, first, the still limited interest in this topic among North American historians, especially when compared to Europeanists. Second, it reflects the failure of his challenge to shake the ideological force of the 'strong' approach to literacy's roles. (Texts and other references to literacy in diverse fields of American history, as for example in economic history, bear out this contention.) Third, a number of Lockridge's (and, indeed, other recent students') findings have not been difficult to assimilate into the traditional, ideological framework. And, fourth, the potential appeal of his analysis was weakened by the overstated manner in which he cast his argument.

Through a careful quantitative analysis of a well-designed sample of colonial wills, Lockridge established the first systematic data base for the history of literacy in North America.[16] Calling his findings 'surprisingly "traditional" ', he reported that the signature rate of those who settled New England and who left wills between 1650 and 1670 was over 60 per cent, perhaps as much as 50 per cent above that estimated for England and indicating migratory selectivity of literate persons and / or persons from more literate areas. Despite the famous Puritan school laws and the presumptions of previous interpreters, little progress was shown over the next half century. For those dying around the years 1705–15, the signature rate remained at about the 60 per cent point.[17]

> The reason seemed to be that a large minority of the scattered population lived in communities small enough to escape the school laws, legally or otherwise. Also, men perhaps saw no pressing need for literacy. Whatever the reason, each locality within New England tended to maintain that exact level of partial literacy with which it had been endowed by its original stream of migrants. Within each area, the differences in literacy between the various occupations and degrees of wealth remained as sharp as they had been among the English migrants.

Over the next two generations, however, literacy levels did leap forward. Of men dying *c.* 1760, over 80 per cent signed; of those dying *c.* 1790, virtually 90 per cent signed their wills. It was the schools, Lockridge avers, that were responsible for this rise to near universality which also all but erased the 'traditional' association of literacy with occupational status, wealth, and type of residence.

Behind the schools as a motive force for male literacy was 'social concentration', the increasing density of settled areas and the maturation of society. The latter gave meaning to the provincial school laws.

Along with other students of literacy in Western Europe, Lockridge finds a sharp ecological correlation between rates and degrees of increase in male literacy on the county level and county population density. He further speculates, in terms that have proved meaningful in European studies, 'More than availability [of schools] may have been involved, for it is often assumed that increasing population density entails greater commercial and legal sophistication and a greater demand for writing and for mathematics.' Nevertheless, Lockridge also reported that in two large counties in which literacy rates rose, no upward shift in patterns of wealth-holding or occupational status took place. Thus, in breaking with previous students, he postulated, 'neither the expectation nor the reality of improved socio-economic condition was involved in the massive rise of literacy in New England. If economic pressure were involved, they probably smacked more of the increasing necessity for literacy in order to maintain one's place in the world, or an increasing need to have literacy to move into any vacancies in the next rung of a relatively fixed social hierarchy.' Even as the forward march in male literacy levels occurred, erasing previous social distinctions by literacy among men, stratification by occupation and wealth was neither narrowed nor erased; it continued and probably increased over time. That, in fact, has appeared as a consistent theme of recent studies of eighteenth and nineteenth-century North America.[18]

In the historiography of literacy, themes of stratification, differentiation, and inequality have emerged forcefully. Specifically, apparent regularity in variations along the dimensions of social class, occupational status and function, community type, ethnicity and race, gender, and perhaps also demands for the use of literacy, stand out in most research. Although such differences were not his primary focus, Lockridge's data and analysis support such a view. In contrast to most areas surveyed, New England's regional variations and wealth and occupational differences in literacy narrowed sharply by the third quarter of the eighteenth century. Both 'backwoods' areas and low-standing labourers rapidly increased their rates of literacy, although the original rank order persisted, if in a constricted form. By contrast, however, women's literacy rose much less than men's, although it too showed improvement (from 33 per cent *c.* 1660, to 40 per cent *c.* 1710 and 45 per cent *c.* 1780).[19] 'Traditional' distinctions and inequalities remained, even in favoured New England. Lockridge slights this dimension of his findings. On one hand, as he argues, literacy's increase was a movement of less literate regions and persons to higher rates. But, on the other hand, inequalities—of place, occupation and wealth, and gender—did not disappear. Although their level increased faster (and of course they had further to progress), the lesser developed places, such as Maine and New Hampshire, did not equal literacy rates in more mature settlements. Similarly, important gaps distinguished literacy rates of labourers and farmers from those of merchants-professionals-gentry and artisans. Wealth and gender differences also continued. Moreover, the lack of progress in Boston's levels, after its high beginnings at 75 per cent literate suggests that very high levels of density and intensive commercialization which engender downward (as well as upward) social mobility and also stimulate the growth of a poor and landless wage labouring class were not conducive to literacy.[20] There were limits to the rise of literacy. Such evidence, I believe, foreshadows key elements of the future. It also hints that New England was less a unique social world than the sponsors of the traditional interpretation or Lockridge himself in rather different terms, believed.

Lockridge placed his New England in a comparative perspective. If there was no uniquely ' "American" social dynamic' there, what was the case elsewhere?, he asked. In fact, neither high rates of literacy growing toward universality nor a 'liberating' literacy appeared in Pennsylvania and Virginia. In two counties of the former colony, estimated male literacy stood, respectively, at 65–70 per cent; in the latter, it was about 62 per cent—comparing more favourably to New England's levels than one might have expected. In large part, this resulted from the relatively high literacy rate among recent migrants from Germany and England, underscoring an important relationship found in many studies between long-distance migration and selectivity by literacy (among other attributes). Migration streams served to raise literacy levels in both places, in contrast to contemporary New England. Literacy, however, did not much increase during the eighteenth century; approximately one-third of men and many more women remained unable to sign their names. Literacy did not march forward with commercialization and social development.[21]

The 'traditional' correlates of literacy (and illiteracy) were, Lockridge found, all but untouched. Literacy levels continued to vary strongly with occupation and wealth. Women's rates were much lower than men's; typically below 50 per cent. Not surprisingly, when Lockridge—ingeniously if not wholly persuasively—attempted to test for literacy's relationship to attitudinal change (as asserted causally by recent social scientists and proponents of the traditional ideological interpretation) by studying the disposition of gifts in wills, he found no more sign of modern or 'liberated', enterprising, optimistic, or cosmopolitan attitudes in Virginia than he had in Pennsylvania or in his sample of English wills. 'Traditional' attitudes predominated wherever he looked regardless of literacy, time or place. To Lockridge, in literacy levels and their associations, Virginia and Pennsylvania strikingly resembled England, more so than they did New England. And, that, contra Morison, Bailyn, or Cremin, is really not so surprising.[22]

American levels of literacy, it seems, compared favourably to England's in large part as a result of migration and the lack of a large population of poor, landless labourers. It is possible that 'This points to an irony: leaving the mass of laborers behind brought America a higher overall literacy, but American farmers, artisans, tradesmen, and gentry were less literate than their counter-parts in England, so the result was an overall literacy only slightly above that in England. America was progression and retrogression rolled into one. The progression, however, disappears on considering that if slaves were included in the analysis, not only the level of literacy by occupation, but also the overall level of male literacy would be lower in America.'[23] New World literacy was not so novel. And, it seemed that a new interpretation was needed.

Lockridge essayed just that. Rejecting ideological interpretations of the American colonists' unique response to the wilderness and the modernizing impact of literacy, he emphasized another ideology: that of intense Protestantism. Comparing New England with Sweden and Scotland (I would add parts of Germany, Switzerland, Holland, etc), he portrayed the educational thrust, signified and codified in the school laws, as a traditional religious impetus for whose success was required 'social concentration'—a maturing, developing society. The 'limited dynamism' of literacy in New England, as compared with the other colonies or with England, stemmed from the conservative force of piety. With Scotland and Sweden, New England shared not only small size, but also state action promoting Protestantism: 'The motive force behind this action was the common Protestant impulse to bring to all men the Word of God, implemented by the intensity of the local Protestantism in terms of its depth, breadth, and uniformity.'[24] This is what was lacking elsewhere.

Lockridge took pains to establish the importance of what he termed 'social concentration' and under which he subsumed such key factors as density, socioeconomic and institutional development, and commercialization, and he feelingly speculated about the limits of literacy in times of transition and confusion. His over-riding emphasis, nevertheless, fell upon the conservative force of intensive Protestantism. Although the data and their discussion refer to 'interaction', his sweeping introduction and conclusion lose sight of the seemingly crucial roles of social development: commerce, density, wealth, institutions, and the like. Intriguingly, and importantly, it seems that rising rates of literacy tended perhaps more to follow the forces of 'social concentration' than to precede or cause them. These suggestions await their full and fair evaluation, with due recognition of the contribution of Puritanism. Lockridge, however, lent himself more toward a monocausal and ideological interpretation: 'Puritanism had finally made schools available to men regardless of their station in life, with a little help from social concentration but without any evident assistance from increasing social mobility or other extreme dynamisms in the society. Availability was perhaps all the religion had even intended and from the evidence it is all it here achieved.'[25]

This form of monocausal interpretation has served, unfairly I believe, to reduce the impact that Lockridge's work should have had on North American historians. With few exceptions, his successors have taken several courses: using his estimated rates of literacy to support the 'received wisdom'; actively dismissing the importance of such scholarship because of its monocausal, seemingly reductionistic interpretation; or qualifying his findings with those of local case studies.[26]

Religion, as European studies affirm, deserves major attention. However, as international studies have also shown, it can no longer be viewed as an abstract, virtually autonomous force in the progression or stagnation of literacy levels. Rather, religion, as Johansson's Swedish work in particular has underscored, can only be understood in precise, contextual terms. Here the roles of social development, migratory timing and selectivity, 'social concentration', school availability, and commercial or other social, cultural, or economic necessity complexly interrelate, especially in a New England permeated with Puritanism. And here, the process of rising rates among previously disadvantaged persons and places must be balanced against both the persisting (if reduced) levels of inequality and the changing contours of society and economy. Even if more limited than traditional interpretations have stressed, individual demands and needs for literacy were undoubtedly increasing, especially in growing, developing, and commercializing areas during the eighteenth century. Rates by place and occupation, as well as the influence of wealth levels, all support such a view; so does recognition of continuing, significant degrees of social and educational inequality. In this view, New England and the rest of North American society were shaped by the same dynamics that have been discovered elsewhere in the West—and by the same contradictions of literacy's interaction with social, economic, and cultural development.[27]

What did literacy mean to men and women of the late colonial world? Despite the dominance of the ideological interpretation of literacy's intimate connection with North American enlightenment, modernization, politicization, and mobilization, another view, much more nuanced and less linear and universalistic, seems more likely. Rhys Isaac and Harry Stout, for example, have reasserted the power of the oral culture and oral-aural communications, including ritualistic behaviour, in such a world. Linda Auwers has, in the case of women's increasing literacy, suggested connections with mounting rates of premarital pregnancy and changes in church membership. Lockridge speculates about the growth of a 'literacy gap' despite increasing levels of literacy: 'If the eighteenth century saw a spread of basic literacy without much improvement in its quality, men may have been further than ever from the skills needed to function independently.' Disconnecting literacy from attitudinal modernization, for which there is no direct or persuasive evidence, he suggests that literacy, regardless of functional needs, was insufficient to meet the growing confusion, conflict and contention, and complexity of the last decades of the colonial era and the first of the Republic. 'New England's farmers would have resembled their less literate counterparts throughout the colonies, passive before or frustrated by an environment changing beyond their comprehension. Neither mass literacy nor, in all the colonies, the Revolution could alter this frustration.' Of course, a firm perspective on variation in literacy ability and human response, on one hand, and on socio-cultural contradiction, on the other, is required to proceed further. What is at stake is at once the meaning of the levels of the literacy that students have begun to 'measure', and their variation, *and* of the way in which that literacy is best conceptualized analytically and interpretively. Recent scholarship, if slow to commence and stimulate interest, has nonetheless demonstrated the inadequacy of the traditional ideological interpretation. A 'new world' of literacy's history can be glimpsed, one that reconnects the New World with the Old World.[28]

III

The study and interpretation of the history of literacy in nineteenth-century North America has differed little from that of the earlier period. That is itself no surprise. Here too, ideology, expectation, and assumption long stood for intensive research and fresh interpretation. First, it was assumed, perhaps not wholly erroneously, that levels of literacy were impressively high in the 'New Nation' and also in its British American neighbour to the north. Second, the differences, often major ones, between regions (especially North and South in the United States, and Ontario and Quebec in Canada), races, ethnic groups (especially between the native-born whites and European immigrants), were expected and apparently accountable in terms of the ideological tradition of the 'literacy myth'. Third, the perceived course of social development, long considered to be special and different from that found elsewhere in the West—in terms of commercial and industrial development, educational and institutional structures, political culture, and the like was claimed to derive, at least in part, from the North American tradition and levels of literacy. Until the last few years, in fact, few students felt any need to take up these issues.

Once again, it was Lawrence Cremin who summed up the 'received wisdom'. In the second volume of *American Education: The National Experience, 1783–1876* he played out his interpretive theme: popularization. 'Among the significant direct outcomes of the popularization of education was not only a continuing spread of literacy but a change in the character of literacy.' Although he exempted blacks and Indians from this development, and is little concerned with immigrants or women, Cremin sought support, surprisingly, in census totals of the numbers able to read and / or write. Reporting that the white population of the US compared favourably with other Western nations, he repeated his earlier argument in favour of a spreading 'liberating literacy'. At that point, he recited a historicized version of modernization theory as applied to literacy: explaining access to print; opening minds to change, ideas, and influences; systemizing, individualizing, rationalizing experience; criticizing and reflecting; and stimulating demand for more literacy. All this, previously manifest, expanded, Cremin asserts: 'the literacy environment as a whole expanded impressively'. Deriving from the systems of popular education, this interacted further with the cultures of print, church, and polity, and created a new 'intelligence', especially American and supportive of liberty, equality, comity, community, and common aspiration. Not all persons were so included or so influenced, he reminds us.[29]

Once again, we face a strong and dramatic form of the ideological view, which Cremin casts in terms of literacy as 'agency'. Once more, we find a glaring disparity between assertion and evidential support. As with the colonial period, one is struck by the overall lack of research, the manner in which the ideological interpretation has shaped, in many ways, studies recently published and those now underway, and the interesting ways in which new findings have been accommodated into that framework.[30] Although the terms vary, a similar perspective has also held in Canadian studies.[31] In other dimensions, nineteenth-century literacy studies have differed from those of the preceding era. They have been even more unabashedly quantitative and somewhat more limited in interpretive thrusts. In scope and in number, they are also more restricted. They have tended to follow the revisionist / anti-revisionist split in historical circles. However, especially with the ready availability of literacy data in the form of manuscript census schedules and published census aggregates, North American historians, along with others elsewhere, increasingly include literacy as a (typically independent) variable in research in demographic and economic history. Such studies usually begin with the 'received wisdom', perhaps at least as frequently acquired from social science works as from historical interpretations. Often and sometimes less than convincingly, they also end with such views. Finally, it has become increasingly common for studies in social and economic history to take some account of literacy among their topics and questions.[32]

Nevertheless, the scholarship in the history of literacy, in both the US and in Canada, has begun to challenge the hegemony of the traditional view, although no new orthodoxy has arisen to replace it. This challenge has come largely, but not exclusively from two recent books: my own *The Literacy Myth: Literacy and Social Structure in the Nineteenth-Century City* and Lee Soltow's and Edward Stevens' *The Rise of Literacy and the Common School in the United States: A Socioeconomic Analysis to 1870.*

In *The Literacy Myth,* I attempted a frontal attack on what I identified as the 'received wisdom' and the dominant interpretation of a significant, independent, and overwhelmingly positive impact of literacy, historically seen. After stating the elements and suggesting some of the sources of the 'literacy myth', I presented an interpretation of the 'moral bases of literacy', which in my view constituted the normative, largely conservative and limited contemporary approach to literacy: in conceptualization and in its carefully and properly controlled, ideal form of transmission. The promotion and sponsorship of literacy, increasingly in institutions designed expressly for that purpose, and the approved forms of its use I linked directly to the struggle for cultural hegemony. In this I drew upon the formulations of Antonio Gramsci as well as on recent studies in cultural and educational history.

Part I of the book presented a quantitative analysis of literacy in the social structure of three Canadian cities: Hamilton, Kingston, and London, Ontario, with supporting evidence from US, English, and European studies. Among the findings I emphasized were the social, demographic, and economic characteristics of illiterates, who were in fact surprisingly few (less than 10 per cent of adult populations) in these largely immigrant, commercial cities. Immigrants, especially Irish Catholics and black Americans (many of whom were former slaves) dominated among the illiterates, although no group was primarily illiterate. Seventy per cent of Irish Catholics were recorded able to read or write.[33] Women were more often unable to read or write, as were older persons. Literacy I also found to be related to the selectivity of long-distance migration; I hinted at a special contribution that such selectivity of more literate persons may have meant for the social development of North America, in contrast to the common view of such migrants as the uncultured dregs of their homelands.

Considerable attention was addressed to literacy's relationships to work and wealth. On the whole, I discovered that whereas illiterates commonly held semi-skilled or unskilled low status occupations and ranked poorly in wealth-holding, such a common perspective seriously needed qualification. First, my analysis (limited by the impossibility of completing a multivariate replication of the original cross-tabulations) strongly indicated that social and economic—and class—positions followed more from social ascription (in terms of class, ethnic, racial, and gender origin) than from a lack of achievement of literacy. Second, when compared to literates of the same background and characteristics, illiterates were often more similar than different. Third, I discovered a substantial number of persons who were unable to read or write but who nonetheless had gained occupations of some status and skill and / or moderate or higher levels of wealth. Illiterates who persisted in a city over a period of at least a decade were able to maintain such positions and often to increase their property and wealth. Thus, on one hand, I urged that we must reduce our expectations about the significance of literacy and that literacy's real but more limited than assumed contributions were mediated by other social and economic factors and relationships. On the other hand, and equally importantly, my analysis supported an interpretation that stressed the 'rational', sensible, and adaptive characteristics of men and women who lacked the skills of literacy. In sum, I suggested that the normative wisdom, imbedded in both historiography and in social scientific theories, required basic revision. Literacy's role, while sometimes quite vital to skilled persons, for example, was a limited one which worked its influence through other factors and mediating relationships.[34]

In Part II, I cast my net more widely. I attempted to re-evaluate the common interpretations of literacy's links to criminality and to industrialization. In both cases, I studied Canadian primary sources and compared my findings to recent American, European, and English analyses. In each case, I argued for new frameworks for understanding. The long postulated, but apparently superficial causal connections tying illiteracy to criminality were disputed by careful attention to social reformers' and early criminologists' formulations. Ascriptive social factors, such as ethnicity, class, and gender, were more significant causes of prosecution and conviction, when related to patterns of criminal justice and differential treatment of types of crime, than was illiteracy.

With respect to literacy's presumed causal relationships to industrial development, I cast my voice with those who criticize a direct and linear causal view. I stressed, on one hand, the limited demands for literacy that early industrialization required and, on the other, I urged that forms of commercial development were both more conducive to and more dependent upon literacy's skills than were industry's. Literacy's contribution was not unimportant, but it lay more in the non-cognitive, attitudinal and behavioural domain than in terms of directly productive skills. Finally, I advanced a hypothesis that variations in the timing of the spread of literacy and in the advent and evolution of industrialization marked important international (and inter-regional) differences. Later beginnings of industrial capitalism in North America from a basis in higher rates of literacy (with the important exception of Quebec) resulted, I speculated, in a potentially smoother and less violent transition. That hypothesis awaits elaboration and testing.[35]

Finally, joining the brilliantly original work of Daniel Calhoun, I essayed an approach to the quality of literacy during the middle half of the nineteenth century. Drawing broadly and diffusely on a range of 'indirect' indicators, I suggested that popular *qualitative* levels of literacy were not impressively high and that there was a significant disparity between literacy viewed quantitatively and qualitatively. No sources for North America allow a direct confrontation of this question. In addition, I argued that urban society, which I surveyed across the Atlantic, in the mid- to later nineteenth century was not yet dominated by print or a mass need to confront it with a high level of ability. Class differences, of course, existed, in both dimensions: the working class, while not opposed to literacy, was ambivalent and sometimes critical about forms of provision and sponsorship. Others came to wear their literacy as a badge of respectability. Popular levels of literacy, I concluded, were sufficient for many of the daily and ordinary demands placed upon them, but insufficient for 'higher' demands, from intellectual life or even for radical analysis of the exploitation of the contemporary working class.[36]

So brief a summary must suffice. In part, my interpretation slighted the creative potentials inherent within literacy; in part, my quantitative analysis was less than complete. What follows from that effort suggests that future scholarship must broaden the bounds of literacy history's numerically-based beginnings, attempt to articulate the dialectic that ties the overwhelmingly conservative goals of literacy promotion (and the predominantly conservative ends, too) to the more radical possibilities among literacy's outcomes, maintain an international and comparative focus, and pay even closer attention to patterns of differentiation and inequalities and to the variable uses of literacy. Literacy can only be understood with consistent attention to its contradictions.

Some of these themes, as well as others, comprise the focus of Soltow's and Stevens's *The Rise of Literacy*.[37] Quantitative analysis and investigation of changing configurations of differentiation from the colonial era constitute the main features of this work. The analysis is set in the explicit context of nineteenth-century promotion of an 'ideology of literacy'—of morality and citizenship—and the expansion of common schooling. Eschewing sweeping interpretative terms, the authors carefully analyze a variety of sources, attending to the 'rise of literacy', the modes of its transmission, and their correlates.

Soltow and Stevens add to our knowledge of levels and variations in literacy *before* the censal era. For the colonial period, they examine a wide range of petitions and probate records and point to a pattern of almost extraordinary variation (suggesting that Lockridge's estimates may have been optimistic but that literacy was undoubtedly rising). With other students, they focus on the contribution of population density (analogous to Lockridge's 'social concentration'), in this period and in the next. They also attempt a mathematical formulation of its role, which they term 'gradual'. Importantly, their signatory sources indicate a broad level of illiterate participation in the political and economic life of the colonies, regardless of the growing import of literacy and print. From their use and access to them, illiterates were not excluded; they were politically and economically active.[38]

For the important, largely uncharted, early Republican period, 1790–1840, Soltow and Stevens offer fresh data. From enumerations of merchant seamen and military recruits, they deduce a level of illiteracy for men at about 25 per cent *c.* 1800; they also point to significantly higher levels for non-whites, the non-New England-born (especially Southerners), the foreign-born, and labourers (farmers to a lesser extent). Major improvement, however, took place after 1830, which the authors link to the spread of schools (with increasing population density) and the establishment of the 'ideology of literacy'. Social development and literacy promotion went hand-in-hand, they aver. During the preceding four decades, they argue, illiteracy became a 'social problem' and concern with literacy an issue of policy; a 'religious literacy model' was replaced by a 'civil model'. Before 1840, it remains clear that levels of literacy were indeed influenced by ethnicity, gender, race, age, region of birth and residence, occupation, and wealth.[39]

Literacy was important; it was increasingly valued by many in the US. Soltow and Stevens present much testimony in support of the campaign for the promotion of the hegemony of literacy's ideology and for the values and virtues of reading. About that there can be no doubt. Institutionalization followed on the heels of the streams of rhetoric. Newspapers, books, libraries, churches, and, above all, common schools led to rising levels of literacy, according to these scholars. With Ohio and Rochester, New York, case studies, they detail the place of reading and writing in the schools' curricula. Although they discuss the problems that the common school faced in its campaign for literacy, the story they tell is one of achievement: the increasingly successful transmission of literacy. Their approach is original, but the story they tell differs strikingly from that I offered in *The Literacy Myth*. Basic interpretive questions are at issue here. Soltow's and Stevens's perspective does not differ much from that of Cremin and the traditional ideology, despite their novel findings.[40]

Yet, their examination of data on Northern soldiers during the Civil War points directly to great inequalities in educational changes during the preceding period of educational expansion. Whereas only 6–7 per cent reported *no* schooling, almost half were recorded as having a limited elementary education. Least likely to be well-schooled were men from the border states, followed by Canadians (from Quebec) and the Irish-born; the New England-born had the best record among the native-born, but the Scots, Scandinavians, and Germans were most impressive. Those from the most western regions also had less schooling. This was one meaning for the work of the common schools. Another was the major, persisting regional disparity between the North and the South. Yet another was familial economic need and seasonal work that pre-empted for many youths school attendance and literacy's acquisition. Although Soltow and Stevens stress the future earnings lost to an early labouring youth, whose opportunities for learning were sacrificed, they equivocate when they associate literacy with the moral discipline desired by employers, rather than with practical job skills.[41]

The most revealing aspect of *The Rise of Literacy* is the way in which key analyses pivot around issues of opportunities, which the authors term 'meritocratic'. A meritocracy based in literacy—opportunities for it and from it both—represents an ideal to them and they test for its presence in the past. It should be understood, first, that 'meritocracy' is not itself a neutral or objective measure or goal; it represents an ideological category that requires elaboration and justification, especially when applied historically. Unfortunately, nowhere do Soltow and Stevens provide definition or explanation. Equally important, their evidence, I think, less than meets their own criteria. Although they document a 'rise in literacy' among virtually all classes and regions, they find significant levels of inequality persisting in virtually all dimensions. In suggestive analyses, they show that school enrolment and literacy were both correlated positively with wealth, and that as the extent of inequality in enrolment narrowed, especially among those aged five to nine, where they associate most literacy learning, literacy itself remained strongly linked to inequalities of wealth.[42] Their discussion also indicates, impressively, that the bases of inequality were also shifting away from literacy, to pivot more around heavily stratified access to higher levels of education as time passed.[43] Thus, it is likely that levels of inequality were little reduced in the process, one which also pivoted upon class, ethnicity, race, region, and gender. Intergenerational inheritance of inequality continued. The complexity of the relationships is itself revealing; that challenges previous efforts at understanding. In the end, an essential contradiction emerges: at once, literacy and schooling were becoming more equally available and distributed, but the correlates of illiteracy and the levels of class (and ethnic) and economic inequality persisted. That hardly seems meritocratic.

Intriguingly, their pioneering, if preliminary evaluation of the legal standing of the illiterate during the middle one-third of the nineteenth century shows judicial efforts to protect, especially from fraud, those unable to read and write. The social position of the 'unlettered' movingly emerges: 'the dependent position into which the illiterate individual was cast when dealing with contractual agreements. [Yet] it would be inaccurate to describe the illiterates in these instances as "marginal" people, that is, people who had been separated from the mainstream of American society by their illiteracy.' Undoubtedly the level of dependency, and the potential for exploitation and discrimination, had increased since the colonial period. This suggestive discussion, which Stevens continues to research, points to new avenues for literacy research.[44]

The campaign for universal literacy (with the exceptions of blacks, slave and sometimes free, too, and native peoples) continued throughout the century. Progress, as alluded above, was made; this the authors document in aggregate census data and their census random samples. Definite progress, related to changing cultural emphases, came in women's levels of literacy, although more slowly for the foreign-born. Geographic differentials, always pronounced in North America, were harder to transform; north-south variation proved more deeply-rooted (in history, culture, settlement patterns, institutions and communications, and economic development and need) than either east-west or urban-rural differences. Over time, however, areas of high levels of illiteracy became fewer; 'there was much less dispersion in areal inequality'. Population density, institution building, access to printed materials, nativity of population, and, especially, per capita wealth were associated with declining rates of illiteracy. There was, however, an upper limit (20,000–30,000) to density's positive contribution.[45] Soltow's and Stevens's demonstration of social and economic development's importance for the 'rise' of literacy is conclusive—particularly in the roles of 'urbanity', wealth, and schools—but in the aggregate level of analysis, it raises more questions than it answers. For example, other studies indicate that combining indicators of commercial and manufacturing activity, rather than distinguishing them, may distort instead of advance understanding of the forces conducive to literacy's promotion; 'urbanity' is too gross a measure for variations in types of communities. A finer set of indicators and a more precise specification of areas is required.

Illiteracy, Soltow and Stevens show, was increasingly inversely related to indices of social and economic development. The form of their inquiry suggests that literacy followed from the fact of such development, although their evidence also hints that in some ways it also preceded it: in terms of migratory selectivity and promotional activities, for example.[46] Thus, a reciprocal multidimensional causal path is indicated, rather than a linear, one-way influence. That probability has yet to receive the kind of testing it merits.

Individual patterns are analogous to the areal, it seems, though the analysis stops short of complete causal analysis here too. Wealth and literacy were strongly related, as Soltow and Stevens have demonstrated.[47] No meritocracy is apparent in their data, however; nor was it impossible for many illiterates to succeed economically, despite the increasing importance of that ability in social and cultural as well as economic terms. Not surprisingly, the literacy-wealth relation was stronger in the North than in the South and in more urban than in rural places. Illiteracy, the authors indicate, tended to be transmitted from generation to generation. Intervention of agencies outside the family, in the US as elsewhere (with the important historical exception of preindustrial Sweden), was required for the 'rise' of literacy.[48] That, too, along with the other factors, mitigated against any form of 'meritocracy', as it underlay the complicated and sometimes contradictory parameters and meanings of literacy.

The Rise of Literacy is an important addition to understanding North American literacy and its relationship to social development. Limits of the research design and the interpretation prevent Soltow and Stevens from breaking firmly with the traditional ideological understanding—best revealed in their treatment of 'meritocracy' and inequality—and moving toward a new conceptualization of the subject.[49] That, I urge, is precisely what is required. The 'received wisdom' has outlived its usefulness as a paradigm for the history of literacy. Ironically, as it has continued to stimulate and to organize important new research over the past decade, the results of these studies have continually underminded it.

IV

Those studies, as I have suggested, have begun to erect an outline, if still a limited and sometimes narrow one, of the historical course and contours of literacy. They have demonstrated conclusively that normative conceptions are inadequate to accommodate their results. Importantly and coincidentally, research in other aspects of social, family, demographic, economic, working-class, immigrant and ethnic, and cultural history—typically beginning from normative bases with respect to the role of literacy—not only has begun to take literacy more seriously as a variable but has also documented unexpected complexities and contradictions in its relationships. The links between illiteracy or literacy and fertility provide one set of good examples, as do studies of the pay-offs of literacy for black Americans or many working-class families. Present day research is moving in the same direction.[50]

A new agenda for historical studies of literacy in North America is just emerging. That is suggested here. Our understanding of the past demands it. Perhaps even more importantly, our understanding and our action, today and tomorrow—for which we have much to learn from historical analysis—mandate it.[51]

Notes

1 See my *Literacy in History: An Interdisciplinary Research Bibliography*. New York, 1981; my 'The Legacies of Literacy', *Journal of Communication* 32 (1982); my *The Legacies of Literacy: Continuities and Contradictions in Western Society and Culture*. Bloomington, 1986.

2 For a discussion, see my *The Literacy Myth: Literacy and Social Structure in the Nineteenth-century City*. New York, 1979; *Literacy in History*. See also KENNETH A. LOCKRIDGE, *Literacy in Colonial New England: An Enquiry into the Social Context of Literacy in the Early Modern West*. New York, 1974, and 'Literacy in Early America, 1650–1800', in *Literacy and Social Development in the West*. (Ed.) HARVEY J. GRAFF, 1981.

3 See, as key examples, BERNARD BAILYN, *Education in the Forming of American Society*. Chapel Hill, 1960; LAWRENCE A. CREMIN, *American Education: The Colonial Experience*. New York, 1970 and *The National Experience*. New York, 1980, both discussed below. See also, LEE SOLTOW and EDWARD STEVENS, *The Rise of Literacy and the Common School in the United States: A Socio-Economic Analysis to 1870*. Chicago, 1981, also discussed below; MARIS A. VINOVSKIS, *Fertility in Massachusetts*

from the Revolution to the Civil War. New York, 1981; studies in economic and working-class history for additional examples.

4   See esp. the works of GRAFF and LOCKRIDGE above.

5   For recent efforts, see my *Legacies of Literacy*, 'The Legacies of Literacy': LOCK-RIDGE, *Literacy*, 'Literacy in Early America'; the work of EGIL JOHANSSON on Sweden; GERALD STRAUSS on Reformation Germany; FURET and OZOUF and NATALIE Z. DAVIS on France; M.J. MAYNES' comparative analysis of France and Germany; the research on England by R.S. SCHOFIELD and W.B. STEPHENS, among others.

6   This point applies less to Canadian history than to American. There are basic and deep historiographical, and ideological, divisions among students of Canada's past about these issues and their relevance. This of course makes for special interpretive problems.

7   For additional comment, see the works of GRAFF and LOCKRIDGE above.

8   References to CREMIN and BAILYN above; SAMUEL E. MORISON, *The Intellectual Life of Colonial New England.* Ithaca, N.Y. 1961 (1936). See also, RICHARD D. BROWN, 'Modernization and the Modern Personality in Early America, 1600–1865', *Journal of Interdisciplinary History* 2 (1972), and *Modernization: the Transformation of American Life, 1600–1865.* New York, 1976; and many texts in US history.

9   MORISON, *Intellectual*, 82, 84, 85.

10 *Ibid.*, p. 83n, quoting P.A. BRUCE's data on Virginia literacy levels. With men at about 60 per cent and women about 25 per cent, this was no surprise. The early studies commonly cited are: W.H. KILPATRICK, *The Dutch Schools of New Netherlands and Colonial New York.* Washington, DC, 1912; P.A. BRUCE, *An Institutional History of Virginia in the Seventeenth Century.* New York, 1910; CLIFFORD K. SHIPTON, 'Secondary Education in the Puritan Colonies', *New England Quarterly* 7 (1934). Now see, DAVID GALENSON, 'Literacy and the Social Origins of Some Early Americans', *History Journal* 22 (1979); and "Middling People" or "Common Sort"; the Social Origins of Some Early Americans Re-examined', with a rebuttal by Mildred Campbell, *William and Mary Quarterly* 35 (1978) and a reply by Campbell, *ibid.*, 36 (1979); 'Literacy and Age in Preindustrial England', *Economic Development and Cultural Change* 29 (1981).

11 BAILYN, *Education*, pp. 14, 15, 43, 45, 48–9. See also LOCKRIDGE, *Literacy*, pp. 28–9, 103–8; GRAFF, *The Legacies*, Ch. VI.

12 CREMIN, *American Education: the Colonial Experience*, pp. 526, 533, 540, 543.

13 *Ibid.*, p. 545, 546, 548–9, 549. The story is carried forward in his *National Experience*, see below. CREMIN'S view is usefully compared not only with LOCKRIDGE'S and my own, but also with RHYS ISAAC, 'Dramatizing the Ideology of Revolution: Popular Mobilization in Virginia, 1774 to 1776', *William and Mary Quarterly* 33 (1976); 'Preachers and Patriots: Popular Culture and the Revolution in Virginia', in *The American Revolution: Explorations in the History of American Radicalism*, ed. A.F. YOUNG, DEKALB, Ill, 1976; *The Transformation of Virginia*, Chapel Hill, 1982; HARRY S. STOUT, 'Culture, Structure, and the "New" History: a Critique and an Agenda', *Computers and the Humanities* 9 (1975); 'Religion, Communications, and the Ideological Origins of the American Revolution', *William and Mary Quarterly* 34 (1977); ALAN TULLY, 'Literacy Levels and Educational Development in Rural Pennsylvania, 1729–1775', *Pennsylvania History* 39 (1972). But see also DAVID D. HALL, 'The World of Print and Collective Mentality in Seventeenth-Century New England' in *New Directions in American Intellectual History* (ed. JOHN HIGHAM and PAUL K. CONKIN, Baltimore, 1979).

14 See LOCKRIDGE, *Literacy*, 'Literacy'; the works cited in note 13 above. Note, first, Lockridge's documentation of his influence by and close association with European students of literacy's history, and, second, the qualifications introduced to his work by ROSS W. BEALES, Jr, 'Studying Literacy at the Community Level: A Research Note',

Journal of Interdisciplinary History 9 (1978); LINDA AUWERS, 'Reading the Marks of the Past: Exploring Female Literacy in Colonial Windsor, Connecticut', *Historical Methods* 13 (1980); WILLIAM J. GILMORE, 'Elementary Literacy on the Eve of the Industrial Revolution: Trends in Rural New England', *Proceedings, American Antiquarian Society* (1982); Isaacs (as cited in note 13); Hall (as cited in note 13); Stout (as cited in note 13); SOLTOW and STEVENS, *Rise of Literacy*, Ch. 2.

15 See LOCKRIDGE, Literacy, *Literacy;* Beales, 'Studying'; AUWERS, 'Reading'; Gilmore, 'Elementary Literacy'; SOLTOW and STEVENS, *Rise of Literacy.*

16 LOCKRIDGE, *Literacy* and 'Literacy', provides exceptional discussions of source bias and correction procedures. See also my review, 'Literacy and History: an Essay Review', *History of Education Quarterly* 15 (1975).

17 LOCKRIDGE, 'Literacy', p. 184; *Literacy,* Section 1, and the graphs in that book on pp. 20, 25, 80.

18 LOCKRIDGE, 'Literacy', p. 186; see also the more complete discussion in his *Literacy,* Sections I, II, and graphs in this book. For the continuities in patterns, see, among others, GRAFF, *Literacy Myth;* Soltow and Stevens, *The Rise of Literacy;* 'Economic Aspects of School Participation in the United States' *Journal of Interdisciplinary History* 8 (1977); MICHAEL B. KATZ, MICHAEL J. DOUCET, and MARK J. STERN, *The Social Organization of Early Industrial Capitalism.* Cambridge, Mass., 1982. LOCKRIDGE provides an illuminating discussion of the intricacy of the causal relations between literacy and occupation and literacy and wealth, *Literacy,* pp. 144–7 and the text itself.

19 LOCKRIDGE, *Literacy, passim.,* and especially his graphs (pp. 20, 25, 80). But see also BEALES, 'Studying'; AUWERS, 'Reading'; GILMORE, 'Elementary Literacy'.

20 Both confirmation and qualification of Lockridge's findings are presented by BEALES, AUWERS, and GILMORE. Their data and arguments should be consulted.

21 On PENNSYLVANIA, see also the work of ALAN TULLY (cited in note 13); on Virginia, see that of BRUCE (cited in note 10) in addition to Isaac's interpretations. LOCKRIDGE draws explicitly on the data of Tully and Bruce. LOCKRIDGE, *Literacy,* pp. 72, 46–7, 72–83, *passim.* On migration, see also the studies of GALENSON (cited in note 10); GRAFF, *Literacy Myth,* Ch. 2, and the citations presented there.

22 On attitudes, see LOCKRIDGE, *Literacy,* Section II. In fact, this aspect is the most original of his book; it has not stimulated the critical attention that it merits as a historian's retrospective 'opinion poll'. There are hints in his data, however, that run counter to the argument; see my 'Literacy and History', for an initial discussion. Evidence and discussion are found in *Literacy,* pp. 32–8, 84–7, 94–7. For comparative discussion, see *Literacy,* pp. 87–101. LOCKRIDGE'S stress on tradition and slow change and the struggle for continuities, is an aspect of a recent, important thrust in early American historiography.

23 LOCKRIDGE, *Literacy,* p. 93. For Quebec, LOUISE DECHENE, in *Habitants et marchands de Montréal au XVII siècle* (Montreal, 1974). pp. 467–8, presents comparable evidence.

24 LOCKRIDGE, *Literacy,* p. 100.

25 *Ibid.,* p. 69, *passim.* Cf, e.g., pp. 1–7, 42–7, 97–101, with 48–68; see also his 'Literacy in early America'. It might be noted that much of the interpretation is indirect and inferential and without confirming support outside the series of literacy rates and the correlations. That is one reason why it is so imperative that LOCKRIDGE'S research and speculations be explored further. See also his 'Social Change and the Meaning of the American Revolution', *Journal of Social History* 6 (1973); 'The American Revolution, Modernization, and Man: a Critique' in *Tradition, Conflict, and Modernization: Perspectives on the American Revolution,* ed. RICHARD MAXWELL BROWN and DON E. FEHRENBACHER, New York, 1977, pp. 103–19. The latter is especially illuminating for students of literacy.

26 Among the exceptions, I include ISAAC and STOUT; among those with limited impact, SOLTOW and STEVENS; among the assimilators, R.D. BROWN and HALL; among the dismissals CREMIN (see his review, 'Reading, Writing, and Literacy', *Review of Education,* 1 (1975); and among the qualifiers, BEALES, AUWERS, GILMORE, and STEVENS and SOLTOW. All citations appear above.

27 Compare Lockridge's work, Auwer's article, and, to some extent, Hall's paper with the emphases of recent European scholarship in the history of literacy. See also, my *Legacies of Literacy.* Then contrast with the views of CREMIN and R.D. BROWN; the results are instructive, I believe. See also, for Canada, DUCHENE, *Habitants;* ALAN GREER, 'The Pattern of Literacy in Quebec, 1745–1899', *Histoire Sociale* 11 (1978). But see any debate with GREER, *ibid.,* 12 (1979).

28 LOCKRIDGE, *Literacy,* 37; see also, his 'Social Change', 'American Revolution'; ISAAC (cited in note 13); STOUT (cited in note 13); AUWERS, 'Reading'; GRAFF, *Legacies of Literacy.* Again, compare with Cremin's interpretation. See, finally, the essential SYLVIA SCRIBNER and MICHAEL COLE, *The Psychology of Literacy.* Cambridge, Mass., 1981. Obviously, this is a large and crucial aspect of the subject; recent historical writing reflects that.

29 CREMIN, *American Education: the National Experience,* pp. 490, 492–3, 496; and cf. p. 492 with the passage from *The Colonial Experience,* quoted above and the pages cited.

30 See, e.g., the studies of SOLTOW and STEVENS, cited above, and the many papers in demographic history by MARIS VINOVSKIS. Economic history provides many other examples.

31 See GREER, 'The Pattern'; HERBERT MAYS and H.F. MANZL, 'Literacy and Social Structures in Nineteenth-century Ontario: An Exercise in Historical Methodology', *Histoire Sociale* 7 (1974); DAVID ALEXANDER, 'Literacy and Economic Development in Nineteenth Century Newfoundland', *Acadiensis* 10 (1980); Graff, *Literacy Myth,* 'Towards a Meaning of Literacy: Literacy and Social Structure in Hamilton, Ontario', *History of Education Quarterly* 12 (1972); 'Literacy and Social Structure in Elgin County, Canada West', *Histoire Sociale* 6 (1973), 'What the 1861 Census can tell us about Literacy', *Histoire Sociale,* 8 (1975), among my other relevant studies. For further references, see my *Literacy in History.*

32 Full citations exceed space limitations. See, however, the relevant works in demographic history by VINOVSKIS, VINOVSKIS and TAMARA HAREVEN, EDWARD MEEKER, MICHAEL HAINES, DON LEET, RICHARD EASTERLIN, LEE SOLTOW, and CLAUDIA GOLDIN; in economic history by GOLDIN, HAINES, GAVIN WRIGHT, ROBERT HIGGS, RICHARD RANSOM and RICHARD SUTCH; in working-class history by PAUL FALER, BRUCE LAURIE, MICHAEL KATZ, WILLIAM SHADE, and IAN DAVEY; immigrant and ethnic history by HIGGS, JOHN BRIGGS, JOHN BODNAR, VIRGINIA YANS MCLAUGHLAN, DAVID HOGAN, or in black history by LAWRENCE LEVINE, LEON LITWACK, EUGENE GENOVESE, VERNON BURTON, D.S. SMITH, GOLDIN, MEEKER, JAMES MCPHERSON, ELIZABETH PLECK, THOMAS WEBBER, HERBERT GUTMAN. These are only examples; citations to 1980 are found in my *Literacy in History.*

33 *Literacy Myth,* p. 57. On the census as a measure of literacy see my 'What the 1861 Census', *Literacy Myth,* Appendix B.

34 See *Literacy Myth,* pp. 73–4, 85–6, 337–9.

35 On nineteenth-century Quebec literacy, and especially its differentials by ethnicity (French and English) and urban-rural residence, see GREER, 'The Pattern'. GREER'S study suffers from several basic problems, which I discussed in my critique (note 27 above). GREER does present interesting data on occupational differences: p. 304. On literacy and economic development in Newfoundland, see ALEXANDER, 'Literacy'.

36 DANIEL CALHOUN, *The Intelligence of a People*. Princeton, 1973, 'The City as Teacher', *History of Education Quarterly* 9 (1969). See also my *Legacies of Literacy;* studies of working-class literacy.

37 On US literacy, see also CALHOUN, *The Intelligence:* RICHARD GRISWOLD DEL CASTILLO, 'Literacy in San Antonio, Texas, 1850–1860', *Latin American Research Review* 15 (1980); MICHAEL WEISS, 'Education, Literacy and the Community of Los Angeles in 1850', *Southern California Quarterly* 60 (1978); SOLTOW and STEVENS, 'Economic Aspects'.

38 SOLTOW and STEVENS, *Rise of Literacy*, Ch. 2.

39 *Ibid.*, 50–4, Ch. 2, *passim.*

40 *Ibid.*, 92–6, Chs. 3–4.

41 *Ibid.*, 115–18, 122–8.

42 *Ibid.*, 178.

43 *Ibid.*, Chs. 4–5 and the tables therein. Their discussion of ethnicity and schooling and their questions about acculturation are innovative, see pp. 130–4, 135–41.

44 *Ibid.*, 151, 148–55.

45 *Ibid.*, 166, 156–8, 159–76 (analysis by states and counties).

46 *Ibid.*, Ch. 5.

47 *Ibid.*, p. 178.

48 *Ibid.*, 176–88.

49 *Ibid.*, esp. Conclusion, pp. 195–201.

50 See, as examples, the work referred in note 32, above. See also, my 'Literacy, Education, and Fertility—Past and Present: A Critical Review', *Population and Development Review* 5 (1979); 'Literacy Past and Present: Critical Approaches in the Literacy-Society Relationship', *Interchange* 9 (1978), 'Legacies of Literacy', (Chapters 4, 2 and 1 in this book), *Legacies of Literacy*. Stimulating examples of recent research include SCRIBNER and COLE, *The Psychology*, among their work; SHIRLEY BRICE HEATH, 'The Functions and Uses of Literacy', *Journal of Communication* 30 (1980): MARCIA FARR WHITEMAN (ed.), *Writing; the Nature, Development, and Teaching of Written Communication, Vol. 1, Variation in Writing.* Hillsdale, NJ, (1981).

51 This I attempt, at least preliminarily, in *Legacies of Literacy;* a sketch appears in 'Legacies of Literacy'. Some of the critical work of R.S. SCHOLFIELD and EGIL JOHANSSON points in related directions. See also IAN WINCHESTER, 'How Many Ways to Universal Literacy?', unpublished paper presented to the Ninth World Congress of Sociology, Uppsala, Sweden, 1978 and to the Leicester University Conference on the History of Literacy in Post-Reformation Sweden, 1980.

4   Exaggerated Estimates of Reading and Writing as Means of Education (1867), by W. B. Hodgson

William Ballantyne Hodgson stands as a typical, but also a special Victorian. His unheralded but important essay, "Exaggerated Estimates of Reading and Writing as Means of Education," also combines the typical with the special. It informs our understanding of nineteenth-century attitudes toward education, adding a complexity and a critical edge usually not accorded to reformers. It also reveals a special depth to that most Victorian of obsessions: the faith in the power and efficacy of schooling for the improvement of society and of the individual within it. The document, reprinted here, not only has a historical value which should be apparent to readers, but it may also be seen as speaking to concerned persons of the late twentieth century.

Hodgson is not well known among mid-nineteenth-century educational activists. Although he merited a full-page entry in the *Dictionary of National Biography* and his *Life and Letters* was edited in fine contemporary style by J. M. D. Meiklejohn in 1883, his name and manifold activities only occasionally appear in educational and intellectual histories of the period. In part, the typicality of his life and work accounts for this neglect.

Born in 1815 in Edinburgh, Hodgson was known primarily as an educational reformer and political economist. The son, appropriately, of a working printer, he studied at Edinburgh High School and then worked for a short time in a lawyer's office. In 1829, at the age of fourteen, he matriculated at Edinburgh University, although he took no degree as a student. For several years, he was employed as a lecturer, speaking on literature, education, and phrenology in Scottish towns. On June 1, 1839, he became the secretary of the Liverpool Mechanics' Institute, beginning a career of associations with formal educational institutions that occupied the remainder of his life and revealed the eclecticism of the active reformer. While at Liverpool, Hodgson was instrumental in the addition of a girls' school to the Institute in 1844, the same year he ascended to the principalship. Taking an LL.D. degree from Glasgow University in 1846, he next stood as principal of Manchester's Chorlton High School from 1847 to 1851. In 1848, he agitated for the education of women at the Royal Institution of Manchester.

During the period 1851–52, Hodgson traveled abroad; he spent most of his time in Paris. Returning to Edinburgh in 1853, he taught popular courses in physiology, having qualified by attending classes at the College of Surgeons. In 1854, he lectured at the Royal Institution, London, on economic science, a subject that he continued to pursue and whose study he long promoted. Hodgson's work and interests were further combined in 1858 when he was appointed an assistant commissioner of inquiry into primary education and moved to London. From 1863 to 1868, he served as examiner in political economy at London University and took a place on the council of University College. That position he resigned in 1867, upon the rejection of James Martineau's nomination to the vacant chair of mental philosophy.

In 1870, Hodgson moved to Bournemouth, but one year later, the Merchant Company of Edinburgh elected him the first occupant of the new chair in commercial and political economy and mercantile law at Edinburgh University. His efforts in this field had led to the establishment of this position. For the remainder of his life, he occupied this professoriate, and was successful in stimulating formal, academic study of economics until his death in 1880. He frequently participated in the Social Science Association's meetings, and was president of the education section in 1873. In 1875, Hodgson was made president of the Educational Institute of Scotland. He died on 24 August 1880, of angina pectoris, while attending an international educational congress in Brussels. Hodgson was survived by his second wife and two sons and two daughters.

As this brief sketch shows, Hodgson's life was rich and varied. He combined work in education, medicine, political economy, and law into a "career"; he changed positions and places of residence frequently. This was possible at a time in which professionalization and more rigid vocational paths were only emerging. Throughout his life and work, he was busy and engaged, indeed a representative middle-class Victorian social and educational reformer. A strong liberal, he was not active in formal politics. Lecturing, writing, agitating within institutions, promoting, and administering constituted his methods of reform as well as his occupations. As the essay reprinted below suggests, "Hodgson was a remarkably lucid lecturer and speaker, and his humorous illustrations relieved a monotonous delivery. Somewhat reserved in his manner, his conversation was rich in terse anecdote and in jocose suggestion."[1] He was also, not surprisingly, a prolific writer on a variety of contemporary topics. His *Dictionary of National Biography* entry lists publications on mechanics' institutes, the secular and the religious (he was a man of religion), economics, public schools, classical education, education of women and girls, the English language, as well as a biography of Turgot, a translation of Count Cavour's *Thoughts on Ireland*, and an edition of William Johnson Fox's *Works*. Although a special individual, he was clearly a person of his times. Interestingly, "Exaggerated Estimates of Reading and Writing as Means of Education" is not listed among his works in the *DNB*.

Biographical data prepare us for William Hodgson's neglected paper on reading and writing. This ten-page essay was originally presented to the 1867 annual meeting of the Social Science Association in Belfast. Hodgson was then an assistant primary education commissioner, so he spoke from first-hand knowledge. The Social Science Association, along with its counterpart in the United States, was a transitional forum for reformers, early social and political scientists, concerned civil servants, and interested lay persons, who met to discuss current social problems and to air and debate proposals for their solution. Poverty and welfare, health, sanitation and other urban problems, political economy, crime, governmental organization, and, of course, education were central, vital issues.[2]

This was obviously the appropriate body for Hodgson's acerbic comments on contemporary education and popular attitudes toward it and its reform. One can only imagine the excitement and controversy that his presentation stimulated. Presented to the Association in 1867, the paper was published first in London by W. W. Head's Victoria Press in 1868; there was sufficient interest to merit a second edition, printed in Reading, in 1875.[3]

The text requires little preliminary comment. Its critical, often scathing stance is clear; Hodgson establishes his context well. The tone is strong and striking. The author's representative faith in education and fears—about the present system of schools and its recent reforms are not blunted. His concern for proper moral education is equally clear. But most important, as historical source and as "lesson" from the past, are Hodgson's strictures on the limits of literacy and the conceptualization of literacy as part and parcel of education. This struck at the core of most contemporary formulations, yet it also spans almost a century and a quarter in underscoring the inherent limitations of any view that focuses narrowly on the presumed "basics." In that, "Exaggerated Estimates of Reading and Writing" has more than a solely historical significance.

Hodgson notes that the introduction of the Revised Code gave "a new or renewed prominence to reading, writing, and arithmetic . . . under the name of payment for results, as tested by individual examination." This "reform" he unhesitantly brands as both retrogressive and insulting to the "masses of the people." He explains, in a rare moment of critical insight for his time and for our own: "Of reading and writing, then, we are often enough told in words that they do not constitute education. . . . in spite of the currency of this truism, I venture to think that reading and writing are far too much regarded not as all education, but as all of education that can be secured for and by the children of the mass. . . . " That, however, is not all. Hodgson also strikes out generally at the limits of reading and writing as independent, autonomous skills, from whose basis a true education will doubtlessly follow. For most students, he opines, "teaching must be adapted. . . . for such natures reading and writing will be master-key to all or much beyond, is not to be thus proved, or without proof to be accepted." He also draws attention to larger, social and cultural limitations and misconceptions that accord to literacy unbridled provenance for individual and social advancements.

Most importantly, in a way that present-day researchers are just beginning to grasp, Hodgson focuses on reading and writing as discrete skills: "Reading is a mechanical means, one of several means, of gaining knowledge and ideas. . . . [reading and writing] are at most, not knowledge, but means of knowledge. I say not *the* means, but means of knowledge." In and of themselves, they lead neither necessarily nor alone to either knowledge or to the many cognitive or attitudinal attributes long assigned to them. This is powerfully indicated in the enormously important and suggestive new study by Sylvia Scribner and Michael Cole, *The Psychology of Literacy*.[4] That literacy and its uses and development are bound by individual and social context and do not, apparently, wield a transforming power all their own flies in the face of centuries of western assumptions, expectations, and theories to the contrary. Hodgson, indicating a pedagogical debate that has raged for centuries, also draws attention to the key distinction between oral reading ability and reading for and with understanding.

"Reading is but one means, if, in the long run, the most important, for acquiring knowledge," the author nonetheless concludes, maintaining the faith. That faith remains with us, and in another time of perceived societal crises and transformations—as in Hodgson's day—we focus on literacy with special concern, taking it once more as an indicator of the state of our civilization and an omen for the future. That, if we heed Hodgson, is risky indeed. W. B. Hodgson had no complete answers of his own. The past does not provide that. Yet, it is instructive that we are now in the midst of repeating precisely that process of debate, criticism, and censure about the place of literacy in learning and in life. How sadly reminiscent are Hodgson's words to us. Perhaps it is time to listen to such views and to struggle toward a new approach to literacy. The past can be of some help in that endeavor, I believe.

In these days much is said about progress, and I am not disposed to deny its reality in various regions, or to disparage its extent. But, admittedly, general and ultimate progression is compatible with partial or temporary retrogression; and there are occasions which tempt one to doubt whether the alleged progress be not a delusion—whether the too obvious retrogression be not final and enduring. Or, to take the somewhat hackneyed simile, which tells us that the advance of the tide is not inconsistent with the retirement of individual waves after they have reached the shore, let us but continue the analogy, and we find that the tide itself, after it has reached its highest, its appointed limit, retires also, leaving a wide waste of dreary sand; and that, though it returns again, it retires again, so that we have, on the whole, not progress, but only oscillation and repetition. The history of popular education tends to confirm the notion that movement is by flux and reflux, and that there is now a season of low water and ebb tide.

Not much more than half a century divides us from the state of social opinion which denounced, or dreaded, or ridiculed any and all teaching of the great masses, which prompted even intelligent and kindly men to predict the entire overturning of society as the inevitable result of the teaching of "the lower orders," as if society depended, for its very existence, on the domination of one small class more or less enlightened, and on the unquestioning subserviency of all other classes, whom any glimmering of light could not fail to render discontented, insubordinate, insurrectionary.

Then came the period which may be called, for a well-known reason, the era of the three R's, *Reading, Riting,* and *'Rithmetic*. The inconveniences of total darkness were more and more recognized, and the advantage of, at least, a sort of twilight state of mind was more and more perceived; but it may well be questioned whether the noonday blaze of knowledge was not more dreaded by the educational patrons of the lower classes than even the midnight blackness of total ignorance. Teaching was encompassed with many limitations and precautions. It might be well for all to be able to read their Bible, according to the famous wish of George III.; but no other literature was encouraged. A good plain hand-writing, with a certain knowledge of ciphering, as it was called, might be useful for the taking of business-orders, and the keeping of accounts. But a too facile or graceful penmanship might be dangerous; it might even lead to forgery, and through that to the gallows. With acquirements so restricted, it was not unlikely that the lower classes would still demean themselves with due humility towards their superiors in station, and believe and act and suffer according to the will of those placed in authority over them, whether spiritual or secular.

By degrees, the scope of popular education was widened, so far, at least, as regards the admission of other subjects of instruction. I cannot think that there was generally a more philosophic estimate of the true nature of education; but the frequent modern examples of individuals rising from humble station to wealth and rank, familiarized men's minds with the thought that so much culture should be generally given as would assist the exceptionally clever boy in his social ascent, rather than improve the condition of the great body of the working classes. Geography, and history, and sundry other things, were more and more generally introduced. It may well be doubted whether these additions were always or commonly improvements. Time was consumed in committing to memory the events of so-called history, one half of which was probably false, while of the other half, one half was probably doubtful, while a large proportion of the whole was unimportant. History must, of course, be begun at the beginning, and the ancient Britons, and the Danes, and the Saxons, and the Normans must have due attention, though, probably, the pupils had passed away from the schools before they had gone down the stream of history below the time of Henry VIII., the names of whose wives, with the order of their execution, furnished excellent material for questions,—or of Elizabeth, whose character was summed up and recited in the pithiest phrases of the Pinnock order of historians. As for geography, such facts as the height of the Himalayas, and the length of the Brahmapootra, were stored up for reproduction at the stated examinations, where the effect was striking, in proportion to the recondite nature of the information, and in inverse proportion to its utility. The barrenness of this kind of teaching, for which, in some cases, no doubt, things of more importance were neglected, did much to damage popular education in the esteem of many, and to give occasion to those previously so disposed to disparage or deny the efficacy and the value of all popular education whatsoever. This tendency was brought to a crisis by the fact that the Educational Department of the Government was in danger of breaking down from an accumulation of routine work, while the annual cost of the educational grant had risen to an amount that shocked the frugal temper of the House of Commons; and the opportunity afforded by the complaint of the Royal Commissioners of 1858–9, that reading, writing, and arithmetic were in some cases neglected, and especially in the younger classes, was readily seized for the introduction of the Revised Code. Of that I need say little more here, than that it gave a new or renewed prominence to reading, writing, and arithmetic, confining practically its rewards to a certain measure of proficiency in these branches, under the name of payment for results, as tested by individual examination.

As to the actual result, opinion is considerably divided, and I cannot here weigh the conflicting testimony. My own belief, however, is that, as might have been expected, it has injuriously affected the higher education, that is, all that deserves the name of education, while it has not generally succeeded in ensuring even mechanical proficiency in the three arts thus specially fostered. It has done much, I venture to think, to throw us back into the second of those stages of national opinion on educational subjects which I have hastily sketched; that, namely, in which this merely elementary sort of teaching was deemed enough for the masses of the people.

And here let me say that it is of reading and writing, and not at all of arithmetic, that henceforth I mean to speak. Arithmetic holds a quite different position from the other two things. Besides its actual uses in the working world, it is a science, capable of becoming the instrument of important training, and though when Baillie Nicol Jarvie said that the multiplication table (i.e. arithmetic) is the root of all knowledge, he had rather in view its application to bills of parcels, and tare and tret, and profit and loss, than to cosmic harmonies, or numerical proportions in the framework of the universe, the doctrine of numbers may truly be regarded as at once a root science and a great power in education. I would rescue it from the slur cast on it by the company in which it is usually found.

Of reading and writing, then, we are often enough told in words that they do not constitute education. By many this is considered a mere truism, but a truism quite as often means a truth neglected as a truth made real. It is with words as with things, (though words too are things), "Too much familiarity breeds contempt." The coin which passes from hand to hand, loses gradually the clearness, and finally the traces, of its image and superscription. Now, in spite of the currency of this truism, I venture to think that reading and writing are far too much regarded not as all education, but as all of education that can be secured for and by the children of the mass, nay, as all that it is important for them to obtain; and that thus a low, unworthy, and mischievous estimate of education, so far as concerns the masses, prevails among us.

In last Friday's meeting one speaker drew forth strong expressions of dissent, by saying that often it is thought enough to apportion knowledge to the station in which the pupil happens to be born, and in which it is assumed that he is likely to remain. I must confess that my own experience supports this statement. Thus, not many years ago I visited a school for female orphans in London, and I was told distinctly by the secretary that only a very plain education was even aimed at, "because," said he, "they are destined to be domestic servants, and it would not do for them to be too near the level of their employers' attainments!" It may not be necessary here to speak in condemnation of that spirit which would keep back those who have so few and so slight opportunities of culture for the supposed sake of those who have so many and so great advantages within their reach; or to contend that the lot to which human beings are really and truly called by Providence (that Providence so often appealed to as a justification of existing evils which it is sought to maintain), is not the condition in which they are born, or in which their parents live, but that of which by the best culture of all their faculties, they qualify themselves adequately to do the work; or to argue that the education of the lower classes is in the interest even of the upper. But that this spirit prevails largely beyond the circle of such an association as this I cannot doubt. There are persons who, as I once heard Archbishop Whately say, embark in the ship of knowledge in order to delay the voyage, being quite willing to appear as promoters of education if they can but gain the power to limit it within what they consider to be safe bounds.

Even among those who regard education with very different feelings, and who have no unworthy jealousy of others less favoured by fortune than themselves, a similar estimate of the sufficiency of the mere elements of knowledge in schools for the people may be traced. "Teach a child to read and to write, and he will educate himself," this is a common saying. No doubt, your Stephensons, and your Faradays, and those with large natural capacity for any kind of mental effort, will, with this simple help, do all besides for themselves. Nay, even without this help, their innate energy would still surmount every obstacle in their way. But such men are the exceptions, not the rule; and the frequent appeal to such cases in evidence of the sufficiency of reading and writing in humble schools, is one more proof of the prevalence of the error which looks at popular education rather as a means of enabling the peculiarly gifted to rise into a higher station, than of enabling and disposing all efficiently to discharge the duties of their actual station, even though they should rise to none higher. It is to the average capacity, the average disposition of ordinary school pupils, that teaching must be adapted, and it is by its success in dealing with that average capacity, that average disposition, that its efficiency is to be judged. Now, that for such natures reading and writing will be a master-key to all or much beyond, is not be thus proved, or without proof to be accepted.

Another sign of the current estimate of reading and writing may be cited. We are all familiar with the statistical tables about criminals, and the proportions among them of those who can read and write well, imperfectly, or not at all. Crime, we are told, flourishes most rankly among the last, less among the second, least among the first. What, then is the natural inference from such statements? Of course, diminish the ignorance, and you diminish the crime.[5] But the ignorance of what? of course, of reading and writing. Ignorance of reading and writing is productive of, or accompanied by, a great amount of crime. Knowledge of reading and writing will, therefore, diminish crime! There may be fallacies more palpable than this; there can be few more gross or serious. The inability to read and write argues, in our present state, it may be freely granted, great ignorance of all beyond that it is good or useful to know. But the ability to read and write, (not to cavil about the degree of ability), by no means argues the knowledge of aught beyond. Negatively, the ignorance implies much, positively the knowledge implies little. Let us take an obvious illustration. If a man does not possess a penny, he is undeniably very poor; if he does possess a penny, is he therefore rich? Is he that, with even one penny, a man may begin to increase his store; but his doing so, his striving, or desiring to do so, depends on considerations widely apart from the mere possession of the penny. The tabulation of such statistics may be useful in various ways. It is not in the facts or in the figures, but in the application of them that the danger lies. By all means let those tell-tale columns make us blush for the deplorable and disgraceful national ignorance that they reveal; let them spur our determination to remove it; but do not let them lull us into the delusive fancy that the presence of the *minimum* of knowledge will cure the evils which the absence of that *minimum* indicates, if it does not cause.

We will now test a little more closely the real educational value of reading and writing.

1.   Reading is a mechanical means, one of several means, of gaining knowledge and ideas. Writing is one mechanical means of conveying knowledge or ideas to others, as well as a means of recording them for either others or ourselves. What is the educational value of either? There is, I am well aware, a high sense, in which it may be contended that he who can read easily, intelligently, appreciatively, pleasurably, even one valuable book, especially if he can read it aloud with due "emphasis and discretion," correct intonation, and utterance at once expressive and impressive; and who further can give written form to his thoughts and knowledge, if, that is, we take writing to mean not merely penmanship, but what is called composition also,—may be said to have received no mean or narrow, though it may still be a defective education. But it is obvious that we are here concerned with such measure of the powers of reading and of penmanship, as is commonly obtained in our cheap and general schools. Now, the first thing that strikes us, is, that they are at most, not knowledge, but means of knowledge. I say not *the* means, but means of knowledge. They are no more knowledge or education, as has often been said, than a knife, fork, and plate constitute a dinner. Given the dinner,—the knife, fork, and plate are useful in enabling us to deal with it. But, though the combination is best, it is better to have the dinner without the implements, than the implements without the dinner. That the two can be separated is undeniable; and so it is quite possible, though not common, to find a man shrewd, sagacious, even well informed, who can neither write nor read, and it is not only possible but very common to find the grossest ignorance and the greatest dulness associated with ability to read and write.[6] But it may be said that a knife, fork, and plate are instruments not for gaining a dinner, but for helping us to consume it when gained; whereas reading and perhaps writing are instruments for actually gaining knowledge. Let us grant that they are tools for gaining knowledge; they are not crop, but plough and harrow. Now, given the plough and the harrow, the mode of using them remains to be taught; the disposition to use them remains to be encouraged. Neither of these things follows inevitably from the mere conferring of the tools; the workman may still be unskilful, or indolent or both. To give a man a loom is one thing; to teach him to weave well and industriously is quite another thing.

This leads me, dropping metaphors, in which fallacy may lurk, to say in the second place—

2.   That the power of reading and of writing often rusts unused, if it is not wholly lost, through neglect and apathy after leaving school. The attainments are not usually carried far enough to render their use either easy or pleasant, and the power gradually decays.[7] For, in the third place—

3.   A knowledge of the sounds and forms of the letters, the syllables and words made up by the letters, is too commonly confounded with knowledge of the things read about, with the taking in of the ideas verbally expressed. An extreme instance may be given. The late Principal Baird, of Edinburgh University, reported that on an official visit which he made to some schools in the remote highlands and islands of Scotland, he was greatly surprised and pleased by the

fluency and correctness with which the children read some verses from the New Testament in English. He ventured to put some question, and then discovered that the children knew nothing whatever of English, that they spoke Gaelic solely, and that they read the English words aloud, by imitation, as mere sounds, without any sense to which they could be echo. Let me cite another instance less extreme. In a school in Hampshire I once heard some girls read, as I thought, with rather unusual correctness, a description of a crab. I happened to ask, as it was an inland place, if any of them had ever seen a crab. After a pause, one girl acknowledged her having seen a crab; but, on inquiry, it appeared that it was a crab-apple she had seen, and it never had occurred to her that the description did not at all fit the object supposed to be described! So, after reading about the straining out of gnats, and the swallowing of camels, one of the pupils (as Miss Cobbe vouches) being asked what was the great sin of the Pharisees, answered, not hypocrisy, but "eating camels." These are detached examples of misapprehension of the things for which the equivalent words are given: but thousands escape detection, and, whether it is through the eye or through the ear that the words reach the sensorium, it is a sad truth, that in innumerable cases they excite no ideas, or false ideas. For such condition of mind is it wonderful that reading should be an irksome, not a pleasing task, one to be soon laid aside, and as seldom as possible resumed? The great mass do not, like the few, persevere sufficiently to surmount those hampering difficulties and earn the reward which such perseverance brings. But, in the fourth place, as I have already said,—

4. Reading is but one means, if, in the long run, the most important, for acquiring knowledge. On Saturday last I had a letter from home which, by an apt coincidence, illustrates what I mean. My little boy, not yet four years old, says to his mother, "Mamma, why does cousin Bella learn lessons?" "That she may grow up to be wise and useful." "But don't I learn by asking questions?" "Out of the mouths of babes." The radical fallacy is in supposing that no knowledge or improvement is obtainable except from books, and the result is the confounding of means with ends. A child is a living, restless, never ceasing interrogator, "perpetually wanting to know, you know," perpetually asking, What? and how? and when? and where? and above all (as I have observed with some surprise) why? perpetually putting all around it "to the question." This is to nurses and parents and teachers a disturbing, fatiguing, and exasperating process, and questions are commonly discouraged, or evaded, if not forbidden. "Children ought not to ask questions:" "Children should be seen, not heard:" such are the ethics of the nursery. I willingly allow for the difficulty of at once carrying on, at least in school, a continuous course of teaching with many pupils simultaneously, and of caring for individual differences of mental state. But principles do not cease to be principles because their application is difficult; and it cannot be doubted that one intelligent answer to such a question as a child will ask and at the time when it asks it, when its interest is aroused and the mental soil is prepared, does more good, has more suggestive and stimulative power than pages of "useful knowledge" which are not *"en rapport"* with the child's mental state, and which respond

to nothing then active within its little brain. A child of average health and capacity sucks in knowledge at every pore; its craving for knowledge is truly insatiable. "It is as natural," says Quintilian, "for the human mind to learn as for the bird to fly, or the fish to swim." But many who spend dreary years in seeking the power to read Quintilian in the original, and most frequently without succeeding in the endeavour, tell us a very different tale. The youthful mind, they say, is averse from knowledge, that is, what they call knowledge, or, at best, indifferent to it, and it must be artificially coaxed, or bribed, or threatened into the semblance of interest. A child eagerly examines every object around it, or, in lack of objects, then the pictures or images of objects. But between the child and nature we interpose an opaque medium called a book, and we expect the child to profit by symbols which to us, indeed, are full of meaning, but which to it are mysteries, whose significance it is slow to discover. Pedants snort disdainfully at the thought of teaching science to children. Yet what is science, in great part, but observation methodized? A child cannot be easily kept from observing and even from generalizing. The question is whether it shall do both ignorantly, of its own wild fancy, or under the guidance of maturer judgment and ampler knowledge. As all children, not wholly stupified by the compression and distortion of the school, form for themselves a kind of science, draw inferences and make generalizations, probably erroneous, certainly incomplete, shall they be left without guidance, as without encouragement?[28]

Even attempts to teach science are often marred by confounding it with literary or verbal knowledge. Nature is treated on the system of the Eton Latin grammar. Technical names and lists of genera and species are committed to memory without due explanation of the grounds of distinction. I have before me a catechism for the young, entitled "First Lessons in Physiology." All the knowledge runs freely from the pupil, when tapped by the teacher with a question. The teacher says: "How many varieties of absorption are there, and name them?" The pupil answers: "Interstitial, cutaneous, recrementitial, respiratory, venous, excrementitial, and lacteal." Such are the new husks upon which babes are fed! Without a revolution in method no mere change of subject can do much good.

5.   Again, the learning of the art of reading, being treated as an end, is made much more difficult than it needs to be. The letters are taught by their names, not by their sounds; in the arbitrary order of the alphabet, instead of in the natural order of the organs by which they are pronounced. Spelling is still taught by means of columns of long, hard, unconnected words, selected for their very difficulty and rarity, to be learned by rote, or, as is said with unconscious irony, "by heart." At a large and well-endowed school in London, I have seen dozens of boys engaged simultaneously in laborious efforts to learn to spell badly, with the aid of a most ingenious book, in which every word was incorrectly spelled. Then the process of teaching to read begins too early, as it is continued too long. I know well the difficulty in a school, where the minds of the pupils may be, nay must be, in different stages of development; still, the first thing being to rouse an appetite for knowledge, and the second to gratify it when roused, all attempts to reverse

this order, or even to anticipate its evolution, must be injurious. A child that, eager to hear a story over again, puts to its ear the book in which it is told, is in a fair way learning to read swiftly, easily, gladly. Before it reaches that stage, the instruction might have been tedious and ineffectual. These are but hints which it is impossible here to follow out in detail.

6. Then, what is the literature by means of which reading is too often taught? In Scotland still, the shorter Catechism of the Westminster Assembly of Divines (in my boyhood I used to wonder what the longer could possibly be), has prefixed to it an alphabet which is learned as a preliminary to plunging into the depths of Calvinistic divinity. Even in London I have visited a "respectable" school, in which reading is taught from the Bible, and so soon as the pupil is tolerably proficient, he is promoted to the dignity of secular reading! And this is done in the supposed interests of religion! It is as if we were to begin the teaching of our children with Milton's Paradise Lost, and then advance them into Robinson Crusoe, or Miss Edgeworth's Tales. In many Scotch schools the Bible is almost the only reading book; the junior and senior classes are called respectively the Testament class and the Bible class. I have heard of a boy so taught who, having been asked by his mother to read a passage in a newspaper, was suddenly roused from his monotonous chaunt by a box on the ear, accompanied by these words— "How dar ye, ye scoundrel, read the newspaper with the Bible twang?"

7. With such a spirit in the school, is it wonderful that the whole teaching should have a narcotic tendency, that it should crush intelligence, and breed disgust, weariness, hatred of all study? At a former meeting of this Association, I heard one of Her Majesty's Inspectors of Schools (since dead), declare that in certain schools he could tell pretty accurately by the pupils' faces how long they had been at school. The longer the period, the more stupid, vacant, and expressionless the face. Another school inspector (Diocesan), has told me that when, examining a class in the Acts of the Apostles, he asked:—"Why did the eunuch go away rejoicing,"—the answer frankly was—"Please, sir, because Philip had a done o' teaching on him." What hours of weariness and waste are summed up in this brief story! Such teaching defeats its own end; the power to read is gained at the cost of the desire to read. This, if, in spite of false quantity, I may adapt the words of the Roman poet, is *"propter legendum legendi perdere causas,"* for the sake of reading to lose that which makes reading to be desired.

8. Lastly, it ought never to be forgotten that the power to read does not in the least determine the use to which it is to be put. What will be the nature of the books or journals read? How much of mischievous, not to speak of idle, literature is there in the world that must all find readers, admirers, purchasers! With the diffusion of the mere power of reading, without intellectual and moral culture, must we not expect that this sort of literature will be multiplied? The increased numbers of cheap "sporting" papers, of papers devoted to police reports, with coarse and exciting woodcuts, and of the literary master-pieces of the "singing saloon," have of late attracted notice. Nay, the power to read and write arms with greater force the disposition for evil, as well as that for good. In every

wicked enterprise such attainments are helps to its success. It used to be argued that writing ought not to be taught to the people, lest it should lead to the commission of forgery, or other fraud; but this sort of argument, if futile against teaching to write, supplies a reason why the power of writing, or of reading, should be associated with such training and guidance as will tend to ensure its beneficial employment.

As I rejoice to see in this Association, and elsewhere, a growing tendency to regard the teaching of all classes, and of both sexes, from the same points of view, and to apply to all alike the same fundamental principles, I will here briefly say that what I think to be the exaggerated estimate of reading and writing in the instruction of the poor has its exact counterpart in the hitherto far too exclusively literary character of the instruction of the rich. In this aspect, how pregnant with meaning is the title, "Grammar school," so almost universal as the designation of our upper schools! Not to insist on the practical identification of "Grammar" with the teaching of Latin and Greek, what a petrifaction is this term of the whole cast of opinion, which viewed all instruction as an affair of books and words! What a record it preserves of the habit of regarding even Science as a knowledge less of things than of what men have written about things, and of the style in which they have written! Widen as we may the sense of grammar, far beyond the scope and practice of schools, past or present, till it become, if you will, coextensive with philology, and even literature, (and far be it from me to disparage such studies), how lamentably does this title fall short of what ought to be the aim of education in such a country, in such an age as ours! Over the door of the Bradford Grammar School stands this inscription:—

"Quod Deus optimus maximus bene vertat
Aedificium hocce ad literarum antiquarum
Studium promovendum juventutemque doctrina
Elegantiore imbuendum extructum est atque
Musis in perpetuum consecratum."
—"For promoting the study of ancient literature, and for imbuing youth with elegant learning, this building has been raised, and for ever consecrated to the muses."

A noble part of a liberal education, the polished and graceful capital of the educational column, but assuredly neither its shaft nor its base! Try mentally to realize what Bradford or Belfast is, and what it needs for the instruction and guidance of the youth who are to do its actual work, to maintain and to extend its prosperity, to remove its evils, to raise the character of its people, to improve their sanitary and social condition, to teach them how to lead a clean, healthy, happy, human life—and how painfully one-sided and defective it is! How it ignores the essential! How it magnifies the less important! How it subordinates strength, solidity, and service to grace and ornament and surface-show! Assuredly the time is coming, I think it is at hand, when such a title as that of "Spelling school" will be regarded as scarcely less expressive of the purposes, grand and manifold, at which our upper schools, aye, all our schools, ought to aim. Even in our higher, even in our highest schools, improvement is slowly but surely creeping in; slowly but surely is it being recognized that any school which ignores the knowledge of man himself, of the objects animate and inanimate with which he is surrounded, and of the relationship between him and them, his social duties, his economic interests, and the reciprocal bearing of the individual and the social well being is radically, deplorably, disgracefully defective. Every improvement in our lower schools will react upon the upper, and *vice versâ*. And when the instruction of our higher classes is what it ought to be, and in proportion as it shall be what it ought to be, will the problem of our lower education be practically solved. Had our upper classes ever been really educated, they would not, and could not, so long and so complacently have endured the ignorance and consequent degradation of the masses of their fellow citizens, of those whom, as if in mockery, they style their fellow immortals, their brothers and their sisters.

It is, however, of the lower schools that I here speak. It is even fortunate that narrow and selfish fears are beginning to urge on what enlarged conceptions and generous impulse have failed hitherto to effect. Thus (1) the recent extension of the suffrage is opening the eyes of many to the necessity of training the masses to the judicious and beneficial exercise of the power thus conferred. One whose name will be, in history, connected as well with the political changes that he resisted as with the educational changes that he introduced, has said that we must now teach our future masters their letters. That this was said in bitter irony there can be little doubt; and it cannot be taken to mean that in the opinion of the speaker that amount of teaching will suffice. Those who have already had the suffrage can, for the most part, read and write. But they, too, need enlightenment, and moral as well as intellectual training; so do those whom they elect to represent them. On the one hand, reading and writing have not prevented dishonest voters in thousands from selling their votes for bribes, solid or liquid; on the other, reading and writing, and much besides, have not prevented unscrupulously ambitious millionaires from debauching whole constituencies by lavish expenditure, or from masking their immoral and demoralising practices by liberal donations to charities, to schools, and even to churches. Nevertheless, the fear of the large classes now admitted within the pale of the constitution for the first time has given no slight impulse to the general zeal for education. It is for us to see that the movement now begun be turned to good account. Let us help to educate, but in what? That is the question of questions.

Then, again (2), foreign nations, we are told, are beginning to beat us at our own weapons. They have learned more than their letters. They are, it is said, driving us out of the markets which, with insular arrogance, we have fancied should for ever be ours exclusively. A cry of alarm is raised for more and better technical instruction; and, though this is narrow enough in the thoughts of many who raise it, more and better general culture will certainly come out of it; a greater development of general mental power, and the formation of better social habits, will ere long be discovered to be the things really needful.

Again (3), our industry is partially paralyzed, our capital is wasted, our prosperity, our very national existence, are endangered by strikes and trade combinations and restrictions, which check production, often by means as unscrupulous and truculent as the end sought is false and mischievous. The masses have been suffered to grow up in ignorant and angry defiance of the elementary principles of economic science, and reading and writing will not cure this long rankling sore. Broadhead, who could read and write (as he has amply shown), believing at the time that the introduction of a certain machine would injure his craft, instigated an act of criminal violence. He confessed that he had discovered his error; but the discovery came too late. Had he made it sooner, one outrage less would have been attempted. With wider knowledge others, perhaps all, might have been prevented. Knowledge is not merely power; it is restraint and guidance, if not impulse. It is the rudder, if not the sail; the fly-wheel, if not the steam-boiler. It is true that there have not been wanting men of so-called education to defend such blunders, and even to extenuate such atrocities; but their education has lacked the special direction which alone could save from error in this matter. It is true that the employers are often not more intelligent in this respect than the employed; but the enlightenment of the latter, who are the many, and from whose ranks the former, hitherto the few, must largely come, will extend to, and react upon the former also, and do much to soften their mutual relations, to make all see their common interest, and to fuse them together, so as in time to modify, if not, as some hope, to obliterate the distinction itself.[9]

For such reasons as these, a new educational agitation is arising, or the old is reviving with fresh vigour. One and all point to something far beyond reading and writing. I am, I must say, hopeful of the ultimate, if not of the early, issue. The now swelling call for "compulsory" education will force on the public mind the fundamental inquiry, what ought education to be. If, by compulsion, what now passes under the name of education were rendered even universal, I presume to think that the existing mass of pauperism, crime, vice, misery and disease, would scarcely be perceptibly abated. But it is no small gain to have recognized the claim of even the poorest, still more even because the poorest, to something that is called education. Bad or grossly defective education in any quarter cannot continue long after education has ceased to be regarded as the heritage of the few. Just as air becomes stagnant and foul when confined, so education when restricted to the few loses its vital freshness. To diffuse education of any kind is indirectly to improve it. Make education general, universal, and the (so called) higher education will be rationalized, and, as I think, liberalized.[10] Youths will no longer be sent into active life from costly seminaries, accomplished it may be in Greek metres, but ignorant of the structure of their own bodies, the constitution of their own minds; filled with mythologic lore, but unaware of their social duties; primed with verbal scraps of inconsistent moral precept, but less ashamed of debt than of honest industry; looking on the world as a spoil for the lucky, or the crafty, or the strong, not as a field for useful and ennobling labour to the benefit of all as well as of self; of self just in proportion as it tends to the good of all. Then, instead of the rich being fed on intellectual sweetmeats, while the poor are starved, or gather up the crumbs that fall from the others' table, all, rich and poor alike, shall be nourished with plainer, more substantial and wholesome diet, not without such lighter fare as may be obtainable by either. As knowledge will be no longer confounded with books, or with words about knowledge, so morals, of which the laws are as eternal as they are simple, as universal as they are strong, the morals in which all sects and conditions of thinking men agree, will be dissociated from the verbal and dogmatic formularies about which men differ, and, while becoming less sectarian and theological, will become more widely Catholic, more truly religious.[11] We, or our survivors, will then look back with a smile, not of contempt or pride, but of joy and pity, on the time when there was so great a pother about so small a matter as reading and writing, and when even this beggarly amount of teaching was found to be a tremendous national difficulty, just because so little more was aimed at, or desired, or perhaps conceived. The less is included in the greater, and the little becomes easy from the effort to do much.

Notes

1 *Dictionary of National Biography*, 9 (1917): 967. All biographical information is taken from this source. [HJG]

2 See, for example, REBA N. SOFFER, *Ethics and Society in England; The Revolution in the Social Sciences, 1870–1914* (Berkeley, Calif., 1978): PHILIP ABRAMS, *Origins of British Sociology 1834–1914: An Essay with Selected Papers* (Chicago, 1968); THOMAS L. HASKELL, *The Emergence of Professional Social Science: The American Social Science Association and the Nineteenth-Century Crisis of Authority* (Urbana, Ill., 1977). Both the Social Science Association and Hodgson himself call for further study; there are signs of new interest in the former. [HJG]

3 The 1868 London edition provides the text reprinted here. The British Library kindly supplied me with a photocopy. I acknowledge their assistance as well as that of the inter-library loan librarian, ISOBEL GIBB, at the Ontario Institute for Studies in Education. [HJG]

4 SYLVIA SCRIBNER and MICHAEL COLE, *The Psychology of Literacy* (Cambridge, Mass., 1981). For an elaboration on this point, see HARVEY J. GRAFF, *The Legacies of Literacy: Continuities and Contradictions in Western Society and Culture* (Bloomington, Ind., 1986), Introduction: for précis, see idem, "The Legacies of Literacy." *Journal of Communication* 32 (Winter 1982): 12–26; idem, *The Literacy Myth: Literacy and Social Structure in the Nineteenth-Century City* (New York, 1979). *The Literacy Myth* sets the trans-Atlantic context, see esp. chs. 1, 7. These views should be contrasted with the more normative approaches of, especially, MARSHALL MC-LUHAN, JACK GOODY and IAN WATT, G.H. BANTOCK, DANIEL LERNER, ALEX INKELES, among others. [HJG]

5 "A Maiden Session.—At the Salisbury Quarter Sessions, just held, there was not a single prisoner for trial. The Mayor of the city (Mr. S. Eldridge) had therefore the pleasing duty of presenting the Recorder (Mr. J. D. Chambers), the clerk of the peace, and the governor of the gaol with pair of white kid gloves each, according to custom on occasions of this sort. The Recorder, in addressing the grand jury, said that he had read the other day in *The Times* that Wiltshire was one of the best educated counties

in England, and *it was highly satisfactory to learn therefore that the decrease of crime had been in proportion to the spread of education.*" (!)—*Times*, 2nd Jan., 1868.

6 "Although the perusal of such works must, in strictness of speech, be denominated reading, yet, so far as the cultivation of mind is concerned, it is little else than the sheer act of deciphering so much letter press, without the acquisition of a single new idea that can at all conduce towards improvement."—REV. THOS. PRICE, "Tour in Brittany, Literary Remains." 1854, vol. 1, p. 81. "No doubt the power of reading is a key to the whole literature of England. But in the hands of persons ignorant how to use it, a key is of little use."—*Saturday Review*, 4th Jan., 1868, p. 20. In the very same article the writer says:—"What is wanted is that every child should be able to read and write fairly before he goes to work: that he should be enabled to turn this knowledge to more intellectual account while he is at work; and that, in cases where his parents' means, or his own industry, can defray the cost, he should be further enabled to perfect himself in the various branches of study which have a bearing, general or special, on his professional occupation." It is too obvious that the reviewer does not expect the child to turn the ability to read and write to any "intellectual account" during the school period!

7 "The imperfect instruction given to the children in factories, under the half-time system, is retained by them during a year or two at most, when it is forgotten, and many intelligent young overlookers are unable to keep correctly the simple accounts which should form a part of the duties of their position."—MR. SAMUELSON, M.P. (speaking of Bradford, Yorkshire).

8 "Why are the people who notice what comes before them to be marked by a separating name, and called naturalists? Why are we ashamed of a failure in what comes to us through books and the costly instrumentality of masters and teachers? Why do we blush at any flagrant slip in history, or science, or language, and keep cool and easy under any extravagance of error in what nature, through our own observation, might teach us."—*Saturday Review*, 28th July, 1863. Article on "Ignorance." Yet Canon Moseley, who is deservedly an authority in education, would keep out of schools (not merely elementary schools) all "the sciences of observation," specially so called. At Clifton College, on 30th July, 1867, he is reported to have said:—"The subjects of human knowledge, which claimed to be considered and taught in our schools, might be divided into four groups. First of all," (why 'first?') "there were the languages and the subjects allied to them; secondly, the pure mathematical sciences, which were pursued in the exercise of pure thought and rested upon abstractions; thirdly, the sciences of experiment, including physics and chemistry; and fourthly, the great sciences of observation, such as natural history and the like. He thought they might put the last out of consideration, as they had had quite enough to do with the three others." In like manner, I once heard it contended that any new poetry is superfluous, because there is more poetry already written than any human being can possibly read! In like manner, it has been urged that the discovery of new planets is absurd, because we have as many already as we well know what to do with! But, perhaps, we ought less to regret that the subjects in the fourth class are thus shut out, than rejoice that those in the third are admitted. Too often both classes are still visited with the same arbitrary sentence of exclusion, and on the same ground, that there is quite enough to do without them! It is not very long since subjects of even the second class ceased to be regarded as unlicensed intruders on the traditional monopoly of the first.

9 To the three reasons given in the text a fourth may well be added. Society is, not without reason, more and more alarmed by the rapid increase of outrages which threaten its very existence. "Education" is hailed as the sure if slow, remedy. The adult ruffian is probably beyond its influence, but the embryo garotter may be tamed if only he can be taught to spell "gallows;" and on the juvenile pickpocket a course of alphabet, with exercise in pothooks and hangers, may have a salutary effect, deterrent

or emollient! By all means let trial be made. Its failure will open the eyes of many to the need of something better, though it may also lead many to say, "Education has been tried, and tried in vain."

10 "Coleridge, when he predicted that the effect of popularizing knowledge would be to plebify it, erred in his vision of the future, as many seers have done before and since. He uttered that predication on the assumption that knowledge, in its higher portions, was confined to the regions of theology and psychology; and he overlooked the fact that, in proportion as these branches of knowledge have been cultivated by the few, ignorance has prevailed among the many. He failed to observe that, if thousands rushed to Abelard's lecture room, millions outside of it were immersed in the grossest superstition."—*Saturday Review*, 26th Oct., 1867, p. 544.

11 "As Sir R. Palmer reminded his audience, the line between 'religious' and 'secular' is purely conventional. 'All knowledge, all instruction, in whatever is honest and of good report, is essentially religious.' Dogmatic theology concerns itself with creeds; but religion has to do with common life; and its sphere, though not identical, is co-extensive with that of education. The clergyman and the schoolmaster are inevitably working together, whether they are working in concert or not."—*Times*, 2nd Nov., 1866.

Part III
The Social Relations of Literacy

Introductory Note to Part III

In its examples of empirical exercises and critical reviews of the literature, Part III forms one pole of this book. The other pole is the conceptual and agenda-setting, which dominate Parts I and IV, and to a certain extent Part II as well. It is important that Chapters 5–14 be read and interpreted in the terms of those that precede and follow them.

I want first to stress the common ground of these chapters. Each is committed to a critical evaluation of empirically based research, by myself and other writers. Second, each essay takes up a theme that ties past with present, from fertility in Chapter 6 through economic development in Chapter 9 and criminality in Chapter 10. Each of these themes was of great concern to our ancestors and remains so today: linking not only past with present but also popular thought with social theory and social/political policy. Third, those relations underscore the limitations of views that conceptualize literacy apart from its larger contexts and without recognition of the breadth of its associations. Fourth, each of the chapters highlights the contradictions that beset most formulations about the social relations of literacy—past and present both—*and* that emerge from close analysis within those social relations themselves.

The contrapuntal nature of these connections and their echoes is unmistakable. Neglect of historical dimensions mutes and even erases that illuminating circumstance. Thus we see the questions and problems of the present without a full context and without the kinds of precedents that encourage alternative theoretical *and* polity approaches. That kind of short-sighted and self-limiting perspective can be both paralyzing and self-destructive, as recent 'back to basics' reforms reveal. Without knowing the course of history and how it has shaped the world today, we cannot even know which 'basics' were in fact basic or evaluate the significance—or even the possibility itself—of such a 'return.'

Controversy wracks a number of the issues that these chapters confront. A revealing example is Chapter 6 on the relations between literacy and/or education and the course of human fertility. Conceived originally as a critique of the theory and practice of fertility studies, the chapter takes a strongly negative stance toward the dominant tendencies in empirical study and interpretation.

Despite continuing empirical and conceptual support, my views have sometimes been cited without taking note of their implications (by Maris Vinovskis, for example) or rejected, most prominently by John Caldwell in his reassertion of demographic transition theory from a modernization perspective. Disturbing in these latter works is an unwillingness to explore the contradictory nature of research results and to confront criticisms of presuppositions and conceptualizations. That only obstructs advancement.

Chapters 9 and 10, cast primarily in historical terms, are committed to the same tasks of linking past and present issues and showing the linkages among the normative, the popular concepts, social theoretical concerns, and policy issues. Here the issues are economic development for individuals and nations, and causes and preventions of criminality and punishment with respect to literacy. The limitations, theoretical and empirical, of normative constructions and empirical examinations, form one thrust; discussion of new approaches constitutes another.

Chapter 7, on the Renaissance, demonstrates one kind of 'explanation sketch' of the historical conceptualization of literacy in society and culture during a time of transitions. The continuities and contradictions, the legacies from its own past and for the future, and the variations among different kinds of literacies are core elements of this exercise.

Chapter 11, on literacy, in literature as in life, is a different kind of undertaking. In part a playful exercise in the social history and the social relations of literature and popular culture, the essay claims some methodological import but also shows how one might reciprocally move between the 'hard evidence' of statistical data and the so-called 'soft data' of cultural sources. I stress the need to embrace both for the comprehension of literacy and also recommend Robert Tressell's *Ragged Trousered Philanthropists* to readers.

Finally, Chapters 8 and 12 originated as review essays. My evaluations focus on method and sources as well as conceptualization and execution. For the terms I attempted to develop, perhaps more than for the materials themselves, these remain integral to the larger project of this book.

Chapters 5, 12, and 14 newly join this section. They expand it in directions critical and empirical by supplementing and refining the focus. Chapter 5 provides a revealing beginning. It amplifies and refocuses key ideological issues aired in Part II in its effort to contextualize and criticize E. E. Hirsch's *Cultural Literacy*. Among the chapter's purposes is the historical location of a renewed 'cultural literacy' movement and a historical view of its appeal and contradictions. It bridges intellectually and chronologically my mid- to late-1970s concerns as reflected in Chapters 1, 2, and 4, with, on one hand, the more empirical approaches of Chapters 7, 9, 10, 11, 12, and 14, and, on the other hand, the more general evaluation and agenda-setting of Part IV.

Chapter 12 joined new research in first-person testimonial sources with longstanding concerns about literacy's acquisition and uses. The contradictions between literacy's often exaggerated but nonetheless real possibilities and the more restricted patterns of its common uses and practices permeate the revealing human testaments. The social history of literacy's uses is in its very early phases. A history of reading but not yet writing gradually emerges, threading its way through the obstacles of overly enthusiastic assumptions and expectations. This essay, along with Chapters 9, 10, and 11, points toward new sources, research approaches, questions, and conceptualizations. First-person sources, with their literate bias and problems of representativeness recognized and admitted, provide reasonably precise evaluations of reading and/or writing practices.

Although very different, Chapter 14 (co-authored with Robert Arnove) is dedicated to the same goals. It also stands as a synthetic introduction to and overview of a collection of separate investigations of national literacy campaigns that Arnove and I solicited and edited. That volume considered significant campaigns, six historical, and six after the mid-twentieth century. Opening a fascinating and vital path toward new comparisons, this essay only begins to point the way. Underscoring the power and the import of explicit comparison in literacy studies, it raises new questions not only about theories and generalizations but also about cross-national, cross-cultural, and longtime comparative perspectives and the potential applications of the fruits of research which mandate renewed collaboration.

(1993)

5   *Critical Literacy Versus Cultural Literacy: Reading Signs of the Times?*

Cultural Literacy: What Every American Needs to Know
by E. D. Hirsch, Jr.
Boston: Houghton Mifflin, 1987

A great malaise haunts the land. Rising to epidemic proportions in the United States, but perhaps only a bit less dramatically elsewhere in North America and the Western World, this is the spectre of the "great literacy decline" and the dire consequences imagined to follow in the wake of an apparent contemporary loss of literacy. The perceived plight elicits so much commentary that we need do no more than name it to evoke its many dimensions and imputed causes and effects. Sadly, despite its ubiquity, misunderstanding and confusion accompany this profusion of notions, and indeed may be said to drive them. This is especially the case for a recent book that I take as my central text in these comments: E. D. Hirsch, Jr.'s extraordinarily popular, celebrated, and all but canonized *Cultural Literacy: What Every American Needs to Know*.[1]

In these comments I take Hirsch's *Cultural Literacy* as a key text for our times. In the tradition of the humanities, I present a reading of it. Whereas I will focus closely on Hirsch, my intentions are not fixed on his prolegomena or program. Hirsch, to this reading, is a symbol and a symptom of issues that form *assumptions* in his book but are more telling on a larger socio-cultural and political economic plane; of *contexts*, historical as well as contemporary, in which his moral lessons are heard, and in which we must read him; and of a *critical discourse* about literacy which his work obstructs rather than promotes. The phrase "cultural literacy" is the totem and banner for Hirsch and his allies in the current educational reform movements[2]; more revealing than they themselves recognize, the term cries out for deconstruction. To it, I wish to counter-pose another term, that of "critical literacy."

In English professor E. D. Hirsch, Jr.'s capable hands, the promotion of cultural literacy becomes a powerful position. His presentation is carefully constructed to brook no criticism and to disarm, sometimes by homily, sometimes by caricature, any potential quibbles. Hirsch thus proclaims:

> Although mainstream culture is tied to the written word and may therefore seem more formal and elitist than other elements of culture, that is an illusion. Literate culture is the most democratic culture in our land: it excludes nobody; it cuts across generations and social groups and classes; it is not usually one's first culture, but it should be everybody's second, existing as it does beyond the narrow spheres of family, neighborhood, and region. (p. 21)

How dare anyone object! As rhetoric, *Cultural Literacy* is even more impressive than it is as ideology.

To the extent that the book captures and organizes and newly legitimizes preexisting concern and the hopes and goals of many different persons today, it needs to be read as much more than one volume representing the proposals of one professor. It is an icon as well as a banner to be waved with pride.[3] Like all such cultural icons, the closer one examines it the more slippery it becomes; this is at once a strength and a weakness. Like the notions of modernity that the book takes as its bases, but also struggles to reject and replace, "all that is solid melts into air" (with apologies to Marx).[4] These aspects need to be grasped firmly and critically.

That is my task here. Hirsch's *Cultural Literacy* is my vehicle to raise a series of questions about contemporary views and practices of literacy that are absolutely central to an understanding of conditions of contemporary culture, education, and policy. I begin with major questions concerning assumptions, definitions, conceptions, and theory; contexts, including historical forces and traditions; fallacies, limits, and dangers. I argue that "cultural literacy" represents the last long gasp of a complex of historical legacies surrounding literacy that received major endorsement in the 18th-century Enlightenment. Clarity was neither then nor later a hallmark of the Enlightenment, but the power to shape conceptions and policies of literacy was.[5]

Hirsch, apparently unknowingly, has rediscovered this tradition. In the reification, reductionism, and approach of his work—he presents a *list* that presumes to define the "contents" of cultural literacy—Hirsch evokes the spirit of the writers of the *Encyclopédie* with their misplaced utopianism, elitism, goals of cultural homogeneity, and obfuscation. In his appeal to science and the spirit of progress (and fear of cultural regression), his stated desire to raise up the lower elements in society to higher levels, and his focus on early schooling and the development of a minimal level of common cultural knowledge, he joins their ideological ranks. In uncritically equating "knowledge" and "values," he shares their platform. Perhaps most tellingly, in seizing a rhetoric of democracy and of social mobility in the face of clear snobbery, he rests comfortably among them. And, of course, in the endorsement of "universal" training in literacy, and presumptions of great transformations in the wake of that success, is Hirsch marked most of all. The ironies and contradictions in this circularity exceed my ability to enumerate them. So, too, do the manifold ways in which our current imputed crisis is the legacy of that tradition in its original guise. Hirsch's repeated targeting of Jean-Jacques Rousseau and John Dewey (as well as school administrators and teachers) as the villains of the melodrama fits perfectly here.[6]

We may applaud Hirsch's forthrightness; he hides little. He prefaces *Cultural Literacy* with these words:

> To be culturally literate is to possess the basic information needed to thrive in the modern world. The breadth of that information is great, extending over the major domains of human activity from sports to science. It is by no means confined to "culture" narrowly understood as acquaintance with the arts. Nor is it confined to one social class. Quite the contrary. Cultural literacy constitutes the only sure avenue of opportunity for disadvantaged children, the only reliable way of combating the social determinism that now condemns them to remain in the same social and educational condition as their parents. (p. xiii)
>
> Only by piling up specific, communally shared information can children learn to participate in complex cooperative activities with other members of their community. (p. xv)
>
> Literacy, an essential aim of education in the modern world, is no autonomous, empty skill but depends upon literate culture. Like any other aspect of acculturation, literacy requires the early and continued transmission of specific information.... Only by accumulating shared symbols, and the shared information that the symbols represent, can we learn to communicate effectively with one another in our national community. (p. xvii)
>
> Why is literacy so important in the modern world? Some of the reasons, like the need to fill out forms or get a good job, are so obvious that they needn't be discussed. But the chief reason is broader. The complex undertakings of modern life depend on the cooperation of many people with different specialties in different places. Where communications fail, so do the undertakings. (That is the moral of the story of the Tower of Babel.) The function of national literacy is to foster effective nationwide communications. Our chief instrument of communication over time and space is the standard national language, which is sustained by national literacy. Mature literacy alone enables the tower to be built, the business to be well managed, and the airplane to fly without crashing. (p. 2)

The inflation of literacy and the import of its simple and direct consequences receive few more soaring proclamations. The problematics that confute many other students of literacy, whether of oral versus written languages, cultural differences, pedagogy, measurement, or definition, simply do not exist for Hirsch.

Although Hirsch explicitly evades the issue of defining cultural literacy and strategically disallows any imperative to do so, the book presents definition by way of seeming synonyms. A Hirsch "lexicon" of cultural literacy thus includes: "mature literacy," "true literacy," "network information," "competent reading," "background information," "effective [nationwide] communications," "national literacy," "the essence of literacy," "effective use of standardized literate language"/"mastery of the standard instrument of knowledge and communication," "shared information," "an enabling competence," "cultural values," "intergenerational information," and "universal literacy." This lexicon is not complete; the listing of these synonyms merely follows the order in which they appear in the text. Similarly, Hirsch decries any notion of literacy as "skill," but he himself resorts regularly to a rhetoric of skills in his discussion (see pp. 5 et seq. for examples). Contradiction appears to be a central feature (function?) of cultural literacy.

I don't want to caricature this table of interchangeable elements. Nor do I wish to subject it to criticism that it cannot fairly stand. Nevertheless, we should observe not only its surface confusions, but also its traditionalist and ritualistic tendencies. In the face of great change, disruption, and decline, we naturally hew our way back to those foundations of culture seen as most stable and "conservative," in the etymological sense of that abused term. We have no need to inquire into the presumed "golden age" of shared knowledge and values, the foundation of our new programs. In this, the first *philosophes* had a firmer command than Hirsch; they also appreciated the necessity for historical and contextual understanding, something which Hirsch's approach demands but which he, sometimes astonishingly, does not provide. In raising concerns about citizenship, as one significant example, he takes regular recourse to traditions of nation-founding, crises of polity, and longing for community without serious consideration of meanings, possibilities, limits, or constraints. Anthropology, called on for legitimation, serves the most meager of rhetorical purposes. History and myth, genuinely difficult to distinguish, are conflated and confused virtually with glee. (On this, see both the text and "The List." The footnotes are equally revealing.) Progress and communications offer parallel examples.

Hirsch is neither so naive nor so ignorant as this might suggest. His rhetoric depends upon an epistemology that he attempts to root in science, specifically educational psychology, another legacy of the Enlightenment. That is, the need for national background knowledge as the foundation of cultural literacy derives its support from something in addition to examples of tribal society, Hirsch's father's business letters, presumptions of authors about audiences of readers, and quotations from social scientists.

First of course is a formula or equation: communication rests upon knowledge, knowledge upon literacy, and literacy upon cultural literacy (see, for example, pp. 12–13). This is, for Hirsch, axiomatic. It depends nevertheless upon formal schooling and interestingly the stuff of the foundation, of cultural literacy itself, is "necessarily vague," "superficial," and "limited in extent." It requires nevertheless the support of science; here Hirsch brings forward the notion of "schema," or the role of background knowledge for effective reading, devoting a lengthy chapter to a review of presumably relevant research.

As rhetorical support, this is fascinating. As evidence—scientific, logical, or contextual—it is at best problematic; at worst it exposes one of the central epistemological fallacies of cultural literacy according to Hirsch. First, it is not clear, nor does Hirsch really argue, that background schema for learning to read can bear the weight of the all-important goal of cultural literacy. The roles of memory, and distinctions between long- and short-term memory, and the retention of vague, often superficial gists of meaning simply do not function in an analogous manner for reading by itself and for developing an overarching, "mature," "competent," and "comprehending" cultural literacy. Distinctions between literacy and language, of great concern to linguists, are totally ignored. Ironically, in seeking this kind of support, and in placing his own case on its foundation, Hirsch risks his larger effort.

Among the many complications two stand out: the issue of individuals bringing "meaning" to texts, written or otherwise, and the implications of the necessarily superficial foundations of knowledge. It is equally significant that Hirsch misses completely the crucial roles of *practice* and *content* of learning, reading encounter, and usage, despite the central place they occupy in the relevant psychological literatures on reading and other forms of everyday competence and cognition.

With respect to the first complication, note that Hirsch writes about how language is understood: "we construct an elaborated model of what the words *imply* and store that. . . . we always go beyond a text's literal meanings to supply important implications that were not explicitly stated by the words of the text" (pp. 38–39). To recognize this *without* considering the nature of and necessary conflicts in interpretation muddies the waters. It drastically reduces the value of Hirsch's use of the psychology of reading as a foundation for cultural literacy. Even if it were possible for a primary school curriculum to be built on and transmit the elements of cultural literacy, unless their *meaning* and *interpretation* in different contexts and in various combinations were also systematically and uncritically taught, "acculturation" in "cultural literacy" would not succeed in promoting the seemingly complementary goal of a "mature literacy."

At this juncture, we must ask: how do the avowed goals of "standard" or "shared" relate to those of "mature," "true," "comprehending"? if the contradiction is more than superficial, the concept and construct themselves are contradictory and self-limiting. In Hirsch's approach, there are simply no grounds on which to believe that the former goals would lead to or promote the latter, or that a useful, critical literacy would result.

As to the second complication, Hirsch plumbs the depths of American culture more deeply than he seems to realize. If Daniel Calhoun's brilliant archeology of dominant tendencies in learned intelligence in the United States is accurate (and I believe it to be largely so), formulaic approaches and skills to problem solving have long been the desired outcome of schooling and a central feature of the curriculum. In the midst of the so-called golden age of a shared culture, Calhoun concludes that children did gain the bare mechanics and yet "once they progressed to more complex matter, [they] relied on these elements and little more. They called out the words in a selection rapidly, and articulated them plainly for a listener who had the printed words to follow. But whether he understood whole passages and ideas was hardly doubtful. He did not." What the young mind demanded and was presumed to need were "automatic responses and rule-of-thumb techniques" enabling one to become "a productive member of society."[7] Perhaps this is what Hirsch wishes to regain; perhaps this is what all the to-do is about—a "national" literacy that is acculturating, superficial, and vague.

There is another epistemological fallacy that completes the circle surrounding and imprisoning Hirsch's cultural literacy. This is what we might call the linear or teleological fallacy, that *if* children in schools acquire some familiarity with the lengthy, arbitrary list constituting the national culture and thus achieve cultural literacy, then all else will follow: from a higher, mature literacy and communications competence, to civic, national, and economic progress, to individual advancement, and to the attainment of the good life. How this rings of the 18th- and 19th-century faith in institutionalized schooling; how poorly we cope with such legacies today![8]

Can we but conclude that the assumption on which this house of cards is erected—the common, early acquisition of long lists of approved bits of vague, superficial information—is naive, faulty, and dramatically misconceived? Only such a misconception would permit the absence of key concepts of practice, use, context, and criticism with respect to literacy. Conversely, it is the only way that Hirsch's cultural literacy can evolve into such a functionalist, reductionist, and self-defeating program. And only in such an approach can a national culture rooted in conflict and struggle be viewed as benign, democratic, and pluralist. Perhaps literacy in the form of a 5000-item list is the only possible conclusion! My fears far exceed those voiced by Hirsch himself at the end of his book about the sorry, stale, and confused results of a curriculum thus defined. Anachronism is only one quality it will assume.

In pursuit of cultural literacy and a dictionary (without definitions) of its contents, any sense of literacy as a dynamic and critical ability is lost. To Hirsch and company, we must ask, with Johan Galtung:

> What would happen if the whole world became [culturally] literate? Answer: not so very much, for the world is by and large structured in such a way that it is capable of absorbing the impact. But if the whole world consisted of literate, autonomous, critical, constructive people, capable of translating ideas into action, individually or collectively—the world would change. (1976, p. 93)

Reviewers critical of *Cultural Literacy* have branded Hirsch's views as "academic pipe dreams" and "cocktail party views of education."⁹ Those perspectives miss the point and fail to grasp the truly limiting, alienating, and subversive dimensions of the project.

With no concept of literacy as practice, critical or useful in any larger sense, or as dynamic for individuals and groups, Hirsch offers no solution to problems of present-day schooling or educational policy. He unknowingly repeats the efforts and errors of the past 200 years. He also misunderstands the nature of culture and of learners who influence their own learning. Emphasizing the pursuit of shared information, he neglects the kinds of politically and culturally agreed-upon meanings and interpretations, the result of conflict and struggle among the visions and values of differing persons and groups, that in fact constitute a political culture. But that of course is *not* the goal of cultural literacy, which willfully ignores politics, social structure, and social relations as well as cultural change and conflict.

Those of us who struggle for an alternative approach—deem it for now, critical literacy—must turn our energies elsewhere. The approach we are seeking requires a broadly based literacy that connects critical thinking with the skills of critical reading and writing in politics, economics, and social relations as well as in a larger cultural sphere, a literacy no longer limited to alphabetic abilities and to a historical basis that is static and acculturative. A critical literacy of course recognizes the significance of common knowledge, but it sees it as a consequence of criticism, as changing and transforming, not as inflexible and timeless. It does not separate "skills" from "content" but strives to link them dynamically. The critical literacy we are seeking must be based not only on a radically revised and more demanding curriculum, but also on an epistemology and theoretical critique that grasps the centrality of ambiguity, complexity, and contradiction to literacy and to life itself.¹⁰

Notes

1   See for example "A Dunce Cap for America," *Newsweek*, April 20, 1987, pp 72–74; "Scholar Decries Cultural Illiteracy in America," *Chronicle of Higher Education*, April 22, 1987, p. 3; "Ideas People Think With," *New York Times Book Review*, April. 26, 1987, p. 36; *Dallas Times Herald*, April 12, May 11, June 21, September 28, 1987; *D-The Magazine of Dallas*, June, 1987, p. 160.

2   I refer here to the writings and prognostications of those who identify themselves with movements ranging from "back-to-basics" to "excellence in education," most prominently WILLIAM BENNETT (now U.S. Secretary of the Department of Education), DIANE RAVITCH, and CHESTER FINN. See among a plethora of statements, as relevant examples, RAVITCH and FINN (1987): FINN, RAVITCH, and ROBERT T. FANCHER (1984): FINN, RAVITCH, and P. HOLLEY ROBERTS (1985); and RAVITCH (1985).

3   Note here HIRSCH's creation of a foundation to "create standardized tests of students' general knowledge" with a board of experts offering "a 'Good Housekeeping-type seal of approval' to textbooks and other curricular materials that properly attempt to im-

prove students' cultural literacy" (*Chronicle of Higher Education*, August 5, 1987, p. 2) and the JOHN D. and CATHERINE MACARTHUR Foundation's new program of "grants to boost literacy."

4   The phrase, of course, is from *The Communist Manifesto*; the complete passage is, "All fixed, fast-frozen relations, with their train of ancient and venerable prejudices and opinions, are swept away, all new-formed ones become antiquated before they can ossify. All that is solid melts into air, all that is holy is profaned, and men at last are forced to face . . . the real conditions of their lives and their relations with their fellow men." The irony in my use of the quotation is completely conscious and intended.

5   See GRAFF (1987); see also CHISEK (1981). HIRSCH's own efforts to use historical interpretations and materials in his Introduction, on educational history, and in Chapter 3 on language history are laughably ignorant.

6   In the latter, HIRSCH, however uncomfortable, joins hands with another "man of our times": ALLAN BLOOM (1987); see my review in *Transaction/SOCIETY*, Nov.–Dec., 1987, among the many critiques now appearing.

7   CALHOUN (1973), pp. 80–85, 130–131, Chapter 2, passim.; see also GRAFF (1979), Chapter 7, and GRAFF (1987).

8   See GRAFF (1979, 1987).

9   See, for example, PATTISON (1987) and BROOKFIELD (1987).

10 I refer readers to two fine new books that are not receiving the attention they merit: FRAATZ (1987) and TUMAN (1987). TUMAN comments intelligently and critically on HIRSCH's essays preceding *Cultural Literacy*.

References

BLOOM, A. (1987). *The closing of the American mind*. New York: Simon & Schuster.

BROOKFIELD, S.D. (1987, September 16). E. D. Hirsch's cultural literacy: A cocktail party view of higher education. *Chronicle of Higher Education*, p. B2.

CALHOUN, D. (1973). *The intelligence of a people*. Princeton: Princeton University Press.

CHISICK, H. (1981). *The limits of reform in the Enlightenment*. Princeton: Princeton University Press.

FINN, C., RAVITCH, D., & FANCHER, R. T. (1984) *Against mediocrity*. New York: Holmes & Meier.

FINN, C., RAVITCH, D., & ROBERTS, P. H. (Eds). (1985). *Challenge to the humanities* New York: Holmes & Meier.

FRAATZ, J. M. B. (1987). *The politics of reading: Power, opportunity and prospects for change in America's public schools*. New York: Teachers College Press.

GALTUNG, J. (1976). Literacy, education and schooling. In L. Bataille (Ed.), *A turning point for literacy: Adult education for development. The spirit and declaration of Persepolis*. Oxford: Oxford University Press.

GRAFF, H. (1979). *The literacy myth: Literacy and social structure in the nineteenth century city*. New York: Academic Press.

GRAFF, H. (1987). *The legacies of literacy: Continuities and contradictions in western society and culture*. Bloomington: Indiana University Press.

PATTISON, R. (1987, May 30). On the Finn syndrome and the Shakespeare paradox. *The Nation*, 710–720.

RAVITCH, D. (1985). *The schools we deserve*. New York: Basic Books.

RAVITCH, D., & FINN, C. (1987). *What do our 17-year-olds know?* New York: Harper & Row.

TUMAN, M. C. (1987). *A preface to literacy: An inquiry into pedagogy, practice, and progress.* Tuscaloosa: University of Alabama Press.

6 Literacy, Education, and Fertility, Past and Present: A Critical Review

Among the accomplishments of social scientists and historians, the explanation of demographic events and behavior certainly does not rank high. Of the varieties of demographic variables to which sustained attention and major efforts have been directed, fertility remains among the most inexplicable, even though it has received the most attention. Immense efforts have gone into the analysis of both historical and contemporary data on fertility patterns and their changes; a literature truly daunting in its size and sometimes in its technical virtuosity has resulted. The changing course of the birth rates—marital and nonmarital—of different racial, ethnic, age, and socioeconomic groupings has been relatively well charted for recent centuries in much of the western world. The rises and falls and many of the correlates and associations of fertility rates have been documented too. Nevertheless, our understanding of the causal structure of fertility and of changes in birth rates is far from clear; confusion, problems of data comparability, definitions, and often unstated assumptions mark the relevant discussions. Explanation has not been achieved to the satisfaction of many (see References and Selected Bibliography, esp. Hawthorn, 1970; Easterlin, 1969, 1974; Leibenstein, 1974).

It is not the purpose of this chapter to wade fully into the morass of fertility studies past and present; the author would surely sink rapidly into the swamp. We shall instead examine a small, but quite significant piece of the larger puzzle: the relationships that join education and literacy to fertility patterns, or, perhaps more accurately, those relationships that are sometimes said or found to relate these factors.

The explication of the causal structure of fertility decisions, as well as fertility goals and ideals, is far from clear, and competition rather than consensus or cooperation all too often marks the various theories and accounts of this form of vital behavior (Leibenstein, 1974; Hawthorn, 1970). In addition, the numerous attempts to present causal models and explanations draw on a wide range of factors, including those taken to represent societal and individual modernization;

class and / or status; place of residence; type of work; religious, ethnic, class, racial, and family origins and present status; age and timing of vital events; and educational attainment.[1] Despite the relative lack of agreement on how many of the proposed associations might actually 'fit' together causally and interpretively, one factor appears in a great many studies and summaries as especially significant. If a broad consensus does exist, it revolves around *education,* or *literacy,* which stands as its proxy in most historical-demographic studies and in much contemporary research of less developed areas. As Peter Cox summarized, 'Education has a special value of its own. . . . Literate people are more likely to adopt such measures than illiterate ones' (Cox, 1970, p. 398). Or, in the usual platitudinous terms, the Commission of Population Growth and the American Future proclaimed in 1972, 'There is abundant evidence that higher educational attainment is associated with smaller families in the United States' (US Commission, 1972, pp. 155–156).

In this chapter, I wish to reexamine the proposed relationships between education and literacy and fertility behavior and goals. I discuss both contemporary studies and those few historical attempts to specify and explain the nature of the relationship and the role of literacy and education in changing patterns of fertility. In so doing, I offer a critical commentary on these studies and their results, specifically seeking to elaborate how education is conceptualized as an independent variable. I contend that the common ways, or the paradigmatic manner, in which education is viewed accounts largely for the role it typically is found to play. In this way, critical questions about the analysis of fertility data are raised, and critical perspectives on the role of literacy and education discussed. Through such a prism, the results of different studies will be reviewed, and an attempt made both to reexamine the relationships found commonly and to inquire into the important differences in patterns of results. We begin with a review of the 'received wisdom,' the rather general consensus on education or literacy in fertility studies and its qualities.

The Received Wisdom: An Overview and Discussion

A review of a large sample of fertility studies that attempt to include the role of education within their parameters (statistical, theoretical, or programmatic) is a fascinating exercise. The researcher finds first a huge literature, sprinkled liberally with a variety of types of data and definitions, statistical techniques, and formulations. At first glance, there seems to be a surprising and apparently reassuring degree of consensus on the importance of education, as well as on the directionality of its contribution to the resulting patterns. Nevertheless, when the surface is broken much of this agreement and consistency begins to blur, if not in fact disappear. Problems of comparability of data, definitions, and, perhaps more importantly, contradictory results provide a first warning. Beyond that point, caution and skepticism increase when the reader finds longitudinal and time-series results compared with analysis of differential fertility patterns, educational attainment of husbands and wives used sometimes interchangeably, and a wide variety of qualifications and exceptions introduced into interpretive attempts with astonishing frequency. Skepticism begins to turn to doubt when we find that changing levels of education and / or literacy seem to lead sometimes to lower fertility and at other times to increasing birth rates. Finally, the pattern of results and analytical attempts begins to suggest that education, usually conceptualized and specified as an independent and quite significant variable, may in fact play a more indirect, mediating role in actual behavioral circumstances. These, I am aware, are sweeping statements even if they derive from a perusal of this vast body of data and literature. We must relate them to the data and analyses available to us, beginning with more recent studies.

The type of discussion I consider to represent the 'received wisdom' is effectively exemplified by Donald J. Bogue in his widely respected *Principles of Demography* (1969). Bogue includes, in his elaborated consideration of the educational impact on fertility, both recent US Census Bureau data and international comparisons, concluding from surveys of both that 'throughout the world there seems to be a strong inverse correlation between the amount of educational attainment and the level of fertility' (1969, p. 693). Although he finds real differences in patterns by contrasting *cumulative* fertility (which correlates in his 'expected' direction) with *current* patterns in 1960 data (which reveal higher fertility both for groups of married women with more and for those with less education), his overall conclusions and emphases stress the role of education in reducing birth rates.[2]

This perspective is revealed much more strikingly in this review of the international fertility pattern. Set within the limitations of the rather outmoded 'demographic transition' paradigm, Bogue finds the roles of both literacy and education, which he uses interchangeably, to be strong indeed. Correlational analysis of national aggregates shows very strong relationships between 'per cent of the demographic transition completed' and per cent educated at 'level 1' or higher and per cent in school (+ .75, + 79). Per cent illiterate has the highly negative, inverted relationship of − .77; impressively, these are the highest coefficients in his results. Bogue therefore concludes:

> Although these results are very crude, they suggest that rising educational levels, increased school attendance, and elimination of early marriage are much more powerful in promoting fertility reduction than simple urbanization and rising levels of income. A major driving force behind fertility control appears to be education.
>
> It is noteworthy that educational level alone accounted for 56 per cent of the total variance in demographic transition. Adding all the other variables managed to account for an additional 16 (1969, p. 675).

Bogue of course is aware that his correlations are less satisfactory than those of others who have applied multivariate techniques (for example, Adelman, 1963;

see summaries of many studies in Hawthorn, 1970). Rather than review a large number of such attempts, it is sufficient to repeat Bogue's conclusions about them: they show a *'negative* relationship between level of educational attainment and fertility' (1969, p. 677). Despite intriguing contradictions in some results and deficiencies in all these studies, to which we return later, Bogue is quite satisfied to rest with his general statement quoted above, extending it in his examination of US data to argue that with each succeeding level of education comes a progressive lowering of birth rates—a pattern of consistent relationships due to educational differentials.

While Bogue reflects the normative conception of education's role in fertility behavior, under the rubric of transition theory, other authors and even 'schools' with particular approaches do not stop at this point of clear, simple, and linear relationships. Indeed, within the broad consensus, we may point to a variety of distinct subapproaches and interpretations. Classification and categorization always risk oversimplification and distortion; the example at hand is no exception. Nevertheless, it is useful to point to the following schools of demographic and fertility interpretations and to discuss previous attempts under these classes: varieties of economic theories, especially those involving 'structural modernization' and the 'new home economics'; demographic transition theory (under which Bogue places his own analysis); and psychological and attitudinal forms of modernization theory, which have been very popular recently, as well as some rather undefined forms. It should be plainly stated that broad (and some not so broad) areas of overlap exist; the distinctions made here are primarily for the basis of discussion and clarity—they are not meant to exaggerate differences, which can in actuality be quite slight. No attempt at a comprehensive survey or enumeration is intended.

Economic Theories

Despite the rejection of economic determinism by most academicians in the United States, economic interpretations of fertility have held a special appeal. Economic considerations of course underlie many of the analytical attempts that have been made, but discussions that stress the primacy of material circumstances and responses to them and their changes among childbearing populations have always had a large following. More recently, in fact, the 'new home economics' has split other students into camps of acclaim and of critical dismissal.

In an important article, Harvey Leibenstein (1974) has reviewed a large number of economic approaches to explanations of fertility, so we need not pursue a detailed summary. His excellent commentary and summary calls attention to the important role accorded to education in many of the economic approaches. Leibenstein points first to the 'profusion of theories' in the area, discussing transition theory (see below), his own work, the 'Chicago School'—the 'new home economics'—and other contributions.

Today, the most widely discussed and debated work results from the efforts of the new home economists, whose work largely derives from the orientation of the neoclassical 'human capital' approach and early efforts by Gary Becker (T.W. Schultz, 1973; Becker, 1960).[3] The hallmark of these approaches is the attempt to reduce virtually all factors and personal decisions to the paradigm offered by the human capital economics, its assumptions about calculating economically oriented decision-making, and the econometric techniques used to 'test' the resulting mathematical formulations. Microeconomic consumption and marginal utility theories underlie these fertility analyses, estimating the changing 'prices' of children to married couples and attempting to determine both 'price effects' and 'quality of children.' Children, finally, are treated as stocks of human capital. Education is almost universally accorded a prominent position in these formulations. As Theodore W. Schultz states:

> The education of parents, notably that of the mother, appears to be an omnibus. It affects the choice of mates in marriage. It may affect the parents' preferences for children. It assuredly affects the earnings of women who enter the labor force. It evidently affects the productivity of mothers in the work they perform in the household, including the rearing of their children. It probably affects the incidence of child mortality, and it undoubtedly affects the ability of parents to control the number of births (1973, S8–9).

Moreover, he is 'impressed by the evidence that the relationship between additional schooling of mothers and the number of children is strongly negative for the early years of schooling of mothers,' a conclusion with which others do not always concur. Nevertheless, the new home economists certainly share an acceptance of the broad outlines of education's perceived contribution to fertility.

Before we delve more deeply into this approach, it is well to note the qualifications that even Schultz raises. 'The task of specifying and identifying each of the attributes of the parents' education in the family context is beset, he warns, 'with analytical difficulties on a par with the difficulties which continue to plague the economic analysis of growth in coping with the advances in technology' (1973, S9). Moreover he seems equally concerned about the lack of a continuing negative relationship between additional education and fertility. This is only one 'puzzle,' to use his term, in the approach's attempt at explanation.

In certain studies, proponents of the new home economics have sought to relate their general theoretical perspective to empirical data and to state mathematical representations that are potentially quantifiable with econometric techniques. Examples include De Tray's efforts at speculative model-building, which assume that 'the effect of a change in female education or wage rates should be larger in absolute terms and contribute more to the explanatory power of the estimated equation than changes in male education or wages' (1973, S79), and his result that female education has a 'significant negative effect' on numbers of children, following however the role of female earnings (S92–93). Other studies find the expected negative relationship between wives' schooling and number of children. Gardner in fact finds a stronger correlation for wives' education than for her wages, family income, and husband's education: -0.42 to -0.56 (1973, S107). Although he is uncertain about just how education contributes, his analysis stresses schooling as 'one of the most consistently significant variables,' with its coefficient showing 'remarkable stability' (S117). Intriguingly, Gardner is skeptical about the strength and consistency he discovers in his rural North Carolina data; the results are 'in a sense *too good* for this interpretation because the effect of schooling remains practically the same when the observed price of the wife's market time is held constant' (S117–118, italics added). Nonplussed, he discusses three ways of relating the results to the theory. These involve alternatives ranging from the effects of schooling on relative prices of kinds of time, increased psychic benefits of work, and increased productivity; the second interpretation seems to him the most 'straightforward.' Yet, problems result from implications hinging on questions of 'tastes,' which bring the explanation outside the model per se. Consequently, he returns to the third option, one consistent with the model, concluding that the education-fertility relationship is nonlinear. In sum, and largely in accord with other studies within the framework of this school, Gardner concludes that increases in wives' schooling decrease family size significantly.

Still within the bounds of the new home economics, Robert T. Michael stresses the role of schooling in creating greater access to fertility-control information and more extensive use and approval of contraceptive technology. He shares with many of the modernization theorists an emphasis on the conscious planning consequences of schooling. In his data from US Census Bureau surveys, he finds a negative relationship with either husbands' or wives' education and an increase with levels of schooling, which he also notes in non-US studies. 'While many of these simple correlations are not high, their consistency over so many groups is corroborative' (1973, S140). He is able to conclude that education 'lowers contraceptive costs by reducing the information costs'—raising effectiveness and aiding in best selection and use—and 'by raising the marginal product of the couple's time used in conjunction with any specific contraceptive device' (1973, S148). Education also has an effect on the marginal benefits, for unwanted children represent a higher cost to more educated couples. Unfortunately, the data analysis does not enable the researcher to make an interpretive choice among these alternative explanations (1973, S160–161). Other studies within the paradigm report similar conclusions, although the strength and consistency of relationships differs by types of data, place and time period, and levels of education. The roles of male's and female's education vary in their contributions too (Ben-Porath, 1973; T.P. Schultz, 1973).

A great many objections have been raised against the approaches, methods, and techniques of the new home economists. Effective general summaries appear in Leibenstein (1974) and Blake (1968), which need not be repeated. Some of these problems (some of which are accepted by the home economists themselves) relate to our concern with the educational variable. Overall, the approach and its assumptions place grave, perhaps debilitating, restrictions on the behavior of human beings; there is no firm evidence that most individuals or couples consciously or unconsciously make the marginal utility and cost 'calculations' that the approach assumes. The roles of culture and tastes and of tradeoffs (for example, between costs of childbearing and rearing, working, and further schooling, especially for women) are never explicitly taken into account. Consideration of children as goods with 'qualities,' or as 'consumer durables' in Blake's words, may retard rather than advance explanations; calculations of gains and losses remain fuzzy. Leibenstein concludes that this theory is both 'potentially falsifiable' and 'an interesting intellectual game' (1974, pp. 466–7).

More specifically, problems result from the use of the variable of education. First, results, as indicated gently above, are often more ambiguous than they might seem. We can point to the tremendous range of correlation coefficients generally relating education negatively to fertility, the mixed pattern of results when both wife's and husband's schooling are introduced into equations, the 'mixed bag' of results on the effects of higher levels of education, and differences with regard to the linearity or nonlinearity of the relationships. Some studies in fact find a *positive* relationship between education and number of children (T.P. Schultz, 1973). Real ambiguity and confusion lurk beneath the apparently smooth surface.

Significantly, these same or quite similar problems also mark other economic approaches, which only partially derive from the specific orientations of the home economics school and its economistic assumptions. Readers should justifiably be disturbed by results that almost alternatively substitute women's work and wage levels and their education with each other as the more significant factor, especially when the critical relationship tying the two is only occasionally discussed. This last consideration leads to a fundamental point: the conceptualization of education as a variable leaves too much to be desired. This crucial failure again encompasses too many of the approaches examined here, as will be seen. In this case, most of the studies mentioned hardly pause to consider the operational role of schooling in influencing fertility patterns, goals, or decisions.

The weakness of discussions relating female education to work presents a telling and representative illustration. Those attempts, such as Michael's (1973), that consider schooling as contributory to increases in information, planning, technological awareness, and skills are both exceptional and severely restricted—and ultimately incomplete, especially when compared with attitudinal modernization approaches. Differences between awareness and use, like those between thought and behavior, can be confused as well as ignored, as Michael himself acknowledges (1973, S141). While he seems content with 'intuitive plausibilities' and limitations of data and interpretation, we perhaps should be more demanding, especially because of consistent findings of weak correlation as 'corroboration.' In sum, education—regardless of level—is hardly conceptualized in either theoretical or empirical terms; its role seems to be assumed (hardly a surprise in itself [Graff, 1975: Introduction]) and more precise 'specification' not to be required. Nevertheless, the variety of problems and complications discussed here, which are more common than exceptional when compared with other approaches, points to a special deficiency and a cloudiness surrounding the precise role of this factor. We return to this point later.

In addition, it is important to recognize that the greatest cost involved in the 'quality' of children is most likely to be education, most of whose costs are provided free or relatively inexpensively by the state. The contribution of education to choices between work, childbearing and rearing, and increasingly more education itself is problematic, as is education's impact on tastes and cultural considerations and 'net opportunity costs' of mothers' time. None of these relationships, potential or read, is directly confronted in the available literature.

Other important attempts at economic explanation include those of Kasarda and Heer. John D. Kasarda recognizes the importance of the educational factor in fertility analysis, but interestingly he relegates it to the position of a 'background variable' along with urbanization and industrialization because he is uncertain whether its contribution is one of causation or correlation. To him formal education is important not simply because of its assumed intrinsic value and significance, but because of its influence on the quantity and quality of women's work (1973, p. 314). 'Moreover, the more years of formal education women have, the more likely they are to be in the modern sector of the working force, i.e. as salaried employees in a modern type of factory, office, or other such employment' (1971, p. 311). His approach is more guarded and cautious than many others, and considers education to play not an independent role but one that prepares, streams, or channels (mediates) female workers into more 'modern' kinds of work. Kasarda's account of declining fertility stresses the rate of female labor force participation outside the home, along with low economic activity rates for children. Education, while still important (a major variable), is reduced in its significance. This seems a more realistic tack to take; nevertheless, education continues to lack conceptual attention, and its own 'modern' qualities, as well as the nature of its contribution to 'modern' work, remain unquestioned and unexamined.

In an important article, David Heer presents what we might term an 'integrated checklist' approach, in order to evaluate the economic developmental relationships of and impacts on changes in birth rates. Education figures in his formulation most directly with regard to children. As do a number of attempts, Heer comments on the rising costs of children's longer stay in school and the cost to parents of continued dependency as contributors to fertility declines (1972, p. 111). He does not mention at all the role of education for either parent, although his presentation includes many of the usual correlates and causes of increasing levels of schooling. Instead, it is the effect of higher costs for children's schooling, a simple and direct factor, that is important to his explanation.

Sweezy (1971) discusses the 'economic explanation' of fertility changes in twentieth-century America in an article largely aimed at introducing qualifications to Easterlin's analysis. To Sweezy, education—again given hardly any conceptual attention—is not a major factor; rather, income changes, and the shifting attitudes that accompany them and direct their expenditure by the households, are more important. He concludes that economic factors alone are too simple to explain fertility changes. Education, while recognized as contributing to change, is seen to increase fertility in specific situations of changing attitudes and increasing incomes, especially during the post-World War II baby boom—an event that has seriously challenged most fertility explanations. We shall shortly observe the various attempts to incorporate such unexpected changes into normative theories.

Other economic theories merit only the briefest attention; largely they either are derivative or comprise aspects of the larger efforts. These include the roles of changing levels of infant mortality, socioeconomic status, threshold levels in income and / or education, and changes in norms and institutions (Leibenstein, 1974, pp. 464–470; Hawthorn, 1970). Education is considered in most, if not all, of the studies that fall under these approximate headings; it is accorded both direct and indirect status. For example, changes in infant mortality rates are certainly related to changing educational patterns: parental education may in some times and places result in declining rates, just as declines may stimulate greater 'investment' in children's education. The issue is far from clearly resolved, as Tilly (1973) makes clear. Education is even more directly related to socioeconomic status; in fact, there is a direct reciprocal relationship. Students seem generally aware of this, and as a result tend to use status or class rather interchangeably with educational attainments—often oversimplifying and confusing the issues as much as advancing their resolution. Indeed, this confusion between education, class, and socioeconomic status and the common lack of specification is certainly a principal failing in much of the literature. Education contributes increasingly to status or class, although its full equivalence is more often assumed than demonstrated. In addition, education's role in reproducing the social structure from generation to generation (and in supporting social mobility) has direct impact on fertility decisions and demographic behavior. It is regrettable that these aspects are never fully recognized in the literature. Attempts at estimating threshold levels at which the effects of schooling are not strongly related to fertility or at which the effects diminish or reverse their contribution are too often circular ways of explaining otherwise contradictory or ambiguous empirical results. They are seldom built into sophisticated analytical or theoretical efforts. Similarly, the use of changing institutional and normative factors, both obviously if not clearly or consistently related to education, is more often circular than sophisticated and insightful. They commonly are seized on after the fact, rather than as initial factors built into research designs. Consequently, their roles can be oversimplified and viewed entirely too linearly, especially when expressed in terms of microeconomic theory. Real complications and confusion arise when tastes are added to norms and institutions in explanatory attempts.

These last considerations take us to our final two examples in the economic analysis of fertility: the work of Leibenstein and of Easterlin. These form the two most sophisticated and, most probably, the best analyses put forward to date. Their stress on the multiplicity of factors and their consideration of education represent a significant advance over most of the literature surveyed here. In some ways, it may be demeaning to their own formulations to place them under this rubric; nonetheless, I merely follow their own labeling in so doing.

Harvey Leibenstein offers an intelligent and honest critique of his own work, as well as a sketch of how it might be adjusted (1974, pp. 460–461, 470–475). Commencing within the then-pervasive influence of demographic transition theory, he had earlier (in 1957) offered a marginal utility interpretation that sought to avoid the limitations of many neoclassical, self-interest maximizing assumptions. From his presumption that families attempt to balance utilities (especially in prices or costs) against disutilities, he concentrated on 'higher-level birth orders,' assuming fully rational decision-making only for 'marginal children.' The approach therefore speculatively balanced utilities against disutilities, inquiring at what point one outweighed the other and relating fertility behavior to that calculation. The problems in application are admitted, even if the economistic assumptions and complexity of relationships are barely hinted (1974, pp. 460–461).

Leibenstein is critical of narrowly construed economic approaches; he considers income differentials more important than increasing 'costs' of children (which, he concludes, are rarely a sufficient basis for explanation). Wisely, if elusively, he finds the determinants of fertility to be 'manifold,' including the 'historically unique,' the socioeconomic, and the cultural as well as the economic ones. As does Easterlin, he chooses to place his explanation under the broad guise of modernization theory. Taking tastes, prices, and household decisions on expenditures as variable, rather than as constants, he postulates the effects of changing socioeconomic and income statuses. Decisions therefore result in fertility or in alternative expenditures, depending on what goals and standards are set by one's defining 'social influence groups' and the pressures and commitments that act on the individual.

The reader can appreciate Leibenstein's efforts to circumvent the limitations of economic assumptions while building on the economic tradition. However, he seems to rest his revisions far too early and not to take into account many of his own criticisms of the approaches of other economists. The context of modernization seems to offer very little, and sociocultural influences play a narrow and artificial role indeed. Most critically for our purposes, he neglects the educational factor almost totally, despite its obvious contribution to socioeconomic and social influence groups and to alternative expenditures and commitments.

Richard Easterlin, especially in his more recent statements, makes the greatest efforts to surmount these and previously discussed failings and limitations and to specify the role of education. The theory is cast explicitly in terms of modernization, stressing the effects of both structural and attitudinal consequences of socioeconomic change. This perspective deviates from many other modernization theories in its explicit economic orientation, although modernization is typically used to cover an array of social, demographic, psychological, political, and economic developments (Easterlin, 1974, p. 262). The modern decline in fertility is seen as an intrinsic part of this process, especially through the rise of attempts to deliberately control and restrict family size. In applying economic analysis to fertility explanation, Easterlin focuses on these principal components: demand for children, potential output of children, and costs of fertility regulation. The demand for children results from the interrelations of income, price of children in relation to goods, and subjective preference for children compared with goods; actual fertility is determined through the impact of income and preference on the price of children (1974, pp. 266–268). Modernization acts on this calculus through innovations in public health and medical care, education and communications, urbanization, new goods, and per capita income growth. Education, of course, is the factor that concerns us most directly here.

Easterlin commences from assumptions embodied within the main traditions; he finds education to be 'one of the most pervasive factors influencing completed family size,' operating on demand, output, and cost of fertility regulation, the three components in his analytics of fertility (1974, p. 269). How does the educational factor operate? It acts on fertility by diffusing improved knowledge of personal hygiene, food care, environmental dangers, and the like, and may also work to break down traditional beliefs and customs and consequently to undermine cultural practices. In some of these ways fertility may well be increased as a result (1974, p. 269). Education, along with mass media, may also work to lower the cost of fertility regulation: providing information, altering cultural norms, challenging traditional beliefs, and encouraging a 'problem-solving approach to life' (1974, p. 269–270). Additionally, education may decrease the price of alternative goods in relation to children by improving the income-earning chances of women and thus increasing the cost of child rearing; compulsory education may also increase the cost of children by reducing their possible contribution to family income (1974, p. 270). In terms of tastes, education may reduce the desire for children by encouraging new lifestyles that compete with traditional values of large family size, as well as by 'liberating' women's lifestyles. Finally, education may contribute to higher standards for child care and child rearing, by both raising the cost of children and emphasizing quality over sheer numbers.

Thus, Easterlin offers a blend of economic theories and more structural and psychological approaches to modernization, setting attitudinal shifts within a context of socioeconomic transformations and importantly placing the role of education well within a larger perspective on change and development (1974, p. 270). The overall emphasis lies in accounting for fertility decline through lower desired family size; the stress falls on regulation opportunities and changing (motivational) relations among costs, demands, and alternatives. Possibly contradicting his exploration of the role of education, he attempts to decrease the normative emphasis on rational calculation and linearity in both experience and causation, offering a model that, ideally, can accommodate a variety of patterns of change and assumptions.

Easterlin's proposal remains untested empirically. His own historical work, which is reviewed below, remains largely outside his theoretical excursions (1976). It remains to be seen how well this model will perform analytically in empirical tests, so it is well to withhold possible criticisms on that side. We may note, however, that he seems to forestall some of the potential criticism in his concluding remarks about the flexibility of this approach to differing assumptions and various patterns of experience. Among these, one might place patterns of rises as well as falls in birth rates, especially as they relate to education as noted above. In this way, we might remain wary about his broad and loose conceptualization of education's contribution. For one thing, the relative failure of family limitation and planning efforts in much of the 'underdeveloped' world should make us less than sanguine about some aspects of his formulation. Moreover, T. Paul Schultz's (1973) findings in Taiwan of a *positive* correlation between increasing levels of schooling and fertility, among others, remain significant and challenging.

In other ways, Easterlin fails to offer a sufficiently elaborated conceptualization of the impact of schooling, preferring an omnibus or pluralistic approach. His language of 'mays' and 'tend'-encies belies much of the confusion and complications in previous conceptual and empirical forays. Education, if we extrapolate from his presentation, can function both directly and indirectly; it can diffuse information and contribute to changes in desires and tastes and can also contribute to work and income. Now, all this is certainly true and germane, and his approach is one of the most efficacious in the literature. It remains, nevertheless, unsatisfactory. It is too diffuse and does not specifically speak to the contradictory findings in data-based studies of the role of schooling; education continues, as in most studies, to be idealized, almost romanticized, in keeping with the western tradition and the received wisdom. Dichotomies of new and old, modern and traditional underlie the formulations, while the many contradictions are not explicitly confronted. Other costs, including simultaneous presence and lack of choice for many women, are not taken into account, nor are the possible accommodations that attempt to blend elements of new and traditional arrangements, as in much of women's work and in many aspects of schooling. Availability or diffusion of information and technology and / or technique are not the same as use, as recent history in much of the world so poignantly reveals. Finally, norms and worldviews do not so swiftly evaporate under the assault of literacy and education or hypothetical modernization 'syndromes.'

Education acts in many ways, directly as well as indirectly, positively as well as negatively; it can liberate or rationalize, but it can just as easily reinforce new patterns of control whose implications remain to be recognized and analyzed more completely. Among these implications fertility must be included. In economic, as in other approaches to fertility, we await new and more appropriate considerations of education and its contribution.

Demographic Transition Theories

Of all the theories advanced to account for changing demographic behavior, transition theory is undoubtedly the most elegant and parsimonious. Over almost half a century, it has tended to dominate analysis and debate, although it remains unclear whether anything near a majority of students was even comfortable with it. Major texts such as Bogue's (1969) and Petersen's (1975) continue to use it as an organizing principle. The theory, or its major variants, is undoubtedly too well known to require summary here. While transition is indisputably in decline, its long hold over discussions and its continuing appeals to many require that we consider the role it assigns to education in the explanation of fertility.

Recall first the strength of the role that Donald Bogue gave to education and literacy in his discussion cited above. Bogue serves well as a representative of this school, which along with others places education very high in its lists of influences and contributions to fertility behavior. Common to many varieties of transition theory is a solid consensus about the critical role of education and / or literacy; considerations of education include that of women and children, contributions to value changes and cultural norms, and diffusion of information and techniques. To some, like William Petersen, education has 'several advantages over occupation as an index of social class,' it applies even to women who are not married, and the expected negative relationship of educational levels with family size may be located in international comparisons (1975, pp. 527–528, 558, 625, 627). Education secularizes populations that undergo its effects: their traditional attitudes are 'refashioned' and they are provided with 'fresh opportunities for putting them to work' (Stolnitz, 1964, p. 34). This effect is perhaps felt most strongly by women (Westoff, 1964, pp. 111–112). Finally, as Steven Beaver argues in his interesting recent attempt at revising and resurrecting demographic transition theory, education, as indexed by either school enrollments or literacy, generally demonstrates the predicted relationship, sometimes emerging as 'notably powerful.' It is one of the 'best predictor variables' of natality and child-woman ratios (1975, pp. 30, 36).

It is important that some of the major failings of transition theory, which count heavily toward its decline in recent years, include the role of education. I think it fair to conclude that, of all those surveyed here, transition theory has had probably the loosest and weakest conceptualization of education; among other problems, levels of formal schooling and literacy have been sweepingly interchanged, despite the problems of definition and comparison inherent in such an enterprise. Education has meant all things and has played a wide variety of roles in the various formulations of demographic transition. It should not be very surprising that complications are so often found.

We can take Beaver's study as one example. We have already noted the prominence accorded to education and literacy. Both in his summaries of other studies (many of which may be found in the References) and in his analysis of Latin American data, he discovers the following: (a) direct negative relationships tying education and / or literacy and fertility; (b) a strong role for urbanization (which many studies qualify or reject), operating through literacy as well as directly; (c) a strong role for female labor force participation, presumably working through the schooling of women; (d) literacy rates associated with fertility 'in the "wrong" directions, even in the whole sample,' with female literacy sometimes having 'a positive association with natality when other variables are controlled';

(e) the distortion of literacy as well as of school enrollment as an indicator, especially with regard to age structures and lag-times; and (f) multivariate analysis revealing education to be very 'weak' (1975, pp. 36, 37, 75, 125). This pattern of results speaks for itself.

There are other difficulties, too. Recall Bogue's recognition of the contradictory patterns that result when current fertility is compared with cumulative. Examinations of longitudinal with cross-sectional or census data reveal similar complications, exacerbated by the fact that some studies seem unknowingly to use both types of data and analysis. Many studies encounter difficulties as a result of confusing the different effects (which are far from clear) of different levels and amounts of education and of levels of educational attainment with literacy, which is not a very discerning indicator when taken alone. Different and often crude measures of fertility often accompany the use of different indexes of education; comparability is then either precluded or totally inappropriately attempted.[4]

Perhaps the most severe challenge to transition theory was the recent post-World War II baby boom in the West. Educational attainments of both men and (especially) women and labor force participation of women reached new heights, but simultaneously birth rates reversed their long-term decline and rose unexpectedly to impressive levels. Much of the data studied to account for this reversal of all predictions made by transition, as well as most other, theorists indicated that highly educated women often led in increasing family size.[5] So, in this historical case, as in some others as indicated above, the expected influence of education on fertility was in fact reversed. Many interesting but relatively unconvincing explanations have been offered for this. Bogue and, to some extent, Petersen, point to postponement as a factor in inducing 'extraordinarily high rates of fertility'; the divergence between current and cumulative fertility is called on too, confusing more than explaining (Bogue, 1969, p. 711; Petersen, 1975).

More often we read about 'convergences' cancelling out the expected role of educational differentials; however, this is more descriptive than explanatory (Petersen, 1975, p. 526; Westoff, 1964, pp. 117–118). Earlier marriage and postponement of contraception (including inefficient use) are also raised in this context (Kiser *et al.*, 1968, pp. 40–49, chapter 9). Class, racial, residential, socioeconomic, as well as educational differentials are brought into this analytical fray (Kiser *et al.*, 1968; Farley, 1972; Bradshaw and Bean, 1972; Davis, 1972). Differential approaches and statistical techniques continue to reveal rather different relations (Kiser *et al.*, 1968: esp. chapter 9). One who wades into this mass of analytic and data confusion is likely to throw up both arms and retreat quickly. Such a reaction, while perhaps a sane one, would be a discredit to some sincere attempts at broader conceptualization and at placing the correlations and associations in a wider context. Nevertheless, whether tastes, lifestyles, ideology, consumption patterns, 'conservative' fertility desires, suburbanization effects, or the like are considered, education continues to play a role quite contradictory to that expected of it and to that accorded in most formulations. No explanation relating theory to empirical data succeeds in building a role for the educational factor that encompasses both positive and negative relationships with fertility. This failing, while perhaps most central to the tradition of the demographic transition theorists, is shared by other approaches as well—this perhaps is the most important of the various relationships.

Modernization Theories

The final group or school to be examined is modernization theory. Clearly, most of the approaches considered thus far place themselves within an overarching notion of modernization, and of course there are overlaps of detail and of larger conceptual issues among many of these perspectives. This last group stresses the social psychological or attitudinal consequences and outcomes of more structural, socioeconomic aspects of the processes of transformation. In some ways, too, these studies seem to share more assumptions and theoretical linkages than those of other schools. The modernization paradigm is today strong and pervasive, as is its impact on historical studies. Of this large and growing literature, only a small number of studies may be reviewed; those of Fawcett, Palmore, Clifford, and Inkeles and his associates (see also Noonan, 1972) have been selected as among the most important.

Fawcett and Bornstein (1973), Fawcett and Arnold (1973), and Palmore (1974) concentrate on social psychological and attitudinal approaches to the study of fertility, although their published studies are certainly more programmatic than empirical. Both therefore tend to be more concerned in their formulations with family size goals and desires than with actions and behavior (and their consequences). Not surprisingly, their presentations also tend to be general and vague; both explicitly place their efforts in the context of individual modernization impacts and are therefore interested in attitudes, values, opinions, and beliefs as these relate to population. Palmore terms this 'population socialization,' while Fawcett uses the language of modernization theory. In their reviews of the literature, finally, both stress the paucity of psychological interpretations (Fawcett and Arnold, 1973; Fawcett and Bornstein, 1973; Palmore, 1974).

Of the two very similar approaches, Fawcett elaborates his position on the functions of education and literacy at greater length and more explicitly. Following earlier, paradigm-setting studies by Daniel Lerner and Alex Inkeles, he conceives of 'modernity' as a 'pattern of psychological characteristics related to societal modernization' (Fawcett and Bornstein, 1973, p. 107). His principal assumption, that of a causal relationship between modernity and fertility, derives from the observation that 'in general people in modern societies have fewer children' (1973, p. 107). If fertility is to be explained, argues Fawcett, studies must include those individual personality traits that form a part of modernization. To do this, cultural and religious values, social-structural effects, perceptions of environment and resources, and personality traits, as they interrelate and cohere, are central to the program. Education, of course, receives a high priority in the resulting conceptual schema. From other studies, he accepts the conclusion that those who are more educated, literate, urbanized, and exposed to mass media also exhibit key aspects of the 'modern' individual. Importantly, Fawcett recognizes that with regard to education and literacy, as well as to other presumed 'socializing' factors, few studies 'have been designed in a manner to permit clear inferences about causality' (1973, p. 125).[6] Nevertheless, previous efforts are apparently sufficient for him to continue:

> It is not surprising, but nonetheless interesting, to note the pervasive influence of formal education. It is not surprising because education is after all a preparation for modern life, and measures of individual modernity are bound to reflect that. There is a built-in relationship between education and some (but not all) of the items on modernity scales. The connection between education and modernity is of particular interest here because education has been shown in other studies to be a major factor affecting fertility. The effect of education on fertility is, of course, not direct: children are not taught in school to have smaller families, but rather the attitudes, values, and behaviors learned in school interact with subsequent life experiences to produce an overall trend toward lower fertility (1973, p. 125).

Intriguingly, Fawcett follows Inkeles and his associates in stressing the educational role of school, city, and factory, while pointing out that women—whose attitudes are seen as the most important—are less involved than men in each of these 'modernizing' settings (1973, pp. 125–128). Another, and related problem is that most studies of fertility center on the education of women, correctly so, while most studies of modernity and its derivations focus on men.

In an empirical study of 'acceptance of family limitation,' Inkeles and Karen Miller, working with the same assumptions and conceptualization as Fawcett, set out to test the formulation. As in many other papers and books, Inkeles first maintains that desires, goals, and especially attitudes are 'good predictors' of behavior; however, this is not confirmed or even tested in the study (Miller and Inkeles, 1974, p. 169). The data at hand derive from Inkeles's massive Modernization Project, a study of psychological modernity in six relatively underdeveloped nonwestern countries; data for *men* in Bangladesh, India, Israel, and Nigeria are analyzed here. Miller and Inkeles report that the median correlation of 'education or literacy' with acceptance of family limitation is highest, although urbanization, occupation, and living standards, which follow, have similar coefficients. However, most important remains the fact that the correlations are quite low, with medians on the order of $+.12$ (1974, pp. 177–181). Education-literacy, their composite variable, ranges from a high of $+.25$ to a low of $+.09$, with a median of $+.19$. The conclusion is contrary to that hypothesized and expected: 'In three out of the four country samples we examined, contact with modern institutions (including the school) in itself had little or no direct influence on the acceptance of family limitation' (1974, p. 183). Still, these researchers are convinced of the pervasive impact of modernity as a coherent syndrome of personality traits. Accepting the patterns of very weak correlations and inconsistencies, they nevertheless conclude that experiences with modern institutions do in fact have 'considerable impact,' evidently producing their effect through influence on the modernity of attitudes and values'—a statement readers must regard as equivocal and tenuous in view of the data analysis. Education, they argue, 'seems to have a more substantial impact on psychological modernity, and through it, on acceptance of family limitation, with some independent effect on the latter . . .' (1974, pp. 183–184). Given the very low correlation coefficients and the patterns of inconsistencies and variations, these statements must be regarded with considerable caution.

A final empirical example comes from Clifford's (1971) study of a sample of women in Lexington, Kentucky. He, too, seeks to determine the role of values and attitudes related to fertility, and presumes that a cluster of attitudes both exists and coheres that may be appropriately termed 'modern.' His analysis shows that both value orientations and socioeconomic status can be related to fertility goals and behavior, although not all the findings are statistically significant and the differences between modern and 'intermediate' women are quite slight. Importantly, and in opposition both to Fawcett and to Miller and Inkeles, socioeconomic status tends to fare better as a predictor than value orientations (1971, pp. 42–45). Although he fails to examine this relationship in multivariate analysis, Clifford concludes that value orientations 'intervene' between position in the social structure and fertility behavior, while status is more closely related to actual fertility decisions (1971, p. 46). He also fails to test for the relationship between these two factors.

Despite their elegant formulations and the promise with which they have been trumpeted, attitudinal-modernization explanations of fertility have yet to reveal their worth in specific tests, unless one is content with Miller and Inkeles's interpretations. There remain a number of problems with the use of modernization perspectives on the educational contribution to fertility actions. Modernization, however one may define it, is not a linear, evolutionary, and irreversible leap forward, nor are its impacts on individual men and women clear and positive, as much of this literature implies. More specifically, virtually all studies cast in this mold continue to report variabilities and inconsistencies; both Fawcett and Bornstein and Miller and Inkeles (1974, p. 167) note that the general trend relating modernization and fertility, and often education as well, 'admits of many variations, irregularities, and even reversals' (Fawcett and Bornstein, 1973, p. 109). The empirical attempts certainly sustain this observation. The 'reversals' remain quite important here, for the problem of education's ability to correlate both positively and negatively with fertility rates plagues all the approaches examined here. Despite education's 'pervasive' influences on fertility and its presumed role in producing modern attitudes, values, and behavior, neither formulations nor tests have proven very satisfactory or confidence-generating. These are elements that tie together the larger problems linking both these studies and the dominant approaches to education-fertility analysis, whether they derive from economic, demographic transition, or modernization bases. Much of the problem lies in the way in which education or literacy is conceptualized as a contributing variable.

Problems Common to Education-Fertility Analysis
Without a full recapitulation, I think it fair to conclude in summary that, despite a tradition of post-Enlightenment faith in education as producer of progress and a heavily weighted received wisdom about the educational contribution to fertility behavior, the empirical results and the explanatory formulations are less than satisfactory. Principal problems lie in the empirical analyses that find education and / or literacy correlating both positively *and* negatively with fertility, the definition of variables and the comparability of data, the analytics (e.g., which confuse literacy with different levels of schooling, men's with women's education, 'modernity,' and status, etc.), and especially in the conceptualization and expectations of the educational factor itself. As Hawthorn reports in his useful survey, some studies 'find no association between mere literacy and fertility, literacy presumably being possible at an educational threshold well below that considered necessary, if not sufficient, to adopt the kind of rationality and orientation to the future that make for successful birth planning and control' (1970, p. 76). Others of course, with their often unstated assumptions about the meaning and significance of literacy and basic education, find the former quite sufficient. Any number of attempts have been advanced to account for this problem, as well as for those that derive from the existence of both positive and negative correlations. None, however, has offered consistent and explicit formulations within which to place the patterns of reversals, inconsistencies, and irregularities.

Beyond these problems, we also encounter those relating to the confusion not only of literacy and higher levels of attainment but also of education and socioeconomic group, class, and income indicators (see, e.g., Hawthorn, 1970; *passim;* studies cited in his annotated bibliography; studies reviewed here; Matras, 1977, pp. 23, 190, 194; Matras, 1973, pp. 344–352). The confusion and complications are too many and too severe to bear excessive recounting here; their existence and importance have undoubtedly been established. The problems impinge, we need to note, on matters far more important than academic understanding and applications of theory to research. The implications weigh on public policy, balanced and appropriate development and planning, and the future of societies and economies (Ridley, 1972; Miller and Inkeles, 1974), whether contemporary or historical.

At the heart of much of this difficulty (which also plagues newer historical studies, as we shortly observe) lies the question of the *conceptualization* of literacy and education. The role of this factor in fertility studies and modernization schemata is not at all exceptional; this problem is found in a wide variety of studies of development and change (Graff, 1975; Introduction; chapters 2 and 5, *passim*). Education and literacy, it is commonly if not universally assumed, have an intrinsic importance and close association with these processes; yet explication, elaboration, or basic questioning is seldom found in this literature. Education, regardless of level, is seen most often as a simplistic quantity / quality, which affects attitudes / behavior directly (or sometimes indirectly) in a linear (sometimes, but relatively rarely, nonlinearly) and overwhelmingly progressive way. It supposedly contributes to value and attitudinal reorientations toward the 'modern,' making for greater self-interest, rationality, planning, and calculating—all of which are expected to influence fertility. Nonetheless, sometimes it affects tastes, desires, and preferences, which in certain, usually too vaguely defined circumstances can influence fertility in rather opposite ways. Yet, as seen above, studies simply do not reveal the expected results; assumptions are not met. Reconceptualization and rethinking, as the historical cases also illustrate, are demanded if our understanding is to be advanced.

Historical Studies of Literacy and Fertility

Historical studies of fertility are relatively few; those attempting to examine empirically the role of education are even fewer. This of course is the reverse of the vast body of more contemporary studies, and the interested student is torn between regret and relief. Before considering the way in which literacy and education might be reconceptualized, it is important to review those few relevant historical forays. We readily observe the pervasive grip of the contemporary approaches and paradigms on the historical studies. Economic interpretations, demographic transition theory, and modernization approaches organize and dominate the historical literature, although given both limitations of data and paucity of work these divisions are sometimes less clear-cut. In fact, I divide, arbitrarily to be sure, the material into only two main categories—the economic and modernization—for the demographic transition theory either underlies the studies (conceptualized in much less rigorous terms than in some of the contemporary literature) or simply is not dealt with to any significant extent.

That a stress on literacy and education pervades these historical studies is easy to establish. Consider Ansley Coale, for example, who writes: 'In European national experience, the only factor apparently always changing at the same time that fertility declined was literacy,' although in a telling qualification he continues, 'but the onset of the fertility decline has no consistent relationship with the proportion literate at the time' (1969, p. 18). Interestingly, Coale concludes his overview by commenting that none of the standard indexes (including literacy and education) confirm by correlation an association with the origins of the European fertility decline. He finds the range of associations to be too 'broad,' despite the fact that he casts his preliminary interpretation explicitly in terms of the key elements of economic, transition, and modernization theories (1969, pp. 17–18).[7]

Economic Interpretations
As with contemporary attempts at explanation, economic perspectives tend also to dominate historical studies. We first consider two studies of the European

fertility decline conducted under the auspices of Coale's major project on that theme at Princeton University's Office of Population Research. The work of Knodel (1974) on Germany and van de Walle (1976) on Switzerland follows quite similar procedures and techniques and is set within the same perspective. John Knodel hypothesizes fully in terms of the received wisdom:

> In general we expect increases in education or literacy to have a depressing effect on fertility, at least during the initial phases of the fertility transition. Education should foster the flow of communications of all types and thus facilitate the diffusion of new information and attitudes towards birth control and family size. Also increased education should contribute to the spread of rationality and secularism, which may be crucial to the acceptance of family limitation (1974, pp. 231–232).

This explicit orientation makes the fact of his rather disappointing findings all the more important. Knodel, as others, is forced to use male literacy (of military recruits) as his educational index. Moreover, his data are deficient for this test because most of Germany had exceptionally high levels of literacy, and those few areas with highest fertility were also areas of highest illiteracy (1974, pp. 235–236). His high negative correlations here are a less than convincing illustration of the expected relationship. In a subsequent multivariate analysis, however, the role of literacy 'practically disappears' (1974, pp. 237–238), and when regional influence is controlled the resulting correlations are much weaker (p. 239). Finally, the role of education is only one of the expectations that go unmet: indexes such as female labor participation, often seen as a by-product of increased education for women, show virtually no relationship with fertility decline. Whether the relationship sought is in fact an incorrect one, or whether Knodel's concerns about 'moving thresholds' and data deficiencies are the main problems, it is impossible to tell. Overall, the performance of educational indicators is not especially noteworthy.

Francine van de Walle's (1976) Swiss analysis is set within the same context. She, too, is forced to use data on male recruits, although her measures allow some differentiation of attainment levels. Interestingly, she finds a definite negative association between education and marital fertility and a decrease in fertility 'concomitant' to a rise in educational level. She also finds this relationship lasting over time. (Note that she used district-level data, not individual-level data; Knodel also employed aggregated data). Van de Walle's findings seem direct and definite; their difference from those of Knodel and others, however, cannot be explained on the basis of the data and relationships made available. Yet, within her brief study there are hints of other important relationships that should not be overlooked. Education in Switzerland, not surprisingly, was highly correlated with urbanization and type of occupations, especially administrative and commercial work; conversely, education and proportion in agricultural work were negatively related. Unfortunately, among her correlations van de Walle does not examine the interrelatedness of education, urbanization and occupation, and marital fertility. It therefore remains impossible to indicate the nature of these relationships, important though they surely are.

In fact, she hints at her own questions in this area: 'Nevertheless we cannot tell whether low fertility was the result of better education or whether both education and low fertility were accepted as new acquisitions of modernity' (1976, p. 5.65). Many factors, she concludes, were at work in reducing levels of fertility; it is difficult to assess precise roles and contributions because they are hard to isolate statistically. Until this is achieved, alternative arrangements of the factors remain possible, and these analyses provide insufficient guidance.

In a historical study Easterlin (1976) examines factors in the decline of farm family fertility in nineteenth-century America, using rural census data on households. Among the variables he examines are the literacy of wives and husbands and school attendance of children. He explicitly tests for the role of education in shaping attitudes and finds, contrary to expectations, that 'the indicators of education, though imperfect, do not show very important differences' between newer and older areas of settlement in fertility rates. Neither do rates of school attendance (1976, pp. 108–109). Similarly, he also rejects hypotheses of increasing 'opportunity costs' of women's time and labor qualifications. Summarily then, in a brief but important examination of key hypotheses, Easterlin finds a remarkably small role for education in accounting for differential fertility in farm populations.

Don R. Leet, a former student of Easterlin, has completed a similar analysis, focusing on a more narrowly defined population, that of ante-bellum Ohio, and reporting on a more sophisticated statistical analysis, in attempting to explain the nineteenth-century fertility transition. He, too, tests for the expected relationship of education (1976, p. 370), and discovers from regression analysis that 'education (as measured by illiteracy) and urbanization had much less effect on fertility than either the agrarian economic situation or the cultural heritage of the settlers' (1976, p. 372). Not only are correlations of literacy and fertility rates rather unimpressive, but they decline as secular trends, so that 'one can only give them a minor role in the overall fertility decline' (1976, pp. 374–376). Finally, this trend in relationship is inconsistent with statewide movements in fertility. Thus, in two important recent analyses of the education-literacy-fertility relationship, attempts to confirm the received wisdom are disappointed. These results, indicative of the problems raised earlier, should serve as guidelines to the cautious and critical. It is important to note that these studies utilized data from cross-sectional analysis of households and trend analysis of cross-sectional county-level aggregates, respectively.

Other analyses of the education-fertility relationship that focus on special groups reveal similar difficulties. Michael Haines (1977), for instance, examines fertility ratios of coal miners, a group traditionally notorious for high fertility and for the female concomitants of early marriage and very low rates of labor force participation. Not surprisingly, low literacy rates were associated with these patterns, for after standardization, comparisons show that 'literate parents had lower fertility than illiterate parents at all dates' (1977, p. 43). Interestingly, though, this result did not obtain when unstandardized child-woman ratios were compared (1977, p. 44). In a multivariate analysis, illiteracy continued to relate negatively with fertility in three of the four census years examined (1850, 1860, 1880). These correlations remain revealingly low: at $+.11$, $+.11$, $-.02$, and $+.06$, only the first two were statistically significant at the 5 per cent level, and the fourth was not significant at 10 per cent (1977, pp. 43–45).

As one who has followed the patterns this far might expect, there is indeed an education-fertility relationship, but its level of significance and strength are not impressive. The other results from correlation, regression, and multiple classification analysis suggest, moreover, that literacy's (or illiteracy's) contribution may well not be direct, but may work through its undoubtedly high interrelationships with such factors as ethnicity, place of residence, occupation, and age at marriage, all of which demonstrate higher degrees of association with fertility. Until analysis of such mediating and indirect relationships is completed, we will continue to read about 'pervasive' influences of education and literacy, accompanied by rather low correlations.

In a second special-group study, Meeker (1977) examined the fertility of black Americans between 1860 and 1910, inquiring about the role of education. This represents an explicit historical test of the 'new' economic models of fertility in which 'literacy and schooling also play a role in determining family size' (1977, pp. 400–403). Coefficients for illiteracy, found to be significant and positive in all but one case, range from $+.18$ to $+.31$ (1977, pp. 405–406). Analysis of 'pooled' regressions shows a similar pattern, if somewhat weaker coefficients (1977, pp. 407–408). Interestingly, Meeker shows that black fertility rates are more sensitive to changes in education than those of whites, yet somewhat less sensitive to influences of urbanization (1977, pp. 408–409). The fact remains that this otherwise important study examines the impact of urbanization, income, and labor force participation along with education. Since the schooling variable once more does not reveal itself to be unique or especially powerful, we might be well advised to consider it contributing through the others, with which it undoubtedly is interrelated. This approach hints at more fruitful formulations.

In a final economic example, Peter Lindert's (1977) data analysis shows the ways in which education's role can vary over time, and also how its contribution can contradict important elements of the received wisdom. Lindert examines US fertility patterns since the Civil War, finding in Census Bureau data that education, up to 1930, related inversely to fertility ratios (1977, p. 263). Interestingly, and in opposition to a central tenet of the standard approach, he discovered that in 1900 education seems to have promoted earlier marriage yet lower fertility; presumably this may be accounted for by increased and more effective mechanical contraception. By 1940, in fact, education is positively associated with marriage and, indirectly, is now positively related to fertility as well (1977, p. 263). With a partial exception in 1950, this relationship holds through the 1960 census and disappears by 1970—obviously as a result of the baby boom.

To explain both the long- and short-term shifts, Lindert uses a multiple-factor economic approach, not too unlike Easterlin's, although their measures differ. The irregular role of schooling must be taken into account, and Lindert is sensitive to this issue. After raising the possibility that education itself might act as a 'mirage' for other variables, he considers that, in changing contexts, education may actually raise the sensitivity of fertility to economic and other changes influencing the desirability of extra births. 'The more educated had achieved a considerably lower fertility than those with less education by 1940. Having greater control over fertility, they were able to raise their birth probabilities more sharply and certainly when the economy revived with World War II' (1977, pp. 266–268). This results in greater instability in the birth rates of educated couples. Despite this promising formulation, data-analysis tests do not provide firm confirmation, especially in terms of relating education to other influential factors, as we might have anticipated (1977, p. 268). We, along with Lindert, are left with a variety of factors, including education—all important, but not yet placed into a theoretical, empirically tested framework offering a persuasive explanation of the education-fertility relationship. The historical study of this connection owes much to contemporary perspectives: it has raised critical questions about the received wisdom while proving unable to either escape or supplant it. Its findings suffer from similar patterns of reversals, irregularities, and inconsistencies.

Modernization Theories

Varieties of economic interpretations of fertility and of education-fertility relationships have long been popular in historical work (Banks, 1954; Banks and Banks, 1964; Eversley, 1959); more recently, modernization theory, imported directly from the social sciences, has become very influential indeed. Modernization approaches are well represented by the studies of Edward Shorter (1973a, 1973b) and Maris Vinovskis (Vinovskis, 1976a, 1976b; Vinovskis and Hareven, 1974). These are instructive examples, for Shorter's approach is highly speculative and interpretive, at some remove from case studies and empirical verification, while Vinovskis's is closely bounded by his cross-sectional case studies. Their use of modernization concepts differ accordingly, yet assumptions and presumptions remain within the same paradigm.

In recent years, Shorter has emerged as a leading theorist of the modern decline of fertility in Western Europe and the making of the modern family; his efforts have sparked considerable controversy, as well as acrimonious debate. In his view, sexual behavior is tied to the changing values and attitudes stimulated by the socioeconomic expansion of the capitalistic marketplace and its impact on individual men and (especially) women (1973a, 1973b). Interestingly, Shorter's earlier work is more explicit in attempting to describe the mechanisms for this modernization of values and attitudes. In an article first published in 1971, he stated, 'The final sensitizing variable crucial in value change appears to be exposure to primary education.' He continued:

Formal education, if only of a rudimentary sort, is calculated precisely to give the individual a sense of self by teaching logical thought. Learning to read requires the acquisition of linear logic, which mode of thought then surely spreads to other intellectual processes and levels of perception, to say nothing of the logical capacities instilled by other kinds of formal education (1973a, p. 63).

This is part and parcel, according to Shorter, of the transformation of lower-class women and men from traditional to modern behavior: acquiring rational, calculating, independent, self-interested, and personally gratifying goals and desires (see also 1973b, pp. 620–622). Most importantly, in sharp contrast to the views of the others, Shorter relates this process rather directly to increasing rates of fertility (both marital and nonmarital) and *not* to fertility decline.

This is a fascinating speculation, albeit as yet undocumented and untested. Despite its impressive deviation from most other interpretations, which stress the negative relations tying fertility and literacy, there are grave conceptual problems with this formulation. To be sure, it does remind us that education can result in 'reversals'; nevertheless, this abstract view of the power of literacy simply does not bear much relationship to either the goals or the methods of reading instruction in the eighteenth or nineteenth centuries. Levels of literacy, especially among those Shorter describes, could be very low; this skill was often of a mechanical and simplistic quality. The mere acquisition of literacy, finally, need not relate to the development of linear or logical thought, or of a sense of selfhood. The common contexts and uses of literacy were often quite different (Graff, 1975, Introduction; chapters 1, 7).

Vinovskis's studies of literacy differ from Shorter's, as we have noted. He also relates education to modernization, but to declining levels of fertility. In this way, he employs the received wisdom to help explain declining birth rates and intergroup differentials in studies of New York State (1976a), mid-nineteenth-century states in the US (1976b), and Essex County, Massachusetts (Vinovskis and Hareven, 1974). Placing nineteenth-century United States in the perspective of a modernizing society, he concludes that the society was becoming 'more modern' in its attitudinal and structural characteristics. Education ranks high among the indicators and causes of such change (1976a, pp. 79–80).

In all three studies, Vinovskis derives his expected relationship, although different measures of education and different forms of fertility analysis are employed. In the New York study, a cross-sectional analysis, school attendance becomes the proxy for the educational attainment of the population. A low negative coefficient of $-.136$ shows the association between rates of those aged 5–16 attending school and the white fertility ratios. He concludes, 'If, in fact, the school attendance of children reflects roughly the relative levels of their parents, then our finding simply confirms the anticipated inverse relationship between education and fertility found in most contemporary studies' (1976a, p. 71). Among all the variables examined, however, the contribution of this proxy for education is not impressive (1976a, p. 65). In his study of the determinants of interstate fertility differentials in 1850 and 1860, Vinovskis again tests for the contribution of education, this time employing adult literacy rates as the value for schooling (1976b, p. 377). Through multiple regression analysis of state-level data, he discovers a very high relationship between illiteracy and fertility ratios in both census years. 'The results,' he concludes, 'were striking—the educational level of the white population was the single best predictor of fertility differentials among the states in 1850 and 1860' (1976b, p. 393). This is a revealing finding.

These findings parallel contemporary studies, as he notes. Moreover, they support my conclusion, from comparisons of findings with different research designs, that the higher the level of aggregation and the further the data are removed from the level of individuals, families, or households, the higher the degree of association. This serves to reinforce my second conclusion, that education is not always, nor necessarily, an independent or direct contributor to fertility levels or behavior. Vinovskis's findings, as others', suggest that its influence may well be through such factors as ethnicity, urbanization or residence, and socioeconomic indicators, all of which commonly are highly interrelated with educational indicators. Considerations such as these, I suggest, are necessary to relate and reconcile findings such as Vinovskis's with those on education alone.

Finally, additional support for this interpretive revision derives from Vinovskis and Hareven's (1974) study of rural-urban differences in marital fertility in Essex County, Massachusetts. In this study, too, fertility is positively related to illiteracy, but the associations between illiteracy and both foreign birth and occupation may also be clearly seen. Although covariate and multicollinear relationships are not specifically analyzed, the overall pattern of results 'predicts' its striking and important role.

Two final studies, by Levine (1977) and Graff (1975, pp. 145–154), point the way toward the reformulation hinted at throughout this chapter. It must be stated clearly that both these studies are limited, by sample size, geographical and chronological span, and by very simple techniques of data analysis. Their findings are far from conclusive; nonetheless, they remain important as indicators. Both studies consider the literacy-fertility relationship in the context of family formation.[8] Although population, place, data, and method differed, Levine and Graff indicate that illiterate men and women probably married earlier than the literate, and may well have begun childbearing earlier as direct consequence. According to Levine, 'The age-specific fertility statistic show that the illiterate couples bore children with below-average frequency, contrast, the fertility of literate couples was higher than the average' (1977, p. 9, table 3). Economic depression, rising mortality rates, deterioration in the expectation at birth, and family limitation are all raised as possible explanatory factors for these eighteenth- and early-nineteenth-century problems. In that context, Levine's findings are more revealing than his highly tentative discussion of them. Graff's data show, however, that the earlier-marry illiterate couples did in fact have higher fertility ratios, although only slightly so, and that illiterate-headed families and households were smaller than that of literates, except in the first years of the family life cycle. He stresses economic problems and structural inequality, high mortality rates, and early ages for children's leaving home as explanatory factors (1975, pp. 146–). Both studies remain very tentative in their conclusion, to be sure.

Toward a Reconceptualization of the Education-Fertility Relationship

This lengthy, but necessary exegesis of specification and empirical examination of the education / literacy-fertility relationship has offered a critical review much of the relevant literature. Accompanying that review, a pattern of observations, deriving from hints in the findings of other studies and problems in the conceptualization of the relationship, has been put forward. The sum of these comments does not yet contribute to a thorough revision of the so-called received wisdom or to a complete reformulation. Nevertheless, it points the way and takes us a few important steps down that path.

To repeat, major difficulties encountered in this review of contemporary and historical writings include: problems of comparability, analysis, and data; results indicating reversals, inconsistencies, and irregularities in relationships, as well as rather weak levels of association; acceptance and reinforcement (perhaps even reification) of traditional assumptions and received wisdom; and—both as cause and consequence and probably most important—inadequate conceptualization of the role of education and literacy.

In keeping with broad forces of western social thought, largely inherited from the twin thrusts of the Reformation and the Enlightenment, we place education among the highest of the various agencies supportive of change and progress for societies, economies, and individuals. For more than two centuries we have maintained, rather uncritically, this faith in the influences of education. More specifically, social changes, events, and popular intellectual responses of the late eighteenth and early nineteenth centuries tied this legacy closely to the problems of birth rates. David Eversley illustrates these developments in his fine book *Social Theories of Fertility and the Malthusian Debate* (1959), illustrating also the origins of economic and attitudinal types of explanations. Faith in education since that time has maintained its impressive hold over assumptions and theoretical forays, apparently deriving sufficient empirical support for its preservation. As we have seen in this chapter, neither negative results nor conceptual deficiencies have led to any significant level of critical attention, despite some dissatisfaction (e.g., Miller and Inkeles, 1974). More often, qualifications and marginal revisions substitute for reconsideration.

The analysis presented here, however, leads to the plausible conclusion that these formulations have outlived their usefulness as interpretive and explanatory modes of approach. Both the needs for and the possibilities of a new and more critical reformulation should be apparent. Education and literacy, to merely begin, might more usefully be considered to be less pervasive and powerful influences on fertility decisions and behavior (and, by implication, on other aspects of belief and action too). Second, their contributions should be viewed as less abstract and as more concretely dependent on contextual and structural correlates of the society under examination, as well as on the context and specific circumstances in which literacy is provided or acquired and the uses to which it is put (see, e.g., Graff, 1975, esp. chapter 7). In other words, a more basic, critical, and realistic conceptualization of the role of education is required. Education in this way should be seen as more often contributing its influence less directly and less linearly, functioning and mediating through and with other structural and attitude-shaping factors. The resolution of the variations in degrees of association among these factors and even in their direction of association may well be found through such an approach.

The next step awaits its takers. The road to revision derives neither from more abstract theories nor from undocumented assumptions; it follows directly from systematic criticism and hints found in many of the findings discussed here. A new conceptualization, finally, may advance from an attempt to collect a number of those hints, to develop a framework for relating them to one another and to the other important factors, and, lastly, to test and recast the new paradigm with comparative data on different levels of aggregation and behavior.

Notes

1   A perusal of the literature, even that part cited in the References and Selected Bibliography below, is illustrative.
2   This points to one not uncommon problem in such studies: different patterns of relationships when essentially different measures are used. Bogue is aware of the problem and its sources, and makes the germane if incomplete comment that 'this is an example of contradictions that can exist between current fertility and cumulative fertility' (1969, p. 711).
3   For cogent criticisms, see LEIBENSTEIN (1974); BLAKE (1968); EASTERLIN (1974); HAWTHORN (1970, chapter 4). The clearest statements and examples of this approach may be found in the 1973 special supplement to the *Journal of Political Economy* 81, no. 2, part 2 (March / April), entitled 'New economic approaches to fertility.'
4   This commentary is based on my survey of many studies and texts; see, for example, HAWTHORN (1970); LEIBENSTEIN (1974); BOGUE (1969, chapter 3 and pp. 678–679), as well as the relevant literature found in the References.
5   It is interesting to note that economic analysis, particularly that which seeks to account for and to measure the impact of changing tastes and preferences, owes much of its emphasis to this event (EASTERLIN, 1969, 1974; LEIBENSTEIN, 1974; SWEEZY, 1971; HAWTHORN, 1970, among a vast literature). Easterlin's most recent formulation, it would appear, attempts to take this into account; however, he does not seem to succeed to this reader's satisfaction.
6   I would question this statement. In my reading of the literature on individual and attitudinal modernization, I have found that many of the studies have attempted to determine causal effects and to weigh relative strengths of causal factors. These efforts have thus far been less than successful; the problem, I would argue, lies more in

conceptualization of the role of such factors as education and literacy than in research designs alone.

7   For further complications as well as an exciting social history of relevant contemporary ideas, see EVERSLEY (1959: passim), especially with regard to the overlap, historically, of economic and attitudinal change arguments, and also the origins of the emphasis on education and literacy in conceptualization.

8   LEVINE (1977) based his discussion on the results of a family reconstitution analysis of a 'proto-industrial' Leicestershire community; GRAFF (1975) examines the characteristics of illiterate- and literate-headed families, from cross-sectional analysis of mid-nineteenth-century manuscript census data in three cities in Ontario, Canada.

References and Selected Bibliography

ABU-LUGHOD, JANET (1965) 'The emergence of differential fertility in urban Egypt,' *Milbank Memorial Fund Quarterly* 43, no. 2 (April), 235–253.

ADELMAN, IRMA (1963) 'An econometric analysis of population growth,' *American Economic Review* 53, no. 3 (June), 314–339.

BAJEMA, CARL JAY (1966) 'Relation of fertility to educational attainment in a Kalamazoo public school population: A follow-up study,' *Eugenics Quarterly* 13, no. 4 (December), 306–315.

BANKS, J.A. (1954) *Prosperity and Parenthood: A Study of Family Planning among the Victorian Middle Classes.* London: Routledge and Kegan Paul.

BANKS, J.A. and BANKS, OLIVE (1964) *Feminism and Family Planning in Victorian England,* Liverpool: Liverpool University Press; New York: Schocken.

BEAVER, STEVEN E. (1975) *Demographic Transition Theory Reconsidered: An Application to Recent Natality Trends in Latin America.* Lexington, Mass.: Lexington Books.

BECKER, GARY S. (1960) 'An economic analysis of fertility,' in *Demographic and Economic Change in Developed Countries.* Universities-National Bureau Committee for Economic Research. Princeton, NJ: Princeton University Press.

BEN-PORATH, YORAM (1973) 'Economic analysis of fertility in Israel: Point and counterpoint,' *Journal of Political Economy* 81, no. 2, part 2 (March / April), S202–233.

BLAKE, JUDITH (1966) 'Ideal family size among white Americans: A quarter of a century's evidence,' *Demography* 3, no. 1, 154–173.

BLACK, JUDITH (1968) 'Are babies consumer durables? A critique of the economic theory of reproductive motivation,' *Population Studies* 22, no. 1 (March): 5–25.

BOGUE, DONALD J. (1969) *Principles of Demography.* New York: Wiley.

BOYDEN, STEPHEN (1972) 'Ecology in relation to urban population structure,' in *The Structure of Human Populations,* (Ed.) G.A. HARRISON and A.J. BOYCE. Oxford: Clarendon Press.

BRADSHAW, BENJAMIN S., and BEAN, FRANK D. (1972) 'Some aspects of the fertility of Mexican-Americans,' in *Demographic and Social Aspects of Population Growth,* (Ed.) CHARLES F. WESTOFF and ROBERT PARKE, Jr. Commission on Population Growth and the American Future, Vol. 1, Research Reports. Washington, D.C.: US Government Printing Office.

CLIFFORD, WILLIAM B., II (1971) 'Modern and traditional value orientations and fertility behavior: A social demographic study,' *Demography* 8, no. 1 (February), 37–48.

COALE, ANSLEY J. (1969) 'The decline of fertility in Europe from the French Revolution to World War II,' in *Fertility and Family Planning: A World View,* (Ed.) S.J. BEHRMAN, LESLIE CORSA, Jr., and RONALD FREEDMAN, ANN ARBOR: University of Michigan Press.

COX, PETER R. (1970) *Demography,* 4th (Ed.) Cambridge: Cambridge University Press.

DAVIS, KINGSLEY (1963) 'The theory of change and response in modern demographic history,' *Population Index* 29, no. 4 (October), 345–366.

DAVIS, KINGSLEY (1972) 'The American family in relation to demographic change,' in *Demographic and Social Aspects of Population Growth*, (Ed.) CHARLES F. WESTOFF and ROBERT PARKE, Jr. Commission on Population Growth and the American Future, Vol. 1, Research Reports. Washington, D.C.: US Government Printing Office.

DAVIS, KINGSLEY and BLAKE JUDITH (1956) 'Social structure and fertility: An analytic framework,' *Economic Development and Cultural Change* 4, no. 3 (April), 211–235.

DE TRAY, DENNIS N. (1973) 'Child quality and demand for children,' *Journal of Political Economy* 81, no. 2, part 2 (March / April), S70–95.

DUNCAN, OTIS DUDLEY (1965) 'Farm background and differential fertility,' *Demography* 2, 240–249.

EASTERLIN, RICHARD A. (1969) 'Towards a socioeconomic theory or fertility: A survey of recent research on economic factors in American fertility,' in *Fertility and Family Planning: A World View*, (Ed.) S.J. BEHRMAN, LESLIE CORSA, Jr., and RONALD FREEDMAN, Ann Arbor: University of Michigan Press.

EASTERLIN, RICHARD A. (1974) 'The effect of modernization on family reproductive behaviour,' in *The Population Debate: Dimensions and Perspectives*. Papers of the World Population Conference, Vol. 2, Bucharest. New York: United Nations.

EASTERLIN, RICHARD A. (1976) 'Factors in the decline of farm family fertility in the United States: Some preliminary results,' *Journal of American History* 63, 600–615.

EVERSLEY, D.E.C. (1959) *Social Theories of Fertility and the Malthusian Debate*, Oxford: Clarendon Press.

FARLEY, REYNOLDS (1972) 'Fertility and mortality trends among blacks in the United States,' in *Demographic and Social Aspects of Population Growth*, (Ed.) CHARLES F. WESTOFF and ROBERT PARKE, Jr. Commission on Population Growth and the American Future, Vol. 1, Research Reports. Washington, D.C.: US Government Printing Office.

FAWCETT, JAMES T., and ARNOLD, FRED S. (1973) 'The value of children: Theory and method,' *Representative Research in Social Psychology* 4, no. 1 (January), 23–36.

FAWCETT, JAMES T. and BORNSTEIN, MARC H. (1973) 'Modernization, individual modernity, and fertility,' in *Psychological Perspectives on Population*, (Ed.) JAMES T. FAWCETT. New York: Basic Books.

FORD, THOMAS R., and DE JONG, GORDON F. (1970) *Social Demography*. Englewood Cliffs, NJ: Prentice-Hall.

FREEDMAN, RONALD (1961–62) 'The sociology of human fertility: A trend report and bibliography,' *Current Sociology* 10 / 11, no. 2, 35–121.

FREEDMAN, RONALD et al. (1977) 'Trends in fertility and in the effects of education on fertility in Taiwan, 1961–74,' *Studies in Family Planning* 8, no. 1 (January), 11–18.

GARDNER, BRUCE (1973) 'Economics of the size of North Carolina rural families,' *Journal of Political Economy* 81, no. 2, part 2 (March / April), S99–122.

GOLDSTEIN, SIDNEY (1972) 'The influence of labour force participation and education on fertility in Thailand,' *Population Studies* 26, no. 3 (November): 419–436.

GRAFF, HARVEY J. (1975) 'Literacy and social structure in the nineteenth-century city,' unpublish PhD. dissertation, University of Toronto. Revised manuscript: *The Literacy Myth: Literacy and Social Structure in the Nineteenth-Century City*. New York and London: Academic Press, Studies in Social Discontinuity Series, 1979.

HAINES, MICHAEL R. (1977) 'Fertility, marriage, and occupation in the Pennsylvania anthracite region, 1850–1880,' *Journal of Family History* 2, no. 1 (Spring), 28–55.

HAREVEN, TAMARA K., and VINOVSKIS, MARIS A. (1975) 'Ethnicity and occupation in urban families: An analysis of South Boston marital fertility and the South End in 1880,' *Journal of Social History* 8, 69–93.

HASS, PAULA H. (1972) 'Maternal role incompatibility and fertility in urban Latin America,' *Journal of Social Issues* 28, no. 2, 111–127.

HAWTHORN, GEOFFREY (1970) *The Sociology of Fertility.* London: Collier-Macmillan.

HEER, DAVID M. (1972) 'Economic development and the fertility transition, in *Population and Social Change,* (Ed.) D.V. GLASS and ROGER REVELLE, London: Edward Arnold; New York: Crane, Russak.

HENRY, LOUIS (1976) *Population: Analysis and Models.* London: Edward Arnold.

HOFFMAN, LOIS W. (1974) 'The employment of women, education, and fertility,' *Merrill-Palmer Quarterly* 20, no. 2, 99–119.

HUGHES, RUFUS B. Jr. (1959) 'Human fertility differentials: The influence of industrial-urban development on birth rates,' *Population Review* 3, no. 2 (July), 58–69.

KANTNER, JOHN F., and ZELNIK, MELVIN (1972) 'Sexual experience of young unmarried women in the United States,' *Family Planning Perspectives* 4, no. 4, 9–18.

KASARDA, JOHN D. (1971) 'Economic structure and fertility: A comparative analysis,' *Demography* 8, no. 3 (August), 307–317.

KISER, CLYDE V., and FRANK, MYRNA E. (1967) 'Factors associated with the low fertility of nonwhite women of college attainment,' *Milbank Memorial Fund Quarterly* 45, no. 4 (October), 427–449.

KISER, CLYDE V., WILSON H. GRABILL and CAMPBELL, ARTHUR A. (1968) *Trends and Variations in Fertility in the United States.* Vital and Health Statistics Monographs, American Public Health Association. Cambridge, Mass.: Harvard University Press.

KNODEL, JOHN E. (1974) *The Decline of Fertility in Germany, 1871–1939.* Princeton, NJ: Princeton University Press.

KUNZ, PHILLIP R. (1965) 'The relation of income and fertility,' *Journal of Marriage and the Family* 27, no. 4 (November), 509–513.

LEET, DON R. (1976) 'The determinants of the fertility transition in antebellum Ohio,' *Journal of Economic History* 36, no. 2 (June), 359–378.

LEIBENSTEIN, HARVEY (1974) 'An interpretation of the economic theory of fertility: Promising path or blind alley?' *Journal of Economic Literature* 12, no. 2 (June), 457–479.

LEVINE, DAVID (1977) 'Immiseration, illiteracy and family life during the first industrial revolution,' paper presented to the History of Education Society and Social Science History Association annual meetings.

LINDERT, PETER H. (1977) 'American fertility patterns since the Civil War,' in *Population Patterns in the Past,* ed. RONALD D. LEE. New York: Academic Press.

MATRAS, JUDAH (1973) *Populations and Societies.* Englewood Cliffs, NJ: Prentice-Hall.

MATRAS, JUDAH (1977) *Introduction to Population: A Sociological Approach.* Englewood Cliffs. NJ: Prentice-Hall.

MAXWELL, JAMES (1969) 'Intelligence, education and fertility: A comparison between the 1932 and 1947 Scottish surveys,' *Journal of Biosocial Science* 1, no. 3 (July), 247–271.

MAZUR, D. PETER (1967) 'Fertility among ethnic groups in the USSR,' *Demography* 4, no. 1: 172–195.

MAZUR, D. PETER (1973) 'Relation of marriage and education to fertility in the USSR,' *Population Studies* 27, no. 1 (March), 105–115.

MEEKER, EDWARD (1977) 'Freedom, economic opportunity, and fertility: Black Americans, 1860–1910,' *Economic Inquiry* 15, no. 3 (July), 397–412.

MICHAEL, ROBERT T. (1973) 'Education and the derived demand for children,' *Journal of Political Economy* 81, no. 2, part 2 (March / April), S128–164.

MILLER, KAREN A., and INKELES, ALEX (1974) 'Modernity and the acceptance of family limitation in four developing countries,' *Journal of Social Issues* 30, no. 4, 167–188.

MORRIS, NAOMI M., and SISON, BENJAMIN S. (1974) 'Correlates of female powerlessness: Parity, methods of birth control, pregnancy,' *Journal of Marriage and the Family* 36, no. 4 (November), 708–712.

NOONAN, JOHN T. Jr. (1972) 'Intellectual and demographic history,' in *Population and Social Change*, (Ed.) D.V. GLASS and ROGER REVELLE, London: Edward Arnold; New York: Crane, Russak.

PALMORE, JAMES A. (1974) 'Social and psychological aspects of fertility in the United States, in *Social and Psychological Aspects of Fertility in Asia: Proceedings of the Technical Seminar, Choonchun, Korea, 7–9 November 1973*, (Ed.) HENRY P. DAVID and SUNG JIN LEE, Washington, D.C.: The Transnational Family Research Institute: Seoul: Korean Institute for Research in the Behavioral Sciences.

PERRUCCI, CAROLYN CUMMINGS (1967) 'Social origins, mobility patterns and fertility,' *American Sociological Review* 32, no. 4 (August), 615–625.

PERRUCCI, CAROLYN CUMMINGS (1968) 'Mobility, marriage, and child-spacing among college graduates,' *Journal of Marriage and the Family* 30, no. 2 (May), 273–282.

PETERSEN, WILLIAM (1975) *Population*, 3rd ed. New York: Macmillan.

POTVIN, RAYMOND H., and WESTOFF, CHARLES F. (1967) 'Higher education and the family normative beliefs of Catholic women,' *Sociological Analysis* 28, no. 1 (Spring), 14–21.

PRESSER, HARRIET B. (1971) 'The timing of the first birth, female roles and black fertility,' *Milbank Memorial Fund Quarterly* 49, no. 3, part 1 (July), 329–361.

RIDLEY, JEANNE CLARE (1972) 'On the consequences of demographic change for the roles and status of women,' in *Demographic and Social Aspects of Population Growth*, (Ed.) CHARLES F. WESTOFF and ROBERT PARKE, Jr. Commission on Population Growth and the American Future, Vol. 1, Research Reports. Washington, D.C.: US Government Printing Office.

ROBERTS, G.W. *et al.* (1967) 'Knowledge and use of birth control in Barbados,' *Demography* 4, no. 2, 576–600.

ROSSI, ALICE S. (1972) 'Family development in a changing world,' *American Journal of Psychiatry* 128, 1057–1066.

SALAFF, JANET W. (1972) 'Institutionalized motivation for fertility limitation in China,' *Population Studies* 26, no. 2 (July), 233–262.

SAMUEL, T.J. (1965) 'Social factors affecting fertility in India,' *Eugenics Review* 57, no. 1 (March), 5–15.

SCHULTZ, T. PAUL (1973) 'Explanation of birth rate changes over space and time: A study of Taiwan,' *Journal of Political Economy* 81, no. 2, part 2 (March / April), S238–274.

SCHULTZ, THEODORE W. (1973) 'The value of children: An economic perspective,' *Journal of Political Economy* 81, no. 2, part 2 (March / April), S2–13.

SHORTER, EDWARD L. (1973a) 'Illegitimacy, sexual revolution, and social change in modern Europe,' in *The Family in History: Interdisciplinary Essays*, (Ed.) THEODORE K. RABB and ROBERT I. ROTBERG. New York: Harper and Row.

SHORTER, EDWARD L. (1973b) 'Female emancipation, birth control, and fertility in European history,' *American Historical Review* 78, no. 3 (June), 605–640.

SLESINGER, DORIS P. (1974) 'The relationship of fertility to measures of metropolitan dominance: A new look,' *Rural Sociology* 39, no. 3 (Fall), 350–361.

SMITH, DANIEL SCOTT (1973) 'Family limitation, sexual control, and domestic feminism in Victorian America,' *Feminist Studies* 1, 40–57.

SMITH-ROSENBERG, CARROLL , and ROSENBERG, CHARLES (1973) 'The female animal: Medical and biological views of woman and her role in nineteenth-century America,' *Journal of American History* 60, 332–356.

SPEARE, ALDEN, Jr., SPEARE, MARY C. and HUI-SHENG LIN (1973) 'Urbanization, non-familial work, education, and fertility in Taiwan,' *Population Studies* 27, no. 2 (July), 323–334.

STERN, MARK (1976) 'Differential fertility in Hamilton, Ontario, 1851–1861,' in *Social History Project Report 2*, (Ed.) M.B. KATZ. Downsview, Ontario: York University.

STOKES, C. SHANNON, CRADER, KELLY W. and SMITH, JACK C. (1977) 'Race, education, and fertility—A comparison of black-white reproductive behavior,' *Phylon* 38, no. 2 (June), 160–169.

STOLNITZ, GEORGE J. (1964) 'The demographic transition: From high to low birth rates and death rates,' in *Population: The Vital Revolution*, (Ed.) RONALD FREEDMAN, Garden City, N.Y.: Anchor Books.

SWEEZY, ALAN (1971) 'The economic explanation of fertility changes in the United States,' *Population Studies* 25, no. 2 (July), 255–267.

TAEUBER, IRENE B., and TAEUBER, CONRAD (1971) 'People of the United States in the twentieth century: Continuity, diversity, and change,' *Social Science Research Council Items* 25, no. 2 (June), 13–18.

TILLY, CHARLES (1973) 'Population and pedagogy in France,' *History of Education Quarterly* 13, 113–128.

US COMMISSION ON POPULATION GROWTH AND THE AMERICAN FUTURE (1972) *Population and the American Future*. New York: Signet.

VAN DE WALLE, FRANCINE (1976) 'Education and the fertility transition in Switzerland,' paper presented to the Annual Meeting of the Population Association of America, Montreal, April.

VINOVSKIS, MARIS A. (1976a) 'The decline of fertility in nineteenth-century America: A model for less developed countries today,' in *Demographic History and the World Population Crisis*. Chester Bland-Dwight E. Lee Lectures in History. Worcester, Mass.: Clark University Press.

VINOVSKIS, MARIS A. (1976b) 'Socioeconomic determinants of interstate fertility differentials in the United States in 1850 and 1860,' *Journal of Interdisciplinary History* 6, no. 3 (Winter), 375–396.

VINOVSKIS, MARIS A. and HAREVEN, TAMARA K. (1974) 'Rural-urban differences in fertility: An analysis of marital fertility, ethnicity, occupation, and literacy in five Essex County towns in 1880,' revised manuscript published as 'Patterns of child-bearing in late nineteenth-century America: The determinants of marital fertility in five Massachusetts towns in 1880,' in *Family and Population in Nineteenth-Century America*, (Ed.) TAMARA K. HAREVEN and MARIS A. VINOVSKIS. Princeton, NJ: Princeton University Press, 1978.

WESTOFF, CHARLES F. (1964) 'The fertility of the American population,' in *Population: The Vital Revolution*, (Ed.) RONALD FREEDMAN, Garden City, NY: Anchor Books.

WESTOFF, CHARLES F. and POTVIN, RAYMOND H. (1967) *College Women and Fertility Values*. Princeton, NJ: Princeton University Press.

WILLIS, ROBERT J. (1973) 'A new approach to the economic theory of fertility behavior,' *Journal of Political Economy* 81, no. 2, part 2 (March / April), S14–64.

WOBER, MALLORY (1973) 'Some areas for the application of psychological research in East Africa,' *International Review of Applied Psychology*, 22, 41–53.

7   On Literacy in the Renaissance: Review and Reflections

Preface and Overview

Renaissance. Literacy. How well these words resound when linked together. How naturally and intimately their relationships strike responsive chords in the minds and, perhaps even more deeply, the hearts of historians. That connection is not in the least surprising—not to persons familiar with the historiographical literature.

The age, or ages, of the great Renaissance rebirth of learning clearly impinges on manifold issues related to the social distributions and cultural conditions of literacy. The Renaissance was, in too many ways to note, profoundly an educational and a pedagogical movement. Although this has long been appreciated, recent scholarship in the Humanities has reinforced the point and deepened our understanding. Furthermore, the era witnessed the diffusion of printing, which also influenced currents in literacy and learning. Finally, this was an age of discovery and invention, marked by exploration and advancement manifest in science, medicine, technological innovations—eyeglasses, the compass, weaponry—and in the spread of what we now term the 'European world system'; all of these helped to reshape the known universe between the fourteenth and seventeenth centuries.

The contribution of literacy to these epochal transformations has been recognized, although its precise roles are not yet well specified. Conversely, the changing configurations of European society, culture, and political economies equally, if not even more dramatically, affected the levels, roles, and meanings of literacy. That, while appreciated, is perhaps less clearly understood.

This chapter was originally presented as a contribution to the Wellcome Institute for the History of Medicine's Conference, 'Medicine. Printing and Literacy in the European Renaissance'. It draws upon and is documented fully in my *The Legacies of Literacy: Continuities and Contradictions in Western Society and Culture*, (Bloomington, 1986), Chs. IV and V.

Despite these recognitions, which have achieved the safe (and sometimes stultifying) harbour of historical commonplaces, far too little is known about the basic facts of literacy during this key transitional era of 'early modernity'. Literacy, as a subject for direct historical analysis, is something of a novelty; its literature, though expanding rapidly, is hardly exhaustive or satisfying. As I have argued at length elsewhere, a general assurance of the nature of literacy's contributions, derived from a post-Enlightenment synthesis of 'normative' humanistic and social scientific 'wisdom', long precluded the direct study of literacy as a historical factor and a fresh questioning and critical stance toward our usual expectations and assumptions of its primacy and provenance.[1] For the 'pre-statistical' era, there remain, in addition, perhaps insoluble problems of evidence, although recent scholarship points to some ways around this complication.[2]

Conceptual problems, part theoretical, part historiographic, and part epistemological, plague efforts to comprehend literacy as a historical factor and force. Briefly put, what I term collectively the 'legacies of literacy'—centuries-old and much more recently—have culminated in expectations that literacy's roles are typically linear, direct, progressive, relatively unmediated, highly pervasive, and requisite and responsible for individual, societal, and national advancement. Literacy, in this common view, is not only intimately associated with progress and modernization, but also inextricably linked with *change.* Indeed, the sheer number of concomitants asserted to accompany changing levels of basic literacy and the processes of its acquisition could fill weighty tomes by themselves. Alas, the evidence—whether statistical or more substantive—typically is revealingly scarce. As an increasing number of students are beginning to recognize, new paths to conceptualization and understanding are needed; given contemporary perceptions of 'crises' and 'declines', the need is no less than urgent.[3]

These kinds of complications confound attempts to explicate the history of literacy during the centuries that comprise the European Renaissance. That is one of my arguments in surveying our knowledge of the contours of that history. There can be no doubt that the years spanning the fourteenth to the sixteenth centuries were critical in the long sweep of literacy's history. In the same way, there can be no doubt that this history differs from its usual presentations, whether in the hands of textbook authors or authorities like Professors Cipolla or Eisenstein.[4]

What I argue here is that literacy's courses, its determinants and its influences during this period can only be grasped with direct attention to (*a*) *contradictions* in the processes of social, economic, political and cultural development; (*b*) *continuities,* as well as *changes,* in thought about literacy, agencies for transmission and dissemination, and realities of changing patterns of distribution, demand, and uses; (*c*) considerations of the variety of *outcomes* (sometimes opposing or conflicting) from such patterns; (*d*) greater than usual attention to literacy's associations with *hierarchies and inequalities;* and, perhaps most importantly for historians, (*e*) more precise specification of what *qualitative levels* and what *different kinds* of literacy(ies) are under discussion. This, it may be noted, is hardly an exhaustive list of cautions. Rather, it is best taken as a set of origin points.

Perhaps the most intractable of all such problems impinges on issues of definitions of literacy, their relationships to levels and utilities of the skills, and, together, their relationship to the limited array of sources available to the student. Given such problems, for which no grand resolution is proposed here, I focus on levels of basic or elementary skills of reading and writing, *except as otherwise specified,* in this chapter. The typical, if far from satisfactory indicator, is of course the presence or absence of a signature; such admittedly problematic sources only become available in a systematic if hardly sufficient fashion in this period.° Signs of literacy in any language, and not solely in the learned Latin, are accepted; indeed, in his era, vernacular literacy not only takes on special importance but constitutes a force in its own right. Evidence of the uses and non-uses of reading and writing lends meaning to such measures. Literacy, finally, is viewed in terms that are not limited solely to the functional or its 'functionalities'. The import of such a perspective should be apparent.

From that beginning, let us consider the subject more directly. If the preceding is granted—and about that there may be some dissent—I wish to argue the following, in brief and highly schematic form.

(i) The centuries that comprise the Renaissance era were a critical period for literacy, but perhaps more so in ways that are not so commonly stressed.

(ii) Many of the major intellectual and broadly 'high' cultural events and advances of the Renaissance age have, perhaps surprisingly, relatively little to do directly with literacy *per se.* That point need not diminish the celebration of the achievements of the era, nor lessen their relevance (if conceived differently) for the history of literacy in that time or in the future.[5]

(iii) Regardless of the usually-emphasized changes and transformations of the period, literacy's history owes a major debt to social and cultural continuities. This does not imply that literacy's contours were unchanging; they were not. Instead, it demands a greater sensitivity to the Renaissance's relations to its own past and precursors. Continuities conditioned, shaped and limited the uses of literacy during the Renaissance. Thus, the simultaneity of change *and* continuity must be grasped and grappled with.

(iv) This was an era of marked advances in rates of literacy and in changing uses of literacy. To appreciate this, in the context suggested here, firm

---

°The deficiencies of this measure are well-known. I shall not rehearse either the case against or in favour of its use in these pages. In the absence of alternatives, the historian must utilize, with caution and criticism, that which is available.

distinction must be made between levels, qualities and uses among elites (intellectual and other), middling persons, and the labouring and peasant orders. For some persons and places impressively high levels were achieved; for others little change transpired. Simple generalizations serve to describe or link neither the experiences of the differents orders of society nor, for that matter, those of different geographic places. To the contrary, unevenness and often sharp differentiation are expected and found.[6]

(v) Change, sometimes major, *is* important in this period, yet it was probably not a common experience if the mass of European populations is considered. The major transformations, with many of which we are all familiar, were often slow to develop, and sometimes gradual, hesitant, and incomplete in their challenges and penetration. The early decades of printing, as well as the onset of pedagogical and cultural reforms, may be taken as examples.[7]

(vi) Literacy's roles, determinants, and influences or associations were seldom direct or unmediated. Literacy's history, in other words, can *never* be an isolated, abstracted history; it is *one* with the larger, complicated histories of society, culture, polity, and economy. This is marked in the case before us.

(vii) Potentially most significant *and* most difficult is the striking possibility that comprehending the history of literacy in this seminal age requires breaking the bounds of traditional definitions of literacy. As usually (and I also argue usefully) termed, literacy refers to reading and writing (decoding and reproducing, if you will, the products of writing and printing). The medium of exchange, to coin a phrase, is alphabetic. That, of course, is what we overwhelmingly signify when employing the term 'literacy', something better captured by the French *l'alpha-bétisation*. I recommend maintaining this usage, but going one step further in delimiting its employment: reserving 'literacy', *if* unqualified by modifiers or adjectives, for basic levels of so-called 'traditional' or alphabetic literacy. References to 'higher' or 'critical' forms of reading and writing skills, for example, can be made by qualifying the term 'literacy'; as one result, much historical (as well as contemporary) confusion may be reduced.[8]

My point with respect to the Renaissance is slightly different. In this, I follow the implications of recent thinking and, ironically, writing, in the arts and in science and technology. This is the significant recognition that there exist very different kinds of types of literacy or literacies: ranging, it seems, from numeracy to graphicacy, to various kinds of artistic, visual, aural, and perhaps even physical skills of and for 'reading' and expressing communicatively and meaningfully. More specifically, what I propose, although not wholly originally, is that some of the greatest achievements in the arts and in technology, and probably also in science and medicine, stemmed from advances in the uses of *non*alphabetic literacy, especially from forms of visual literacy or literacies.

These, then, are my major themes. Obviously, to fully develop or document them is impossible in a brief presentation such as this. That is not my purpose here. Rather, in the remainder of this chapter, I wish to comment selectively on certain aspects of them. In so doing, I wish to suggest the outlines for a new approach to literacy's history and to hint at some speculations and hypotheses that strike one historian as worthy of investigation and reflection. I shall address the trends and levels of literacy, the patterns of uses and demands for literacy's skills, the 'meaning' of the Renaissance for literacy levels; the place of literacy in the contemporary culture(s), and, finally, achievements of 'visual' literacies. (I should note that only brief mention is made of the significance of print.)

Trends and Levels of Literacy

The bewildering variety of literacy levels during the period we call the Renaissance, and the vagaries and limitations of the written record itself, preclude any simple survey or summary, yet that variety and vagary are themselves revealing. First, they reflect in fairly direct ways the uneven and often irregular patterns of socioeconomic, cultural, and political development of the late medieval and early modern eras; that development, often conjointly with the persisting impact of religiosity, underlay—although in no linear or simple causal sense—the contours and conditions of continental literacy. However trite it may seem today, the ages of the Renaissance were part of the epochal passing of a medieval world and worldview, and the onset of an incipient modernity. Levels and uses of literacy, and the forces and motivations that impelled and shaped them, were *transitional*. The meeting of new and old, of beginnings as well as endings, is found in European literacy of the period—not yet a fully literate world.

Variety—variability—is the first point to note, although students are forever limited by the paucity of sources that reveal, directly or indirectly, patterns of individual possession of literacy's skills, typically at an elementary level. That throughout Europe levels of adult elementary literacy cannot have surpassed something on the order of 5 per cent is hardly surprising. That rural and agrarian areas (in a world that was overwhelmingly rural) had a largely non- or illiterate population is not a novel claim. Yet within the countrysides that were home to most Europeans, pockets of literacy and literate men (far less often of women, however) could be found. Although in the mass or aggregate, Renaissance Europe was neither a functionally nor culturally literate society, literacy was evidently expanding and beginning to break medieval bounds; the economies, polities, and cultures that comprised continental society were increasingly marked by the presence of literacy and the written word. Its context, however, more resembled the past than the future, regardless of some scholarly claims to the contrary.[9]

What must be stressed, though, is the *extent* of the diffusion of the skills of basic reading and writing and the *expanding patterns* of their uses. That extent *should* be seen as impressive, if not astonishing, and as unprecedented, despite being persistently restricted and uneven. Two brief examples establish my claim: the great centres of Florence and London. Florentine literacy levels have long, since G. Villani's time (1339), been celebrated; indeed, I believe that they have been exaggerated. Nevertheless, my demographic estimates suggest that perhaps as many as 50 per cent of the school-aged population were in some form of education, with perhaps two-thirds of them male. Many of them gained some post-elementary schooling. Overall, adult basic literacy was conceivably as high as 25–35 per cent, with, to be sure, sharp gender, class, status and wealth differentials. This, I emphasize, was an astonishing achievement for a time before print or public school systems. Opportunities for schooling for local youths abounded, and the city's dynamism attracted migrants who were more likely to be literate than not. Of course, Florence's achievement, not sustained long into the future, was exceptional; it can only be explained in the specific contexts of social structure and relationships, economic developments and opportunities, benefactions, cultural vitality, political structures and the like which made Florence the jewel of the Italian Renaissance. This was perhaps the limits of the possible. In numerous ways, literacy was valuable, or perceived as important to large and growing numbers of Florentines in the Quattrocento.

Whilst Florence's literacy levels were exceptional and precedent-setting, they were not quite unique. Although lacking that plurality of conjunctures that made Florence so distinctive, other important centres of commerce and trade, finance and exchange, small commodity production, administration—civil and clerical, migration, education, religious and cultural production, and surplus wealth and luxury can be located among the *urban* lights of fourteenth-, fifteenth-, and sixteenth-century Europe. One or more such places can be found in most of the regions or incipient nations of the West. Further, these were places, relatively less scarred by the Black Death and other ravages of the first half of the period, which may have seen their literacy levels rise in partial consequence.

London is a good example, well studied in pioneering work by Sylvia Thrupp and more recently David Cressy. Thrupp was able to document impressively high literacy rates for the merchant class of late-medieval London, regardless of her tendency to extrapolate too readily from her rare but limited sources. Economic, religious, and cultural needs all provided a base for high levels of literacy—especially among the merchant class—as for increasing educational opportunities and their direct support—on that foundation were built more needs for cultural consumption, status symbols, and higher levels and more sophisticated uses of literacy. As in Florence and elsewhere, the maturation and more common use of vernacular language also underlay and stimulated such growth. Literacy was also achieving a pragmatic or practical value: a relatively new one for many persons, though 'traditional' uses and motives remained crucial. Crafts, professions, and a women's culture were also positive forces. Thrupp presents evidence of a 40 per cent literacy rate amongst 'employed' males: merchants achieved a significantly high level in a group skewed toward the higher ranking occupations. Cressy's sixteenth-century data suggest continued growth in the distribution of literacy. He stresses, perhaps a bit narrowly, more or less 'functional' or practical motivations as key.[10]

London and Florence, if not unique, were not representative of the fuller expanse of the continent or even their own regional and national territories. Many places continued to experience the presence of at best a small handful of literate persons (regardless of language of literacy); some remained much like LeRoy Ladurie's thirteenth-century mountain village of Montaillou or his largely illiterate Languedoc of the sixteenth and early-seventeenth centuries. In parts of this region, in the 1570s through 1590s, only 3 per cent of agricultural workers and 10 per cent of better-off peasants could sign their names; women were virtually 100 per cent illiterate.[11] Parts of rural England were not much more often literate, as was much of Spain and Eastern Europe. England, was, overall, one of the European leaders in literacy, although it was likely to have been passed by parts of Germany and the Dutch and Swedish lands by the later-sixteenth and seventeenth century, with the penetration of the Reformation.[12]

Europe is perhaps best viewed as extraordinarily variegated 'crazy quilt', especially with regard to literacy levels. Cities and towns were regularly populated by a higher proportion of literates, and attracted more literate immigrants. They held more formal and informal opportunities for learning and for higher education. Literacy was definitely expanding, sometimes significantly. Nevertheless, the countryside was not static in terms of literacy, albeit with substantial, significant variations. Literacy, writing, and later print, and more educational opportunities (often at the level of parish priests and clerks) were penetrating, to some extent, a growing area. Naturally, the more advanced or developed regions moved farthest and fastest; medieval limits were being stretched, if not always broken. Regardless, with the rise of literacy levels (which, it should be noted, did 'take off' from medieval beginnings), real limits remained and were even reinforced. Most important were those of gender, social origins, social status and wealth ('class', if that term be allowed), places or regions of birth and residence, types of work or occupations, and similar factors. The links between literacy and stratification were growing, as were cultural divisions by states and regions. Within such a social framework, numerous forces could push or pull individuals toward or away from literacy. Yet, as Cressy, Spufford, and Laqueur all emphasize, individual motivations began to count for more and were able to overcome some obstacles.[13]

Uses of Literacy

The first generation of literacy studies, now largely completed, paid far less attention to needs for and uses of reading and writing (the two are not always the same as narrow functionalism might otherwise suggest) than to measuring or estimating patterns of distribution. The many careful counts tell us relatively little, alas, about the larger significance and meanings of literacy. The issue is nonetheless vital.

In a nutshell, the Renaissance era can well be seen as a time of changes but also of continuities. In that intersection lies its relevance for literacy's history and that of literacy for it. About both our understanding is far from complete; 'modern' assumptions have sometimes inadequately substituted for critical analysis and historical imagination. We are, I believe, only now gaining a grasp of the simultaneous circumstances of expanding and changing uses of reading and writing, reinforced and amplified by moveable typographic printing after the mid-fifteenth century; a strongly persistent 'traditional' and orally-based cultural mode of communications that limited the uses of literacy while also integrating literate with oral and aural modes, partially reshaping both; the continuing power of religion and the Church; and very real limits to both opportunities and needs for literacy's skills for most Europeans of the period. If this complicated, indeed transitional, cultural conjuncture strikes you as contradictory, that, I believe, lies as much in the history as in this interpreter(!) and constitutes an important recognition in itself.

The plethora of possible and actual uses of literacy defies simple listing or categorization; my commentary nevertheless demands such a simplification. At the grossest level, these observations seem most germane: for the largest mass of the population, there was, practically speaking, no special need for literacy. On one hand, rural peasants, agricultural workers, and small holders who constituted the greatest share of the people, had no significant pragmatic need for individual access to reading or writing. Their work and welfare did not demand it; neither did religious adherence, especially for those on the land. On the other hand, their culture, as Natalie Davis in particular has argued, placed little primacy on it; and, in any case, the written (and more, perhaps, the printed) work worked its way into their minds through church readings by notables or officials, and by a literate reading to many others who were themselves unable to read in such settings as evening *veillées* and other collective occasions.[14] Readers and scribes seem to have been available in many, if not all places.[15] With the growth of a capitalized, commercialized market and rural production for market exchange and a possible expansion of private property ownership, to the contrary, did come more formal and direct needs for and uses of literacy. This was limited and selective, of course. According to Clanchy, this process of penetration and encroachment was underway in the twelfth through to the fourteenth centuries.[16] It spread even further during the next two to three centuries. The literacy levels of landholding peasants and yeomen in some parts of Europe do show the mounting utilities of literacy's skills: both to protect oneself and one's family and to use reading and writing toward one's own and one's family advantage. Those of power, wealth, and status had many other motives and uses. Not all took up such possibilities, of course.

In addition to social, economic, and political changes that pushed increasing numbers of persons toward literacy, cultural and religious trends pulled more persons toward it. This was true before the Reformation, as Aston has demonstrated for Lollards, and more so after its onset.[17] The relationship tying literacy to such forces worked in complex ways; both sides of any equation are best viewed as at once causes and consequences; few such factors worked independently from one another. In the countryside, literacy's presence was becoming stronger from a number of motives. Yet, illiteracy remained the most common condition. Among other things, this serves to remind us that: (*a*) no linear or narrowly utilitarian interpretations will serve well; and (*b*), as Cressy (among others) observes

> First, it should be stressed that people were capable of rational action, of acquiring and digesting information, and of making well-founded political and religious decisions without being able to read or write. Illiteracy was not necessarily a bar to economic advancement nor did it stand in the way of common sense. Second, we should not assume that people were wiser or more in control of their environment just because they had become literate. The skill could be squandered, used to rot the mind as well as inform it . . ., and might find no exercise beyond scanning an almanac or signing a receipt. . . . We must distinguish the liberating potential of popular literacy from its more mundane reality. . . . Literacy unlocked a variety of doors, but it did not necessarily secure admission.[18]

But that, as critical as it is, is only one dimension of the dialectic that literacy's realities comprised. The other more frequently (though not exclusively) urban pole was changing during this era, for reasons both old and more novel. Density, wealth, and better channels for communications underlay not only more opportunities for using literacy but also stimulated (and required, too) more demands and uses. Economics, politics, popular and scholarly culture, benevolence, concern for social order, and of course religion and its imperatives joined in this, as they came together in different ways and to differing degrees in the cities, towns, and sometimes the villages and countrysides of Europe: before and after the advent of printing. As Natalie Davis notes for sixteenth-century French cities, 'this press for literacy was associated with technological, economic, and social developments'.[19]

For Florence and Venice from the mid-thirteenth through the fourteenth century, J.K. Hyde points to the following uses of literacy: new employment for long-distance commerce and finance: accurate records of transactions in ledgers including the beginnings of double-entry book-keeping, correspondence, bills of exchange, contracts, and means to transport them thus creating a new class of 'professionally literate merchants' whose literacy differed from that of previously literate clergy and lawyers. Not needing Latin, they tended to stress numeracy and some degree of calculation. This could be a literacy active and broad; its remains are of enormous bulk, as the archive of Francesco Datini of Prato demonstrates. These uses of literacy at once overlapped with similar practices of civil and clerical administrators and large landowners as well as diplomats. They differed strikingly, however, from those of literary and scholarly elites. But, as Hyde usefully explicates, in one literary genre of the early Renaissance period, 'mercantile influence is unmistakable. This is the lay autobiographies and citizen family histories which grew directly out of the books of memoranda in which businessmen recorded their personal affairs . . . [and which] being essentially private, could be elaborated with a freedom impossible in more public documents'.[20]

Importantly, the maturation, expansion, and popular (if not always scholarly) acceptance of the vernacular (as in this case, Tuscan) underlay and abetted many of these developments. With printing came a greater possibility for individual and improving uses of literacy. Such personal writing, of course, is only one sign of an emergent lay expressiveness, seen in other literary works of the period. This was also the age of Dante, his peers, and successors: another aspect of the transitional state of the era, and the forms of rhetoric that accompanied it. Diverse aspects of Renaissance culture were influenced, including forms of civic life and artistic creation, although many elites and scholars were revealingly ambivalent. Literacy was by no means an independent stimulus, as factors that propelled its increase also stimulated its diverse and sometimes novel employments. Histories, chronicles, political writings, philosophy, classical translations, in addition to literature—prose and poetic—and perhaps also to some extent medicine and science reflected this, and benefited. Great strides did not await the advent of printing. Importantly, oral culture—rhetoric, as spoken—was at least as great a beneficiary, if not even more so. This was one, but not the only, manifestation of Renaissance humanism. Nevertheless, the predominating religiosity of the age was not replaced; if anything, for prospering as well as popular classes, it may well have *increased* with expanding literacy and its uses. Early printing also demonstrates this. Of course, such important uses of literacy barely touched directly the truly popular classes, the *menu peuple*.

For the more 'ordinary' residents of towns and cities, the changing uses of literacy were different but still significant. Religion was one common, underlying factor. With the multiplication of manuscripts, vernacular writings, including religious materials, block prints, heresies and dissent, and, then, printing and Reform, an earlier foundation typically above that of rural areas expanded. Crafts, by practical needs as well as by 'new' traditions, increasingly required literate workers. Apprentices were either to be able to read upon entry or were, in theory, to be instructed in letters as well as morality as part of their training. Guilds founded and supported schools; and, early welfare efforts by municipalities began to institute tutelage in elementary literacy along with religion and morality for their charges and inmates.

Literacy, not surprisingly, was not evenly distributed among urban workers. In Lyon, for example, according to Davis, in the late-sixteenth century, there was a clear hierarchy of crafts by literacy rate which seems to parallel their status and wealth levels:

Very high: apothecaries, surgeons, printers.
High: painters, musicians, taverners, metalworkers (including gold).
Medium (about 50 per cent): furriers and leatherworkers, artisans in textiles and clothing.
Low to very low: artisans in construction, provisioning, transport; urban gardeners; unskilled dayworkers.

Levels varied from place to place; the facts of distinct hierarchies varied much less.[21]

City and town dwellers were also more likely to understand national vernaculars than rural folk. This not only gave an additional stimulus to their acquisition of literacy, but it also gave them access to more materials, individually or collectively, directly or indirectly. Nevertheless, although this category of evidence is ambiguous, urban artisans seldom owned books, or at least seldom were they listed in their wills. If they did, French studies indicate that the *Book of Hours* or the *Golden Legend,* a vernacular Bible, or a technical work such as a pattern book were most likely. They did not rush to personally acquire the products of the press. Costs, to be sure, limited their buying even after printing's advent, but it is more revealing that they found other ways to gain access to writing or prints. They bought a book, read it until they finished, or until they were broke or needed cash, and then pawned it with an innkeeper or more likely sold it to a friend or to a *libraire'*. Books were also shared in oral reading groups which brought together the literate and the illiterate, and some writings were clearly designed to be read orally rather than to be read silently. Perhaps the most innovative of such reading groups were the secret and secretive bands of religious dissenters: from the Lollards (well discussed by Aston) to Protestants. Such groups formed much deeper bonds, regardless of individual literacy abilities; they also more often crossed neighbourhood and occupational group lines. Cultural divisions were thus reinforced. Literacy was sought by an increasing number among virtually all social groups before the Great Reform of the 1520s and religiosity was both a motive and a consequence. Forms, influences, and results varied, to be sure.[22]

As Davis' French studies have taught us, some few among the urban *menu peuple,* not unlike Hyde's Italian merchants, expanded their literacy into writing. This was furthered by print, but print was not itself a cause. Surgeons and apothecaries wrote on health, medicine, and welfare; sailors on their travels; artisans and traders presented poetry; the potter Bernard Palissy wrote important dialogues on chemistry and agriculture; and there were the justly famed printer-scholars (as recently re-emphasized by Elizabeth Eisenstein). Some women also took to pen and print. On rare occasions, finally, groups spoke collectively through the literate medium, as did for example the *compagnonnages* of the journeymen of Lyon and Paris in a brief to the Parlement of Paris in 1572 objecting to a royal edict on printing and attacking their employers. Literacy, though not actually *causing* politicization or collective action, did prove a valued, useful vehicle for presenting, airing and gaining larger audiences for grievances. This was no less true for advice literature, religious writings, creative literature, or, for that matter, scholarship—all amplified in important new, innovative ways with the addition of printing's technology.[23]

The Renaissance's Relationships to Literacy

Penetrating the textbook glosses of literacy as stimulus to the Renaissance and, conversely, the Renaissance as further stimulus to literacy is no simple task. Beyond the bounds of self-evident, partial truisms, often weak in explanatory or interpretive value—and the fact that the Renaissance was, chronologically, a period of generally rising levels of literacy—the connections are often less than clear or direct. In fact, the case I sketch emphasizes, on one hand, the contradictory nature of many connections, and, on the other hand, the limits of the Renaissance contribution to general levels of literacy; if, that is, we focus on it as a cultural and intellectual movement of the period, as I think we properly should. My position is sceptical, agnostic, if you like; it is not, I hope, heretical.

Several key distinctions must be made. First, we err if we are too latitudinarian in our use of the term 'Renaissance'. I wish to employ it in a fairly precise sense, which I think fits the historical case. Second, although we must be sensitive to variations over time and space, delimiting *too* many different Renaissances over the almost three-century period is as distorting as seeing the currents as constituting a seamless web. With respect to the Renaissance, of course, time and space *do* coalesce in essential ways. Third, and potentially most significant for the historian of literacy, we *must* distinguish (*a*) theory from practice; (*b*) impacts during the times themselves from those felt in later centuries—as in pedagogical reform, for example; and (*c*) actions and influences taken and felt by relatively small numbers of select, often elite, persons from those of and by the many.

With these provisos, the contradictions and the limits of Renaissance relations with literacy may be glimpsed. It should be clear, nevertheless, that literacy *was* very important; among those intellectual, artistic, and political elites who made and shaped the movements and their dynamics, the uses of literacy, novel and more 'traditional', were obviously enormously significant. Of that there can be no doubt; yet, that point is neither surprising nor original. Such uses derived in a general sense from the broadening diffusion of literacy skills and educational opportunities during the later Middle Ages and from the intellectual progress of that period. However, it is exaggerated and inadequate to presume that literacy *per se* 'caused' or stimulated the Renaissance. Such statements not only remove it from its far more complex and interesting historical context, but also misunderstand fundamentally the roles of literacy. What determined selected uses of literacy by special persons is a far more crucial matter.

Specifically, for the purposes of discussion, we may say that the primary emphases of the Renaissance were (i) the rediscovery of antiquity and the classical revival; (ii) civic humanism; and (iii) Christian humanism. These key elements overlap and interrelate, and contain within them most, if not all, of the period's major thrusts. In few direct or immediately consequential ways, however, did these epochal threads influence mass literacy or shape mass uses of reading and writing. In this, their roles differed instructively from those of economic change, trade and commerce, and the incipient expansion of the increasingly capitalized marketplace. This is not to argue, let it be said, that there were *no* impacts or that they were not consequential; rather, it is to postulate a limiting case.

The rediscovery of antiquity and its intellectual / artistic / cultural legacies and products was limited to the efforts and the *direct* benefits of the few. That argument should require the least qualification. This was an activity of the highly literate, whose own and whose successors' and adherents' learning and literacy usage only gained and deepened in the process. Their numbers surely grew, and they influenced much else: but not the conditions or opportunities for the literacy learning or usage of the greater mass of the population. Intellectual and cultural achievements of a high level, history shows, are never in any direct way a simple consequence of the extent of literacy, elementary, or even secondary schooling. They may occur in settings with a low level of literacy; a high rate is no guarantee, though it may assist. As in so much else, literacy was a contributor, *not* a cause; a beneficiary, *not* a consequence.

Indeed, their efforts may be seen as contradictory and limiting in that sense. One important issue is language. The Renaissance took place at a time of diffusing, maturing regional and national vernacular languages. Yet, with some important exceptions among literary figures, the classical revival did little to endorse or contribute to the vernacular's obvious potential for expanding lay and popular literacy and schooling. To the contrary, in many ways and to many influential minds, it was at best hesitant and ambivalent and sometimes actively opposed to use of the vernacular, especially in schooling and scholarly (and often literary) expression and creativity. Major authors in the vernacular (Petrarch, Boccaccio) scorned mass audiences. More popular literary work and more 'practical' kinds of schooling, as well as the persisting powerful presence of church-supervised education, never major thrusts of the Renaissance, were more consequential to general literacy levels. Vernacular translations did increasingly become factors conducive to more popular literacy. A widening cultural divide—based far less on literacy than on its uses and its linguistic vehicles—must also be associated with this period. Printing in no way reduced this widening split.

Civic humanism, the keystone of the great cultural contributions, had a wider scope than the classical revival and touched more lives. It too was limited and could be contradictory. Lauro Martines, in his *Power and Imagination*, presents an impressive case that humanism was a 'program for the ruling class'. Though he may overstate his thesis, he is not seriously in error, for that was not only the overarching emphasis of humanism, especially but not exclusively in Italy, but it was also the dominant, if not the sole impact. This is seen perhaps most starkly in humanist educational and pedagogical thought and theories, which dealt remarkably little with either elementary or literacy learning or training of the many. This is also seen in the practice of humanist education.[24]

If not the case for all such writing, this was the dominant perspective. Classical languages and their use was one prime theme; rhetoric, revealingly, was another. It was the pinnacle of education, toward whose advancement virtually all else was addressed. And rhetoric, a highly-valued political as well as cultural tool, reminds us that orality and aurality were hardly erased or eclipsed by literacy's increasing impact on the culture and communicative modes, nor by print's penetration for that matter. Walter Ong's seminal, idiosyncratic *The Presence of the Word* illustrates the persisting presence and power of oral speech and oral exchange into the early modern era. Much of formal education was so shaped, as was much of literature. Martines, among others, suggests the applications to power and control.[25]

Of course, humanism selectively but firmly fostered literacy's acquisition and uses, from sponsoring the upward mobility through schooling for some talented persons to increasing women's education and expanding job opportunities in administration, teaching, the professions, and cultural production. Investment in education was indeed promoted; although primary concern and support were addressed to post-literacy or post-elementary schooling, that foundation needed to be secured too. Surplus wealth, cultural consumption, political stability and ambitions, flowering of genius, and other factors equally underlay that set of developments. They were not the primary interests of leading humanists and their patrons.

Christian humanism is generally associated more with northern Europe and its later, so-called Northern Renaissance. Such dichotomizing from the 'classical' or Italian Renaissance is only partially accurate, yet differences remain and were often significant. In some ways, Christian humanism had, at least in potential and theory, a greater relevance and relationship to literacy. That potential, I believe, lay more in the future than in the age itself. In most respects, the breadth of concern and action of Christian humanists, regardless of their geographic locations, were little broader than those of their Italian predecessors. Their programmes overwhelmingly related to the shaping of elites for properly enriched, cultivated, responsible, and godly-goodly works and lives. The writings of the major English, French, Dutch, Spanish, and German humanists all illustrate this. Formal religion was also very important to them. Precious little attention was accorded literacy and primary schooling, especially for the commoners and the masses; the vernacular received only slightly less hostility and ambivalence than earlier in the south of Europe. Eramus of Rotterdam is a fitting case in point.

There is another side to Christian humanism, more important for literacy then and later both. More broadly mass or popular themes, more often proposed than enacted, are found here than in the more 'classical' thrusts of Renaissance humanism. They ranged from the bitterly-debated but nonetheless innovative vernacular schools and publishing of the Brethren of the Common Life, to municipal welfare and 'social reform' efforts—Catholic and Reformation Protestant—which sometimes included formal, required instruction of the poor charges in letters, along with moral and religious indoctrination. Such activities looked more to the future than the past. They also included farseeing, unprecedented, 'utopian' plans for mass welfare and mass education symbolized radically by Thomas More's *Utopia*, with its peculiar combination of modernity and medieval vistas, or by Vives' plans. A renewed focus on children and the young was part of these conceptions. Herein lay important seeds for the future of literacy—at once demonstrating its potential uses for control and hegemony and for individual and collective advancement and initiative and roles for formal institutions and the State—if relatively few strong initiatives before the sixteenth and seventeenth centuries. Precedents were being set for State and private philanthropic actions.

The Reformation of course attempted, on occasion came to compel, sometimes with striking success, mass campaigns and organizations for instilling literacy, in tandem with religion and morality, to large and growing populations. Counter-reformers made similar, if smaller efforts in these directions. Gerald Strauss' magnificent *Luther's House of Learning* demonstrates this and the contributions—and indeed contradictions—of humanism to the process. Regardless of place or sponsorship, however, a truly 'useful' literacy was seldom the goal. To be sure, as Strauss, among others, also illustrates, more than a few among the target populations took advantage of, and worked to expand, such opportunities for reasons not always dominated by concerns religious or humanistic.[26]

In either case, literacy's social and cultural relationships were expanded and reinforced. Furthermore, literacy's growth was indeed fostered. Numerical data available only from the mid-sixteenth century show this result. That this should derive from the diverse but often overlapping emphases of the Renaissance, in the ways it did, suggests the indirectness and contradictoriness of many of the most import relationships. For the Renaissance's and humanism's major interests lay elsewhere and were more narrow socially. That should be one aspect of any interpretation of the period. For the endorsement of literacy, of differing levels and types, for differing persons and classes, and for divergent purposes, was cumulatively strengthened, and a set of legacies endowed for succeeding centuries.

Literacies: Alphabetic and Visual

Mention of 'differing literacies' leads to my final theme and to another dimension of the Renaissance experience. This is the import of 'non-alphabetic' or, more precisely, 'visual literacy', a subject whose significance and scope, past or present, we are just coming to appreciate. As the strikingly original studies of Eugene Ferguson, William Ivins, and Peter Burke (and A.F.C. Wallace for a later period) together can teach us, Renaissance achievements, especially in the plastic arts and technology and probably also in science and medicine, owed a major debt to forms of literacy other than the traditional alphabetic type.[27] This is a difficult, largely uncharted area; we are, for example, ignorant of the relations that may tie visual with alphabetic skills. My comments are therefore hypothetical, but the significance of the subject demands its note.

Regardless of the connections among differing literacies, the visual, or what Ferguson has called, 'The mind's eye; nonverbal thought', seems both highly relevant and potentially seminally important to the Renaissance. Very different dynamics seem at work as compared to those with alphabetic literacy. And, if Burke's prosopographical data are representative, there may well have been strikingly different social origins, training and career patterns, and paths to productiveness and accomplishment between the two fields of endeavour, which may relate to, derive from, and result in acquisition of very different forms of literacy and their employment.

William Ivins notes:

> While both words and pictures are symbols, they are different in many ways of the greatest importance. So little are they equivalent to each other that if communication were confined to either alone, it would become very limited in its scope. All words need definition, names for them. Verbal definition is a regress from word to word, until finally it becomes necessary to point to something which we say is the last word in the verbal chain of definition means. Frequently the most convenient way of pointing is to make a picture. The word then receives definition, or, if one likes, the thing receives a name, by the association of a sensuous awareness with an oral or visual symbol.[28]

More specifically, after establishing striking distinctions in the social origins of 320 Italian Renaissance painters, sculptors, and architects, when compared to to 231 writers, scientists, and humanists (much more artisanal), and also in their form of education, orientations, influences, and outlets, Peter Burke points to two rather distinct 'cultures': one rooted in a lengthy apprenticeship and workshops, the other in formal, higher education. Such differences likely resulted in different abilities and manners of 'reading' and 'expression'. (In grasping these possibilities, we should not be led astray by the virtually unique cases of a Michaelangelo or a da Vinci). Living with their masters, such artists obviously emphasized the visual. Although they surely had uses of the alphabetic, it was not primary to their forms of expression. Burke observes, 'an important part of the training was the study and copying of the workshop collection of drawings, which served to unify the shop style and maintain its tradition. A humanist described the process in the early fifteenth century: "When the apprentices are to be instructed by their master . . . the painters follow the practice of giving them a number of fine drawings and pictures as models of their art" '.[29] How different this was from the training and practice of scholars and authors.

Ferguson, in a brilliant speculative article on technology and its cognitive concomitants, has taken this perspective a step further. Attempting to understand inventiveness and innovativeness during the Renaissance, and later, he explores their 'non-scientific' modes of thought, or the nonverbal thinking of the 'mind's eye'. He notes that many features and qualities of the objects that 'technologists' think about are not reducible to unambiguous verbal statements; 'they are dealt with in his mind by a visual, nonverbal process'. The developed, practised, and trained, 'mind's eye', he postulates, reviews one's visual memory and seeks to form new images as thought requires.

> If we are to understand the development of Western technology, we must appreciate this important, if unnoticed mode of thought. It has been nonverbal thinking, by and large, that has fixed the outlines and filled in the details of our material surroundings. Pyramids, cathedrals, and rockets exist not because of geometry, theory or structures, or thermodynamics, but because they were first a picture—literally a vision— in the minds of those who made them.

After reviewing the nature of design and invention, including important examples from the Renaissance and noting contemporary picture books, he concludes, 'Yet, science, when applied to engineering, is analytical . . . [Whereas] Nonverbal thinking, which is a central mechanism in engineering design, involves perceptions, the stock-in-trade of the artist not the scientist'.

> Much of the creative thought of the designers of our technological world is nonverbal, not easily reducible to words; its language is an object or a picture or a visual image in the mind. It is out of this kind of thinking that the clock, printing press, and snowmobile have arisen. Technologists, converting their nonverbal knowledge into objects directly . . . or into drawings that have enabled others to build what was in their minds. . . . This intellectual component of technology, which is nonliterary and nonscientific, had been generally unnoticed because its origins lie in art and not in science.[30]

My speculation, my hypothesis, leads me to ask: how much of science itself and indeed of medicine, too, derives from the same or similar dynamics? Common sense, which I employ however misleadingly since I have no expertise in either field, suggests that it should be a great deal indeed. Burke's linking of Italian scientists with the scholars and writers, however justified on many grounds (a point that *is* significant), may mislead us on this one. By the sixteenth century, more and more scientists, physicians, and technologists, though certainly not all, were acquiring a relatively formal and advanced form of education; in this they differed from artists. In other ways and in key aspects of their training, it is possible that the difference remained less than might otherwise seem apparent. If that is in fact the case, a large number of important questions is opened to historians of science, medicine, and technology, as well as to those of the arts, and, of course, to students of literacy or, shall I now say, litera*cies*. The roles of illustrations, and of printing's impact on reproduction, precision, accuracy, and like, recently pointed to by Elizabeth Eisenstein (though not considered in depth), is highly suggestive here. So is that of training. It may be the case that major scientists and physicians, among others, employed and practised, as they needed, visual as well as alphabetic literacies. Studies aimed at this question may provide one important path towards the relations and interactions of these, and perhaps other, literacies—an urgent priority on the scholarly (and contemporary) agenda.

A discussion like this one requires no conclusion or summation. Suffice it to emphasize the mixing and intricately interrelating variety of media, or communicative modes, that I have sought to introduce. In so far as literacy, traditional alphabetic literacy, that is, my major focus, is concerned, its understanding and interpretation can be achieved *only* with the appreciation of the other important modes, especially the oral and aural and the visual. Ong suggested something of this, when he wrote

> The Renaissance fell heir to the medieval preoccupation with texts and to its lingering predilection for oral performance. In terms of the presence of the word to man, the Renaissance is one of the most complex and even confused periods in cultural history, and by that token perhaps the most interesting up to the present in the history of the word. An exacting devotion to the written text, a devotion which has been the seedbed of modern humanistic scholarship, struggled in the subconscious with commitment to rhetoric and to dialectic, symbolic of the old oral-aural anxieties and a sense of social structure built to a degree intolerable today on personal loyalties rather than on objectification of issues. Humanistic rhetoric as such was opposed to scholastic dialectic, and yet both belong to the oral-aural culture which typography was to transmute.[31]

Yet, to assume a complete transformation is to misread (to use a word) both literacy and communicative change.

Notes

1 See my 'The legacies of literacy', *Journal of Communication*, 32 (1982), 12–26. 'Reflections on the history of literacy', *Humanities in Society*, 4 (1981), 303–333, and *The Legacies of Literacy, passim.*, esp. Introduction.

2 As examples, see FRANZ BAUML, 'Varieties and consequences of medieval literacy and illiteracy', *Speculum*, 55 (1980), 237–265; MICHAEL CLANCHY, *From Memory to Written Record: England, 1066–1307*, London and Cambridge, Mass., 1979; DAVID CRESSY, *Literacy and the Social Order*. Cambridge, 1980; NATALIE Z. DAVIS, 'Printing and the people', in her *Culture and Society in Early Modern France*. Stanford, 1975, 189–226; FRANCOIS FURET and JACQUES OZOUF, *Lire et écrire*, 2 vols., Paris, 1977; J.K. HYDE. 'Some uses of literacy in Venice and Florence in the thirteenth and fourteenth centuries'. *Transactions*, Royal Historical Society, 5th ser., 29 (1979), 109–129; THOMAS LAQUEUR, 'Cultural origins of literacy in England, 1500–1850', *Oxford Review of Education*, 2 (1976), 255–275; JOAN H. MORAN's forthcoming book on late medieval York; and of course LAWRENCE STONE, 'Literacy and education in England, 1640–1900', *Past and Present*, 42 (1969), 61–139, among a growing literature. For

bibliography to 1980, see my *Literacy in History: An Interdisciplinary Research Bibliography*. New York, 1981. For a selection of major studies, see my reader, *Literacy and Social Development in the West*. Cambridge, 1981.

3 See, for example, my *The Literacy Myth: Literacy and Social Structure in the Ninteenth-Century City*. New York and London, 1979, esp. Introduction; as well as the literature cited above.

4 CARLO CIPOLLA, *Literacy and Development in the West*. Harmondsworth, 1969, ELIZABETH EISENSTEIN, *The Printing Press as an Agent of Change*, 2 vols. Cambridge, 1979.

5 *The Legacies of Literacy*, Introduction and *passim*.

6 See, for example, BAUML 'Varieties and consequences'; DAVIS, 'Printing'; CRESSY, *Literacy*; forthcoming work of MORAN. Compare with, for example, EISENSTEIN, *The Printing Press*; HYDE. 'Some uses'.

7 On printing, see EISENSTEIN, *The Printing Press*. Compare with LUCIEN FEBVRE and H.-J. MARTIN, *The Coming of the Book*. London, 1976; RUDOLPH HIRSCH, *The Printed Word*, London, 1978. See also, ANTHONY GRAFTON, 'The importance of being printed', *Journal of Interdisciplinary History*, 11 (1980), 265–286; MICHAEL HUNTER, 'The impact of print', *The Book Collector*, 28 (1979), 335–352; ROGER CHARTIER, 'L'Ancien Régime typographique: reflexions sur quelques travaux recents', *Annales; e., s., c.*, 36 (1981), 191–201; SUSAN NOAKES. 'The development of the book market in late quattrocentro Italy', *Journal of Medieval and Renaissance Studies*, 11 (1981), 23–55; ANNE JACOBSON SCHUTTE, 'Printing, piety, and the people in Italy, *Archive for Reformation History*, 71 (1981), 5–19.

8 Compare for example with the radically relativist viewpoint expressed in ROBERT PATTISON, *On Literacy: The Politics of the Word from Homer to the Age of Rock*. New York, 1982; see also my comments in a review forthcoming in *Language and Society* (Chap. 10, this volume).

9 Fuller documentation of this argument is presented in *The Legacies of Literacy*, esp. chs. IV and V; see also the literature cited above.

10 SYLVIS THRUPP, *The Merchant Class of Medieval London*. Ann Arbor, Mich. 1962 (1948); CRESSY, *Literacy*

11 E. LEROY LADURIE, *Montaillou: The Promised Land of Error*. London and New York, 1978, *The Peasants of Languedoc*. Urbana, Ill., 1974.

12 EGIL JOHANSSON, *The History of Literacy in Sweden, in Comparison with Some other Countries*. Umeå. Sweden, 1977, 'The history of literacy in Sweden', in *Literacy and Social Development*, ed. GRAFF, 151–182; GERALD STRAUSS, *Luther's House of Learning*, Baltimore, 1979.

13 CRESSY, *Literacy*; MARGARET SPUFFORD, 'First steps in literacy: the reading and writing experiences of the humblest seventeenth-century spiritual autobiographers', *Social History*, 4 (1979), 407–435 (reprinted in *Literacy and Social Development*, [Ed.] GRAFF). *Contrasting Communities*. Cambridge, 1974, and *Small Books and Pleasant Histories: Popular Fiction and its Readership in Seventeenth-Century England*, London, 1981.

14 DAVIS, 'Printing'; see also, PETER BURKE, *Popular Culture in Early Modern Europe*. New York, 1978.

15 See SPUFFORD, *Contrasting Communities*; articles on scribes, for example, in *Local Population Studies*; KEITH WRIGHTSON and DAVID LEVINE, *Poverty and Piety*. New York and London, 1979.

16 CLANCHY, *From Memory*.

17 MARGERET ASTON, 'Lollardy and literacy', *History*, 62 (1977), 347–371.

18 CRESSY, *Literacy*, 189; DAVIS, 'Printing'; ASTON, 'Lollardy'; DAVID LEVINE, 'Illiteracy and family life in early industrial England', *Journal of Family History*, 4 (1979), 368–380, 'Illiteracy and family life in the first industrial revolution', *Journal of Social*

History, 14 (1980), 25–44; GRAFF, *The Literacy Myth,* BURKE, *Popular Culture;* ROGER S. SCHOLFIELD, 'The measurement of literacy in pre-industrial England', in *Literacy in Traditional Societies,* (Ed.) JACK GOODY (Cambridge, 1968), 311–325, 'Dimensions of illiteracy in England, 1750–1850', *Explorations in Economic History,* 10 (1973), 437–454 (reprinted in *Literacy and Social Development,* ed. GRAFF). Compare with SPUFFORD, 'First steps'; *Small Books;* LAQUEUR, 'The cultural origins'; EISENSTEIN, *The Printing Press.*

19 DAVIS, 'Printing', as reprinted in *Literacy and Social Development,* (Ed.) GRAFF, 83.

20 HYDE, 'Some uses of literacy', 116, and *passim.*

21 DAVIS, 'Printing'. See also, FURET and OZOUF, *Lire;* CRESSY, *Literacy;* GRAFF, *The Legacies of Literacy,* for additional data.

22 DAVIS, 'Printing', as reprinted, 85; ASTON, 'Lollardy'; LEROY LADURIE. *Montaillou;* CARLO GINZBURG, *The Cheese and the Worms.* Baltimore, 1980.

23 DAVIS, 'Printing'.

24 LAURO MARTINES. *Power and Imagination: City-States in Renaissance Italy,* New York, 1979; GRAFF, *The Legacies of Literacy.*

25 WALTER J. ONG, S.J., *The Presence of the Word.* New York, 1970; BAUML, 'Varieties and consequences'; MARTINES, *Power and Imagination;* among the literature.

26 STRAUSS, *Luther's House;* JOHANSSON, *History of Literacy;* KENNETH LOCKRIDGE, *Literacy in Colonial New England.* New York, 1974, the major contributions of NATALIE DAVIS, HAROLD GRIMM, BRIAN PULLAN, and ROBERT KINGDOM on the development of social welfare in early modern Europe.

27 EUGENE FERGUSON. 'The mind's eye: nonverbal thought in technology'. *Science,* 197 (1977), 827–836: WILLIAM IVINS, *Prints and Visual Communications* Cambridge, Mass., 1969; A. HAYETT MAYOR, *Prints and People.* Princeton, 1981; ANTHONY F.C. WALLACE, *Rockdale,* New York, 1978. On the psychology of literacy, the major work to date is SYLVIA SCRIBNER and MICHAEL COLE, *The Psychology of Literacy,* Cambridge, Mass., 1981.

28 IVINS, *Prints,* 158–159.

29 BURKE, *Culture and Society in Renaissance Italy,* London, 1972, 53, *passim.*

30 FERGUSON, 'The mind's eye', 827, 834, 835, *passim.*

31 ONG, *Presence,* 63.

Literacy in History: Review Essay

Popular Education in Eighteenth Century England
by Victor E. Neuburg
London: Woburn Press, 1971

Literacy in Society
by Victory E. Neuburg (Ed.)
London: Woburn Press, 1971

*Literacy in Colonial New England: An Enquiry into the Social
Context of Literacy in the Early Modern West*
by Kenneth A. Lockridge
New York: Norton, 1974

The historical study of literacy is in a major 'take-off' period today. Once a merely peripheral concern of historians and educational researchers, treated anecdotally in passing, if at all, literacy now features as the major theme of several large projects as well as an important variable in many other studies. Not only has the spread of literacy been recognized as a modern development of vast importance in itself, literacy has been associated with attitudinal modernization, industrialization, urbanism, political radicalism, and revolution. In fact, contemporary correlations reveal that literacy relates, to some degree, with literally scores of social, economic, and demographic variables. With these relationships in mind, historians have recently begun to chart the growth and transmission of literacy—its rise to near universality in the West, social and regional variations in its distribution, the social and economic demands for literacy, and the changing importance of possessing literacy.[1]

One of the most interesting and instructive aspects of the new literacy studies is the variety of sources and approaches currently utilized. In fact, the books under review provide sharply contrasting examples of this point. To a large degree, however, much of the work on literacy is based upon quantitative and demographic analyses of a handful of data bases which pertain to reading and / or writing. An international phenomenon, research (largely unpublished) is being conducted in England, Sweden, France, the Netherlands, Canada, and the United States. Researchers have exploited the range of sources from marriage registers, wills, deeds, legal depositions, catechetical examinations, military recruits' dossiers, goal registers, employment contracts to census manuscripts and library records, as well as aggregated sources.[2] The disparate nature of materials makes this an exciting field for its practitioners, while, simultaneously, it does raise severe problems in comparison which have yet to be satisfactorily solved.[3] Nevertheless, this work represents one of the few areas in which the concerns of the historians of education and the 'new' social historian have been fortuitously blended, and in which a rich cross-fertilization of concept, method, and hypotheses has occurred. Indeed, the study of literacy has involved both historians of education as well as social economic historians.

The books reviewed here are very much a part of the trend discussed. Although their chronological focus, their topics, and questions are quite similar, the resulting monographs are as different as night and day. Both authors focus in large part on the eighteenth century: Lockridge on the American Colonies (with some comparison with England) and Neuburg on England alone. Each is explicitly concerned with literacy, and with its transmission over time; each addresses popular education, that is, schooling of classes other than upper and middle orders. In addition, both Lockridge and Neuburg define literacy as the ability to read, centering on its place in social change in their conclusions. Finally, each treatment is imaginative and clearly written.

The comparison stops here, and, admittedly, these points of similarity are superficial. The books deviate from one other in their data sources, methodology, level and style of conceptualization, range of generalization, and, perhaps most importantly, in their assumptions and conclusions, which are intertwined in both cases. For reasons which I will elaborate below, the volumes are ultimately unsatisfying, albeit for different reasons. Lockridge admits his work has this consequence; Neuburg, however, does not.

Victor Neuburg's *Popular Education in Eighteenth Century England* attests to the fact that the proponents of numerical history have not yet captured the field of literacy; nor, I would add, should they. Neuburg's research, in fact, represents one genre of what might be termed 'literary' literacy studies, and may be grouped with R.D. Altick, Leslie Shepard, Paul Kaufman, Robert Collison, and Alvar Ellegard's studies of literacy and readership.[4] Neuburg deviates from past scholars in explicitly asking 'to what extent was the ability to read a common achievement amongst working men and women in eighteenth century England?' (p. 1). The remaining 150 pages elaborate the evidence which suggests to him that the ability to read was spreading among the poor throughout the century and that by 1800 there was a 'considerable' amount of literacy among working men and women. Neuburg, as we will see, eschews the possibility of the explicit quantification to literacy; but, nevertheless, he engages in the common habit of making numerical judgments without statistical evidence, or implicit quantification.[5] This, then, is Neuburg's thesis; how does he establish it and how satisfactory is his interpretation?

Neuburg's approach to historical evidence is highly impressionistic, almost as deliberately non-analytical as it is anti-quantitative. His method is highly traditional, and not in the best sense of that abused term: he argues from strings of quotations and examples, relatively unconcerned with questions of context, development, change, typicality, or representativeness. This fault leads him through a great amount of data (too often poorly or even unreferenced in the irritating English manner), which is often either inconclusive or contradictory. He seems at times to be wearing blinders in order to prove his thesis at all costs, and as a direct consequence the reader becomes frustrated and irritated with lack of questioning and of a logic of inquiry. This defect appears perhaps most obviously in the chapters on 'Education in Practice' and 'The Art of Reading'. In the former, Neuburg examines teachers and pupils, and his evidence about the former hardly represents a propitious portrait which might advance his central case. He first provides opinion about the low esteem, lack of preparation, transiency, and poor quality of teachers (five examples); then he brings forth evidence of some few serious-minded, dedicated teachers (seven examples). His conclusion after twenty-odd pages of examples: 'It does seem clear, however, that in fact there were more teachers who were able to impart at least the elements of reading than this lack of training would suggest.' (p. 38) He deals with pupils in a similar fashion—this reader, for one, remains unconvinced; faced with conflicting evidence, ignorant of its representativeness or of a framework for comparison or change, I must declare it at best inconclusive, at worst. . . . What he does not prove is that the children of the poor and working classes had the chance for a schooling which would have provided them with a useful literacy. This failure weighs heavily on his argument.

Literacy itself features more directly in succeeding chapters on 'The Act of Reading' and 'Approaches to Literacy'. Yet Neuburg continues his impressionistic and vague presentation of quotations first from reading texts of which he offers a brief history, illustrating the important point that the impulse toward the transmission of literacy was religious and socially conservative. Unfortunately, in his attention to texts, he neglects the question of the classroom: how were they used, how successful were teaching methodologies? He gives precious little space to actual learning or the quality of the educational product, and crucially Neuburg fails to confront his conclusion of no methodological advance with a presumed increase in literacy. Rather he assumes that a documented increase in number of charity schools led to a demand for primers which in turn indicates an increase in literacy (pp. 89–90). This causal statement rests in his own admission upon 'presumptive' evidence; moreover, it courts the dangers of several logical fallacies. Specifically, Neuburg never addresses these problems: an increase in facilities does not mean an increase in either aggregate attendance, regular attendance, or in the skills obtained; educational provision does not mean effective instruction or that learning to read was a common result; reading instruction which focussed on Bible and catechism through memory and rote learning does not necessarily suggest that a 'fluent' reader comprehended much of what he or she enunciated.[6] Finally, increasing numbers of texts and several editions say nothing definite about reading habits, size of the audience or size of editions; in fact, rather than indicating demand, it may merely relate to technological innovations in printing, distribution or size of print-runs.[7]

Indeed, his failure to confront this last fallacy mars his key chapters on literacy, chapbooks, and cheap literature. Evidence of more volumes simply is insufficient to prove advances in readership, or 'indicate the existence of a considerable and growing reading public amongst the working class throughout the century' (p. 91). Where is the evidence that they were bought by this class, that they were individually and not orally read, that the number of readers per copy was not changing, or that printing and book-selling were not changing. Instead of attempting to discover some more direct indicator of literacy or reading, Neuburg resorts again to 'presumptive' evidence and argument. First, he cites several examples of books belonging to peasants (were they read? was this typical?); then he admits that while this does not prove the case, the increase in books available 'suggests strongly that existence of a growing number of readers' and 'the balance of probability suggests that [the books] were read' (p. 95). Is this a valid level of argumentation; are 'balances of probability' without estimates convincing as evidence to the central argument—I would suggest that the answer must be no.

Do such indicators exist? This is an issue of contention to be sure; however measures do exist which may be cautiously employed to estimate the number of *potential* readers in a society. Marriage registers are the principal source in England, yet Neuburg eschews them as valid historical evidence. He finds their evidence misleading, at best 'only a partial and unsatisfactory solution' (pp. 96–98). His attitude on this issue is particularly disturbing, for Neuburg is quite ready to castigate other scholars for ignoring his evidence, but he himself prefers not to confront his thesis with even an approximate test. He not only ignores Roger Schofield's 1968 discussion of the registers and frank admission of these limitations, but he forecloses the opportunities for a fortuitous marriage of approaches; one demanded, I would urge, if literacy's historical importance is to be truly evaluated.

The remainder of the volume suffers from the same inadequacies. Neuburg's discussion of the motives and working assumptions of SPCK and other tract societies is unbalanced and unconvincing, as are his naive assumptions about the simplicity of maintaining proficiency in the skill of reading. Similarly, his most original contribution, the notion of the existence of a pervasive print culture in the late eighteenth century, is contradictory and unproven. He never attempts to balance the simultaneous existence of a traditional oral culture with one shaped by modern print media, or of its meaning for social life and attitudinal change.[8] The discussion of chapbooks fails on these same points; indeed, it is inferior to his 1968 essay on that topic.[9] Moreover, chapbooks' appeal—that they were escapist, unsophisticated and traditional matter—tradition was petrified in print—is somehow overcome in the development of a working class consciousness and identity. I, for one, would be extremely interested in an explanation of this seemingly mystical process, whose development somehow proves that it was poor judgement on the part of conservative agencies to teach the poor to read. How, for example, did traditionally oriented chapbooks smooth the transition into literate society from a pre-literate one (or is this itself an artificial distinction?) and how did popular reading of escapist, entertaining literature help individual workers' 'sense of a group concept?' (pp. 141–142).

Neuburg errs as others have by giving the mere possession of literacy too much credit. The source of literacy has historically been a conservative, religious, moral one to aid in the maintenance of a stable and cohesive society. This was as true of the nineteenth as of the seventeenth and eighteenth centuries. Moreover mass literacy is not a prerequisite to radicalism or revolution, as the cases of China and Cuba will attest. Moreover, in Neuburg's England, to cite one example, the activities of Captain Swing were greatest in the least literate counties.[10] Class consciousness, cohesion, and action depend upon much more than literacy, and, as E.P. Thompson has argued, literacy is only the elementary technique; the ability to handle abstract and consecutive argument are very different matters. Indeed, the literacy of but a few readers can provide news and argument to a much greater number, and even illiterate men have been known to own books, whether the Bible or Tom Paine.[11] The final irony for Neuburg's case, alas, is that, statistically-speaking, levels of literacy were falling in the last decades of the eighteenth-century.[12]

Neuburg's selections in his anthology, *Literacy and Society,* make sense only in light of his assumptions elaborated above. With the barest attention to interpretation or context, he has reprinted W.H. Reid's *The Rise and Dissolution of the Infidel Societies in This Metropolis* (1800) and W.J. Linton's *James Watson: A Memoir* (1879). The former essay is meant to illustrate the last vestiges of eighteenth-century fears of an educated poor as subversive. To my reading, however, Reid fears not a literate poor but a threat to religion and social order stemming from middle class-inspired reading clubs and propaganda. There is no evidence that Reid feared a properly, morally educated poor; moreover, he finds that atheism and deism had a limited and brief appeal even upon the susceptible working class and that infidelity never took firm hold among the common people (e.g., p. 33). Reason and maturity, Reid concludes, led the masses to Christianity; certainly no democrat or supporter of the masses, W.H. Reid apparently does not represent those who feared that an educated poor would be a dangerous and subversive class. James Watson's story, however, is cast in terms of the struggle against political censure and is an important one. Clearly, as Neuburg states, Watson was out to exploit the spread of literacy; additionally he had his own political axe to grind which he did in sales, printing, and activism. Nevertheless, the link with mass literacy remains indirect and ambiguous, and in interpretation

Neuburg does little more than restate his opinion that literacy led to radicalism and 'was to prove an important factor in the re-ordering of society which followed the Industrial Revolution' (p. v). The meaning and dimensions of this 're-ordering' remains a matter of great contention among social and economic historians; nevertheless, the role of literacy was less than paramount.

Kenneth Lockridge, in *Literacy in Colonial New England,* has written a very different kind of book—really an essay—on literacy in the American colonies. It is a bold and challenging volume, forthright in its judgments, explicit in its conceptualization and argument, and explicitly aware of its limitations. (I might add too, as my students this year convinced me, it can be a difficult book.) Indeed, Lockridge's awareness of these limitations makes review a difficult task. In sharp contrast of Neuburg, his data is quantitative and his measure of literacy is a direct test: the signature, which is no more than the ability to sign, a level of skill commonly presumed to be mid-way between elementary reading and writing ability.

Lockridge's frankly tentative exercise in numerical estimation of literacy is based upon a revisionist assumption. His purpose is to debunk claims of American uniqueness, Bailyn's and Cremin's (among others) contentions of an indigenous educational response to the wilderness and notions of literacy serving a 'liberating' or modernizing function. Toward this end, he has analyzed thousands of colonial wills, the majority drawn from New England with smaller comparative samples from Pennsylvania, Virginia, and England. Lockridge handles the evidence cautiously and clearly discusses his procedures in the footnotes. The results may be summarized as follows: literacy was possessed by about 50 per cent of the settlers of New England and levels of literacy grew slowly (hardly a frenetic response) until the earlier decades of the eighteenth-century, whereupon the rate of increase more than doubled, creating a nearly universal literate population by the eve of the Revolution. This expansion, the result of educational provision following a minimum level of population concentration needed to support a school (about 1000 per town, he hypothesizes), largely erased the social structure of literacy, that is, its association with occupation and wealth. Status and class differentials, however, were maintained—a very significant point which was true a century later as well. In fact, occupation, wealth, and literacy were so closely interrelated that imputation of causation is nearly impossible. Nevertheless, the rise of 'universal' literacy was overwhelmingly a male phenomenon; female literacy barely changed.

How is New England's literacy trend explained? Lockridge does this by external argument bolstered with comparative data. Universal male literacy, he shows, was achieved by the eighteenth -century by only three societies: Sweden (men and women), Scotland, and New England. These were small, intensely religious societies, dominated by a Protestant impulse which led to active encouragement or compulsion of education for 'the conservation of piety.' Thus, the impetus to literacy was conservative, and as a result, social attitudes (in so far as they can be measured by wills) remained traditional in orientation. Moreover, literacy 'moved glacially' in societies lacking an intense religious fervor, such as England, Pennsylvania, or Virginia. Sympathetic to his approach and assumptions, I would conclude that Lockridge is probably correct. However, some severe complications do arise, making his account less than satisfactory.

The first problem involves his measure: signatures on a will (others no doubt will question his sample sizes and sampling procedures; this I will ignore here). Wills are selective sources. Lockridge acknowledges as much in text, notes, and appendices, and he attempts to estimate the biases in age, sex, wealth, and occupation. His conclusion that biases may well cancel out, however, is a tenuous one, for the extent of under-representation of the poor is probably much greater than he allows. As D.S. Smith has recently demonstrated, 67 per cent of the wealthiest forty per cent left a will, while only eight per cent of the poorest twenty per cent did so.[13] This means, first that Lockridge's sample is more upwardly biased than he expected, and, second, that with increasing poverty in the eighteenth-century, the association between literacy, wealth, and status may remain strong.

A second problem involves the use of signatures on wills themselves. Wills are not as broadly-based a source as English marriage registers, Swedish catechetical examinations, or nineteenth-century censuses, as only a quarter to a third of men dying left them. Moreover, while the signature is a valid test of literacy, it remains an approximation of a level of fluent reading, as Lockridge and Roger Schofield admit. It is a comparative measure of only the ability to sign and in itself implies little about the level of reading ability or comprehension. Many markers, too, may have been readers, especially in a society such as Sweden where signatures were quite rare and literacy was overwhelmingly transmitted in reading (oral proficiency—not comprehension) alone.[14]

Lockridge's most original use of his data involves an attempt to measure attitudes as traditional or modern from the charitable bequests listed in wills. Testing theories about the modernization of attitudes, he nowhere finds evidence of literacy bringing forth attitudes which may be described as innovative, active, aware, optimistic, worldly, and abstract, as modern researchers have sometimes found. Rather, the charitable gifts reveal no such orientation to extra-village activities or instrumental gifts; they remained traditional. In part, Lockridge's categories may be too broad to reveal subtle differences, and, as well, he tends to ignore a 20 per cent increase in gifts to village causes (see Table 1, p. 34). Nevertheless, his results should open a new series of historical questions as well as cast some qualifications upon the current faddish adoption of modernization theory by historians. With many others, moreover, Lockridge is uncertain about what to make of social development as modernization and the difference between economic, institutional, and individual modernization. The result is a confusing sketch of the role of literacy in eighteenth-century political development. Lockridge hypothesizes increasing homogenization and contentiousness as a prelude to revolution. The questions of how and why remain open as does the role of attitudinal change.

Sketchy at best is his brief discussion of the social and economic needs for the demands of literacy, and here inattention to quality of literacy leaves a large gap in his interpretation of a frustrated populace unable to deal with a changing world. Nevertheless, his conclusion that 'in the long run the level of basic literacy in the colonies, and the advent of mass literacy in New England may appear of little relevance in the face of a society whose demands far outpaced what either colonial literacy or colonial culture prepared men to understand' (p. 38) seems a logical one, if literacy's use for daily life is assessed differently.

Finally, many readers will find unsatisfactory Lockridge's dependence upon numbers and his ignorance of local variations, inconclusive analyses of cause and effect, and too brief treatment of the level and demands for functional literacy (as well as a valid definition of that ambiguous concept). The importance of this brief book ultimately rests not on its own conclusions, which remain suggestive at least, but in the new questions raised, the approach and data employed, and in the fact that more questions than answers exist at the end. I hope, as does Lockridge, that his work will become a stimulus to others, regardless of motivation to refute, verify, or qualify, for these questions are among the most crucial in social, economic, and educational history. Moreover, I would suggest that an explicit quantitative approach, with more attention to local and social variation and more traditional sources, has much more to offer the student of literacy than the approach of Victor Neuburg.

Notes

1 On these and related points, see my 'Literacy and Social Structure in the Nineteenth-Century City,' PhD. dissertation submitted to the University of Toronto, 1975.

2 For a more complete discussion, see *ibid.*, esp. Introduction and Bibliography.

3 *Ibid.*, 'Preface to Part One: The Census as a Measure of Literacy;' my 'What the 1861 Census Tells Us About Literacy,' *Histoire Sociale*, forthcoming, 1975; LOCKRIDGE, *Literacy in Colonial New England*, Appendix B; and R.S. SCHOFIELD, 'The Measurement of Literacy in Pre-Industrial England,' in *Literacy in Traditional Societies*, (Ed.) JACK GOODY, Cambridge, 1968, 311–325. [Ed. note. For an informative review of Goody's book, see DANIEL F. McCALL, 'Literacy and Social Structure, *HEQ*, 11 (Spring 1971): 85–92].

4 R.D. ALTICK, *The English Common Reader*. Chicago, 1957; LESLIE SHEPARD, *The History of Street Literature*, Detroit, 1973; ROBERT COLLISON, *The Story of Street Literature*. London, 1973, PAUL KAUFMAN, *Libraries and Their Users*. London, 1969; and ALVAR ELLEGARD, 'The Readership of the Periodical Press in Mid-Victorian Britain, *Gotesborgs Universities Arsskrift*, 63 (1957).

5 See ROBERT W. FOGEL, 'The Limits of Quantitative Methods in History, '*American Historical Review*, 80 (1975); 329–350.

6 See my 'Literacy and Social Structure,' Chap. 7 for a discussion of the quality of literacy in the past; see also, DANIEL CALHOUN, *The Intelligence of a People* Princeton, 1973.

7 *Ibid.*, Introduction: SCHOFIELD, 'The Measurement of Literacy in Pre-industrial England.'

8   NEUBURG'S 'The Literature of the Streets,' in *The Victorian City*, (Ed.) H.J. DYOS and MICHAEL WOLFF. London, 1973. 191–210, is much more sophisticated in its argument: indeed, it is more relevant to the later period.

9   VICTOR NEUBERG, *The Penny Histories*, Oxford, 1968.

10 GEORGE RUDE and E.J. HOBSBAWM, *Captain Swing*. New York, 1969.

11 E.P. THOMPSON, *The Making of the English Working Class*, New York, 1967.

12 R.S. SCHOFIELD, 'Dimensions of Illiteracy, 1750–1850,' *Explorations in Economic History*. 10 (1973), 437–454, and MICHAEL SANDERSON, 'Literacy and Social Mobility in The Industrial Revolution in Britain.' *Past and Present*, 56 (1972): 75–104.

13 DANIEL SCOTT SMITH, 'Underregistration and Bias in Probate Records,' *William and Mary Quarterly* (1975): 100–110.

14 See GRAFF, 'What the 1861 Census Tells Us About Literacy;' SCHOFIELD, 'The Measurement of Literacy in Pre-industrial England' and LOCKRIDGE Appendix B.

9   *Respected and Profitable Labour:*
     Literacy, Jobs and the Working Class in
     the Nineteenth Century

In 1848, Egerton Ryerson, The Chief Superintendent of Education for Canada West, addressed himself to, 'The Importance of Education to a Manufacturing, and a Free People.' Commencing from the premise that a system of mass education was prerequisite to a system of manufacturing—the symbol of the incoming social order—he proclaimed that 'education is designed to prepare us for the duties of life.' While moral principles and values of social order dominated among these duties, the importance of proper preparation for work was not lost to Ryerson. Moreover, he asked, 'how is the uneducated and unskilled man to succeed in these times of sharp and skilful competition and sleepless activity?' Education he must have; it was a natural right of each child 'to receive such an education as will fit him for the duties of life.'[1]

One year later, Ryerson enlarged upon his view, bringing the role of literacy more specifically into play. Discussing 'Canadian Mechanics and Manufactures,' he claimed that the mechanic 'will be a member of society; and, as such, he should know how to read and write the language spoken by such society. . . . This supposes instruction in the grammar or structure of his native tongue.' Social order and society were the supreme beneficiaries of all education in Ryerson's archetypical Anglo-American world-view. To his eyes and mind, 'educated labour is more productive than uneducated labour.' Workers with a common school grounding were thus thought to be less disruptive, superior workmen, orderly, punctual, and of good conduct. In all, the 'proper education of the mechanic is important to the interests of society as well as to his own welfare and enjoyment.'[2]

Yet, the key question was more complex than Ryerson's statements would allow. Just how important have literacy and education been to occupational and economic success? Traditional wisdom, modern sociology, the canons of modernity and nineteenth century school promoters all sang out the praises of education and the skills of literacy in the determination of success. Yet, not all the evidence, past or present, lends credence to this view. Consider this:

> Wanted immediately FORTY ABLE BODIED MEN, to serve as JUSTICES OF THE PEACE, for the COUNTY OF HURON. A plain

> English Education is desirable but not indispensable—each candidate
> however must be able to make his mark, unless he has learned to write
> his name, and will be expected to produce a character signed by the
> Deputy Commissioner of the Board of Works and the Collector of Cus-
> toms Goderich.

and

> [For all children,] except the 10 per cent who will earn a living by the
> use of their verbal ability there is a case for substituting practical for
> academic education.[3]

The relationship of education in general, and the skills of literacy in particular, to
work and occupation remains an imprecise one, complex and often contradictory.
This chapter is devoted to an explication of the relationship, examining both the
real and perceived connections surrounding the economic value of education.
The views of middle class school promoters and reformers and those of the working class will be examined. The literacy levels and differentials of the urban Ontario working class will be explored, as well as the intellectual context of the
discussion of the economic importance of education. Finally, a case study based
on the employment contract ledgers of an Ontario lumbering firm will be offered:
an attempt to isolate the importance of literacy to working men in a specific social
situation. The thrust of the chapter is to illuminate the contradictions in the
perceived connections between education, as measured by literacy, and employment level, to show that literacy was not always so central to jobs and earnings in
the nineteenth century.

The terms *education* and *literacy* thus far have been employed interchangeably. This has been done purposefully. However, they do not have the same
meaning. Education implies the broader process of socialization and acculturation
in addition to mere schooling, while literacy applies much more specifically to
the cognitive skills of reading and writing. It is essential that this difference in
meaning be understood. However, measures of education, necessary to test the
opinions of the value of schooling to a workingman, are scarce at best. Literacy
has the advantage, although it correlates indirectly with years of schooling and
regularity of attendance, of providing a simple index of the presence or absence
of some education in the individual case. In this way it serves as a proxy for
education, and will be employed as that symbol as well as in its more specific
connotation.

Industry, skill, and wealth could be individually obtained without education,
yet education itself was viewed as central to the development and the maintenance
of the economic system, as it was to the social order. This was the claim of the
nineteenth century schoolman: educated and literate labour was more productive
and of more benefit to both society and the individual. As Egerton Ryerson
claimed, 'every man, unless he wishes to starve outright, must read and write,
and cast accounts, and speak his native tongue well enough to attend to his own
particular business.'[4]

Ryerson long felt that education underlay any of the main branches of career pursuits. In his first report, of 1846, he laid the foundation.

the establishment of a thorough system of primary and industrial education, commensurate with the population of the country, as contemplated by the Government, and is here proposed, is justified by considerations of economy as well as of patriotism and humanity.

He further argued, employing evidence from Switzerland, that uneducated workers have neither logic, power of systematic arrangement, capacity for making sound deductions, nor collecting observations. Furthermore, 'this want of capacity of mental arrangements is shown in their manual operations.' Quite simply, it was the well-informed, well-educated workers who were thought to produce the most and the best, to possess superior moral habits, and to save. Uneducated, illiterate workers did not.[5]

There was little doubt or hesitation in proclaiming the benefits of education to the individual worker or the economic system. Yet, it is important to note as does Alison Prentice that 'statements relating specific occupational groups to social status tended to be vague and contradictory.' To Ryerson there were but two kinds of labour. Workers were either 'rude, simple or uneducated' or they were educated. These were the classes of society, as status increasingly included demeanour and gentility as well as the skills obtained. 'And by skills, few school promoters meant manual dexterity.' Literacy was just one such skill, an important one but not the only one. The benefits of education were not to be simple or direct, following from the advantages of literary training. They involved the inculcation of the proper code of behavior, which included morality and savings. Literacy revealed that process had begun.[6]

More than upward mobility through education, Ryerson emphasized the loss of status and downward mobility which he claimed would accompany the lack of schooling. Educated men might advance; the uneducated would surely fall. The burden he placed on the shoulders of the fathers:

Does a man wish his sons to swell the dregs of society—to proscribe them from all situations of trust and duty in the locality of their abode— to make them mere slaves in the land of freedom? Then let him leave them without education, and their underfoot position in society will be decided upon.

Additionally, Ryerson taught that all men were not to be educated to despise their occupations. Not all should aspire to the highest statuses of work. Practical men were needed too, and the supply of farmers and mechanics must not diminish. Education therefore could not alienate labour; it should not, for labour, he claimed, did not deaden the mind. The ideal mechanic then would combine 'in his own person, the qualifications and skills' of both the manufacturing superintendent and the operative.[7] In sum, all members of the working class required that which 'is essential to the successful pursuit of any one of the several departments of human activity and enterprise.' This was 'what is rudimental, or elementary in education.' In addition to this—reading, writing, arithmetic, and grammar—'each must learn that which will give him skill in his own particular employments,'[8] all the while making for more productive and more easily managed labour, advancing the nation's development. The individual came not first, in the benefits of education.

Ryerson of course was not an isolated spokeman for the economic benefits of education, for he was joined by many others throughout Anglo-America.[9] To a certain extent the spokesmen of the labour movement in Canada (and the United States) tended to agree with the voices of the middle-class school promoters when the benefits of education were discussed. Yet, to an important degree, labour's views were marked by a tension between a hunger for public schooling and doubts about the value of that form of education. As well, education represented to them something more than the making of better workmen.

That workmen desired educational provisions cannot be doubted. Their case was put forth in the first issue of the *Ontario Workman* in 1872: 'a thorough and general system of education we consider to be one of the first duties of the state; to see that in all its branches it is placed as near as possible within the reach of every son and daughter of the land.' The whole body of workmen should be raised by education and mental training to a higher intellectual level, not merely to permit isolated cases of social advancement. As the Hamilton *Palladium of Labor* claimed, 'an education is the practical side of American industrial success. In the industries where your working people have the best common school education, there you will find them earning the best wages.' This situation, however, was related to the absence of child labour and therefore to the absence of cheap competition. Education cut two ways in its benefits for working men: education was valuable in raising and maintaining wages and standards of labour, all the while it restricted the supply of workers. Yet, simultaneously, 'educated workmen, skilled workmen, and moral workmen . . . [made] labor respected as well as profitable.' Can we doubt that respect was less important than profit.

To make better workers was not the sole emphasis of the labour press, and their educational program was not quite that which Ryerson *et al.* had urged. Education ought to be mechanical, scientific, and technical: for the hand and body as well as the mind. They recommended a combination of work and study, four hours of each per day, certainly not the common school education of Ryerson. Literacy was at best a part of this process.[10]

Yet education was not primarily viewed as job preparation; it represented a higher ideal. A boy 'should be regarded, rather as the man that will be, than as the future doctor, lawyer, tradesman, farmer or mechanic.' Would such education intersect with economic productivity? The *Workman* suggests that workers were not to be educated to increase the value of capital through their labours. They were not simply *to be* educated: 'they must educate themselves to think; they must also learn to think for themselves.' To a large degree, education was to instil a direction, a goal, and the correct set of personal qualities—all more important than either skills or a mere hunger for gold. Education was, in one sense, character-building: it enabled workers to see their calling as useful and dignified. Morals, wisdom, and honourable careers ranked above the skills of the job. Were such men to be the loyal, punctual, non-disruptive workers the mill-owners desired, and Egerton Ryerson had promised if allowed to fashion a system of common schools? Education could lead to a rather different direction as the *Palladium* saw it:

> Educate first, agitate afterwards. Ignorance, superstition and timerity are the weapons which our oppressors have used most effectively against us in the past. Secure an education at any cost, put the ballot to its proper use, and then the fall of the venerable structure of legal robbery, alias monopoly, will shake to its centre. . . .[11]

Furthermore, the working class was more than a bit ambivalent about education and its value; this tension brought contradiction to their apparent endorsement of mass education:

> 'A self-made man' awakens in most all a glow of appreciation and regard which we do not feel for the man, equally distinguished for ability and learning he has got, who has been regularly taught in the schools. The one has had the countersign, and has been invited into the fort, the other has scaled the ramparts and conquered his place.

Success without the benefit of education was admired above that 'aided' by the schools, sharply contrasting with Ryerson's view. A curious tale related in the *Workman* indicates a further lack of regard for education-related skills. A man in England, the story went, had been jailed. To obtain bail, he was advised that he must sign his name. Overnight he taught himself to do so. The implications drawn were important; there was no *a priori* reason for illiterates or poor workers to be barred from the ballot. Inability to read or write need not disqualify a man from exercising his rights nor did it signify an inability to carry them out. A final point is implied. When needed, one could quickly and easily gain the skills of literacy.[12]

Ambivalence went even further. For example, *Fincher's Trades Review* reprinted 'Proverbs of the Billings Family,' which included 'if you kan't git clothes and education too, git the clothes.' A more interesting notice came from the Lawrence, Massachusetts, Mutual Benefit Society. The society began its operations with a system of bookkeeping for accounts, but:

> We are now doing it with checks. Our checks are printed on cardboard, of the following denominations . . . fifty cents, white; one dollar, blue; two dollar, pink; three dollar, yellow; five dollar, orange; ten dollar, salmon color. We find that this system is much easier than booking. . . .

Storemen and members need not even know the decimal system or how to read numbers; the colours differentiated for them. Literacy or schooling need not figure in workers' everyday transactions.

More important, perhaps, was the view that the present system of education was beset with certain evils. The *Palladium* urged its readers to learn a trade, not to be seduced by class education, with its examples in school of millionaires, for 'schools love to dwell too much on the achievements of professional men.' The school curriculum itself was found to be class-biased and the ideas of classical literature anti-workingmen; 'it is generally felt that our educational methods are one-sided.' Or, as Phillips Thompson expressed it, education 'if perverted by the inculcation of the untruths and half-truths of bourgeois political economy, is a hindrance rather than a help.' This he called 'wrong education,' tempting the worker with self-aggrandizement and wealth. And, the system of state education, compulsory by the 1870s, taught reading and 'then gives them dime novels for perusal, having previously given them a taste for such reading.' Such an education was not desirable; it would not benefit the workingman.[13]

The greatest evil of all rested at the pinnacle of the educational system—the university, which all working-men supported by taxation, but whose expense was prohibitive to most:

> It is an injustice that all the farmers, mechanics, and laborers should be taxed to teach the sons of the wealthy merchants and professional men Greek and Latin, and to support a lot of imported professors at high salaries to inculcate false and undemocratic notions of social caste, and teach an obsolete system of political economy. As a training for practical life and usefulness the ordinary university education is well-nigh value-less.

The educational system, from the top down, was biased against the working-man and his children. Lest the working class be falsely accused of anti-intellectualism, we must note that the *Palladium* urged that as good an education could be secured by well-directed reading.[14]

Reading, moreover, was often discussed (particularly in the pages of *The Ontario Workman*) in terms of amusement, enchantment, comfort, consolation, and leisure. 'Let the torch of intelligence be lit in every household.' The family hearth was the place for reading to begin, for the taste for reading ('one of the true blessings of life') to be found, and where parents were to guard against the taint of bad books, magazines, or newspapers. Relief from toil came through literature, making 'study the more refreshing,' and the delights of reading and contemplation brought wisdom 'in common with all mankind.' Here lay one real value of literacy to the workman. Knowledge is 'always power,' but this sense was not economic or material.[15]

Similarly, there were reasons more important than book-learning in the establishment of mechanics' institutes, working men's reading rooms and ancillary public institutions. Workmen needed a place to become better acquainted with one another, where their various interests could 'harmonize,' where committees could meet. Two hours of leisure each day spent in mental and physical culture 'would result in the shame and discomfiture of our opponents. . . .' Knowledge was power, in the purely political sense, much as Phillips Thompson would have it. Yet mass literacy need not be a requirement for the development of a shared consciousness, political culture, or the exchange of ideas or information. Merely a few readers could enlighten a greater number given the chance of congregation. As E.P. Thompson argued, 'Illiteracy by no means excluded men from political discourse.' They could listen and discuss. Activities such as those of 'Captain Swing' give validity to the argument, for it was the areas lowest in literacy that experienced the greatest amount of action. Moreover, it can not be obscured that 'the ability to read was only the elementary technique. The ability to handle abstract and consecutive argument was by no means inborn; it had to be discovered amid almost overwhelming difficulties. . . .' Much more than literacy or education is related to cohesion, consciousness, and activity; factors of social structure, economics, psychology, leadership and organization, numbers, and opportunity are equally if not more important. Easier communications, which literacy may advance, may aid the process, but literacy is hardly the key variable.[16]

Labour, in spite of an apparent clamour for equal educational opportunity, deviated from the premises of leading schoolmen who sought more education of the workforce for greater productivity. Ambivalent about the proper role, form, and content of education, and often placing its benefits and applications quite aside from their jobs, they sought to be free and independent, powerful in ways which would not please the men who desired to have the masses educated. More fundamentally, they did not always equate education with the skills required to gain a good job. Their notions of education and the uses of literacy were hardly the same as those of the schoolmen.

In the face of these discussions and arguments about the needs, uses, and benefits of education and literacy, what was the social distribution of literacy and what rewards did it bring? The question will be approached on two levels: first, the urban Ontario workforce at large, as revealed in routinely-generated census records, and second, the worker in a specific setting, the lumber industry.

Ontario in the 1860s and 1870s was an overwhelmingly literate society. Adult (twenty years and older) literacy ranged over ninety per cent as measured by the censuses of those years. In terms of wealth and occupation, there was a significant amount of stratification relating to illiteracy, for the majority of illiterates were employed as semi- and unskilled workmen. Yet, large numbers of men, lacking education, assumed positions of skill. These positions, moreover, were maintained over the course of the decade 1861 and 1871.[17]

One hundred and thirty-five illiterates in Hamilton, Kingston, and London, Ontario, held skilled labouring and artisanal occupations in 1861; forty-four held higher ranking jobs. Open to at least some illiterates were the occupations of blacksmith, builder, cabinetmaker, carpenter, clergyman, clothier, constable, customs collector, engineer, grocer, bailiff, innkeeper, joiner, mason, merchant, manufacturer, moulder, plasterer, printer, stonecutter, tailor, farmer, tavernkeeper, tinsmith, wheelwright, shoemaker, and watchmaker (see Tables 9.1 and 9.2).

Table 9.1   Occupational Structure of Literacy

		Hamilton literates	Hamilton illiterates	Kingston illiterates	London illiterates	Hamilton illiterates as a percentage of adult workforce
Professional/	N	306	3	1		
Proprietor	%	7.4	0.8	0.4	—	0.9
White Collar	N	768	21	13	6	
	%	18.6	5.4	5.4	3.9	2.7
Skilled	N	1467	72	34	29	
	%	35.4	18.6	14.2	19.2	4.7
Semi-skilled	N	959	75	85	32	
	%	23.2	19.4	35.4	21.2	7.3
Unskilled	N	638	216	107	84	
	%	15.4	55.8	44.6	55.6	25.3
Total Number		1138	387	240	151	

Source: Census, 1861.

In fact, no single occupation in Hamilton was comprised of a majority of illiterates; only one-fourth of the adult common labourers, fifteen per cent of seamstresses, and five per cent of female servants could not read or write. The remainder of those occupying these positions—low on the social order—were literate. Seventy-five per cent of the unskilled and ninety-three per cent of the semi-skilled possessed the skills of literacy, yet they had climbed no higher in occupational class. Their literacy was no advantage; to some illiteracy was a dis-advantage—but not to all illiterates.

The distribution of wealth held by illiterates strikingly parallels that of oc-cupation. The majority of illiterates whose wealth (as measured by total annual value on the 1861 city assessment rolls) could be determined were poor: below a poverty-line struck at the fortieth percentile of the assessed population (see Table 9.3). Nevertheless, sizeable numbers of illiterate workers achieved middle-class or higher economic ranking. Illiteracy did not consign all men to poverty. Similarly, many literate workers remained poor.

More important, though, than either the occupational or economic ranking of illiterate workmen was the relationship of literacy to the economic rewards of occupation. Among the unskilled and the semi-skilled, little economic advantage accrued to the more literate (see Table 9.4). However, stratification appears at the artisanal or skilled level of work, a line at which literacy's perceived advantages bespoke of reality. Yet, some illiterates fared well, especially those in white collar or small proprietor positions.

Possession of literacy did have its rewards, though its benefits were not clear or unambiguous ones. The relationship of basic education to work and earnings was very complex, complicated moreover by other social structural determinants,

Table 9.2   *Illiterates: Selected Occupations*

	Hamilton	As percentage of Hamilton adult workforce	Kingston	London
Barber	2	10.5	3	1
Blacksmith	8	10.3	—	2
Builder	2	7.2	—	1
Cabinet maker	1	1.9	—	—
Carpenter	14	4.7	4	4
Clergymen	1	3.2	—	—
Clothier	2	13.3	—	—
Constable	1	11.1	—	—
Customs Collector	1	33.3	1	—
Dealer	1	9.1	1	—
Dressmaker	1	1.4	2	—
Engineer	1	2.1	1	1
Farmer	3	10.0	3	2
Grocer	1	1.1	1	1
High Baillif	1	50.0	—	—
Innkeeper	1	6.7	3	—
Joiner	1	5.9	—	—
Labourer	205	25.2	105	83
Mail conductor	2	50.0	—	—
Mariner	1	2.0	10	—
Merchant	1	0.9	—	—
Mason	2	3.9	3	1
Moulder	2	3.6	—	—
Painter	2	3.2	—	—
Pedlar	2	6.1	1	1
Printer	1	2.5	1	—
Seamstress	8	15.1	2	—
Servant (f)	33	6.1	34	—
Tailor	8	6.2	8	—
Tavernkeeper	7	9.3	1	—
Tinsmith	2	5.1	—	—
Wagonmaker	2	18.2	—	—
Wheelwright	1	50.0	—	—
Gentleman	1	1.5	1	—
Watchmaker	1	7.2	1	—
Porter	3	4.8	1	2
Teamster	4	13.3	—	—
Plasterer	3	6.9	—	2
Clerk	—	—	1	—

such as age and ethnicity. Illiterate workers were far from a homogeneous lot; indeed, they possessed a social ordering within their own ranks, one which duplicated that of the larger society. As such, Irish Catholics, illiterate or not, (though the larger group of illiterates) and the aged (again, most often illiterate) are generally found in the lowest classes, occupational or economic. Much more than

Table 9.3 Economic Structure of Literacy

$		Hamilton literates	Hamilton illiterates	Kingston illiterates	Hamilton illiterates as percentage of Hamilton assessed heads	Percentile
			Total Annual Value-Linked Heads of Household			
0–23	N	329	76	16		0–19
	%	12.9	40.6	22.2	18.8	
24–42	N	609	62	36		20–39
	%	23.9	33.2	50.0	9.2	
43–71	N	477	22	11		40–59
	%	18.7	11.8	15.3	4.1	
72–168	N	593	15	8		60–79
	%	23.2	8.0	11.1	2.5	
169–375	N	230	10	1		80–89
	%	9.0	5.3	1.4	4.2	
376–700	N	141	1			90–94
	%	5.5	0.5	—	0.7	
701–2367	N	117	1	—	—	95–98
	%	4.6	0.5			
2368–9999	N	55	—	—	0.9	99–100
	%	2.2	—			
Total		2551	187	72		
Mean		$98.8	53.6	38.9		

Source: Census and Assessment. 1861

mere literacy operated in the establishment and maintenance of the stratification system of the nineteenth century. Education alone would not often dramatically affect class or social status.[18]

Lack of education similarly would not reduce status or class as the society modernized and industrialized. The social mobility of persistent illiterates (1861 to 1871) directly contradicts any such notions. Occupationally, stability was the normative experience as skilled workers held their positions, not slipping to lower class ranks. Economically, improvement and acquisition of wealth was the dominant experience, exclusive of occupation or ethnicity.[19]

Lack of education and absence of the tools of literacy did not remove all opportunity for higher-ranking occupations, wealth, or social mobility. Ethnicity favoured some illiterates, hindered others; often it required more years for their success. Factors such as chance and personality figured too, undoubtedly countering some of the disadvantages that illiteracy could bring. An illiterate could then achieve some success in the working world of the nineteenth century. These conclusions form a crucial baseline against which to assess the rhetorical economic claims of middle-class school promoters and against which to test the publicly-enunciated educational aspirations and criticisms of the working class. Far more

Table 9.4   Illiterates: Occupation and Wealth Percentiles of Total Annual Value (linked heads of household)

		0–19	20–39	40–59	60–79	80–89	90–94	95–98	99–100
					Unskilled Labour				
Hamilton	N	150	143	44	24	10	3.0	—	—
Literates	%	40.1	38.2	11.8	6.4	2.7	0.8	—	—
Hamilton	N	47	35	8	5	1	—	—	—
Illiterates	%	49.0	36.5	8.3	5.2	1.0	—	—	—
Kingston	N	9	20	5	1	—	—	—	—
Illiterates	%	25.7	57.1	14.3	2.9	—	—	—	—
					Semi-skilled Labour				
Hamilton	N	25	56	43	33	8	4	1	—
Literates	%	14.7	32.9	25.3	19.4	4.7	2.4	0.6	—
Hamilton	N	1	4	5	1	—	—	—	—
Illiterates	%	9.1	36.4	45.5	9.1	—	—	—	—
Kingston	N	2	7	1	2	—	—	—	—
Illiterates	%	16.7	58.3	8.3	16.7	—	—	—	—
					Skilled Labour				
Hamilton	N	68	257	222	198	56	33	28	8
Literates	%	7.8	29.5	25.5	22.8	6.4	3.8	3.2	0.9
Hamilton	N	13	14	7	2	2	—	1	—
Illiterates	%	33.3	35.9	17.9	5.1	5.1	—	2.6	—
Kingston	N	—	5	4	2	1	—	—	—
Illiterates	%	—	41.7	33.3	16.7	8.3	—	—	—
					White Collar				
Hamilton	N	17	52	54	154	58	29	23	8
Literates	%	4.3	13.2	13.7	39	14.7	7.3	5.8	2
Hamilton	N	—	2	1	1	6	—	—	—
Illiterates	%	—	20.0	10.0	10.0	60.0	—	—	—
Kingston	N	2	2	—	1	—	—	—	—
Illiterates	%	40.0	40.0	—	20.0	—	—	—	—

than the skills of literacy were fundamentally at issue; other matters were thought to be as central to the curriculum for the future worker.

The schoolmen's emphasis on the advantages of schooling, as illustrated by literacy, did not hold true for many workers. Literacy did not benefit all who possessed it nor handicap many who did not. Class, status, and discrimination functioned to prevent the direct rewards of education for some individuals, if not for the larger society. Perhaps the workers had a better vantage point from which to view the social order and realized that education did not guarantee a better position and its commensurate reward. Perhaps they saw the possible economic limits of literacy as well. Education, no doubt, could aid in economic life to a not insignificant degree—this they recognized—but it was not the morally dominant middle-class education. Moreover, to them literacy did have other important uses.

The paradoxes of literacy's relationship to work may be further explored, this time in a specific work setting focusing on one large lumbering concern, the Hawkesbury Lumber Company, located in the rich timberland of the Ottawa

River Valley.[20] Hawkesbury was in important ways a common larger-scale nine-teenth century firm. Lumbering was firstly a primary extractive industry, yet had a large component of secondary processing (or more properly industrial) func-tions. Lumbering, certainly capitalist-based, may be viewed as a transitional op-eration, between traditional and seasonal rhythms of work, and the discipline and internal control of the factory which milling would represent.[21] It was a mixture of two historical developments of economic organization, preindustrial and in-dustrial structures. Yet, it represents the large work setting, as 795 men were employed, or rehired, during the years, 1887–1903. The number hired varied from year to year from a maximum of 208 in 1880 to a low of six in 1906. Rather than indicating the introduction of new technology or mechanization, or a drastic response to the business cycle, this fluctuation illustrates the stability of the work-force, as most hands retained their positions.

The Hawkesbury Lumber Company is of special interest, as its detailed re-cords of employment contracts have survived. Ledgers of annual contracts were maintained, for 1887–1888 (Hamilton Brothers) and 1889–1903 (Hawkesbury). Exceptional records, they provide for each employee, contract date, occupation, name, wage rates, and a signature or mark—a measure of literacy.[22] From these records, the occupational hierarchy, wage structure, and the distribution of lit-erate and illiterate workers may be reconstructed.

The functional structure of occupations is readily discernible from these re-cords (see Table 9.5). The largest group of workers were the semi-skilled, al-though the group 'millmen' may well have included some skilled workmen. Skilled workers comprised the second largest group, twice the number of white collar, three times the unskilled. The diverse processes of work are easily seen from the list, including the extractive and the processing. The larger number of factory occupations (millman, ironworker, mechanic, millwright, etc.)—perhaps a third of the total—reveals the industrial side of operations.

Large variation existed in monthly rates of earnings, from $1.00 (day's work) to $87.00. The mean wage was $24.00, the median $22.50, certainly not atypical for the area or the period. (see Table 9.6).[23]

How did literacy intersect with the structure of earnings and occupations, our key concern? Fifty-two per cent of employees were literate and forty-eight per cent were not, though the measure underestimates the level of reading ability (Table 9.7). This was a high rate of illiteracy for Ontario, Canada, and North America for the last quarter of the century, but it reflects the traditionally high rates of Eastern Ontario and Quebec, and the French Canadian origins of the great mass of the workers.

Importantly, literacy did not always represent higher earnings, supporting the general outline presented above. Among the lowest-paid, ten or fewer dollars per month, illiterates dominated. The succeeding levels represented near parity, how-ever. These ranges, $21–30, which encompassed a plurality of the workforce, and $11–20 together comprised over eighty per cent of employees and herein illit-erates were hardly disadvantaged. With the exception of the lowest paid (probably

Table 9.5   Occupational Classification and Literacy: Hawkesbury Lumber Company (N = 672)

White Collar (8.5%)	N	Percentage literate
Foreman	17	88.2
Clerk	27	100.0
Timekeeper	6	83.3
Jobber	5	40.0
Lumber Inspector	1	100.0
Contractor	1	100.0
Total	57	89.5
Skilled Labour (17.7%)		
Blacksmith	11	81.8
Carpenter	19	52.6
Cutter	28	64.3
Millwright	14	57.1
Watchman	5	100.0
Mechanic	11	90.9
Gardener	2	100.0
Painter	1	0.0
Saddler	6	100.0
Sawyer	4	50.0
Trimmer	1	100.0
Wheelwright	1	100.0
Miller	1	0.0
Plasterer	1	0.0
Filer	1	100.0
Edger	6	50.0
Ironworker	7	0.0
Total	119	63.9
Semi-Skilled Labour (68.8%)		
Handyman	21	47.6
Teamster	149	36.9
Courier	1	100.0
Lumberman	2	0.0
Cook	1	0.0
Blockmaker	1	100.0
Fuller	1	100.0
Housekeeper	1	100.0
Stableman	3	66.7
Chainer/Raker	9	66.7
Picket	8	50.0
Spareman	3	0.0
Barkman	5	40.0
Pileman/Piler	69	40.6
Stabber	7	71.4
Slideman	16	31.3
Chopper	21	28.6
Loader/Striker	6	0.0

Table 9.5   Continued

Semi-Skilled Labour (68.8%) (*continued*)		
Boorman	8	50.0
Butter	3	0.0
Millman	99	32.3
Road Cutter	13	23.1
Logmaker	14	21.4
Total	462	36.8
Unskilled Labour (5.1%)		
Labourer	28	35.7
Choreman/Boy	6	16.7
Total	34	32.4

Table 9.6   Rates of Wage and Literacy (N = 752)

Rate Month	N	Percentage	Percentage literate
$ 1–10	12	1.6	25.0
11–20	298	39.6	43.3
21–30	341	45.4	49.0
31–40	48	6.4	89.6
41–50	40	5.3	72.5
51–60	2	0.3	50.0
61–70	7	0.9	100.0
70 +	4	0.5	50.0
mean	$24.12		
median	22.53		

Table 9.7   Literacy (N = 795)

	N	Percentage
Literate	413	51.9
Illiterate	382	48.1

casual or part-time), literate workmen fared little better than did their illiterate colleagues. Yet, there was a limitation on the level of earnings to which the majority of illiterates could achieve, much as the tabulations for assessed wealth revealed earlier. Here, however, it was the top twelve per cent from which illiterates were largely excluded, as they comprised just one-fifth of those earning $31 or more each month. Yet, some illiterates did make it to these higher levels (see Table 9.6). What such men lacked in education or booklearning, they no doubt compensated for with skill, experience, or common sense.[24] Presumably their employers did not find that their illiteracy made them less productive, and their skills were rewarded.

The rewards of illiterate workers were also illustrated by the benefits of rising wages. The contracts in some cases (24 per cent of all) provide two rates of remuneration for a workman: the initial wage used above and a subsequent higher rate (see Table 9.8). These men often were employed to hold more than one occupation, often a seasonal variation, showing a versatility of skill if not neces- sarily a high initial wage or occupational status. Illiterates dominated among men exhibiting this flexibility. One-and-a-half times as many illiterates increased their earnings than did literate employees, encompassing 70 per cent of all increases $1–10, 50 per cent of those above that line. These wage differentials strikingly demonstrate the ability of the uneducated to both perform a variety of skills and to benefit directly in the rewards.

Skills mean occupation, a matter of less interest than economic rewards in the determination of literacy's roles and an inadequate measure of skill or status.[25] As in the larger society, literacy related directly to occupational status in the Hawkesbury operation. Literacy increased directly with occupational class, with large differences separating the white collar from the skilled, and the skilled from the rest. However, these sharp divisions did not carry over into wages, certainly

Table 9.8   Wage Differentials and Literacy (N = 794)

Change in Wages	N	Percentage	Percentage literate
– $1	2	0.3	50.0
0	605	76.1	57.6
1–5	125	15.7	31.5
6–10	42	5.3	30.9
11–30	20	2.6	50.0

contradicting analyses of social or class structure based solely on occupation, a quite common sociological procedure. In fact, skilled workers were more highly paid than white collar and several semi-skilled workers attained high salaries. Important, as well, the obvious factory occupations were not all marked by high levels of literacy.

Moreover, some illiterates were able to achieve higher ranking occupations: 11 per cent of white collar and 36 per cent of skilled labour were unable to sign their names. Blacksmiths, carpenters, cutters, millwrights, mechanics, millers, and iron-workers could be illiterate. Though largely disadvantaged in occupation, il- literates held a great variety of jobs, only slightly handicapped in earnings. Lack of schooling did not significantly restrict them in the pay envelope or pocket.

Ninety-six men, longer-term employees, signed more than one contract. The influence of literacy on both this form of persistence within the firm and on the changing wage rates, advances the argument. Illiterates outnumbered literate workers in this category, and they dominated among those who increased earn- ings. Illiteracy, it would seem, was not the salient factor; more probably it was factors involving skills and performance about which the ledgers are silent. Illiterates' greater persistence is important; their greater volatility is intriguing (see Table 9.9A). Literacy's importance is seen more in the magnitude of the changes, as literate workmen gained a greater proportion of larger increases and larger decreases. Illiteracy may have placed restraints once more on mobility, but the restraints operated in both directions. Such limitations regulated that frequency of changes (see Table 9.9B).

Analysis of literacy's role in a specific occupational situation, the Hawkesbury Lumber Company, reveals the limits of illiteracy. These operated largely in the occupational sphere, but not in wages, flexibility, or salary increments. Literacy related to occupation strongly, but not completely, and very little to remuneration.[26] The Hawkesbury experience contradicts the expectations and perceptions of Ryerson and other middle-class school reformers and some working class opinion. Yet, it provides support for working class claims that education figured not always or necessarily in work, but could relate more directly to other aspects of life.

Table 9.9   Changing Wage Rates: Employees with Two or More Contracts (N = 96)

			Literate		Illiterate	
A	Same rate		9	20.9%	7	13.2%
	Increasing rate		27	62.8%	34	64.2%
	Decreasing rate		7	16.8%	12	22.6%
			43		53	
B	Increase	$1–5	15	55.6%	23	66.7%
		6–10	7	25.9%	10	29.4%
		11–18	5	18.5%	1	2.9%
	Decrease	$1–5	4	57.2%	9	75.0%
		6–8	3	42.8%	3	25.05%

Horace Mann, Secretary of the Massachussetts State Board of Education, was a middle-class reformer and a correspondent of Ryerson. In his *Fifth Report* (1842), he argued that education brought labour economic rewards. From a survey of manufacturers, he estimated that literate labour received 50 per cent more in pay than illiterate workers. Mann's estimate of a 50 per cent greater return from educated labour cannot be accepted, and a 10–20 per cent differential puts the question into a radically different light. Such a difference need not seem significant to the average working man, and key questions surround the reasons why he chose—and the majority did—to acquire some education and to send his children to school. An answer must lie with the contradictions inherent in the working class attitudes as well as the perceived non-economic benefits of education. Equally important questions pertain to how much schooling made a significant difference in wages.

We must ask, moreover, why discussions of the productivity of education so rarely spoke to specific job skills, those beyond abstract thought processes. Certainly a partial answer derives from an awareness of the moral virtues and behavioural traits which Egerton Ryerson, Mann, and his manufacturers all found central in the making of a contented and productive working class. In this, they were undoubtedly correct; as Gintis has found and Dreeben has argued, it is precisely the non-cognitive functions of schooling which most directly relate to the creation of a workforce acceptable to modern industrial capitalism. Toward this end their schools were designed to control, to prepare the masses.[27] And the schools were attended. Yet this does not sufficiently answer the basic query of how education related to the skills of individual occupations. Neither schoolmen nor labour spokesmen addressed this question to any meaningful degree. So we do not yet know, beyond educated guesses or modern analogies, how much education a carpenter, shoemaker, mechanic, painter, storekeeper, or hotelkeeper would need to do his job. They might need arithmetic, but, this could be gained without schooling.[28] Examples of the self-taught, to read or to write, are almost legendary. Yet, to what extent these skills, the tools of literacy, were required remains questionable for those not employed in professional clerical endeavours.

Moreover, it is very possible that reading was not often required in the search for employment. Advertisements for jobs are rarely found amidst the plethora of announcements and solicitations in nineteenth-century newspapers. Work was most often gained informally. Gareth Stedman Jones reported on the labour market of London, England, in the second-half of the century. Workers circulated among the trades, from one to another in a seasonal pattern:

> Skilled workers could gain information about the availability of work either from press announcements or from local trade union branches. But neither of these channels was really open to the casual worker. The only way he could find out about work was either by chance conversations in pubs or else by tramping around the yards and workshops in his districts . . . being known at local centres of casual work was more important than degree of skill and where character references were not required.[29]

Reading and writing were to such men—a sizeable proportion of the workforce in nineteenth century cities—relatively inconsequential to their quests for work, perhaps relatively unimportant in doing a good job. Jones' conclusions may hold for many skilled workers, journeymen, and artisans as well. The benefits of literacy lay elsewhere.

In the partly industrial setting of Hawkesbury, literacy did not significantly relate to individual rewards and presumably it did not relate to productivity. In this section, the more general question of the connection between education, literacy, and industrialization will be discussed. Recent research in economic history and development has begun to contradict the received wisdom that primary education is central to the process of industrialization and that it must logically precede 'take-off into sustained growth.' However, education and economic development need not be collateral or sequential processes. Productivity and wealth do not necessarily follow from mass literacy, as the history of Sweden and Scotland demonstrate. Both achieved mass literacy before the nineteenth century, yet remained desperately poor.

The larger issue is taken up by Roger Schofield who remarks, 'today literacy is considered to be a necessary precondition for economic development (and this one may question); but the historian might well ask himself whether this was so in England at the end of the eighteenth century' or in North America in the nineteenth. Schofield continues:

> The necessity of literacy as a precondition for economic growth is a persistent theme running through many UNESCO publications. Correlations between measures of industrialization and literacy both in the past and in the present are established in UNESCO *World Illiteracy at Mid-Century* (Paris, 1957), pp. 177–89. These measures are very general and throw no light on the question of why literacy should be considered essential to economic growth.[30]

In various studies, C. Arnold Anderson and Mary Jean Bowman have attempted to demonstrate the ways in which literacy should be considered essential to economic development.[31] Operating from the premise that education is one of the few sure roads to economic growth, they find increasingly a tendency to 'justify' education in economic terms.[32] In 1965, Anderson claimed that 'about 40 per cent of adult literacy or of primary enrolment is a threshold for economic development.'[33] Of course, he added that a level of education alone is an insufficient condition in a society lacking other prerequisites. Throughout their writings, Bowman and Anderson have stressed the necessity, if not the sufficiency, of a literacy threshold for sustained growth, a stage to be maintained until a level of 70–80 per cent is attained. Yet, they have not shown with any precision that these thresholds have meaning with historical evidence.

David McClelland, on the other hand, finds in his data that investment in education at the elementary or literacy level is inadequate; investment in education does not correlate positively with growth rates. He concludes:

> Primary school attendance has a doubtful relationship to significant improvements, in the labor force or even to literacy itself. That is, the marginal product of a primary school education would seem likely to be low, because skilled artisans may function as well without being literate. Furthermore, primary school attendance is not enough by itself to lift a person to the level of being able to perform jobs characteristic of the middle class.

A strong relationship, however, derives from post-primary education, if the lag-time between training and effect on the economy is considered. 'Education is a long-term investment from the economic point of view.' This approach seems more sound, in historical context, though problems do remain, especially within the industrial revolution.[34]

What about the past, and the transition to the factory itself as the work-setting for industrial capitalism? In the most general sense, John Talbott has remarked, 'in the first decades of industrialization, the factory system put no premium on even low-level intellectual skills. Whatever relationships existed between widespread literacy and early industrial development must have been quite roundabout.'[35]

Ironically for those who perceived the productive value of educated and literate labour, the relationship, at least in England, was less than direct. Early industrialization was, first of all, disruptive to education, and adult literacy levels fell as a result. The demand for child labour, in England and in North America, greatly reduced the chances for a lower-class child to attend school.[36] Factory schools were, on the whole, rare, ineffectual, and irregularly attended. Secondary education was unheard of for the children of the working class.

The logical result, Roger Schofield and Michael Sanderson have concluded, was reflected directly in the literacy rates of late eighteenth- and early nineteenth-century England. Sanderson discovered that 'the English Industrial Revolution cannot be seen as one nourished by rising educational standards at least at the elementary level . . .'[37] The decline in literacy did not impede the upsurge of economic growth because the nature of industrialization was such to make very low literacy demands on the educational system. Or, as Schofield expands:

> Thus, insofar as economic growth in this period entailed the acquisition of a large number of practical skills by a growing proportion of the population, developments in literacy and education were probably largely irrelevant to it. And, insofar as economic growth resulted from the increased productivity of labor brought about by the shift from domestic to factory production, literacy and education were also probably largely irrelevant for many of the new industrial occupations recruited a mainly illiterate work force . . .[38]

Knack, as Sanderson calls it, was of greater importance than booklearning in the process of industrialization.

In the historical case, then, of English industrialization, there is good evidence to part from the company of those who must relate mass education directly to economic development. England had reached the 40 per cent 'threshold' level of literacy by 1750 (at least for males); it remains for researchers to isolate an exceptional case to that rule of thumb. The threshold level may well be so general as to be meaningless. The relationship of higher levels of education to development continues to be obscure, though post-primary education played no role at this early stage. As Roger Schofield ably expressed it, 'for England, at least, the usual causal relationships between literacy and economic growth might probably be reversed. In this alternative perspective the reduction in illiteracy in nineteenth-century England would appear more as a cultural change brought about by economic growth than as the cause of growth.'[39]

If not education as preparation for productive labour, what then? Sidney Pollard and Edward Thompson, in pathbreaking analyses, have revealed that the labouring population had to be trained to the workings, of the factory, broken to industrial spirit, rhythm, and pace in ways to which literacy was far from central. As Pollard demonstrates, it was not necessarily the better worker, but the stable one who was worth more to manufacturers; 'often, indeed, the skilled apprenticed man was at a discount because of the working habits acquired before entering a factory.'[40] The problem was of course one of discipline, and factory-owners suffered great difficulties in training men to 'renounce their desultory habits of work, and identify themselves with the unvarying regularity of the complex automation.' Discipline was needed to produce goods on time. To orient the hands to this routine, rules became the norm: 'Work rules, formalized, impersonal and *occasionally printed,* were symbolic of the new industrial relationships.'[41] No primacy for literacy, here, in solving the most difficult of capitalism's conundrums.

To 'educate' the workers was necessary. But it was not an education in reading and writing, but

> the need to educate the first generation of factory workers to a new factory discipline, [part of] the widespread belief in human perfectability . . . but one of their consequences was the preoccupation with the character and morals of the working class which are so marked a feature of the early stages of industrialization.[42]

This view resembles rather closely that of many North American manufacturers, yet their desire for provision of schooling and the timing of provision made for one crucial difference.

Thompson focuses more closely at the importance of time in the transition to the factory, the place of precise and mechanically-maintained clock-time. Whether or not literacy was needed to tell time, 'the bell would also remind men of [time's] passing. . . . Sound served better than sight, especially in growing manufacturing districts.' The first generation of factory workers was taught the importance of time by its masters. But there was an area to which the school could contribute; as we remarked above and as Thompson notes as well, schools could be useful in circulating 'time-thrift.' Charity schools, for example, were praised for teaching industry, frugality, order, regularity, and punctuality. By the time a child reached six or seven years of age, he or she should be 'habituated, not to say naturalized, to Labour and Fatigue;' the socialization of the children of the poor should commence at age four. The parallels between the rules of the school and the rules of the factory must not be overlooked either. 'Once within the school gates, the child entered the new universe of disciplined time. . . . Once in attendance, they were under military rule.'[43]

Some Englishmen, along with Ryerson, were aware of the values of the school. Its importance in the accommodation to the factory was certainly not in terms of literacy or skills, but in morals, discipline, and social values. As R.P. Dore concluded for a different culture, Tokugawa Japan:

> But what does widespread literacy do for a developing country? At the very least it constitutes a training in being trained. The man who has in childhood submitted to some processes of disciplined and conscious learning is more likely to respond to further training, be it in a conscript army, in a factory, or at lectures arranged by his village agricultural association.[44]

Training in being trained, as Dore aptly puts it, is the crucial job preparation and the problem for industrialism. The English examples have been very instructive in this manner, yet the North American experience differed greatly in timing and the sequence of events. England industrialized well before literacy reached universal proportions (not much beyond a 40 per cent 'threshold'); education seems not an integral part of the transition, and there is no role for a lag-time for educational investments. The transition to the factory itself was far from easy—marked by riots, strikes, disruption, luddism, Chartism.

On the contrary, North American development, particularly Canadian industrialization, came comparatively much later. Importantly, it followed the establishment of systems for mass elementary education, though not much secondary schooling, and the attainment of new universal levels of literacy. As well, I would advance the hypothesis that in North America the transition to industrial capitalism was a smoother one.[45] There is, I would now suggest, an intimate connection between the timing of mass educational provision and the subsequent patterns of industrialization. Schooling, in this formulation, paved the way for the economic transformation and here is the function of lag-time at the elementary level. This is the purpose of education of which Ryerson and other middle-class reformers spoke: this is how they sought to control the masses in the cause of productivity and national development.

To do so, it was essential to break pre-industrial work habits, to 'Canadianize' the immigrant worker, removing him from his traditional origins and patterns. As might be expected, the transmission of literacy's cognitive skills was of secondary importance. Yet literacy, in virtually all cases, came with schooling and had its uses, some of which labour grasped. Print had important socializing functions; literacy served to regularize behaviour and to discipline man. In the North American case, education could replace much of the coercion of English labour to strict factory rules and internalized self-discipline. As J.F.C. Harrison has argued, 'the process of assimilation was closely related to the spread of literacy. . . .' And, in the long run, he concluded, education was much more effective in instilling the necessary discipline.[46] Provision of mass schooling; the working class's acceptance, though a questioning one, of them; increasing rates of attendance; and compulsory education all featured in this direction; promoting discipline, moral values, and the 'training in being trained' which mattered most in the preparation of a modern industrial workforce. These were the purposes of the school.[47]

Notes

1 *Journals of Education for Upper Canada,* I (1848), pp. 289–301; for English parallels, see Central Society of Education, *Papers,* (London, 1837–1839); on the centrality of morality in nineteenth century education, see ALISON PRENTICE, 'The School Promoters: Education and Social Class in Nineteenth Century Upper Canada', (PhD thesis, University of Toronto, 1974), and my 'Literacy and Social Structure in the Nineteenth Century', (PhD thesis, University of Toronto, 1975), Chapter I.

2 *Journal of Education,* II (1849), pp. 19–20.

3 *Hamilton* (Ontario) *Spectator and Journal of Commerce,* December 6, 1848; JOHN DUNCAN, *The Education of the Ordinary Child,* London, 1943, p. 60.

4 *Journal of Education,* VII, (1854), p. 134.

5 'Report on a System of Elementary Instruction for Upper Canada, 1846', in *Documentary History of Education for Upper Canada,* (Ed.) J.C. HODGINS, Vol. 6, Toronto, 1899, pp. 143, 144–145.

6 PRENTICE, *op cit.,* pp. 150, 174.

7 *Journal of Education,* I, (1848), p. 297; *Documentary History of Education,* pp. 11, 45.

8 'The Importance of Education to an Agricultural People', in *Documentary History of Education,* Vol. 7, p. 141.

9 In Canada, for example, CHARLES CLARKE. See his 1877 address to the South Wellington, Ontario, Teachers Association: *Teachers and Teaching (and) Then and Now.* Elora, Ont., 1880, p. 2. For British examples, see RICHARD JOHNSON, 'Educational Policy and Social Control in Early Victorian England', *Past and Present,* No. 49, (1970), pp. 96–119. The major spokesman for these ideas was Horace Mann, Secretary of the Massachusetts State Board of Education. He had a direct influence on RYERSON: DAVID ONN 'Egerton Ryerson's Philosophy of Education: Something Borrowed or Something New?', *Ontario History,* Vol. LXI, (1969), pp. 77–86; and 'Report Upon a System', *op. cit.* On MANN: *Annual Report of the Secretary of the Board of Education,* 5, (Boston, 1842); MARIS A. VINOVSKIS, 'Horace Mann on the Economic Productivity of Education', *New England Quarterly,* Vol. 43, (1970), pp. 550–571: Also see: FRANK TRACEY CARLETON, *Economic Influences upon Educational Progress in the United States, 1820–1850* (reprinted, New York, 1965). Chapter 4; GRAFF, 'Literacy and Social Structure', Chapter 5; HERBERT GINTIS 'Education, Technology, and the Characteristics of Worker Productivity', *American Economic Review,* Vol. 61, (1971), pp. 266–279; ROBERT DREEBEN, *On What is Learned in School.* Reading, Mass., 1968; ALEX INKELES, 'Making Men Modern', *American Journal of Sociology,* Vol. 75, (1969), pp. 208–225. On another spokesman for the ideas, EDWARD JARVIS of Dorchester, Massachusetts, see: EDWARD JARVIS, MD, 'The Value of Common-School Education to Common Labour', *Report of the United States Commissioner of Education,* Washington, 1872, pp. 572–585.

10 *Ontario Workman,* April 18, 1872, March 13, 1873 (hereafter cited as *OW*); *Palladium of Labor.* Hamilton, Ont., May 16, 1885; see also Feb. 7, 1885 (hereafter cited as *POL*). See also *Fincher's Trades Review* (1863–66), a Philadelphia weekly, read by and concerned with Canadian labour, which included letters from Canadian workmen; September 24, 1864, February 4, 1865 (hereafter cited as *FTR*); *OW,* May 2, 1872, January 16, 1873, February 12, 1874; *POL,* December 22, 1883, February 23, 1883, September 19, 1885.

11 *OW,* February 13, 1873; January 22, 1873, *FTR,* June 27, 1863, October 22, 1864, September 17, 1864, July 11, 1863, *POL,* November 24, 1883, November 22, 1884, January 5, 1884. See also PHILLIPS THOMPSON, *The Politics of Labor.* New York, 1887, pp. 11–14, who claimed that reading would open the eyes of the working man

to the injustices of the system. THOMPSON, a Toronto radical journalist, often contributed on the *POL* under the pseudonym Enjolras.

12 *OW,* April 2, 1874 and October 14, 1872.

13 *FTR,* June 27, 1863, February 11, 1865; *POL,* November 10, 1883, August 29, 1885, August 16, 1884; THOMPSON, *op. cit.,* pp. 17, 58, 83, 151; *POL,* February 2, 1884.

14 *POL,* December 1, 1883; see also THOMPSON, *op. cit.* pp. 61, 171.

15 *OW,* November 22, 1872, December 19, 1872, January 2, 1873, February 12, 1874, March 19, 1874; *POL,* March 1, 1884, September 1, 1883; *FTR,* October 22, 1864, September 17, 1864, July 11, 1863.

16 *FTR,* March 18, 1865, April 8, 1865, *FTR,* November 7, 1863, January 16, 1864; See also October 3, 1863, and *POL,* September 8, 1883. Ironically, in fact, mechanics' institutes in Canada, as in Britain, tended to be middle class in inspiration and in membership; see J. DONALD WILSON, 'Adult Education in Upper Canada before 1850,' *The Journal of Education* (U.B.C.), 19 (1973), pp. 43–54; FOSTER VERNON, 'The Development of Adult Education in Ontario, 1790–1900' (unpublished PhD thesis, University of Toronto, 1969); and E. ROYLE, 'Mechanics Institutes and The Working Classes, 1840–1860,' *The Historical Journal,* 14 (1971), pp. 305–321. See also JOHN FOSTER, 'Nineteenth Century Towns—A Class Dimension,' in *The Study of Urban History,* (Ed.) H.J. DYOS (London, 1968), pp. 281–300. See, in particular, E.P. THOMPSON, *The Making of the English Working Class,* New York, 1967 pp. 712–713; R.K. WEBB. *The British Working Class Reader, 1790–1848,* London, 1955; and HOBSBAWM and GEORGE RUDE, *Captain Swing,* New York, 1969; JOHN FOSTER, *Class Struggle and the Industrial Revolution* London, 1974.

17 See H.J. GRAFF, 'Towards a Meaning of Literacy: Literacy and Social Structure in Hamilton, Ontario,' *History of Education Quarterly,* 12 (1972), pp. 411–431; and 'Literacy and Social Structure in Elgin County, 1861' *Histoire sociale / Social History,* 6 (1973), pp. 25–48, as well as my dissertation.

18 'Literacy and Social Structure in the Nineteenth Century,' Chapters 2 & 3 provide full detail.

19 *Ibid.,* Chapter 3.

20 The company was begun by GEORGE and WILLIAM HAMILTON of Quebec in 1797 and transformed into a joint-stock venture upon its sale to Blackburn, Egan, Robinson, and Thistle in 1889, taking on the new name of Hawkesbury. A few summary statistics suggest the scope: by 1885 30 million feet of timber were cut annually and milled by 350 hands, by 1909 the annual yield was 50 million feet. Hawkesbury continued to operate until 1936. The records are found in the Archives of the Province of Ontario (Toronto).

   On the lumber industry, in general see MICHAEL S. CROSS. 'The Dark Druidical Groves: The Lumber Community and the Commercial Frontier in British North America to 1854,' unpublished PhD Thesis, University of Toronto, 1968; EDWARD McKENNA 'Unorganized Labour versus Management: The Strike at the Chaudiere Lumber Mills, 1891,' *Histoire Sociale / Social History,* 5 (1972), pp. 186–211; and A.R.M. LOWER *The North American Assault on the Canadian Forest* (Toronto, 1938).

21 See, E.P. THOMPSON, 'Time, Work-Discipline, and Industrial Capitalism,' *Past and Present,* No. 38 (1967), pp. 56–97; and SIDNEY POLLARD, 'Factory Discipline in the Industrial Revolution,' *Economic History Review,* 16 (1963), pp. 254–271.

22 On signatures and literacy, see ROGER SCHOFIELD, 'The Measurement of Literacy in Pre-Industrial England,' in *Literacy in Traditional Society,* (Ed.) JACK GOODY. Cambridge, 1968, pp. 311–325; and KENNETH A. LOCKRIDGE, *Literacy in Colonial New England.* New York, 1974. Signatures, it should be noted, slightly underestimate the level of reading literacy, as some men would be able to read and not write.

23 For comparative wage data see McKENNA, *op. cit.,* p. 190, and *Royal Commission on the Relations of Labor and Capital.* Ottawa, 1889, Ontario Evidence.

24 Information on worker's age could be very revealing in this regard.
25 See, on this point, MICHAEL B. KATZ, 'Occupational Classification in History,' *Journal of Interdisciplinary History*, 3 (1972), pp. 63–88.
26 This analysis may be largely confirmed and supplemented by an examination of the receipt book of the Madawaska Improvement Company (1888–1903) in the Provincial Archives of Ontario. This too shows little disadvantage in wages for illiterates, although data is less complete than the Hawkesbury material.
27 Of the important literature of the social control functions of education, see PRENTICE, *op. cit.*: JOHNSON, *op. cit.*: CARL KAESTLE. *The Evolution of an Urban School System.* Cambridge, Mass. 1973; STANLEY SCHULTZ, *The Culture Factory*, New York, 1973; MICHAEL B. KATZ, *The Irony of Early School Reform.* Cambridge, Mass., 1968; RUTH MILLER ELSON, *Guardians of Tradition.* Lincoln, 1964; J.M. GOLDSTRUM, *The Social Context of Education, 1808–1870.* Dublin, 1972; SAMUEL BOWLES, 'Unequal Education and the Reproduction of the Social Division of Labor,' in *Schooling in a Corporate Society*, (Ed.) MARTIN CARNOY. New York, 1972, pp. 36–64; and the Special Issue of the *History of Education Quarterly*, 12 (Fall, 1972).
28 See above 9. *Massachusetts Teacher*, 15 (1862), p. 210 and Rev. JOHN MAY, *Essays on Educational Subjects* (Ottawa, 1880), p. 5.
29 JONES, *Outcast London.* Oxford, 1971, pp. 82–83; See also E.J. HOBSBAWM, 'The Tramping Artisan,' in his *Labouring Men* New York, 1967, pp. 41–74. Skilled literate, and organized, workingmen could of course read about economic conditions, and therefore employment opportunities, in the working class press. The development, circulation (including oral transmission of news and group readership), and impact of the developing Canadian labour press in this period is obviously crucial and merits detailed and separate study.
30 SCHOFIELD, *op. cit.*, p. 312.
31 ANDERSON, 'Literacy and Schooling on the Development Threshold: Some Historical Cases,' in *Education and Economic Development*, (Ed.) ANDERSON and BOWMAN. Chicago, 1965, pp. 347–362; BOWMAN and ANDERSON. 'Concerning the Role of Education in Development,' in *Old Societies and New States*, (Ed.) CLIFFORD C. GEERTZ. New York, 1963, pp. 247–279; and BOWMAN and ANDERSON, 'Human Capital and Economic Modernization in Historical Perspective' paper presented to the Fourth International Congress of Economic History, 1968. For a critical analysis of approaches in the economics of education, see W.G. BOWEN, 'Assessing the Economic Contribution of Education,' in *The Economics of Education*, I, (Ed.). MARK BLAUG. Harmondsworth, 1968, pp. 67–100.
32 Such were the roots of the human capital school of economists, largely dominated by GARY BECKER and THEODORE SCHULTZ.
33 'Literacy and Schooling,' p. 347.
34 'Does Education Accelerate Economic Growth?' *Economic Development and Cultural change*, 14 (1966), pp. 262, 266.
35 'The History of Education,' *Daedalus*, 100 (1971), p. 141.
36 MICHAEL SANDERSON, 'Education and the Factory in Industrial Lancashire, 1780–1840.' *Economic History Review*, 20 (1967), p. 266 and 'Social Change and Elementary Education in Industrial Lancashire, 1780–1840,' *Northern History*, 3 (1968), pp. 131–154. The labour press cited above made many of the same points, as did both the commissioners and the evidence in *The Royal Commission on the Relations of Labor and Capital*. Ottawa, 1889. An excellent compendium of its four volumes has been edited by GREGORY KEALEY (Toronto, 1973).
37 'Literacy and Social Mobility in the Industrial Revolution,' *Past and Present*, No. 56 (1972), pp. 75, 102.
38 'Dimensions of Illiteracy, 1750–1850,' *Explorations in Economic History*, 10 (1973). pp. 452–453.

39 *Ibid.,* p. 454.
40 POLLARD, *op. cit.,* 255, see also his *Genesis of modern Management* Harmondsworth, 1968, esp. Chapter 5; THOMPSON, 'Time, Work-Discipline,' KEITH THOMAS, 'Work and Leisure in Pre-Industrial Societies,' *Past and Present,* No. 29 (1964); ROBERT MALCOLMSON, *Popular Recreation in English Society, 1700–1850.* Cambridge, 1973; and HERBERT GUTMAN, 'Work, Culture, and Society in Industrializing America, 1815–1919,' *American Historical Review,* 78 (1973), pp. 531–588.
41 RICHARD ARKWRIGHT, quoted in POLLARD, 'Factory Discipline,' p. 258 (emphasis mine).
42 *Ibid.,* p. 268.
43 THOMPSON, 'Time, Work-Discipline,' pp. 64, 84–85.
44 *Education in Tokugawa Japan.* London, 1967, p. 292.
45 At this stage of research this contention must remain hypothetical. We know all too little about the transition in Canada, and comparative studies of Anglo-America are sadly lacking. Recent work by CHARLES TILLY and EDWARD SHORTER on strikes in France suggests one approach, though an exclusive focus on strike action would obscure some issues.
46 *The Early Victorians, 1832–1851.* London, 1971, pp. 135–136. See also the work of MARSHALL MCLUHAN.
47 This is, of course, the mere skeleton of a theory, for many questions surrounding the actual experience of schooling remain unanswered. There is, for example, the problem of irregular attendance which was widespread. Did this militate against the schools' success? Quite simply we do not yet know how much exposure to the routine and the message of the schools was required for sufficient training.

For a fascinating argument on a closely related theme, that of the sanitation movement, see RICHARD L. SCHOENWALD, 'Training Urban Man' in *The Victorian City,* (Ed.) H.J. DYOS and MICHAEL WOLFF. London, 1973, pp. 669–692.

The experience of Quebec in the nineteenth century illustrates vividly the problems of the transition in a society without mass literacy; see, *Royal Commission on the Relations of Labor and Capital,* Quebec Evidence. See also MICHAEL BLISS' interesting attempts to explain manufacturers' lack of understanding of these problems; 'Employers, as representative as anyone else of prevailing social mores, were often confused and puzzled when faced with insistence that the familiar rules of the game should be changed, and not in their favour.' 'A Living Profit: Studies in the Social History of Canadian Business, 1883–1911' (unpublished PhD thesis), University of Toronto, 1972; see also pp. 137, 148, 157; published as *A Living Profit.* Toronto, 1974, see esp. Chapter 3.

10 'Pauperism, Misery, and Vice': Illiteracy and Criminality in the Nineteenth Century

'First, such a system of general education amongst the people is the most effectual prevention of pauperism, and its natural companions, misery and vice.'[1] With this statement, made early in his career as Chief Superintendent of Education for Upper Canada, Egerton Ryerson embraced a central tenet of the mid-nineteenth-century school promoter. That education could prevent criminality, if not cure it, was integral to school promoters' programs: they marshalled reams of evidence, rhetorical and statistical, to prove the perceived relationship between ignorance or lack of education and criminality. In their formulations, ignorance and crime were associated not only with each other, but also with illiteracy, a visible and measurable sign of the lack of schooling.

The prominence accorded formal schooling and instruction in literacy for the masses as social insurance against criminality and disorder forms one significant example of the broad new consensus about education which emerged throughout Anglo-America by mid-century. In a period of massive social change, of urban-industrial modernization, education increasingly was seen as the dominant tool for social stability for societies in which stratification by social class had replaced traditional paternalistic control by rank and deference. The changing scale and bases of society demanded the creation of new institutions, like the school, to aid in the inculcation of restraint, order, discipline, integration: the correct rules for social and economic behavior in a changing and modernizing context. No longer could proper social morality and values be successfully transmitted by informal and traditional means; the forces of change necessitated formal institutions to provide morally grounded instruction aided, eased, and speeded by carefully structured provision of literacy. Literacy became the vehicle for the efficient training of the population. Morality without literacy was more than ever seen as impossible, and literacy alone was potentially dangerous. The nineteenth century educational consensus was therefore founded upon a 'moral economy' of literacy. Agencies created to prepare men and women for their future places in society seized upon the controlled transmission of literacy. The potential of printing was to achieve the desired and expected ends in the inculcation of a morally ordered and religiously rooted behavioral code: the guarantee of conservative and orderly social and economic progress.[2]

Despite the existence of this unified attitude to the place of the school in society and the goals of education, the connections advanced between the provision of proper education, literacy, and the reduction of disorder and criminality, or conversely, illiteracy and criminality, were often less than satisfactory or conclusive.

Egerton Ryerson's statements, consequently, were not always clear and unambiguous, especially regarding the role of illiteracy. To a significant extent, of course, the moral importance of schooling represented the critical factor, but in their use of the statistics of illiteracy, school promoters in Canada and elsewhere confused their arguments, uncertain at times about what form of schooling would best serve their purposes. Their focus on schooling, moreover, obscured the role of other factors which contributed to criminality and made their notions of causality less than convincing. In spite of their explanations, criminality, or more properly arrest and conviction, related to much more than illiteracy. Illiteracy, to be sure, was often symptomatic of poverty and lower class status, which were also associated with arrest and punishment, but it was only one element in a complex of factors. Ethnicity, class, sex, and the suspected crime, rather than illiteracy alone, determined conviction, as those with fewest resources were most often convicted. Systematic patterns of punishment, apparently, might relate to factors other than guilt.

The link between social inequality as well as the distribution of literacy, on the one hand, and factors of ethnicity and sex on the other, was vital. Ascribed characteristics thus determined social stratification, access to economic opportunity, social discrimination, and apparently judicial treatment as well, contradicting much of the school promoters' rhetoric about the advantages of educational achievement in countering factors of birth (one key premise of modern society). Literacy, the evidence suggests, in spite of the schoolmen's arguments, did not relate directly to individual advancement or to social progress as exemplified by a reduction of criminality. Similarly, illiteracy, in isolation from ethnicity, or sex, did not relate solely or unambiguously to criminality, nor to poverty or immobility. The centrality of literacy in educational rhetoric and the promise of schooling itself, past as well as present, demand revision.[3] The case of criminality, significantly, supports the emerging outlines of a new historical sociology of education.

This chapter focuses upon the relationship between criminality and illiteracy perceived and discussed by school promoters. First, their causal notions and their evidence will be examined, and then tested through an analysis of a nineteenth-century gaol register which included literacy among its data.

I

The extent of criminality was among the most pressing social concerns of Upper Canadians in the mid-nineteenth century.[4] With other Anglo-Americans, they asked: what had caused the apparent increase in crime and violence; what produced criminality in the populace? The complex answers given to these questions included immigration, poverty, urbanism, immorality, ignorance, and, of course, illiteracy. These forces, all at work in Upper Canada as elsewhere, were woven into a causal explanation of criminality. In these explanations, the connection between ignorance, illiteracy, and criminality, always crucial, formed a central assumption of men who attempted to build and expand systems of mass schooling. To them, education was fundamental to the prevention of crime and disorder.

Crime in Upper Canada, it was thought, was intimately connected to 'an influx of criminal elements from outside the country, and particularly from Ireland.'[5] To Ryerson, immigrants were 'notoriously destitute of intelligence and industry, as they are of means of subsistence.'[6] Lack of schooling, idleness, and poverty were the causes of this social problem, and foreigners were the greatest offenders. Cities, moreover, were the scene of the greatest difficulty; they represented the seed-bed of crime and were of course the centers of reform attention. Crime, according to Ryerson, 'may be said in some sort to be hereditary, as well as infectious, . . . to multiply wretchedness and vice . . . [as] the gangrene of pauperism in either cities or states is almost incurable.'[7] The city, especially Toronto, provided his common examples, and throughout his tenure in office he regularly provided evidence from gaols and prisons to show that most inmates came from the most populous places. Summarizing this widely held belief, Michael Katz has concluded, 'in the lexicon of reformers the first fact about crime was its urban nature.'[8] Agreement was joined on this point throughout Anglo-America and in much of the West.[9]

These factors were associated with causes of criminality; ignorance, however, was the source. Consequently, Ryerson and many of his contemporaries urged that their systems of popular education were the most effective preventatives of ignorance, pauperism, misery, and vice.[10] How schooling was to accomplish this, and, conversely, how lack of schooling resulted in criminality were points, on which the school promoters were less than clear. At least this was where their statements became vague. To document an apparent relationship and to urge prevention was one thing; to explain it was quite another.

Egerton Ryerson enunciated the commonly perceived connection in its starkest and most direct form in his first report.

> Now the Statistical Reports of Pauperism and crime in different counties, furnish indubitable proof that ignorance is the fruitful source of idleness, intemperance and improvidence, and these the fosterparents of pauperism and crime. The history of every country in Europe may be appealed to in proof and illustration of the fact . . . that pauperism and crime prevail in proportion to the absence of education amongst the labouring

classes, and that in proportion to the existence and prevalence of education amongst these classes, is the absence of pauperism and its legitimate offspring.[11]

To this he would soon add the history of Upper Canada. Here, however, Ryerson succinctly stated that ignorance—the lack of schooling—was the first factor in a life of crime. Simply, 'the condition of the people and the extent of crime and violence among them follow in like order,' from the state of education. Among other evidence, he cited English Poor Law Commissioners ('a principal cause of [Northumberland's lack of crime] arises from the education they receive' and the example of Prussia's school system.[12] Others in Upper Canada concurred. The Toronto *Globe,* which disagreed with Ryerson on many issues, declared: 'educate your people and your gaols will be abandoned and your police will be disbanded; all the offenses which man commits against his own peace will be comparatively unknown . . .'[13] Thus education was not only effective; it was the cheapest agency of prevention: 'The education of the people forms part of the machinery of the State for the prevention of crime.'[14] Costs and public expenses were important as well, and often central to the school promoters' arguments. To them, schools were both cheaper than gaols and prisons and a better investment. Naturally, they felt 'it is much better to prevent crime by drying up its sources than by punishing its acts.'[15]

Ignorance and illiteracy, as Ryerson argued, were the first causes of poverty and crime, which in turn were inextricably linked. Each was seen to cause the other, particularly among immigrants and in cities.[16] The result was a simple causal explanation or model of criminality: ignorance caused idleness, intemperance, and improvidence, which resulted in crime and poverty.[17] Ryerson and other promoters saw crime not only as the 'legitimate' child of this chain of factors, they also labelled each factor a crime itself. For example, idleness and ignorance were more than causes, they also were offenses: 'If ignorance is an evil to society, voluntary ignorance is a crime against society . . . if idle mendicancy is a crime in a man thirty years of age, why is not idle vagrancy a crime in a boy ten years of age? The latter is the parent of the former.'[18]

Ignorance also led to poverty, and education, conversely, led to success. Again the *Globe* agreed: 'If we make our people intelligent, they cannot fail to be prosperous.'[19] The poor, therefore, were ignorant, often living lives of crime and withholding their children from school—preparing the future class of criminals.[20] In fact, families and parents were blamed for the prevalence of ignorance, nonattendance, and the resulting illiteracy, and neglectful parents were as guilty as their children. Indeed, they were 'bringing up and sending abroad into the community [children] who are prepared by ignorance, by lawlessness, by vice, to be pests to society—to violate the laws, to steal, to rob, and murder . . .'[21] The crime was not only against the victim alone, for 'training up children in ignorance and vagrancy, is a flagrant crime against Society,' depriving it of 'examples, labours, and talents . . . and inflicting upon it serious disorders and expenditures.'[22]

The eradication of ignorance through education was the solution, a characteristically Victorian one. Schooling was the right of each child and the preparation of each citizen, as well as the security of the rich.[23] Consequently, neglect of education was itself a crime, and social order would be 'better conserved by having [Toronto's] thousands of idle boys industriously and appropriately receiving instruction in her hitherto empty schoolhouses than in contracting vicious habits in the streets and on the sidewalks of the city.'[24] Nevertheless, crime persisted, especially among the young, after the founding of mass public school systems. Rather than re-examining his premises, Ryerson maintained that further provision for schooling was needed and that the schools were not full, thus not reaching all the children.[25] Arguments explaining criminality, therefore, continued to be stated negatively, stressing the results of non-schooling and not the specific ways in which education would prevent crime.

In their explanations, moreover, reformers seldom considered other factors, or whether their factors might be reordered. Disregarding the social and economic realities which determined school attendance, poverty, for example, was not considered a cause of ignorance or illiteracy. Chief Justice Robinson made this clear in addressing a Grand Jury: 'I am satisfied that no proper excuse can be given for the Children of the poor not being sent to the Schools ready to receive them in Towns and Cities.'[26] It is difficult to censure schoolmen for ignoring problems of immigration, poverty, and neglect, for they saw these as all too real. Their notions of causality, however, may be questioned, for they were unable to recognize poverty as a structural feature of society or capitalism. To them, pauperism and idleness emanated from ignorance; economic failure derived from moral weakness, and many were considered paupers by choice, not by chance or structural inequality.[27] Ignorance, idleness, and intemperance, then, remained the result of individual behavior, and the reformers' answer, a Victorian one, was education to prevent illiteracy, ignorance, and criminality: in one sweep this was the role of the state.

Schoolmen were certain that ignorance and illiteracy lay at the heart of criminality. Statistical evidence was gathered as proof: data which described the educational condition of prisoners assumed guilty of criminal offenses. Ignorance of course meant more than illiteracy, but this latter was taken to be its measurable sign. From these statistics, educational promoters derived their arguments, and reciprocally, in them they found continuing support. As a result, illiteracy itself was raised to a causal factor in their explanations, along with ignorance. Indeed, wherever in the West promoters inquired, the same results were found: the periodic examination of the literacy of the arrested and convicted served to bolster the cause of education. As direct evidence of ignorance and the lack of schooling, these tabulations became the statistical foundation upon which the rhetorical house explaining criminality was built.

Indeed, it is significant that gaols and prisons, as well as reformatories, regularly inquired into the educational condition of their inmates, and that literacy was the universal measure chosen. Since illiteracy was accepted as the sign of ignorance, the knowledge of the prisoners' achievement or status was an essential concern. Moreover, efforts were made in Upper Canadian prisons to provide instruction in reading and writing, and J. George Hodgins, Ryerson's lieutenant, pressed for the establishment of prison libraries. Not only did annual prison reports detail the literacy of all inmates, chaplains and school-masters told of their repeated efforts to instruct and tabulated the numbers and progress of their pupils.[28] They too linked criminality with ignorance and sought to replace it with literacy; 'such being the almost barbarous ignorance in which the great majority of convicts have been raised, it would seem an unnecessary cruelty to deprive them of the means of the "limited education" which the humanity of Christian legislation has provided for them in this institution.'[29] R.V. Rogers, a chaplain who failed to secure funds for either library, schoolroom or schoolmaster, summed up their goal in instruction: 'a Professed School of Reform, without the needed Machinery for Reformation—a Penitentiary in Name—A Jail in Fact!!'[30]

Egerton Ryerson referred to English and European statistics in his first report, and often included them in his *Journal of Education*. A decade after that report, he presented the evidence for Upper Canada itself: 'How intimate and general is the connexion between the training up of children in ignorance and vagrancy and the expenses and varied evils of public crime may be gathered from the statistics of the Toronto Gaol during the year 1856, as compiled by the Governor of the Gaol from the Gaol Register.' As on other occasions, he reproduced the statistics of literacy for the inmate population. For 1967 prisoner, the registers presented this distribution:

	Male	Female
Neither read nor write	401	246
Read only	253	200
Read and write imperfectly	570	198
Read and write well	68	—
Superior education	1	—

Just what literary abilities these categories may have described will be considered below; regardless, Ryerson's conclusions from them rang familiarly in support of his stated assumptions. To him, they revealed that more than 95 per cent of the incarcerated 'had grown up without the advantages of a good common school education; and that less than 5 per cent of the crimes committed, were committed by persons who could even read and write well.'

Here then was the evidence for his causal model and for the centrality of illiteracy; but what was to be done? Ryerson continued, arguing prescriptively, that these were 'facts which show that had a legal provision been made, such as would have secured to all these 1967 prisoners a good common school education, the number of prisoners committed to the Toronto Gaol would scarcely have exceeded one hundred . . . their crimes would have been prevented, and the time, trouble, and expenses attending their detection and punishment would have been saved.'[31] Of course their was a certain circularity in these common arguments, for it was assumed that in keeping the potential youthful offenders off the streets and in the schoolrooms the prisons would be emptied of the great bulk of their numbers (95 per cent to Ryerson). Funds saved on one would then become freed for the other.

Ryerson was far from alone in recognizing the importance of literacy in the educational prevention of crime or in the use of illiteracy statistics in support of his argument. Either summary statistics or the more common practice of presenting raw numbers of prisoners at each level of education was a standard feature, significantly, of both the educational and the penitentiary report of the last century. Massachusetts reports, for example, frequently cited them, whether the discussion related to prisons, juvenile reformatories, or schools, which all were seen as weapons attacking the same social problems.[32] Standard also was the reproduction of foreign statistics to illustrate the universality of the problem, or to demonstrate that progress could occasionally be made, either to censure or to applaud the situation at home.

Others in fact went further than Ryerson in their investigations of the relation between illiteracy and crime, continuing of course to equate ignorance in criminals with illiteracy. Reformers in the United States, in particular, scoured the records to produce statistical summaries which rang with the truth of arithmetic exactness. One summary was a report by James P. Wickersham to the National Educational Association, which investigated the charge, 'that a very high proportion—60 per cent, I think—of the convicts then confined in the prisons of Philadelphia, were high school graduates.'[33] His response, 'Education and Crime,' concluded to the contrary, in 1881,

1 that about one-sixth of all the crime in the country is committed by persons wholly illiterate.
2 that about one-third of it is committed by persons practically illiterate.
3 that the proportion of criminals among the illiterate is about ten times as great as among those who have been instructed in the elements of a common-school education or beyond.[34]

These facts led Wickersham to conclude that the amount of crime is about as uniform from year to year as the amount of ignorance or illiteracy. Ten years earlier, another commentator established an even stronger relationship between illiteracy and criminality. E.D. Mansfield surveyed Europe as well as the United States, finding a strong connection between illiteracy and criminality wherever he looked. His mathematical relationships led him to conclude.

First. That one-third of all criminals are totally uneducated, and that four-fifths are practically uneducated.
Second. That the proportion of criminals from the illiterate classes is at least tenfold as great as the proportion from these having some education.[35]

Despite the certainty with which education was advanced as the best preventative of criminality and the evidence which repeatedly revealed that the criminals were largely ignorant, the eradication of illiteracy did not always seem to reduce crime. Of course, schools, as Ryerson argued, are 'not responsible for defects in criminal laws, or police or municipal regulations.'[36] Nevertheless, as attendance increased, Ryerson continued to reprint the gaol statistics, and it was significant that he never reported a diminution in crime. The happy result of expanding educational provision in reducing offenses was not often to be found. In Massachusetts, for example, Frank Sanborn, the first Secretary of the State Board of Charities, discovered that the number of illiterates in the prison population fell by 50 per cent, 74 per cent to 38 per cent, from 1854 to 1864. In spite of such apparent progress, he was startled. First, he discovered that in England and Wales, without a system of common schools, only 33 per cent of prisoners could neither read nor write, and in Ireland only 50 per cent.[37] More importantly, while Massachusetts' figures led him to believe that the proportion of illiterates among the prison population was far greater than among the entire population, the decadal decrease in criminal illiteracy had not been accompanied by a corresponding decrease in crimes.[38]

Sanborn and Ryerson were not alone in making unsettling discoveries, which ran counter to their models and expectations. Some resorted to explanations of continuing high rates of crime by referring to improved enforcement and enlightened judicial systems. Commonly, however, the situation led to a confused, sometimes contradictory, posture by school reformers and public officials who used the illiteracy statistics to demonstrate that ignorance was a primary cause of criminality. Witness the efforts of Wickersham on this quandary, as he discussed the hypothetical possibility that Prussia possessed more criminals than France in spite of better schooling and higher rates of literacy. 'It will be found that the cause is not in her schools but in spite of her schools, for in Prussia, as in all other countries, an illiterate man is many times more likely to commit crime than one who is educated.' This alone was not a sufficient reason for continuing criminality; the cause could also be 'a crime-producing factor in his nature or in the circumstances that surround him which his education has not been able to eliminate.' Education could then fail to achieve its goal. With this information in mind, however, Wickersham could conclude securely and optimistically, 'were it not for the restraining effects of intellectual, moral, and religious factors, our opinion is that [crime] would completely disrupt society and resolve its broken fragments into chaos,'[39] Ryerson, of course, argued the same point.

In fact, school promoters covered themselves nicely. If education failed to decrease criminality as they predicted, they retreated to explanations which stressed a poor environment, immigration, poverty, heredity, the wrong sort of education, or non-attendance. If, however, ignorance, as discovered by statistics of illiteracy, was the cause, educational provisions would protect order, with training in literacy the essential aim. Some spokesmen attempted to use both arguments and to have their claims accepted both ways, seemingly unaware of the potential for circularity or contradiction. The way around problems of argument and evidence often centered upon their definitions of ignorance, and as a result the applicability of literacy statistics varied according to the chosen meaning. Illiteracy, then, represented either *the fact* of ignorance or merely *one possible* symptom of the lack of a proper education. To the former, statistics of prisoners' literacy were relevant and germane evidence. To the latter, however, measures of literacy—or of intellectual education—were insufficient and inappropriate proof to connect illiteracy with ignorance and criminality. Literacy, if unrestrained by morality, could be very dangerous, and an individual's literacy alone was hardly a guarantee of his or her orderliness.[40] In spite of the clear differences in the role of literacy in their discussions, schoolmen turned to both models, revealing their confusion and the contradictions inherent in their uses of literacy.

By the mid-nineteenth century, the school was more than ever before seen as the vehicle required to replace the traditional roles of moral training of family and church, and its success, moreover, was sometimes determined by the proportion of literate men and women produced for the society. Literacy, then, indicated that the expected training had occurred; illiteracy, conversely, meant a lack of schooling or the presence of a deeper ignorance rooted in personal deviance which schooling could not eradicate. The provision of schools to properly teach literacy was sufficient for the *Globe:* 'give the child the simple rudiments of education and to him all else is opened . . . if we make our people intelligent, they cannot fail to be prosperous: intelligence makes morality, morality industry, industry prosperity as surely as the sun shines.'[41] The process was automatic; intelligence, prosperity, and morality followed from literacy. Prison chaplains and masters agreed. J.T. Gardiner claimed, 'reading and studying of books is a powerful means of leading men to consider and abandon the evil practices by which their youth may have been contaminated.'[42] Or, as a Kingston Penitentiary schoolmaster exclaimed, 'to be a reading man, is to be a powerful man, . . . a moral man and a useful member of society.'[43] Here, illiteracy was equated with ignorance, and statistics of prisoner illiteracy were relevant and necessary to the arguments.

Simultaneously, though, arguments were advanced which stressed the insufficiency of literacy as a preventative of crime. Ryerson, for one, remarked that schooling did not always end in moral training, as 'much of this moral degradation and social danger must be charged on the neglected or perverted, culture of the Schools.' False education, 'which severs knowledge from its relations to duty,' could be found in many schools, and as a result, 'a reading and writing community may be a very vicious community, if morality be not as much a portion of education as reading and writing.'[44] Henry Mayhew, in England, was even more vehement in his critique of Ragged Schools. These institutions, he concluded, 'may be, they are, and must be, from the mere fact of bringing so many boys of vicious propensities together, productive of far more injury than benefit to the community. If some boys are rescued many are lost through them.'[45] Some schools could stimulate rather than prevent crime, and if schooling prevailed without morality at its core, illiteracy could decrease while crime did not, much as Frank

Sanborn had discovered. The result then of educational expansion can be no more than more clever and skillful criminals.

This issue was directly confronted by the *Christian Guardian*, which under Ryerson's editorship addressed earlier fears about the dangers of over-education. Responding to the question, 'Does Mere Intellectual Education Banish Crime?,' the *Guardian* noted that 'the only ascertained effect of intellectual education on crime is to substitute fraud for force, the cunning of civilized for the violence of savage life.' To increase intellectual power without inculcating moral principles made men restless and dissatisfied, 'hating those that are above him, and desirous of reducing all to his own level.' To convince their audience of the truly conservative nature of proper schooling, as Ryerson continued to do, the *Guardian* explained that intellectual and secular education alone were insufficient. The formation of the Christian character was the only proper end, and literacy itself did not erase the crucial ignorance. The fault of the age, they concluded, was that men have hitherto been prone to take for granted, that it was only necessary to teach the Art of reading, and before this new power all vice and error would flee away.' Education such as this might not cause crime, but it did not prevent it.[46] This was the argument which Ryerson made central to his discussions and promotions in the succeeding decades. Schooling, he often urged, included the moral as well as the intellectual; literacy, the tool of training, was to be provided in carefully structured institutions. The pace of social change demanded no less a solution; the maintenance of the social order mandated it. Prison chaplains and instructors agreed too, contradicting their other statements. Reading and writing, while important, were not education; further instruction in morality was necessary and the moral faculties must be directly trained.[47] The role of literacy was to provide the vehicle for the efficient transmission and reinforcement of morality and restraint.

These were the principal lines of argument, then, in the relationship joining ignorance and criminality. Forming two poles in the elaboration of the perceived connection, they were not seen as exclusive or contradictory. Each was used as it fit the situation, and definitions and processes differed with the argument chosen, both functioning toward the same end. School promoters vacillated between the two, and they continued in many cases to employ the statistics of literacy regardless of their line of argument. If the first formulation were expounded, that learning to read led naturally to the inculcation of restraint and morality, the use of literacy and the prisoners' statistics was both necessary and appropriate as proof. If, however, the second argument were advanced, stressing morality as independent of literacy or intellectual training, the use of literacy as a measure of proper education was highly problematic. For, 'the moral must advance contemporaneously with the intellectual man, else we see no increased education, but an increased capacity for evil doing.'[48] In the formulation, literacy was hardly the crucial element; its role was unclear, and individuals could be ignorant whether literate or illiterate. Its importance instead lay in its usefulness for efficient mass schooling in a growing and changing society. Nevertheless, those who argued in this way continued to draw upon the statistics of criminal literacy, while their words denied the relevance of this evidence. Thus, Egerton Ryerson, within the span of several pages, could recognize the potential immorality and viciousness of the literate *and* employ the gaol registers as proof for his explanations, contradicting himself with his own data. So did Wickersham and Mansfield. Apparently, they never realized that the literacy statistics simply could not be used to prove both arguments. In attempting to do so, school promoters confused their efforts, reducing their credibility and forcing a reexamination of both their assumptions and their explanations. The questions about which they were so certain, in fact, bear reopening.

Some contemporaries realized the contradictory employment of literacy tabulations and not all accepted the use of their evidence. From Great Britain came a scathing attack on their application to demonstrate the relationship between education and crime. W.B. Hodgson, addressing the social Science Association in 1867, declared that although there may be 'fallacies more palpable than that ignorance of reading and writing is productive of, or accompanied by, a greater amount of crime there can be few more gross or serious.' While granting that the inability to read or write may represent the ignorance of all that lies beyond, he concluded that 'the ability . . . (not to cavail about the degree of ability), by no means as gives the knowledge of aught beyond. Negatively, the ignorance implies much, positively the knowledge implies little.'[49] Twenty years later another English commentator, Rev. J.W. Horsey, continued the attack on the role of literacy and education in the equation which accounted for criminality. 'One can get no clear evidence or trustworthy statistics,' he discovered, 'to prove that the greater attention to educational matters has largely diminished even juvenile crime. There are fewer boys and girls sent to prison happily, but this arises from various causes, and *not entirely from their increased virtue and intelligence.*'[50] The statistics did not prove the case; the explanation was faulty. The expansion of educational provision, it would seem, did not prevent crime. If the convicted were and continued to be illiterate or if more were literate, there must be other causes, or the factors must be differently ordered. Illiteracy simply could not represent the first cause of criminality and their relationship must be mediated by other factors.

Other problems, moreover, result from the use of literacy statistics. First, and most superficially, school promoters simply found what they were looking for; the statistics became part of a self-fulfilling prophecy. And they could be manipulated; for example, if one-third of prisoners were illiterate, it was then claimed that one-third of all crimes were committed by the illiterate (a questionable deduction in itself), of course disproportionate to their share of the population. This does not negate, however, the fact that the criminals may have had a lower rater of literacy than the population at large. But the degree of difference could vary radically from place to place and from year to year. Comparisons between prisoners and those who could 'neither read nor write' are very difficult, and entire populations, enumerated only by censuses, were never questioned about their *levels* of education or literacy, only about literacy or illiteracy. The very ambiguity of the classifications for the different levels obscures their meaning as well as their comparability, for nowhere were they defined.

Several difficulties are apparent here. First, we are never told how prisoners compared with the population on levels of education above that of simple literacy. Nor are we told how they compared with the arrested but not convicted or with the unapprehended criminal. The reinforcing role the statistics played obscured attention from these questions. Moreover, there is no *a priori* reason for contemporaries' ceaseless combination of the illiterate with those of imperfect education in applying this evidence to their explanations. This too was done without regard to the wider distribution of educational skills in the society.

Problems with the employment of criminal statistics are exacerbated by the irregularity of the statistical relationships found for the past century. Stability in rates of crime could be accompanied by increases or decreases in rates of inmate literacy. Similarly, rises or falls in rates of crime need not correspond with changes in criminal literacy rates which seem to have been remarkably stable in the face of movement in rates of other relevant factors.[51] As the century passed, more children enrolled in and attended school and rates of adult literacy increased. Yet there remained little discussion of crime's reduction as a result; at best reformers claimed that more offenses would have been committed or that the situation was worse elsewhere. In sum, too many paradoxes and contradictions exist among the relationships in the simple causal models of Ryerson and other reformers, who consequently failed to prove that illiteracy caused criminality, that the association was either direct or casual, unmediated by other factors of potentially greater significance.

II

The data used by the reformers, the extraordinarily detailed nineteenth-century gaol registers, have survived for places in Upper Canada, allowing us to move beyond the rhetoric and to directly re-examine the relationships claimed by educational promoters. In discussions of the relationship between education and crime, the low level of literacy of the inmate population represented, as we have seen, the most commonly cited characteristic of the annual tabulations, to the neglect of other regularly collected information about the prisoners. The registers, in fact, on an annual and individual basis, inquired about birthplace, religion, age, sex, occupation, moral habits, crime or offense and judgment by the authorities, all in addition to the educational condition of each arrested person.

With this information, patterns of arrest and conviction may be recreated. As we will see, conviction in fact was associated with illiteracy, but the clearest patterns of successful prosecution related directly to ethnicity, occupational class, and sex, when the effects of illiteracy are controlled. These important factors, largely ignored in nineteenth-century explanations of criminality, blur a direct connection between illiteracy and conviction, for they intervened to form patterns of a systematic discrimination and prosecution by the judicial system. Illiteracy, of course, was often symptomatic of factors which made for high rates of punishment, as both were rooted in social inequality;[52] however, the most illiterate groups did not always fare the worst in judgments. Illiteracy's role was in many ways, then, a superficial one, acting through its associations with poverty and social structural inequality, and not necessarily with guilt. The crime for which one was apprehended was an important determinant as well, and the interaction of variables was more complex than the causal explanations of men like Ryerson would allow, forcing us to develop a new, more subtle understanding of crime and punishment in the past and a re-evaluation of the role played by literacy. School promoters' use of aggregate tabulations obscured the complex interrelationship of variables; to them the literacy statistics served as blinders.

The manuscript gaol registers of Middlesex County, Ontario, for the year 1867–1868, were selected for this analysis. The earliest registers located, they provide complete information on all persons arrested, permitting us to distinguish between the convicted and acquitted, and to analyze their characteristics.[53] Urban crime and prosecution form the core of this discussion, as Middlesex County was dominated by the fledgling metropolis of London, a source of the majority of the country's 48,000 in 1861. The city and the county were growing, prosperous centers of trade and transportation in western Ontario.

In the thirteen months the register spans, 535 men and women were arrested, their profiles and characteristics recorded. Overwhelmingly urban residents, 64 per cent claimed London as their home with an additional 3 per cent reporting other Ontario cities. They were arrested for a broad range of crimes (over sixty in all) and two-thirds of them were convicted. Arrest and conviction, however, were far from random, as certain groups (Irish and English) were disproportionately arrested and the Irish were most often convicted. Similarly, those holding lower-class occupations, the officially unoccupied, and women were dealt with severely, as were those arrested for crimes related to drink and vagrancy.[54] Illiteracy related to these patterns in both reinforcing and contradictory ways.

Differences in educational background existed among the convicted, the acquitted, and the arrested. (See Table 10.1) Among the arrested, though, the number who read well and very well exceeded the number of illiterates, as more educated than uneducated persons were apprehended as suspects. Reformers, of

Table 10.1   Literacy of Middlesex Criminals (percentages)

	All Arrested	Convicted	Acquitted
Neither read nor write	17.8	22.7	7.2
Read and write imperfectly	62.6	63.5	60.8
Read and write well	16.3	11.9	25.9
Read and write very well	3.2	1.7	6.0
N	535	362	173

Source: Manuscript Gaol Registers, County of Middlesex, Ontario, 1867–1868.

course, would not accept this statement, for as we have seen, they readily combined the numbers with an imperfect grounding in literacy with the illiterates. For Middlesex, therefore, they would have observed, rather, that 80 per cent of the arrested and 86 per cent of the convicted lacked a good common-school education. If their combination were justified, it remains interesting that 68 per cent of those acquitted had not been well educated and that over 60 per cent of those released as innocent were imperfectly educated; many supposedly ignorant individuals, then, had not been found guilty. More important, however, was the slight difference in educational achievement between those suspected and those convicted; the proportion largely uneducated diverged marginally from one group to the other, though somewhat more from those released. Ignorance, as defined by those who assumed it to be the first cause of crime, apparently did not significantly differentiate suspects from convicts, and was only slightly better in distinguishing the acquitted from the accused.

It is far from clear, however, that the reformer's combination of the lowest educational classes was justifiable in the first place. The representativeness of the imperfectly educated, in comparison with the larger population, is the key to an answer, and, in fact, there proves little reason to consider them disproportionately represented among suspects or criminals. They were arrested, convicted, and acquitted with the same frequency as the better educated, and indeed, the published tabulations of prisoners' illiteracy in the province's *Sessional Papers* did not even include them in their statistical tables, presenting *only* county totals of those who could not read or write at all. Moreover, it is possible that the imperfectly educated were broadly representative of popular levels of education. As other research suggests, the high statistical level of literacy in Upper Canada may belie a lower qualitative level of achievement.[55]

Direct evidence on this question comes from research in progress in the extraordinary Swedish sources, conducted by Egil Johansson of Umea University. The parish catechetical examination registers include, for some years and on an individual basis, measures of both oral reading ability and comprehension. For Bygdeå parish in 1862, Johansson discovered that of those who achieved the highest grade in oral ability, 77.6 per cent comprehended only partially at best. Of those who read orally with less proficiency, 28 per cent had poor comprehension, while less than 4 per cent read with 'passable' understanding. The ability to read well did not correlate with an ability to understand or to use one's literacy, and regardless of literacy, few comprehended even passably and only a tiny proportion totally understood what they read.[56]

The implications of these findings for a country with a long heritage of high levels of literacy cannot be minimized. Not only do they effectively contradict the efforts of Ryerson and others to combine the imperfect with the illiterate as without education, they suggest that the imperfect range was a broad one which encompassed a large proportion of the population. In this way the close correspondence of the imperfectly skilled's distribution among the arrested, convicted, and acquitted persons is significant, and should be expected. In all probability, they were individuals generally representative of the city's and county's educational condition. They cannot simply be combined with the illiterate in the effort to prove that paucity of education or ignorance contributed directly to criminality, its apprehension and conviction. Rejection of the school promoters' categorization radically revises the statistical relationship that supposedly joined ignorance with crime. No longer might they claim that more than five-sixths of the convicted were exceptional persons without education; only 23 per cent remain fairly within those ranks.

That fewer than one-fourth of the convicted criminals were illiterate, and that fewer than one-fifth of the arrested were uneducated, severely modifies the contentions of the reformers. The weight of numbers shifts to individuals who were at least partially educated, who may now be seen as the great majority of the supposed offenders. Among the arrested, as noted, the well-educated, in fact, equalled the illiterates. Among those convicted, the illiterates outnumbered those with a good education, but the margin is not large (10 per cent). As well, the illiterates convicted only slightly over-represented their distribution among all arrested. Nevertheless, the balance shifts when the convicted are compared with the acquitted: the illiterates form a small proportion of those released, representing only one-third of their strength among the convicted. This difference, however, must be qualified too; the illiterates, significantly, were not under-represented among the acquitted, for their proportion corresponded closely to the 1861 rate of adult illiteracy in London, home of the majority of those arrested.[57] Although they were somewhat over-represented among all arrested, a direct causal relationship linking illiteracy with criminality should have led to a far greater under-representation of illiterates among those found innocent and released rather than only a proportionate representation.

Illiterates, then, in Middlesex and London, were not the most frequent offenders; nevertheless, they were punished with greater regularity than others.[58] While their place in the criminal population was far from the extraordinary one reformers claimed, five-sixths of them were convicted if brought to trial, and frequency of conviction related directly to level of education. Does this imply some measure of truth in reformers' arguments; that although the convicted were not overwhelmingly illiterate, the uneducated suspects were almost certainly guilty? In fact their incredible rate of conviction was related first of all, to patterns of discrimination and social prejudice against the Irish, the lower class, and women—these individuals were convicted most often regardless of their level of literacy. Punishment was of course more frequent for the least educated members of these groups, and illiteracy related more directly, perhaps, to arrest and successful prosecution than it did to guilt or criminality. Social inequality was the root of both illiteracy and conviction, and the actions of the courts were based in the social hierarchy.

Moreover, we cannot doubt that the agencies of law enforcement and justice, the constabulary and the courts, accepted the dominant explanations of criminality, naturally accusing the ignorant and the illiterate, who were very often poor, and expecting them to be guilty. The ideology of criminality and its causes, and the mechanisms of inequality, were thus operationalized, as illiterates, with their supposedly unrestrained ignorance and immorality, were perceived as a threat to social order. Their other characteristics, of class, sex, and ethnicity, only reinforced their social marginality and the severity with which respectable society would react to them. As a result, their vulnerability was increased. No doubt they were visible, not hidden in ghettos like the poor today, working outdoors when employed, living near the rich, or perhaps begging in the streets. As well, they would have few resources to employ for their defense, whether for legal aid or for a bribe. They also lacked the formal training and experience to deal with the procedures and the language of a courtroom. Prepared by life in the streets or work place, rather than the school, a formal institution, illiterates could perhaps be intimidated, unable to respond properly, or to make themselves understood in a situation where their guilt might be presumed. Some of them, too, might welcome the gaol as a refuge, a warm shelter with food regularly provided. Expectations, ideology, inequality, and physical circumstances all combined in conviction.

Ethnicity was one factor upon which the wheels of justice turned, as the courts meted out judgments of varying severity to arrested members of different groups, with extraordinary frequency, the Irish (Catholic and Protestant) were arrested and convicted well above the mean rate of conviction, and more often than any other ethnic group (see Table 10.2). Significantly, however, the Irish were not marked by the highest levels of illiteracy. Among the arrested, five ethnic groups had greater proportions unable to read or write than the Irish Catholics, and three counted more than the Protestants; yet these groups were not convicted as regularly (see Table 10.3). Conversely, native-born Canadians (Protestant and Catholic) were most often illiterate, and they were acquitted most frequently. Clearly conviction was determined by more than measurable ignorance.

Among all the ethnic groups, rate of conviction corresponded to level of education, as illiterates were most often convicted. Nevertheless, Irish Catholics, and Protestants to a lesser extent, were convicted most frequently regardless of their educational attainments. Moreover, Catholics who read and wrote well were successfully prosecuted with greater frequency than those who were imperfectly skilled. These patterns point directly to systematic conviction for Irish men and women in mid-nineteenth-century London and Middlesex, to discrimination against them regardless of their literacy. Illiterates of course were isolated for severe prosecution, and Irish illiterates, especially Catholics, were certain to be convicted, but ethnicity was the key, as it was in the economic and occupational stratification of mid-nineteenth century urban society. As social inequality often derived from the facts of ethnic ascription, successful prosecution apparently did too. Irish men and women, especially Catholics, faced inequality in courtroom as in marketplace. Concomitant poverty and illiteracy could only reinforce their precarious position; illiteracy was hardly a prior or first cause in itself. Their acqui-

Table 10.2 *Middlesex Criminals: Rate of Conviction for Each Ethnic Group, Controlling for Level of Literacy*

Literacy Level		Irish Catholic	Irish Protestant	Scottish Presbyterian	English Protestant	Canadian Protestant	Canadian Catholic	Others	Total
Neither read nor write	N	5	7	3	3	24	16	24	82
	%	100.0	87.5	100.0	75.0	75.0	94.1	92.3	86.3
Read and write imperfectly	N	35	29	13	38	39	23	53	230
	%	85.4	80.6	72.2	63.3	54.9	51.1	82.8	68.7
Read and write well	N	10	4	1	7	15	0.3	6	43
	%	90.9	66.7	16.7	50.0	46.9	37.5	49.4	
Read and write very well	N	1	0	2	2	0	1	—	6
	%	50.0	0.0	100.0	40.0	0.0	33.3	—	35.3
Total arrested	N	59	53	29	83	137	64	110	535
Total convicted	%	86.4	75.5	65.5	60.2	56.9	60.9	77.3	67.7

Table 10.3 *Middlesex Criminals: Ethnicity by Literacy*

	Irish Catholic	Irish Protestant	Scottish Presbyterian	English Protestant	Canadian Protestant	Canadian Catholic	Others	Total	Percentage Convicted
Neither read nor write	5 / 8.5	8 / 15.1	3 / 10.3	4 / 4.8	32 / 23.4	17 / 26.6	26 / 23.6	17.8	86.3
Read and write imperfectly	41 / 69.5	36 / 67.9	18 / 62.1	60 / 72.3	71 / 51.8	45 / 70.3	64 / 58.2	62.6	68.7
Read and write well	11 / 18.6	6 / 11.3	6 / 20.7	14 / 16.9	32 / 23.4	2 / 3.1	16 / 14.5	16.3	49.4
Read and write very well	2 / 3.4	3 / 5.7	2 / 6.9	5 / 6.0	1 / 1.5	—	3 / 2.7	3.2	
N	59	53	29	83	137	64	110	535	
Percentage	11.0	9.9	5.4	15.5	25.6	12.0	20.6	100.0	35.3
Percentage convicted	86.4	75.5	65.5	60.2	56.9	60.9	77.3	67.7	

sition of literacy, moreover, neither guaranteed their economic success nor their security from criminal conviction.[59]

Class, status, and wealth, as signified by occupational rank, represented a second factor which determined the course of justices.[60] Lower-class workers, the unskilled and the officially unoccupied, predominantly women, were both arrested and convicted far more often than those more highly ranked, (see Table 10.4). Here there was a direct relationship with illiteracy, for literacy corresponded with occupational class as it did in the larger society; and, within each occupational rank, the uneducated were punished most frequently. Nevertheless, the class convicted most often, the semi-skilled, was not the most illiterate (10.3 per cent illiterate). The unskilled, moreover, with slightly higher illiteracy (13.3 per cent), were punished far less often, and those with no occupation, and much greater illiteracy (30.5 per cent), were convicted no more often.

As with the Irish, lower-class workers were selected for severe judgments; the poor and unemployed with least resources for defense were disproportionately arrested and convicted. Their numbers included many Irish and women as well as illiterates, and these factors combined to produce swift pronouncements of guilt. Indeed, they were by and large precisely those expected to be offenders by theories of criminality. Lower-class status and poverty could be synonymous conditions, and they could cause illiteracy as well as the need to resort to crime. Idleness was equally an offense. By contrast, in the formulations of the reformers poverty or structural features of society or economy did not cause illiteracy or ignorance. Yet, in fact, inequalities of social stratification, with their basis often in ethnicity, were an important source of convictions, whether reinforced by illiteracy or not.

The courts' decisions to convict also pivoted upon the sex of the suspect, as women were convicted in 80 per cent of their cases compared to 60 per cent of men (see Table 10.5). Regardless of literacy, ethnicity, or crime, women received harsh judgments, and this was related to both their lack of occupation or idleness and their rate of illiteracy (27 per cent). Falling into categories which were severely adjudged (10 per cent were semi-skilled, as well), they no doubt were seen as failing in the society's expected standards of feminine behavior.[61] They were not at home, nurturing a family or properly domesticated; their perceived deviance endangered the maintenance and propagation of the moral order, the family, and the training of children. While Irish and illiterate women were convicted most often, women were punished if arrested more often than men within each ethnic group and for virtually all crimes. Pervasive inequality had deep roots in sexual stratification.

The crimes for which individuals were most often arrested and found guilty, not surprisingly, were moral offenses, and most striking was vagrancy: an offense marked by high rates of conviction and of illiteracy (see Tables 10.6 and 10.7). This was of course the crime of idleness, to which ignorance and illiteracy were presumed to lead. Perceived as dangerous, rather than as the poor in need of aid, arrested vagrants were largely women (77 per cent, while only 35 per cent of all

Table 10.4 Middlesex Criminals: Rate of Conviction for Each Occupational Category, Controlling for Level of Literacy

Literacy Level		Professional, Proprietor	White Collar, Small Proprietor, Farmer	Skilled Artisanal	Semi-Skilled	Unskilled	None	Total
Neither read nor write	N	—	0	2	6	15	59	82
	%	—	0.0	66.7	100.0	83.3	88.1	86.3
Read and write imperfectly	N	—	8	27	37	59	99	230
	%	—	44.4	65.9	86.0	59.6	73.9	68.7
Read and write well	N	1	4	17	2	8	11	43
	%	100.0	30.8	51.5	28.6	57.1	57.9	49.4
Read and write very well	N	0	5	1	0	—	—	6
	%	0.0	62.5	20.0	0.0	—	—	35.3
Total arrested	N	4	40	82	58	131	220	535
	%	0.8	7.5	15.4	10.7	24.5	41.2	
Total convicted	%	25.0	42.5	57.3	79.3	62.5	76.8	67.7

Table 10.5   Middlesex Criminals: Rate of Conviction for Each Sex Controlling for Level of Literacy

Literacy Level		Male	Female	Total
Neither read	N	33	49	82
nor write	%	76.7	94.2	86.3
Read and write	N	132	98	230
imperfectly	%	62.6	79.0	68.7
Read and	N	37	6	43
write well	%	50.0	46.2	49.4
Read and write	N	6	—	6
very well	%	35.3	—	35.3
Total arrested	N	345	190	535
Total convicted	%	60.3	81.1	67.7

arrested) who were visible and seen as moral and social failures. Indeed, vagrancy would be a charge quite easy to prove, and it is unlikely that poor, homeless women, unaware of legal subtleties, could plead other than guilty. Moreover, the shelter of the gaol might often be welcome, for there were few other institutions to care for them.

Crimes related to drink, the offense of intemperance, which could also be easily proved, illustrate the discrimination against the Irish. Perhaps an operationalization of the myth of the drunken Irishman, these offenses were severely judged, and Irish were arrested for drunkenness twice as often as they were for all other crimes combined (43 per cent to 20 per cent). Nevertheless, those suspected of drunkenness were among the least illiterate of all arrested (11.4 per cent) yet they were among the most often punished (82 per cent). A severe moral offense, intemperance was convicted regardless of the literacy of the suspects; other causes were more direct.

Even the relationship between immorality, illiteracy, and criminality, so central to explanations of deviance, was ambiguous. Moral offenses were certainly harshly judged, but contrary to Ryerson's formula, immorality was not always related to illiteracy. Significantly, when the moral habits of those arrested are examined, the intemperate included fewer illiterates (14 per cent) than the temperate (22 per cent).[62] Moreover, prostitution, clearly a moral offense, was marked by neither high illiteracy nor a high rate of conviction. Prostitutes, furthermore, were among the most literate of arrested women, and they were convicted less often than virtually all other female offenders.

The fact that for any crime illiterates were disproportionately convicted obscured the ambiguities behind this first and most obvious relationship, though the superficial connection no doubt only reinforced the popular views. Blurred from school promoters' vision, or perhaps ignored as contrary to expectations or even incomprehensible, were the literacy of the suspected and acquitted as well as the convicted, patterns of discrimination, and varying rates of conviction for different

Table 10.6 Middlesex Criminals: Rate of Conviction for Each Category of Crime, Controlling for Level of Literacy

Literacy Level		Against Property	Against Persons	Crime Drink-Related	Related to Prostitution	Vagrancy	Against By-Laws	Others	Total
Neither read nor write	N	16	7	5	7	39	7	1	82
	%	72.7	77.8	100.0	70.0	100.0	77.8	100.0	86.3
Read and write imperfectly	N	41	42	22	22	82	10	11	230
	%	43.6	70.0	81.5	61.1	95.3	76.9	61.1	68.7
Read and write well	N	10	11	7	1	6	2	6	43
	%	33.3	57.9	77.8	12.5	85.7	66.7	54.5	49.4
Read and write very well	N	1	0	2	—	—	—	3	6
	%	16.7	0.0	66.7	—	—	—	42.9	35.3
Total arrested	N	152	89	44	54	133	25	38	535
Total convicted	%	44.7	67.4	81.8	55.6	96.2	76.0	51.5	67.7

Table 10.7 Middlesex Criminals: Crime by Literacy

	Against Property	Against Persons	Drink-Related	Prostitution	Vagrancy	Against By-Laws	Others	Total	Percentage Convicted
Neither read nor write	22	9	5	10	39	9	1	82	
	14.5	10.1	11.4	18.5	29.3	36.0	2.6	17.8	86.3
Read and write imperfectly	94	60	27	36	86	13	19	230	
	61.8	67.4	61.4	66.7	64.7	52.0	50.0	63.5	68.7
Read and write well	30	19	9	8	7	3	11	43	
	19.7	21.3	20.5	14.8	5.3	12.0	28.9	16.3	49.4
Read and write very well	6	1	3	—	—	—	7	6	
	3.9	1.1	6.8	—	—	—	18.5	3.2	35.3
N	152	89	44	54	133	25	38	535	
Percentage convicted	44.7	67.4	81.8	55.6	96.2	76.0	51.5	67.7	

offenses. Indeed, the crime for which most arrests were made, property offenses, was least often convicted and was marked by the literacy, not the illiteracy, of the suspects. Most judicial attention, it would seem, was focused on crimes of idleness, intemperance, and disorder (by-laws violations), crimes which were expected to follow directly from ignorance, even though they did not constitute a majority of supposed offenses. Both educational promoters and the judiciary presumed the illiterate, or ignorant, the Irish, and the idle to be guilty of social offenses; it is not surprising that they were found guilty so often. Expectations, then as now, influenced justice, even though the perceived connection between illiteracy and criminality was neither the only nor the most important relationship.

Criminal prosecution, and probably apprehension as well, derived from the facts of inequality. Punishment, stratification, and illiteracy too were rooted in the social structure; pervasive structures of inequality which emanated from ethnic and sexual ascription ordered groups and individuals in mid-nineteenth century urban areas. Achievement of literacy, or education, had little impact upon these structures, and in many cases only reinforced them. Despite the superficial relationships linking literacy and status and illiteracy and criminality, social inequality represented the primary determinant of criminality. Stratification by ethnic or sexual factors influenced the hierarchy of class, status, and wealth; in similar fashion, they turned the wheels of justice. Rather than illiteracy or ignorance leading directly to lives of crime, ethnicity, class, and sex lay behind and strongly mediated the relationships most commonly drawn.

Notes

1 RYERSON, "Report on a System of Public Elementary Instruction for Upper Canada," in *Documentary History of Education in Upper Canada* (D.H.E.) (Ed.) J.G. HODG-INS, 6, Toronto, 1899, 143.

2 For an evaluation of the educational consensus and an extended discussion of the 'moral economy' of literacy, see my 'Literacy and Social Structure in the Nineteenth-Century City,' unpublished PhD thesis., University of Toronto, 1975, esp. Chapter 1, and the documentation provided there.

3 *Ibid.,* esp. Chapter 2, for the analysis of literacy and social structure. The data presented there demonstrate broadly that as the allocation of literacy followed the structure of ethnic stratification the achievement or acquisition of literacy did remarkably little to alter the structure of inequality or the ranking of individuals and groups. Success in occupation and wealth derived from the factors of ethnicity, age, and sex; ascription dominated over achievement. Literacy, moreover, tended to reinforce rather than counter the effects of stratification, with some few exceptions. See also, MICHAEL B. KATZ, *The People of Hamilton, Canada West.* Cambridge, Mass., 1975, esp. Chapter 2.

4 J.J. BELLOMO, 'Upper Canadian Attitudes towards Crime and Punishment,' *Ontario History,* 64 (1972), 12, 13.

5 *Ibid.,* 12.

6 *Journal of Education,* I (1848), 300. (hereafter cited as *J.E.*)

7 RYERSON, 'Report,' 143.

8 KATZ, *The Irony of Early School Reform.* (Cambridge, Mass., 1968), 170–171.

9   BELLOMO, *op. cit;* J.H. TOBIAS, *Crime and Industrial Society in the Nineteenth Century.* Harmondsworth, 1972; SUSAN HOUSTON, 'The Victorian Origins of Juvenile Delinquency,' *History of Education Quarterly,* 12 (1972), 254–280.

10 See ALISON PRENTICE, 'The Social Thought of Egerton Ryerson,' unpublished paper, 1970, and 'The School Promoters: Education and Social Class in Nineteenth Century Upper Canada,' unpublished PhD thesis, University of Toronto, 1974. See also WALTER HOUGHTON, *The Victorian Frame of Mind.* New Haven, 1957 and SUSAN HOUSTON, 'The Impetus to Reform,' unpublished PhD thesis, University of Toronto, 1974.

11 RYERSON, 'Report,' 143.

12 *Ibid.,* 143–144.

13 *Toronto Globe,* Dec. 11, 1851.

14 *Globe,* Dec. 11, 1862; RYERSON, *Annual Report of the Chief Superintendent of Education,* 1857, 17. On their disagreements, see J.M.S. CARELESS, *Brown of the Globe,* 2 vols, Toronto, 1959, 1963, and C.B. SISSONS, *Egerton Ryerson, His Life and Times,* 2 vols, Toronto, 1937, 1947.

15 *JE,* 10 (1857), 9; *Globe,* Dec. 11, 1851; 'Truancy and Juvenile Crime in Cities, 1859–1860,' in *DHE,* 15, Toronto, 1906, 1–5.

16 KATZ, *op. cit.* found the same in Massachusetts, 180.

17 The stark simplicity of the causal model is striking:

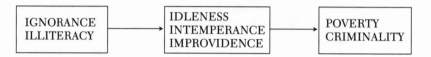

18 *Annual Report,* 1857, 47; and PRENTICE, 'The School Promoters,' 66.

19 *Globe,* Dec. 11, 1851; 'Address of Dr. Daniel Wilson to the Teachers Association, 1865,' *DHE* 19, 48.

20 'Truancy and Juvenile Crime,' 4.

21 *Ibid.,* Globe, *op. cit.*

22 *JE,* 10 (1857), 9.

23 *JE,* 1 (1848), 151.

24 *JE,* 2 (1849), 96; on these points see also 'Truancy and Crime' and 'Address of Wilson.'

25 'Truancy and Crime,' 2.

26 'Truancy and Juvenile Crime,' 2, 1–5.

27 'Address of Wilson.'

28 Report of the Board of Inspectors of Asylums, Prisons, & etc., Penitentiary Reports, Canada, *Sessional Papers,* esp. 1841, 1846–1849, 1852–1858, 1862.

29 *Ibid.,* 1852–1853.

30 *Ibid.,* 1847.

31 *JE,* 10 (1857), 9; see also *ibid.,* 20 (1867), 64, and 'Truancy and Juvenile Crime.'

32 See KATZ, *op. cit.,* and DAVID ROTHMAN, *The Discovery of the Asylum.* Boston, 1971.

33 WICKERSHAM, 'Education and Crime,' *The Journals and Proceedings and Addresses of the National Education Association of the United States,* Session of the Year 1881. Boston, 1881, 45; see also 45–55.

34 *Ibid.,* 50.

35 'The Relation Between Crime and Education,' *Report of the U.S. Commissioner of Education.* Washington, D.C., 1872, 586–595; see also his 'The Relation Between Education and Pauperism,' *ibid.* 596–602 on the role of poverty. Mansfield states,

'Pauperism and crime are so closely allied that the same individuals belong to both fraternities . . . steals when he cannot beg, and begs when he cannot steal,' 602.

36 *JE*, 10 (1857), 9; see also 'Truancy and Crime.'

37 These statistics must not be confused with national rates of literacy for the British Isles determined by the percentages of signatures on marriage registers. There is no necessary relationship.

38 Board of State Charities, Massachusetts, *Secretary's Report*, 1865 (Public Document Supplementary, No. 19), quoted in KATZ, *op. cit.*, 184.

39 WICKERSHAM, *op cit.*, 50.

40 On the meaning and relationship of literacy to education and the inculcation of morality and restraints, see again, my 'Literacy and Social Structure . . .,' esp. Chapter 1.

41 *Globe*, December 11, 1851.

42 Report of the Board of Inspectors of Asylums, Prisons, & etc., *op. cit.*, 1857.

43 *Ibid.*, 1860.

44 RYERSON, 'Report,' 150, and THOMAS WYSE, *School Reform*, as quoted, 151.

45 *Morning Chronicle*, March 29, 1850, quoted in TOBIAS, *op. cit.*, 207. See also, M. HILL and C.F. CORNWALLES, *Two Prize Essays on Juvenile Delinquency.* London, 1853, 220, quoted in TOBIAS, *op. cit.*, 207. See also G. STEDMAN JONES, *Outcast London* Oxford, 1971.

46 *Christian Guardian* (CG), July 2, 1834; see also *The Church.* Oct. 12, 1839, May 15, 1851. See also, GRAFF, *op. cit.*, esp. Chapter 1.

47 Reports of the Inspectors, 1862, 1852–1853.

48 *CG*, July 2, 1834; see also RYERSON, 'Report,' *passim.*

49 HOGGSON, *Exaggerated Estimates of Reading and Writing as a Means of Education* London, 1867, 6–7.

50 J.W. HORSEY, *Jottings from Jail* London, 1887, 57, quoted in TOBIAS, *op. cit.*, 206 (emphasis mine).

51 See V.A.C. GARELL and T.B. HADDEN, 'Criminal Statistics and their Interpretation,' in *Nineteenth-Century Society*, (Ed.) E.A. WRIGLEY, Cambridge, 1972, 363–396, Statistical Tables and *passim.*

52 See again, GRAFF, 'Literacy and Social Structure . . .' esp. Chapter 2, for the data and argument linking illiteracy to inequality and stratification to ascription.

53 I must acknowledge my gratitude to EDWARD PHELPS, Regional History Library, University of Western Ontario, who not only saved these records from destruction, but drew my attention to them and made them available to me. I have discussed the general patterns found in the analysis of the registers in 'Crime and Punishment in the Nineteenth Century: The Experience of Middlesex, County, Ontario,' Canadian Social History Project, *Report*, 5 (1973–74) 124–163, and I have described the registers in 'Crime and Punishment in the Nineteenth Century; A New Look at the Criminal,' *Journal of Interdisciplinary History*, VII (1976–77), 477–491. This latter paper includes, as well, a complete listing of all crimes of apprehension and their categorization.

    The history study of criminality remains in a primitive condition. Most attention to date has centered on either attitudes toward crime or criminality or on the establishment of permanent police forces in the 19th century. While some recent work has now been completed on the irrascable problem of estimating rates of crime for the past (only now appearing in print), precious little energy has been focused on the criminals themselves. See, however, the important study by ERIC MONKKONEN, *The Dangerous Class* (Cambridge, Mass., 1975) and the special issue of the *Journal of Social History* 8 (Summer, 1975), among a newly blossoming literature.

54 GRAFF, 'Crime and Punishment . . .'

55 See GRAFF, 'Literacy and Social Structure . . .,' esp. chapter 7, for argument and evidence; see also the important and fascinating study of DANIEL CALHOUN, *The Intelligence of a People* Princeton, 1973.

56 JOHANSSON, 'Literacy Studies in Sweden: Some Examples,' in *Literacy and Society in a Historical Perspective: A conference report,* (Ed.) JOHANSEN UMEÅ, 1973, 56. The incomparable Swedish parish registers provide date on annual examinations on the quality of literacy as determined by either oral ability or comprehension. Sponsored by the state church, the examinations record individual and community progress over the years as well as demographic and socio-economic data. Available from the 17th to the 19th centuries, they allow more detailed analysis of literacy's transmission, dimensions, and correlates, as well as distinguishing levels of literacy, than any other Western source. JOHANSSON has begun a large-scale project, but unfortunately little work has focused on the relationship of reading to comprehension.

57 On illiteracy in London, See GRAFF, *op. cit.*, Part One.

58 Conviction rates for each group are as follows: Neither read nor write, 86.3%, read and write imperfectly, 68.7%, read and write well, 49.4%, read and write very well, 35.3%.

59 See again, on ethnic stratification, GRAFF, *op. cit.*, and KATZ, *op. cit.*

60 The classification of occupations is based on the International Association of Social History Project rankings, as developed by MICHAEL KATZ, THEODORE HERSHBERG, LAURENCE GLASCO, CLYDE GRIFFEN, and STUART BLUMIN, for comparative urban social structural analysis. See their discussion in 'Occupation and Ethnicity in Five Nineteenth-Century Cities,' *Historical Methods Newsletter,* 7 (1974), 174–216. Of course, we know that occupation is an imperfect proxy or approximation of social class, status, or wealth. On this problem, see, KATZ, 'Occupational Classification in History,' *Journal of Interdisciplinary History,* 3 (1972), 63–88, and GRIFFEN, 'Occupational Mobility in Nineteenth-Century America,' *Journal of Social History,* 5 (1972), 310–330.

61 See for example BARBARA WELTER, 'The Cult of True Womanhood,' *American Quarterly,* 18 (1966), 151–174, among a growing literature; see also the recent studies of CARROLL SMITH-ROSENBERG and CHARLES ROSENBERG.

62 All arrested men and women were classified by 'moral habits,' defined by temperate or intemperate.

11 Literacy in Literature and in Life: An Early Twentieth-Century Example

Ironically perhaps, *literary* evidence has often proved a misleading or inadequate basis for the study of popular *literacy* in the past.[1] The reasons for this observation include the approaches and assumptions of researchers, the types of literary sources examined, biases of both students *and* their data, researchers' misplaced emphases and expectations, inadequate notions of the meaning of 'literacy' as well as that of the 'popular' among reading publics, and the literary materials available for perusal.

The issues central to these points impinge on questions well beyond those of the history of literacy alone. They belong properly to considerations of disciplinary boundaries and relations, epistemology, methodology and interpretation, and source criticism. These are areas in which the 'human sciences,' whether social or humanistic, have far to go; the road is long and crossing the path has barely begun. That the relations between historical and literary research—always close, but not overlapping or synonymous—are problematic is well known, despite past and ongoing practice in both fields. Regardless of the cavils of the 'new critics' or the prognoses of 'scientific' historians, it is undeniable that just as students of literature and its history need the evidence of history, historians require that of literature.

The relationships between 'history' and 'literature' are many and diverse, if not always well understood or elaborated in practice. Although researchers in both disciplines regularly draw upon the sources and, increasingly, the methods of the other, neither parameters nor paradigms nor questions are the same. Readers are undoubtedly aware of some of the strengths and limitations of scholarship that crosses the boundaries of these interdisciplines.

Literary sources have not been fully or well utilized for research into the history of education or schooling. Of course, *The Hoosier Schoolmaster, Glen-*

This essay was written while I was a Research Associate at the Newberry Library. I would like to acknowledge funding for the research from the National Endowment of the Humanities and the Spencer Foundation.

garry School Days, Tom Brown's School Days, and passages in Dickens are often quoted and employed heuristically in the classroom. Nevertheless, the extant scholarship that draws on literary evidence seldom reflects much concern with its central complications or with the problems that plague the use of literary sources in historical research. Within the history of literacy,[2] for example, one researcher aptly notes,

> Another consequence of the vague use of the concept of literacy in history has been that research on the extent of literacy has been conducted on a wide, and at times ill-defined, front. This has been most marked in the case of studies which present evidence of a literary or anecdotal kind. Here some contemporary comment as to the proportion able to read is taken as an indication of literacy, without any examination either of the representativeness of the observation, for example the sex, status, and residence of the people concerned, or of the level of reading ability in question.[3]

Consider an example. A student of literacy interested in the employment of popular literacy may well turn to the evidence of the history of publishing, on one hand, or, more narrowly, existing records of circulation tallies and print runs, in order to estimate audience sizes and patterns of readership. Such common practice risks committing several fallacies. Despite the tendency among literary historians and bibliographers to assume that the appearance of some new form of publication or an increase in the volume of existing forms is associated with an increase in the level of literacy, no such relationship necessarily exists. As Roger Schofield comments, 'difficulties prevent any inference being drawn from changes in either the volume or the nature of literary productions to changes in the level of literacy.' The number of readers per copy cannot be assumed to remain constant; changes in volume of production also are influenced by factors other than literacy levels: technological innovations in printing, changes in legal status of printers or laws respecting size of editions, and changes in fiscal policies such as rates of stamp duties.[4]

Those are only one set of fallacies common to historical literacy research, whether by historians or literary critics.[5] Seminal and 'standard' works on this subject, by scholars from both disciplines, commit these and other fallacies. Marshall McLuhan's writings are perhaps the most blatant example. The well-known books by Richard Altick (*The English Common Reader*), Victor Neuberg (*Popular Literature, Popular Education in Eighteenth-Century England*), Russell Nye (*The Cultural Life of the New Nation, Society and Culture in America*), Louis B. Wright (*Culture on the Moving Frontier, The Cultural Life of the New Nation*) among others, old and new, may be cited in this respect without distorting or demeaning their other qualities. In United States studies, the ground-breaking volumes of Lawrence A. Cremin on *American Education: The Colonial Experience* and *The National Period* are recent cases in point.[6]

Another example comes from Victor E. Neuberg's many observations on popular literature. A special case of the fallacies criticized by Schofield, Neuberg flirts with what I term an 'ecological' fallacy in the history of literacy. In a fascinating paper on 'street literature' in the first half of the nineteenth century, this author argues, poetically but without basis, that the 'massing of people in cities . . . meant not only higher densities on the ground but also new opportunities for communication on many different levels.' The new mass, of itself, to Neuberg, provided the demand for new kinds of 'mass journalism', of which the most characteristic was street literature.[7] A simple correlation in time or space is not evidence of a causal or any other kind of historical association.

Despite the difficulties involved in the historical use of literary evidence, the importance of these sources remains undisputable. Literary evidence has provided human perspectives, textures, and nuances that other kinds of data—quantitative sources *or* more traditional varieties of manuscript and print—have not supplied. For this reason, the use of such evidence represents an ongoing challenge to the student of culture and society to integrate it with other bodies of evidence and to develop new techniques to evaluate its utility and potential.

Certain kinds of literary evidence are more useful to social and cultural historians than others. Researchers in literary history and historians who have attempted to work with literature often agree that the 'best' literature is neither the easiest to work with nor the most accurate source of historical evidence. The authorial voice is strong and subtle, the depiction of the times often nuanced and filtered or highly personal. It is 'realistic' fiction, instead, often didactically presented, that serves better for historians' purposes. For example, such literature as nineteenth-century domestic fiction is useful for fleshing out details that derive from the analysis of other sources, confirming insights from other evidence, revealing varieties of human responses including disjunctures and discontinuities, and leading to new questions.[8] Often, it is precisely the novels and stories disdained by traditional students of 'high' literary culture that are best-suited to social or cultural research into the past.

An excellent example is *The Ragged Trousered Philanthropists*. A novel accorded little attention outside circles of English working-class historians, it nevertheless achieved the status of a minor 'underground' classic. *The Ragged Trousered Philanthropists* was written by Robert Tressell about 1910; it was first published by Grant Richards Ltd. in England in 1914, three years after the author's death from tuberculosis. The publisher of the first complete edition in 1955 described the book as 'the first account in English of the lives and opinions of a group of working men, written with realism and passion, not by an outside observer, but by 'one of themselves.' 'The book has had a fascinating publishing history. The complete original manuscript was not the version published in 1914 but was rediscovered only in 1946 and published in the mid-1950s. The altered 1914 and subsequent editions were successively abridged. Yet, according to the recent publisher, 'In our lifetime it has become a classic of the Labour movement.'[9]

The novel is important for many reasons: as historical source, document of the working-class and Labor movements, portrait of working-class life, and an example of working-class art. The author himself was a house painter by trade. His purposes followed his political commitments and permeated the text, which should be read as a piece of didactic literature. His biases have not reduced its significance for students of history or of literature. As Tressell wrote in his original Preface, 'In writing this book my intention was to present, in the form of an interesting story, a faithful picture of working-class life. . . .' He wished to describe the relationships between the men and their employers, the attitudes and feelings between the two classes, the varying conditions of workers, and 'their pleasures, their intellectual outlook, their religious and political opinions and ideals.' The story takes place in a period just longer than a year, but Tressell attempted to encapsulate the life cycles of the workers and their families, 'to show the conditions resulting from poverty and unemployment: to expose the futility of the measures taken to deal with them and to indicate what I believe to be the only true remedy, namely—Socialism.'

Robert Tressell has not camouflaged the ideological orientation of the book. However, he has emphasized that his epic 'is not a treatise or essay, but a novel. My main object was to write a readable story full of human interest and based in the happenings of everyday life, the subject of Socialism being treated incidentally.' Urging that the book's success was 'for others to say,' Tressell asserted that 'whatever their verdict, the work possesses at lease one merit—that of being true.'

> I have invented nothing. There are no scenes or incidents in the story that I have not either witnessed myself or had conclusive evidence of. As far as I dared I let the characters express themselves in their own sort of language and consequently some passages may be considered objectionable. . . . The scenes and characters are typical of every town in the South of England and they will be readily recognized by those considered. . . . Because it is true it will probably be denounced as libel on the working classes and their employers, and upon the religious-professing section of the community. But I believe it will be acknowledged as true by most of those who are compelled to spend their lives amid the surroundings it describes, and will be evident that no attack is made upon sincere religion.[10]

The forcefulness of this claim is felt vigorously as the novel's 621 pages are read.

The principal attraction of *The Ragged Trousered Philanthropists* for historians is more narrow than the author's sweeping literary and political goals. It is the portrayal of the roles and meanings of literacy and schooling and the attitudes of the working class toward literacy's skills and schooling's place, as depicted in a number of the book's detailed sketches of working-class life, thought and feeling, particularly in struggles during the early years of the twentieth century—before the 'welfare state'. Important for the social historical use of this text, these subjects are central to the novel's detail and example, rather than to its main themes or arguments. That increases the probability of accuracy and veracity, and its value as a historical source.

The Ragged Trousered Philanthropists has vividly portrayed the roles and meanings of working-class literacy and primary schooling, on one hand, and, on the other hand, the working-class characters' opinions about them. His illustrations have paralleled the conclusions reached in my own analyses of very different historical sources, principally census, tax roll, and wage records and the periodical press of the nineteenth century. *The Literacy Myth: Literacy and Social Structure in the Nineteenth-Century City* reported those findings.[11] These parallel lines of depiction and argument serve to raise key questions about the uses of literary sources in historical study and about the relations between sources, approaches, and disciplinary perspectives. This relationship provided a basis for one type of evidence to reflect back upon the other, deepening and extending the analysis and interpretation. (The absence of parallels would also raise key questions and issues, though of an opposing stripe.)

Tressell has set *The Ragged Trousered Philanthropists* in Hastings (called Mugsborough in the novel) and has concerned himself primarily with a group of painters and decorators and their families around the year 1906. The English novelist, Alan Sillitoe, has written in his Introduction to the 1955 edition: 'It describes the workman's life of that time, the subjection, deception, and destitution of the people whose labor helped to create the luxury and glitter of the Edwardian age.' In the novel, Owen, the main character, struggled to enlighten his fellow workmen about the oppression and exploitation of their lives and about the hopes for change under socialism. Alas, they did not listen to him,

> so he calls them philanthropists, benefactors in ragged trousers who willingly hand over the results of their labor to the employers and the rich. They think it is the natural order of things that the rich should exploit them, that 'gentlemen' are the only people with a right to govern.

This issue is the heart of the novel, but Sillitoe agreed, 'a mass of personal detail keeps it a novel and not a tract.'

Sillitoe considered *The Ragged Trousered Philanthropists* the 'first good novel' of English working-class life. He has noted that working people who are familiar with the book speak about it as if they knew the characters, and they lived the incidents themselves. 'What makes Tressell's work unique,' he has insisted, 'is the author's sense of humor and sense of honor. You can laugh at the way tragic things are told, while being led through the fire, only to weep when cold blasts you at the other end. He is utterly unsentimental.'[12] The struggle to survive, to get one's daily bread, became central themes without losing sight of the quest for self-respect and human dignity, as historians recognize as essential themes in working-class history. Yet, Tressell has not elevated them in order to mythologize them.

Literacy has figured vividly in the story told by Robert Tressell. For example, early in its pages, one of the workmen, Easton, and his wife discussed their weekly budget and its severe limitations. Verbally, they each enunciated their material needs and the costs and their debts. The recital quickly became lengthy. Easton paused and stated:

'Wait a minit,' said Easton, 'The best way is to write out a list of everything we owe; then we shall know exactly where we are. You get me a piece of paper and tell me what to write. Then we'll see what it all comes to.'

'Do you mean everything we owe, or everything we must pay tomorrow.'

'I think we'd better make a list of all we owe first.'. . .

'It seems to me,' said he, as, after having cleared a space on the table and arranged the paper, he began to sharpen his pencil with a table-knife, 'that you don't manage things as well as you might. If you was to make out a list of just the things you must have before you went out of a Saturday, you'd find the money would go much farther. Instead of doing that you just take the money in your hand without knowing exactly what you're going to do with it, and when you come back it's all gone and next to nothing to show for it.'[13]

The Eastons made their list; the total rose astonishingly before their eyes. At that point, Ruth, the wife, showed her husband notices from the City Corporation about rent in arrears and from the furniture dealer about the next monthly bill.

In this scene, Tressell has revealed much about working-class domestic life, gender relations (and conflicts), the struggle to make ends meet, and the interconnections of print, literacy, and the cash economy. Simply but richly, the author has sketched the basic literacy skills of husband and wife in the early twentieth-century working class, which contemporary statistics led us to expect. He has shown common uses of reading, writing, and counting skills. Whether or not the Eastons were slow to turn to list-making and written accounting in this household conference, this basic, practical everyday use of literacy was not alien to them. They grasped simple uses of literacy and recognized the benefits.

From this passage, we have understood the ways in which print penetrated the daily and intimate lives of the working poor. With bills, notices, and list-making becoming prevalent by the early twentieth century and indeed somewhat earlier—for example, with railroad schedules and the postal service—we no longer need refer to evidence of literacy's use via ballads, broadsides, pamphlets, posters, and cheap literature, all of which were quite important.

This simple scene has revealed one result of common, elementary schooling. Its goals were to teach a pupil to 'spell correctly the words he will have to use; he shall read a common narrative—the paragraph in the newspaper that he cares to read—with sufficient ease to be a pleasure to himself and to convey information to listeners . . . write his mother a letter . . . legible and intelligible; he knows enough of ciphering to make out, to test the correctness of a common shop bill. . . .' These skills could be difficult to learn well, given the short and irregular periods of schooling common to working-class youths of the period. The pupils learned some of them and these skills proved to be useful in their later lives; of this Tressell's novel provided examples. As I argued in *The Literacy Myth,* many did not require a high degree of literacy and few acquired it. About the final aim of schooling in Victorian and Edwardian England—'Underlying all, and not without its influence, I trust, upon his life and conversation, he has acquaintance with the Holy Scriptures . . . to know what are the duties required of him toward his Maker and his fellow men'—there may be greater doubt. *The Ragged Trousered Philanthropists* also has addressed this issue; the thrust of Tressell's narrative has illustrated in rich detail the articulation and development of a cultural hegemony of the 'moral bases of literacy' as purpose and often as result of popular, formal schooling.[14]

Tressell's characters spoke to this crucial issue. In another domestic scene, mother, father, and son explicitly discussed the function of schooling for the working class. This interchange happened at Owen's home, whose head is the chief protagonist of the book. Owen serves as a model of a respectable but conscious member of the working class. Young Frankie, his son, has just picked up his toys, as the question of who shall speak to and for the workers was broached. The lad asserted:

> 'I should think the workers will be jolly glad when they see me coming to tell them what to do, shouldn't you, Mum?'
>
> 'I don't know dear; you see so many people have tried to tell them, but they won't listen, they don't want to hear. They think it's quite right that they should work very hard all their lives, and quite right that most of the things they help to make should be taken away from them by the people who do nothing. The workers think that their children are not as good as the children of the idlers, and they teach their children that as soon as they are old enough they must be satisfied to work very hard and to have only very bad food and clothes and homes.'
>
> 'Then I should think the workers ought to be jolly well ashamed of themselves, Mum, don't you?'
>
> 'Well, in one sense they ought, but you must remember that that's what they've always been taught themselves. First, their mothers and fathers told them do; then, their schoolteachers told them so; and then, when they went to church, the vicar and the Sunday School teacher told them the same thing. So you can't be surprised that they now really believe that God made them and their children to make things for the use of the people who do nothing.'[15]

This passage, I emphasize, was *not* written during the past decade by revisionist historians! It was written during the first decade of this century by an astute observer and participant in working-class life. One of the clearest and most dramatic statements of the sources and results of cultural and ideological hegemony that I have encountered in primary or secondary literature, it enumerates the agencies that work to support the functioning of social order and promote cohesion and integration: home and family, school and church. Its consequences, apparently common, were outlined, as well as the causal agencies. Tressell also has depicted the course and nature of their relationships.

Antonio Gramsci has described such a process, when he wrote that hegemony was the consent of the masses arising in response to 'the direction imposed on social life by the dominant fundamental group.' Involving neither conscious choice nor coercion or deliberate deception, the resulting predominance derived from consent, 'the spontaneous loyalty that any dominant social group obtains from the masses by virtue of its social and intellectual production.' Hegemony obtained from correct and proper moral schooling, in part. This was one way in which a concept of reality was diffused throughout society and informed tastes, morality, customs, religious and political principles, and all social relations, 'particularly in their intellectual and moral connotations.' Tressell's view, 'close to the ground', put schooling in its contemporary perspective and indicated how it joined with home, family, and other social relations in creating and supporting cultural hegemony.[16] Tressell also underscores that a net of agencies—and not the schools or formal institutions alone—and their interactions worked toward that purpose. The novel in this way can serve as a guide to historians.

'But,' precocious Frankie responded to his mother, 'you'd think their own sense would tell them! How can it be right for the people who do nothing to have the very best and most of everything that's made, and the very ones who make everything to have hardly any. Why even I know better than that, and I'm only six and a half years old.' Mum explained his basic difference to the lad, and in so doing, also commented on the social functions of education and the manner in which hegemony was maintained.

> 'But then you're different, dearie, you've been taught to think about it, and Dad and I have explained it to you, often.'
>
> 'Yes, I know,' replied Frankie confidently. 'But even if you'd never taught me, I'm sure that I should have tumbled to it all right by myself; I'm not such a juggins as you think I am.'
>
> 'So you might, but you wouldn't if you'd been brought up in the same way as most of the workers. They've been taught that it's very wicked to use their own judgement, or to think. And their children are being taught so now.'

To clarify what she meant, his mother illustrated the process by an example:

> 'Do you remember what you told me the other day, when you came home from school, about the Scripture lesson?'
>
> 'About St. Thomas?'
>
> 'Yes, What did the teacher say St. Thomas was?'
>
> 'She said he was a bad example: and she said I was worse than him because I asked too many foolish questions. She always gets in a wax if I talk too much.'

'Well, why did she call St. Thomas a bad example?'

'Because he wouldn't believe what he was told.'

'Exactly: well, when you told Dad about it what did he say?'

'Dad told me that really St. Thomas was the only sensible man in the whole crowd of Apostles. That is,' added Frankie, correcting himself, 'if there ever was such a man at all.'

'But did Dad say that there never was such a man?'

'No; he said *he* didn't believe there ever was, but he told me to just listen to what the teacher said about such things, and then to think about it in my own mind, and wait till I'm grown up and then I can use my own judgment.'

'Well, now, that's what *you* were told, but all the other children's mothers and fathers tell them to believe, without thinking, whatever the teacher says. So it will be no wonder if those children are not able to think for themselves when they're grown up, will it?'[17]

A very special set of supports and education was apparently required to combat successfully the force of literacy's and schooling's moral bases or the likelihood of another consequence: anti-intellectual, self-deprecating obscuranticism.

Later in *The Ragged Trousered Philanthropists* Tressell added to this depiction of the roles of the schools and their place in civil society and working-class life in a passage which is part of a larger description of the degradation of labor, the insecurities of work and welfare, and the implications for workers' selfhood and their families' well-being. In particular, the author focused on the intergenerational reproduction of the social and class structure and the active-passive roles of the present generation of workers in the process. The schools, literacy, and hegemony appeared as parts of that complex process of social reproduction.

Tressell wrote movingly:

It was a pathetic and wonderful and at the same time a despicable spectacle. Pathetic that human beings should be condemned to spend the greater part of their lives amid such [work] surroundings, because it must be remembered that most of their time was spent on some job or other. . . . Wonderful, because although they knew that they did more than their fair share of the great work of producing the necessities and comforts of life, they did not think they were entitled to a fair share of the good things they helped to create! And despicable, because although they saw their children condemned to the same life of degradation, hard labour and privation, yet they refused to help to bring about a better state of affairs. Most of them thought that what had been good enough for themselves was good enough for their children.

But he did not stop at this point. The author elaborated instructively:

It seemed as if they regarded their own children with a kind of contempt, as being only fit to be the servants of the children of such people as

235

Rushton and Sweater [the painters' employers]. But it must be remembered that they had been taught self-contempt when they were children. In the so-called 'Christian' schools they attended then they were taught to 'order themselves lowly and reverently towards their betters', and they were not actually sending their own children to learn the same degrading lessons in their turn! They had a vast amount of consideration for their betters, and for the children of their betters, but very little for their own children, for each other, or for themselves.

That was why they sat there in their rags and ate their coarse food, and cracked their coarser jokes, and drank the dreadful tea, and were content! So long as they had Plenty of Work and plenty of—Something—to eat, and somebody else's cast-off clothes to wear, they were content! And they were proud of it. They gloried in it. They agreed and assured each other that the good things in life were not intended for the 'Likes of them', or their children.[18]

Here too, this passage from a novel spoke more eloquently than do many historians about working-class life and culture and their relationship to education and schooling. This was the working class that had been to publicly-sponsored and provided schools, although typically for a short stay.[19] There, and sometimes elsewhere, they acquired the rudiments of literacy, a literacy sometimes useful to them. That acquisition of some literacy and schooling, however, did not often change their lives or their minds, despite the prognostications of social and psychological theorists about the 'modernizing' and 'transforming' impacts of literacy. Rather, it was most often a cultural process that reinforced their lowly, underfoot positions in the class, social, and economic hierarchies, and thus *taught* many a fair measure of grudging acceptance of their stations. For the most part, expectations were not hopes for the improvement or mobility of selves or children stimulated. Instead, the opposite held true: hopes were not created, stability was largely maintained, little respect for learning or the tools for it were gained, and acceptance of the status quo was emphasized. These were the moral bases of literacy: the social morality, the message, that accompanied the processes of learning to read and to write, and which constituted the transmission of cultural hegemony.[20]

Working-class attitudes toward education were—and are—varied and complex. They defy simple summary. Many hungered after literacy and opportunities for schooling; this craving appeared dramatically in the working-class autobiographies that David Vincent has studied.[21] Quests for respectability and mobility competed with those for the keys to knowledge and freedom, although they could overlap uncomfortably. Many others were uninterested in attending school, in learning, or in using literacy. They accorded education a relatively low priority in their hierarchies of needs and values—for themselves or their children. In it, they saw little value or relevance. Still others were actively and consciously hostile: for reasons ranging from political and ideological opposition to the 'bourgeois political economy' of the curriculum, to the ways in which their children were treated and mistreated, to opposition to state or even private efforts to intervene into working class life and culture. For a great many reasons, a deep and pronounced ambivalence punctuated the working-class' approach toward their opportunities for education.[22] Ambivalence, tension, and variation in responses were all richly illustrated in Tressell's story.

The story of Owen and his family and Owen's struggle for his own education plus that of his workmates was central to *The Ragged Trousered Philanthropists.* Tressell illuminated the great respect that many in the working class held for *self-*learning, above and outside that provided by the schools. Not only a sign of initiative, self-learning also represented the potentials inherent but not necessarily or often realized in the uses of literacy. (Too often the potentials for action and transformation that many follow from learning and *using* literacy are confused with the technique itself or the more common, reinforcing results.) A variety, indeed a hierarchy, of possibilities forms what David Vincent, for example, has referred to, in ascending order, as the struggle for 'Bread, Knowledge and Freedom,' to which literacy might contribute.

Owen, the protagonist of the novel, succinctly stated the political economic critique of public schooling found on both sides of the Atlantic during the nineteenth and early twentieth centuries.[23] One occasion was a discussion among the workmen on the job site, and Owen replied to Slyme's claim that Socialists, if in power, would steal the savings held in the Post Office Savings Bank. Another man picks up the point, and related one common attitude toward schooling:

'And there's another thing I objects to,' said Crass. 'And that's all this 'ere talk about hignorance: wot about all the money wots spent every year for education.?'

Owen took this as his point of entry:

'You should rather say—"What about all the money that's wasted every year on education?" What can be more brutal and senseless than trying to "educate" a poor, little, ill-clad child? Such so-called "instruction" is like the seed in the parable of the Sower, which fell on stony ground and withered away because it had no depth of earth; and even in those cases where it does take root and grow, it becomes like the seed that fell among thorns and the thorns grew up and choked it, and it bore no fruit.

'The majority of us forget in a year or two all that we learnt at school because the conditions of our lives are such as to destroy all inclination for culture or refinement. We must see that the children are properly clothed and fed and that they are not made to get up in the middle of the night to go to work for several hours in the evening after school, or all day and till nearly midnight on Saturday. We must first see that our children are cared for, as well as the children of savage races, before we can expect a proper return for the money that we spend on education.'[24]

Education of this type, offered in this way, was no education at all.

Thus spoke Owen to his peers. Not surprisingly, they proved unwilling to discuss this issue, which they had introduced, any further. Subsequent conversation, focusing on wealth and the distribution thereof, only increased the contradictions. Rather than attending to Owen's analysis and examples, his fellow workers equated money with intelligence, the former standing as a sign of the latter.[25] Obviously, working men were confused, partly as a result of their schooling, about the sources of power and wealth, the meaning of 'intelligence', and the functions and correlates of education. The skills taught in school, including literacy, were of little use, as acquired—qualitatively, cognitively, and noncognitively—and as commonly employed, for the goals that Owen propounded. Such intelligence, of course, was not the purpose of schooling or of the sponsored transmission of literacy. Neither the conditions or content of schooling nor the maintenance of hegemony encouraged it.

The literary analysis accorded with the contradictory stance toward education and its agencies expressed by North American working-class spokesmen a few decades earlier. On one hand, they stressed the need to educate first. That formed the necessary precondition to agitation and the erasing of ignorance, superstition, and temerity. This solution looked toward the use of the ballot. But, on the other hand, force and action were emphasized; the hammer, the symbol of labor, was seized as more powerful than the pen, the symbol of thought.[26] In the second formulation, education, especially that provided publicly, was decidedly not primary.

Owen was the sympathetic hero of the novel. His knowledge, his struggles and plight, his noble wife and child, and his active concern with the enlightenment and consciousness-awakening of his peers served as lynch-pins for the tale. 'His experiences included regular lunchtime informal lecture discussion sessions with his workmates, who, appropriately but revealingly called him the 'Professor'. On the one hand, the other workers, including their foreman, valued his discussions and all but begged him to speak to and with them, in part because they enjoyed it as entertainment. But on the other hand, they simultaneously and contradictorily mocked and jeered and insulted him, and did all in their power to deny his arguments, ignore his logic, and undercut his points. *The Ragged Trousered Philanthropists* is filled with examples of this.[27] They add to our understanding of working-class culture, literacy, and schooling.

Tressell, for example, ended an account of a typical day's session of lecture and discussion by noting forcefully:

> For some moments an oppressive silence prevailed. The men stared with puzzled, uncomfortable looks alternatively at each other and at the drawings on the wall [Owen's illustrations of points in his presentation]. They were compelled to do a little thinking on their own account, and it was a process to which they were unaccustomed. In their infancy they had been taught to distrust their own intelligence and to leave 'thinking' to their 'pastors' and masters and to their 'betters' generally. All their lives they had been true to this teaching, they had always had blind, unrea-

soning faith in the wisdom and humanity of their pastors and masters. This was the reason why they and their children had been all their lives on the verge of starvation and nakedness, whilst their 'betters'—who did nothing but the thinking—went clothed in purple and fine linen and fare sumptuously every day.

Though they sought out Owen and commanded him to speak to them, they were unwilling to confront his message on any reasonable grounds, whether to accept, reject, or qualify it. Calling him the 'Professor' was two-edged, blending respect with scorn and paralleling their evaluation of education and its uses. Both were filled with tension; they reflected the results of schooling and assimilation of the process of hegemony. In the end, they rejected analysis of the current system and proposals or hopes for its alteration as beyond the realms of their notions of possibility, beyond their understanding, and beyond their sense of agency. As two of the men responded to Owen, the silence that followed the conclusion of the lecture showed:

> 'Well,' interrupted Crass, with a self-satisfied chuckle, 'it'll take a better bloody man than you to enlighten *me!*'
> 'I don't want to be henlightened into Darkness!' said Slyme piously.[28]

Owen, as a representative of 'Knowledge' and as a fitting hero, persevered. Socialism, of course, was a very real and vital movement in England at this time; much discussed in virtually all quarters of society, it was also a legitimate political force and party struggling for supporters, adherents, and voters. As a movement, it believed deeply in the efficacy of literacy and education; it was a product of the time.

In context, however, Owen employed a number of approaches, drawing upon different media in his efforts to reach the minds of his peers. Despite the increasing levels and penetration of print into ongoing social, economic, political, and cultural life, that life was neither dominated nor reshaped by print and literacy.[29] Owen *spoke* frequently, formally and informally, to his fellow workmen and to others he encountered. Oral means of communication remained basic to the flows of communication, information, and discourse, regardless of social theories to the contrary. He also used primitive visual aids in his discussions in order to clarify and extend his points in the best possible manner.

And of course, he also used print, his own source of much information and opinion. Despite the great power contemporaries accorded to print, it was perhaps not the most effective media for the task. Attempting to educate the other men and to convert them, he shared with them the volumes in his small library of Socialist books and pamphlets. Some of the men took the books, sometimes acting as if *they* were doing *him* a favor, and promised to read them. The men, however, were neither good nor great readers of the printed page. In part, this was one consequence of their schooling as well as of conditions in their homes and lack of leisure. Thus, when they returned the books, 'it was with vague expressions of approval, but they usually evinced a disinclination to discuss the contents in detail because, in nine instances out of ten, they had not attempted to read them. Of those who attempted to read, 'in the majority of cases their minds were so rusty and stultified by long years of disuse, that, although the pamphlets were generally written in such simple language that a child might have understood, the argument was generally too obscure to be grasped by men whose minds were addled by the stories told them by their Liberal and Tory masters.' Others, when offered material by Owen, refused; some who took the loans later boasted of using them as toilet paper![30]

A person like Owen was shown to be exceptional, among the working class, and perhaps among the middle class as well. The latter were not portrayed as frequent readers or pursuers of knowledge or self-improvement, despite stereotypes to the contrary. Again, this depiction agreed with and extended my conclusions derived from very different kinds of evidence. For regardless of the level of print's penetration and literacy's diffusion to near universality, reading was apparently not a typical use of one's time, either on the job or at leisure. In *The Ragged Trousered Philanthropists,* Robert Tressell illustrated the workers who had other, more important uses for their time away from work. He helps us to understand why. He wrote of how the men had formerly taken all their wages home to their wives each Saturday and how 'in a moment, yea, even in the twinkling of an eye, it was all gone!' Sick and tired of that and desiring a little pleasure, excitement, and fun, the men took to spending on quart pots in the pub. 'They knew they were not the genuine articles, but they were better than nothing at all, so they gave up the practice of giving all their money to the old girl to give to the landlord and the other harpies, and bought beer with some of it instead.'[31] This was a common use of time, more common than reading, it seems. Of course, there was more to popular recreations than drink, despite stereotypes to the contrary. They included the increasingly popular music hall, street life, gambling, horseracing, and even reading of newspapers and cheap literature. Outings and street life figured in *The Ragged Trousered Philanthropists,* in addition to drink and pub sociability, but reading was not prominent. Nor, beyond newspaper perusal, did other sources suggest that it was a very popular pastime.

Politics, especially Parliamentary elections and electioneering, did capture significant interest and attention. Politics also stimulated newspaper reading, it seems. As Tressell indicates, political and electoral life was most prominently expressed in oral settings of speeches and orations and in ritualized public encounters and dramas. Print and literacy, as in other aspects of life, were only one medium among others. Their meaning is only found in the interaction of many media.[32] Efforts to isolate them not only obscure their understanding, but also that of working-class life and culture.

But for all that, the novel ends on a note of hope. Tressell saw, or thought he saw, rising from the ruins, 'the glorious fabric of the Co-operative Commonwealth,' with humanity 'at last looking upward to the light that was riving asunder and dissolving the dark clouds.' That 'Golden Light' was the rays of 'the risen sun of Socialism.'[33] His hopes have yet to bear fruition. Neither, of course, have those, held by whatever class, for the potentials of universal literacy and schooling.

The Ragged Trousered Philanthropists is rich in its other testimony and descriptions. It speaks to many issues other than those discussed in this essay. Nevertheless, its importance should be clear. The close, paralleling, humane, and texturally illuminating relationship between this self-consciously realistic portrayal of the English working class uses of literacy and attitudes toward education and the analysis presented in recent historical works is significant. The support it provides to the interpretation based on other, rather different kinds of primary sources is more than coincidental; it has many implications for strategies of historical and literary research and for interdisciplinary scholarship. The ways in which this literary presentation extends, illustrates, and indeed sharpens an understanding based on other kinds of evidence make the point deeply. The richness of the human textures and the details of daily life is one basic complement. Contradiction would be no less important, of course; it would raise a challenge to the initial understanding, and perhaps suggest underlying discontinuities and disjunctures. Literary evidence such as this, however, cannot of itself negate independent evidence; that is one of its limitations. More than support or, for that matter, contradiction is therefore at issue. Analyses that derive from very different lenses or perspectives illuminate understanding by the manner in which they reflect upon each other, under intellectually and historically-controlled conditions, constitute important lessons and significant problems.

Should we be surprised by this overlap and parallel? If we heed Peter Laslett's well-known strictures *against* the use of literary evidence in social historical research, we perhaps should be.[34] Laslett, of course, used examples like the marriage ages of characters like Romeo and Juliet almost hyperbolistically to attack traditional historical dependence on literacy sources and imagery and Aries, *Centuries of Childhood's* reliance on art as well as literature. His point, if excessive, remains well taken. Literary evidence, *if taken alone*, often does represent 'The wrong way through the telescope'.

Yet, the use of literature in historical work continues to be significant; that is one purpose of the present exercise. One is on far sounder grounds with literature that is, first, realistic and highly descriptive and, second, that does *not* necessarily meet many of the canons of 'great' works of art. Detail and example, third, are often most useful for social historical interpretation. Whereas a very important novel for many reasons, *The Ragged Trousered Philanthropists* will never meet inflated standards of literary critics. That ranking, I believe, does not diminish its value to social and cultural historians; it may actually enhance it. Not only may such literature confirm, which is important in itself, interpretations and analyses based on different kinds of data and methods, but it also serves to qualify, extend, and elaborate such conclusions. Of course, a lack of agreement would in itself be important and worthy of investigation and asking of additional and new questions.

In this case, it was confirmation and extension rather than disjuction or contradiction that resulted.

The uses of literature in historical study are many and important. Traditional social and cultural history drew heavily upon such testimony. In reaction to this, among other things, 'new' social historians have strongly distrusted and often avoided such evidence. Michael Anderson's important *Family Structure in Nineteenth-Century Lancashire,* with its systematic analysis of Elizabeth Gaskell's novels, is a major exception to this trend. Avoidance of essential testimony about the textures of life, attitudes, sentiments, and mentalities, however, constitutes an *over-*reaction, not a methodological advance or innovation.

Literature must be employed cautiously and carefully as evidence, like any other document. It must be criticized and evaluated; its testimony must be compared with that of other sources. Yet, literature is a different kind of source in many of its intrinsic and extrinsic qualities and characteristics. This makes it exceptional in its ability to aid the *experienced* student of any topic or period, but it also makes its evaluation all the more demanding and difficult. The point is that the needs of historians for a truly human and 'scientific' (in the European sense of science as systematic study) understanding of the past demand its fullest employment. In that task, we have far to go. This exposition is only one beginning step on that long path.

Notes

1 I have in mind principally the examples of the work of NEUBERG, ALTICK, and EN-GELSING, See VICTOR E. NEUBERG, *Popular Literature: A History and Guide.* Harmondsworth. 1977 and *Popular Education in Eighteenth-Century England.* London, 1971; R. ENGELSING, *Analphabetum und Lekture, Zun Sozialgeschichte des Lesen in Deutschland Zwischen feodaler und industrielle Gesellschaft.* STUTTGART, 1973 and *Der Burger als Leser: Lesergeschichte in Deutschland, 1500–1800.* Stuttgart, 1974; RICHARD ALTICK, *The English Common Reader,* Chicage, 1957. Many of the French 'histoire du livre' studies are best classified here too.

2 For intelligent use of the genre of autobiographies, see DAVID VINCENT *Bread, Knowledge and Freedom: A Study of Nineteenth-Century Working Class Autobiography.* London, 1981. The work of BARBARA FINKELSTEIN is also interesting in this respect. See her 'Reading, Writing, and the Acquisition of Identity in the United States. 1790–1860,' in *Regulated Children / Liberated Children: Education in Psychohistorical Perspective,* (Ed.) B. FINKELSTEIN. New York, 1979, 114–139, 'The Moral Dimensions of Pedagogy.' *American Studies,* 15 (1974): 79–89, and 'Pedagogy as Intrusion: Teaching Values in Popular Primary Schools in Nineteenth-Century America," *History of Childhood Quarterly,* 2 (1975): 349–378. See also, note 22, below.

3 ROGER SCHOFIELD, 'The Measurement of Literacy in Pre-industrial Societies,' in *Literacy in Traditional Societies,* (Ed.) JACK GOODY. Cambridge, 1968, p. 314.

4 SCHOFIELD, 'Measurement,' 314–315. See also, as examples, the work of NEUBERG, ENGELSING, and ALTICK cited above, among many other examples.

5 For further examples and analysis, see HARVEY J. GRAFF, *The Literacy Myth Literacy and Social Structure in the Nineteenth-Century City.* New York and London, 1979 and *The Legacies of Literacy: Continuities and Contradictions in Western Society and*

Culture. Bloomington: Indiana University Press 1986; DAVID CRESSY, *Literacy and the Social Order* Cambridge, 1980; KENNETH A. LOCKRIDGE, *Literacy in Colonial New England.* New York, 1974; FRANÇOIS FURET and JACQUES OZOUF, *Lire et Ecrire.* Paris, 1977; EGIL JOHANSSON, *The History of Literacy in Sweden Umeå, 1977;* LEE SOLTOW and EDWARD STEVENS, *The Rise of Literacy and the Common School,* Chicago, 1982. For specific examples, see my review of NEUBERG and LOCKRIDGE, 'Literacy in History,' *History of Education Quarterly,* 15 (1975): 467–474.

6 On Cremin's approach to literacy, see LOCKRIDGE, *Literacy;* GRAFF, *The Legacies of Literacy.*

7 'The Literature of the Streets,' in *The Victorian City,* (Ed.) H.J. DYOS and MICHAEL WOLFF. London, 1973. I: 191. See also, for other examples, THOMAS W. LAQUEUR. 'The Cultural Origins of Literacy in England. 1500–1850.' *Oxford Review of Education,* 2 (1976): 255–275; MARGARET SPUFFORD, *Small Books and Pleasant Histories.* London, 1981. This approach is usefully compared with those of DAVID LEVINE and KEITH WRIGHTSON. *Poverty and Piety in an English Village.* New York, 1979; LEVINE, 'Illiteracy and Family Life in the First Industrial Revolution,' *Journal of Social History,* 14 (1980): 25–44 and 'Education and Family in Early Industrial England.' *Journal of Family History,* 4 (1970): 368–380: GRAFF, *The Literacy Myth,* esp. ch. 7; DANIEL CALHOUN, 'The City as Teacher,' *History of Education Quarterly,* 9 (1969): 311–325 and *The Intelligence of a People* (Princeton, 1973). The second set of citations offer differing, but suggestive paths to grounded and controlled analysis.

8 My own thinking on these issues has been influenced by the experience of team-teaching a graduate seminar on 'Women in the Nineteenth-Century,' at The University of Texas at Dallas with LILIAN FURST, a professor of comparative literature. Professor FURST deserves my thanks but none of the responsibility for my conclusions. ELLEN DWYER, Indiana University; JILL MILLING, University of Texas at Dallas; and PAUL MATTINGLY, New York University, offered critical readings which I appreciate. Women's history offers important parallels to this approach.

9 Publisher's Forward to the 1955 British Edition, p. 6. The edition used here and cited throughout is the Monthly Review Press edition, published in New York, 1962 a reprint of the Lawrence and Wishart edition, 1955.

10 ROBERT TRESSELL, *Ragged Trousered Philanthropists* (1914) pp. 11–12. See also Alan Sillitoe's Introduction to the novel. For important information on the author and the novel, see F.C. BELL, *One of the Damned.* London, 1979.

11 See also *The Legacies of Literacy.*

12 TRESSELL, *Ragged Trousered,* p. 1, 2, 3.

13 Ibid., p. 54, 54–55.

14 Commission on Popular Education, *Report,* 1861, p. 243. See also, *The Literacy Myth,* Chs. 1, 7, and the literature cited there.

15 TRESSELL, *Ragged Trousered,* pp. 86–87.

16 GRAMSCI, *Selections from the Prison Notebooks,* (Ed.) and tr. QUENTIN HOARE and GEOFFREY NOWELL SMITH, London, 1971, p. 12; JOHN M. CAMMETT, *Antonio Gramsci and the Origins of Italian Communism.* Stanford, 1967, p. 204; GWYN WILLIAMS, 'The Concept of "Egemonia" in the Thought of Antonio Gramsci,' *Journal of the History of Ideas,* 21 (1960), 587. See also GRAFF, *The Literacy Myth,* esp. 34–36, 28, Ch. 1, and the literature cited there. The best exposition of GRAMSCI's thought in English is WALTER L. ADAMSON, *Hegemony and Revolution,* Berkeley, 1980.

17 TRESSELL, *Ragged Trousered,* pp. 87–88.

18 Ibid, p. 223. See also RICHARD HOGGART, *The Uses of Literacy* (Boston, 1961); PAUL WILLIS, *Learning to Labour,* Farnborough, 1977.

19 See, on schooling, for example, J.S. HURT, *Elementary Schooling and the Working Classes, 1860–1918,* London, 1979; PHILLIP MCCANN (Ed.), *Popular Education and*

Socialization in the Nineteenth Century. London, 1977; DAVID REEDER (Ed.), *Urban Education in the 19th Century.* London, 1977, among a large literature.

20 See *The Literacy Myth, The Legacies of Literacy.* See also the brilliant nineteenth-century criticism of W.B. HODGSON, *Exaggerated Estimates of Reading and Writing as Means of Education.* London, 1867. I am reprinting this in a forthcoming issue of the *History of Education Quarterly.* See also the new and important book, SYLVIA SCRIBNER and MICHAEL COLE, *The Psychology of Literacy.* Cambridge, Mass., 1981.

21 VINCENT, *Bread, Knowledge and Freedom;* see also, VINCENT (Ed.), *Testaments of Radicalism.* London, 1977; *The Autobiography of a Beggar Boy.* London, 1978; VICTOR NEUBERG (Ed.), *Literacy and Society.* London, 1972: JOHN BURNETT (Ed.), *Useful Toil.* Harmondsworth, 1974; MARGARET SPUFFORD, 'First Steps in Literacy: The Reading and Writing Experiences of the Humblest Seventeenth-Century Spiritual Autobiographers,' *Social History,* 4 (1979); 407–435. The latter is reprinted in my *Literacy and Social Development in the West.* Cambridge, 1981.

22 See for example, HURT, *Elementary Schooling;* GRAFF, *The Literacy Myth,* Chs. 5, 7. For a literacy example of contemporary evidence and tension, see JERZY KOSINSKI. *Being There,* New York, 1972. The novel, as usual, is a much better source than the film. Other evidence today is legion.

23 See, for example, *The Literacy Myth,* Chs. 5, 7: VINCENT, *Bread, Knowledge and Freedom;* RICHARD JOHNSON, 'Really Useful Knowledge,' *Radical Education,* 7–8 (1975–1976): TRYGRE R. THOLFSEN, *Working Class Radicalism in Mid-Victorian England.* New York, 1977; the work of BRIAN SIMON, among many other examples.

24 TRESSELL, *Ragged Trousered,* pp. 514–515.

25 Ibid., p. 515.

26 Hamilton, Ontario, *Palladium of Labour* (24 November 1883); *Fincher's Trades Review* (18 March 1865). See also the *Literacy Myth,* Ch. 5.

27 TRESSELL, *Ragged Trousered,* pp. 223–230, for example.

28 Ibid., pp. 299–300.

29 GRAFF, *The Literacy Myth,* Ch. 7. There is also a rising amount of contemporary evidence, for example. SHIRLEY HEATH'S studies and WALTER J. ONG's several papers on 'orality' in 'literature' culture. WALTER J. ONG, 'The Literate Orality of Popular Culture Today,' in his *Rhetoric, Romance and Technology* (Ithaca, 1971), pp. 284–303 and 'Literacy and Orality in Our Time,' *Journal of Communication,* 30 (1980): 197–204; HEATH, 'The Functions and Uses of Literacy,' *Journal of Communication.* 30 (1980): 123–133. 'Protean Shapes in Literary Events,' in *Spoken and Written Language,* (Ed.) D. TANNEN, Norwood, NJ, forthcoming, and her forthcoming monograph.

30 TRESSELL, *Ragged Trousered,* pp. 394–395; see also, pp. 424–425. CALHOUN, *The Intelligence;* IAN DAVEY, 'Educational Reform and the Working Class,' Unpub. PhD. Diss., University of Toronto, 1975.

31 TRESSELL, *Ragged Trousered,* p. 495.

32 See, on these issues, for example, GARETH STEDMAN JONES, 'Working-Class Culture and Working-Class Politics in London, 1870–1900,' *Journal of Social History,* 7 (1974): 460–508; PETTER BAILY, *Leisure and Class in Victorian Society.* Toronto, (1978); GEOFFREY BEST, *Mid-Victorian Britain, 1854–1875,* New York, 1972; PAUL THOMPSON, *The Edwardians.* Bloomington, 1975; STANDISH MEACHAM, *A Life Apart* Cambridge, Mass., 1977; ROBERT MALCOLMSON, *Popular Recreations in English Society,* Cambridge, 1973; BRIAN HARRISON, 'Religion and Recreation in Nineteenth-Century England,' *Past and Present,* 38 (1968): 98–125; LYNN H. LEES, 'Getting and Spending: The Family Budgets of English Industrial Laborers in 1980,' in *Consciousness and Class Experience in Nineteenth-Century Europe,* ed. JOHN M. MERRIMAN, New York, 1979; GRAFF, *The Literacy Myth,* Ch. 7, *The Legacies of Literacy,* esp. Ch. 7. See also TRESSELL, *Ragged Trousered,* p. 496.

33 TRESSELL, *Ragged Trousered,* p. 630.
34 PETER LASLETT, *The World We have Lost.* London, 1965; 2nd ed., 1971, 'The Wrong Way through the telescope: A note on literary evidence in sociology and historical sociology.' *British Journal of Sociology,* 27 (1976): 319–342. But, see also MICHAEL ANDERSON, *Family Structure in Nineteenth-Century Lancashire.* Cambridge, 1971 Laslett's article is must reading for all concerned. It should be noted though that his posture is self-contradictory, and his calls for theoretical perspectives are piously empty in this presentation. The concern for 'confidence' and assumption that one ought best, but not always, begin with historical rather than literary evidence, I want to underscore. For a new effort at social historical use of literature related to the history of literacy, see SPUFFORD, *Small Books.*

12   Literacy, Libraries, Lives: New Social and Cultural Histories

Addressing Library History Seminar VII in 1985, British publishing historian John Feather drew explicit attention to the relevance of library history for the history of the book and, conversely, the history of the book for library history. Aptly, he wrote, "Like the history of the book, the history of libraries has been transformed in recent years by a more general historical awareness and a broader social and cultural approach. Library history is no longer a tedious catalog of the good deeds of benefactors, the enacting of laws, and the opening of buildings." More specifically, Feather noted, "There is one aspect of library history that can be particularly informative to the historian of the book"—and there I add, emphatically, the *historian of literacy*, too—"the study of the use of libraries.... the book historian needs to know something about who read books...."[1]

Not at all unrelatedly, in their generous review of my *The Legacies of Literacy: Continuities and Contradictions in Western Society and Culture*, library historians Cynthia Peterson and Donald Davis commented, "readers of *Libraries & Culture* will soon discover to their disappointment that libraries are relegated to the status of scattered, random footnotes—somewhat more significant in brief mentions than the half-dozen specific index references.... For one who emphasizes the *use* of literacy, Graff might have provided a more serious treatment of, at the very least, popular libraries."[2] Although we might quibble about the nature and implications of that criticism, there is no doubt that the relevance and the relations of library history to the history of literacy bear far more serious attention and study than they have thus far received. Peterson and Davis—Feather too, I suspect—would join me in asserting that the responsibility for the limited appearance of libraries in my *Legacies of Literacy* is only partly mine alone. The contours and condition of the practice of library history, especially in North America, cry out for constructive criticism and novel approaches.

My purpose here is not to elaborate the lacunae of library history at the time I wrote my histories of literacy, or now, however interesting or relevant that might be for this seminar. Nor is it to intervene in detail in the "great debates" among

American library historians.[3] Instead, I offer another approach to the questions implied in the quotations from Feather and Peterson and Davis and the relative silences in my prior work. In embracing the tripartite theme of my title—*literacy, libraries, lives*—I will seek out a series of relationships of varying kinds that connect these large subjects. In the context of my previous writings on literacy's history and in offering a gloss on the practice and promise of library history, I draw directly on a database of first-person testimonies—diaries, memoirs, autobiographies, letters, and the like—that forms the foundation of my current research, and writing, on the history of growing up in Anglo-America, c. 1750–1920 and beyond.[4] In terms of critical approach and in terms of the kinds of primary sources consulted, I essay a novel perspective for library—and other—historians. This I do in part by linking recent emphases in different domains of social and cultural history with directions my own work currently follows.[5]

Advancing from the critical, dialectical conceptualization of literacy developed over the last decade and a half, and also from a sociocultural, constructivist, life course perspective central to the "growing up" project, I examine through individual, personal testimony concrete *uses* of literacy's reading skills in their relationships to libraries in the historical context of the shaping of the lives of relatively ordinary persons, and the social and cultural relations of which they were part, from the late eighteenth to the early twentieth century. Cutting across the limiting dichotomies that mark most of the "great" interpretative and ideological debates that characterize both literacy's and libraries' historical study, such evidence propels us toward wider and deeper viewpoints and recognition of greater complexity and contradictoriness in historical relationships that range from the most mundane to the truly astonishing.

Conceptualization of these relationships takes us well beyond linear, progressive or evolutionary frameworks and turgid questions of "social control" versus democracy and progress. Indeed, no simple or single formulation accommodates these patterns. Not only are the *uses* of literacy and of libraries extremely variable and broad, but so, too, are the range of libraries encountered and the modes of those encounters. Notions of passages from private to public sponsorship or control, from restrictedness to boundlessness or popularization, barely hint at the depth or, indeed, the fascination and the significance of the historical process.

These interactions intersect with central themes of historical development to an extent generally unappreciated: *from* institution and community building; individual human development and the life course; study, work, and recreation; *to* the lines connecting public and private spheres; the political economy; cultural formations; and the making and remaking of ever sharpening lines of social class, gender, and race. In other words, practices in the exploitation of literacy and libraries lay near the very heart of the complicated human historical process, with all the ironies, paradoxes, and contradictions that that implies. We cannot neglect, however, the fact that the far greatest number of personal accounts make absolutely *no* mention of reading or library usage. That fact, too, cries out for study and interpretation.[6]

Silas Felton's "Life or Biography . . . Written by Himself" warms the heart of any Whiggish historians among us.[7] Born to an old Massachusetts farming family in Marlborough in 1776, Silas read Benjamin Franklin's autobiography at age eighteen and, in drafting an account of his life, at least self-consciously modeled himself after Franklin's. Fittingly, Silas moved from farming to school teaching, which he began at age nineteen, later combining teaching with running a store and holding local and state political offices until his death in 1828. He wrote the 50-page autobiography in 1801–1802. His student, Rena Vassar, enthusiastically asserts:

> Silas Felton was an ordinary American growing up in the early national period in a small town in central Massachusetts. . . . The man who emerges from the autobiography, however, is a remarkable individual. Here is a self-educated man with varied interests and abilities. . . . Benjamin Franklin was Felton's principal teacher, and one concludes from reading the autobiography that he was an apt pupil. His formal training was meager, only a limited common school education which he received rather sporadically; yet because he wished to excel in learning, he read widely and voraciously, as his list of titles attests. He applied his knowledge to the world around him. . . .[8]

Silas grew up as many rural children of his era did: combining familial labor with schooling on a seasonal basis when schools were kept. Less commonly, he early grew fond of school and reading.

> Being more fond of School than of work I generally had more praises bestowed on me at school than at home. When at home I was call'd rather lazy, but at School I almost always was at the head of the Class of which I belonged. At the age of 9 or 10 I was very fond of reading entertaining stories, and borrowed all the books within my reach. These I perused evenings and Stormy Days. Becoming more fond of books, I used at every convenient opportunity to take my book and step ought [sic] of sight; by often repeating this and being out of the way when wanted caused the people often to bestow the name of Lazy upon me, which I acknowledge was not altogether misplaced. . . . Strictly following my old practice of reading, I used generally to have some book or newspaper every evening and Stormy Day, except when I was roving about on the evenings, which is generally the case with boys from 10 to 21 years old.[9]

From age fourteen to nineteen, ambition more than compensated for sporadic schooling. Silas "practised carrying my book home on the evenings, to study, because I was generally ambitious to excel in learning."[10]

In his sixteenth year, a major new opportunity came to Marlborough and to Silas Felton. This was the formation in 1792 of "a Society, by the name of The Marlboro Library."[11] Sixty "proprietors" subscribed to establish the institution, first investing $2.50 and agreeing to pay 25 cents per year. "This sum purchased books sufficient to be call'd a handsome library." Not surprisingly, Silas, "by frequent Solicitations, caused my father to join as one of the first proprietors, and he not being fond of reading, I had the books to myself; this gave me an excellent opportunity of improving my mind."

The availability of the "handsome library" did not resolve all complications. No simple "supply side" solution, it created other problems for the lad. First, teenage sociability competed with reading for Silas's time and energy; "possessing a strong desire to [partake] of the fountain of youthful pleasures, like the rest of my companions, which was commonly done by visiting each together in the evening—by practicing these, I soon found they interfered with each other, which lessened my chance for reading." Seeing that he could part with neither, Silas learned to divide his time more wisely in pursuit of learning and of society—no need to choose one over the other for him (despite, perhaps, the wishes of historians!). Some evenings along with Sundays he reserved for his reading.[12]

Competition for his time and inclinations was one problem. Choice of appropriate reading material was another complication, hardly Silas's or his era's alone.

> Some of the books, which fell into my hands, appeared to me to contain dark and mysterious passages, which my reason (though small at that time) caused me to doubt very much, especially some passages of the Scriptures. About this time the Age of Reason, written by Thomas Paine appeared; I perused it very attentively; although many advised me not to read it. A number of Answers were immediately written with an Intention of confuting the sentiments advanced by Paine. . . . These had a contrary effect with me, than what the authors intended. The ministers also appeared zealously engaged in preaching against the Deists, or as they stiled [*sic*] them, Infidels. Almost every one, which I heard, carried their points to such a pitch that I think I may safely say that they advanced many large strides beyond the truth. . . . And in contemplating, I thought it right to judge by the Doctrine itself, not by the pretended actors.[13]

This was the moment, fortuitously, that Franklin's writings entered the eighteen-year-old's life. Silas "perused them attentively, and found many very valuable precepts, which I endeavored to treasure up and follow. And I believe I may safely say they kept me from many Errors, for from that time I determined to *adhere strictly to Reason, Industry, and Good Economy, to Always examine both sides, to keep my mind free from prejudice of any kind whatever, always to practice reason and truth. . . .*"[14] Interestingly, the struggle for people's minds did not result in Paine's removal from the library, but in the competition of print and oral arguments in the marketplace of dogma and doctrine.

Books, and print more generally, the young man discovered, did not of them-selves simply and directly admit or contribute to reason and truth. They were at least equally the grounds for bias, distortion, and conflict. Still, at least for Silas in developing Massachusetts: "Situated in a land of Liberty, books being plenty and Newspapers circulating freely, I not only confined myself to Morality and Religion, but made Politics no small part of my study." Silas himself saw no potential for contradiction or hypocrisy in concluding that *his* study of print con-firmed by practice of reason and truth *his* "true genuine Republicanism" and antipriestly rational religion. More realistically, if no more rationally perhaps, his faith in and attention to reading did not make him a hermitlike bookworm: "To see one thus early engaged in the study of religion, morality, and politics, we might suppose sufficient to employ his mind; but I assure you that the Desire for pleasure and amusement, also that still stronger one for the fair sex, implanted in man will not permit him to sit silently at home studying into the knowledge of futurity, especially me—who, although fond [of] reading, yet was fond of other recreations, and did as opportunities presented partake of youthful joys, like other young people." At age eighteen, Silas began to court Lucretia Fay, whom he later wed.[15]

Silas Felton's Franklinesque path of intellectual self-improvement also had utilitarian implications, although he claimed some surprise at this. In 1795, nine-teen-year-old Silas unexpectedly was asked by the Selectmen to teach the town's eastern school. With a candor and self-deprecation alien to his idol, Silas consid-ered declining the offer due to his ignorance of English grammar. With his father's willingness for him to "do as I pleased" and others assuring him of his prepar-edness, he passed the oral examination of a local minister and was certified to teach. The preparation Silas lacked, however, did not stem from his condition of learning; keeping order and discipline and constantly attending to the correction of lessons was a greater challenge than the intellectual one—with the partial exception of his need to master arithmetic faster than his pupils.

The rewards of learning when applied to teaching—such as they were and are—Silas found were personal and psychological, not financial. Disappointing his "enemies" by his classroom success, from "adhering to truth and reason," his wage was raised for a second term to $9.00 a month. Teaching two terms from March to July, Silas farmed with his father until October. The practice of learning, and teaching, remained for many a seasonal routine. No more surprising was Silas's wish to continue to improve himself, especially in grammar. Once again, he "solicited" his father and "at length gained his consent" to attend an academy for a few months. Choosing this path, he also thought, meant ending his courtship of Miss Lucretia: "Considering my circumstances and knowing that I was not in any condition to marry, that if I attended school it was necessary to have my mind fix'd there, that if I followed the same course much longer it would be difficult to part with each other." So he bid her farewell, seemingly forever. That was not to be; soon reunited, our young scholar-teacher one morning "found myself where a few days I could almost have sworn I should not have been. . . . " A second but no more final farewell followed.[16]

Completing his time at the academy, Silas mastered grammar and arithmetic. He returned to the farm qualified to teach an English school. This he did the next spring and summer, for $10.00 and then $10.50 per month. By fall, his suit of Lucretia resumed; after haying he taught for $12.00 a month.[17] Entering his maturity, Silas turned to another use of print: a Franklinesque, precise keeping of personal accounts of income and expenses and of books read. Later he "made me a book, and kept it for the purpose of extracting any thing remarkable, or any thing, which very pleased or displeased my fancy. This I entitled Extracts from different authors by Silas Felton."[18]

Inclination and reading intertwined not only in career path but in its practice: "Adhering strictly to the principle I laid down when I first engaged in school, I constantly studied what would be advantageous to the scholars."[19] He learned, too, to support his growing family by leaving teaching for storekeeping and town office-holding. Silas ended his memoir, his anthem to reading and its rewards, with the "public" subscription library's place at its center, by listing the books he had read. Of this remarkable roster, he characteristically wrote, "Having before hinted my inclination for reading and the perseverance I continued it. I will now, for my own gratification, and also as a tablet of memory, insert the Titles of the books, which I have read previous to the 1st of April 1802, arranged under the different professions or arts to which they belong. But it is with sorrow, I here must remark: that had I studied particular authors more and read fewer pages daily, and upon those pages I did read examined and re-examined I believe I should now have been more, and better informed."[20] That, of course, is one risk of reading and of intensive library use. There are others. "But on the other hand, what great and useful advantages, not only so, but what pleasure I now derive, by looking back, and contemplating upon the time I have spent in studying, while others were roving, gaming, employed in what was not only spending their time heedlessly, but to their very great damage. . . . "[21]

Almost ringing of the stuff of which cultural mythologies are made, Silas Felton was exceptional but not unique. There were also men like Dr. Daniel Drake, learning from a neighborhood doctor in Kentucky and later founding civic cultural institutions in Cincinnati, Ohio, and women like Catharine Sedgwick, learning from her family's private library as well as those of family friends and boarding schools.[22] *Most* among Felton's contemporaries and successors who left accounts of their growing up (and later lives) made little or no mention of active employment of literacy's skills or use of libraries. We may presume that in this they were typical in their lesser use of print, perhaps encountering and examining little more than schoolbooks and periodicals.[23] Yet Silas was not alone in expressing his significant relationship to reading and libraries. In pointing to new relationships, he redirects our attention.

John Griscom, New York City teacher, physician, social reformer, and institution founder, identified other relationships with libraries.[24] A self-styled rustic youth, Griscom left his parents' New Jersey home at age twenty in 1794 to teach in the neighboring town, Burlington. He, too, developed an early liking for reading; Griscom's irregular schooling exceeded Felton's. To supplement his income, Griscom also became town librarian with the salary of £5 a year. One dimension of this relationship was pecuniary and utilitarian. There were others, and they were mixed. "Of the reading privileges which this situation offered him, he eagerly availed himself; to such a degree, in fact, that the sedentary habit thus engendered endangered his health—an effect which he, however, counteracted by riding on horseback, and other exercises."[25] Literacy and libraries do have their dangers.

Looking back on his formative years, Griscom pointed to at least two great benefits for his subsequent life from his stay in this town. First, the impressive local library held "the works of the best standard writers of England and America. The Encyclopedia Britannica claimed my earliest attention, and every volume of it was perused with avidity, so far as the subjects were within my comprehension. It served materially to enlarge my views of general science, and to enhance my love for exact knowledge. History was, very much, a new theme; and the productions of the best English poets were also within my reach."[26] Science was one domain in which he made future contributions.

At the same time, "among the most valuable advantages incident to my position in Burlington, was the acquaintance I early made with the most respectable and wealthy inhabitants."[27] Some of these persons were learned, in science and languages. From their private libraries and from their conversation, Griscom gained much, cautioning us against too rigid a distinction between public and private, and print and interpersonal, oral sources of learning. He also learned from the library and the headmaster of the town's academy. This included foreign languages, ancient and modern, which he later found quite useful: "Could I have duly foreseen the vast advantages which the acquisition of these languages would certainly have afforded me, in the various duties of teaching, speaking, and writing—the greater confidence it would have inspired, and the reputation which it adds to the profession of a teacher. . . . " He was keenly aware of the benefits from the signs, the trappings of learning. Not surprisingly, his tastes ran to science and books that required "*study*, rather than simple perusal," decidedly not to fiction. Simultaneously, Griscom lamented his lack of "a more prudent foresight"—his great error—and also that "I was ever so much prone to reading as to neglect the use of bodily exercise." The latter contributed to "so much debility" as to alarm his friends.[28]

No less consequential to his advancement were the benefits of influential personal contacts among his acquaintances. This included the benefits of association. Griscom organized a reading club, which subscribed to European journals. "Promiscuous reading (unrestrained within the bounds of sound morality) although somewhat unfavorable to the acquisition of thorough or profound knowledge, has the advantage of diversifying the talent, improving the taste, and preparing the individual for more enlarged usefulness and influence in society." In this spirit, "one of the first *set* of books with which I supplied my first book-case was the 'British Classics.' . . . These have furnished a fund of profitable reading, as well as the finest examples of style and composition, and the richest display of learning, taste, and talent."[29] Not least of all, these influential persons paved Griscom's path to New York City, where he opened an innovative school, gave public science lectures, associated with Columbia's medical school, and founded his fame in science and reform. The contributions from print and libraries' collection and access to it seldom exist by themselves. John Griscom gained conjointly from his acquaintances' libraries, knowledge, and personal influence—within specific historical circumstances—crossing many lines along the way.

Chance and happenstance also played major parts. Consider Devereux Jarratt, English-ordained Episcopal minister of late colonial and early national Virginia.[30] Common-born Virginian, Jarratt was transformed, in part by serious religious reading from private domestic libraries and by a profound religious conversion partially stimulated by this reading, in part by the Great Awakening. Both in turn stemmed from his association with pious possessors of private libraries; these included persons for whom he worked who were also sympathetic to his desire for learning and improvement. One woman, for example, read a sermon each evening. Over a year's time, this made its impress on the young man, who then sought to foster his own further education. Historian Douglass Adair concluded, "He was not born a gentleman, did not strive directly to become one, and only achieved that honorific status as a by-product of his deep thirst for knowledge and his driving intellectual ambition." Jarratt, moreover, did not succumb to the hegemony of gentry culture; "after this self-made gentleman crossed to the upper side of the class line he repudiated many of the traditional genteel virtues of his new station as unworthy. . . . Jarratt's driving intellectualism, his determination to make a vocation of letters, of speculative thought, also mark him as a maverick."[31]

The role of chance, his own background and personality, the fortuitous commingling of his wanderings for work with goodly influences of persons and their books, and the singlemindedness of Jarratt's pursuit after conversion to his new path in his mid- to late twenties prevent any simple generalizations about the roles of literacy or libraries. That private libraries were in an important sense open, not a direct opposite of public, is worth pondering. So, too, were the costs of the struggle to escape both his humble origins and the confines of gentry culture, in part through literacy and libraries: "without doubt the experience was traumatic and left scars," noted Adair. This included his increasing social and moral rigidity. "Would Jarratt have been so fanatical, so exclusive in his final definition of the 'good life' if he had not suffered so in the process of attaining his intellectual and spiritual salvation?"[32] Literacy and libraries, we too often forget, are weapons with two—indeed—many edges. Their costs, individually as well as in the aggregate, can be high; their benefits are never really "free," despite the slogan of Andrew Carnegie's libraries.

More mundane but more typical were the place of literacy and libraries in the life of William Wait Oliver, deputy collector of the Custom House, Salem,

Massachusetts.[33] Oliver belonged to the town social library. In the diary of his twenty-fifth year, 1802–1803, he evidenced his regular reading fare of history, biography, and travel books, often quoting at some length and commenting in his journal. Hardly a week passed without some such entry. Reading very widely, he essayed such judgments as "Monday, 28 [June] . . . Read 60 pages of Johnson's Journey to the Hebrides, entertaining but not variety enough."[34] Others among Johnson's writings he preferred. His response to Thomas Paine, interestingly, was one with Silas Felton's: "Read Common Sense . . . at the time he was in this Country he was much courted, but now matters are changed. . . . Though I can not myself admire his mans [*sic*] conduct I can not approve of the many frivolous assertions thrown out against him. . . . "[35] Oliver, significantly, seemed to see his reading habit and level of library usage as unworthy of comment. That his contemporaries also did so underscores his minority status and his significant use of libraries and literacy.

For neighboring Archelaus Putnam of New Mills, the library occupied rather a different position than it did for his peers discussed here.[36] In a diary kept from age eighteen to just prior to his death in 1818 at age thirty-one, Putnam showed himself to be an unfortunate young man with great ambitions, but with great difficulty in making decisions about his career path and even more trouble in acting upon them. He died soon after his marriage, and the diary was among his few accomplishments. As his editor noted, in terms of occupation, Archelaus "met with indifferent success. He was handicapped from the first by ill-health, which was aggravated by an over-sensitive and somewhat morbid nature. He had little business capacity and chafed under the confinement of 'keeping shop.' . . . He had aspirations toward a literary or professional career. . . . "[37]

Among his ambitions was establishing a social library in New Mills. To Archelaus, this was a cause that credited both the town—founding an important institution—and its founder—himself. From it, he could draw satisfaction and status in town as well as in his own eyes. At the end of March 1808 the nineteen-year-old mentioned that he had drawn up a proposal to establish a social library. There is no further word until 22 October when he wrote hyperbolically, "It is with the keenest sorrow and regret that I state the expected unsuccessful result of my ardent endeavors to have a library established in this place. All that is wanting is for some person of influence and respectability to advertise for a meeting. I have solicited many to take that little trouble but they refuse. I have drawn up a paper & obtained a sufficient number of subscribers & I think in my grade that is presumption enough. For me to head this business any further would be very improper, especially when I see persons so cold in co-operation."

Only three weeks later, on 15 November, a meeting of subscribers for a library was called and convened. Measures required to establish and operate it were taken, with five men of sufficient "grade" chosen trustees and a minister, chaplain. "[P]erhaps unfortunate for the proprietors, by misdirecting their confidence," Putnam was chosen treasurer.[38] In three months, by February 1809, Archelaus's labors bore fruit. In this, he took immoderate pride: "It is with the greatest pleasure and satisfaction that I am at length permitted to see the establishment of a public library in this place fully effected, not that I expect to reap any considerable advantages from it myself, but for the benefit & improvement of the minds & manners of the people of the place. I consider it no acquisition to one's merit in recording his own good doings, but I hope I shall be pardoned when I say that I feel conscious that the establishment of the library would have been delayed had it not been for my exertions."[39] A library could carry much personal psychological return and status conferral, quite aside from intellectual or literary aspects. Archelaus wrote nary a word about its contents. "Social" libraries had a plethora of social meanings and benefits, including conferring status on their founders.

Lives and libraries intersected in many ways, we begin to grasp. The usual formulations and questions are too narrowly cast. Consider Elihu Smith's early association with another significant library type: college student society libraries.[40] After attending a variety of schools and gaining a love of reading by his fifth year, at the precocious age of twelve the future literary light entered Yale College. His reading teeth were cut early on books from home including the Scriptures, from clerical libraries in the vicinity, and schoolbooks classical and modern. His father was "a man of a more cultivated taste"; before the age of eight, Elihu recalled, "I became so passionately attached to reading. I was familiar with the adventures of 'Jack Hick-a-thrift,' 'Valentine & Orson,' renowned heroes! & with all the tales contained in Mr. Newberry's little book intituled 'Entertaining Stories' (many of which are truly excellent,) which I had been presented with by my aunt Elizabeth; but they had not triumphed over my love of play. This was an honour reserved for 'The Fool of Quality'—a work that, with many exceptions it is true, I still read with pleasure & approbation." Looking back, Smith also grasped "the extreme folly of impossing [*sic*] certain kinds of reading as a duty—which are tiresome to all, who are not wedded to them by principle & habit, & are peculiarly detestable to children." Happily, he escaped that dire danger.[41]

Given both the curriculum and the resources of colleges of the late colonial and early national eras, the extracurriculum was fundamental to Elihu's—and countless others'—college learning. Joining with his Litchfield School associates one of the two literary societies at Yale, the Brothers in Unity, he not only formed lifelong friendships within a group interested in literature and drama but also gained greater access to its library than students had to the college's library. There he found a collection of novels, travel books, and works of the major poets. Graduating from Yale at age fifteen, young Smith next attended Timothy Dwight's Greenfield Hill Academy before beginning to study medicine with his father, attending medical school at the University of Pennsylvania, joining the "Connecticut Wits" literary circle, and then moving to New York City seeking his way ostensibly in medicine but much more in literary activities. His early love of literature dominated his pursuits and complicated his efforts to support himself. Yet another danger of literacy and libraries to which some succumb! The lad did find a place in American literary history, although, alas, he died of yellow fever in September 1798, at the age of twenty-seven.

Elihu Smith is one of countless college students who turned by necessity and fraternal sociability to student society libraries. Some shared his drive to read and learn; others did not. Some benefited greatly; some did not. None of them had much choice about conducting their studies as college students: a point to ponder for library historians.[42] For a young man like Lucien Boynton, who attempted careers and their preparation in the ministry, teaching, and then the law, the variety of libraries and relatively informal, personal means of access available— at least to a middle-class, Anglo-Saxon, and ambitious man—made his lengthy series of studies and sometimes overwrought quest for advancement and self-promotion much more possible than they might otherwise have been. Class origins counted. In his search for the status and stature that he considered appropriate for himself, Lucien exploited school, seminary, private, and personal libraries. Establishing his legal practice, he purchased for himself a law library. Consuming an impressive and lengthy list of books, often in an apparent frenzy alternately to advance or to compensate for some deficiency, did not, however, lead Lucien to the satisfaction, security, or success he deeply desired. His subsequent marriage to a widow may have better served him in that.[43]

Some persons found in libraries—of different kinds, to which they gained access in different ways—means of intellectual advancement. For some of them this meant an opportunity for further secondary and sometimes higher education. A great deal depended on chance, too, though the idiosyncrasies of individual's stories can misleadingly exaggerate an apparent randomness or frequency. The personal testimonies themselves often are much more interesting and challenging than formulaic notions of rising through acquisition and use of literacy in libraries that complement comforting if distorting myths surrounding both libraries and literacy.[44]

For John Albee, the path from family hardship and a series of incomplete apprenticeships and menial jobs to further study came from acquaintance in his teen years with a student preparing to become a missionary and from access to a private library. "For the first time I heard of Greek and Latin books. . . . Here were other things of which I knew nothing, and I began at this period to be oppressed continually by the more and more frequent discovery of the extent of my ignorance. Luckily I knew how to read. My rustic mentors had warned me against girls, but never of books. I found in the Professor's library a queer assortment of odds and ends of learned works." Of these, two in particular made a lasting impress: the story of Alexander the Great in Whelpley's *History* and Emerson's *Representative Men*. Reading Byron led young Albee to imitate his moods and fashions—in Worcester, Massachusetts, in the 1840s! "I began to turn down my Sunday linen collar which had stood up to my ears, and to wear my hair long and careless. . . . I let it hang as it would over my forehead and neck." The book also served as his pillow.

Pursuit of learning changed Albee's life, but not in any one firm direction. "In turn one book after another held me like a captive lover, and I endeavored to conform my life to what I read, no sooner enthralled by one than I found another more enchanting."[45] Literacy and exploitation of libraries, he recognized, can make for capricious lovers. Silliness aside, here Albee formed a lifelong taste for serious reading and a stimulus to further schooling at the local academy and in its library, where Todd's *Student's Manual* was the text read most carefully by the boys. Along with striving Jeremiah Curtin, twenty-four years old from the Wisconsin frontier, Albee strove to gain admission to Harvard. Ill health and misfortune obstructed his path, but not Curtin's, who traveled from farm to foreign service.

Elihu Smith is also one of a number of exceptional, precocious young persons of the period. Growing up in the late eighteenth and early nineteenth century when precocity was not yet damned as a disease to guard resolutely against, these young persons illustrate further relationships in their early life courses between literacy and libraries.[46] New Hampshire-born Cyrus Bradley was the son of the state librarian. His quick mastery of that library brought him to the attention of influential citizens eager to assist the lad in quenching his thirst for the classical education his father could not afford to give him. In the words of the journal's editor, "The literary citizens of Concord, thereupon, united in securing for him, admission to Exeter Academy as a 'charity scholar.'" Completing his preparatory course in one year, he entered Dartmouth. Also teaching and producing literary work, his studies and achievements expanded boundlessly. He published a variety of pieces before completing college, where he was deemed the peer of Daniel Webster, Rufus Choate, and Salmon P. Chase. He died shortly thereafter, succumbing to a lasting illness.[47]

Merrill Ober, of Monkton, Vermont, is even more astounding. Writing in his journal at age sixteen, he admits, "I have spent my life mostly in mental occupation. I have been to school a great deal. . . " Having studied arithmetic, geometry, chemistry, Latin, Greek, grammar, geography, French, history, literature and poetry, music, and shorthand, he had an avid interest in politics and took part in electioneering. He also wrote songs, played flute and violin—and played boys' games. As he put it, "I am now 16 & have not decided what business I shall follow through life. But I shall probably teach for a spell anyway. I must keep on studying & learn all I can. A man can not learn too much. If what he learns is of no temporal use it certainly will be of mental use." In his amazing advance, young Merrill was assisted by his access to G. P. Marsh's 15,000-volume library in Burlington and Marsh's willingness to send books to Monkton as well as to welcome Ober in his home. Merrill Ober died at the age of twenty-one.[48] We draw no connections between young Merrill's and Cyrus's extreme and early love of libraries and learning and their premature deaths, of course.

Others grew up amidst all the trappings of literary culture and the great favors of social class and family fortunes. For them, private libraries, at home and among family friends, joined with advantaged institutional settings—public, private, or those that blurred such lines—encouragement for the development of reading skills and their literary application, and more leisurely, comfortable growing up.[49] That this crossed gender lines, albeit with all the contradictions of the developing class-gender system of the nineteenth century, is revealed in the life histories of authors Catharine Sedgwick and Caroline Dall.

Ralph Waldo Emerson's children were brought books to peruse from the Boston Athenaeum. They also had Emerson himself. Daughter Ellen recalled that when she was eleven, "About this time he used to let me bring a French book and sit on his knee and try to translate it, without knowing more than ten words of French. . . . That was delightful. . . . He brought home Michelet's books and others from the Athenaeum, and would let me sit by him and look over while he read to me—scraps of French history they were, which made me love it, or about Savonarola and Michael Angelo. I think I never had any Latin with him, but as soon as Eddy began to translate it, he used to read Erasmus's Colloquia with him, . . . and when he and Edith studied Vergil they quite regularly read the lesson with Father." When she attended school in Lenox a few years later, he took an active interest in her studies. The children also attended his lectures.[50] Well-heeled Granville Norcross's diaries, kept from age six to twenty-two, record not only his avid reading of light and serious literary fare, but also paternal gifts of books and bookshelves, use of public as well as private libraries, and familial pressures to excel in prep school and at Harvard.[51] For Caroline Dall, her family's position in Boston and her precociousness gained her access to private libraries, institutions, and persons that those lacking in status, class, and connection could not achieve. Not all young women had fathers who actively educated them from early childhood.[52] Bookishness and femininity, however, intricately intertwined in the shaping of modern American culture, one of the more contradictory episodes in this history.

Comparatively high rates of basic literacy, extensive networks of schooling opportunities, a wide range of library settings, and the massive, competing volumes of print of the nineteenth century are the findings familiar from the last generation of research on these topics. Their causes, meanings, and consequences, to be sure, are subjects of great debate.[53] The personal testimony of relatively ordinary persons, like apprentice artisans and clerks, both challenges and grounds scholarly generalizations and debates.[54] Although most personal records make little or no mention of the use of their authors' obvious literacy in reading or libraries, those who do provide a variety of untapped perspectives.

Greenfield, Massachusetts, apprentice carpenter Edward Carpenter read much but apparently never from libraries. Newspapers were a favorite of his and of other young men of the mid-nineteenth century. His reading included the novels of T. S. Arthur and other popular writers, and he all but devoured the stories in papers like the *Washingtonian* and *Rural Repository*. He also attended the local literary club and many lectures, showing no sign of differentiation between his learning and pleasures from print and oral means. In the 1830s, orphaned teenage schoolboy and apprentice cabinetmaker Joseph Dwinnell borrowed Fenimore Cooper's *Last of the Mohicans* from the Salem Mercantile Library (well-born Granville Norcross found his copy forty years later in the Boston Public Library). Sixteen-year-old, Charlestown-born, Boston bank apprentice James Whittier recorded his reading in his Sunday school library and also his proud teenage sense of responsibility when asked to take care of the library. Similarly, when asked to be assistant librarian at his school, sixteen-year-old James Fiske, student and part-time job holder in Holliston, Massachusetts, "like[d] the business so far very well indeed." School activities and reading religious periodicals helped this lad cope with and sometimes escape from his problematic relations with young women. No doubt his library work was also good practice for the future town postmaster.[55]

More self-consciously, Henry Seidel Canby felt the permeation and import of reading in middle-class Wilmington, Delaware, at the end of the century. Books were as much displayed as read; they undergirded, rather than challenged, a culture "narrow and not often deep." After reciting the many omissions from usual reading and purchase, and pointing to the rising role of the public library, Canby emphasized the lack of contemporary poetry, criticism, drama, and the domination of a superficial "wide reading" over "deep reading." Of the latter, he pointed to "Scott and the other romancers." What was learned in this way was that "sentiment, in our society, was distinctly literary." That he later deemed a costly restriction. Nonetheless, reading was "confident": "Nothing critical came our way, especially in fiction. . . . Our reading was what so many today advocate for cynical realism—positive, whole-hearted, largely unliterary and unintellectual. We took as we took our meals, asking nothing of the cook, and less of the quality, if its taste was right."[56]

Despite the exaggerations and clichés to which they gave rise, the powerful memoirs of Lowell mill girls Lucy Larcom and Harriet Hanson Robinson speak poignantly to our concerns and the intricately intertwining play of class and gender and concrete social conditions. Family necessity, in its many forms, drove girls like eleven-year-old Lucy to the new textile mills in the 1830s and 1840s. That experience was itself educational, but for some among them at least, it provided opportunity and outlet for other uses of literacy and libraries.

Young women like Lucy and her sister alternated reading with work, for its solace and transcendence of their material condition as well as for more mundane reasons. "Work, study, and worship were interblended in our life," she wrote of her family. Her minister suggested worthwhile books and aided in study. "The two magazines published by the mill-girls, the 'Lowell Offering' and the 'Operatives' Magazine' "—special exercises of literacy they were, Lucy tells us—"originated with literary meetings in the vestry of the two religious societies," the Universalist and Congregational churches. The editors and many of the contributors were public schoolteachers who had worked in the mills. Lucy's active involvement in the *Offering* followed her return to Lowell at age sixteen and her sister's involvement, too. They became regular contributors.

It did not occur to us to call these efforts "literary." I know that I wrote just as I did for our little "Diving Bell,"—as a sort of pastime, and because my daily toil was mechanical, and furnished no occupation for my thoughts. Perhaps the fact that most of us wrote in this way accounted for the rather sketchy and fragmentary character of our "Magazine." It gave evidence that we thought, and that we thought upon solid and serious matters; but the criticism of one of our superintendents upon it, very kindly given, was undoubtedly just: "It has plenty of pith, but it lacks point."

Lucy, in fact, was much more critical of her own early writing when she reflected back upon it. She was also critical of the fame this literary fare attracted. She grasped the historical specificity of the enterprise: "It would hardly be worth while to refer to it particularly, had not the Lowell girls and their magazines been so frequently spoken of as something phenomenal. But it was a perfectly natural outgrowth of those girls' previous life. For what were we? Girls who were working in a factory for a time, to be sure; but none of us had the least idea of continuing at that kind of work permanently. . . . That they should write was no more strange than that they should study, or read, or think."[57]

Also learning to dislike her mechanical work intensely, Lucy left the mills' machines with the goal of having time to study. In response to the paymaster's quip "time is money," she thought, "time is education." Working in the cloth room, a fellow worker, "quite a poet, and a fine singer also," loaned her a volume of Whitman. She soon developed a taste for American verse. With no machinery, cloth-room workers were permitted to have books, and a circle of readers and lenders grew. Aided by suggestions of older workers, Lucy also borrowed from the public library, as did Harriet Hanson Robinson. Her choices on occasion, like the library copy of Mather's *Magnalia*, drew compliments from the superintendent which she found satisfying. Many among Lucy's peers toiled for money to spend, for example, on their clothes. "For myself, no amount of money would have been a temptation, compared with my precious daytime freedom. Whole hours of sunshine for reading, for walking, for studying, for writing, for anything I wanted to do!" Unable to pursue her dream of a better education directly, she took the path of public library-assisted self-study through English literature and beyond.[58] She and her peers read contemporary literary journals as they appeared, formed classes, sought tutors.

In time, Lucy's dream materialized. But it came less directly than even she expected. "So the pleasantly occupied years slipped on, I still nursing my purpose of a more systematic course of study, though I saw no near possibility of its fulfillment. It came in an unexpected way, as almost everything worth having does come. I could never have dreamed that I was going to meet my opportunity nearly or quite a thousand miles away, on the banks of the Mississippi. And yet, with that strange, delightful consciousness of growth into a comprehension of one's self and of one's life that most persons must occasionally have experienced, I often vaguely felt new heavens opening for my half-fledged wings to try themselves in."[59]

Reading and libraries sometimes contribute to such a path. Many women write of them in their personal testimonies, attesting to special connections with gender. They also write movingly, though sometimes with no more explicit recognition than Larcom, of the obstacles, limits, and contradictions in their paths due to gender (and with others to social class, race, ethnicity). Indeed, about race, I have been silent—for the record of the nineteenth century is largely silent, too. Literacy and reading there were—that is exceptionally important; access to libraries there was not, whether public or private, free or for pay. African-Americans are not alone. They are joined by the poor, most immigrants, many women, among countless others. These are silences to which we must listen, the great costs of the historical development of reading and libraries, and major contradictions, among others.

Nancy Cott writes of Lucy Larcom's personal story—and I emphasize for literacy: they are contradictory. For some, like Lucy, "these contradictory impulses resolve themselves in the larger theme of individualistic self-invention. . . . Her contradictoriness is a Whitmanesque largeness and encompasses multitudes: the worker, the poet, the student, the teacher, the stay-at-home, the traveler, the adult, the forever-child, the woman, and the individual."[60] To that resolution, contradictory at its core, reading and libraries also contributed. For others, many others, the contradictoriness is not, could not be, resolved in self-invention, individualism, or encompassing multitudes; it probably is never resolved. To all dimensions of these contradictions, literacy, reading, and using libraries contributed, positive and negative, progress and loss, gain and cost, and more. We now begin to see the import and complexity of these connections and the questions to which they give rise. That is a history not yet written.

Notes

1 JOHN FEATHER, "The Book in History and the History of the Book," in *Libraries, Books & Culture: Proceedings of Library History Seminar VII* (6–8 March 1985, Chapel Hill, N.C.), ed. DONALD G. DAVIS, JR. (Austin: Graduate School of Library and Information Science, University of Texas at Austin, 1986), p. 24.

2 HARVEY J. GRAFF, *The Legacies of Literacy: Continuities and Contradictions in Western Society and Culture* (Bloomington: Indiana University Press, 1987); PETERSON and DAVIS, review, *Libraries & Culture* 23 (1988): 219.

3 In preparation for this essay, I scanned the pages of library journals, bibliographies, anthologies, monographs, and the like to gain some measure of the field. For a social historian not centrally concerned with libraries, and their histories, this was revealing. One cannot but be struck by the struggle for new approaches and new levels of sophistication—or, however, by the derivative character and relative immaturity of much of the work when compared to other fields of *historical* (not library, that is) scholarship. See, for one example, JOHN CALVIN COLSON, "The Writing of American Library History, 1876–1976," *Library Trends* 25 (1976): 7–21. The kinds of debates I refer to prominently include the position papers of and responses to MICHAEL H.

HARRIS. See his "The Purpose of the American Public Library: A Revisionist Interpretation of History," *Library Journal* 98 (1973): 2509–2514; PHYLLIS DAIN, "Ambivalence and Paradox: The Social Bonds of the Public Library," *Library Journal* 100 (1975): 261–266; and ELAINE FAIN, "Manners and Morals in the Public Library: A Glance at Some New History," *Journal of Library History* 10 (1975): 99–105, with responses by HARRIS, 106–110, and DEE GARRISON, 111–116. See HARRIS, "The Dialectic of Defeat: Antimonies in Research in Library and Information Science," *Library Trends* 34 (1986): 515–531; "State, Class, and Cultural Reproduction: Toward a Theory of Library Service in the United States," *Advances in Librarianship* 14 (1986): 211–252. Comparison with recent French and British studies is also revealing. See, for contrast, ROGER CHARTIER, *The Cultural Uses of Print in Early Modern France,* tr. LYDIA COCHRANE (Princeton: Princeton University Press, 1987); PHILIP CORRIGAN and VAL GILLESPIE, *Class Struggle, Social Literacy and Idle Time: The Provision of Public Libraries in England,* Studies in Labour History/Librarians for Social Change (Brighton: John L. Noyce, 1978). See, too, DAVID VINCENT, *Bread, Knowledge and Freedom: A Study of Nineteenth-Century Working Class Autobiographies* (London: Europa, 1981), and *Literacy and Popular Culture: England, 1750–1914* (Cambridge: Cambridge University Press, 1989).

4   These data derive from a major long-term project that commenced with the publication of two articles in *History of Education Quarterly* (1986) and *Journal of Early Adolescence* (1985) and continued with *Growing Up in America: Historical Experiences* (Detroit: Wayne State University Press, 1987). *Conflicting Paths: The Transformations of Growing Up, 1750–1920/90* is published by Harvard University Press. Most of the first draft was prepared in 1989 while I was an American Antiquarian Society/National Endowment for the Humanities Fellow in residence at AAS. My appreciation goes to both institutions. Earlier research was conducted with the support of the American Antiquarian Society, the Newberry Library, and The University of Texas at Dallas.

5   I refer here to the recent and exciting work of scholars like DOMINIC LaCAPRA, ROGER CHARTIER, ROBERT DARNTON, WILLIAM GILMORE, JEFFREY BROOKS, JANICE RADWAY, and others, among a rapidly developing literature that crosses several disciplines. Note here, as well, that this essay aims at opening questions and connections, not at exhaustive, definitive, or conclusive treatment.

6   In what follows, readers should remain aware of the limitations as well as the possibilities of first-person testimonial sources. They provide exceptional access and data that no other primary materials can supply, but they also demand critical assessment. Like all other sources, they are biased; questions of representativeness, memory, and reliability stand among the many complications. The biases of producing and preserving such evidence exclude many persons, by education, race, class, age, and so forth. Their silences merit careful listening, too. So do memory and the literary creative process. My treatment here does not probe these points at length or in detail. *Conflicting Paths* will deal with these issues in requisite detail. The organization of the sections that follow combines a topical and chronological approach. The examples chosen are selective and exemplary; they make no pretense of representativeness of any kind.

7   RENA L. VASSAR, "The Life or Biography of Silas Felton Written by Himself," *Proceedings,* American Antiquarian Society, 69 (1959): 119–154. The original autobiography is in the Manuscript Division of the New York Public Library.

8   VASSAR, "Felton," pp. 121–122. See also William J. Gilmore, *Reading Becomes a Necessity of Life: Material and Cultural Life in Rural New England, 1780–1835* (Knoxville: University of Tennessee Press, 1989)

9   VASSAR, "Felton," pp. 126–127. From this passage Silas continues, presenting his "progressive" views on childrearing by following the young's inclinations. On growing

up, see JOSEPH KETT, *Rites of Passage* (New York: Basic Books, 1977); and GRAFF, *Conflicting Paths*, in progress.

10   VASSAR, "Felton," p. 127.

11   On subscription libraries, the major work is PAUL KAUFMAN's for eighteenth-century England; for example, his "The Community Library: A Chapter in English Social History," *Transactions*, American Philosophical Society, 57/7 (1967). The seminal U.S. work, of course, is JESSE H. SHERA, *Foundations of the Public Library: The Origins of the Public Library Movement in New England, 1629–1855* (Chicago: University of Chicago Press, 1949; Shoe String Press, 1965). See also recent studies of private, public, and mixed libraries by MICHAEL HARRIS for Indiana, EDWARD STEVENS for Ohio, WILLIAM GILMORE for Vermont, ROBERT GROSS for Concord, Massachusetts, and JOSEPH KETT for Virginia, among other studies in this and later periods. These studies are diverse and often very suggestive.

12   VASSAR, "Felton," p. 128.

13   Ibid., pp. 128–129. More generally, see my *The Literacy Myth: Literacy and Social Structure in the Nineteenth-Century City* (New York: Academic Press, 1979) and *Legacies*; and GILMORE, *Reading Becomes*.

14   VASSAR, "Felton," p. 129 (emphasis in her text).

15   Ibid., p. 130.

16   Ibid., pp. 132–133.

17   Their courting continued on again off again until they married in January 1799. At that time, Silas taught school near his father's home, where he and his bride first resided. Silas had also learned surveying by this time.

18   VASSAR, "Felton," p. 154.

19   Ibid., p. 139.

20   Ibid., pp. 151–152.

21   Ibid., p. 152.

22   DANIEL DRAKE, *Pioneer Life in Kentucky: A Series of Reminiscential Letters from Daniel Drake, M.D. to His Children*, ed. CHARLES D. DRAKE (Cincinnati: R. CLARKE, 1870); MARY E. DEWEY (ed.), *Life and Letters of Catharine M. Sedgwick* (New York: Harper and Bros., 1871).

23   See, for this argument, my *The Literacy Myth* and *Legacies*. Contrast with GILMORE, *Reading*. See below for more ordinary, everyday reading and library use.

24   *Memoir of John Griscom, LL.D.: with an Account of the New York High School; Society for the Prevention of Pauperism; the House of Refuge; and Other Institutions, Compiled from an Autobiography, and Other Sources* (New York: Robert Carter and Bros., 1859).

25   GRISCOM, *Memoir*, pp. 32–33.

26   Ibid., p. 33.

27   Ibid.

28   Ibid., pp. 33–35, 44–46.

29   Ibid., p. 47.

30   "The Autobiography of the Reverend Devereux Jarratt, 1732–1763," with an introduction and notes by DOUGLASS ADAIR, *William and Mary Quarterly* 9 (1952): 346–393. On Jarratt, see RHYS ISAACS, *The Transformation of Virginia* (Chapel Hill: University of North Carolina Press, 1980).

31   "The Autobiography," p. 347.

32   Ibid., pp. 347–348, *passim*.

33   "Journal of William Wait Oliver of Salem, 1802–1803," *Essex Institute Historical Collections* 81 (1945): 124–137, 227–256, 348–353.

34   Ibid., p. 127.

35   Ibid., p. 131.

36 "Diary of Archelaus Putnam of New Mills," *Historical Collections*, Danvers Historical Society, 4 (1916): 51–72; 5 (1917): 43–69; 6 (1918): 11–29.

37 Ibid., pp. 51–52.

38 Ibid., p. 68.

39 Ibid., 21 February 1809, p. 11.

40 DAVID E. CRONIN (ed.), *The Diary of Elihu Hubbard Smith (1771–1798)*, Memoirs, American Philosophical Society, vol. 95 (Philadelphia: American Philosophical Society, 1973). On college and college student society libraries, see esp. JAMES MCLACHLAN, "The *Choice of Hercules*: American Student Societies in the Early 19th Century," in *The University in Society*, ed. LAWRENCE STONE (Princeton: Princeton University Press, 1974), vol. 2, pp. 449–494. See also below.

41 CRONIN, *Diary*, September 1779, pp. 24–25.

42 See, for example, SOLON J. BUCK, "Selections from the Journal of Lucien C. Boynton, 1835–1853," *Proceedings*, American Antiquarian Society, 18 (1933): 329–380; WILLIAM DITTO LEWIS, "The Diary of a Student at Delaware College, August, 1853, to November, 1854," *Delaware Notes*, University of Delaware, 24th series (1951): 1–81; CLAUDE M. FUESS, "An Amherst Graduate of the 1840s [William Gardiner Hammond]," *Amherst Graduates Quarterly* 23 (1933): 1–10.

43 BUCK, "Selections from the Journal."

44 See for my early formulation *The Literacy Myth*, refined and broadened in *Legacies of Literacy*. Library history follows no more smoothly the same currents of founding myths, revisionism, and refinement. For relevant examples, see JOHN ALBEE, *Confessions of Boyhood* (Boston: Badger, 1910); JOSEPH SCHAFER (ed.), *Memoirs of Jeremiah Curtin*, Wisconsin Biography Series, vol. 2 (Madison: State Historical Society of Wisconsin, 1940); WILBUR J. COHEN, "Growing Up in Milwaukee: 1913–1934," *Milwaukee History* 7 (1984): 82–92; and of course the classic accounts of immigrants and their children.

45 ALBEE, *Confessions*, pp. 222–226, *passim*.

46 On precocity and its dangers, see JOSEPH KETT, "Curing the Disease of Precocity," in *Turning Points: Historical and Sociological Essays on the Family, American Sociological Review*, Supplement 84 (Chicago; University of Chicago Press, 1978): S183–211. For examples, see "Journal of Cyrus P. Bradley," *Ohio Archaeological and Historical Society Quarterly* 15 (1906): 207–270; WILSON O. CLOUGH, "A Journal of Village Life in Vermont in 1848," *New England Quarterly* 1 (1928): 32–40; CAROLINE DALL, "Alongside," *Being Notes Suggested by "A New England Boyhood" of Doctor Edward Everett Hale* (Boston: Privately printed, 1900).

47 "Journal of Bradley," pp. 210–213.

48 CLOUGH, "A Journal," pp. 32, 34, *passim*.

49 See, for example, MARY E. DEWEY (ed.), *Life and Letters of Catharine Sedgwick* (New York: Harper and Bros, 1871); EDITH EMERSON WEBSTER GREGG, "Emerson and His Children: Their Childhood Memories," *Harvard Library Bulletin* 28 (1980): 407–430; DALL, *"Alongside"*; and GRANVILLE HOWLAND NORCROSS, Diaries, 1860–1876, ms., American Antiquarian Society. See also HENRY SEIDEL CANBY, *The Age of Confidence: Life in the Nineties* (New York: Farrar and Rinehart, 1934). SEDGWICK is mentioned above.

50 GREGG, "Emerson," p. 412.

51 NORCROSS, Diaries, *passim*.

52 DALL, *"Alongside"*. That CAROLINE DALL explicitly chose to write her memoir as a female parallel and implicit response to EDWARD EVERETT HALE's a A *New England Boyhood* is striking and cries out for consideration.

53 See and compare, only as beginning examples, GRAFF, *The Literacy Myth, Legacies*; GILMORE, *Reading*; and LAWRENCE A. CREMIN, *American Education: The National Experience, 1783–1876* (New York: Harper and Row, 1980). See also DAVID D. HALL

and JOHN B. HENCH (eds.), *Needs and Opportunities in the History of the Book: America, 1639–1876* (Worcester: American Antiquarian Society, 1987); and WILLIAM L. JOYCE, DAVID D. HALL, RICHARD D. BROWN, and JOHN B. HENCH (eds.), *Printing & Society in Early America* (Worcester: American Antiquarian Society, 1983). The literature relating to these points is not only voluminous but continues to grow rapidly. See CARL F. KAESTLE, "Literacy and Diversity: Themes from a Social History of the American Reading Public," *History of Education Quarterly* 28 (1988): 523–550, his contribution to Library History Seminary VIII and his larger project on this topic. See also my "Whither the History of Literacy? The Future of the Past," *Communication* 11 (1988): 5–22.

54 See, for rich examples, in addition to those cited above, EDWARD JENNER CARPENTER, Journal, 1844–1845, ms., American Antiquarian Society, now edited and published by CHRISTOPHER CLARK with the assistance of DONALD M. SCOTT, "The Diary of an Apprentice Cabinetmaker: Edward Jenner Carpenter's 'Journal' 1844–46," *Proceedings*, American Antiquarian Society, 98 (1988): 303–394; "Extracts from Diary of Joseph Porter Dwinnell, 1837–1838," *Collections*, Danvers Historical Society, 26 (1938): 23–41; JAMES LAWRENCE WHITTIER, Diary, 1830–1831, ms., American Antiquarian Society; JAMES FERDINAND FISKE, Diaries, 1857–1860, ms. 5, American Antiquarian Society; RAY BINNS, Diary, 1910, ms., copy in my possession; LUCY LARCOM, *A New England Girlhood, Outlined from Memory* (Boston: Northeastern University Press, 1986 [1889]); and HARRIET H. ROBINSON, *Loom and Spindle or Life among the Early Mill Girls with a Sketch of "The Lowell Offering" and Some of Its Contributors* (New York: Thomas Y. Crowell, 1898). It bears repeating, once more, that the greatest number of such records make little or no mention of using their obvious literacy in reading or in libraries. I thank Donald Scott for sharing a prepublication typescript of the Carpenter Diary with me.

55 FISKE, Diaries, 12 July 1857, *passim*.

56 CANBY, *Age of Confidence*, pp. 186, 190–191, 195, 206–207. CANBY's distinctions between "wide" and "deep" reading, interestingly, are echoed by German scholar ROLF ENGELSING's "intensive reading" and "extensive reading," a designation followed by DAVID HALL, WILLIAM GILMORE, and ROBERT DARNTON, among others.

57 LARCOM, *New England*, pp. 209, 211, 222–223. See pp. 105ff, 128ff., for Lucy's childhood "appetite" for reading from age four.

58 Ibid., p. 236, chapter II, *passim*.

59 Ibid., pp. 245–246. Following her sister west, Lucy prepared to teach at a women's seminary near St. Louis. She returned to Massachusetts, continuing to teach, in 1852.

60 COTT, foreword to *New England*, p. xvii, *passim*. Other important women's writings include DALL, *"Alongside"*; ANZIA YEZIERSKA, *The Bread Givers* (New York: Persea Books, 1975 [1925]); KATE SIMON, *Bronx Primitive* (New York: Harper and Row, 1982), and *A Wider World* (New York: Harper and Row, 1986); and ANNIE DILLARD, *An American Childhood* (New York: Harper and Row, 1987). Obviously, gender demands more systematic and sustained attention than given here.

13 On Literacy: Review Essay

On Literacy: The Politics of the Word from Homer to the A of Rock
by Robert Pattison
New York: Oxford University Press, 1982

'We are inadequately literate in part because we have inadequate ideas about literacy. This book seeks to improve our literacy by defining the term accurately' (v). Thus writes Robert Pattison, a humanities professor at Southampton College of Long Island, in beginning his bold new book *On Literacy*. What follows is a 'critique radical of the term literacy and its popular uses which are usually unfounded in fact and destructive in practice' (vii). To Pattison, his critique, one which he claims is rooted in historical analysis, on one hand, and in sociocultural, historical relativism, on the other, is radical politically and historically both. (That historically based paths of understanding must be justified as 'radical' is a sad commentary on our times, for which the author is hardly responsible.)

On Literacy is, to say the least, an ambitious book. Not only does Pattison attempt to encapsulate the history of literacy over the past 5000 years within the confines of 213 pages of text, but he also struggles to evaluate the changing linguistic consciousness of humanity and to reorient definitions and the views that follow from that reorientation. The result is a bold, indeed a brash book, which depends more often on assertions and short-circuited logic than on developed argument and evidential support. It is a book, it must be stated, about which specialists—including the present reviewer—are certain to be less than pleased. The problem lies, I believe, at least as much with the book's genre, form, and style of presentation, as with the author himself. In following the author's own views, at least for the moment, we might well consider both as signs, symbols, and forms of literacy. This also reflects on the relations between scholarly literacy and popular literacy, about which Pattison has definite opinions. That is a point to which I will return. Pattison, I suspect—despite the contradictions of his (limited) scholarly apparatus and stylistic habits of dropping the names of so-called authorities with the barest of descriptions, explanations, or evaluations—aims at a largely nonscholarly, 'popular audience.'

On Literacy is difficult to summarize. It has no simple thesis or hypothesis. Rather, it has a set of 'general conclusions' around which the text is shaped, often repetitively and sometimes contradictorily. They are to replace the unfounded faith in equally general axioms, which Pattison terms the 'same old whine.' In the place of views that equate literacy with skill in reading and writing; the use of that 'standard' as an indicator of a person's cultivation or civilization; the propagation of reading and writing to the poor as a first step toward social and economic advancement; and preservation and expansion of reading and writing skills as a bulwark of democracy, morality, and rationality, he offers his four substitutes:

> (I) that literacy is foremost consciousness of the problems posed by language, and secondarily skill in the technologies, such as rhetoric and writing, by which this consciousness is expressed; (2) that different cultures may have different concepts of language and different technologies to express these concepts; thus there can be no universal standard of literacy; (3) that economic and social development depends on a pragmatic concept of the uses of language shared among the leadership of the evolving community, and therefore imposition of narrow Western ideas about literacy on developing populations at home or abroad is not automatically beneficial; (4) that literacy changes in step with changing notions about language and with new technologies, and American literacy is currently undergoing a fundamental redefinition of literacy (vi–vii).

To Pattison, the latter is 'Neither good nor bad'; rather the problem lies in 'mindless resistance to it in the name of preserving deliquescent concepts of language.' This is 'almost certainly fatal,' he warns, 'to the preservation of culture.' Obviously, the author takes his business seriously.

Unlike most persons who discuss literacy, Pattison is explicitly concerned with the all important roles of definition, variations across time and space, and historical transformations. This is to his credit, and as one result, he gains this social historian's sympathy. The uses he makes of these crucial principles of literacy study, however, raise numerous issues of method, interpretation, and, indeed, epistemology; and, in the end, Pattison is tangled tightly in the web that he has sought to create to liberate all of us. This irony, in fact a key contradiction, is itself revealing.

The problems begin at the onset, first with the approach to definitions, second with the reading of history and perspective on change. In his preface, as quoted here, Pattison asserts that there are no universals with respect to literacy; several pages later, in the first chapter, he declaims the necessity for a universal definition that links consciousness of language (about which one, interestingly, apparently need not be conscious!) with mastery of skills for its expression. This contradiction—of his own use of language (the expression of his consciousness?), of conceptualization, and of logic—provides a first warning to the wary. It is a clue to the looseness of the web spun throughout the book, and hints at the dangling ends, flying fragments, and untied knots. Imprecision in word usage, particularly at the conceptual level, is another sign, surprising in such a book.

In part, the key issue is epistemological, especially as it relates to the author's assumptions, concepts, and subsequent methodology. This can be seen in the simple fact that Pattison, on occasion, professes a dialectical view of both historical change and linguistic media interactions (e.g., the oral and the written, the 'high' cultural and the 'popular,' the traditional alphabetic and the electronic), when his conception is overwhelmingly linear, evolutionary, and sequential. Perhaps the best examples of this failing appear in his superficial and highly abstracted readings and rewritings of historical works, especially in Chapters 2, 3, and 4. His ignorance of the role of specific historical contexts—the discipline's supreme contribution—greatly weakens the interpretations proffered. (This historian is skeptical of his familiarity with the literature often bizarrely and misleadingly summarized in his bibliographic essay.) Whereas history does serve fundamentally as a tool toward understanding the present and clarifying complex relations, misappropriations of historical interpretations are no better than none. Pattison begins on the correct path; the problems lie more in his execution.

In part, too, the key issue is Pattison's ideational first principles. The sentences from *On Literacy* with which I began this review return to haunt the wary reader, regardless—or indeed in spite—of my own sympathies with a great deal of what Pattison wishes to tell us. Instructively, they connect intimately with his redefinition of literacy as language consciousness. Although his historical sources and sometimes apparently his own gut instincts run to the contrary, the dominant perspective shaping the book—nay, determining—is an endorsement of the ideational, the idealist rather than a materialist or a more interactive, truly dialectical point of departure and overarching perspective. If consciousness is assumed to be determinant—if, in a phrase, 'We are inadequately literate in part because we have inadequate ideas . . .'—the mental, and its roots, shape all else. The troubling and tricky question of human consciousness—whose study, understanding, and discussion is highly problematic and controversial, as Pattison notes but does not embrace in his waffling positions around virtually all major areas of contention—then comes to the fore.

If, however, other aspects of human history and relations are *at least* as important as the ideational, if, indeed, the material, for example, (as *this* historian believes) is primarily though not exclusively or solely determinant in its shaping power and impact on key relations, then the terms of discussion and the balance of interpretation fall, on balance, elsewhere. In terms which Robert Pattison should accept, if not approve, this point is surely not only academic. And the proof, I posit, lies in *the* history, with which Pattison claims to be familiar and which is found in his book. Literacy thus may be a form of consciousness and its expression. But surely it is not equivalent with consciousness of language itself.

The narrowness and the circularity of that viewpoint reappear throughout the pages of *On Literacy*. They are seen in the confusion about language and its uses and in the focus on verbal expressions as the key to linguistic consciousness. They are seen again in the profoundly ahistorical relativism into which Pattison's assumptions and convictions regularly lead him. And, amazingly in 1982, they appear in his complete neglect of the other largely nonverbal 'new' literacies of mathematics, geography, visual arts, music (beyond the lyrics to which Pattison does listen), and the dance, to cite only the most prominent. Whereas the author is concerned, however superficially, with the relations between the alphabetically literate and the oral or rhetorical modes of expression, he ignores the other increasingly crucial dimensions of literacy, or more properly litera*cies*. In his call, at the end, for a 'new literacy,' explicitly reconnecting the formal with the supposedly more spontaneous and lively 'popular,' this is a glaring omission. It weakens the power of Pattison's proposals for the future: 'To reach that point ['the kind of literacy implied in Marx's utopian vision'] we need a curriculum that besides teaching utilitarian skills also demonstrates the connection between language and life. One way to achieve this end is to allow the nascent literacy of the people to emerge' (211). This, alas, is not the most exaggerated or hyperbolistic of his prose's leaps.

My criticism, which has been suggestive in its selectivity, rather than exhaustive, must *not* detract from the importance of the project that Robert Pattison seeks to initiate in his small book. Nor must it negate the many insights which he presents to readers. The book is powerful; it forces its audience to respond, to examine their own thoughts, to compare their versions of the 'received wisdom' with Pattison's partial and incomplete challenge to it. His failings, shortcomings, and contradictions are neither his alone, nor are they uninstructive. (I am at a loss, however, to account for his use of sexist language in allowing masculine terms and pronouns to stand at *all* points throughout the text.) He has much of importance to tell, including his critique of the 'liberal' tradition with respect to literacy, discussion of the exaggerated pragmatism in terms of instruction and expectations relating to literacy, and his willingness to look to history, however inadequately.

The dangers with *On Literacy* are twofold. Not surprisingly, they are contradictory. On the one hand, there is the danger of many readers' unwillingness to confront his challenge, to take seriously his positions. His prose style will not draw them in. That would be a serious loss. But on the other hand, there is the danger of other readers' accepting uncritically his critiques. That, I fear, would be little better. In sum, this is not a book for the uncritical, regardless of their own orientations to the issues. It is, in many important ways, a book to be considered carefully and selectively, and most of all consciously critically. That, I think, would only be in keeping with Robert Pattison's own spirit. Most of all, it should *not* be read in isolation from the growing body of writings and other expressions equally of a critical spirit but often more firmly grounded: in history, anthropology and linguistics, literary studies, psychology, and increasingly elsewhere. Then, a 'new' relationship between scholarly and popular literacies may be relocated and explored.

14 National Literacy Campaigns in Historical and Comparative Perspective
(with Robert F. Arnove)

History has shown that, up to the present time, revolutionary regimes have been the only ones capable of organizing successful mass literacy campaigns. From the Soviet Union to China, from Vietnam to Cuba, all revolutionary governments have given high priority to the war on illiteracy.[1]

The magnitude of the problem in many countries calls for massive efforts. Only specific campaigns with clearly defined targets can create the sense of urgency, mobilize popular support and marshal all possible resources to sustain mass actions, continuity, and follow-up.[2]

The idea of a campaign to promote massive and rapid increases in rates of literacy is not unique to the twentieth century. We contend, and this work illustrates, that major and largely successful campaigns to raise levels of literacy have taken place over the past four hundred years from the time of the Protestant Reformations, and that they share common elements. Our belief is that contemporary literacy campaigns can be better understood in a historical and comparative perspective.

Historically, large-scale efforts to provide literacy have not been tied to the level of wealth, industrialization, urbanization, or democratization of a society, nor to a particular type of political regime. Instead, they have been more closely related to efforts of centralizing authorities to establish a moral or political consensus, and over the past two hundred years, to nation-state building.[3]

What may be said of literacy campaigns is that, both historically and comparatively, they have formed part of larger transformations in societies. These transformations have attempted to integrate individuals into more comprehensive political and/or religious communities. They have involved the mobilization of large numbers of learners and teachers by centralizing authorities, who have used elements of both compulsion and social pressure to propagate a particular doctrine.

Campaigns, since the Protestant Reformations of the sixteenth century in Western Europe, have used a variety of media and specially developed materials, commonly involving a special cosmology of symbols, martyrs, and heroes. They often have been initiated and sustained by charismatic leaders and usually depend on a special "strike force" of teachers to disseminate a particular faith or world view.

A belief in the efficacy of literacy and the printed word itself has been an article of faith. Then as now, reformers and idealists, shakers and movers of societies and historical periods, have viewed literacy as a means to other ends—whether a more moral society or a more stable political order. No less today than four hundred years ago, individuals have sought and used literacy to attain their own goals.

In the twentieth century, particularly during the period from 1960 on, pronouncements about literacy deem it a process of critical consciousness-raising and human liberation. Just as frequently, such declarations refer to literacy, not as an end itself, but as a means to other goals—to the ends of national development and to a social order that elites, both national and international, define.[4]

This work examines continuities as well as changes in literacy campaigns over the past four hundred years. It also points to persisting issues related to literacy campaigns, their goals, organization, processes, and outcomes. The overarching goal of this work is a historically, comparatively, and dialectically based reconceptualization of the idea of a literacy campaign. By implication, we also call for a reconceptualization of literacy in theory and practice.

The Idea of a Campaign

In a Unesco-commissioned review of twentieth-century national literacy campaigns, H.S. Bhola defines the literacy campaign as "a mass approach that seeks to make all adult men and women in a nation literate within a particular time frame. Literacy is seen as a means to a comprehensive set of ends—economic, social-structural, *and political*." According to Bhola, "a campaign suggests urgency and combativeness; it is in the nature of an expectation; it is something of a crusade." Sometimes, this becomes the moral equivalent of war. By contrast, a " 'literacy program', which even though planned, systematic and designed-by-objectives, may lack both urgency and passionate fervor."[5]

Although a limited time frame is considered to be a defining characteristic of a mass campaign, those national cases frequently pointed to as exemplars of twentieth-century literacy mobilizations commonly took two or more decades. Bhola's examples include the USSR (1919–1939), Vietnam (1945–1977), the People's Republic of China (1950s–1980s), Burma (1960s–1980s), Brazil (1967–1980), and Tanzania (1971–1981). Only the Cuban literacy campaign spanned a period of one year or less. The Nicaraguan Literacy Crusade of 1980, not studied by Bhola, lasted but a brief five months. Despite the variable time spans, they all had "an intensity of purpose expressed in a series of mobilizations and were highly combative in trying to achieve their goals."[6]

What distinguishes twentieth-century literacy campaigns from earlier educational movements (such as those of Germany, Sweden, and Scotland, which spanned over two hundred years) is the telescoped period of time in which the mobilizations occurred, stemming from the fact that political power can be more effectively centralized than in earlier periods. The transformation of communications, including electronic technologies and economies of scale in the publishing industry, further facilitates printing and dissemination of literacy texts, and transmission of messages and symbols relating to a campaign. The combination of technology and concentration of political power also may portend greater opportunities for the monitoring of, and social control over, the uses of literacy.

There also are international dimensions to the types of literacy activities characterizing the second half of the twentieth century, and increasing opportunities for countries to learn from one another. Despite these differences, the similarities between literacy campaigns over the past four hundred years are strongly evident. Insufficiently recognized among these similarities is the increasing tendency of countries to borrow from other campaigns, a process of mimesis. This is what Graff terms the "legacies of literacy."

In the following pages, we review similarities between contemporary campaigns and the literacy drives and movements of the sixteenth through nineteenth centuries. The characteristics on which we focus are the contexts, goals, mechanisms, organization, materials and methods, teachers, and consequences of campaigns. Another important common feature is the relationship between literacy efforts and the institutionalization of schooling. The chapters contained in this book place literacy efforts in historical context while also searching for common patterns over time and across different social, economic, and political configurations. Theorists and planners of literacy campaigns may learn much of value from these patterns, from the past successes and failures documented in the national case studies.

Context and Triggering Events

Historically, the initiation of a literacy campaign has been associated with major transformations in social structures and belief systems. Typically, such campaigns have been preceded and accompanied by more gradual changes, such as the spread of religious doctrine, the growth of market economies, the rise of bureaucratic and legal organizations, and the emergence of national political communities. But usually there is a profound, if not cataclysmic, triggering event: a religious reformation or a political revolution, the gaining of political independence and nationhood.

The German, Swedish, and Scottish campaigns from the middle of the sixteenth century were intimately connected to the Protestant Reformations and the subsequent Catholic Counter-Reformation. In the German case, the Treaty of Augsburg of 1555 established that the religious preference of the ruling elite of each city or territory determined whether the population of that political entity would adhere to the Catholic or the Lutheran Church. Shortly thereafter, the Catholic Church, reinvigorated by the Council of Trent and the founding of the Order of Jesuits, responded to the threat of religious heterodoxy. According to Gawthrop, the Protestant rulers, in conjunction with religious authorities, systematically set out to establish schools "to indoctrinate the general population and thereby ensure religious conformity."

For Scotland, the Reformation of the 1560s is described by Houston as a political event with religious overtones. Anti-French and anti-Catholic nobility, concerned with the establishment and protection of their faith, advocated a national effort to educate the population in the principles of Protestantism.

Literacy efforts in Sweden, according to Johansson, must also be understood in the context of the Protestant Reformation. The Swedish experience should be taken as part of a process of nation building following a series of great wars. Military defeat contributed to renewed emphasis on mass literacy in Prussia in 1807, France in 1871,[7] and Russia in 1905.

Literacy efforts in the nineteenth century, for example in the United States, represent a convergence of various social forces and widely held beliefs: the competition of various religious denominations to capture souls and a belief in republican government, with its need for an educated citizenry. But a key catalyst was the extension of the franchise to the working class during the first three decades of the century, a trend which coincides with the beginning of the common school movement.

In Russia, the abolition of serfdom in 1861 unleashed enormous energies, both at the local and state levels, that were channeled into literacy activities. At the same time, national elites, of both progressive and conservative tendencies, began to make linkages between literacy and the process of modernization and the strengthening of the Russian State.[8]

The campaigns of the twentieth century are usually associated with revolutionary upheavals and attempts by state authorities to create a new political culture and accelerate the process of economic development. The most striking cases of massive mobilization that pivot on the provision of literacy and adult education are the USSR, following the October 1917 revolution; the People's Republic of China, following the 1949 "liberation"; Cuba, following its 1959 revolution; and Nicaragua, after the "triumph" of 1979. Other notable cases involving large-scale literacy as part of the struggle for independence from colonial domination include Vietnam from 1945 on, and the actual attainment of independence followed by the restructuring of a society in accordance with a new model of development—Tanzania after 1967.[9]

The wealth and resources of a country have not been the critical factor in shaping the scope and intensity of a war on ignorance. Rather, the political will of national leaders to effect dramatic changes in personal beliefs, individual and group behaviors, and major institutions emerges as the key factor. Cases in which a strong political will has been lacking include India, with approximately one-half of the world's more than 800 million illiterate adults, and the advanced industrialized countries of the U.S., the U.K., and France, which, according to Limage, have profound illiteracy problems.[10]

Goals

The transformations that provide the context for most mass literacy campaigns usually embrace the formation of a new type of person in a qualitatively different society. In the contemporary period, there is frequent reference, for example, to the creation of the "New Socialist Man [Woman],"[11] in a society organized according to principles of cooperation, egalitarianism, altruism, sacrifice, and struggle (the USSR, the People's Republic of China, Vietnam, Cuba, Ethiopia, Nicaragua). In the period of the great Protestant reforms, educational goals were joined, according to Strauss, "to that grand design of a spiritual renewal of state, society, and individual which endowed earlier Lutheranism with its strongest source of appeal."[12] The Lutheran Reformation in Germany, Strauss continues, was particularly important because

> It embarked on a conscious and, for its time, remarkable systematic endeavor to develop in the young new and better impulses, to implant inclinations in consonance with the reformers' religious and civic ideals, to fashion dispositions in which Christian ideas of right thought and action could take root, and to shape personalities capable of turning the young into new men—into the human elements of a Christian society that would live by evangelical principles.[13]

An important legacy of the German campaign is Luther's shift in attention to shaping the young, as opposed to his earlier focus on all members of the community. The dilemma faced by Luther, whether to concentrate literacy efforts on the young or on adults, is a strategic issue in almost all subsequent mass campaigns. In twentieth-century campaigns, despite initial large-scale efforts aimed at entire populations, a narrowing eventually occurs with greater emphasis placed on the formal education of the young. Literacy and basic education, over time, become conflated (confused?) with state-organized and regulated systems of schooling.

Luther's emphasis on youth reflects the widespread and persisting belief that youth is less corrupt and more easily molded. Gawthrop points to the pessimistic views of German religious reformers concerning the malleability of human beings. Whereas many of the earlier reformers did not believe it was possible to effect any permanent, positive alteration in human nature—given their belief in the imminence of the Day of Judgment—they embraced, according to Gawthrop, "the molding power of education only in so as it assisted their efforts to combat the spread of heretical doctrine." The early Protestant reformers attempted to make basic instruction available to the largest possible number of youths, not only for the sake of their salvation, but for the common welfare.

In Scotland, political order and doctrinal conformity were the goals of centralizing authorities. In Sweden, according to Johansson, all educational efforts were concentrated on comprehending, understanding, and putting the word into practice in everyday life.

In the nineteenth-century United States, the rapid spread of literacy served similar purposes of religious propagation, maintenance of political order, and the formation of a national character. According to Stevens, "the process of becoming literate was itself a process of socialization promulgated by those interested in using the school to resolve social, economic, and political tensions arising from a culturally pluralistic and emerging industrial society. The process of schooling and hence the process of becoming literate are seen in relation to nation-building, a fervent evangelical Protestantism, and technological innovation." What is of special significance in the U.S. case is that the reformers advocated a republican form of government, based on more active citizen participation in political governance.

In Russia, following the 1917 Revolution, Lenin noted that "the illiterate person stands outside politics. First it is necessary to teach the alphabet. Without it, there are only rumors, fairy tales, prejudice, but not politics."[14] The society of worker collectives ("soviets") that the socialist reformers envisioned depended on a literate citizenry that could understand the nature of their past exploitation, grasp the organizing principles of the new society, and participate in the necessary transformations.

In all the above cases, literacy is almost never itself an isolated or absolute goal. It is rather one part of a larger process *and* a vehicle for that process. Literacy is invested with a special significance, but seldom in and of itself. Learning to read, possibly to write, involves the acquisition or conferral of a new status—membership in a religious community, citizenship in a nation-state. Literacy often carries tremendous symbolic weight, quite apart from any power and new capabilities it may bring. The attainment of literacy per se operates as a badge, a sign of initiation into a select group and/or a larger community.

Historically, there has been constant tension between the use of literacy for achieving individual versus collective goals. Inseparable are the questions of (a) whether to select the individual or the group as the target of a campaign and (b) whether to aim at transforming individuals in order to change societies or at transforming collectivities in order to reform individuals. Changes at one level do not necessarily bring about a corresponding transformation at the other.

Throughout history, the provision of literacy skills to reform either individuals or their societies rarely has been linked to notions of people using these skills to achieve their own ends. To the contrary, reformers advocating the extension of education to the populace have attempted to restrict the ability to read to learning a particular text or doctrine. They commonly feared that unbridled literacy would lead people to new visions, to new ways of perceiving and naming the world that were not acceptable.[15]

Houston notes that in the sixteenth- to eighteenth-century literacy campaigns, "The individual [had] no right to learning for its own sake. The overall aim was societal advancement." John Knox, the great Protestant divine, stressed that "all should be educated in the doctrines of Calvinism . . . the preservation and extension of Protestantism was central to the literacy campaign."[16] Similarly, Resnick and Resnick note that the goal of Protestant religious instruction in the United States was not enlightenment in the general sense, but rather "a particular way of viewing the world."[17]

In the contemporary period, especially in those mobilizations that occur in socialist societies, the acquisition of literacy is linked integrally to "political education" in a particular ideological doctrine, Marxism—Leninism or (Mao-Zedong Thought) or nationalist variations such as Sandinismo. In the People's Republic of China, Mao Zedong stressed "political literacy," even though, as Hayford points out, peasants and workers remained unable to read books, magazines, and newspapers. Lenin noted, "As long as there is such a thing in the country as illiteracy it is hard to talk about political education." Even prior to the 1917 revolution, political elites in Russia, who were promoting literacy efforts as part of modernization, evinced, according to Eklof, a fear of "wild" popular literacy. Eklof's analysis of literacy campaigns after the revolution shows that it was precisely at the time of massive extension of education in the early 1930s that Stalin also drastically tightened up censorship and surveillance to control the uses of literacy.

The post-World War II era is particularly interesting because of a change in the rhetoric, and sometimes the ideology, of literacy campaigns and the goals that are announced in international conferences such as that of Tehran in 1965. The Tehran Conference declared that literacy, rather than being an end in itself, "should be regarded as a way of preparing man for a social, civic and economic role . . . reading and writing should lead not only to elementary general knowledge but to training for work, increased productivity, a greater participation in civil life and a better understanding of the surrounding world, and should . . . open the way to basic human culture."[18]

A year before the Unesco-sponsored Tehran Conference, the 1964 session of Unesco's General Conference called for a "five-year experimental world literacy program designed to pave the way for the eventual execution of a world campaign in the field of literacy."[19] The Experimental World Literacy Campaign (EWLP, 1967–73) was distinguished both by its selectivity (reaching one million adults in eleven countries) and by its stress on "functionality." As Gillette notes, the central criterion in the program was narrowly oriented functionality—with major emphasis being given to industrial, agricultural, and craft training for men, and homemaking and family planning for women.

The only country to expand immediately its EWLP pilot project into a major campaign was Tanzania. The goals of the Tanzanian campaign are noteworthy, for they reflect a different conceptualization of the methods and outcomes of literacy. They also reflect the pedagogical ideas of leading adult educators like Paulo Freire, who focus on literacy as a process of individual consciousness-raising and social change. Tanzanian declarations on the goals of literacy and adult education, for example, state that "one of the most . . . significant functions of adult education is to arouse consciousness and critical awareness among the people about the need for and possibility of change." The goal of adult education programs, according to Kassam and Hall, was to "help people in determining the nature of the change they want and how to bring it about."[20]

Paulo Freire's conception of the adult literacy process as "cultural action for freedom" is relatively open-ended. It is also clear that those countries that have embraced Freire's language and some of his pedagogical methods in their national campaigns, for example Tanzania and Nicaragua, have a more specific notion of the desired end-state of literacy promotion and acquisition. Literacy and adult education efforts are always informed and oriented by particular political world views of societal elites and dominant groups. In Tanzania and Nicaragua, as in other mass campaigns such as those of Vietnam and Ethiopia, literacy promotion is predicated upon socialist and populist notions. In Brazil, Freire's native country, a literacy campaign has been underway for years, frequently employing the rhetoric of "conscientizacion" but also very much tied to gaining acceptance for a technocratic, statist, and capitalistic approach to development.

The most eloquent international statement on the goals of literacy campaigns appears in the 1975 Declaration of Persepolis (Iran):

> literacy . . . [is] not just the process of learning the skills of reading, writing, and arithmetic, but a contribution to the liberation of man and to his full development. Thus conceived, literacy creates the conditions for the acquisition of a critical consciousness of the contradictions of society in which man lives and of its aims; it also stimulates initiative and his participation in the creation of projects capable of acting upon the world, of transforming it, and of defining the aims of an authentic human development.[21]

Such goals are articulated by a number of national literacy campaigns (Cuba, Tanzania, Nicaragua, Guinea Bissau). Nagging questions remain. The translation of these goals into outcomes very much depends on the mechanisms, methods, materials, and teachers that are employed in large-scale literacy efforts. Given the transformations and mobilizations that generally precipitate and accompany such campaigns, or "crusades," it is unlikely that literacy will be used only for ends exclusively determined by the individual or individuals collectively organized at the base. It is to these mechanisms and mobilizational strategies that we now turn.

Patterns of Mobilization

The initial literacy campaigns in Western Europe—Germany, Scotland, and Sweden—from the mid-sixteenth century on, and the nineteenth-century United

States education movements reveal several distinctive patterns of mobilization. These patterns may be viewed in relation to (a) the degree of centralization of political and religious authority exercised over a campaign, and (b) the extent to which a literacy campaign's activities are institutionalized in schooling.

One legacy—that of state-directed activities—was established by the German literacy drives. Initially, literacy activities promoted by the followers of Luther were decentralized, domestically based, and informal. But by the 1550s, according to Gawthrop, there was an unmistakable trend toward coordination and direction of primary education by centralizing political and ecclesiastical authorities, and movement toward a uniform system of education. There was a corresponding shift to formal institutions and "carefully trained cadres of pastors and teachers operating under the aegis of benevolent, but strong willed, governments." Among the reasons offered for this shift are the disillusionment of Luther and his followers with the results of "uninformed enthusiasm." Gawthrop notes that "peasants justifying their rebellion of 1525 by misrepresenting (in Luther's eyes) his religious message turned the Great Reformer against any fostering of unsupervised book learning."[22]

Similarly, Scotland's literacy efforts were state-directed and even more comprehensive in scope. According to Houston, the literacy campaign "initiated in Scotland at the time of the Reformation and carried through by legislation in the seventeenth century (1616) was the first truly *national* literacy campaign." It was universal in coverage, religiously oriented, and school-based. Educational activities directed at literacy involved joint action of the Scottish State and the Protestant Kirk. What distinguishes the Scottish case from that of the German—as well as that of seventeenth-century New England—campaigns was that the latter were essentially more localized efforts.[23]

Another distinctive pattern was that of the Swedish campaign. Launched in 1686, it was national in scope but was carried out almost entirely *without* the use of schools. Sweden offers an example of a domestically based but politically and religiously sponsored and enforced campaign. The primary focus was on informal activities supervised by local religious authorities. Its unique features included a literacy based in reading ability but seldom in writing, and also a special stress on the mother's educational role in the home. In early modern Sweden, as a result, the exceptional pattern of women's rates of literacy paralleling men's was achieved. This represents a historical and indeed a contemporary anomaly.[24]

The nineteenth-century United States represents another pattern. Unlike the German, Swedish, and Scottish cases, according to Stevens, there was no centrally orchestrated policy that brought the power and resources of the nation-state to bear on the problem of literacy. Instead, the competition of religious denominations, the proliferation of religious and secular presses, the exhortation of leading secular and clerical authorities, and local civic initiative came together to promote literacy activities. Most activity was organized and directed by the individual states rather than the federal government.

These patterns may be represented graphically as in Figure 1. The lower right hand cell of centralized, non-school-based literacy campaigns essentially remains a highly preliminary stage from which campaigns pass as they develop. Historically and comparatively, state and religious authorities strive to move literacy promotion away from unregulated, unschooled situations.

In the twentieth century, the most striking examples of mobilization involve national, centrally organized efforts that are waged in terms of a "war on ignorance." But these efforts have also depended heavily on local initiative and popular organizations to recruit teachers and students and to implement instructional activities. The People's Republic of China, with the most massive mobilization of people (over 48 million), was, according to Bhola, "centrally instituted and nationally orchestrated, but carried out in a decentralized manner, leaving much to local choice and initiative."[25]

From the sixteenth century onward, political and religious authorities have used exhortation and appeals to moral and patriotic sentiments, as well as compulsion and social pressure, to induce people to acquire literacy. State legislation

		Centralization	
		High	Low
	Yes	Scotland	USA
School-based		Germany	
	No	Sweden	Germany initially

Figure 1. Patterns of mobilization

requiring local municipalities and religious institutions to offer instruction, hire teachers, and ultimately require illiterate individuals to attend schools or demonstrate knowledge of certain texts characterizes the early German, Swedish, and Scottish cases.

In the twentieth century, the Soviet Union stands out as the first case of a country adopting a war-seige mentality to combat illiteracy. The December 29, 1919 Decree on Illiteracy, for example, required all illiterates eight to fifty years of age to study, empowering local Narkompros (People's Commissariats of Enlightenment) to draft literate citizens to teach, and making it a criminal offense to refuse to teach or study.[26] In June 1920, the All-Russian Extraordinary Commission for the Eradication of Illiteracy was created and given the power to issue regulations with the force of law. During the 1917–1921 period, as detailed by Eklof, an institutional framework was created to set up Likpunkty ("liquidation points") from which to attack illiteracy. The likpunkty were to provide 6–10 week literacy courses.[27] The "New Committee" that was established to conduct literacy efforts was called the *gramCheka* (*gram* being the abbreviation for literacy, and

Cheka the initials for the secret police). And, as Eklof notes, looming large in adult literacy efforts was the Red Army.

Interestingly enough, the Russian army, at the end of the nineteenth century, also played an important role in state efforts to promote literacy. New recruits who could produce a primary school certificate or demonstrate reading ability had their terms of enlistment reduced. The French and U.S. armies, in the nineteenth century, also conducted significant literacy instruction among recruits.

However, social control and compulsion, as well as positive inducements to acquire literacy, are not unique characteristics of twentieth-century campaigns. In the case of Sweden, a church law of 1686 required children, farm hands, and maid servants "to learn to read and see with their own eyes what God bids and commands in His Word."[28] Every household person and villager was gathered once a year to take part in examinations supervised by the local clergy in reading and knowledge of the Bible. The adult who failed the examination could be excluded from communion, and denied permission to marry.

In Scotland, as in Sweden, the Church had the right to refuse admission to communion to the grossly ignorant. Other social pressures included efforts to shame illiterates.

In the German states of Saxony (1772) and Bavaria (1802), pastors were forbidden to confirm anyone who had not spent enough time in school to have learned reading and a certain amount of religious knowledge. Throughout the German states, according to Gawthrop, a series of regulations restricted numerous categories of jobs from the state administration to those who could read, write, and do sums. Prussia imposed such limitations on those who wished to enter a craft guild.[29]

Compulsion is frequently counterproductive. The history of education in Western Europe and North America, as in other parts of the world, offers striking evidence of local initiatives of communities and grassroots movements to acquire literacy skills and establish schools. These efforts run parallel to and, in some instances, counter to the authority of state and religious authorities.[30]

In Scotland, for example, "adventure" or private fee-paying schools, although putatively illegal, comprised a parallel education system to the state-sponsored parish schools. These schools, as Houston indicates, were extremely important in extending education as the Scottish population increased.

In pre-1917 Russia, most peasants learned to read and write outside the formal school network. As Eklof documents, peasants set up informal village schools founded either by payments from individual households or by the entire commune. Formal school expansion in the 1861–1914 period was, according to Eklof, eventually a process of formal recognition and registration of extant peasant schools.[31]

By contrast, more recent campaigns tend to originate with centralized authorities, thus raising the question of the intent and will of national leaders. In his review of twentieth-century campaigns, H. S. Bhola stresses the importance of national political will in mass literacy campaigns:

The political will of the power elite actualized by the institutional power of the state can work wonders—resocialize each and every member of the society, transform the fabric of a society and invent a new future. Cultural revolutions can be brought about; literacy campaigns can be launched and ensured of success.[32]

In the Soviet Union, five years after the passing of comprehensive legislation, the establishment of liquidation points, and the creation of gramCheka, Minister of Education Lunacharskii complained that "the society for the liquidation of illiteracy passes wonderful resolutions but the concrete results of its work are despicable."[33] Krupaskaya, Lenin's wife and a renowned educator, complained ten years after the 1919 literacy decree that not a single article had been implemented. More aptly, Bhola notes:

> There are no substitutes for the twin process of organization and mobilization. On the one hand, the government must undertake both the administrative and technical organization of its decision making in the implementation system. On the other hand, people must be mobilized; learners must be motivated to learn; those who can teach and contribute in other ways, must be enabled to do so.[34]

But how? A review of past campaigns suggests that the creative use of symbols, a variety of media, the sponsorship of charismatic figures, and the availability of relevant and interesting materials all contribute to the diffusion of literacy. Moreover, opportunities for grass roots organizations (mass organizations in socialist societies) to participate is critical to the success of a mass campaign.

Motivating Learners

As literacy campaigns—historically and comparatively—have been associated with major social movements and transformations, they have benefited from the unleashing of energies and the opening of opportunities that occur in periods of social transition. Concomitantly, they have suffered from the dislocations, disorganization, and upheavals that characterize such periods.

The Soviet Union reveals both the revolutionary zeal with which populations may be mobilized for educational purposes and the debilitating conditions of civil war, external aggression, and widespread famine that also typified post-1917 Russia. Post-1949 China, similarly, was wracked by the legacy of war, but also by mobilizations such as the Great Leap Forward (1958) and the Great Proletarian Cultural Revolution (1966–1976). Among other goals, these mobilizations sought to extend education to larger numbers. Yet they contradictorily resulted in more than 100,000,000 people being added to the ranks of illiterates due to schools being closed and literacy skills being frowned upon and therefore not used.[35] The cases of Vietnam, Ethiopia, and Nicaragua also underscore the twin phenomena of enormous energies being channeled into literacy efforts and to the necessity of diverting resources into national defense and reconstruction—with extreme difficulty in meeting both sets of demands at the same time.

In all of the major twentieth-century campaigns, as in past campaigns of the previous three centuries, charismatic figures have been associated with literacy campaigns. Notable among the early Protestant reformers are Martin Luther, John Calvin, and John Knox; among Americans of the early republican and common school era, Thomas Jefferson, Noah Webster, and Horace Mann; in the twentieth century, Vladimir Illich Lenin, Mahatma Gandhi, Mao Zedung, Ho Chi Minh, Fidel Castro, And Julius Nyerere.[36]

The stature of these figures and the symbols that they represent to their followers are tied to notions of salvation, redemption, recreation. Notions attached to the saving of individual souls in the Reformation and Post-Reformation periods of Western Europe, and the common school "crusade" of nineteenth century U.S., become linked in the twentieth century (especially in the post-World War II period) to the goals of redemption of a society that had suffered under colonialism, to the birth of a nation, and to the creation of a new and more just (moral?) society.

In the twentieth-century campaigns, to mention some of the more salient cases, literacy workers have been variously designated as *kultarmeitsy* (cultural soldiers) in the Soviet Union and as *brigadistàs* (brigade workers) in the Cuban and Nicaraguan campaigns. Posters and billboards portray literacy workers as fighting a war with pencils, blackboards, and notebooks as their weapons against the "dark forces" of ignorance. (Pencils had very real meaning as weapons of war in Nicaragua: counter-revolutionaries who attacked literacy workers as agents of the transformations occurring in the country actually drove pencils through the cheeks of some of the "brigadistas" whom they had killed.)

Arnove describes the symbolization of the 1980 Nicaraguan National Literacy Crusade (CNA) in this way:

> The imagery and vocabulary of struggle and a national war loomed large in the symbolism of the SNA. Just as six guerrilla armies victoriously converged on Managua on 19 July (1979), in the wake of Somoza's flight from the country, so, on 24 March 1980, six "armies" left Managua to wage war on illiteracy. The six national fronts of the people's Literacy Army consisted of some 55,000 brigadistas (literacy workers), mostly high-school students, who would live in the rural areas of the country. . . . The six fronts were divided into "columns" at the hamlet level. The columns had four "squadrons" of thirty brigadistas each.[37]

Emotionally charged words and generative themes characterize the literacy primers in societies that are undergoing radical change. Appropriately, the first words of the Nicaraguan primer are *la Revolución* (the Revolution), which also contain all the vowels of the Spanish alphabet. Other key words include *liberación*, *genocidio*, and *masas populares*. Similarly, significant words are found in the Cuban literacy primer. The Soviet literacy text began with this dramatic exclamation:

"My ne raby, ne raby my." ("We are not slaves, slaves we are not.") The campaigns of early modern Germany, Sweden, and New England all had parallel features. Scribner shows this especially well in the German Reformers' use of pictorial imagery.[38]

In the twentieth-century campaigns, slogans abound and frequently are very similar. (Whether this indicates mutual borrowing or similar phenomena is difficult to determine.) In Cuba, various slogans centered on the notion that "if you were literate you could teach; if you were illiterate you could study."[39] In Ethiopia, the saying was: "Let the educated teach the uneducated, and the uneducated learn."[40] In Nicaragua, billboards and posters proclaimed:

En cada casa un aula
En cada mesa un pupitre
En cada Nica un Maestro!

Every home a classroom.
Every table a school desk
Every Nicaraguan a teacher!

Billboards, posters, flyers, specialized newspapers and publications—and, historically, pamphlets, handbills, and boards—have been an integral part of literacy campaigns. For example, pamphleteering littered early-to-mid-sixteenth-century Germany; in the second half of the seventeenth century, as Gawthrop documents, governments and private reformers disseminated leaflets to parents extolling the benefits of education. In Germany, as later in the United States, religious messages as well as technical information were disseminated widely in the form of simply written works and tracts for adults. Print media included specialized periodicals, calendars, almanacs, and also cheap novels and newspapers. This glut of print enjoyed great popularity but did not necessarily represent the interests of societal elites and their designs for literacy in the masses.

Print assumed a symbolic power and significance aside from individuals' ability to read it. For example, possession of a Bible, and its location in a prominent place in the home, was a goal of many. In the late eighteenth and early nineteenth centuries, in England and the U.S., Tom Paine's works held such power among literates and illiterates alike.

In many countries, traditional art forms—theatrical groups, dance troups, and musical ensembles—have been used to arouse popular interest in the literacy campaign. In China, wall murals, bulletin boards, and public blackboards have been used to raise interest in reading. Historically, wall plaques, printed cards, and pictorial icons played this part.

Tanzania, which has emphasized postliteracy maintenance and development activities more than most countries in recent years, has imaginatively used a variety of media and vehicles to promote reading and writing skills: the radio, mobile book libraries, and locally and inexpensively produced newspapers. Critical to the success of the Tanzanian program has been the development of textbooks that represent different areas of interest to learners and that are designed according to level of reading difficulty.[41]

Linguistically suitable reading materials and appropriate forms of adult education have not always characterized literacy campaigns.[42] Continuities that derive from the German campaign, however, include the attempt to impart a uniform and socially significant message (world view) to all students, the selection of teachers with special traits, and the use of a common language to do so.

Materials and Methods

In Germany, following the Treaty of Augsburg (1555), government leaders supported the clergy of their territories in creating an expanded network of primary schools. School ordinances set forth a standard curriculum—consisting above all of catechism, drill, and psalm saying—followed, in descending order of importance, by reading, writing, and much less often arithmetic. Gawthrop notes that in his concern with religious conformity, Luther created a pedagogical instrument, the shorter catechism, to guide teaching efforts of parish sextons "to gather the children at least once a week to teach them the commandments, the Creed, the Lord's Prayers, and some hymns." Emphasis was also placed on selecting carefully trained cadres of pastors and teachers. But generally, the level of knowledge required of the teachers was little more than "that which their pupils would learn if their instruction were successful." In Württemberg, nominees for teachers were required to pass an examination testing their literacy, singing ability, and knowledge of the catechism. It was not until the mid-eighteenth century that emphasis was placed on teacher training and the comprehension of teachers. Pedagogy consisted of "constant reiterations of immutable formulas."[43]

In Sweden, materials consisted of special psalm books (combining catechism, biblical motifs, and texts of the ecclesiastical calendar). Special syllabary were developed, such as "The Golden ABCs" with 24 verses, each of which began with a letter of the alphabet. The most widely distributed book was the 1689 Catechism with Luther's "Explanations." The text included 303 questions and answers, scriptural passages, questions for young persons and bridal couples, and rules for home worship.

In Scotland, according to Houston, "Because of its religious and moral emphases, the form of education was dictated by the wish to transmit an approved body of knowledge and doctrine to the pupil rather than to stimulate critical understanding." Rote learning involved catechism, reading, writing, and, especially for girls, training in domestic vocational skills such as sewing, knitting, and weaving. In the United States, as Resnick and Resnick have observed, the earliest mass literacy effort, Protestant religious instruction, was intended to develop, not a generalized capacity to read, but mastery of a very limited set of prescribed texts.[44]

From viewing these earlier campaigns, we learn that new and carefully crafted materials were developed to convey prescribed content. Attempts were made to simplify texts and also to use mnemonic and other heuristic devices. Concomitantly, most pedagogy was dominated by basic drill and repetition, with a goal of uncritical internalization of revealed truth or doctrine or unquestioning patriotism. Aligned with this pedagogy was an experience of "training to be trained," a socialization in discipline, orderliness, and obedience.

While state and religious authorities were concerned with the uniformity of messages, religious groups also vied to place their particular view before the public. The result of this competition, and the increasing availability of inexpensive print materials—novels, vocational manuals and guides, religious materials, as well as fairy tales and political tracts—contributed to the diversity of information available to the literate. Sometimes, state and church pursued contradictory ends. Propagation of one particular religion or sectarian doctrine over another could, and did, conflict with the promotion of common citizenship in a nation-state supposedly based on consensus values. Important examples of this conflict include Scotland and England and, to a lesser extent, the United States and Canada.

Other issues surfaced in these early campaigns that still trouble planners of literacy campaigns. One problem—the language of instruction—emerged in the Scottish campaign. In the Lowlands, the more urbanized, economically developed, and Protestant section of the country, English was spoken; in the rural, relatively undeveloped, and Catholic Highlands, Gaelic was the primary language. Since the Lowlands were politically dominant, English was the language of instruction. As Houston points out, "The drive for conformity in beliefs and language usage was harmful to literacy attainment in Scotland." If anything, the language problem was even more complex in Ireland.

The language issue poses serious problems in twentieth-century campaigns. Gillette, in his essay on the Experimental World Literacy Program, notes that the opposition within various participating countries to "the use of international funds to promote literacy as a means of spreading the national language to assimilate (subdue?) minority groups . . . raised sensitive cultural, and thus political questions in certain instances." Among the eleven participating countries, Tanzania used Kiswahili, the official language, as the medium of instruction; in fact, the literacy campaign contributed to the dissemination and standardization of the use of Kiswahili in the school system and throughout the country. In India, Kenya, and Ethiopia various languages have been used. In Indonesia, learning in the national language was supplemented by materials in local languages.[45] The language problem is highly reminiscent of bilingualism and trilingualism that plagued literacy campaigns in the West from the late medieval period through the twentieth century.

In Vietnam, efforts to extend literacy to various ethnic minorities may be viewed in terms of "cultural uplift" and the creation of a common culture bene-fitting all persons.[46] It may also be seen as cultural imperialism, attempts to undermine traditional cultures.

In some cases, the nature of the language itself—Chinese, for example— poses serious problems for the widespread dissemination of literacy. Hayford's essay notes the long history of attempts to simplify the Chinese language system of orthography, and how literacy, in the past, was confined to elite stratum and was very much related to limited mobility opportunities for the gentry and to political rulers.[47] Hayford examines pre-1949 literacy efforts to design new readers in a simplified language with themes that appealed to mass and middle-brow audiences. The James Yen Movement of the 1930s and 1940s developed, for example, the "People's Thousand Character Primer," based on frequency of words in selected texts, street signs, and standard contracts. Mao Zedong, who was involved in the movement, employed many of the same methods but introduced socialist content into the texts. In Ya'nan, by 1939, he had introduced a new writing system and a phonetic alphabet to teach literacy to populations under the control of the Chinese Communist Party.[48]

The language of instruction leads to the question of *whose* language and values form the medium and content of a literacy campaign. The power of dominant groups to shape language policy and educational content is similarly reflected in what skills are developed in what populations as part of the literacy process. Historically and comparatively, rural populations, the working class, ethnic and racial minorities, and women have been the last to receive literacy instruction and to gain access to advanced levels of schooling. As various Unesco publications reiterate, "The world map of illiteracy is the map of poverty."

Women have been the most disadvantaged group. From the time of the Protestant Reformation, when household heads were held responsible by the state for literacy instruction and for supervising reading, men typically have benefitted most from education campaigns. Moreover, when reading was extended to women, men received preference in the teaching of writing.[49] However, in early modern Sweden and the nineteenth-century United States, perceptions of women's special educational "mission" at home, as mothers, and as school teachers propelled their rates of literacy upward, sometimes rivaling those of men.

Do significant differences in materials and methods characterize contemporary literacy campaigns? Over the past two decades, there has been a shift to concepts of literacy as individually or collectively empowering and liberating. In some cases, this has meant developing different literacy primers that appeal to different interests. In Tanzania, for example, twelve different literacy primers were prepared—all but two, according to Kassam and Hall, based on the economic and social activities of the people of that country.[50] Elsewhere, it has meant the use of emotionally charged themes that awaken people to examine their past exploitation and to their role as agents of change in a society now reorganized along radically different principles.

Campaigns of the last two decades, in addition to employing notions derived from Paulo Freire's "pedagogy of the oppressed," are also based on borrowings from other countries. Current literacy programs take from the declarations of international conferences such as those of Persepolis and Udaipur. According to Gillette, the Experimental World Literacy Program, for example, contributed to instructional methodology specifically for adults. Appropriately designated as "andragogy," adult literacy efforts increasingly stress (1) an inductive approach, which starts with adults' own ideas and insights; (2) experiential learning, which derives from and relates to the prospects of applying newly acquired knowledge and skills; and (3) a variety of techniques and a flexible approach in which it is realized that there is "no magical solution to the problem." Other approaches, of course, focus on children and youth.[51]

Interestingly enough, statements by Lenin and Ho Chi Minh cautioned against too impetuous and inflexible an approach to literacy instruction. Both were aware of the dangers of authoritarian, and—in the case of Lenin—excessively political, instruction that ignored learners' interests and needs in the initial stages of literacy. Revealingly, Lenin, along with Marx and Gramsci, held to rigorous, very sound, seemingly traditional, education for all. Only a broadly based education would end the cultural dominance of previous elites and their social system.

Although contemporary campaigns seem to differ from past campaigns in their more learner-oriented approaches and their emphasis on participatory teaching methods, similarities also are important. An examination of mass mobilizations, such as that of Nicaragua, reveal, on the one hand, attempts to engage the learners in dialogue and to design texts that respect the linguistic universe and social interests of illiterates. But, on the other hand, national uniform texts were used, instruction was frequently teacher-centered and directive, and the acquisition of basic literacy skills was often based on various repetitive and mechanical means of teaching and learning.[52] Moreover, in mass mobilizations, teachers are often chosen for their allegiance to a particular party or regime, rather than for their pedagogical preparation.

In the mass mobilization literacy campaigns, all elements—materials, media, symbols, methods, instructional personnel—work together in theory to socialize the population into a new faith, sometimes a conserving one, sometimes a revolutionary one. Outcomes, however, may be something else.

Outcomes

Outcomes may be studied at the individual, group, and collective levels. Consequences may be assessed as immediate or over a longer term. They may be studied in quantitative or qualitative terms. The quantitative side generally refers to numbers of individuals reached by a campaign and the numbers who achieve literacy and continue on to postliteracy adult educational activities. Frequently, these figures are impressive, involving millions of people who participated in a campaign and dramatic decreases in illiteracy levels.[53]

As a result of earlier campaigns, an estimated eighty-five percent of the German population could read by 1850. A base had been established for the subsequent industrialization of the country. Similar figures are noted for Scotland and for much of the developed West.[54] In the twentieth century, the Soviet campaign claimed to have raised literacy levels to approximately eighty-two percent by 1939. In the post-World War II period, the studies in this volume note a decline in illiteracy in Tanzania, from sixty-seven percent in 1970 to fifteen percent in 1983; in Cuba, from twenty-four percent to four percent as the result of the 1961 campaign; and in Nicaragua, from fifty percent to approximately fifteen percent, as the result of the 1980 campaign in Spanish and the follow-up campaign in indigenous languages. A striking pattern emerges: with the exception of Cuba, the results are essentially the same. Regardless of date, duration, or developmental level, approximately eighty-five percent adult literacy is achieved. Nevertheless, an irreducible minimum remains of at least ten to twenty percent. This is a point to ponder.

Such figures tell little about the levels of literacy achieved or the uses and implications of literacy acquisition. The more interesting analyses, from our point of view, are those of a more qualitative nature. Literacy itself is too often viewed in only a dichotomous way: either a person is literate or not. But literacy may also be viewed along a continuum: a set of skills that may become more complex over time in response to changing social contexts, shifting demands on individuals' communication skills, or individuals' own efforts at advancement. Only in Tanzania did the campaign actually define as many as four levels of literacy acquisition that involved increasingly more complex uses of reading and writing skills.

Historically, reading has not always related closely to either comprehension or writing. In seventeenth-century Sweden, emphasis was placed on reading Holy Scripture, not on being able to use the skills of writing. Limage similarly draws attention to the difference between reading and writing skills in France. For the Soviet Union, Eklof distinguishes between literacy and "true education," which means use of reading and writing skills to understand the nature of one's society and being able to contribute to improvements in it—perhaps even to alter its very premises and structures. If comprehension, understanding what one reads, is a critical feature of literacy, then, even in the more wealthy school districts of the United States many teenagers may be classified as illiterate; they do not understand their school texts or major stories in newspapers. Arnove and Arboleda remark that if illiteracy refers to the ability to understand the basic issues confronting individuals in contemporary society, then illiteracy is pervasive in many industrially advanced nations with extensive systems of schooling.[55]

The relations between quantity and quality within campaigns, more generally, are represented schematically in Figure 2. That mass literacy campaigns almost invariably—indeed, virtually by definition—aim at quantitative rather than qualitative goals is grasped immediately. The contrasting strategy of emphasis on the quality of literacy skills, as the figure also illustrates, take the individual as the target.

	Quantity	
Low		High
Low		Mass campaigns: collective advancement and individual benefits; political socialization and moral development
Quality		
High	Selective campaigns: individual (often upper or middle class) benefits; cognitive skills; "gatekeepers"	

Figure 2. Quantity and quality in national literacy campaigns.

The goal of many literacy campaigns has been changes in individuals' belief systems as part of transformations in social systems. The outcomes that merit study include changes in self-concepts, ideological orientations, political dispositions, feelings of efficacy, and commitments to engage in social action. There have been some attempts to measure these outcomes using questionnaires and interviews.[56] Assuming that countries are willing to examine critically the course and outcomes of their campaigns, there are a number of serious problems. Changes in individuals are extremely difficult to assess, particularly with regard to the role of literacy as a causal factor. The instruments tend to be limited in their reliability and validity. For example, positive sentiments aroused by the experience of participating in a campaign may be reversed as government policies and circumstances change.

Importantly, the very process of participating in a campaign and achieving literacy may confer a new status on individuals, removing a stigma of inferiority.[57] The opposite side of the coin is that those who do not participate in a campaign or who continue to be illiterate may be labeled as deviant and denied full membership rights in a religious or political community. Historically as well as more recently, those who oppose literacy efforts may be viewed as dissident, unassimilated, counterrevolutionary, or enemies of the state.

The community-level outcomes of expanded literacy are more difficult to measure. Nevertheless, we must ask how diffusion of literacy affects the practices that traditionally have held communities together, if such practices are to be supplanted or reinforced by the cultural policies of new political regimes, how the spread of literacy modifies orality and other traditional means of communication, and whether or not, as Bhola claims, literate communities "by definition, will have to have a higher fund of symbolic skills."[58]

Historically, collective transformations have been sought through literacy campaigns. Therefore, outcomes must also be examined at the societal level. This level has up to now been studied least.[59]

The case studies in this book suggest a number of (intended as well as unintended) structural and cultural outcomes. Among these outcomes are the institutionalization of school systems, standardization of national languages, incorporation of marginal populations into national societies, and legitimation and consolidation of political regimes. Another consequence is the resistance of individuals and groups to centralizing tendencies on the part of national authorities. Despite apparent high-level generalizations across time and space, what is most important resides in specific contexts. Each social context shapes and conditions relations that can only be viewed as dialectical—tying all factors and actors together in complex fashion.

Institutionalization of Schooling

The development of state-controlled or sponsored school systems is one legacy of the Reformation German and Scottish campaigns. The dissemination of literacy in most of Western Europe and North America, from the late seventeenth century, is the sometimes torturously slow and gradual story of the establishment of schools—and systems of schooling. Lurie testifies to the culmination of this history:

> Literacy education for adults and the provision of schooling for children must be seen as two sides of the same coin, and that consequently, the planning of education and the subsequent facilities of educational systems . . . must be redirected as to serve the aims of these two objectives more effectively.[60]

At times, literacy activities (as in late nineteenth-century Russia) outran the establishment of schools by state authorities. But the long-term historical trend has been for formal institutionalized education to either replace or incorporate nonformal (out-of-school) activities that also provided literacy.

Campaigns of the last three decades, such as those of Cuba and Nicaragua, have consciously attempted to develop a postliteracy system of adult education outside the formal school system. They nonetheless have contributed to tens of thousands of youths and young adults entering higher levels of the formal system after completing the adult education cycles. In many respects, the "popular education" system in Nicaragua, with progressively more levels being added to it, comprises a parallel, increasingly institutionalized education system.[61]

Literacy provision and socialization of individuals over time have merged and been institutionalized in state systems of formal education. From the earliest campaigns, the goals of literacy provision have been the propagation of a particular faith or world view, the reading of prescribed texts, under the supervision of teachers of a certain moral persuasion and of an upright character. Historically, the religious orientation of school systems has given way to a more secular faith in the nation-state and/or the propagation of an ideology such as capitalism or socialism.

Standardization of Languages

The widespread dissemination of mass literacy depends not only on common texts (hence inducements to all facets of publishing) but on the use of a common language. The histories of England, France, and Italy illustrate the importance of creating linguistic commonality as part of nation-state formation.[62] School systems in many countries today are viewed by national authorities as contributing to the forging of consensus values as well as teaching a national language. Gillette points out, for example, that one of the effects of the EWLP in Mali was standardization of the national language. In Tanzania, the literacy campaign that followed the EWLP helped develop a new written literature in Kiswahili. In pre- and post-1949 China, according to Hayford, literacy movements often attempted to simplify, and even romanize, traditional Chinese orthography.

Incorporation and Integration

One of the intended outcomes of recent campaigns, such as those of Cuba and Nicaragua, is also the integration of countryside and city. Not only recently, but also historically, literacy campaigns have been an important device for attempting to overcome geographical and social divisions within a society.

In twentieth-century campaigns, sending tens of thousands of urban high school and university students to live and teach in the countryside is a manifestation of a new political regime's intent to extend basic social services to marginal populations and to incorporate them into national efforts. These mobilizations also seek to teach urban, largely middle-class youths about the realities of rural life, and make them more appreciative of their rural brothers and sisters and more committed to rural development.[63]

Attempts to integrate society by means of literacy campaigns are not unique to the twentieth century. Describing the German literacy drives of the eighteenth and nineteenth centuries, Gawthrop remarks that "by the early nineteenth century the vast majority of peasants were receiving the same basic education as that given to all but the elite elements of Germany's middle classes." There was a narrowing of cultural disparity between town and countryside as people of different social strata had access to the same books—Bible, catechism, and hymnal.

The publication of scores of editions of the same religious texts—in the millions—in Germany, Sweden, and the United States, as well as popular books such as the McGuffey readers in the United States and Chairman Mao's Little Red Book in China, contributed to the population's reading common texts. But the inducements to diversification as well as economies of scale in publishing also contributed to specialized publications. This specialization resulted in the proliferation of tracts aimed at a multitude of audiences, with their differing belief systems and points of view. The proliferation and specialization of print materials has at times contributed to consensus building but at other times to the deepening of divisions within a society.

Legitimation and Consolidation of Regimes

The incorporation of people into a new moral or political order is always a desired outcome of mass campaigns. Regime legitimation at the national level is certainly an intended goal of nineteenth- and twentieth-century campaigns. Legitimation at the international level is a more recent and less studied phenomenon. According to Unsicker, campaigns apparently may contribute to a nation's standing in the international community and may facilitate greater readiness on the part of international technical assistance and donor agencies to provide aid.[64]

The success of large-scale mobilizations is often the function of mass organizations, such as youth, worker, neighborhood, defense, and women's associations. In turn, one structural outcome of literacy campaigns in mobilizational regimes, such as Nicaragua, Cuba, Ethiopia, the Soviet Union, and the People's Republic of China, has been the strengthening of these mass organizations.

A national campaign, by mobilizing large numbers of people and strengthening mass organizations, creates opportunities for large-scale citizenship participation in decision making. But such mobilizations and organizations may also serve as instruments for exercising cultural and political hegemony by dominant groups or the state apparatus. The history of efforts at social control, of dominant groups trying to control the uses of literacy and expanded communication skills, offers countless examples of people, individually and collectively, resisting efforts at either imposition or control.

Resistance

As literary provision commonly forms part of efforts to impose centralizing authority and attempts to change people's beliefs, it is not unusual to discover instances of individuals and groups resisting perceived threats to their identity. The German literacy drives elicited such responses from peasants from as early as the sixteenth century. Russia offers abundant instances before and after the 1917 revolution of peasant populations setting up their own schools and employing reading materials that did not accord with the designs of state authorities. Eklof chronicles peasant attacks on state-appointed teachers in the late 1920s and early 1930s. He also describes how, despite intense efforts at censorship, readers pursue their own interests, frequently of an escapist nature: "Library subscribers took out books on politics in far smaller number than their availability. Books checked out were concentrated in the areas of travel, biography and history (primarily on World War II, military memoirs, spy documentaries, regimental histories)."

Similar accounts of reading habits from Tanzania and the People's Republic of China indicate that peasants and workers may be less interested in reading about how to construct a latrine or organize a cooperative than they are in romance and adventure stories. Gillette sums up the difficulty of controlling outcomes of literacy campaigns: "Happily, literacy like education more generally cannot be reduced to behavioral conditioning. It endows people with skills that they can (although do not always) use to receive and emit messages of an almost infinite range, a range that in any event escapes the control of those who imparted literacy. . . . Literacy is potential empowerment."

Persisting Problems

In addition to the resistance of people to control, and the unpredictable outcomes of literacy campaigns, there are other seemingly intractable problems. Class, ethnic, racial, geographical, and gender differences in literacy acquisition have been ubiquitous over the past four hundred hears. The recent Cuban and Nicaraguan campaigns, however, reveal a new potential for breaking this pattern. One particularly important change is the extent to which women are participants in and beneficiaries of literacy campaigns. In Cuba and Nicaragua, a majority of the literacy workers were women. As Arnove notes, one of the changes accelerated and magnified by the latter literacy crusade has been the liberation of women from their marginal positions in society. The results from other campaigns, such as Tanzania, further indicate that women predominate at the lower levels of literacy attainment; at the highest levels, corresponding to functional literacy, males predominate.[65]

Lessons

To ask of literacy that it overcome gender discrimination, integrate a society, eliminate inequalities, and contribute to political and social stability is certainly too much. Literacy may be empowering, especially when it can work in conjunction with other changes. Ultimately, the retention and uses of literacy depend on the context on the environment of opportunities available to people to use their literacy skills, transformations in social structures, and the ideology of leaders. Whether the materials and methods of literacy and postliteracy campaigns are truly designed to equip people to play more active roles in shaping the direction of their societies or, to the contrary, are intended to induct people into roles predetermined by others, is a telling indication of ideology and intent.

Literacy planners and political leaders are aware of a number of the factors that contribute to the success—as well as limitation—of current and past campaigns. The extent to which international and national authorities involved in literacy campaigns have fully grasped the implications of these lessons and are committed to applying them remains in question. One basic reason for doubting the resolve of political and educational leaders in many countries is that widespread possession of literacy by a populace may lead to unpredictable, contradictory, and conflictive consequences.[66]

There is a dialectic, an interaction, between individuals and the environment as they gain literacy, and between them and centralizing authorities. The dialectic is an ongoing process with the nature of that interaction being shaped by the expansion—and sometimes the transformation—of literacy itself. In the last thirty years, there has been a change in the ideology of literacy toward an emphasis on empowerment. Contributing to this shift have been the seminal work of Paulo Freire, the example of the Cuban literacy campaign, Unesco-sponsored conferences and declarations, and the emergence of a more critical and political scholarly literature. Whether this shift to empowerment and grass-roots determination of literacy development will effectively counter long and strong traditions of top-down centralized direction of literacy efforts remains to be seen.

The tension between the base and the top, between the masses and elites, between those who are the supposed beneficiaries of literacy and those who envision and organize for the populace, has been heightened by the telescoped period of time, the scale of mobilization, modern technologies and communication, and the refined instruments of state power. Also contributing to the tension is the new awareness of base and top alike of the political nature of literacy—not surprising given the rhetoric and ideology of recent campaigns concerning education for critical consciousness and liberation. This tension, as the essays in this volume illustrate, has a long history. We can perhaps understand the nature of the tension; it is very difficult to predict or prescribe the manifold outcomes of a campaign and the uses of literacy.

Notes

All textual references below to essays by Richard Gawthorp, Rab Houston, Egil Johansson, Edward Stevens, Ben Eklof, Charles Hayford, Jeff Unsicker, Marvin Leiner, Arthur Gillette, H. S. Bhola, Robert F. Arnove, and Leslie Limage refer to their contributions to *National Literacy Campaigns in Historical and National Perspective*, ed. Arnove and Graff (New York: Plenum, 1987), unless otherwise noted. This chapter originally served as the introduction to that book, hereafter cited as *NLC*.

These essays examine most of the important examples of national literacy campaigns over the past four hundred years; any major omissions are due to our inability to secure a contribution. We do think that we deal with the essential cases, however. In all that follows, the term "literacy," when used without qualification, refers to basic or elementary levels of alphabetic reading and/or writing. We also wish to note that, although we discuss "wars on ignorance" and use other such terminology derived from various historical campaigns, we firmly believe that individual adults who cannot read or write have a rich reservoir of knowledge and skills. Similarly, largely illiterate societies with oral traditions have a richness of culture, involving alternative ways of perceiving, interpreting, and communicating views of the world, that should not be downplayed or denigrated.

1 LÊ THÀNH KHÔI, "Literacy Training and Revolution: The Vietnamese Experience," in *A Turning Point for Literacy*, ed. LEON BATAILLE (Oxford: Pergamon), 1976, pp. 125–26.

2 Udaipur Conference, "Campaigning for Literacy: Proceedings," International Council for Adult Education, Unesco, Uadiapur, India, January 1982.

3 HARVEY J. GRAFF, *The Legacies of Literacy: Continuities and Contradictions in Western Society and Culture* (Bloomington: Indiana University Press, 1986); see also RANDALL COLLINS, "Some Comparative Principles of Educational Stratification," *Har-*

vard Educational Review 47 (February 1977), pp. 1–27, JOHN BOLI, FRANCISCO O. RAMIREZ and JOHN W. MEYER, "Explaining the Origins and Expansion of Mass Education," *Comparative Education Review* 29 (May 1985), pp. 145–70, YEHUDI COHEN, "Schools and Civilization States," in *The Social Sciences and the Comparative Study of Educational Systems*, ed. J. FISCHER (Scranton, PA: International Textbook, 1970).

4   G. CARRON and ANIL BORDIA, *Issues in Planning and Implementing National Literacy Programmes* (Paris: Unesco and IIEP, 1985), esp. p. 18.

5   H. S. BHOLA, *Campaigning for Literacy: A Critical Analysis of Some Selected Literacy Campaigns of the 20th Century, with a Memorandum to Decision Makers* (Paris: Unesco/ICAE Study, 1982), p. 211.

6   Ibid.

7   BOLI, RAMIREZ, and MEYER, p. 165.

8   BEN EKLOF, *Russian Peasant Schools: A Social and Cultural History, 1861–1914* (Berkeley: University of California Press, 1986); see also his "Russian Literacy Campaigns" in *NLC*.

9   See BHOLA, *Campaigning*, LÊ THÀNH KHÔI, "Literacy Training," and JEFF UN-SICKER, "Tanzania's Literacy Campaign" in *NLC*.

10   See Chapters 11 and 13 in *NLC*. See also GRAFF, *Legacies*, BRIAN STREET, *Literacy in Theory and Practice* (Cambridge: Cambridge University Press, 1984), JONATHAN KOZOL, *Illiteracy in America* (Garden City: Doubleday, 1985), and KENNETH LEVINE, "Functional Literacy: Fond Illusions and False Economies," *Harvard Educational Review* 52 (1982), p. 252.

11   Whatever the reasons, revolutionary societies following the socialist path to development almost invariably refer to the formation of the new "socialist man," equating the masculine gender with humanity. We feel uncomfortable with this formulation and therefore purposely refer to the new "socialist female" as well. The terminology used by new revolutionary regimes merits considerably more examination and discussion, and the sexist implications of key expressions should not be glossed over.

12   GERALD STRAUSS, *Luther's House of Learning: Indoctrination of the Young in the German Reformation* (Baltimore: Johns Hopkins University Press, 1978), p. 8.

13   Ibid., p. 2; see also STRAUSS, "Lutheranism and Literacy: A Reassessment," in *Religion and Society in Early Modern Europe*, ed. KASPAR VON GREYERZ (London: Allen & Unwin, 1984), pp. 109–23, and RICHARD GAWTHROP and GERALD STRAUSS, "Protestantism and Literacy in Early Modern Germany," *Past and Present* 104 (1984), pp. 31–55.

14   PETER KENEZ, "Liquidating Illiteracy in Revolutionary Russia," *Russian History* 9 (1982), p. 175, quoted in EKLOF, "Russian Literary Campaigns"

15   HARVEY J. GRAFF, *The Literacy Myth: Literacy and Social Structure in the Nineteenth-Century City* (New York: Academic Press, 1979).

16   See RAB HOUSTON, *Scottish Literacy and the Scottish Identity* (Cambridge: Cambridge University Press, 1986). See also KENNETH LOCKRIDGE, *Literacy in Colonial New England* (New York: Norton, 1974).

17   DANIEL P. RESNICK and LAUREN B. RESNICK, "The Nature of Literacy: An Historical Explanation," *Harvard Educational Review* 47 (1977): 370–85.

18   United Nations, Educational, Scientific and Cultural Organization, *World Conference of Ministers of Education on the Eradication of Illiteracy, Final Report* (Tehran, Iran, 1965).

19   13th Session of Unesco's General Conference, quoted in *The Experimental World Literacy Program: A Critical Assessment* (Paris: Unesco Press and UNDP, 1976), p. 9.

20   YUSSAF KASSAM and BUD HALL, "Tanzania's National Literacy Campaign: A Journey of Imagination, Energy, and Commitment," unpublished paper, International Council for Adult Education, Toronto, 1985, p. 7.

21   United Nations Food and Agricultural Organization (FAO), "The Declaration of Persepolis," *Ideas and Action* 10 (1975), p. 43; also see BATAILLE, *Turning Point*.

22   See also GERALD STRAUSS, Luther's House of Learning.

23   See also HOUSTON, *Scottish Literacy*; LOCKRIDGE, *Literacy*.

24   EGIL JOHANSSON, "The History of Literacy in Sweden," in *Literacy and Social Development in the West*, ed. HARVEY J. GRAFF (Cambridge: Cambridge University Press, 1981), pp. 151–83.

25   See BHOLA, *Campaigning*, pp. 89–990; see also Chapter 7 in *NLC*, and ROBERT F. ARNOVE, "Education in China and India," *Comparative Education Review* 28 (August 1984), pp. 378–401.

26   KENEZ, "Liquidating Illiteracy," pp. 180–81, quoted in EKLOF, "Russian."

27   There was similar imagery and sloganeering in the Cuban and Nicaragua campaigns, with territories being declared free of "illiteracy" when more than eighty percent in a hamlet, village, or city had achieved literacy. Illiteracy was viewed as a scourge to be eliminated by a conquering army of literacy brigades.

28   JOHANSSON, *The History of Literacy in Sweden* (Umeå: School of Education, Umeå University, Sweden, 1977), p. 11.

29   See MAX WEBER's essay on "The Rationalization of Education and Training" for a later view of the reasons for educational requirements in the German civil service, in *From Max Weber*, Ed. H. H. GERTH and C. WRIGHT MILLS (Oxford: Oxford University Press, 1946).

30   On compulsion, see M. J. MAYNES, *Schooling for the People: Comparative Local Studies of Schooling History in France and Germany, 1750–1850* (New York: Holmes and Meier, 1985), DAVID TYACK, "Ways of Seeing: An Essay on the History of Compulsory Schooling," *Harvard Educational Review* 46 (1976), pp. 355–389, W. M. LANDES and LEWIS C. SOLOMAN, "Compulsory Schooling Legislation," *Journal of Economic History* 32 (1972), pp. 36–61; CARL KAESTLE and MARIS VINOVSKIS, *Education and Social Change in Nineteenth-Century Massachusetts* (New York: Cambridge University Press, 1980), an the two books by MICHAEL B. KATZ, *The Irony of Early School Reform* (Cambridge, MA: Harvard University Press, 1968) and *Class, Bureaucracy and Schools*, 2nd ed. (New York: Praeger, 1975).

31   On formal vs. informal and nonformal learning of literacy, see SYLVIA SCRIBNER and MICHAEL COLE, *The Psychology of Literacy* (Cambridge, MA: Harvard University Press, 1981).

32   BHOLA, *Campaigning*, p. 57.

33   ROGER PETHYBRIDGE, *The Social Prelude to Stalinism* (London: 1974), p. 152, cited in Chapter 6 this volume.

34   BHOLA, *Campaigning*, p. 57.

35   ARNOVE, "Education in China and India," p. 382.

36   R. W. SCRIBNER, "Incombustible Luther: The Image of the Reformer in Early Modern German," *Past and Present* 110 (1986), pp. 38–68.

37   See ARNOVE, "The 1990 Nicaraguan National Literacy Crusade," in *NLC*.

38   R. W. SCRIBNER, *For the Sake of Simple Folk: Popular Propaganda for the German Reformation* (Cambridge: Cambridge University Press, 1981); see also "History of Literacy" in JOHANSSON, *The History of Literacy in Sweden*.

39   RICHARD FAGEN, *The Transformation of Political Culture in Cuba* (Stanford: Stanford University Press, 1969), p. 56; see also JONATHAN KOZOL, *Children of the Revolution* (New York: Delacorte, 1978 and Chapter 8 below.)

40   BHOLA, *Campaigning*.

41 KASSAM and HALL, "Tanzania's Campaign." For historical situations, see SCRIBNER, "Incombustible Luther," PETER CLARK, *English Provincial Society from the Reformation to the Revolution* (Hassocks: Harvester, 1977), and E. P. THOMPSON, *The Making of the English Working Class* (New York: Pantheon, 1963).

42 On the notion of "andragogy," see ARTHUR GILLETTE, "The Experimental World Literacy Program," in *NLC*.

43 GERALD STRAUSS, *Luther's House of Learning*, pp. 22; see also RICHARD GAWTHORP, "Literacy Drives in Preindustrial Germany," in *NLC*, GAWTHORP and STRAUSS, "Literacy and Protestantism," STRAUSS, "Lutheranism," and MAYNES, *Schooling*.

44 RESNICK and RESNICK, "Nature," LOCKRIDGE, *Literacy*; see also LEE SOLTOW and EDWARD STEVENS, *The Rise of Literacy and the Common School* (Chicago: University of Chicago Press, 1982). For English comparisons, see DAVID CRESSY, *Literacy and the Social Order* (Cambridge: Cambridge University Press, 1980) and RICHARD ALTICK, *The English Common Reader* (Chicago: University of Chicago Press, 1957). In general, see GRAFF, *Legacies*.

45 See GILLETTE, "Experimental"; CARRON and BORDIA, *Issues*.

46 See CARON and BORDIA, *Issues*, chapter on Vietnam.

47 CHARLES W. HAYFORD, "Literacy Movements in Modern China," in *NLC*. See also COHEN, "Civilizational States," EVELYN RAWSKI, *Education and Popular Literacy in Ch'ing China* (Ann Arbor: University of Michigan Press, 1979), KATHLEEN GOUGH, "Implications of Literacy in Traditional China and Indiana," in *Literacy in Traditional Societies*, ed. JACK GOODY (Cambridge: Cambridge University Press, 1968), pp. 69–84. RAWSKI and GOUGH, in particular, argue that the orthographic obstacle to literacy has been exaggerated.

48 See also RAWSKI, *Education*.

49 See chapter 13 this volume; see also FRANCOIS FURET and JACQUES OZOUF, *Lire et écrire: L'alphabètisation des français de Calvin à Ferry* (Paris: Editions de Minuit, 1977), esp. Vol 1 (translated into English as *Reading and Writing* (Cambridge: Cambridge University Press, 1983).

50 See KASSAM and HALL, "Tanzania's Campaign."

51 See, e.g. ARTHUR GILLETTE, *Literacy and Youth*.

52 See ARNOVE, "1980 Nicaraguan."

53 Sometimes the quantitative outcomes are not impressive. The results of the EWLP indicate that little more than ten percent of the one million individuals who participated in the program in eleven countries completed a test of literacy attainment; see GILLETTE, "Experimental."

54 See following discussions and GRAFF, *Legacies*.

55 See following discussions, JOHN BORMUTH, "*Illiteracy in the Suburbs*," mimeograph. Department of Education, University of Chicago, October 1970. ROBERT F. ARNOVE and JAIRO ARBOLEDA, "Literacy: Power or Mystification," *Literary Discussion* 4 (December 1973), pp. 389–414, STREET, *Literacy*, and KOZOL, *Illiteracy*.

56 On evaluation as a component of the ELWP, see GILLETTE, "Experimental"; see also JAN L. FLORA, JOHN McFADDEN, and RUTH WARNER, "The Growth of Class Struggle: The Impact of the Nicaraguan Literacy Crusade on the Political Consciousness of Young Literacy Workers," *Latin American Perspectives*, 36 (Winter, 1983), pp. 49–53, and KASSAM, *Illiterate No More: The Voices of New Literates from Tanzania* (Dar es Salaam: Tanzania Publishing House, 1979). For earlier works on literacy, education and modernization, see ALEX INKELES and DAVID SMITH, *Becoming Modern: Individual Change in Six Developing Countries* (Cambridge, MA: Harvard University Press, 1974) and DANIEL LERNER, *The Passing of Traditional Society* (Glencoe: Free Press, 1958).

57 See BHOLA, *Campaigning*, p. 25 and ARNOVE, "1980 Nicaraguan."

58 Bhola, *Campaigning*, p. 22.
59 Carron and Bordia, *Issues*, p. 35.
60 S. Lurie, "Preface," in Carron and Bordia, *Issues*.
61 Arnove, *Education and Revolution in Nicaragua* (New York: Praeger, 1986), esp. Chapter 3.
62 Historically, social class formation has been part and parcel of the same process; see Graff, *Legacies*.
63 See Fernando Cardenal and Valerie Miller, "Nicaragua 1980: The Battle of the ABCs," *Harvard Educational Review* 51 (1981): 1–26.
64 Conversely, a regime may lose legitimacy if it fails to mount a successful literacy campaign. This issue also merits study.
65 Kassam and Hall, "Tanzania's Campaign."
66 Henry M. Levin on "The Identity Crisis of Educational Planning," *Harvard Educational Review* 51 (1981): 85–93.

Part IV
Ends and Beginnings

15 Whither the History of Literacy?
The Future of the Past

The history of literacy, as a regular, formal, significant, and sometimes central concern of historian of a wide range of topical, chronological, and methodological inclinations, is certainly well established. The publication of a special issue of *Communication* on the history of literacy reinforces the point. But it also raises a key question: for the necessary relationship between the historical study of literacy and that of communications (past *or* present both) cannot fairly be said to have commenced, let alone grown to fruition. Exchanges between historical and contemporary literacy specialists and between historians of literacy and scholars in communications take place much too rarely for all involved. The active thrust and exceptional growth in historical literacy studies over the past decade and a half has propelled the subject to new prominence; yet, disciplinary and interdisciplinary linkages barely have advanced.

The maturation of the historical study of literacy has been enormously beneficial inside the academy and, on occasion, beyond its walls. Nevertheless, this significant body of scholarship demands attention more broadly: both in terms of what it may contribute to other researchers, planners, and thinkers, and in terms of its own growing needs for interdisciplinary cooperation and criticism. For example, historical literacy studies have been marked by their use of quantitative data and attention to issues of measurement. As important as the quantitative approach has been to initial advances, it also has been, or begins to become, a limitation toward new conceptualizations and, especially, interpretations. (There are instructive parallels here with communications studies.)

My principal concern in this essay is the present state of historical literacy studies, and their possible relations to scholarship in communications. For literacy studies, I think the present is an "awkward age," or stage of development. That I should sense this aspect of the moment is perhaps not surprising, for historical studies in general, after almost two decades of proliferating "new histories," are themselves in something of an awkward age. The recent appearance of a hefty number of books and articles proposing new emphases and directions all underscore this condition.¹ As the history of literacy joins the historiographical mainstream, it encounters similar challenges and questions. Communications research offers a parallel situation, and literacy's students sit, more or less uncomfortably, between these two (and perhaps other) disciplines. (Literacy studies, though, may be an exceptional case: for example, the distinctions between *quantities* and *qualities*, to use one dichotomy, exacerbate all questions of interpretation and meaning. Here, the quantitative record, no matter how essential to literacy's complete study and no matter how cleverly exploited, may have inherent limits at least as severe as those in other areas of historical or communications analysis.)

I referred to "an awkward age" for the historical study of literacy. I am tempted to conceive the field's development in terms of life courses or cycles, at least metaphorically, and to posit the present situation as one of late adolescence or youthfulness. But a *generational* perspective is more accurate than a life cycle one. In these terms, for the purposes of discussion and assessment, we might conceive of three *modern* generations of historical literacy studies.

The *first generation* includes principally the late-1960s work of Stone (1969), Cipolla (1969), and Schofield (1968), and was foreshadowed by the 1950s studies by Fleury and Valmary (1957) in France and Webb (1955) in England. The contributions here were several: to advance a strong case for the historical study of literacy—its direct study, that is—and for its import and significance as a historical factor; to review the general course of literacy's chronological trends and principal transitions and passages; to identify sources for fuller systematic exploitation— primarily (but not exclusively) numerical sources; to advance the case(s) for the utility of routinely-generated, systematic, and sometimes comparable and "direct" measures; and to posit, sometimes speculatively, the factors most closely tied to and responsible for changes in the course of literacy over time, its dynamics, distributions, impacts, and consequences.

A *second generation* grew directly from and was clearly stimulated by these earlier more sweeping and speculative students. Major studies of the second generation include Schofield's (1973) later work, Egil Johansson's studies (1977), and book-length reports by Lockridge (1974), Furet and Ozouf (1977), Cressy (1980), Stevens and Soltow (1981), Rab Houston (1985), Stephens (1987), and myself (1979). In addition, there exist numerous articles, monographs, local and regional studies, and theses and dissertations, mostly unpublished, especially in Great Britain and France.²

The emphasis became a larger, more detailed erection and exploitation of the quantitative record, usually but not always from signatory or census sources; greater concern for a more evidentially and sometimes also more contextually grounded historical interpretation of changing patterns—especially of distributions and differentiations in levels of literacy; relating literacy's trends to social and economic developments, institutional interventions, and state activities (especially factors like the availability of formal schooling and public school, systems, political transformations and events like the French Revolution, and the ideological aspects of the subject; concern with class formation; attention to the uses of literacy in terms both of patterns of reading and of individual and group attitudinal and psychological changes; and increased awareness of the contradictory nature of the subject and alertness to the difficulties in building historical interpretations upon a quantitative analysis of secular trendlines and patterns of distribution and differentiation (among many other aspects). The value of comparative frameworks also was recognized, though comparative studies remained rare.

As a result of this second generation of work, we know much more about literacy's social patterns over time and the fairly systematic and patterned variations in its distributions over time and place. We are perhaps also more hesitant and cautious in explanation and attribution of meaning (Graff, 1987a).

At the same time as the maturing of this "second generation," literacy also was "discovered" by an increasing number of historians, especially those employing quantitative methods and numerical sources which included some information on literacy (either on an aggregative, an ecological, or an individual level) or which were fairly easily linked to information sources on literacy. Thus, literacy increasingly was featured in studies of economic change, demographic trends, cultural development and conflict, class formation and stratification, collective actions of all kinds, family formation and structures, and the like, as the literature on all these key subjects now reflects. Interestingly, in this sphere of studies, literacy tended to be conceptualized most often as an *independent* variable, presumably useful in the explanation of another, dependent variable which was itself the object of more direct and sustained study. (In the history of communications, in partial but not complete contrast, literacy is now more often mentioned but infrequently directly examined: see Stevens and Garcia, 1980; Garcia, 1977.).

In the growing numbers of studies which took literacy itself as the central object of study and discussion, literacy could be and was conceptualized as either or both *dependent* or *independent* variable. At once a source of analytic and conceptual flexibility, this could also be a problem and a source of interpretive confusion and weakness: the nature of literacy as a (historical) variable is rarely examined critically. (Here too, the epistemological, methodological, and interpretative parallels to topics in communications studies should be clear.)

Finally, another group of historians, most interested in cultural, publishing, or literary topics, also tended increasingly to consider literacy within their purview. Although they rarely studied literacy's levels and patterns directly, they took it as a central factor or parameter for their own work: here one thinks of press and newspaper histories, *l'histoire du livre*, studies of popular culture which include new interest in oral culture and its interaction with literacy, and histories of print and publishing. Some of this work, such as that of Robert Darnton (1982, 1983, 1984) and Elizabeth Eisenstein (1979), is relatively closely allied to communications frameworks. We have learned much from such work, too much to summarize. Most of it, unfortunately, often remains unconnected to work focused directly on literacy itself. (For a new, interesting effort, see Gilmore, 1988.) (Martin, 1968–70, 1975, 1977; Burke, 1978; Febvre and Martin, 1958; Eisenstein, 1979; Joyce *et al.*, 1983; Carpenter, 1983; the journals *Revue français d'histoire du livre* and *Publishing History*; Feather, 1985; and critiques by Davis, 1975, and Darnton, 1972, 1982, 1983, 1984.)

Virtually all such work, it should be underscored, has labored under the spectre and shadows of *modernization theories* with their strong assumptions of literacy's role, powers, and provenance—an issue that must be confronted critically. Some students have chosen to challenge the assumptions of modernization's links to and impacts upon literacy (or *vice versa*); others have assimilated their work within the traditions of modernization theories, suffering conceptual and interpretive difficulties (which the empirical record alone seldom meets squarely and which remain to be examined). In some cases, the assumption of modernization actually substitutes for empirical, as well as critical research. Problems also include the persisting presence of obstructive dichotomies such as literate versus illiterate, print versus oral, and the like, none of which are interpretively rich or complex enough to advance our understanding.

The *third generation* now awaits us. It has barely raised its head, although I shall relate my thoughts about its agendas and emphases. In part, I believe, discussion must now focus upon the "needs and opportunities"—questions, sources, methods—of the third generation. In fact, the most recent studies begin to point the way;[3] ground-breaking work in contemporary studies usefully demonstrates the basic areas and aspects of interdisciplinary collaboration, especially respecting historians of literacy and students of communications.

In part, two new and original directions in the social scientific study of literacy offer intriguing and tantalizing leads to historians (as well as to contemporary students). Here I think, in particular, of the social-psychological work—sometimes brilliant and often path-breaking in its implications—of the experimental, ethnographic, and comparative cognitive psychologists, Sylvia Scribner and Michael Cole, especially in their *The Psychology of Literacy* (1981) and in Scribner's continuing studies of the skills, including reading and writing, required and utilized in different kinds of work settings and demands. I also refer to the community-based ethnographies of literacy and education brought together by anthropologist and linguist Shirley Heath in *Ways with Words: Language, Life and Work in Communities and Classrooms* (1983). Together, they underscore the import for literacy of *context* of learning and use, nature of *acquisition, culture,* and *tradition,* and the like. Especially striking are their focus on communication, in theory and in practice, and on ethnography. They offer much to historians by example and analogy and conceptualization and indicate one possible agenda for the "third generation."

Several other recent studies lead us into different and wider terrains. Janice Radway's *Reading the Romance: Women, Patriarchy, and Popular Literature* (1984; see also Radway, 1986) proposes, and with a contemporary group of romance readers illustrates, that reading *can* be usefully and critically (and as her work in particular evidences, sympathetically) studied in contexts social, cultural, and political economic. Her imaginative practice is jointly informed by anthropological and literary critical perspectives; Radway also hints at the possibilities for historical efforts at this direction. In fact, creative research by David Vincent (1981) and Sally Mitchell (1981) shows potential for historical applications, via autobiographical and literary sources, for working-class and middle-class women, respectively. In this respect, the pioneering and idiosyncratic, if not always persuasive, writings of Carlo Ginzburg (1980) and Robert Darnton (1984) suggests the depths and insights that close study of reading practices set into socioculturally-informed communicative contexts may yield. In these examples, I add, the limits of the work are as rich as are the real achievements. (See also Scribner, 1981, 1984; Burke, 1978, 1987; Davidson, 1986; Isaac, 1976a, 1976b, 1982; Stout, 1977; Kaplan, 1984; Goody, 1986, 1987; Thomas, 1986; Muchembled, 1986.)

The occasion for these reflections, happily, coincides with a highly significant moment for historical studies of literacy—and perhaps for communications research, too. If my surmises are at least partially accurate, the field of inquiry is today at a crossroads. We ask, not at all frivolously or lightly: Whither historians of literacy? If the second-generation—having firmly established the field of the history of literacy—is winding down now, and if my sensing a diminishing of new researchers and research projects focused directly on literacy is also an accurate reading, and if we assume that literacy deserves and demands further study and consideration, we also recognize that 1) many gaps in the record remain to be completed; 2) many questions—some only relatively recently posed—remain to be answered; and 3) key problems in conceptualization, interpretation, and explanation mark these efforts. Consideration of the outlines and agendas of a hypothetical "third generation" is of more than academic interest.

In part, we need to shift our dialogue from quantitative methods to critical questions applied to quantitative findings. We do well to ponder the links in terms of both continuities and changes between the second generation (represented so strongly in the literature) and my proposed "third generation." I propose that we take stock and assess recent studies with an aim toward future studies conceived and designed in novel ways. It is that discussion these discursive reflections aim at stimulating.

The achievements of historical literacy studies are many and clear. (No simple summary of that richness is possible or necessary here.) Persisting patterns of limitations also mark the field. Increasingly, we recognize limits of quantitative analysis alone—and of aggregative and ecological methods and research designs. In some ways, I aver, we are only now coming to the most important questions and issues: that perhaps, in addition to time series and patterns of variation, will be seen as one of the major contributions of generations one and especially two. In part, there has been a shattering of "received wisdom" (as in "literacy myths"), expectations, assumptions—that, it should be underscored, is no small accomplishment. The obverse, however, is the question of what will replace it—in part a theoretical issue. This is reflected in the "great debates" about literacy's relationships to economic (i.e., commercial and/or industrial) and social development, political mobilization, religion, social mobility, social class formation, work and leisure life patterns, and social change more generally. Questions about method, such as those of dependent versus independent variables, levels of aggregation, and problems of correlational analysis, follow. The demand for critical reflection now falls upon conceptualization, method, and interpretation.

Historian Rab Houston (1983, p. 279) captures the spirit of this moment when he usefully comments,

> If attempts to explain structures and trends in illiteracy have been less satisfactory than simple expositions of them, analysis of the meaning of literacy is even more rudimentary. The field has seen a proliferation of merely statistical analyses of which it seems trite to say that the well-established structural measures such as regional or male-female difference must be seen in the context of social and political institutions, attitudes surrounding class and gender, but above all of the ways in which power is ordered and preserved. . . . The study of education and literacy has become less anecdotal and parochial but the lack of a proper context prevents us from understanding its place in social development. Education is dealt with too much in its own terms. Even those studies which purport to analyze the interaction of education, literacy and society tend to select only a few simple aspects such as the way educational provision reflected the demands of different groups or how wealth, status and literacy overlap. Literacy can certainly be used as a valuable indicator of social divisions, but in what way did it help to preserve and perpetuate them?

In one way, the path lies in moving beyond literacy as a dichotomous variable, perceived either as conservative and controlling or as liberating. This might constitute moving toward a cultural politics and a political economy of literacy in history. There are a number of possible avenues. Very synoptically, I will suggest some now, with an eye toward setting an agenda for the elusive "third-generation"—and toward bridging historians to other students of literacy and communications.

Most generally, historical literacy studies must build upon their own past while also breaking away from it. The work of the "second generation," such as that for example of Furet and Ozouf (1977), Cressy (1980), or Soltow and Stevens (1981), delineates parameters, baselines, and key interrelationships that offer opportunities to investigate more precisely the linkages and to seek refinements in the specifications of factors and their interactions. These range from literacy's relations with class, sex, age, and culture to larger themes of economic development, social order, mobility and stratification, education and schooling, the actual uses of literacy, language and culture, and so forth. One demand falls upon much sharper contextual grounding, often in clearly delineated localities. Others encompass the completion of time series, among other quantitative analyses.

Second is the advancement of *comparative study*. This requires a greater appreciation and emphasis on source criticism and recognition of the different meanings of different measures of literacy among different populations as evidenced from varying sources. Contextualization here is also critical for comparisons, as Johansson's and Houston's work in particular illustrates. Also critical is the further search for indicators of the levels and the quality of literacy, allowing us to advance beyond the limiting dichotomy of literate versus illiterate. Novel approaches to the combination of records and to record linkage stand out on the agenda.

Third is the major need for new conceptualizations of *context* in the historical study of literacy. Recognizing that literacy acquires meaning and significance only within specified historical contexts does not in itself reduce the risks of abstracted analysis. Novel work in anthropology and psychology, like that of Heath (1983) and Scribner and Cole (1981), mentioned above, provides important suggestions and guidelines for historians. The tasks lie not only in defining and specifying context for study and interpretation but also in delineating the varying levels of context—vertically or horizontally, for example—and in experimenting with ways to operationalize them. Stevens' (1985) focus on illiterates in judicial settings and Johansson's (1977, 1981, 1985) perspective on church and community suggest two opportunities to probe more intensively. Carlo Ginzburg's (1980) writings may provide another; so too may those of Radway (1984), Darnton (1972, 1982, 1983, 1984), Davidson (1986), Vincent (1981), Burke (1987), and Mitchell (1981). Gilmore's (1988) localized case study reiterates the richness of the records. For the recent past, oral histories, library use records, and participant observation or ethnographies of communication offer other possibilities.[4]

Contexts for analysis are many and diverse. They range from those of acquisition, use, and action, to those of individual, family, group or community, gender, or social class. The scope for defined study is itself variable, but should include material conditions, motivations, opportunities, needs and demands, traditions, and transformations. In this way, linguistic forms, dialects, communication channels and networks, "pushes" and "pulls" from religion, culture, politics, the economy, and so forth, may be incorporated. Literacy's relationship to personal and/ or collective efficacy and activism—a source of much debate—may also be further explored, in part in analysis of specific events and processes and in part in terms of patterns of communications and mobilization within defined contexts. Class formation and vital behavior are just two of the many key topics calling for examination.

Are "historical ethnographies"—conceptualized fully in terms of literacy among the modes and relations of communications—of literacy possible? Recent work, such as that noted here, contains fascinating hints in that direction which merit fuller examination. A number of recent studies in popular culture—for example, those of Carlo Ginzburg (1980), Peter Burke (1978, 1987), Emmanuel LeRoy Ladurie (1978), Bob Scribner (1981, 1984), Keith Wrightson and David Levine (1979), Cathy Davidson (1986), Harry Stout (1977), and Rhys Isaac (1976a, 1976b, 1982)—may prove stimulating beginning models. Clearly, the subject and its significance stimulate a fair test. The current interests (within anthropology and elsewhere) in an anthropology of communications in ethnographies of reading and writing at varying levels of context and generality are guides to follow. (See, for example, Heath, 1983; Whiteman, 1981.)

On one hand, literacy may be viewed as one among other "media" and its roles and impacts evaluated. On the other hand, ethnographic and communicative approaches have the potential to expand perspectives while simultaneously grounding them more precisely for meaningful interpretation. Novel contextualization can also be a boost to the renewal and refinement of quantitative studies. Context, in sum, offers both new and better cases for study, opportunities for explanation, and approaches to literacy's changing and variable historical meanings and contributions.

A fourth consideration follows. This is the difficult but severe demand for critical examination of the *conceptualization of literacy* itself. The "second generation" has taught us about the contradictions central to literacy's history, while also revealing the problems in treating literacy as an independent variable and the confusions that inhere in treating literacy as either or both dependent and independent (Graff, 1979). Questions of contextualization may well limit analysis of literacy as independent; they will also, I think, stimulate new formulations of the nature of literacy as a dependent factor. In the process, new considerations about levels and quality of literacy must transcend the related limits of the tradition of conceptualizing literacy as a dichotomous variable. The psychological and anthropological studies promise to contribute here too. The body of work of the "second generation" collectively underscores the special complications whose resolution ranks high on any agenda. To transcend it requires excavation of other relevant aspects of communicative culture—always including the oral and visual—among which literacy, in shifting degrees and mediations, takes its place.

Fifth is the question of literacy and what might well be termed the "creation of meaning." Historical study of literacy has been little influenced by recent debates in intellectual and cultural history, literary criticism, cognitive psychology, cultural anthropology and ethnography, or critical theories of communication. In some manner, the origins of these current emphases stem from dissatisfaction with traditional approaches to "texts," their understanding, and their communication. More recently, the entire enterprise of grasping the "creation," maintenance, and communication of "meaning" has changed in major respects potentially relevant to issues central to literacy. Cultural and intellectual history are themselves, along with major aspects of the humanities and the social sciences—together, the human sciences—in a significant time of ferment and wider exploration of their parameters; so too, importantly, are literary criticism, cognitive and cultural psychology, and some areas of philosophy. Concerns about interactions between readers and texts, responses to writing and print, shaping of individual and collective processes of cognition, and the ways in which "meaning" is created, influenced, transmitted, and changed are common, if not always clarified.[5] Possibly to its detriment, the history of literacy stands in isolation from interdisciplinary rapprochement. Questions about literacy's contribution to individual, class, and collective awareness, patterns of cognitive (and also noncognitive) attitudinal formation, and cultural behavior more generally all underscore this need. The nagging issue of the uses of literacy, and their consequences, deserves new exploration.

The need for a sharper theoretical awareness of the relevance of the history of literacy for many important aspects of social, economic, and psychological theory, constitutes a sixth point. This is implied in the foregoing. Historical studies of literacy do provide significant opportunities for testing theories, and insofar as their results continue to raise criticisms of "normative" theoretical expectations and assumptions, there may be prospects for essaying new formulations. Communications—study and practice—itself can only gain from this encounter.

A seventh consideration, raised as a question of methodology, indeed of epistemology, links all of the above. Has the tradition, from two generations of studies, of taking literacy as primary object of analysis—"the history of literacy" per se—approached an end point? Should a "third generation" rooted at least in part in the foregoing refocus itself in terms of literacy as a significant—indeed a necessary—aspect of other relevant investigations? The question, simply put, is that of shifting from "historical studies of literacy" to "histories that encompass literacy within their context and conceptualization," from "the history of literacy" to "literacy in history." There is reason to argue, I think, that the limits of the "second generation's" conceptualization encourage the exploration of what that transformation would entail. To move in this direction is no simple task: I call for the reconceptualization and the mutual interaction not only of the history of literacy but of the history of communications as well.

Finally, I call attention to the relevance of the history of literacy for a number of policy areas in societies "developed" and "underdeveloped" today, and to the additional contributions that reconceptualization might bring. Historical analysis can contribute to understanding and fashioning responses to deal with those problems that are sometimes deemed "literacy crises." In grasping that there are many paths to literacy, that literacy's relations to social and economic development are complex, that the quantity and the quality of literacy (and literacy's possession and its use) are not linearly related, that the consequences of literacy are neither direct nor simple, and that literacy is never neutral, historians have much to share with their fellow students and to offer those who formulate social policies. That in itself is no small contribution.

Consider for example the concept of multiple paths to the making of literate societies and states. The historical study of literacy shows clearly that there is *no one* route to universal literacy, and there is *no one* path destined to succeed in the achievement of mass literacy. In the history of the Western world, we may distinguish the roles of private and public schooling in various configurations in the attainment of high rates of popular literacy, as well as the operation of informal and formal, voluntary and compulsory schooling. Mass literacy was achieved in Sweden, for example, without formal schooling or instruction in writing (Johannson, 1981). High rates of literacy have followed from all of these approaches in different cases and contexts. The developmental consequences are equally varied. The importance of this discovery lies precisely in that:

> perhaps the most striking feature of UNESCO discussions on literacy, since 1965 when a campaign to wipe out illiteracy got going, is that it is little based on either experiment or historical precedents. Rather, in spite of Adam Curle's careful warnings in 1964, action seems as much based on self-evident axioms and hopes as on anything else. UNESCO assumes that literacy is a good thing—more latterly functional literacy. Furthermore, in no clearly believed or understood way poverty, disease, and general backwardness are believed connected with illiteracy; progress, health, and economic well-being are equally self-evidently connected with literacy. UNESCO is committed to what amounts to a modernization theory to the effect that economic progress follows upon a change in many from illiterate to literate, preferably in one generation, and, even better, in the very same man. It is presupposed that such a change will lead, if not immediately then inevitably, to such changes and values in a society that economic progress—and in its train good health, longevity, and, perhaps, peace—is possible. (Winchester, 1978, 1980: 1. See also Arnove and Graff, 1987.)

The past provides, importantly, a different set of experiences than those behind these common expectations. Although neither all of the research nor the balance sheet of historical interpretation is in, we may argue that historical experiences provide a better guide to such crucial questions as how and to what extent basic literacy contributes to the economic and individual well being of persons in different socioeconomic and cultural contexts, and under what circumstances universal literacy can be achieved. The costs and benefits of alternative paths can be discerned, and estimated, too. Thus, the connections and disconnections between literacy and commercial development, a generally positive relationship, and literacy and industrial development, often an unfavorable linkage at least in the short run of decades and half-centuries, offer important case studies and analogs for analysis. The data of the past strongly suggest that a simple, linear, modernization model of literacy as prerequisite for development and development as stimulant to increased levels of schooling will not suffice. Too many periods of lags, backward linkages, setbacks, and contradictions exist to permit such cavalier theorizing to continue without serious challenge and criticism.

The example of Sweden is especially significant in this regard. This case provides the most richly documented illustration of a transition to mass literacy in the Western world, and thus has much to teach us. As shown by the pioneering researches of Egil Johansson (1977, 1981, 1985), near-universal levels of literacy were achieved rapidly and permanently in Sweden in the wake of the Lutheran Reformation. Under the joint efforts of Church and State, from the seventeenth century reading literacy was required under law for all persons. Within a century or so, remarkably high levels of literacy among the population existed—without any concomitant development of formal schooling or economic or cultural change that demanded functional or practical employment of literacy skills. Moreover, literacy grew in a manner that led to its being defined by reading and not by writing. Urbanization, commercialization, and industrialization had virtually nothing to do with the process of making the Swedish people perhaps the most literate in the West before the eighteenth century. Contrary to paths to literacy taken elsewhere, this campaign, begun by King Charles IX, was sponsored by the State Church. By legal requirement and vigilant supervision that included regular personal examinations by parish clergy, the church stood above a system rooted in home education. The rationale for the literacy campaign, one of the most successful in history before the nineteenth century, was conservative: piety, civility, orderliness, and military preparedness were the major goals. The former were as important as the others, and in the end, they were the decisive ones.

Significantly, the home and church education model fashioned by the Swedes not only succeeded in training up a literate population, but it also placed a special priority on the literacy of women and mothers. This led to Sweden's anomalous achievement of female literacy rates as high as male rates or higher, a rare pattern in the Western history of transitions to mass literacy. Sweden also marched to its impressive levels of reading diffusion without mass achievement of writing—alerting us to the variable roles and mixes of different media, literate and others; it was not until the mid-nineteenth-century erection of a state-supported public school system that writing, in addition to reading, became a regular part of popular literacy and a concern of educationists and teachers. Finally, note that the only other areas that so fully and quickly achieved near-universal levels of literacy before the end of the eighteenth century were places of intensely pious religion, usually but not always Protestant: New England, Huguenot French centers, areas of Germany and Switzerland, and parts of Scotland. There are lessons in these histories.

Literacy's relationships to paths to economic development, mentioned above, are another case in point. So, too, are the connections of literacy with social development. In this case, we discover again a history of continuities and contradictions, and of variable paths to societal change and development. From the classical era forward, leaders of polities and churches, reformers as well as conservers, have recognized the uses of literacy and schooling. Often they have perceived unbridled, untempered literacy as potentially dangerous, a threat to social order, political integration, economic productivity, and patterns of authority. Increasingly, however, they came to conclude that literacy, if provided in carefully controlled, structured, formal institutions created expressly for the purposes of education and transmission of literacy and supervised closely, could be a powerful and useful force in achieving a variety of important ends. Precedents long predated the first systematic mass efforts to put this conception of literacy into practice, in Rome, for example, and in the visionary proposals of the fifteenth- and sixteenth-century Christian humanists. For our purposes, the Reformations of the sixteenth century represented the first great literacy campaigns. They were hardly homogeneous efforts, as Sweden reminds us, in either design or degree of success. Nonetheless, they were precedent-setting and epochal in their significance for the future of social and educational development throughout the world.

With the Enlightenment and its heritage came the final ideological underpinnings for the "modern" and "liberal" reforms of popular schooling and institutional building that established the network of educational-social-political-cultural-economic relationships central to the dominant ideologies and their theoretical and practical expressions for the past two centuries. Prussia, revealingly, took the lead, and provided a laboratory that United States, Canadian, English, French, and Scandinavian school promoters and reformers regularly came to study. North Americans and Swedes followed in Prussia's wake, and, in time and in their own ways, so did the English, French, Italians—and recently vast areas of the developing world.

Of course, other important uses of literacy—for personal advancement, entertainment, study, collective action, and the like—must not be slighted. The significance and potential of literacy to individuals and to groups throughout history, even if sometimes taken out of context and exaggerated, is undoubted. The role of social class and group-specific demands for literacy's skills, the impact of motivation, and the growing perceptions of its value and benefits are among the major factors that explain the historical contours of changing rates of popular literacy. In other words, "demand" must be appreciated, as well as "supply," stimuli from "below" as well as force and compulsion from "above" in intricately reciprocal and dialectical relationships. Literacy's limits, history reminds, and its roles in promoting and maintaining hegemony, merit emphasis too. And their deeper exploration and understanding may depend on the new approaches suggested above.

Especially with the transitions from preindustrial social orders based in rank and deference to the class societies of commercial and then factory capitalism, the integrating and hegemony-creating purposes of literacy provision through formal schooling only increased. Schooling, with its transmission of a morally-leavened and often qualitatively low level of skills, became a more and more vital aspect of the maintenance of social stability—particularly during times of massive if confusing social and economic transformations—and a regular feature of the young's life course. Many persons, most prominently social and economic leaders and social reformers, grasped the uses of schooling and the vehicle of literacy for promoting the values, attitudes, and habits deemed essential to order, integration, cohesion, and certain forms of progress. The people's acceptance of literacy's import—not a simple process—forms the other dimension of this historical equation.

The issue of *quality*, as opposed to quantities, of literacy merits comment in conclusion. Because of the nature of the evidence, virtually all historical studies of literacy have concentrated on the measurement of the extent and distribution of reading and writing; issues concerning the qualitative levels, utilities, and actual uses, of the skills have attracted less attention. (This, of course, stems directly from considerations discussed earlier and its remedy on the proposed new agenda.) What research has been conducted, however, does point to a common conclusion that qualitative abilities cannot be deduced simply or directly from quantitative assessments of literacy's distribution. Studies of early modern England, eighteenth- and nineteenth-century Sweden, and urban areas through the West in the nineteenth century all indicate that there has long been a significant disparity between the popular levels of possession of literacy and the qualities and usefulness of those skills. In Sweden, for example, a great many persons who had attained high levels of *oral* reading ability did not have comparable skills in *comprehending* what they read. North American, English, and French data allow the wider generalization of this point.

The implications of these findings are many. First, the measurement of the distribution of literacy in a given population may in fact reveal relatively little about the uses to which such skills could be put and the degree to which the different demands on personal literacy could be satisfied with the skills commonly held. Second, it is also possible that with increasing rates of popular literacy did not come ever-rising capabilities or qualitative abilities—or ever-declining levels, as some would have it, either. Third—and potentially most important today—such evidence places the often-asserted contemporary decline of literacy in a new and distinctive context and encourages a fresher, historically-rooted perspective: mass levels of abilities to use literacy may have, over the long term, lagged behind the increases in literacy rates themselves. For some, like black Americans, great progress has occurred. This recognition also forces us to consider the impacts of changing communications modes and media, of which literacy in its alphabetic elements is just one. That is a task barely begun.

The recent decline, so often proclaimed, but so ineffectually measured and understood, may be *less* a major change than we are told. We need to pay more attention to longer term trends, changes in popular communicative abilities and channels, compositional factors within populations (in and outside of schools), and cultural changes in relation to media and technologies, than to "functional" or "competency" test results or "back to basics" movements.

This, of course, does not imply that real problems do not exist. Rather, it underscores the import of historical perspectives and understanding, actively and publicly joined to other disciplines and major contemporary issues of problems and policies. In this respect, recognition of the emergence of the history of literacy's "third generation" and of its relevance to nonhistorians is at once a first step and a paradigmatic one. Then we may speak of the future of the past, and that of the present, too.

Notes

These reflections on the state of research in the historical study of literacy originated with my comments presented at the session on literacy at the May, 1984, Bellagio Conference of the International Commission for the Application of Quantitative Methods to History on "The Transformation of Europe." For reasons of economy and space, I shall not present complete bibliographic citations for the text; interested readers may refer to my *Literacy in History: An Interdisciplinary Research Bibliography* (New York: Garland, 1981); *The Legacies of Literacy: Continuities and Contradictions in Western Society and Culture* (Bloomington: Indiana University Press, 1987); and *The Labyrinths of Literacy* (Sussex: Falmer Press, 1987). Some of the major examples of historical scholarship are collected in my *Literacy and Social Development in the West: A Reader* (Cambridge: Cambridge University Press, 1981). I thank Konrad Jarausch for inviting me to the conference, and John Nerone for asking me to contribute to this special issue of *Communication*.

1   For example, STONE's calls for retreats from social scientific and quantitative studies and hopes for "new narratives," attacks on social history, among many others. STONE (1979); ABRAMS (1980); HOBSBAWM (1980); KAMMEN (1980); RABB and ROTBERG (1982).
2   See GRAFF (1981a); references in GRAFF (1987); and in HOUSTON (1983).
3   The work in progress by EGIL JOHANSSON for Sweden and EDWARD STEVENS for nineteenth-century United States underscores this point.
4   See the articles by JOHANSSON and STEVENS in the special issue of *Historical Social Research*, No. 34 (Cologne, Germany, 1985) based on their contributions to the Bellagio Conference mentioned above. See also SCRIBNER (1981, 1984) LEROY LADURIE (1978); GRAFF (1979, 1981c, 1987); ISAAC (1976a, 1976b, 1983); GINZBURG (1980); STOUT (1977); BURKE (1987).
5   This literature—actually several different bodies of it—is much too vast to cite here. See for introductions, LACAPRA and KAPLAN (1982); HIGHAM and CONKIN (1979); RABB and ROTBERG (1982); and such journals as *Critical Inquiry*; *New Literary History*; *Representations*. See also KAPLAN (1984).

References

ABRAMS, PHILIP (1980). "History, Sociology, Historical Sociology." *Past & Present* 87:3–16.

ARNOVE, ROBERT F. and GRAFF, HARVEY J., eds.(1987). *National Literacy Campaigns: Historical and Comparative Perspectives*. New York: Plenum.

BURKE, PETER (1978). *Popular Culture in Early Modern Europe*. New York: Harper and Row.

—— (1987). *The Historical Anthropology of Early Modern Italy*. Cambridge: Cambridge University Press.

—— and PORTER, ROY, eds.(1987). *The Social History of Language*. Cambridge: Cambridge University Press.

CARPENTER, KENNETH E., ed. (1983). *Books and Society in History*. New York: R. R. Bowker.

CIPOLLA, CARLO (1969). *Literacy and Development in the West*. Harmondsworth: Penguin.

CRESSY, DAVID (1980). *Literacy and the Social Order*. Cambridge: Cambridge University Press.

DARNTON, ROBERT (1972). "Reading, Writing, and Publishing in Eighteenth-Century France." In *Historical Studies Today*. FELIX GILBERT and STEPHEN R. GRAUBARD (eds.). New York: Norton 238–250.

—— (1982). *The Literary Underground of the Old Regime*. Cambridge, MA: Harvard University Press.

—— (1983). "What is the History of Books?" In *Books and Society in History*. KENNETH E. CARPENTER (ed.). New York: R. R. Bowker. 3–28.

—— (1984). "Readers Respond to Rousseau: The Fabrication of Romantic Sensitivity." In DARNTON, *The Great Cat Massacre and Other Episodes in French Cultural History*. New York: Basic Books. 215–256.

DAVIDSON, CATHY N. (1986). *Revolution in the Word: The Rise of the Novel in America*. New York: Oxford University Press.

DAVIS, NATALIE Z. (1975). "Printing and the People." In DAVIS, *Society and Culture in Early Modern France*. Stanford: Stanford University Press. 189–226.

EISENSTEIN, ELIZABETH (1979). *The Printing Press as an Agent of Change*. 2 vols. Cambridge: Cambridge University Press.

FEATHER, JOHN (1985). *The Provincial Book Trade in Eighteenth-Century England*. Cambridge: Cambridge University Press.

FEBVRE, LUCIEN and MARTIN, HENRI-JEAN (1958). *L'apparition du livre*. Paris: Editions Albin Michel.

—— (1976). *The Coming of the Book*. London: New Left Books.

FLEURY, M. and VALMARY, P. (1957). "Les progrès de l'instruction élèmentaire de Louis XIV à Napoléon III." *Population* 12:71–92.

FURET, F. and OZOUF, J. (1977). *Live et ècrire*. 2 vols. Paris: Editions de Minuit.

—— (1983). *Reading and Writing*. Cambridge: Cambridge University Press.

GARCIA, HAZEL DICKEN (1977). "Communications in the Migration to Kentucky, 1769–1792." Ph.D. Dissertation, University of Wisconsin-Madison.

GILMORE, WILLIAM J. (1988). *Reading Becomes a Necessity of Life*. Knoxville: University of Tennessee Press.

GINZBURG, CARLO (1980). *The Cheese and the Worms*. Baltimore: Johns Hopkins University Press.

GOODY, JACK (1986). *The Logic of Writing and the Organization of Society*. Cambridge: Cambridge University Press.

—— (1987). *The Interface Between the Written and the Oral*. Cambridge: Cambridge University Press.

GRAFF, HARVEY J. (1979). *The Literacy Myth: Literacy and Social Structure in the Nineteenth-Century City*. New York and London: Academic Press.

—— (1981a). *Literacy in History: An Interdisciplinary Research Bibliography*. New York: Garland.

——, ed.(1981b). *Literacy and Social Development in the West*. Cambridge: Cambridge University Press.

—— (1981c). "Reflections on the History of Literacy: Overview, Critique, and Proposals." *Humanities in Society* 4:303–333.

—— (1987a). *The Legacies of Literacy: Continuities and Contradictions in Western Culture and Society*. Bloomington, IN: Indiana University Press.

—— (1987b). *The Labyrinths of Literacy: Reflections on Past and Present*. Sussex: Falmer Press.

HEATH, SHIRLEY BRICE (1983). *Ways with Words: Language, Life, and Work in Communities and Classrooms*. Cambridge: Cambridge University Press.

HIGHAM, JOHN and CONKIN, PAUL, eds. (1979). *New Directions in American Intellectual History*. Baltimore: Johns Hopkins University Press.

HOBSBAWM, E. J. (1980). "The Revival of Narrative: Some Comments." *Past & Present* 86:3–8.

HOUSTON, RAB (1983). "Literacy and Society in the West, 1500–1800." *Social History* 8:269–293.

—— (1985). *Scottish Literacy and the Scottish Identity: Illiteracy and Society in Scotland and Northern England, 1600–1800*. Cambridge: Cambridge University Press.

ISAACS, RHYS (1976a). "Dramatizing the Ideology of Revolution: Popular Mobilization in Virginia, 1774 to 1776." *William and Mary Quarterly* 33:357–385.

—— (1976b). "Preachers and Patriots: Popular Culture and the Revolution in Virginia." In *The American Revolution*, ed. ALFRED F. YOUNG. Dekalb: Northern Illinois University Press. 125–156.

—— (1982). *The Transformation of Virginia* Chapel Hill: University of North Carolina Press.

JOHANSSON, EGIL (1977). *The History of Literacy in Sweden*. Educational Reports, Umeå, no. 12. Umeå, Sweden: Umeå University and School of Education.

—— (1981). "The History of Literacy in Sweden." In *Literacy and Social Development in the West*, ed. HARVEY J. GRAFF. Cambridge: Cambridge University Press. 151–182.

—— (1985). "Popular Literacy in Scandinavia about 1600–1900." *Historical Social Research* No. 34:60–64.

JOYCE, WILLIAM L., HALL, DAVID D., BROWN, RICHARD D., and HENCH, JOHN B., eds. (1983). *Printing and Society in Early America*. Worcester, MA: American Antiquarian Society.

KAMMEN, MICHAEL, ed. (1980). *The Past Before Us*. Ithaca: Cornell University Press.

KAPLAN, STEVEN L., ed. (1984). *Understanding Popular Culture: Europe from the Middle Ages to the Nineteenth Century*. Berlin: Mouton.

LeCAPRA, DOMINIC and KAPLAN, STEVEN L., eds. (1982). *Modern European Intellectual History*. Ithaca: Cornell University Press.

LeROY LADURIE, EMMANUEL (1978). *Montaillou: Promised Land of Error*. New York: Braziller.

LEVINE, DAVID (1979). "Education and Family Life in Early Industrial England." *Journal of Family History* 4:368–380.

LOCKRIDGE, KENNETH A. (1974). *Literacy in Colonial New England*. New York: Norton.

MARTIN, HENRI-JEAN (1975). "Culture écrite et culture orale, culture savante et culture populaire dans la France d'Ancien Regime." *Journale des Savants*: 225–282.

—— (1977). "Pour une histoire de la lecture." *R'evue française d'histoire du livre* 16:583–609.

—— (1968–70). *Le livre et la civilisation écrite*. 3 vols. Paris: Ecole nationale superieure des bibliotèques.

MITCHELL, SALLY (1981). *The Fallen Angel: Chastity, Class and Women's Reading, 1835–1880*. Bowling Green, OH: Popular Press.

MUCHEMBLED, ROBERT (1985, 1978). *Popular Culture and Elite Culture in France, 1400–1750*. Baton Rouge: Louisiana State University Press.

RABB, THEODORE K. and ROTBERG, ROBERT I., eds. (1982). *The New History: 1980s and Beyond*. Princeton: Princeton University Press.

RADWAY, JANICE A. (1984). *Reading the Romance: Women, Patriarchy, and Popular Literature*. Chapel Hill: University of North Carolina Press.

—— (1986). "Identifying Ideological Seams: Mass Culture, Analytic Method, and Political Practice." *Communication* 9:93–123.

SCHOFIELD, ROGER S. (1968). "The Measurement of Literacy in Preindustrial England." In *Literacy in Traditional Societies*, ed. JACK GOODY. Cambridge: Cambridge University Press. 311–325.

—— (1973). "The Dimensions of Illiteracy in England, 1750–1850." *Explorations in Economic History* 10:437–454.

SCRIBNER, R. W. (1981). *For the Sake of Simple Folk: Popular Propaganda for the German Reformation*. Cambridge: Cambridge University Press.

—— (1984). "Oral Culture and the Diffusion of Reformation Ideas." *History of European Ideas* 5:237–256.

SCRIBNER, SYLVIA and COLE, MICHAEL (1981). *The Psychology of Literacy*. Cambridge, MA: Harvard University Press.

SOLTOW, LEE and STEVENS, EDWARD (1981). *The Rise of Literacy and the Common School in the United States*. Chicago: University of Chicago Press.

STEPHENS, W. B. (1987). *Education, Literacy, and Society, 1830–1870*. Manchester: Manchester University Press.

STEVENS, EDWARD (1985). "Literacy and the Worth of Liberty." *Historical Social Research* No. 34:65–81.

STEVENS, JOHN D. and GARCIA, HAZEL DICKEN (1980). *Communication History*. Beverly Hills: Sage.

STONE, LAWRENCE (1969). "Literacy and Education in England, 1640–1900." *Past & Present* 42:69–139.

—— (1979). "The Revival of Narrative: Reflections on a New Old History." *Past & Present* 85:3–24.

STOUT, HARRY S. (1977). "Religion, Communications, and the Ideological Origins of the American Revolution." *William and Mary Quarterly* 34:519–541.

STRAUSS, GERALD (1978). *Luther's House of Learning*. Baltimore: Johns Hopkins University Press.

—— (1984). "Lutheranism and Literacy: A Reassessment." In *Religion and Society in Early Modern Europe*, ed. KASPAR VON GREYERZ. London: Allen and Unwin. 109–123.

—— and GAWTHROP, RICHARD (1984). "Protestantism and Literacy in Early Modern Germany." *Past & Present* 104:31–55.

THOMAS, KEITH (1986). "The Meaning of Literacy in Early Modern England." In *The Written Word: Literacy in Transition*, ed. GERD BAUMANN. Oxford: Oxford University Press. 97–131.

THOMPSON, PAUL (1975). *The Edwardians*. Bloomington: Indiana University Press.

—— (1978). *The Voice of the Past: Oral History*. Oxford: Oxford University Press.

VINCENT, DAVID (1981). *Bread, Knowledge and Freedom: A Study of Nineteenth-Century Working Class Autobiography*. London: Europa.

WEBB, ROBERT K. (1955). *The British Working Class Reader*. London: Allen and Unwin.

WHITEMAN, MARCIA FARR, ed. (1981). *Writing: The Nature, Development and Teaching of Written Composition. Vol. 1: Variation in Writing*. Hillsdale, NJ: Lawrence Erlbaum.

WINCHESTER, IAN (1978, 1980). "How many ways to universal literacy?" Paper presented to the Ninth World Congress of Sociology, Uppsala, 1978, and Seminar on the History of Literacy in Post-Reformation Europe, University of Leicester, 1980.

WRIGHTSON, KEITH AND LEVINE, DAVID (1979). *Poverty and Piety*. New York and London: Academic Press.

16   Literacy, Myths, and Legacies:
Lessons from the History of Literacy

Unlike many discussions, the circumstances that prompted these comments was *not* the proclamation of an imminent "crisis" or "decline." With respect to literacy today—or education or development—this is unusual. Nevertheless, I fear, that sense accompanies us closely, shadowing our critical and creative work, offering scant illumination, often leading us astray. Consider, on the one hand, today's sirens of "cultural" or "historical literacy." On the other hand, superficially more germane to our deliberations, there are notions of "functional" illiteracy and "non-functional" literacy.[1]

Among the many "signs of our times," they mark our mood as they (often over)heat the crucibles of our deliberations. Contemporary cultural conjunctions, they are also clear culminations of critical historical currents that constitute no less than the origins of the modern world. They incorporate the contradictions of that epochal historical process (Graff, 1987a). Failure to appreciate the provenance of the past, of history, in the present and the possibilities for the future makes us its prisoners, bound to repeat the past, rather than to learn from it and to break its bonds. With respect to literacy, in theory and in practice, this is powerfully the case. Indeed, as a historian I know of few other topics about which this is so true or so significant—or about which failure to embrace the opportunities for novel learning is so telling.

That is not all that we must embrace. Among those "signs of our times" are tireless but tiresome claims of ubiquitous "crisis" (or "crises") of education higher and lower, of math and science, of the humanities and social sciences, of literacy functional and other, indeed, of cultures and polities and economies, national and international. Not only are these threads densely intertwined, but they are highly relevant to discussions of literacy attainment and standards. Sadly, they typically confuse the conversation more than they provide useful or heuristic contexts for discussion or understanding. In a revealingly self-contradictory essay, "The Storm Over the University," the philosopher John Searle (1990, 34) aptly begins his professorial notes for the 1990s: "I cannot recall a time when American education was not in a 'crisis.' We have lived through Sputnik (when we were 'falling behind the Russians'), through the era of 'Johnny can't read,' and through the upheavals of the Sixties. Now a good many books are telling us that the university is going to hell in several different directions at once." As a student of literacy for two decades, I can not recall a time when literacy was not in a crisis.

In that diagnosis, higher education newly joins other levels of schooling. Crises in literacy at least putatively accompany (regardless of their own relationships) those of more elevated learning. Schools and universities readily serve as attractive targets assigned responsibility and blame in difficult, confusing times. Of course, so too does literacy. With revealing contradiction, levels of literacy abilities serve simultaneously as symptoms and symbols, causes and consequences. By themselves, they prove convenient, easy symbols for wholesale criticism rather than central sources of failure or, for that matter, successful transformations (Graff, 1987a; Levine, 1985; "Education," 1981). With respect to American schools, the historian Michael Katz (1988, 183) notes, "for about 150 years, education has been proposed as a solution to every major social problem." With respect to the Western world more generally and to literacy, my research establishes a longer historical connection of several millennia and an active association for at least five centuries from the Renaissance and the Enlightenment (Graff, 1987a). This is one among a series of critical historical linkages and legacies we encounter and must challenge. It is also a burden that the institution perhaps—not unlike literacy—cannot bear.

John Searle's (1990, 34) sense of a "crisis" in American higher education shares a basic understanding—a hope, an agenda—with the goals of many: "I believe that, at least in part, the crisis rhetoric has a structural explanation: since we do not have national consensus on what success in higher education would consist of, no matter what happens, some sizable part of the population is going to regard the situation as a disaster. As with taxation and relations between the sexes, higher education is essentially and continuously contested territory. Given the history of that crisis rhetoric, one's natural response to the current cries of desperation might reasonably be one of boredom." (Implicitly, perhaps knowingly, Searle raises the spectre of "cultural literacy.") Between the Scylla of desperation and the Charybdis of boredom, consensus and standards are sought. This gives the lie to Searle's attributions of "American uniqueness," along with his resigned pessimism and unimaginative solutions.[2]

Perception of "crisis" thus links Searle's and my concerns. Both are indeed contested territory. Those perceptions in various formulations underlay the post–World War II rise of notions, concepts, programs, and measures of "functional" literacy. Much like Searle's and many others' cavails, as Levine observed in 1982, "current notions of functional literacy . . . obscure the identification of appropriate targets, goals, and standards of achievement in the education of adults by promising, though failing to produce, a quantitively precise, unitary standard of 'survival' literacy. . . . these varying conceptions of functional literacy encourage the idea that relatively low levels of individual achievement . . . will directly result in a set of universally desired outcomes, such as employment, personal and economic growth, job advancement, and social integration."[3]

More impressive but unremarked is the frequency and commonality of literacy (and schooling) "crises." Not only are they ubiquitous during recent decades, but their presence across an expanse of historical time encompassing centuries commands attention; their recognition may lead to fresh perspectives. In resisting the temptations to boredom cited by Searle, we discover a rhetorical discourse of "crisis" and "decline" seldom far from historical consciousness, or at least from expression. This discourse increased its presence and certainly its visibility/audibility from the time of the "Age(s) of Progress" and those of "Enlightenment," although it long predates them. Its sources and its uses are many and diverse. The relationships of this discourse to and implications for literacy and for schools are enormous, especially in difficult, critical periods of historical transformation, among which we must include our own.

My overarching point is *historical*. Historical interpretation offers potentially innovative approaches—*paths*, I call them—to reforming questions and problems, understanding, criticism, and alternative conceptualizations and perspectives.[4] In this approach, *both* continuities and transformations are critical, as are the specific circumstances in which they appear or are claimed to develop. Their comprehension, explanation, and resolution require great care, and close, contextual investigation. As Michael Katz observes with respect to what he terms "the new educational panic," "By ignoring history, we have replicated the same unsuccessful reform strategies over and over again" (Katz, 1988, 191).[5]

Among literacy's intertwining multiple strands, I distinguish three. Each is claimed to be declining and achieving the status of "crisis." Each of the three (and there are others) is construed, more or less reflexively—but in fact fundamentally *historically*—within the intersecting discourses of literacy and "crisis." Legacies from literacy's history, singly and conjointly, they influence our thinking and actions today. Encompassing uncomfortably a huge and revealing range, they are:

1 "Elementary" or "basic" literacy, typically taken as equivalent to the results from a variety of standardized, "objective" (i.e., "scientific") tests that presume unproblematically (however inadequately) to measure quantitatively and comparatively "schooled" and/or "functional" *reading and writing abilities* (e.g., high school competency, National Assessment of Educational Progress, Armed Forces Qualifying, "skills," etc., tests).

2 Recurrent association, direct and strong to the point of virtual equivalency or synonymy, and unproblematically, of the presumed condition of literacy—including but never limited to basic literacy, but in close connection with visible personal moral, attitudinal, and behavioral characteristics—with the *condition of civilization* (read: morality, order, democracy, progress, productivity, among other things). The association typically implies a great danger to those vested characteristics and the social order itself.

3 The more recently proliferating *many "literacies"* in addition to or "beyond" "traditional" alphabetic literacy—from those of science and numeracy, to the spatial that some geographers term "graphicacy," to the loudly touted and seemingly highly vulnerable "cultural literacy," "historical literacy," and "moral literacy." Some among the lengthening lists are long established in presumption but much more novel discursively or semantically: ecological literacy, "teleliteracy" and other media literacies, food literacy, emotional literacy, sexual literacy.[6]

(The extent to which the newly proliferating literacies signify little more than a semantic "name game" or a feature of the politics of literacy and education or professional specialization raises hard questions. This is central to contemporary considerations of "functional literacy" among the many literacies proclaimed. An enormously important set of critical developments, whose potentially revolutionary consequences for learning and teaching are largely unappreciated, thus far remain prisoner to scholarly, cultural, and pedagogical fragmentation. Major new advances in the study of human learning processes, cognition, and development have much to tell us about schooling and learning. If there are indeed, as I am convinced, a number of distinct "literacies," the manner in which their elements overlap or coincide has, at least in the abstract, the revolutionary potential for reconstructing primary, and perhaps higher, education in order to develop and practice those distinct but not completely differentiated abilities.)[7]

These three threads stand out among the many. They stand out more clearly than they (co)exist together or separately as significations of literacy and as essential elements of education. Not only does each of them represent a case claimed for "crisis" and "decline." They also illustrate how hard it is to deal with literacy, discursively and critically as well as practically. More disparate and different than proverbial apples and oranges, it is not clear which of the three may be horses and which may be carts. No one leads directly to another; none is interchangeable with the others. Recognizing this implicitly contending plurality is only a halting first step, albeit a necessary one. Beset with numerous conceptual complications, literacy is an exceptionally slippery subject *and* object whether the goal is theoretical, critical, or practical. These three strands only begin to suggest the pervasive powers of deeply rooted and widely shared assumptions and presumptions about literacy.

The nature of the relationships imputed or expected among the three strands underscores the point. The broad appeals of the discourse, indeed, the mentality, of "crisis" and "decline," heighten sensitivity. In this respect, our own epoch has many precedents from which we may learn if we are attentive, patient, and bold. Those connections are fragile, fragmentary, partial; neither necessary nor sufficient. At best they are coterminous, often but not always culturally and socially hierarchical; at worst, they are virtually nonexistent, conceptually and empirically fraudulent. In either case, they can be dangerous—to both human subjects and school subjects, to social and cultural relations, to collective and individual developments—especially when unrecognized and unchallenged. The (sometimes insidious) breadth, power, and attraction of this discourse and its practices is nonetheless established and maintains its hegemony despite the presence of widely differing, even opposing, ideologies and philosophies and practices. In that way these diverging threads are awkwardly but commonly and instructively joined under the title of *Literacy* (capital L).

The hegemony of the rhetoric of crisis and decline among the legacies of literacy, is more than ever before challenged, shaken by criticisms social and cultural, political and economic, as well as theoretical and practical (Graff, 1979, 1987a; Botstein, 1990; Winchester, 1990a, 1990b). It has no single or shared resolution or replacement. In the face of confusing challenges and at a time of disconcerting societal and global transformations, efforts evoking "functionalities" and "non-functionalities," "cultural" and "historical literacy," canons old and new, skills of survival and of humanity speak to the same conclusion: the legacies of literacy must be reconsidered and literacy/literacies reconstructed. That would provide a necessary beginning.

Regardless of rhetoric or misunderstanding to the contrary, the ways in which these contemporary conjunctures emerge are fundamentally *historical*. They stand prominently among the historically produced conceptions, assumptions, expectations, arrangements, and relationships surrounding literacy, learning, education, and schooling. They are the "legacies" and "myths" of literacy.

At least as important, as the three strands illustrate, are the *presumed* connections between basic literacy (reading and writing) on the one hand, and both schooling and education—at various levels—on the other hand. The connections, historically produced and derivative, function as assumption, presumption, expectation, sometimes inflated to the level of "theory," more often as received wisdom/accepted truth. Presumed or perceived to be concrete consequences of human action including the historical process, they undergird institutional arrangements, everyday practices, policy construction, and terms of evaluation. These relations, for good reason, almost invariably remain unstated, almost unnoticed. Under scrutiny, they appear much less firm, albeit impressively sturdy and long-lasting for "fictions." Both history and criticism demand their explicit formulation in order to (1) identify and trace their shifting but sometimes contradictory, sometimes seminal intersections, and (2) explore and expose their fallacies and fault lines. We owe that much to the young and not so young, as the subjects of our ministrations change—today and tomorrow. That can be accomplished usefully by renewing our own critical connections to the past, in this case the histories of literacy and education.

Lessons from the History of Literacy[8]

The history of literacy and its relationship to the history of education—learning and schooling—if harvested carefully, present a rich crop of "lessons" for today and tomorrow. Regardless of the terms of my offering—the menu is selective—they are the fruits of rigorous historical research and interpretation. And, as that kind of product, they are contested terrain with much to argue. For me, the import of the cultivation only heightens the stakes.

Not only is the historiography of literacy sometimes an interpretive battlefield, but so too are large questions about the nature of the relationships tying literacy to learning, schooling, and education on various levels and in varying subject matters. Of this morass, the three literacy-related threads alerted us. Common assumptions of simplicity, directness, or linearity in sequence of teaching or learning and of advancement fall quickly to the quagmire that obstructs the progress of the harvester. In the "lessons" that follow, I emphasize those in which there are important—*but not necessary*—parallels, on the one hand, between the domains of literacy and those of schooling (among a larger universe) and, on the other hand, between historical foundations and developments and contemporary configurations and their "crises." Often constituting lessons more negative than positive, they are no less significant, constructive, or potentially critically liberating.

Lesson 1

Although seldom stated, less often contemplated, present-day conceptions, arrangements, and practices of literacy as well as schooling and learning are *historically founded and grounded*. They are also strong and powerfully resistant to change. Encompassing the domain from basic literacy to higher education, this recognition constitutes necessarily a *first* lesson whose regular neglect by university-based (and other) "experts" only increases the likelihood of failures in communication, understanding, and reform in the means and modes of education. Ian Winchester (1990a, 1990b), for example, refers to the "standard picture of literacy"! We willfully neglect the historical roots and courses of our major goals and the manner in which we seek to achieve them. How often have we seen at great cost, unsuccessful efforts to transplant the presumed products—often an image—of Western historical development to other parts of the world?

The limits posed by neglect of the (often quietly present) past mark what passes for their historical record as impressively as what is claimed for their achievements. Repetition is least among the costs of failing to learn from history; if only we might repeat the course! More seriously, ignorance of the circumstances in which crucial concepts, notions, arrangements, or expectations were fashioned, the means by which they have been maintained, and their consequences severely limits, if not contradicts, contemporary analysis, diagnosis, and prescription. (Use of the medical metaphor is itself part of this history.) Many more lessons—minor and major, specific and general—derive from the historical cornerstone. The point encompasses ideas, assumptions, and expectations equally with programs, institutions, and administration (Graff, 1987a).

Lesson 2

That subjects such as literacy, learning, schooling, and education are simple, unproblematic notions is a further historical myth. Experience, historical and more recent, to the contrary jointly underscores their *fundamental complexity*—practically and theoretically. Long persisting problems—in learning and using the elements of learning—follow from this legacy. Among them are the many "great debates" surrounding, for example, human language acquisition and usage; literate as opposed to oral, among other communicative modes—and their presumed "consequences"; relations of literacy to hierarchies of power and wealth as opposed to egalitarian democracy; literacy's contributions to developments economic, political, social; and the status of "texts." Even elementary literacy as learned and practiced is quite complex physiologically, neurologically, and cognitively. Its social and cultural dimensions add on numerous layers of complex meanings—among them "continuities and contradictions," as I term them. How little we know about learning—and about teaching, too, especially respecting the level of literacy.

Especially prominent among the central complications of our traditions or legacies of literacy are (1) the extraordinary frailty of conceptions and conceptualizations of literacy, and (2) the contradiction of expected consequences from its acquisition. With respect to the first, presumption of literacy's unproblematic simplicity accompanies "naturally" or "essentially" the assumptions that emphasize its strong, uniform, universal, unitary, unwavering nature and impact. With respect to the second, "strong" theories of literacy directly and linearly associate rising levels (sometimes once a specified "threshold" is achieved) with large-scale impacts, especially the advancement of both individuals and societies. Termed in various formulations the "consequences," "correlates," or "implications" of literacy, the dizzying number and variety of imputed effects span the individual and societal, including the psychological, cognitive, attitudinal, social-relational, behavioral, symbolic, motivational, participatory, and productive. Literate persons, for example, are said to be more empathetic, innovative, achievement-oriented, cosmopolitan, media and politically aware, identified with a nation, aspiring to schooling, "modern," urban in residence, and accepting of technology. Literacy, it is claimed, correlates with economic growth and industrialization, wealth and productivity, political stability and participatory democracy, urbanization, consumption, and contraception.[9] Equally strong traditions of expectations and expert prescriptions surround higher levels of education, sharing with literacy concerns about, for example, moral character, discipline and order, security, and productivity.

Suffice it to say that these wholesale claims rarely stand up to either empirical or conceptual probing historically or contemporarily. The "strong theory" of literacy—despite its hold on popular and policy opinions—turns out to be much weaker, with literacy's impacts seldom so direct, unmediated, abstract, or universal. Constituting much of what I call literacy's central contradictions, these legacies taken together constitute "the literacy myth," a powerful force despite its massive criticism and rejection in some circles. The contradictions nevertheless give the lie not only to "strong" theories but also to proclamations of a "Grand

Dichotomy" and "Great Divide" rhetorically erected between literate and non-literate persons, societies, and civilizations.

Such powerful formulations rest far more on expectations and faith than they do on ambiguous evidence of complex, usually context-dependent relations and more complicated, oblique connections. Great damage is done to individuals and larger collectivities, positively and negatively, in the name of "development" stemming from expectations about mass provision and possession of literacy in worlds developed and underdeveloped. they include what Leon Botstein (1990) evocatively terms "damaged literacy" and Elspeth Stuckey (1991) movingly calls "the violence of literacy." They are also what Kenneth Levine (1985), Jonathan Kozol (1985), and others link with specific programs for "functional" and other out-of-school literacy campaigns.

Unfortunately but critically, assertions like Bhola's that "fortunately, hardly anyone today allocates such powers [a *deterministic* role in transforming social realities] to literacy" are contradicted too often, for example by claims within the same volume, co-edited by Bhola ("Adult Literacy," 1990, 138; cf. p. 4). It is neither accurate nor especially helpful to declare sweepingly, "Literacy is rightly seen to act in dialectical relationship with social change, and its emancipatory role in societies is now being well understood." Exaggerating, overvaluing, or inflating consequences expected from shifts in literacy levels among either individuals or larger populations stand among the attendant risks. Notions of literacy as a human right join with those of literacy as "functional," economic or utilitarian, in courting disappointment or even more negative responses due to overloading what might fairly be presumed from changes in literacy levels. History holds powerful lessons in disappointment and misplaced expectations.

Paradoxically but instructively, the first formulation rests on an epistemology assuming literacy's effects to be universal, unmediated, unitary—monocausal in effect. The second, in contrast, derives from and undergirds a whole series of simplistic dichotomies—from literate/illiterate to written/oral and civilized/barbaric. Confusion about the nature of literacy itself follows, reflected, for example, in questions concerning "quantity" versus "quality," attitudes versus abilities, substance versus "skills" or "tools," or, to paraphrase Ronald Dore, training versus "training in being trained." Self- and other-contradictory, neither position proves itself useful. To the contrary, both underwrite thinking and arrangements whose limits have not only been demonstrated, but which are anachronistic and destructive. What is at issue, of course, is seldom admitted: it is the purpose of literacy, and other learning. Those issues are inseparable from their historical course, as are the underlying conceptions of literacy and formulations of its presumed powers.

Lesson 3

Literacy and other levels of learning share not only their unproblematical status, but also the presumption of their central value neutrality (that is often represented, ironically, as beneficial, a "good"). To the contrary, *no mode or means of learning is neutral*. Not only does all "knowledge," however elementary, incorporate the assumptions and expectations, the biases of emphases of its production, association, prior use, maintenance, and preservation. So too do the so-called tools or skills.[10] With them, there are biases with respect to their transmission—the circumstances of learning and practice—and quite likely fundamental biases in their very nature, for example, the newly appreciated textual biases of formal schooling—"school" literacy—and most reading and writing shaped by such formative encounters, tutelage, and generally restricted or regulated practice at relatively early ages. Studies of the "media" of literacy, from script to print and beyond, only begin to suggest the intricately interacting relationships; contemporary confusion about the "future of print" compared to the visuality and aurality of electronic media have an impressively lengthy set of precedents.[11] The history, only partially studied and understood, challenges all presumptions of unmediated, linear relations and impacts.

Studies in cognitive psychology like Scribner and Cole's *Psychology of Literacy* (1981) demonstrate the consequences for literacy of the specific circumstances of acquisition, practice, and uses—and of its place in the culture. Raising more questions than they answer, and challenging the legacies of received wisdom, such research joins with other cognitive, linguistic, and historical studies in pointing toward more refined conceptions of skills, abilities, competencies, and knowledge in relatively precise but flexible learning, social, cultural, and communicative contexts.

That alphabetic literacy is one, albeit exceptionally valuable, set of abilities and competencies, among others, slowly influences thinking about schooling and learning, and much else. Here, for example, confusions between long-standing, theoretically touted, and all but boundless *potentials* of literacy when contrasted with more common levels of ability and everyday practices can be excessive and egregious. Here, too, we find contradictions in literacy's and education's history, in part from overvaluing alphabetic literacy *by itself* and slighting (or worse) other "literacies." Enormous implications for teaching and learning, for developing more effective litera*cies*, follow from placing "traditional alphabetic" literacy within its appropriate communicative context along with, say, numeracy and scientific literacy, oral and aural abilities, spatial literacy or graphicacy, visual and aesthetic literacies, and so on. Historians of science suggest that invention and discovery may owe more to visual than alphabetic literacy. How little we know about these "many literacies" sadly corresponds to poor instruction in a limited range of literacy and ignorance of the extent of common elements among different literacies that might support a potentially revolutionary remaking of schooling.[12] It may be difficult to formulate satisfactory notions of literacy(ies) without expanding our understanding of communicative contexts and channels. For such study, history provides a rich laboratory. The challenges of precise comparison across space as well as time, while absolutely mandated, loom large. Any useful notion of literacy or literacies must confront them.

Similarly, we neglect to our loss the extent to which "school" literacy is a very special use of literacy and language. Words are not only taken out of "the context for action," but they are also removed from other, nonschool uses, including much of oral language usage and writing. "School" literacy of course is highly prized, rewarded—but also criticized for its biases and limitations. As David Olson (1977, 75, 86) notes: "To take explicit written prose as the model of a language, knowledge and intelligence has narrowed the conception of all three, downgrading the general functions of ordinary language and commonsense knowledge," much of speech, too. School literacy, predominantly textually based and biased, is often cut off from other modes of verbal communication which are evaluated as inferior regardless of their place in everyday life. Structures of authority are erected on these bases and lines as certain forms of literacy and language abilities support social differentiation, social stigmatization, reinforcement of inequality—and school failure among the young, and not so young. These "literate biases" are another of literacy's legacies, as are the typically inadequate level and form of literacy—of any kind—taken from schools. Neither lower nor higher learning, or students themselves, is served. Yet knowledge of the environment and media of teaching and learning, in relationship to social contexts in which variously literate or nonliterate lives are lived, provides a rich arena for sophisticated study, past and present, that we are only beginning to explore.[13]

Lesson 4

More than excessive are the excesses and damages—massive human costs in domains developed and undeveloped—that follow from the long domination of theoretical presumptions that elevate the literate, the written (as proposed to the nonliterate) to the power and status of the dominant partner in what Jack Goody calls the "Great Dichotomy" and Ruth Finnegan the "Great Divide." In part the arrogance of the imperial West but more the triumph of Goody's "technology of the intellect" over the intellect and the human spirit themselves, traditions of narrowly construed intellectualism rationalized their reification of light over darkness, civilization over barbarity, developed over primitive, formally schooled over natural, written over spoken, literate over oral.

The urge toward a totalizing universality in literate-based conceptions of the world and the superiority of its "consequences" or "implications" sits proudly, if increasingly insecurely over the gap presumed between the halves of the "great dichotomy." Long-standing historically, with massive contributions during Renaissances, Enlightenments, and nineteenth-century "Eras of Progress," the divide, to late-twentieth-century reinterpretations crossing virtually all the human and biological sciences, threatens to widen into a cavernous earthquakelike fault as intellectual equivalents of tectonic plates shift and reconfigure.

Lesson 5

Hand in hand with simplicity and superiority went presumed ease of learning and expectation of individual, along with societal, progress. Despite our inability to

327

recognize its enormous implications, historical perspective repeatedly reiterates the *difficulties* regularly, perhaps normally, experienced in gaining, practicing, and mastering the elements of alphabetic literacy as well as higher learning. Acquiring even basic elements of abilities that may—or may not—prove necessary and useful in acquiring further skills, information, knowledge, or mentalities is seldom easy, for reasons both obvious and devious. Learning literacy, and whatever lies beyond it, is *hard work*. Granting that should lead to appreciation and value of every learner's struggles and triumph, not the condemnation of the slower pupil (especially when granting the limiting or restricted bias of "schooled" literacy and the hierarchical educational systems erected upon it).

Only in part a matter of instructional media, technology, pedagogy, institutional setting, age, or social circumstances, *motivation*—perception of need, sometimes defensively or fearfully, sometimes with great pleasure and satisfaction—is undoubtedly a greater goad than biological age and social station. Sometimes this is a matter of the individual—the rhetorical focus of our formal efforts—sometimes it is collective, with pushes and pulls incorporating the political, economic, social, or cultural, the radical or the conserving. Historical study and contemporary psychology both show this—a very rare occurrence. Alas, scholars, those of us who live by and depend upon our manipulation of the tools of traditional learning, are perhaps least well placed to appreciate common experiences and include them in revised or reconstructed approaches to learning and teaching.

Lesson 6   \

Missing from our common operational and legitimizing myths and legacies is the more complicated historical and richly human set of images: of *multiple paths of learning literacy* and much more; the employment of an extraordinary range of instructors, institutions and other environments, and beginning "texts"; and the diversity of sometimes conflicting motivations. Missing too is the informality and possibility of elementary and higher learning *without* the lock-step enforced march of age-grading and wholesale psychologies of human cognition and learning based on their simplistic presumptions. In this respect, the early modern "discovery" of children and a "special" state of "childhood" and the last two centuries' efforts to institutionalize them constitute more complicated relationships than usually accorded them.[14]

In contrast, the great reforming dream was to create formal, compulsory, mass public schools as expected sites for virtually universal transmission of a minimal level of literacy along with the tenets of secular morality. This was a literacy presumed nonetheless useful *and* also socially secure, as opposed to literacy gained without the proper leavening agents of carefully crafted learning environments with methods and materials created expressly for their employment. The first dreamers long predated the massive nineteenth-century efforts to construct school systems, which awaited the present century for many areas. Distrust, even fear, of the unwashed masses united them, although for centuries fear of schooled masses dominated over fear of the ignorant or those who learned outside the bounds of formal educational institutions. Before that reversal and the subsequent achievement of mass schooling, and long accompanying its development in many places, looser arrangements continued whose poor press was written by reformers who sought to destroy them. Those arrangements, I suspect, have much to tell us.[15]

While underscoring the relative recency and historical constructedness of the means of mass literacy provision and most of other education—as opposed to notions of their inevitability or destiny—caution and hindsight also demand that we not romanticize nostalgically the "premodern" past. (In higher education, age-grading and notions of the "college-aged," along with major "modernizing" reforms, also took shape in the nineteenth century.) Mass public school systems, despite their great limitations and failings, have undoubtedly increased opportunities and elevated typical educational achievement. The price paid, a high one, included culturally and individually restricted literacy and other learning levels and uses, in contexts that led many pupils to disdain or at least undervalue higher levels of literacy and learning. It also included persistent inequalities of opportunity and outcomes, greater rewards for the well-off than for the poor, among much else. Limits of dependence on literacy, itself restricted and likely poorly disseminated, set rigid constraints on the contribution from schools to polity and culture as well as economy. And of course, nearly universal elementary schooling never halted popular cultural practices that included "improper" use of literacy to read scorned or censured writing! This is not to deny that for many individuals exceptional avenues were opened; to be sure, they were never the "common" scholars. Most surprising, perhaps, is how long the legitimacy of mass public schools lasted until its recent erosion.

Among the prices paid, and ranking high among those we seek to redevelop in recent and new approaches to *adult* literacy, has been the historical condemnation, then obscuring and forgetting that, for a great many persons, traditional alphabetic literacy was acquired in the widest variety of informal, as well as formal circumstances, and at a wide range of chronological ages. These included self-teaching and learning in homes, dame schools, work places, fields, class and political domains, cultural settings, carceral institutions, and chance occurrences, at ages sometimes younger but far more commonly older than the limited span of childhood and early adolescence that came to be defined as the "critical period." Modernization of schooling into mass systems rested in part on the denial of previously common paths. Just as importantly and perhaps as powerfully, approved practices respecting institution and age hardened into expectations, policies, and theories (Spufford, 1979; Laqueur, 1976b; Galenson, 1979, 1981). Impressive is the degree to which novel innovations in flexible and innovative literacy programs and campaigns involve the (sometimes unacknowledged, sometimes unknown) rediscovery or reinvention of historical configurations. We have much more to learn (Arnove and Graff, 1987).

Lesson 7

Literacy *as part of elementary education*—all the formal schooling that most common scholars experienced over the historical long term, until the late nineteenth and early twentieth centuries—is a form of "foundationism," to use today's buzz word. In close association with the legacies and myths aired so far, this presumption holds that given the availability of written texts and elementary instruction, simple abilities of reading and writing were in themselves fully sufficient for further development of an individual's literacy and subsequent education, and, of course, for the advancement of that individual. In other words, for anyone or everyone, no serious obstacle to achieving a desired degree of literacy or additional learning need trouble those hungry for more. Learning and using literacy, the "foundation," were, after all, easy. No matter that the cognitive and psychological place of reading and writing as foundations is not well understood, or that reading has so long been poorly taught, and that debates over reading methodologies persist with much heat and little light over centuries. Among the corollaries, also shared, is that failure to acquire literacy reflected overwhelmingly on that individual and her or his race, ethnicity, class, and so forth, not on schools, society, culture, or polity. "Blaming the victim," this pattern is called. It, too, has a long, sorry history, in which the victims are not individuals alone but rather social classes or groups defined by race, ethnicity, gender, nationality, age, or other characteristics. Until recently, in the wake of these legacies, tutelage of adults attracted relatively little effort. Ironically, there are indeed long traditions of adult education seldom called into play (Levine, 1985; Hautecoeur, 1990).

Among the major complications is massive evidence of unequal opportunities and school beginnings from radically different foundations for children of different classes, races, and ethnicities; and teachers' expectations about the abilities of different young persons all but guarantee their level of accomplishment. Gender figures in complexly, too. Motivations among youngsters vary greatly, both within and across social lines. Competency, proficiency, mastery, and levels of literacy sufficient on which to build further: these qualities are neither easy to achieve or typical products of schooling, nor guarantees of normative advances.

Lesson 8

Just as individuals followed different paths to literacy and learning, societies historically and more recently took *different paths* toward achieving rising levels of popular literacy. When the focus falls on the societal, as opposed to the individual, we learn that in emphasis and in impacts the two are not necessarily synonymous, sometimes quite contradictory. Historically and contemporarily, too, regardless of democratizing rhetoric about individual progress, far greater concern and attention derive from considerations of the collectivity and aim at its improvement, than of individuals within its realm.

Despite massive expectations of one sure road to progress, inscribed in "strong" theories and "standard versions," historical research emphasizes that there is *no* one route destined to culminate in universal literacy *and* its associated "modern" concomitants politically, economically, socially, culturally. In various configurations, private and public, formal and informal, compulsory and voluntary factors, and others, have combined to elevate mass literacy. Similarly, with respect to the contributions of literacy and education, there has been *no* one route to economic development, industrialization, political democracy, or other parcels of the "modernization" complex. In some cases, at some times, literacy worked as causal agent indirectly or directly. In others, it did not. In some circumstances, literacy was influenced by development, an effect rather than a contribution. And in others, the impact on literacy and education was negative—in European early industrialization, for example. Sequencing and timing—chronologically and causally—may be very important, say, in the nature and degree of social unrest during industrialization in different places, or the adaptation of large numbers of immigrants. Still, those relationships seem to vary widely. Often, literacy and higher levels of schooling have served noncognitively, attitudinally, behaviorally, and symbolically in furthering social and economic development. That is no small contribution; it is not, however, the one typically touted (Graff, 1979, 1987a, 1993a; "Education," 1981; "Adult Literacy," 1990).

In General

The great danger, one which twentieth-century education on all levels shares with literacy models, is the simple presumption that economic development in particular depends directly on investment in and high rates of productivity from systems of formal education. Whereas education and the economy are undoubtedly related, sometimes intimately, the nature of those connections is anything but simple, direct, unmediated. The role of the market in schooling at all levels is only one broad example. Only disappointment and today's invidiously negative and self-flagellating international comparisons—and censure of teachers, institutions, and students (in that order)—ensue. Quantity and quality are confused; educational purpose is distorted. The consequent fears of "crisis" and "decline" typically and rigidly narrow the frame of education—including literacy itself—and all but guarantee the repetition of the cycle (see, e.g., Barrett, 1990). The legacies of literacy stand close at hand.

Urban Perspectives

Part and parcel of these historical relationships are the twisted links between cities and literacy, a critical subset of the larger connections and a source of major social myths. As hinted above, this history, and its persisting legacies, is contradictory to its very core. That relationship appears at the general level of historical macrosociology. Attend to French scholars Furet and Ozouf: "We had set out with the quiet assurance of the Directory Commissioners, who were convinced that the gathering together of men fostered the contagion of Enlightenment. Indeed, statistically speaking our study bears out their intuition; as a rule, towns improve literacy rates. But what we have discovered in addition is that this is not everywhere, not uniformly, so: the superiority of the towns over the surrounding countryside only becomes really impressive when the regional level of education is wretched; when the *département* as a whole is well-educated, the town-country differential shrinks, and it sometimes even happens that the countryside does better than the towns."

The size of urban places is one pivot on which the connections turn. In their study of France from the sixteenth through nineteenth centuries, Furet and Ozouf found that for places not the *chef-lieu* of their area, at population levels of ten to twenty thousand "literacy begins to mark time, or even slither backwards." More important, "urban literacy rates depended mainly on the nature of the town's functions, economic or administrative, and hence on the socio-occupational make-up of its population."

With industrialization and rapid urban growth, literacy was neither required nor were urban circumstances able to meet the press of numbers and needs. "Certain conditions had to be fulfilled before this new urban population could begin to imitate the cultural behaviour of the traditional city-dwellers: firstly, the occupational composition of the population had to have achieved diversity and equilibrium, mingling the 'middle managers', clerks and shopkeepers with modern industrial workers and the 'elites' of the older urban society; secondly, the town had to have had time to 'digest' its untrammelled growth and to acquire the amenities—school obviously being one of these—they needed to catch up culturally" (Furet and Ozouf, 1983, 225, 224).[16]

Furet and Ozouf's rhetoric speaks as clearly as their apparent surprise that such central developmental myths of Western (and later worldwide) modernization are disappointed in concrete cases. The myths persist, we know too well.[17] Yet difficult questions relate to the extent that Furet and Ozouf's "certain conditions" were in fact "fulfilled," whether historically or in many parts of the world, developed or underdeveloping, today. The formulation itself requires revision.

Not only do urbanization and literacy levels relate complexly and contradictorily, but so do realities of literacy levels *within* different urban places. Historically and contemporarily, striking and sometimes long-lasting variations and inequalities follow the dividing lines of gender, race, ethnicity, geography, migration streams, language, and other factors. Neither are they "historical survivals" in the West, nor simple signs of "new" or "immature" development elsewhere in the world where the press of numbers, poverty, density, inequalities, and the raw struggle for survival far outshadows western historical parallels to the point at which comparisons can be more misleading than useful precedents. Needs for survival, adaptation, and familial traditions together limit use of what reformers and developers view as "opportunities" and "amenities," especially by women and the young. Others old and new to cities see the "opportunities" very differently: as alien, potentially dangerous, irrelevant.

Historically and today, cities simultaneously pull their populations toward rising levels of literacy and schooling, and push them away. Scholars do not grasp well these relationships. On the one hand, urban places often (but not always) offer greater opportunities for learning literacy both formally and informally. In cities, print is more often present and accessible. On certain levels, too, functional demands for work, daily life, political or cultural participation, and the like lead many to literacy and its practice. None of those connections is surprising to our late-twentieth-century expectations.

On the other hand, cities also obstruct schooling with inadequate, unappealing, overcrowded institutions that have little latitude with which to make schooling more attractive to pupils young or old. Cities for some simply offer fewer and less adequate ways in which to attain survival, thus distracting or foreclosing educational options for many. Demands of living and making a living are hard and occupy many hands. Differences and discriminations of ethnicity, religion, ideology, language, race, class, gender, age, and the like also rebuke and repel. Even in situations in which some schooling is compulsory, urban places make evasion easier. In cities, it is not only easier to secure the message of print from oral sources, directly or indirectly, but both traditional and new communicative modes and media replace its value for many whose own literacy sometimes is "lost" through non-use. Motivation, "seizing opportunities," or "helping one's self" are hardly the issue. Regardless of ideology and myths to the contrary, many low-level jobs require very little in the way of literacy- or school-based skills. Literacy requirements may signify the desire for formal tutelage in noncognitive attitudinal and behavioral lessons. Finally, survival in cities may well depend on an ability to "read the city," a kind of "urban literacy," that bears only a partial relationship to traditional, alphabetic abilities.[18]

The great danger for cities and their dwellers, one which twentieth-century education on all levels shares with literacy models, is the simple presumption that economic development in particular depends directly on investment in, and high rates of productivity from, systems of formal education. Whereas education and the economy are undoubtedly related, sometimes intimately, the nature of those connections is anything but simple. The role of the market in schooling at all levels is only one broad example. This, too, is the case with respect to cities. Only disappointment and today's invidiously negative and self-flagellating international comparisons—and censure of teachers, institutions, and students and their families (in that order)—ensue. Quantity and quality are confused; educational purpose is distorted. The consequent fears of "crisis" and "decline" rigidly narrow the frame of education—including literacy itself—and all but guarantee the repetition of the cycle.[19] The legacies of literacy stand close at hand.

Critical Literacy
Reflecting notions current at the time and ideas still developing, I wrote abstractly and sketchily for a 1988 conference presentation:

> Those of us who struggle for an alternative approach [to E. D. Hirsch's cultural literacy]—deem it for now, critical literacy—must turn our energies elsewhere. The approach we are seeking requires a broadly based literacy that connects critical thinking with the skills of critical reading and writing in politics, economics, and social relations as well as in a larger cultural sphere, a literacy no longer limited to alphabetic abilities

and to a historical basis that is static and acculturative. A critical literacy of course recognizes the significance of common knowledge, but it sees it as a consequence of criticism, as changing and transforming, not as inflexible and timeless. It does not separate "skills" from "content" but strives to link them dynamically. The critical literacy we are seeking must be based not only on a radically revised and more demanding curriculum, but also on an epistemology and theoretical critique that grasps the centrality of ambiguity, complexity, and contradiction to literacy and to life itself (Graff, 1989, 51).[20]

Among the key elements to which I was insufficiently attentive is what Freire eloquently phrased as the relation between the "word" and the "world": "Reading the world always precedes reading the word, and reading the word implies continually reading the world. . . . this movement from the word to the world is always present; even the spoken word flows from our reading of the world. In a way, however, we can go further and say that reading the word is not preceded merely by reading the world, but by a certain form of *writing* it or *rewriting* it, that is, of transforming it by means of conscious, practical work. For me, this dynamic movement is central to the literacy process" (Freire in Freire and Macedo, 1987, 35).

Critical literacy today sways uncomfortably between its emancipatory potential and a range of dangers and fallacies some of which I have noted. Possibilities for individual and collective transformations confront misplaced utopianism and exaggerated expectations. A critical literacy at the core of a radical critical consciousness engaged in revolutionary social reconstruction faces problems of inattention to context, insufficient criticism, and undertheorization—and neglect of history's lessons. Conceptualization of critical literacy is itself often fuzzy, as is the relationship of literacy to other aspects of the radical educational agendas of which it is a part, and of different "literacies" within critical literacy to one another and to traditional alphabetic abilities. Critical literacy also risks semantic and conceptual confusion with and cooptation by conservative "critical thinking" or "critical education." Major dangers stem from overloading concepts and expectations, rending them from contexts theoretical and practical—to the extent of conceiving literacy autonomously or universalistically, in and by itself—and confusing parts and wholes. Half steps backward threaten advances, quite apart from contemporary political and economic "realities" that I must ignore now. These dangers include an unknowing repetition of literacy's history.[21]

My explicit intent, as I conclude, lies not in this negative vein. I underscore these points, these questions of criticism, because I do think that literacy's history has a great deal to teach us, and because I find a general absence of sympathetic criticism in the literature on critical literacy. Paulo Freire's writings and his example are seminal. Freire is seldom accorded the highest respect in the form of rigorous constructive criticism, just as his expositors seldom confront the practical and theoretical complications of "translating" his project to very different societies and polities.[22]

Among those most active in this arena, Ira Shor stands out. Deeply influenced by Freire, Shor strives toward a practical pedagogy aimed at "the desocialized thinking called critical consciousness [which] refers to the way we see ourselves in relation to knowledge and power in society, to the way in which we use and study language, and to the way we act in school and daily life to reproduce or to transform our conditions" (1982, 128). Crucially, Shor conceptualizes and situates critical literacy as one among other "qualities" that constitute critical consciousness. They are power awareness, permanent desocialization, self-education/organization, and critical literacy. None stands or is taught alone; each takes its place among the others. Together, they contribute toward curricular practices large and small.

Among proponents of critical literacy, Shor's exposition has a rare, and fresh, specificity descriptively as well as conceptually and theoretically. His critical literacy is recognizable as literacy, no small feat. He writes:

> *Critical literacy:* Habits of thought, reading, writing, and speaking which go beneath surface meaning, first impressions, dominant myths, official pronouncements, traditional cliches, received wisdom, and mere opinions, to understand the deep meaning, root causes, social context, ideology, and personal consequences of any action, event, object, process, organization, experience, text, subject matter, policy, mass media, or discourse; thinking-in-depth about books, statements, print and broadcast media, traditional sayings, official policies, public speeches, commercial messages, political propaganda, familiar ideas, required syllabi; questioning official knowledge, existing authority, traditional relationships, and ways of speaking; exercising a curiosity to understand the root causes of events; using language so that words reveal the deep meaning of anything under discussion; applying that meaning to your own context and imagining how to act on that meaning to change the conditions it reflects (1982, 129).

Shor's project, to condense it unfairly, differentiates rather than universalizes in its critique, approaches, and practices. Attentive to specific contexts of students and their everyday lives, it is impressively sensitive to the age, race, gender, and goals of students and their social and educational conditions. "Desocialization should fit the students as well as the subject matter and the political climate surrounding the classroom. The students' diverse cultures, speech, and thoughts make up the ground on which a desocializing curriculum first plants its feet. Some students are more open than others to transformative learning due to their age or political maturity or to the permissiveness of the local authorities" (1982, 130–31).

The program is explicitly interdisciplinary. Shor refers to "interdisciplinary literacy" as integrating reading, writing, critical dialogue, and cooperative learning across the curriculum while also linking content areas to "collaborative language arts." Ending the "disabling separation" of language studies and academic subjects boosts the practice of literacy in closer connection to students' full range of studies.

Shor calls his program an "activist education." On the one hand, "crossing academic boundaries is curricular action that challenges the dominant structure of education." And, on the other hand, "critical pedagogy is activist in its questioning of the status quo, in its participatory methods, and in its insistence that knowledge is not fixed but is constantly changing" (1982, 1988–89). Central to Shor's program for learning and practicing critical literacy is "problem-posing." Literacy dialogically takes its place within an activist education dedicated to studying life in order to change it, and to students transforming themselves within history. That is a literacy appropriately critical, attentive if properly critical of its own past and that of others, to their limits as well as their possibilities, and therefore to their future.

Thoughts for the Future

In airing a series of key legacies and myths in which the history of literacy resonates and culminates in present-day problems my goal was to show the benefits of historical perspective. Historical analysis and interpretation, applied carefully and knowingly, often have great power in stimulating fresh views, novel questions, and new understandings. No antiquarian search for "origins" or claims for antiquity of lineage, this is the past alive in the present and shaping the future, not a dead hand hanging over us. It is a "human science" that is relevant and public, in the best sense of those hackneyed and contested terms. In the series of conjunctures discussed here are paths for rethinking literacy, schooling, learning, and education. We might usefully construe them as a significant, perhaps necessary challenge for notions and concepts of literacy and paths toward its attainment.

If we wish to take this challenge from history with the seriousness I think it demands, breaking traditional disciplinary and curricular divisions becomes a major requirement. That would follow from accepting the provenance of the past for grappling better with the present and future, and from recognizing the limiting historical legacies from academic disciplines whose foundations were constructed largely during the nineteenth and earlier twentieth century but have outlived their usefulness and require fundamental transformation. Among the lessons from the legacies of literacy is not only that no one discipline may claim fairly to understand literacy, but also that novel combinations of multi- and interdisciplinary study are now more than ever before needed. To make this claim is certainly not unprecedented. To assert that the discipline (in the several meanings of that word) of history should be central to reconstructing the study of literacy is more novel.

Some recent observers point, in part, to the reorientation I propose and its possibilities. With respect to contemporary cultural currents and current debates about texts, Charles Newman (1985, 129–30) writes: "The electronic media fear nothing so much as the historical sense: its contemplativeness, its revisionism, its circumlocution, the inevitable corrections and abrasions of contrasting perspective. Commodity values are threatened by the historical reflection which has always represented the beginning of fiction's territory—memory resuscitated by the imagination."[23]

Sharing the understanding that today's crises in education and literacy are one of "historical purpose and meaning," the educational critic Henry Giroux and the historian Harvey Kaye write with a different end—the college curriculum—in mind. What they articulate might well, with due qualification, stand as a platform for reconstructing literacy(ies):

> We would urge a commitment to *historical* education and the development of humanities and liberal-arts curricula that cultivate perspective, critique, consciousness, remembrance, and imagination. By *perspective* we mean the awareness that the way things are is not the way they have always been nor the way they must necessarily be in the future. *Critique* is more specific, entailing a deliberate notion of unveiling and de-reification in order to comprehend and reveal the social origins of the prominent economic, and cultural orders in which we live and have lived. *Consciousness* refers to an appreciation of the making of history or, as the Italian political theorist Antonio Gramsci once put it, an awareness of "the sum of effort and sacrifice which the present has cost the past and which the future is costing the present." *Remembrance* acknowledges that while the past is not for dwelling in, it is a reservoir of experience—both of tragedy and hope—from which we draw in order to act. And *imagination* commands that we recognize the present as history and thus consider the structure, movement, and possibilities in the contemporary world that show us how we might act to prevent the barbaric and develop the humanistic (Giroux and Kaye, 1989, A44; see Aronowitz and Giroux, 1988).

That perhaps provides a place to pause, and reflect again.

Notes

This chapter is based on a series of keynote addresses, public lectures, and articles developed in the early 1990s, arguing for a set of clear and useful "lessons" from the historical study of literacy that address key "myths" and "legacies," in my lexicon, from the history of literacy that continue to speak to contemporary concerns. Versions with different focuses and direction were presented at the Bard College Conference on Education for Complexity in the 21st Century, 1991; International Conference on Attaining Functional Literacy: A Cross-Cultural Perspective, Tilburg University, The Netherlands, 1991; New Hampshire Humanities Council Conference on Literacy, Myths, and Lessons, 1991; Tema, Linkoping University, Sweden, 1992; Conference on Adult Literacy: An International Urban Perspective, The United Nations, New York, 1992; The Literacy Centre, Montreal, 1993; National Literacy Secretariat, Multiculturalism and Citizenship Canada, Ottawa, 1993; American Educational Research Association, Basic Research on Reading and Literacy

Group, Atlanta, 1993; Conference on Literacy and Power: Difference, Silence and Textual Practice, Griffith University, Australia, 1993; Institute on Literacies, Language, and Social Justice, Melbourne, Australia, 1993; Australian Reading Association, Melbourne, 1993; and a number of Australian universities during a tour in July 1993. I thank all those who solicited my participation and who responded critically and helpfully. Different published versions acknowledge specific individuals and institutions, a list too long to include. The version printed here reflects those different occasions, audiences, and focuses by incorporating three distinct sets of applications by way of conclusions.

The title reflects rhetorically and substantively my principal books on the history of literacy as well as my historical-based epistemology: Graff, 1979, 1987a, 1987b. Interested readers may also consult, among a large literature, my bibliography, Graff, 1981a; anthology, Graff, 1981b; and Graff, 1987a. Recent works are cited in Graff, 1988, 1993a, and Graff, 1979 (1991). No complete bibliography appears here. The lengthy reference list, however, includes the most important historical work to date and some of the best contemporary writing. It is meant to serve as a guide to the literature.

Unless otherwise specified, usage of the word "literacy" in this chapter refers to *basic* levels and skills of *alphabetic* literacy—reading and writing. Inflation, exaggeration, and confusion of literacy with various other forms and modes of practice, learning, and schooling is a regular feature—and a great danger—of many discussions of these timely and critical subjects. Our knowledge of the relationships among different modes of literacy, their acquisition, practice, and uses is astonishingly poor. That is one inordinately important set of questions crying out for study today. So, too, is the question of the very expansiveness and inclusiveness of concepts and notions of "literacy" itself. I fear that we too often overload it rather than qualifying more precisely our usage and expectations. That is among the historical legacies and myths of literacy.

Readers should also note that this essay attempts to draw comparisons between literacy and other, "higher" levels and forms of education—whose connections are often far from simple, linear, or direct despite assumptions to the contrary—and between past and present and future arrangements of schooling and education, levels and uses of learning. This is no easy task. Although I may occasionally seem to violate my own (and no doubt others') dicta, I believe the risks are worth taking. *Caveat lector.* For efforts similar and complementary in spirit if not always in detail and emphasis, see Leon Botstein, 1990; Ian Winchester, 1978, 1990a, 1990b.

1   This obviously is a complicated cultural conjunction. See, as symbol and substance of entanglement and resulting confusion, the fascinating issue of *Daedalus* on "Literacy in America," 1990. Illuminating about many things, on literacy the issue is more revealing in unintended ways than its title might otherwise lead readers to expect. More directly relevant to deliberations with respect to "functional literacy," see for example, "Adult Literacy," 1990; HAUTECOEUR, 1990; K LEVINE, 1982, 1985. For my earlier critique of the 1975 Persepolis symposium, relevant here, see GRAFF, 1978, reprinted above. The extent to which common complications with notions of "function-ality(ies)" respecting literacy (for example, aired by LEVINE), among other things, are transcended forms one key criterion for the success of our deliberations.

2   See LEVINE, 1982, 1985; WAGNER, 1990.

3   LEVINE, 1982, p. 250, passim. See also, among a large and growing literature, LEVINE, 1985; HAUTECOEUR, 1990; "Adult Literacy," 1990. Revealing is the first page of GABRIEL CARCELES, "World Literacy Prospects at the Turn of the Century," in the latter, and contradictory pronouncements by H. S. BHOLA, "Literature on Adult Literacy," also in the latter.

4   I recognize, but will not take up the epistemological swamp on which I tread—lightly, I hope, for now—in proposing novel uses of the past and of historiography, in pursuing formative, but not deterministic, relationships tying present and future to past. Examples of more sustained approaches on these topics include GRAFF, 1979, 1987a,

1987b. Once again, *caveat lector!* At this juncture, too, note the implications for curricular and pedagogical revision toward a fundamentally and thoroughgoing historical basis, an experiment well worth the effort, I think, if historians and other "human scientists" (in the Continental sense, that is) began to take themselves and their potential pedagogical and extracurricular contributions more seriously than we typically do. A contextually rooted program, that includes historical context among its major domains, offers, perhaps, one way around the destructive dichotomies (in the debates over the "canons," for example, but elsewhere, too) and other complications that plague educational debates today. The plasticity and flexibility that characterize historical and other contextual approaches to understanding at their best, with traditions of rigorous research methods and practices (old and new), traditional concern for clarity of communication, new attention to both rhetorical and epistemological issues combine to present elements of a program. The vision of history I hold is an interdisciplinary one that ranges widely among the arts and humanities, social and behavioral sciences, and aspects of natural and mathematical science as well.

5 See also GRUBB and LAZERSON, 1982; LINDBLOM and COHEN, 1979; LINDBLOM, 1990.

6 See, of course, HIRSCH, 1987, 1988; and the loud debates that persist, among them GRAFF, 1989, reprinted in this collection; I find HIRSCH's conceptualization faulty, epistemological foundations inadequate, and history alarmingly anachronistic. For "historical literacy," see GAGNON, 1989. Nowhere in that book is "historical literacy" defined; perhaps we should appreciate rather than deprecate that omission! Regardless, it is incriminating. Among the former, see the recent issue of *Daedalus* cited above along with earlier issues: "Scientific Literacy," 1983; "Reading Old and New," 1983; TUMAN, 1993, among a large and growing literature. Very relevant here are IAN WINCHESTER's recent writings, cited above. See also, alas, ALLAN BLOOM's writings and responses, what amount in themselves to a sorry "cultural phenomenon." Notions of "cultural" or "historical" literacies, and their as yet "unborn"—legitimate or bastard—siblings cry out for extended criticism. I lack the space for that in this essay.

7 Suggestive here are, for example, HEATH, 1983, and her more recent formulations; SCRIBNER and COLE, 1981; SCRIBNER's more recent studies of nonverbal, nonliterate workplace skills, competencies, or "literacies," among current revisionist research in cognitive psychology formulating and probing multiplicities of "competencies." Her work is joined increasingly by others within that field who are redefining our understanding of intelligences and competencies—and perhaps, in time, of literacies as well. HOWARD GARDNER's work with young children holds important promise too.

8 I make no effort to document what follows. My conclusions derive from almost two decades of reading and research in this field. Interested readers may consult my general works and also HOUSTON, 1988. There are many worthwhile historical studies that merit consultation. HOUSTON, 1985, is an excellent analysis in the tradition of "literacy myths." IAN WINCHESTER's (1990a, 1990b) recent articles treat the implications of new historical—and other—research concerning literacy. For the United States, an important new work is CARL KAESTLE et al., 1991.

9 The best known "strong case" is JACK GOODY and IAN WATT, 1968, originally published in 1963. By 1968, GOODY withdrew from the language of causal consequences to looser formulations. For a critical discussion and bibliography, see GRAFF, 1987a, esp. Epilogue. Anthropologist RUTH FINNEGAN's (1988) writings are very important among this literature.

10 The almost cyclical "debate" over "skills" versus "content," which spans the entire educational realm from literacy learning to graduate training, is another version of this. Today's war over undergraduate "core curricula" in such terms is especially silly and wasteful of time and energy. IAN WINCHESTER (1990a, 1990b) relates this issue to the philosophy of science and its revision. There is a large literature on vocational

schooling, among the functional and/or utilitarian literacies. For recent years, see LEVINE, 1985, among others.

11 The many works of WALTER ONG, MARSHALL MCLUHAN, and ELIZABETH EISEN- STEIN provide the starting point on these typically misunderstood issues.

12 CHARLES LINDBLOMS's (1990) major attack on the kinds of "knowledge" and under- standings among social scientists and policymakers represents a clear analogy to the situation with literacy. A fascinating set of examples that stress the import of visual abilities in technological invention appears in several papers by the historian EUGENE FERGUSON (1977). Some of PETER BURKE's (1972) work on artistic orientations in the Renaissance is also complementary.

13 The still novel field of ethnographies of literacy, popularized first by educational an- thropologists like SHIRLEY BRICE HEATH, among others, has tremendous promise. See also BOYARIN, 1993; GOWAN, 1992; STREET, 1993; Historians have just begun to attempt research influenced in these directions. See for example GRAFF, 1988, 1993a.

14 See GRAFF, 1995.

15 Suggestive here, for example, are the studies of LAQUEUR, 1976, and SPUFFORD, 1979. The example of early modern Sweden where exceptionally high levels of reading but not writing literacy and of female literacy were achieved largely without mass institutional schooling is told by JOHANSSON, 1977, 1981, 1985.

16 See also HOUSTON, 1988; MAYNES, 1985a, 1985b; GRAFF, 1979, 1987a, 1993a; STE- PHENS, 1987.

17 The literature on the economics of literacy, including foundational scholarship, for example, by CARLO CIPOLLA, C. ARNOLD ANDERSON, MARY JEAN BOWMAN, DAN- IEL LERNER, ALEX INKELES, MARIAN LEVY, and many others, shows the strong hold of these connections, relatively impermeable but capable of endless qualifications. For one typical case in point, see among his works, HARMAN, 1974, pp. 11–12.

18 On "reading" cities, see CALHOUN, 1969; DE CERTAUX, 1984; MARCUS, 1973, 1974; NEUBERG, 1973; KASSON, 1984. Obviously, these few paragraphs only begin discus- sion of very large and difficult subjects. Indeed, my own use of "cities" and "urban places" is hardly adequate to that task.

19 A neat example of this appears in BARRETT, 1990.

20 See also MCLAREN, 1988; ARONOWITZ and GIROUX, 1985.

21 See, in general, for both dimensions and mixture of success and failings in these terms, "Literacy, Culture," 1988; ARONOWITZ and GIROUX, 1985; EDELSKY, 1991; FERD- MAN, 1990; FREEBODY and WELCH, 1993; FREIRE and MACEDO, 1987; GEE, 1990; GIROUX, 1988; LANKSHEAR with LAWLER, 1987; LANKSHEAR and MCLAREN, 1993; MCLAREN, 1988; ROSE, 1989; SINGH, 1989; SHOR, 1982; WILLINSKY, 1990.

22 Compare FREIRE and MACEDO, 1987, for example, with FERDMAN, 1990; GIROUX, 1988; MCLAREN, 1988.

23 Some of E. L. DOCTOROW's essays are also relevant to these issues.

References

For reasons of economy and space, I shall not attempt a complete bibliography for this text. Citations herein bias books over articles and published over unpublished items.

ABRAMS, PHILIP (1980) "History, sociology, historical sociology," *Past & Present* 87: 3–16.

"Adult Literacy" (1990) Special issue. *Comparative Education Review* 34, 1.

ALLEN, JAMES SMITH (1991) *In the Public Eye: A History of Reading in Modern France.* Princeton: Princeton University Press.

ARNOVE, ROBERT F., and GRAFF, HARVEY J., eds. (1987) *National Literacy Campaigns: Historical and Comparative Perspectives*. New York: Plenum.

ARONOWITZ, STANLEY, and GIROUX, HENRY (1985) *Education Under Siege: The Conservative, Liberal, and Radical Debate Over Schooling*. South Hadley, Mass.: Bergin & Garvey.

—— (1988) "Schooling, culture, and literacy in the age of broken dreams: A review of Bloom and Hirsch," *Harvard Educational Review* 58: 172–194.

BARRETT, MICHAEL J. (1990) "The case for more schooling," *The Atlantic*, November: 78–106.

BARTOLI LANGELI, A., and PETRUCCI, A., eds. (1978) "Alfabetismo e cultura scritta." *Quaderni Storici* 38.

BARTOLI LANGELI, A., and TOSCANI, X., eds. (1991) *Istruzione, alfabetismo, scrittura: Saggi di storia dell'alfabetizzione in Italia*. Milan: Franco Angeli.

BARTON, DAVID, and IVANIC, ROZ, eds. (1991) *Writing in the Community*. Written Communication Annual, vol. 6. Newbury Park, Calif.: Sage.

BAUMANN, GERD (1986) *The Written Word*. Oxford: Oxford University Press.

BAUML, FRANZ (1980) "Varieties and consequences of medieval literacy and illiteracy," *Speculum* 55: 237–265.

BHOLA, H. S. (1990) "Literature on adult literacy: New directions in the 1990s," *Comparative Education Review* 34: 139–144.

BLOCH, MAURICE (1989) "Literacy and enlightenment." In *Literacy and Society*, ed. KAREN SCHOUSBOE and MOGES TROLLE LARSEN, pp. 15–37. Copenhagen: Akademisk Forlag.

BOTSTEIN, LEON (1990) "Damaged literacies and American democracy," *Daedalus* 119, 2: 55–84.

BOYARIN, JONATHAN, ed. (1993) *The Ethnography of Reading*. Berkeley and Los Angeles: University of California Press.

BRANDT, DEBORAH (1990) *Literacy as Involvement: The Acts of Writers, Readers, and Texts*. Carbondale: Southern Illinois University Press.

BRODHEAD, RICHARD H. (1993) *Cultures of Letters: Scenes of Reading and Writing in Nineteenth-Century America*. Chicago: University of Chicago Press.

BROOKS, JEFFREY (1985) *When Russia Learned to Read: Literacy and Popular Literature, 1861–1917*. Princeton: Princeton University Press.

BURKE, PETER (1972) *Culture and Society in Renaissance Italy*. London: Batsford.

—— (1978) *Popular Culture in Early Modern Europe*. New York: Harper and Row.

—— (1987) *The Historical Anthropology of Early Modern Italy*. Cambridge: Cambridge University Press.

—— and PORTER, ROY, eds.(1987) *The Social History of Language*. Cambridge: Cambridge University Press.

CALHOUN, DANIEL H. (1969) "The city as teacher," *History of Education Quarterly* 9: 312–325.

CARCELES, GABRIEL (1990) "World literacy prospects at the turn of the century," *Comparative Education Review* 34: 4–20.

CARPENTER, KENNETH E., ed. (1983) *Books and Society in History*. New York: Bowker, 1983.

CHARTIER, ROGER (1987) *The Cultural Uses of Print in Early Modern France*. Princeton: Princeton University Press.

—— (1989a) "Texts, printing, readings." In *The New Cultural History*, ed. LYNN HUNT, pp. 154–175. Berkeley and Los Angeles: University of California Press.

——, ed.(1989b) *The Culture of Print*. Princeton: Princeton University Press.

CIPOLLA, CARLO (1969) *Literacy and Development in the West*. Harmondsworth: Penguin.

CLAMMER, J. R. (1976) *Literacy and Social Change: A Case Study of Figi*. Leiden: Brill.

CLANCHEY, MICHAEL T. (1979, 1993) *From Memory to Written Record: England, 1066–1307.* Cambridge, Mass.: Harvard University Pres; revised ed., Oxford: Blackwell.

COOK-GUMPERZ, JENNY, ed. (1986) *The Social Construction of Literacy.* Cambridge: Cambridge University Press.

CORNELIUS, JANET D. (1991) *When I Can Read My Title Clear: Literacy, Slavery, and Religion in the Antebellum South.* Columbia: University of South Carolina Press.

CRESSY, DAVID (1980) *Literacy and the Social Order.* Cambridge: Cambridge University Press.

DARNTON, ROBERT (1972) "Reading, writing, and publishing in eighteenth-century France." In *Historical Studies Today,* ed. FELIX GILBERT and STEPHEN R. GRAUBARD, pp. 238–250. New York: Norton.

—— (1982) *The Literary Underground of the Old Regime.* Cambridge, Mass.: Harvard University Press.

—— (1983) "What is the history of books?" In *Books and Society in History,* ed. KENNETH E. CARPENTER, pp. 3–28. New York: Bowker.

—— (1984) "Readers respond to Rousseau: The fabrication of romantic sensitivity." In *The Great Cat Massacre and Other Episodes in French Cultural History,* pp. 215–256. New York: Basic Books.

DAVIDSON, CATHY N. (1986) *Revolution in the Word: The Rise of the Novel in America.* New York: Oxford University Press.

——, ed. (1989) *Reading in America.* Baltimore: Johns Hopkins University Press.

DAVIS, NATALIE Z. (1975) "Printing and the people." In *Society and Culture in Early Modern France,* pp. 189–226. Stanford: Stanford University Press.

DE CERTAUX, MICHAEL (1984) "Walking in the city" and "Spatial stories." In *The Practice of Everyday Life.* Berkeley and Los Angeles: University of California Press.

EDELSKY, CAROLE (1991) *With Liberty and Justice for All: Rethinking the Social in Language and Education.* London: Falmer.

"Education as Transformation: Identity, Change, and Development" (1981) Special issue. *Harvard Educational Review* 51, 1.

EISENSTEIN, ELIZABETH (1979) *The Printing Press as an Agent of Change.* 2 vols. Cambridge: Cambridge University Press.

ENGELSING, ROLF (1973) *Analphabetentum und lekture.* Stuttgart.

—— (1974) *Der berger als leser: Lesergeschichte in Deutschland, 1500–1800.* Stuttgart.

FEATHER, JOHN (1985) *The Provincial Book Trade in Eighteenth-Century England.* Cambridge: Cambridge University Press.

FEBVRE, LUCIEN, and MARTIN, HENRI-JEAN (1958) *L'apparition du livre.* Paris: Editions Albin Michel.

—— (1976) *The Coming of the Book.* London: New Left Books.

FERDMAN, BERNARDO (1990) "Literacy and cultural identity," *Harvard Educational Review* 60: 181–204.

FERGUSON, EUGENE (1977) "The mind's eye: Nonverbal thought in technology," *Science* 197: 827–836.

FINNEGAN, RUTH (1988) *Literacy and Orality.* Oxford: Blackwell.

FLEURY, M., and VALMARY, P. (1957) "Les progrès de l'instrucdtion élèmentaire de Louis XIV à Napoléon III," *Population* 12: 71–92.

FREEBODY, PETER, and WELCH, ANTHONY R., eds. (1993) *Knowledge, Culture and Power: International Perspectives on Literacy as Policy and Practice.* Pittsburgh: University of Pittsburgh Press.

FREIRE, PAULO, and MACEDO, DONALDO (1987) *Literacy: Reading the Word and the World.* South Hadley, Mass.: Bergin & Garvey.

FURET, F., and OZOUF, J. (1977) *Lire et écrire.* 2 vols. Paris: Editions de Minuit.

—— (1983) *Reading and Writing.* Cambridge: Cambridge University Press.

GAGNON, PAUL, and the Bradley Commission on History in Schools, ed. (1989) *Historical Literacy: The Case for History in American Education*. New York: Macmillan.

GALENSON, DAVID (1979) "Literacy and the social origins of some early Americans," *Historical Journal* 22: 75–91.

—— (1981) "Literacy and age in preindustrial England," *Economic Development and Cultural Change* 29: 813–829.

GEE, JAMES (1990) *Social Linguistics and Literacies: Ideology in Discourses*. London: Falmer.

GERLIN, GORDON, and SUM, ANDREW (1988) *Toward a More Perfect Union: Basic Skills, Poor Families, and Our Economic Future*. New York: Ford Foundation Project on Social Welfare and the American Future.

GILMORE, WILLIAM J. (1989) *Reading Becomes a Necessity of Life: Material and Cultural Life in Rural New England, 1780–1835*. Knoxville: University of Tennessee Press.

GINZBURG, CARLO (1980) *The Cheese and the Worms*. Baltimore: Johns Hopkins University Press.

GIROUX, HENRY A. (1988) "Literacy and the pedagogy of voice and political empowerment," *Educational Studies* 38: 61–76.

GIROUX, HENRY A., and KAYE, JARVEY J. (1989) "The liberal arts must be reformed to serve democratic means," *Chronicle of Higher Education*, 29 March: A44.

GOODY, JACK (1986) *The Logic of Writing and the Organization of Society*. Cambridge: Cambridge University Press.

—— (1987) *The Interface Between the Written and the Oral*. Cambridge: Cambridge University Press.

——, ed. (1968) *Literacy in Traditional Societies*. Cambridge: Cambridge University Press.

GOODY, JACK, and WATT, IAN (1968) "The consequences of literacy." In *Literacy in Traditional Societies*, ed. JACK GOODY. Cambridge: Cambridge University Press.

GOWEN, SHERYL GREENWOOD (1992) *The Politics of Workplace Literacy: A Case Study*. New York: Teachers College Press.

GRAFF, HARVEY J. (1978) "Literacy past and present: Critical approaches in the literacy/society relationship," *Interchange* 9: 1–21.

—— (1979, 1991) *The Literacy Myth: Literacy and Social Structure in the Nineteenth-Century City*. New York and London: Academic Press. Reprinted with a new introduction, New Brunswick, N.J.: Transaction.

—— (1981a) *Literacy in History: An Interdisciplinary Research Bibliography*. New York: Garland.

——, ed. (1981b) *Literacy and Social Development in the West*. Cambridge: Cambridge University Press.

—— (1981c) "Reflections on the history of literacy: Overview, critique, and proposals," *Humanities in Society* 4: 303–333.

—— (1987a) *The Legacies of Literacy: Continuities and Contradictions in Western Culture and Society*. Bloomington: Indiana University Press.

—— (1987b) *The Labyrinths of Literacy: Reflections on Past and Present*. London: Falmer.

—— (1988) "Whither the history of literacy? The future of the past," *Communication* 11: 5–22.

—— 1989) "Critical literacy versus cultural literacy: Reading signs of the times," *Interchange* 20: 46–52.

—— (1993a) "Assessing the history of literacy in the 1990s: Themes and questions," presented to the Conference on Writing and Reading in Western Europe, Universidad internacional Menendex Pelayo, Valencia, Spain, forthcoming in volume of conference essays.

—— (1993b) "Literacy patterns in historical perspective." In *Reading Across the Life Span: Recent Research in Psychology*, ed. STEVEN R. YUSSEN and M. CECIL SMITH, pp. 73–94. New York and Berlin: Springer-Verlag.

—— (1994) Literacy, myths, and legacies: "Lessons from the history of literacy," pp. 37–60. In *Functional literacy: Theoretical Issues and Educational Implications*, ed. LUDO HERHOEVEN. Amsterdam: John Benjamins.

—— (1993) *Conflicting Paths: Growing Up in America* Cambridge, Mass.: Harvard University Press.

GRENDLER, PAUL (1989) *Schooling in Renaissance Italy: Literacy and Learning, 1300–1600*. Baltimore: Johns Hopkins University Press.

GROSS, ROBERT A. (1988) *Books and Libraries in Thoreau's Concord: Two Essays*. Worcester, Mass.: American Antiquarian Society.

GRUBB, W. NORTON, and LAZERSON, MARVIN (1982) *Broken Promises: How Americans Fail Their Children*. New York: Basic Books.

HALL, DAVID D. (1979) "The world of print and collective mentality in seventeenth-century New England." In *New Directions in American Intellectual History*, JOHN HIGHAM and PAUL CONKIN, pp. 166–180. Baltimore: Johns Hopkins University Press.

—— (1983) "The uses of literacy in New England, 1600–1850." In *Printing and Society in Early America*, ed. WILLIAM JOYCE, et al., pp. 1–47. Worcester, Mass.: American Antiquarian Society.

—— and HENCH, JOHN, eds. (1987) *Needs and Opportunities in the History of the Book: America, 1639–1876*. Worcester, Mass.: American Antiquarian Society.

HALL, OSWALD, and CARLTON, RICHARD (1977) *Basic Skills at School and Work: The Study of Albertown*. Toronto: Ontario Economic Council.

HARMAN, DAVID (1974) *Community Fundamental Education*. Lexington, Mass.: Lexington Books.

HARRIS, WILLIAM V. (1989) *Ancient Literacy*. Cambridge, Mass.: Harvard University Press.

HAUTECOEUR, JEAN-PAUL, ed. (1990) *Alpha 90: Current Research in Literacy*. Quebec: Unesco Institute for Education.

HAVELOCK, ERIC (1963) *Preface to Plato*. Cambridge, Mass.: Harvard University Press.

—— (1973) *Prologue to Greek Literacy*. Cincinnati: University of Cincinnati.

—— (1976) *Origins of Western Literacy*. Toronto: Ontario Institute for Studies in Education.

—— (1986) *The Literate Revolution in Greece and Its Cultural Consequences*. Princeton: Princeton University Press.

—— (1986) *The Muse Learns to Write*. New Haven: Yale University Press.

HEATH, SHIRLEY BRICE (1983) *Ways with Words: Language, Life, and Work in Communities and Classrooms*. Cambridge: Cambridge University Press.

HEBRARD, JEAN (1980) "Ecole et alphabéisation au XIXe sièle (approche psychologique de documents historiques)," *Annales: e.s.c.* 35: 66–80.

HIGHAM, JOHN, and CONKIN, PAUL, eds. (1979) *New Directions in American Intellectual History*. Baltimore: Johns Hopkins University Press.

HINDMAN, SANDRA L., ed. (1991) *Printing the Written Word: The Social History of Books, circa 1450–1520*. Ithaca: Cornell University Press.

HIRSCH, E. D., JR. (1987) *Cultural Literacy*. Boston: Houghton Mifflin.

—— (1988) *The Dictionary of Cultural Literacy*. Boston: Houghton Mifflin.

HOBSBAWM, E. J. (1980) "The revival of narrative: some comments," *Past & Present* 86: 3–8.

HOUSTON, RAB (1983) "Literacy and society in the west, 1500–1800," *Social History* 8: 269–293.

—— (1985) *Scottish Literacy and the Scottish Identity: Illiteracy and Society in Scotland and Northern England, 1600–1800*. Cambridge: Cambridge University Press.

—— (1988) *Literacy in Early Modern Europe: Culture and Education, 1500–1800*. London: Longman.

HYDE, J. K. (1979) "Some uses of literacy in Venice and Florence in the thirteenth and fourteenth centuries," *Transactions, Royal Historical Society*, 5th series, 29: 109–129.

ILLICH, EVAN, and SANDERS, BARRY (1988) *The Alphabetization of the Popular Mind*. San Francisco: North Point Press.

ISAACS, RHYS (1976a) "Dramatizing the ydeology of revolution: Popular mobilization in Virginia, 1774 to 1776," *William and Mary Quarterly* 33: 357–385.

—— (1976b) "Preachers and patriots: Popular culture and the revolution in Virginia." In *The American Revolution*, ed. ALFRED F. YOUNG, pp. 125–156. Dekalb: Northern Illinois University Press.

—— (1982) *The Transformation of Virginia*. Chapel Hill: University of North Carolina Press.

JOHANSSON, EGIL (1977) *The History of Literacy in Sweden*. Educational Reports No. 12. Umea, Sweden: Umea University and School of Education.

—— (1981) "The history of literacy in Sweden." In *Literacy and Social Development in the West*, ed. HARVEY J. GRAFF, pp. 151–182. Cambridge: Cambridge University Press.

—— (1985) "Popular literacy in Scandinavia about 1600–1900," *Historical Social Research* 34: 60–64.

JOYCE, WILLIAM L.; HALL, DAVID D.; BROWN, RICHARD D.; and HENCH, JOHN B., eds. (1983) *Printing and Society in Early America*. Worcester, Mass.: American Antiquarian Society.

KAESTLE, CARL F. (1985) "The history of literacy and the history of reading," *Review of Educational Research* 12: 11–53.

KAESTLE, CARL F., et al. (1991) *Literacy in the United States: Readers and Reading Since 1880*. New Haven: Yale University Press.

KAMMEN, MICHAEL, ed.(1980) *The Past Before Us*. Ithaca: Cornell University Press.

KAPLAN, STEVEN L., ed. (1984) *Understanding Popular Culture: Europe from the Middle Ages to the Nineteenth Century*. Berlin: Mouton.

KASSON, JOHN (1984) "Civility and rudeness: Urban etiquette and the bourgeois social order in nineteenth-century America," *Prospects* 9: 143–167.

KATZ, MICHAEL B. (1988) "The new educational panic," in *America in Theory*, ed. LESLIE BERLOWITZ, DENIS DONOGHUE, and LOUIS MENAND, pp. 178–194. New York: Oxford University Press.

KIRSCH, IRWIN S.; JUNGEBLUT, ANN; JENKINS, LYNN; and KOLSTAD, ANDREW (1993) *Adult Literacy in America*. Educational Testing Service under Contract with National Center for Education Statistics, Office of Educational Research and Improvement, U.S. Department of Education.

KOZOL, JONATHAN (1985) *Illiterate America*. Garden City: Doubleday.

LACAPRA, DOMINIC, and KAPLAN, STEVEN L., eds. (1982) *Modern European Intellectual History*. Ithaca: Cornell University Press.

LANKSHEAR, COLIN, with LAWLER, MOIRA (1987) *Literacy, School and Revolution*. London: Falmer.

LANKSHEAR, COLIN, and MCLAREN, PETER, eds. (1993) *Critical Literacy: Politics, Praxis, and the Postmodern*. Albany, N.Y.: SUNY Press.

LAQUEUR, THOMAS W. (1976a) "Working-class demand and the growth of English elementary education, 1750–1850." In *Schooling and Society*, ed. LAWRENCE STONE, pp. 192–205. Baltimore: Johns Hopkins University Press.

—— (1976b) "The cultural origins of popular literacy in England, 1500–1800," *Oxford Review of Education* 2: 255–275.

LEROY LADURIE, EMMANUEL (1978) *Montaillou: Promised Land of Error*. New York: Braziller.

LEVINE, DAVID (1979) "Education and family life in early industrial England," *Journal of Family History* 4: 368–380.

—— (1980) "Illiteracy and family life during the first industrial revolution," *Journal of Social History* 14: 25–44.

LEVINE, KENNETH (1982) "Functional literacy: Fond illusions and false economies," *Harvard Educational Review* 52: 249–266.

—— (1985) *The Social Context of Literacy*. London: Routledge and Kegan Paul.

LINDBLOM, CHARLES (1990) *Inquiry and Change*. New Haven: Yale University Press; New York: Russell Sage Foundation.

LINDBLOM and COHEN, DAVID (1979) *Usable Knowledge*. New Haven: Yale University Press.

"Literacy in America" (1990) *Daedalus* 119, 2.

"Literacy, Culture, and the Dilemmas of Schooling" (1988) *Journal of Education* 170, 1.

LOCKRIDGE, KENNETH A. (1974) *Literacy in Colonial New England*. New York: Norton.

MACHOR, JAMES L., ed. (1993) *Readers in History: Nineteenth-Century American Literature and the Contexts of Response*. Baltimore: Johns Hopkins University Press.

MARCHESINI, DANIELE (1987) *Il bisogno di scrivere: Usi dela scrittura nell'Italia modera*. Rome: Laterza.

MARCUS, STEVEN (1973) "Reading the illegible." In *The Victorian City*, ed. H. J. DYOS and MICHAEL WOLFF, pp. 257–276. London: Routledge.

—— (1974) *Engels, Manchester, and the Working Class*. New York: Random House.

MARTIN, HENRI-JEAN (1968–70) *Le livre et la civilisation écrite*. 3 vols. Paris: Ecole nationale supérieure des bibliothèques.

—— (1975) "Culture écrite et culture orale, culture savante et culture populaire dans la France d'Ancien Régime," *Journale des Savants*: 225–282.

—— (1977) "Pour une histoire de la lecture," *Revue française d'histoire du livre* 16: 583–609.

MARTINEZ, PEDRO LUIS MORENO (1989) *Alfabetizacion y cultura impresa en Lorca (1760–1860)*. Murcia: Universidad de Murcia.

MAYNES, MARY JO (1985a) *Schooling for the People: Comparative Local Studies of Schooling History in France and Germany, 1750–1850*. New York: Holmes and Meier.

—— (1985b) *Schooling in Western Europe*. Albany: SUNY Press.

MCKITTERICK, ROSAMOND (1989) *The Carolingians and the Written Word*. Cambridge: Cambridge University Press.

——, ed. (1991) *The Uses of Literacy in Early Medieval England*. Cambridge: Cambridge University Press.

MCLAREN, PETER L. (1988) "Culture or canon? Critical pedagogy and the politics of literacy," *Harvard Educational Review* 58: 213–234.

MELTON, JAMES VAN HORN (1988) *Absolutism and the Eighteenth-Century Origins of Compulsory Schooling in Prussia and Austria*. Cambridge: Cambridge University Press.

MITCH, DAVID (1992) *The Rise of Popular Literacy in Victorian England*. Philadelphia: University of Pennsylvania Press.

MITCHELL, CANDACE, and WEILLER, KATHLEEN, eds. (1991) *Rewriting Literacy*. New York: Bergin and Garvey.

MITCHELL, SALLY (1981) *The Fallen Angel: Chastity, Class and Women's Reading, 1835–1880*. Bowling Green, Ohio: Popular Press.

MORAN, JO ANN HOEPPNER (1985) *The Growth of English Schooling, 1340–1548: Learning, Literacy, and Laicization in Pre-Reformation York Diocese*. Princeton: Princeton University Press.

MUCHEMBLED, ROBERT (1985) *Popular Culture and Élite Culture in France, 1400–1750*. Baton Rouge: Louisiana State University Press.

NEUBERG, VICTOR (1973) "The literature of the streets." In *The Victorian City*, ed. H. J. DYOS and MICHAEL WOLFF, pp. 191–210. London: Routledge.

NEWMAN, CHARLES (1985) *The Post-Modern Aura*. Evanston: Northwestern University Press.

OECD (1992) *Adult Illiteracy and Economic Performance*. Paris: Centre for Educational Research and Development, OECD.

OLSON, DAVID (1977) "The languages of instruction: On the literate bias of schooling." In *Schooling and the Acquisition of Knowledge*, ed. RICHARD C. ANDERSON AND WILLIAM E. MONTAGUE. Hillsdale, N.J.: Lawrence Erlbaum.

ONG, WALTER (1958) *Ramus, Method, and the Decay of Dialogue*. Cambridge, Mass.: Harvard University Press.

—— (1967) *The Presence of the Word*. New Haven: Yale University Press.

—— (1977) *Interface of the Word*. Ithaca: Cornell University Press.

—— (1982) *Orality and Literacy*. London: Methuen.

PELIZZARI, MARIA ROSARIA, ed. (1989) *Sulle vie della scrittura: Alfabetizzazione, cultura scritta e istitzioni in eta moderna*. Naples: Edizioni Scientifiche Ialiane.

PETRUCCI, ARMANDO (1987) *Scrivere e no: Politche della scrittura e analfabetismo nel mondo d'oggi*. Rome: Riuniti.

RABB, THEODORE K., and ROTBERG, ROBERT I., eds. (1982) *The New History: 1980s and Beyond*. Princeton: Princeton University Press.

RADWAY, JANICE A. (1984) *Reading the Romance: Women, Patriarchy, and Popular Literature*. Chapel Hill: University of North Carolina Press.

—— (1986) "Identifying Ideological Seams: Mass Culture, Analytic Method, and Political Practice," *Communication* 9: 93–123.

"Reading Old and New" (1983) *Daedalus*, Winter.

ROCHE, DANIEL (1987) *The people of Paris*. Berkeley and Los Angeles: University of California Press.

ROSE, MIKE (1989) *Lives on the Boundary: The Struggles of America's Under-prepared*. New York: Free Press.

SALJO, ROGER, ed. (1988) *The Written World: Studies in Literate Thought and Action*. Berlin: Springer-Verlag.

SCHENDA, RUDOLF (1970) *Volk ohne buch . . . 1770–1910*. Frankfurt.

—— (1976) *Die lesestoffe der kleinen leute*. Munich: Beck.

SCHOFIELD, ROGER S. (1968) "The measurement of literacy in pre-industrial England." In *Literacy in Traditional Societies*, ed. JACK GOODY, pp. 311–325. Cambridge: Cambridge University Press.

—— (1973) "The dimensions of illiteracy in England, 1750–1850," *Explorations in Economic History* 10: 437–454.

"Scientific Literacy" (1983) *Daedalus*, Spring.

SCRIBNER, R. W. (1981) *For the Sake of Simple Folk: Popular Propaganda for the German Reformation*. Cambridge: Cambridge University Press.

—— (1984) "Oral culture and the diffusion of reformation ideas," *History of European Ideas* 5: 237–256.

SCRIBNER, SYLVIA, and COLE, MICHAEL (1981) *The Psychology of Literacy*. Cambridge, Mass.: Harvard University Press.

SEARLE, JOHN (1990) "The storm over the university," *New York Review of Books*, 6 December: 34–42.

SEWELL, WILLIAM H., JR. (1985) *Structure and Mobility: The Men and Women of Marseille, 1820–1870*. Cambridge: Cambridge University Press.

SHOR, IRA (1982) *Empowering Education: Critical Teaching for Social Change*. Chicago: University of Chicago Press.

SINGH, MICHAEL GARBUTCHEON (1989) "A counter-hegemonic orientation to literacy in Australia," *Journal of Education*, 171: 35–56.

SOLTOW, LEE, and STEVENS, EDWARD (1981) *The Rise of Literacy and the Common School in the United States*. Chicago: University of Chicago Press.

SPUFFORD, MARGARET (1979) "First steps in literacy: The reading and writing experiences of the humblest seventeenth-century spiritual autobiographers," *Social History* 4: 407–435.

—— 1981) *Small Books and Pleasant Histories: Popular Fiction and Its Readership in Seventeenth-Century England*. London: Methuen.

STEEDMAN, CAROLYN (1987) *The Tidy House*. London: Virago.

STEPHENS, W. B. (1987) *Education, Literacy, and Society, 1830–1870*. Manchester: Manchester University Press.

——, ed. (1983) *Studies in the History of Literacy: England and North America*. Educational Administration and History Monographs No. 13. Leeds: Museum of the History of Education, University of Leeds.

STEVENS, EDWARD (1985) "Literacy and the Worth of Liberty," *Historical Social Research* 34: 65–81.

—— (1988) *Literacy, Law, and Social Order*. Dekalb: Northern Illinois University Press.

STOCK, BRIAN (1983) *The Implications of Literacy: Written Language and Models of Interpretation in the Eleventh and Twelfth Centuries*. Princeton: Princeton University Press.

—— (1990) *Listening for the Text*. Baltimore: Johns Hopkins University Press.

STONE, LAWRENCE (1969) "Literacy and education in England, 1640–1900," *Past & Present* 42: 69–139.

—— (1979) "The revival of narrative: Reflections on a new old history," *Past & Present* 85: 3–24.

STOUT, HARRY S. (1977) "Religion, Communications, and the Ideological Origins of the American Revolution," *William and Mary Quarterly* 34: 519–541.

STRAUSS, GERALD (1978) *Luther's House of Learning*. Baltimore: Johns Hopkins University Press.

—— (1984) "Lutheranism and Literacy: A Reassessment." In *Religion and Society in Early Modern Europe*, ed. KASPAR VON GREYERZ, pp. 109–123. London: Allen and Unwin.

STRAUSS, GERALD, AND GAWTHROP, RICHARD (1984) "Protestantism and literacy in early modern Germany," *Past & Present* 104: 31–55.

STREET, BRIAN (1984) *Literacy in Theory and Practice*. Cambridge: Cambridge University Press.

——, ed. (1993) *Cross-cultural approaches to literacy*. Cambridge: Cambridge University Press.

STUCKEY, ELSPETH (1991) *The Violence of Literacy*. Portsmouth, N.H.: Boynton/Cook.

SVENBRO, JESPER (1993) *Phrasikleia: An Anthropology of Reading in Ancient Greece*. Ithaca: Cornell University Press.

SWEARINGEN, JAN (1991) *Rhetoric and Irony: Western Literacy and Western Lies*. New York: Oxford University Press.

TANNEN, DEBORAH, ed. (1982) *Spoken and Written Language: Exploring Orality and Literacy*. Norwood, N.J.: Ablex.

THOMAS, KEITH (1986) "The meaning of literacy in early modern England." In *The Written Word: Literacy in Transition*, ed. GERD BAUMANN, pp. 97–131. Oxford: Oxford University Press.

THOMAS, ROSALIND (1989) *Oral Tradition and Written Record in Classical Athens*. Cambridge: Cambridge University Press.

—— (1992) *Literacy and Orality in Ancient Greece*. Cambridge: Cambridge University Press.

THOMPSON, PAUL (1975) *The Edwardians*. Bloomington: Indiana University Press.

—— (1978) *The Voice of the Past: Oral History*. Oxford: Oxford University Press.

TODD, EMMANUEL (1987) *The Causes of Progress*. Oxford: Blackwell.